EIPGRAMS OF OSCAR WILDE

EPIGRAMS OF OSCAR WILDE

Wordsworth Reference

For my husband
ANTHONY JOHN RANSON
with love from your wife, the publisher.
Eternally grateful for your unconditional love,
not just for me but for our children,
Simon, Andrew and Nichola Trayler

3

Readers who are interested in other titles from
Wordsworth Editions are invited to visit our website at
www.wordsworth-editions.com

For our latest list and a full mail-order service, contact
Bibliophile Books, 5 Thomas Road, London E14 7BN
TEL: +44 (0)20 7515 9222 FAX: +44 (0)20 7538 4115
E-MAIL: orders@bibliophilebooks.com

First published in 2007 by Wordsworth Editions Limited
8B East Street, Ware, Hertfordshire SG12 9HJ

ISBN 978 1 84022 275 3

Text © Wordsworth Editions Limited 2007

Wordsworth® is a registered trademark of
Wordsworth Editions Limited,
the company founded by Michael Trayler in 1987

Typeset in Great Britain by Antony Gray
Printed and bound by Clays Ltd, St Ives plc

Contents

I

All Men Are Monsters

❦ All men are monsters. The only thing to do is to feed the wretches well. A good cook does wonders.

❦ Man is a being with myriad lives and myriad sensations, a complex, multiform creature that bears within itself strange legacies of thought and passion, and whose very flesh is tainted with the monstrous maladies of the dead.

❦ Man is complete in himself.

❦ Men become old, but they never become good.

❦ I don't think man has much capacity for development. He has got as far as he can, and that is not far, is it?

❦ The world was made for men and not for women.

❦ MRS ALLONBY: I delight in men over seventy. They always offer one the devotion of a lifetime.

❦ I sometimes think that God in creating man somewhat overestimated His ability.

❦ How many men there are in modern life who would like to see their past burning to white ashes before them?

❦ Bachelors are not fashionable any more. They are a damaged lot. Too much is known about them.

9

❦ I pity any woman who is married to a man called John. She would probably never be allowed to know the entrancing pleasure of a single moment's solitude.

❦ Formerly we used to canonise our heroes. The modern method is to vulgarise them. Cheap editions of great books may be delightful, but cheap editions of great men are absolutely detestable.

❦ No man is rich enough to buy back his past.

❦ MRS ALLONBY: Man, poor, awkward, reliable, necessary man belongs to a sex that has been rational for millions and millions of years. He can't help himself. It is in his race. The history of woman is very different. We have always been picturesque protests against the mere existence of common sense. We saw its dangers from the first.

❦ The evolution of man is slow. The injustice of man is great.

❦ Men are such cowards. They outrage every law of the world, and are afraid of the world's tongue.

❦ One is tempted to define man as a rational animal who always loses his temper when he is called upon to act in accordance with the dictates of his reason.

❦ A man who moralises is usually a hypocrite, and a woman who moralises is invariably plain. There is nothing in the whole world so unbecoming to a woman as a nonconformist conscience. And most women know it, I am glad to say.

❦ He must be quite respectable. One has never heard his name before in the whole course of one's life, which speaks volumes for a man, nowadays.

By persistently remaining single, a man converts himself into a permanent public temptation. Men should be more careful; this very celibacy leads weaker vessels astray.

CECILY: A man who is much talked about is always attractive. One feels there must be something in him, after all.

Rich bachelors should be heavily taxed. It is not fair that some men should be happier than others.

Men are horribly tedious when they are good husbands and abominably conceited when they are not.

If a woman wants to hold a man, she has merely to appeal to the worst in him.

The fact is that men should never try to dictate to women. They never know how to do it, and when they do it, they always say something particularly foolish.

The home seems to me to be the proper sphere for the man. And certainly once a man begins to neglect his domestic duties he becomes painfully effeminate, does he not? And I don't like that. It makes men so very attractive.

Personality is a very mysterious thing. A man cannot always be estimated by what he does. He may keep the law, and yet be worthless. He may break the law, and yet be fine. He may be bad without ever doing anything bad. He may commit a sin against society, and yet realise through that sin his true perfection.

LADY WINDERMERE: I don't like compliments, and I don't see why a man should think he is pleasing a woman enormously when he says to her a whole heap of things that he doesn't mean.

❦ When a man acts he is a puppet. When he describes he is a poet.

❦ He has one of those terribly weak natures that are not susceptible to influence.

❦ A red-cheeked, white-whiskered creature who, like so many of his class, was under the impression that inordinate joviality can atone for an entire lack of ideas.

❦ Like all people who try to exhaust a subject, he exhausted his listeners.

❦ A man with a hideous smile and a hideous past. He is asked everywhere. No dinner party is complete without him.

On a view from an hotel window:
❦ Oh, that is altogether immaterial, except to the proprietor, who of course charges it in the bill. A gentleman never looks out of the window.

❦ A bad man is the sort of man who admires innocence, and a bad woman is the sort of woman a man never gets tired of.

❦ A man's life is of more value than a woman's. It has larger issues, wider scope, greater ambitions.

❦ The husbands of very beautiful women belong to the criminal classes.

❦ He had that curious love of green which in individuals is always the sign of a subtle artistic temperament and in nations is said to denote a laxity if not a decadence of morals.

❧ Mrs ALLONBY: The ideal man should talk to us as if we were goddesses, and treat us as if we were children. He should refuse all our serious requests, and gratify every one of our whims. He should encourage us to have caprices, and forbid us to have missions. He should always say much more than he means, and always mean much more than he says.

❧ What on earth should we men do going about with purity and innocence? A carefully thought-out buttonhole is much more effective.

❧ Gardenias and the peerage were his only weaknesses.

❧ Mrs ALLONBY: The ideal man should never run down other pretty women. That would show he had no taste or make one suspect that he had too much.

❧ When a man is old enough to do wrong he should be old enough to do right also.

❧ Nothing should be able to harm a man except himself. Nothing should be able to rob a man at all. What a man really has is what is in him. What is outside of him should be a matter of no importance.

❧ . . . one of nature's gentlemen, the worst type of gentleman I know.

❧ Men who are trying to do something for the world are always insufferable; when the world has done something for *them*, they are charming.

❧ Mrs ALLONBY: He should invariably praise us for whatever qualities he knows we haven't got. But he should be pitiless, quite pitiless, in reproaching us for the virtues we have never dreamed of possessing.

❦ Mrs Allonby: Nothing is so aggravating as calmness. There is something positively brutal about the good temper of most modern men. I wonder we women stand it as well as we do.

❦ When men give up saying what is charming, they give up thinking what is charming.

❦ Man can believe the impossible, but man can never believe the improbable.

❦ The true perfection of man lies not in what man has but in what man is.

❦ The man is but a very honest knave, full of fine phrases for life's merchandise, selling most dear what he holds most cheap: a windy brawler in a world of words. I never met so eloquent a fool.

The Very Gold of Their Lives

🐦 Women give to men the very gold of their lives. But they invariably want it back in small change.

🐦 You women live by your emotions and for them. You have no philosophy of life.

🐦 With a proper background women can do anything.

🐦 One should never trust a woman who tells one her real age. A woman who would tell one that, would tell one anything.

🐦 Women – sphinxes without secrets.

🐦 Crying is the refuge of plain women but the ruin of pretty ones.

🐦 Men know life too early; women know life too late – that is the difference between men and women.

🐦 Women are meant to be loved, not to be understood.

🐦 It takes a thoroughly good woman to do a thoroughly stupid thing.

🐦 Never trust a woman who wears mauve, whatever her age may be, or a woman over thirty-five who is fond of pink ribbons. It always means they have a history.

❦ I don't know that women are always rewarded for being charming. I think they are usually punished for it!

❦ No nice girl should ever waltz with such particularly younger sons. It looks so fast!

❦ If a woman really repents, she never wishes to return to the society that has made or seen her ruin.

❦ Repentance is quite out of date and besides, if a woman really repents, she has to go to a bad dressmaker, otherwise no one believes her.

❦ I don't believe in the existence of Puritan women. I don't think there is a woman in the world who would not be a little flattered if one made love to her. It is that which makes women so irresistibly adorable.

❦ Good women have such limited views of life, their horizon is so small, their interests are so petty.

❦ Like all stout women, she looks the very picture of happiness.

❦ She'll never love you unless you are always at her heels; women like to be bothered.

❦ How fond women are of doing dangerous things! It is one of the qualities in them that I admire most. A woman will flirt with anybody in the world as long as other people are looking on.

❦ Plain women are always jealous of their husbands. Beautiful women never have time. They are always so occupied in being jealous of other people's husbands.

❦ My dear Margaret, what a handsome woman your husband has been dancing with! I should be quite jealous if I were you! Is she a great friend of yours?

❦ JACK: I'll bet you anything you like that half an hour after they have met, they will be calling each other sister.
   ALGERNON: Women only do that when they have called each other a lot of other things first.

❦ Ordinary women never appeal to one's imagination. They are limited to their century. No glamour ever transfigures them. One knows their minds as easily as one knows their bonnets. There is no mystery in any of them. They ride in the park in the morning and chatter at tea parties in the afternoon. They have their stereotyped smile and their fashionable mauve.

❦ Women should not be idle in their homes,
   For idle fingers make a thoughtless heart.

❦ A perfect saint amongst women, but so dreadfully dowdy that she reminded me of a badly bound hymn-book.

❦ She has exquisite feet and hands, is always *bien chaussée et bien gantée*, and can talk brilliantly upon any subject, provided that she knows nothing about it.

❦ Thirty-five is a very attractive age. London society is full of women of the very highest birth who have, of their own free choice, remained thirty-five for years. Lady Dumbleton is an instance in point. To my own knowledge she has been thirty-five ever since she arrived at the age of forty, which was many years ago now.

❦ It is perfectly brutal the way most women nowadays behave to men who are not their husbands.

❦ Women forgive adoration; that is quite as much as should be expected from them.

❦ Our husbands never appreciate anything in us. We have to go to others for that.

❦ I wouldn't marry a man with a future before him for anything under the sun.

❦ MRS ALLONBY: We women adore failures. They lean on us.

❦ Women defend themselves by attacking, just as they attack by sudden and strange surrender.

❦ LORD CAVERSHAM: No woman, plain or pretty, has any common sense at all, sir. Common sense is the privilege of our sex.

❦ Women are a decorative sex. They never have anything to say, but they say it charmingly. Women represent the triumph of matter over mind, just as men represent the triumph of mind over morals.

❦ I don't mind plain women being Puritans. It is the only excuse they have for being plain.

❦ Women love us for our defects. If we have enough of them, they will forgive us everything, even our own gigantic intellects.

❦ COLONEL: Can she read and write?
PETER: Ay, that she can, sir.
COLONEL: Then she is a dangerous woman. No peasant should be allowed to do anything of the kind.

❦ My dear young lady, there was a great deal of truth, I dare say, in what you said, and you looked very pretty while you said it, which is much more important.

❦ I don't believe in women thinking too much. Women should think in moderation, as they should do all things in moderation.

❦ American girls are as clever at concealing their parents as English women are at concealing their past.

❦ Women have no appreciation of good looks; at least good women have not.

❦ How hard good women are! How weak bad men are!

❦ No woman should have a memory. Memory in a woman is the beginning of dowdiness. One can always tell from a woman's bonnet whether she has got a memory or not.

❦ The three women I have most admired are Queen Victoria, Sarah Bernhardt and Lily Langtry. I would have married any one of them with pleasure. The first had great dignity, the second a lovely voice, the third a perfect figure.

❦ The one charm of the past is that it is past. But women never know when the curtain has fallen. They always want a sixth act, and as soon as the interest in the play is entirely over they propose to continue it.

❦ I am afraid that women appreciate cruelty, downright cruelty, more than anything else. They have wonderfully primitive instincts. We have emancipated them, but they remain slaves looking for their masters all the same.

❦ Every woman is a rebel, and usually in wild revolt against herself.

❦ Every woman does talk too much.

❦ The English young lady is the dragon of good taste.

❦ What have women who have not sinned to do with me, or I with them? We do not understand each other.

❦ Women are not meant to judge us, but to forgive us when we need forgiveness. Pardon not punishment is their mission.

❦ Most women in London, nowadays, seem to furnish their rooms with nothing but orchids, foreigners and French novels.

❦ She looks like a woman with a past. Most pretty women do.

❦ Women are the most reliable as they have no memory for the important.

❦ No man should have a secret from his own wife. She invariably finds it out. Women have a wonderful instinct about things. They discover everything except the obvious.

❦ GERALD: There are many different kinds of women, aren't there?

LORD ILLINGWORTH: Only two kinds in society: the plain and the coloured.

GERALD: But there are good women in society, aren't there?

LORD ILLINGWORTH: Far too many.

❦ The history of women is the history of the worst form of tyranny the world has ever known. The tyranny of the weak over the strong. It is the only tyranny that lasts.

❦ More women grow old nowadays through the faithfulness of their admirers than through anything else.

❦ Immoral women are rarely attractive. What made her quite irresistible was that she was unmoral.

❦ LORD ILLINGWORTH: What a typical woman you are! You talk sentimentally, and you are thoroughly selfish the whole time.

❦ It is said, of course, that she ran away twice before she was married. But you know how unfair people often are. I myself don't believe she ran away more than once.

❦ I have met hundreds of good women. I never seem to meet any but good women. The world is perfectly packed with good women. To know them is a middle-class education.

❦ Women, as some witty Frenchman once put it, inspire us with the desire to do masterpieces, and always prevent us from carrying them out.

❦ She was made to be an ambassador's wife. She certainly has a wonderful faculty of remembering people's names, and forgetting their faces.

❦ I am sick of women who love me. Women who hate me are much more interesting.

❦ No man has any real success in this world unless he has got women to back him, and women rule society. If you have not got women on your side, you are quite over. You might just as well be a barrister, or a stockbroker, or a journalist at once.

❦ There is one thing infinitely more pathetic than to have lost the woman one is in love with, and that is to have won her and found out how shallow she is.

❦ The only way to behave to a woman is to make love to her, if she is pretty, and to someone else, if she is plain.

❦ GERALD: It is very difficult to understand women, is it not?
LORD ILLINGWORTH: You should never try to understand them. Women are pictures. Men are problems.

❦ I don't think now that people can be divided into the good and the bad as though they were two separate races or creatures. What are called good women may have terrible things in them, mad moods of recklessness, assertion, jealousy, sin. Bad women, as they are termed, may have in them sorrow, repentance, pity, sacrifice.

❦ The most important consolation that women find in modern life is taking someone else's admirer when one loses one's own. In good society that always whitewashes a woman.

❦ MRS CHEVELEY: The strength of women comes from the fact that psychology cannot explain us. Men can be analysed and women . . . merely adored.

❦ Being adored is a nuisance. Women treat us just as humanity treats its gods. They worship us and are always asking us to do something for them.

❦ Men can love what is beneath them – things unworthy, stained, dishonoured. We women worship when we love; and when we lose our worship we lose everything.

❦ She is a peacock in everything but beauty.

❦ Women are never disarmed by compliments. Men always are. That is the difference between the sexes.

❦ That awful memory of woman! What a fearful thing it is! And what an utter intellectual stagnation it reveals! One should absorb the colour of life, but one should never remember its details. Details are always vulgar.

❦ I think there are many things women should never forgive.

❦ To the philosopher women represent the triumph of matter over mind, just as men represent the triumph of mind over morals.

❦ The only way a woman can ever reform a man is by boring him so completely that he loses all possible interest in life.

❦ If a woman can't make her mistakes charming she is only a female.

❦ It is only very ugly or very beautiful women who ever hide their faces.

❦ As long as a woman can look ten years younger than her own daughter she is perfectly satisfied.

❦ Women are wonderfully practical, much more practical than we are. In situations of that kind we often forget to say anything about marriage and they always remind us.

❦ Wicked women bother one. Good women bore one. That is the only difference between them.

❦ A poor woman who is not straight is a prostitute, but a rich one is a lady of fashion.

❦ Women are always on the side of morality, public and private.

❦ A chase after a beautiful woman is always exciting.

❦ In the case of very fascinating women, sex is a challenge not a defence.

❦ There is only one real tragedy in a woman's life. The fact that her past is always her lover, and her future invariably her husband.

❦ A woman whose size in gloves is seven and three-quarters never knows much about anything.

❦ I prefer women with a past. They're always so demned amusing to talk to.

❦ The plain women are very useful. If you want to gain a reputation for respectability, you have merely to take them down to supper. The other women are very charming. They commit one mistake, however. They paint in order to try and look young. Our grandmothers painted in order to try and talk brilliantly.

❦ MISS PRISM: A misanthrope I can understand – a womanthrope, never!

❦ Many a woman has a past, but I am told that she has at least a dozen, and that they all fit.

❦ Lady Henry Wotton was a curious woman, who was usually in love with somebody, and, as her passion was never returned, had kept all her illusions. She tried to look picturesque but only succeeded in being untidy, and her dresses always looked as if they had been designed in a rage and put on in a tempest.

❦ She is still *décolletée*. . .and when she is in a very smart gown she looks like an *édition de luxe* of a bad French novel.

❦ Lady Ruxton, an overdressed woman of forty-seven, with a hooked nose, who was always trying to get herself compromised, but was so peculiarly plain that to her great disappointment no one would ever believe anything against her.

❦ She was one of those people who think that if you say the same thing over and over a great many times it becomes true in the end.

❦ [She] talks more and says less than anybody I ever met. She is made to be a public speaker.

❧ They [women] always want one to be good. And if we are good when they meet us, they don't love us at all. They like to find us quite irretrievably bad, and to leave us quite unattractively good.

❧ When a man does exactly what a woman expects him to do she doesn't think much of him. One should always do what a woman doesn't expect, just as one should always say what she doesn't understand. The result is invariably perfect sympathy on both sides.

❧ A woman who can keep a man's love and love him in return has done all the world wants of women or should want of them.

❧ Talk to every woman as if you loved her, and to every man as if he bored you, and at the end of your first Season you will have the reputation of possessing the most perfect social tact.

❧ When a man has once loved a woman, he will do anything for her, except continue to love her.

❧ Men when they woo us call us pretty children,
Tell us we have not wit to make our lives.
And so they mar them for us. Did I say woo?
We are their chattels, and their common slaves,
Less dear than the poor hound that licks their hand,
Less fondled than the hawk upon their wrist.
Woo, did I say? bought rather, sold and bartered.

❧ If you want to know what a woman really means – which, by the way, is always a dangerous thing to do – look at her, don't listen to her.

❧ No woman should ever be quite accurate about her age. It looks so calculating.

❦ He's entrammelled by this woman – fascinated by her – dominated by her. If a woman wants to hold a man, she has merely to appeal to what is worst in him. We make gods of men and they leave us. Others make brutes of them and they fawn and are faithful.

❦ Perplexity and mistrust fan affection into passion, and so bring about those beautiful tragedies that alone make life worth living. Women once felt this, while men did not, and so women once ruled the world.

❦ These straw-coloured women have dreadful tempers.

❦ Never marry a woman with straw-coloured hair. They are so sentimental.

❦ You flatter her. She has her virtues as most women have, but beauty is a gem she may not wear.

❦ In the art of amusing men they are adepts, both by nature and education, and can actually tell a story without forgetting the point – an accomplishment that is extremely rare among the women of other countries.

❦ Young women of the present day seem to make it the sole object of their lives to be always playing with fire.

That Dreadful Universal Thing

❦ The more one analyses people, the more all reasons for analysis disappear. Sooner or later one comes to that dreadful universal thing called human nature.

❦ There is some flaw in each one of us.

❦ People who count their chickens before they are hatched, act very wisely, because chickens run about so absurdly that it is impossible to count them accurately.

❦ One can always be kind to people about whom one cares nothing. That is why English family life is so pleasant.

❦ It is absurd to divide people into good and bad. People are either charming or tedious.

❦ One's past is what one is. It is the only way by which people should be judged.

❦ There is more to be said for stupidity than people imagine. Personally, I have a great admiration for stupidity. It is a sort of fellow-feeling, I suppose.

❦ In the soul of one who is ignorant there is always room for a great idea.

❦ People who want to say merely what is sensible should say it to themselves before they come down to breakfast in the morning, never after.

❦ When people talk to us about others they are usually dull. When they talk to us about themselves they are nearly always interesting.

❦ People nowadays are so absolutely superficial that they don't understand the philosophy of the superficial.

❦ You ask me what is my feeling towards my audiences – towards the public. Which public? There are as many publics as there are personalities. I am not nervous on the night that I am producing a new play. I am exquisitely indifferent. My nervousness ends at the last dress rehearsal. I know then what effect my play, as presented upon the stage, has produced upon me. My interest in the play ends there, and I feel curiously envious of the public – they have such wonderfully fresh emotions in store for them. It is the public, not the play, that I desire to make a success. The public makes a success when it realises that a play is a work of art. On the three first nights I have had in London the public has been most successful, and, had the dimensions of the stage admitted of it, I would have called them before the curtain. The artist is always the munificent patron of the public.

❦ I am very fond of the public, and, personally, I always patronise the public very much.

❦ To influence a person is to give him one's own soul. He does not think his natural thoughts or burn with his natural passions. His virtues are not real to him. His sins, if there are such things as sins, are borrowed. He becomes an echo of someone else's music, an actor of a part that has not been written for him.

❦ Most women are so artificial that they have no sense of art. Most men are so natural that they have no sense of beauty.

❦ For those who are not artists, and to whom there is no mode of life but the actual life of fact, pain is the only door to perfection.

❦ The public clung with really pathetic tenacity to what I believe were the direct traditions of the Great Exhibition of international vulgarity, traditions that were so appalling that the houses in which people lived were only fit for blind people to live in.

❦ As a rule, people who act lead the most commonplace lives. They are good husbands or faithful wives, or something tedious.

❦ The one thing that the public dislike is novelty. Any attempt to extend the subject matter of art is extremely distasteful to the public.

❦ The English public like tediousness, and like things to be explained to them in a tedious way.

❦ The ugly and the stupid have the best of it in this world. They can sit at their ease and gape at the play. If they know nothing of victory, they are at least spared the knowledge of defeat.

❦ Whenever people talk to me about the weather, I always feel certain that they mean something else.

❦ There are only two kinds of people who are really fascinating – people who know absolutely everything and people who know absolutely nothing.

❦ It is only mediocrities and old maids who consider it a grievance to be misunderstood.

❦ He is fond of being misunderstood. It gives him a post of vantage.

❦ Incomprehensibility is a gift. Not everyone has it.

❦ It is curious how vanity helps the successful man and wrecks the failure.

❦ To be an egoist, one must have an ego. It is not everyone who says 'I, I' who can enter into the kingdom of art.

❦ Humility is for the hypocrite, modesty for the incompetent.

❦ Conceit is one of the privileges of the creative.

❦ Conceit is one of the greatest of the virtues, yet how few people recognise it as a thing to aim at and to strive after. In conceit many a man and woman has found salvation, yet the average person goes on all fours grovelling after modesty.

❦ It would be unfair to expect other people to be as remarkable as oneself.

❦ Philanthropic people lose all sense of humanity. It is their distinguishing characteristic.

❦ The man who sees both sides of a question is a man who sees absolutely nothing at all.

❦ Good people exasperate one's reason, bad people stir one's imagination.

❦ Most men and women are forced to perform parts for which they have no qualifications. Our Guildensterns play Hamlet for us, and our Hamlets have to jest like Prince Hal. The world is a stage, but the play is badly cast.

❦ The private lives of men and women should not be told to the public. The public have nothing to do with them at all.

❦ It is perfectly monstrous the way people go about nowadays saying things against one behind one's back that are absolutely and entirely true.

❦ What is a cynic? A man who knows the price of everything and the value of nothing.

❦ A sentimentalist is a man who sees an absurd value in everything, and doesn't know the market price of any single thing.

❦ Well bred people always stay in exactly the same place as we do.

❦ I'm sure I don't know half the people who come to my house. Indeed, from all I hear, I shouldn't like to.

❦ People are so annoying. All my pianists look exactly like poets; and all my poets look exactly like pianists.

❦ Oh! I don't care about the London season! It is too matrimonial. People are either hunting for husbands, or hiding from them.

❦ You can't go anywhere without meeting clever people. The thing has become an absolute public nuisance. I wish to goodness we had a few fools left.

❦ I like men who have a future and women who have a past.

❦ As for the people, what of them and their authority? Their authority is a thing blind, deaf, hideous, grotesque, tragic, amusing, serious and obscene. It is impossible for the artist to live with the people. All despots bribe. The people bribe and brutalise. Who told them to exercise authority? They were made to live, to listen and to love. Someone has done them a great wrong. They have taken the sceptre of the prince. How should they use it? They have taken the triple tiara of the Pope. How should they carry its burden? They are as a clown whose heart is broken. They are as a priest whose soul is not yet born. Let all who love beauty pity them.

❦ Though they themselves love not beauty, yet let them pity themselves. Who taught them the trick of tyranny?

❦ Nowadays most people die of a sort of creeping common sense, and discover when it is too late that the only things one never regrets are one's mistake.

❦ The inherited stupidity of the race – sound English common sense.

❦ Common sense is the enemy of romance.

❦ Anybody can have common sense, provided that they have no imagination.

❦ I love superstitions. They are the colour element of thought and imagination. They are the opponents of common sense.

❦ I like persons better than principles and I like persons with no principles better than anything else in the world.

❦ I never approve, or disapprove, of anything now. It is an absurd attitude to take towards life. We are not sent into the world to air our moral prejudices. I never take any notice of what common people say, and I never interfere with what charming people do.

❦ LORD HENRY: I like to find out people for myself. But Lady Brandon treats her guests exactly as an auctioneer treats his goods. She either explains them entirely away, or tells one everything about them except what one wants to know.

❦ If a novelist is base enough to go to life for his personages he should at least pretend that they are creations and not boast of them as copies.

❦ Anybody can act. Most people in England do nothing else.

❦ Why should not degrees be granted for good acting? Are they not given to those who misunderstand PLATO and who mistranslate ARISTOTLE?

❦ People go through their lives in a sort of coarse comfort, like petted animals, without ever realising that they are probably thinking other people's thoughts, living by other people's standards, wearing practically what one may call other people's second-hand clothes and never being themselves for a single moment.

❦ Most people are other people. Their thoughts are someone else's opinions, their lives a mimicry, their passions a quotation.

❦ I will predict, accurately, all human behaviour except that which governs the human heart.

❦ The real fool, such as the gods mock or mar, is he who does not know himself.

❦ The great things of life leave one unmoved. We regret the burden of their memory, and have anodynes against them. But the little things, the things of the moment, remain with us.

❦ Every little action of the common day makes or unmakes character . . . what one has done in the secret chamber one has someday to cry aloud on the housetops.

❦ Humanity will always love ROUSSEAU for having confessed his sins not to a priest but to the world.

❦ It is what we fear that happens to us.

❦ Great antipathy shows secret affinity.

❦ Whenever there is hatred between two people there is bond or brotherhood of some kind.

❦ Each of us has heaven and hell in him.

❧ All charming people, I fancy, are spoiled. It is the secret of their attraction.

❧ The public is largely influenced by the *look* of a book. So are we all. It is the only artistic thing about the public.

❧ Public opinion exists only when there are no ideas.

❧ We are never more true to ourselves than when we are inconsistent.

❧ If a man needs an elaborate tombstone in order to remain in the memory of his country, it is clear that his living at all was an act of absolute superfluity.

❧ I would not have about me shallow fools who with mean scruples weigh the gold of life and faltering, paltering, end by failure.

❧ Dullness is always an irresistible temptation for brilliancy, and stupidity is the permanent *bestia trionfans* that calls wisdom from its cave.

The One Thing Death Cannot Harm

❧ Art is the one thing which death cannot harm.

❧ An artist's heart is in his head.

❧ There are moments when art almost attains to the dignity of manual labour.

❧ It is only an auctioneer who can equally and impartially admire all schools of art.

❧ All art is immoral. For emotion for the sake of emotion is the aim of art, and emotion for the sake of action is the aim of life.

❧ All art is immoral, and all thought is dangerous.

❧ The best that one can say of most modern creative art is that it is just a little less vulgar than reality.

❧ Life by its realism is always spoiling the subject-matter of art.

❧ What is abnormal in life stands in normal relations to art. It is the only thing in life that stands in normal relations to art.

❧ A subject that is beautiful in itself gives no suggestion to the artist. It lacks imperfection.

❦ Art is the only serious thing in the world. And the artist is the only person who is never serious.

❦ There is nothing that art cannot express.

❦ No artist is ever morbid. The artist can express everything.

❦ To know the principles of the highest art is to know the principles of all the arts.

❦ It is sometimes said that the tragedy of an artist's life is that he cannot realise his ideal. But the true tragedy that dogs the steps of most artists is that they realise their ideal too absolutely. For when the ideal is realised, it is robbed of its wonder and its mystery, and becomes simply a new starting-point for an ideal that is other than itself.

❦ It is a mistake to think that the passion one feels in creation is ever really shown in the work one creates. Art is always more abstract than we fancy. Form and colour tell us of form and colour – that is all.

❦ An age that has no criticism is either an age in which art is immobile, hieratic and confined to the reproduction of formal types or an age that possesses no art at all.

❦ In art, as in politics, there is but one origin for all revolutions, a desire on the part of man for a nobler form of life, for a freer method and opportunity of expression.

❦ We are overrun by a set of people who, when a poet or painter passes away, arrive at the house along with the undertaker and forget that their one duty is to behave as mutes.

❦ Art is the most intense mode of individualism that the world has known.

❧ Art is to a certain degree a mode of acting, an attempt to realise one's own personality on some imaginative plane out of the reach of the trammelling accidents and limitations of real life.

❧ We have no right to quarrel with an artist for the conditions under which he chooses to present his work.

❧ Varnishing is the only artistic process with which the Royal Academicians are thoroughly familiar.

❧ We can forgive a man for making a useful thing as long as he does not admire it. The only excuse for making a useless thing is that one admires it intensely. All art is quite useless.

❧ An artist should create beautiful things, but should put nothing of his own life into them. We live in an age when men treat art as if it were meant to be a form of auto-biography. We have lost the abstract sense of beauty.

❧ The only people a painter should know are people who are an artistic pleasure to look at and an intellectual repose to talk to.

❧ Mediocrity weighing mediocrity in the balance, and incompetence applauding its brother – that is the spectacle which the artistic activity of England affords us from time to time.

❧ Modern pictures are, no doubt, delightful to look at. At least, some of them are. But they are quite impossible to live with; they are too clever, too assertive, too intellectual. Their meaning is too obvious, and their method too clearly defined. One exhausts what they have to say in a very short time, and then they become as tedious as one's relations.

❧ The facts of art are divine, but the essence of artistic effect is unity.

❦ The true artist is a man who believes absolutely in himself, because he is absolutely himself.

❦ ERNEST: Simply this: that in the best days of art there were no art critics.
GILBERT: I seem to have heard that observation before, Ernest. It has all the vitality of error and all the tediousness of an old friend.

❦ The Renaissance was great because it sought to solve no social problem, and busied itself not about such things, but suffered the individual to develop freely, beautifully and naturally and so had great and individual artists and great and individual men.

❦ I am very fond of the work of some of the impressionist painters of Paris and London. For a class that welcomes the incompetent with sympathetic eagerness, and that confuses the bizarre with the beautiful, and vulgarity with truth, they are extremely accomplished. They can do etchings that have the brilliancy of epigrams, pastels that are as fascinating as paradoxes, and as for their portraits, whatever the commonplace may say against them, no one can deny that they possess that unique and wonderful charm which belongs to pure fiction.

❦ Bad artists always admire each other's work. They call it being large-minded and free from prejudice. But a truly great artist cannot conceive of life being shown, or beauty fashioned, under any conditions other than those he has selected.

❦ Most of our modern portrait painters are doomed to oblivion. They never paint what they see. They paint what the public sees, and the public never sees anything.

❦ Things are because we see them, and what we see, and how we see it depends on the arts that have influenced us. At present, people see fogs, not because there are fogs, but because poets and painters have taught them the mysterious loveliness of such effects. There may have been fogs for centuries in London. I dare say there were. But no one saw them, and so we do not know anything about them. They did not exist till art had invented them. Now, it must be admitted, fogs are carried to excess. They have become the mere mannerism of a clique, and the exaggerated realism of their method gives dull people bronchitis. Where the cultured catch an effect, the uncultured catch cold.

❦ The Academy is too large and too vulgar. Whenever I have gone there, there have been either so many people that I have not been able to see the pictures, which was dreadful, or so many pictures that I have not been able to see the people, which was worse.

❦ Paradox though it may seem – and paradoxes are always dangerous things – it is none the less true that life imitates art far more than art imitates life. This results not merely from life's imitative instinct, but from the fact that the self-conscious aim of life is to find expression, and that art offers certain beautiful forms through which it may realise that energy. It is a theory that has never been put forward before, but it is extremely fruitful, and throws an entirely new light upon the history of art.

❦ It follows, as a corollary from this, that external nature also imitates art. The only effects she can show us are effects that we have already seen through poetry, or in paintings. This is the secret of nature's charm, as well as the explanation of nature's weakness.

❦ The public imagine that because they are interested in their immediate surroundings art should be interested in them also and should take them as her subject matter. But the mere fact that they are interested in these things makes them unsuitable subjects for art.

❦ No great artist ever sees things as they really are. If he did he would cease to be an artist.

❦ She is like most artists; she is all style without any sincerity.

❦ Nature is elbowing her way into the charmed circle of art.

❦ Nobody of any real culture ever talks about the beauty of a sunset. Sunsets are quite old-fashioned. They belong to the time when Turner was the last note in art. To admire them is a distinct sign of provincialism. Upon the other hand they go on. Yesterday evening Mrs Arundel insisted on my going to the window and looking at the glorious sky, as she called it. Of course I had to look at it. She is one of those absurdly pretty philistines, to whom one can deny nothing. And what was it? It was simply a very second-rate Turner, a Turner of bad period, with all the painter's worst faults exaggerated and over-emphasised.

❦ In art, the public accept what has been because they cannot alter it, not because they appreciate it. They swallow their classics whole and never taste them.

❦ Art's first appeal is neither to the intellect nor to the emotions, but purely to the artistic temperament.

❦ There are two worlds – the one exists and is never talked about; it is called the real world because there is no need to talk about it in order to see it. The other is the world of art; one must talk about that because otherwise it would not exist.

❦ Mr Quiller is entirely free from affectation of any kind. He rollicks through art with the recklessness of the tourist and describes its beauties with the enthusiasm of the auctioneer. To many, no doubt, he will seem to be somewhat blatant and bumptious, but we prefer to regard him as being simply British.

❧ Art is not something which you can take or leave. It is a necessity of human life.

❧ It is proper that limitations should be placed on action. It is not proper that limitations should be placed on art. To art belongs all things that are and things that are not, and even the editor of a London paper has no right to restrain the freedom of art in the selection of subject-matter.

❧ Art is the mathematical result of the emotional desire for beauty.

❧ It is through art, and through art only, that we can realise our perfection; through art, and through art only, that we can shield ourselves from the sordid perils of actual existence.

❧ We spend our days, each one of us, in looking for the secret of life. Well, the secret of life is in art.

❧ The work of art is to dominate the spectator: the spectator is not to dominate the work of art. The spectator is to be receptive. He is to be the violin on which the master is to play. And the more completely he can suppress his own silly views, his own foolish prejudices, his own absurd ideas of what art should be, the more likely he is to understand and appreciate the work of art in question.

❧ The meaning of any beautiful created thing is at least as much in the soul of him who looks at it, as it was in his soul who wrought it. Nay, it is rather the beholder who lends to the beautiful thing its myriad meanings, and makes it marvellous for us, and sets it in some new relation to the age, so that it becomes a vital portion of our lives and a symbol of what we pray for, or perhaps of what, having prayed for, we fear that we may receive.

❧ That is the mission of true art – to make us pause and look at a thing a second time.

❦ The aim of art is no more to give pleasure than to give pain. The aim of art is to be art.

❦ There are works which wait, and which one does not understand for a long time; the reason is that they bring answers to questions which have not yet been raised; for the question often arrives a terribly long time after the answer.

❦ There is no mood or passion that art cannot give us, and those of us who have discovered her secret can settle beforehand what our experience is going to be. We can choose our day and select our hour.

❦ All good work looks perfectly modern: a piece of Greek sculpture, a portrait of Velázquez – they are always modern, always of our time.

❦ No art is better than bad art.

❦ It is very curious the connection between faith and bad art: I feel it myself.

❦ In art good intentions are not the smallest value. All bad art is the result of good intentions.

❦ Art must be loved for its own sake, and not criticised by a standard of morality.

❦ The sign of a philistine age is the cry of immorality against art.

❦ No art ever survived censorship; no art ever will.

❦ Diversity of opinion about a work of art shows that the work is new, complex and vital.

❦ It is a consolation to know, however, that such an artist as MADAME BERNHARDT has not only worn that yellow, ugly dress but has been photographed in it.

❧ The gods bestowed on MAX [BEERBOHM] the gift of perpetual old age.

❧ No artist has ethical sympathies. An ethical sympathy in an artist is an unpardonable mannerism of style.

❧ Jimmy [JAMES WHISTLER] explains things in the newspapers. Art should always remain mysterious. Artists, like gods, must never leave their pedestals.

❧ WHISTLER is indeed one of the very greatest masters of painting in my opinion. And I may add that in this opinion MR WHISTLER himself entirely concurs.

❧ WHISTLER left America in order to remain an artist, and MR SARGENT to become one.

❧ MR WHISTLER has found in [biographer] MR WALTER DOWDESWELL the most ardent of admirers, indeed, we might almost say the most sympathetic of secretaries.

❧ MR WHISTLER always spelt art, and we believe still spells it, with a capital 'I'. However, he was never dull. His brilliant wit, his caustic satire, and his amusing epigrams, or perhaps we should say epitaphs, on his contemporaries made his views on art as delightful as they were misleading, and as fascinating as they were unsound.

❧ As for borrowing MR WHISTLER's ideas about art, the only thoroughly original ideas I have ever heard him express have had reference to his own superiority as a painter over painters greater than himself.

❧ Last night, at Prince's Hall, MR WHISTLER made his first public appearance as a lecturer on art, and spoke for more than an hour with really marvellous eloquence on the absolute uselessness of all lectures of the kind.

❦   In fairness to the audience, however, I must say that they
      seemed extremely gratified at being rid of the dreadful
      responsibility of admiring anything, and nothing could
      have exceeded their enthusiasm when they were told by
      Mr Whistler that no matter how vulgar their dresses
      were, or how hideous their surroundings at home, still it
      was possible that a great painter, if there was such a thing,
      could, by contemplating them in the twilight, and half-
      closing his eyes, see them under really picturesque
      conditions, and produce a picture which they were not to
      attempt to understand, much less to enjoy.

❦   Admirable as are Mr Whistler's fireworks on canvas, his
      fireworks in prose are abrupt, violent and exaggerated.

❦   The only artists I have ever known who are personally
      delightful are bad artists; good artists exist simply in what
      they make and consequently are perfectly uninteresting in
      what they are.

❦   We try to improve the conditions of the race by means of
      good air, free sunlight, wholesome water, and hideous bare
      buildings for the better housing of the lower orders. But
      these things merely produce health, they do not produce
      beauty. For this, art is required, and the true disciples of
      the great artist are not his studio-imitators but those who
      become like his work of art, be they plastic as in Greek days
      or pictorial as in modern times; in a word, life is art's best,
      art's only pupil.

❦   Art finds her own perfection within, and not outside of,
      herself. She is not to be judged by any external standard of
      resemblance. She is a veil rather than a mirror. She has
      flowers that no forests know of, birds that no woodland
      possesses. She makes and unmakes many worlds, and can
      draw the moon from heaven with a scarlet thread. Hers are
      the 'forms more real than living man', and hers the great
      archetypes, of which things that have existence are but
      unfinished copies. Nature has, in her eyes, no laws, no

uniformity. She can work miracles at her will, and when she calls monsters from the deep they come. She can bid the almond tree to blossom in winter and send the snow upon the ripe cornfield. At her word the frost lays its silver finger on the burning mouth of June and the winged lions creep out from the hollows of the Lydian hills. The dryads peer from the thicket as she passes by and the brown fauns smile strangely at her when she comes near them. She has hawk-faced gods that worship her and the centaurs gallop at her side.

❧ The public make use of the classics of a country as a means of checking the progress of art. They degrade the classics into authorities. They use them as bludgeons for preventing the expression of beauty in new forms. They are always asking a writer why he does not write like somebody else, or a painter why he does not paint like somebody else, quite oblivious of the fact that if either of them did anything of the kind he would cease to be an artist.

❧ There are fashions in art just as there are fashions in dress, and perhaps none of us can quite free ourselves from the influence of custom and the influence of novelty.

❧ There are two ways of disliking art. One is to dislike it. The other is to like it rationally.

❧ The only portraits in which one believes are portraits where there is very little of the sitter and a very great deal of the artist.

❧ Nature is always behind the age. It takes a great artist to be thoroughly modern.

❧ In a very ugly and sensible age the arts borrow not from life but from each other.

❧ Popularity is the crown of laurel which the world puts on bad art. Whatever is popular is wrong.

Remark on seeing WILLIAM FRITH's *vast painting*, Derby Day:
❧ Is it really *all* done by hand?

❧ The great superiority of France over England is that in France every bourgeois wants to be an artist, whereas in England every artist wants to be a bourgeois.

❧ Most of our elderly English painters spend most of their wicked wasted lives in poaching upon the domain of the poets, marring their motives by clumsy treatment, and striving to render by visible form or colour the marvel of what is invisible, the splendour of what is not seen. Their pictures are, as a natural consequence, insufferably tedious. They have degraded the invisible arts into the obvious arts and the only thing not worth looking at is the obvious.

❧ On the staircase stood several Royal Academicians disguised as artists.

❧ Elsewhere on the walls of this delightful exhibition we notice . . . the [CHARLES] LESLIES and the MARCUS STONES have all that faint and fading prettiness that makes us long for the honest ugliness of naturalism; of the work of that poetic school of artists who imagine that the true way of idealising a sitter is to paint the portrait of somebody else.

❧ The originality which we ask from the artist is originality of treatment, not of subject. It is only the unimaginative who ever invent. The true artist is known by the use he makes of what he annexes, and he annexes everything.

❧ Art never expresses anything but itself. It has an independent life, just as thought has, and develops purely on its own lines. It is not necessarily realistic in an age of realism, nor spiritual in an age of faith. So far from being the creation of its time, it is usually in direct opposition to it, and the only history it preserves for us is the history of its own progress. Sometimes it returns upon its footsteps and revives some antique form, as happened in the archaistic movement of late Greek art and in the Pre-Raphaelite movement of our own day. At other times it entirely anticipates its age and produces in one century work that it takes another century to understand, to appreciate and to enjoy. In no case does it reproduce its age. To pass from the art of a time to the time itself is the great mistake that all historians commit.

❦ All bad art comes from returning to life and nature, and elevating them to ideals. Life and nature may sometimes be used as part of art's rough material, but before they are of any real service to art they must be translated into artistic conventions. The moment art surrenders its imaginative medium it surrenders everything. As a method, realism is a complete failure, and the two things that every artist should avoid are modernity of form and modernity of subject matter. To us, who live in the nineteenth century, any century is a suitable subject for art except our own. The only beautiful things are the things that do not concern us. It is exactly because Hecuba is nothing to us that her sorrows are so suitable a motive for tragedy. Besides it is only the modern that ever becomes old-fashioned. Life goes faster than realism, but romanticism is always in front of life.

❦ Lying, the telling of beautiful untrue things, is the proper aim of art.

❦ No artist desires to prove anything. Even things that are true can be proved.

❦ No spectator of art needs a more perfect mood of receptivity than the spectator of a play. The moment he seeks to exercise authority he becomes the avowed enemy of art, and of himself. Art does not mind. It is he who suffers.

❦ Only mediocrities progress. An artist revolves in a cycle of masterpieces, the first of which is no less perfect than the last.

❦   That curious mixture of bad painting and good intentions that always entitles a man to be called a representative British artist.

❦   To fail and to die young is the only hope for a Scotsman who wishes to remain an artist.

❦   One touch of nature may make the whole world kin, but two touches of nature will destroy any work of art.

❦   The more we study art, the less we care for nature. What art really reveals to us is nature's lack of design, her curious crudities, her extraordinary monotony, her absolutely unfinished condition. Nature has good intentions, of course, but, as ARISTOTLE once said, she cannot carry them out.

❦   It is fortunate for us, however, that nature is so imperfect, as otherwise we should have had no art at all. Art is our spirited protest, our gallant attempt to teach nature her proper place. As for the infinite variety of nature, that is a pure myth. It is not to be found in nature herself. It resides in the imagination or fancy or cultivated blindness of the man who looks at her.

❦   The proper school to learn art is not life but art.

❦   Philosophy may teach us to bear with equanimity the misfortunes of our neighbours, and science resolve the moral sense into a secretion of sugar, but art is what makes the life of each citizen a sacrament.

❦   To reveal art and conceal the artist is art's aim.

❦   He finds that literature is an inadequate expression of life. That is quite true: but a work of art is an adequate expression of art – that is its aim. Only that. Life is merely the motif of a pattern.

❦   The public has always, and in every age, been badly brought up. They are continually asking art to be popular, to please their want of taste, to flatter their absurd vanity, to tell them what they have been told before, to show them what they ought to be tired of seeing, to amuse them when they feel heavy after eating too much, and to distract their thoughts when they are wearied of their own stupidity. Now art should never try to be popular. The public should try to make itself artistic.

❦ It is the spectator, and not life, that art really mirrors.

❦ All art is at once surface and symbol. Those who go beneath the surface do so at their peril. Those who read the symbol do so at their peril.

❦ The artist is the creator of beautiful things.

❦ On the afternoon of Easter Day I heard vespers at the Lateran: music quite lovely; at the close a bishop in red, with red gloves – such as [WALTER] PATER talks of in *Gaston de Latour* – came out on the balcony and showed us the relics. He was swarthy, and wore a yellow mitre. A sinister medieval man, but superbly Gothic, just like the bishop carved on stalls or on portals. And when one thinks that once people mocked at stained-glass attitudes! They are the only attitudes for the clothed. The sight of this bishop, whom I watched with fascination, filled me with the sense of the great realism of Gothic art. Neither in Greek nor in Gothic art is there any pose. Posing was invented by bad portrait painters, and the first person who posed was a stockbroker, and he has gone on ever since.

❦ On the whole, then, the Royal Academicians have never appeared under more favourable conditions than in this pleasant gallery. MR [HARRY] FURNISS has shown that the one thing lacking in them is a sense of humour, and that if they would not take themselves so seriously they might produce work that would be a joy, and not a weariness, to the world. Whether or not they will profit by the lesson, it is difficult to say, for dullness has become the basis of respectability, and seriousness the only refuge of the shallow.

❦ Artists, like the Greek gods, are revealed only to one another.

❦ A really great artist can never judge of other people's work at all, and can hardly, in fact, judge of his own. That very concentration of vision that makes a man an artist limits by its sheer intensity his faculty of fine appreciation. The energy of creation hurries him blindly on to his own goal. The wheels of his chariot raise the dust of a cloud around him. The gods are hidden from each other. They recognise only their worshippers.

❦ The moment that an artist takes notice of what other people want, and tries to supply the demand, he ceases to be an artist, and becomes a dull or an amusing craftsman, an honest or a dishonest tradesman.

❦ Alone, without any reference to his neighbours, without any interference the artist can fashion a beautiful thing; and if he does not do it solely for his own pleasure, he is not an artist at all.

❦ The only thing that the artist cannot see is the obvious. The only thing that the public can see is the obvious. The result is the criticism of the journalist.

❦ The more the public is interested in artists, the less it is interested in art. The personality of the artist is not a thing the public should know anything about.

❦ The English public, as usual hypocritical, prudish and philistine, has not known how to find the art in the work of art; it has searched for the man in it. Since it always confuses the man and his creation, it thinks that to create Hamlet you must be a little melancholy, to imagine Lear completely mad.

❦ How can a man who regards success as a goal of life be a true artist?

❦ Insincerity and treachery somehow seem inseparable from the artistic temperament.

❦ Vice and virtue are to the artist materials for an art.

❦ The young artist who paints nothing but beautiful things misses one half of the world.

❦ Nothing is more dangerous to the young artist than any conception of ideal beauty: he is constantly led by it either into weak prettiness or lifeless abstraction.

❦ The greatest artists are stupid and tiresome men as a rule.

❦ In New York, and even in Boston, a good model is so great a rarity that most of the artists are reduced to painting Niagara and millionaires.

❦ The English models are a well-behaved and hard-working class, and if they are much more interested in artists than they are in art a large section of the public is in the same condition, and most of our modern exhibitions seem to justify its choice.

❦ The word 'natural' means all that is middle class, all that is of the essence of jingoism, all that is colourless and without form and void. It might be a beautiful word, but it is the most debased coin in the currency of language.

❦ The word 'practical' is nearly always the last refuge of the uncivilised.

❦ Psychology is in its infancy as a science. I hope, in the interests of art, it will always remain so.

❦ As long as a painter is a painter merely, he should not be allowed to talk of anything but mediums and megilp, and on those subjects should be compelled to hold his tongue.

❧ The domestic virtues are not the true basis of art, though they may serve as an excellent advertisement for second-rate artists.

❧ As for SIR FREDERICK LEIGHTON, he has rarely been seen to more advantage than in the specimen of his work that MR FURNISS has so kindly provided for him. His *Pygmalion and Galatea in the Lowther Arcadia* (No. 49) has all that wax-doll grace of treatment that is so characteristic of his best work, and is eminently suggestive of the president's earnest and continual struggles to discover the difference between chalk and colour.

❧ MR FRITH, who has done so much to elevate painting to the dignity of photography, sends a series of five pictures exemplifying that difference between virtue and vice which moralists have never been able to discover, but which is the real basis of the great Drury Lane school of melodrama. The whole series is like the very finest platitude from the pulpit, and shows clearly the true value of didactic art.

❧ That an artist will find beauty in ugliness, *le beau dans l'horrible*, is now a commonplace of the schools, the argot of the atelier, but I strongly deny that charming people should be condemned to live with magenta ottomans and Albert-blue curtains in their rooms in order that some painter may observe the sidelights on the one and the values of the other.

❧ The moral life of man forms part of the subject-matter of the artist, but the morality of art consists in the perfect use of an imperfect medium.

❧ He was a painter. Indeed, few people escape that nowadays.

❧ MR BOUGHT's *Newest England, Tarred with an American Brush* is, as the catalogue remarks, somewhat low in tone, though high in price.

❦ In every sphere of life form is the beginning of things. Forms are the food of faith, cried [CARDINAL JOHN HENRY] NEWMAN, in one of those great moments of sincerity that make us admire and know the man. He was right, though he may not have known how terribly right he was. The Creeds are believed not because they are rational but because they are repeated. Yes; form is everything. It is the secret of life. Find expression for a sorrow and it will become dear to you. Find expression for a joy and you intensify its ecstasy. Do you wish to love? Use love's litany and the words will create the yearning from which the world fancies that they spring. Have you a grief that corrodes your heart? Learn its utterance from Prince Hamlet and you will find that mere expression is a mode of consolation and that form, which is the birth of passion, is also the death of pain. And so to return to the sphere of art, it is form that creates not merely the critical temperament but also the aesthetic instinct that reveals to one all things under the condition of beauty. Start with the worship of form and there is no secret in art that will not be revealed to you.

❦ Some resemblance the creative work of the critic will have to the work that has stirred him to creation, but it will be such resemblance as exists, not between nature and the mirror that the painter of landscape or figure may be supposed to hold up to her, but between nature and the work of the decorative artist. Just as on the flowerless carpets of Persia tulip and rose blossom indeed, and are lovely to look on, though they are not reproduced in visible shape or line, so the critic reproduces the work that he criticises in a mode that is never imitative, and part of whose charm may really consist in the rejection of resemblance, and shows us in this way not merely the meaning but also the mystery of beauty, and by transforming each art into literature solves once and for all the problem of art's unity.

❦ Art itself is really a form of exaggeration; and selection, which is the very spirit of art, is nothing more than an intensified mode of over emphasis.

❧ Art creates an incomparable and unique effect, and having done so passes on to other things. Nature, on the other hand, forgetting that imitation can be made the sincerest form of insult, keeps on repeating the effect until we all become absolutely wearied of it.

❧ The popular cry of our time is: Let us return to life and nature, they will recreate art for us and send the red blood coursing through her veins; they will shoe her feet with swiftness and make her hand strong. But, alas! we are mistaken in our amiable and well-meant efforts. Nature is always behind the age. And as for life, she is the solvent that breaks up art, the enemy that lays waste her house.

❧ The spirit of an age may be best expressed in the abstract ideal arts, for the spirit itself is abstract and ideal.

❧ As long as a thing is useful or necessary to us or affects us in any way, either for pain or pleasure, or appeals strongly to our sympathies or is a vital part of the environment in which we live, it is outside the proper sphere of art.

❧ When art is more varied nature will, no doubt, be more varied also.

❧ Art begins with abstract decoration, with purely imaginative and pleasurable work dealing with what is unreal and non-existent. This is the first stage. Then life becomes fascinated with this new wonder, and asks to be admitted into the charmed circle. Art takes life as part of her rough material, recreates it and refashions it in fresh forms; is absolutely indifferent to fact; invents, imagines, dreams, and keeps between herself and reality the impenetrable barrier of beautiful style, of decorative or ideal treatment. The third stage is when life gets the upper hand and drives art out into the wilderness. This is the true decadence, and it is from this that we are now suffering.

❦ Life holds the mirror up to art, and either reproduces some strange type imagined by painter or sculptor or realises in fact what has been dreamed in fiction.

❦ It has often been made a subject of reproach against artists that they are lacking in wholeness and completeness of nature. As a rule this must necessarily be so. That very concentration of vision which is the characteristic of the artistic temperament is in itself a mode of limitation. To those who are preoccupied with the beauty of form nothing else seems of so much importance.

❦ The soul of woman is beauty, as the soul of man is strength. If the two could be combined in the one being we should have the perfection sought by art since art began.

A Mauvais Quart d'Heure

❧ Life is simply a *mauvais quart d'heure* made up of exquisite moments.

❧ Nowadays people seem to look on life as a speculation. It is not a speculation. It is a sacrament. Its ideal is love. Its purification is sacrifice.

❧ One is sure to be disappointed if one tries to get romance out of modern life.

❧ One's own soul and the passions of one's friends – those are the fascinating things of life.

❧ All that one should know about modern life is where the duchesses are; anything else is quite demoralising.

❧ Life is not governed by will or intention. Life is a question of the nerves and fibres and slowly built-up cells in which thought hides itself and passion has its dreams.

❧ In these modern days to be vulgar, illiterate, common and vicious seems to give a man a marvellous infinity of rights that his father never dreamed of.

❧ Life is much too important a thing ever to talk seriously about it.

❧ The Book of Life begins with a man and woman in a garden. It ends with Revelations.

❧ One's real life is so often the life that one does not lead.

❦ To live is the rarest thing in the world. Most people exist, that is all.

❦ No man ever came across two ideal things. Few come across one.

❦ To become the spectator of one's own life is to escape its suffering.

❦ There is no reason why a man should show his life to the world. The world does not understand things.

❦ I hope you don't think you have exhausted life. When a man says that, one knows that life has exhausted him.

❦ Public and private life are different things. They have different laws and move on different lines.

❦ Life is never fair, and perhaps it is a good thing for most of us that it is not.

❦ Death is not a god. He is only the servant of the gods.

❦ Everything is dangerous, if it wasn't so, life wouldn't be worth living.

❦ You must not find symbols in everything you see. It makes life impossible.

❦ The sure way of knowing nothing about life is to make oneself useful.

❦ Life! Life! Don't let us go to life for our fulfilment or our experience. It is a thing narrowed by circumstances, incoherent in its utterance, and without that fine correspondence of form and spirit which is the only thing that can satisfy the artistic and critical temperament. It makes us pay too high a price for its wares, and we purchase the meanest of its secrets at a cost that is monstrous and infinite.

❦ The world has been made by fools that wise men should live in it.

❦ Misfortunes one can endure – they come from outside, they are accidents. But to suffer for one's own faults – ah! – there is the sting of life!

❦ Whatever, in fact, is modern in our life we owe to the Greeks. Whatever is an anachronism is due to medievalism.

❦ To believe is very dull. To doubt is intensely engrossing. To be on the alert is to live; to be lulled into security is to die.

❦ When one is in town one amuses oneself. When one is in the country one amuses other people. It is excessively boring.

❦ Town life nourishes and perfects all the more civilised elements in man – Shakespeare wrote nothing but doggerel lampoon before he came to London and never penned a line after he left.

❦ One can only write in cities.

❦ I don't think anyone at all morally responsible for what he or she does at an English country house.

❦ GWENDOLEN: I had no idea there were any flowers in the country.
CECILY: Oh, flowers are as common here, Miss Fairfax, as people are in London.

❦ You have a town house, I hope? A girl with a simple, unspoiled nature, like Gwendolen, could hardly be expected to reside in the country.

❦ But somehow, I feel sure that if I lived in the country for six months, I should become so unsophisticated that no one would take the slightest notice of me.

❦ One of those utterly tedious amusements one only finds at an English country house on an English country Sunday.

❦ You have nothing to look at but chimney-pot hats, men with sandwich boards, vermilion letterboxes, and do that at the risk of being run over by an emerald-green omnibus.

❦ And then look at the depressing, monotonous appearance of any modern city, the sombre dress of men and women, the meaningless and barren architecture, the colourless and dreadful surroundings.

❦ Art is very difficult in this unlovely town of ours, where, as you go to work in the mornings, or return from it at eventide, you have to pass through street after street of the most foolish and stupid architecture that the world has ever seen; architecture . . . reducing three-fourths of the London houses to being, merely, like square boxes of the vilest proportions, as gaunt as they are grimy and as poor as they are pretentious.

❦ Egotism itself, which is so necessary to a proper sense of human dignity, is entirely the result of an indoor life. Out of doors one becomes abstract and impersonal.

❦ The philistine element in life is not the failure to understand art. Charming people such as fishermen, shepherds, ploughboys, peasants and the like know nothing about art and are the very salt of the earth.

❦ Even the disciple has his uses. He stands behind one's throne and at the moment of one's triumph whispers in one's ear that, after all, one is immortal.

❦ People should not mistake the means of civilisation for the end. The steam engine and the telephone depend entirely for their value on the use to which they are put.

❦ Whenever there exists a demand, there is *no* supply. This is the only law that explains the extraordinary contrast between the soul of man and man's surroundings. Civilisations continue because people hate them. A modern city is the exact opposite of what everyone wants. Nineteenth-century dress is the result of our horror of the style. The tall hat will last as long as people dislike it.

❦ What man has sought for is, indeed, neither pain nor pleasure, but simply life. Man has sought to live intensely, fully, perfectly. When he can do so without exercising restraint on others, or suffering it ever, and his activities are all pleasurable to him, he will be saner, healthier, more civilised, more himself. Pleasure is Nature's test, her sign of approval. When a man is happy he is in harmony with himself and his environment. The new individualism, for whose service socialism, whether it wills it or not, is working, will be perfect harmony. It will be what the Greeks sought for, but could not, except in thought, realise completely, because they had slaves, and fed them; it will be what the Renaissance sought for, but could not realise completely except in art, because they had slaves, and starved them. It will be complete, and through it each man will attain to his perfection. The new individualism is the new Hellenism.

❦ Laughter is the primeval attitude towards life – a mode of approach that survives only in artists and criminals.

❦ Give me the luxuries and anyone can have the necessaries.

❦ It is a very sad thing that nowadays there is so little useless information.

❦ 'Comfort,' said Mr Podgers, 'and modern improvements, and hot water laid on in every bedroom. Your Grace is quite right. Comfort is the only thing our civilisation can give us.'

❦ I have no ambition to be a popular hero, to be crowned with laurels one year and pelted with stones the next; I prefer dying peaceably in my own bed.

❦ A map of the world that does not include Utopia is not worth even glancing at, for it leaves out the one country at which humanity is always landing. And when humanity lands there, it looks out, and, seeing a better country, sets sail. Progress is the realisation of Utopias.

❦ What other people call one's past has, no doubt, everything to do with them, but absolutely nothing to do with oneself. The man who regards his past is a man who deserves to have no future to look forward to.

❦ It is because humanity has never known where it was going that it has never been able to find its way.

❦ When we have fully discovered the scientific laws that govern life, we shall realise that one person who has more illusions than the dreamer is the man of action.

❦ We live in an age that reads too much to be wise and thinks too much to be beautiful.

❦ The two weak points in our age are its want of principle and its want of profile.

❦ There are moments when one has to choose between living one's own life, fully, entirely, completely – or dragging out some false, shallow, degrading existence that the world in its hypocrisy demands.

❦ If one doesn't talk about a thing it has never happened. It is expression that gives reality to things.

❦ Are we not better than chessmen, moved by an unseen power, vessels the potter fashions at his fancy, for honour or for shame?

❦ Many men prefer the primrose path of dalliance to the steep heights of duty.

❦ The longer one studies life and literature the more strongly one feels that behind everything that is wonderful stands the individual, and that it is not the moment that makes the man but the man who creates the age.

❦ There is the same world for all of us, and good and evil, sin and innocence, go through it hand in hand. To shut one's eyes to half of life that one may live securely is as though one blinded oneself that one might walk with more safety in a land of pit and precipice.

❦ I love acting. It is so much more real than life.

❦ Drama is the meeting-place of art and life.

❦ Nowadays we have so few mysteries left to us that we cannot afford to part with one of them.

❦ As for omens, there is no such thing as an omen. Destiny does not send us heralds. She is too wise or too cruel for that.

❦ When the gods wish to punish us they answer our prayers.

❦ Our business is to realise the world as we see it, not to reform it as we know it.

❦ To chop wood with any advantage to oneself or profit to others, one should not be able to describe the process – the natural life is the unconscious life. If I spent my future life reading Baudelaire in a café, I should be leading a more natural life than if I took to hedgers' work or planted cacao in mud-swamps!

❦ We can have in life but one great experience at best, and the secret of life is to reproduce that experience as often as possible.

❦ Ethics, like natural selection, make existence possible. Aesthetics, like sexual selection, make life lovely and wonderful, fill it with new forms and give it progress and variety and change.

❦ If a man treats life artistically, his brain is in his heart.

❦ There are few things easier than to live badly and to die well.

❦ One can live for years sometimes without living at all, and then all life comes crowding into one single hour.

❦ Much is given to some, and little is given to others. Injustice has parcelled out the world, nor is there equal division of aught save sorrow.

❦ How poor a bargain is the life of man, and in how mean a market are we sold.

❦ One's days are too brief to take the burden of another's sorrows on one's shoulders. Each man lives his own life, and pays his own price for living it. The only pity is that one has to pay so often for a single fault. One has to pay over and over again, indeed. In her dealings with man Destiny never closes her accounts.

❦ You always find out that one's most glaring fault is one's most important virtue. You have the most comforting views of life.

❦ Good taste is the excuse I've always given for leading such a bad life.

❦ Try as we may we cannot get behind things to the reality. And the terrible reason may be that there is no reality in things apart from their appearances.

❦ Nothing that actually occurs is of the smallest importance.

❦ Life is terribly deficient in form. Its catastrophes happen in the wrong way and to the wrong people. There is a grotesque horror about its comedies, and its tragedies seem to culminate in farce. One is always wounded when one approaches it. Things last either too long or not long enough.

❦ The chief thing that makes life a failure from this artistic point of view is the thing that lends life its sordid security, the fact that one can never repeat exactly the same emotion.

❦ It is only the gods who taste death. Apollo has passed away, but Hyacinth, whom men say he slew, lives on. Nero and Narcissus are always with us.

❦ You don't know what an existence they lead down there. It is pure, unadulterated country life. They get up early because they have so much to do, and go to bed early because they have so little to think about.

❦ We are each our own devil and we make this world our hell.

❦ Heaven is a despotism, I shall be at home there.

❦ Science can never grapple with the irrational. That is why it has no future before it, in this world.

❦ I am always astonishing myself. It is the only thing that makes life worth living.

❦ The world is simply divided into two classes – those who believe the incredible, like the public, and those who do the improbable.

❦ The world has always laughed at its own tragedies, that being the only way in which it has been able to bear them. Consequently, whatever the world has treated seriously belongs to the comedy side of things.

❦ Memory is the diary that we all carry about with us.

❦ Discontent is the first step in the progress of a man or a nation.

❦ Anybody can be good in the country. There are no temptations there. That is the reason why people who live out of town are so absolutely uncivilised. Civilisation is not by any means an easy thing to attain to. There are only two ways by which man can reach it. One is by being cultured, the other by being corrupt. Country people have no opportunity of being either, so they stagnate.

❦ One can survive everything nowadays, except death, and live down anything except a good reputation.

❦ Vulgarity and stupidity are two very vivid facts in modern life. One regrets them naturally. But there they are.

❦ Death and vulgarity are the only two facts in the nineteenth century that one cannot explain away.

❦ GWENDOLEN: Personally I cannot understand how anybody manages to exist in the country, if anybody who is anybody does. The country always bores me to death.
CECILY: Ah! This is what the newspapers call agricultural depression, is it not? I believe the aristocracy are suffering very much from it just at present.

❦ But the past is of no importance. The present is of no importance. It is with the future that we have to deal. For the past is what man should not have been. The present is what man ought not to be. The future is what artists are.

❦ He to whom the present is the only thing that is present knows nothing of the age in which he lives. To realise one's own century one must realise every century that has preceded it and that has contributed to its making.

❦ I wrote when I did not know life; now that I do know the meaning of life, I have no more to write. Life cannot be written; life can only be lived.

❦ Why does not science, instead of troubling itself about sunspots – which nobody ever saw, or, if they did, ought not to speak about – why does not science busy itself with drainage and sanitary engineering. Why does it not clean the streets and free the rivers from pollutants?

❦ Life is not complex. We are complex. Life is simple and the simple thing is the right thing.

❦ The world will not listen to me now. It is strange – I never thought it possible before – to regret that one has too much leisure: leisure which I used so to lack when I myself was a creator of beautiful things.

❦ I wish to look at life, not to become a monument for tourists . . . Privacy! . . . I have had two years of it . . . save for that other self the man I once was.

❦ Humanity takes itself too seriously. It is the world's original sin. If the cavemen had known how to laugh, history would have been different.

❦ In this world there are only two tragedies. One is not getting what one wants and the other is getting it. The last is much the worst – the last is a real tragedy.

❦ Life itself is an art and has its modes of style no less than the arts that seek to express it.

❦ The aim of life is self-development. To realise one's nature perfectly – that is what each of us is here for.

❦ One should live as if there were not death.

❦ Life cheats us with shadows, like a puppet-master. We ask it for pleasure. It gives it to us, with bitterness and disappointment in its train. We come across some noble grief that we think will lend the purple dignity of tragedy to our days but it passes away from us and things less noble take its place, and on some grey, windy dawn or odorous eve of silence and of silver we find ourselves looking with callous wonder or dull heart of stone at the tress of gold-flecked hair that we had once so wildly worshipped and so madly kissed.

❦ For he who lives more lives than one, more deaths than one must die.

❦ We are all in the gutter but some of us are looking at the stars.

❦ Between the famous and the infamous there is but one step, if so much as one.

❦ It often happens that the real tragedies of life occur in such an inartistic manner that they hurt us by their crude violence, their absolute incoherence, their absurd want of meaning, their entire lack of style. They affect us just as vulgarity affects us. They give us an impression of sheer brute force, and we revolt against that.

❦ Why is it that one runs to one's ruin? Why has destruction such a fascination?

❦ One needs misfortunes to live happily.

❦ To live in happiness, you must know some unhappiness in life.

❦ The secret of life is suffering.

❦ While to propose to be a better man is a piece of unscientific cant, to have become a *deeper* man is the privilege of those who have suffered.

❦   Success is a science; if you have the conditions, you get the result.

❦   In the common world of fact, the wicked are not punished nor the good rewarded. Success is given to the strong, failure thrust upon the weak.

❦   I think that in practical life there is something about success, actual success, that is a little unscrupulous, something about ambition that is unscrupulous always. Once a man has set his heart and soul on getting to a certain point, if he has to climb the crag, he climbs the crag; if he has to walk in the mire, he walks in the mire.

❦   There is something vulgar in all success. The greatest men fail – or seem to the world to have failed.

❦   Sometimes I think that the artistic life is a long and lovely suicide, and am not sorry that it is so.

❦   I don't believe in progress: but I do believe in the stagnation of human perversity.

❦   It is only in voluntary associations that man is fine.

❦   Nothing should be out of reach of hope. Life is hope.

More in One Single Hour

- Are there not books that can make us live more in one single hour than life can make us live in a score of shameful years?

- More than half of modern culture depends on what one shouldn't read.

- Since the introduction of printing, and the fatal development of the habit of reading amongst the middle and lower classes of this country, there has been a tendency in literature to appeal more and more to the eye and less and less to the ear.

- There is no such thing as a moral or an immoral book. Books are well written or badly written. That is all.

- I never travel without my diary. One should always have something sensational to read in the train.

- I have always had grave suspicions that the basis of all literary cliques is a morbid love of meat teas. That makes them sadly uncivilised.

- The ancient historians gave us delightful fiction in the form of fact; the modern novelist presents us with dull facts under the guise of fiction.

- One tires, at the end, of the work of individuals whose individuality is always noisy and generally uninteresting.

- People sometimes say that fiction is getting too morbid. As far as psychology is concerned it has never been morbid enough.

❦ The only link between literature and the drama left to us in England at the present moment is the bill of the play.

❦ In old days books were written by men of letters and read by the public. Nowadays books are written by the public and read by nobody.

❦ The actable value of a play has nothing whatsoever to do with its value as a work of art. It is not by the mimes that the muses are to be judged.

❦ No country produces such badly written fiction, such tedious, common work in the novel-form, such silly, vulgar plays as England.

❦ Well, I found myself seated in a horrid little private box, with a vulgar drop-scene staring me in the face. I looked out from behind the curtain, and surveyed the house. It was a tawdry affair, all cupids and cornucopias, like a third-rate wedding cake.

❦ Every word in a play has a musical as well as an intellectual value and must be made expressive of a certain emotion.

❦ Words have not merely music as sweet as that of viol and lute, colour as rich and vivid as any that makes lovely for us the canvas of the Venetian or the Spaniard, and plastic form no less sure and certain than that which reveals itself in marble or in bronze, but thought and passion and spirituality are theirs also – are theirs, indeed, alone.

❦ Poetry is for our highest moods, when we wish to be with the gods.

❦ Poetry should be like a crystal; it should make life more beautiful and less real.

❦ Poetry may be said to need far more self-restraint than prose. Its conditions are more exquisite. It produces its effects by more subtle means.

❦ There seems to be some curious connection between piety and poor rhymes.

❦ Every century that produces poetry is, so far, an artificial century, and the work that seems to us the most natural and simple product of its time is probably the result of the most deliberate and self-conscious effort.

❦ Most people become bankrupt through having invested too heavily in the prose of life. To have ruined oneself over its poetry is an honour.

❦ Books of poetry by young writers are usually promissory notes that are never met.

❦ Poets are always ahead of science; all the great discoveries of science have been stated before in poetry.

❦ A poet without hysterics is rare.

❦ Little poets are an extremely interesting study. The best of them have often some new beauty to show us and though the worst of them may bore yet they rarely brutalise.

❦ A poet can survive everything but a misprint.

❦ Even prophets correct their proofs.

❦ SHAKESPEARE, in the spirit of the true artist, accepts the facts of the antiquarian and converts them into dramatic and picturesque effects.

❦ This unfortunate aphorism about art holding the mirror up to nature is deliberately said by Hamlet in order to convince the bystanders of his absolute insanity in all art-matters.

❦ In point of fact, there is no such thing as SHAKESPEARE's Hamlet. If Hamlet has something of the definiteness of a work of art, he has also all the obscurity that belongs to life. There are as many Hamlets as there are melancholies.

❦ SHAKESPEARE might have met Rosencrantz and Guildenstern in the streets of London or seen the serving-men of rival houses bite their thumbs at each other in the open square, but Hamlet came out of his soul and Romeo out of his passion.

❦ M. ZOLA is determined to show that, if he has not got genius, he can at least be dull.

❦ Poor, silly, conceited MR SECRETARY PEPYS has chattered his way into the circle of the Immortals.

❦ M. GUY DE MAUPASSANT, with his keen mordant irony and his hard vivid style, strips life of the few poor rags that still cover her and shows us foul sore and festering wound. He writes lurid little tragedies in which everybody is ridiculous; bitter comedies at which one cannot laugh for very tears.

❦ MR RIDER HAGGARD, who really has, or had once, the makings of a perfectly magnificent liar, is now so afraid of being suspected of genius that when he does tell anything marvellous, he feels bound to invent a personal reminiscence and to put it into a footnote as a kind of cowardly corroboration.

❦ Only the great masters of style ever succeed in being obscure.

❦ There is no modern literature outside France.

❦ French prose, even in the hands of the most ordinary writers, is always readable, but English prose is detestable.

❦ To learn how to write English prose I have studied the prose of France.

❦ It was said of TROLLOPE that he increased the number of our acquaintances without adding to our visiting list; but after reading the *Comédie Humaine* [by BALZAC] one begins to believe that the only real people are the people who have never existed.

❦ To introduce real people into a novel or a play is a sign of an unimaginative mind, a coarse, untutored observation and an entire absence of style.

❦ The Celtic element in literature is extremely valuable, but there is absolutely no excuse for shrieking 'Shillelagh!' and 'O'Gorrah!'

❦ No one survives being over-estimated, nor is there any surer way of destroying an author's reputation than to glorify him without judgement and to praise him without tact.

❦ There is always something peculiarly impotent about the violence of a literary man. It seems to bear no reference to facts, for it is never kept in check by action. It is simply a question of adjectives and rhetoric, of exaggeration and over-emphasis.

❦ In the works of our own CARLYLE, whose *French Revolution* is one of the most fascinating historical novels ever written, facts are either kept in their subordinate position or else entirely excluded on the general ground of dullness.

❦ The cynic may mock at the subject of these verses, but we do not. Why not an ode on a knocker? Does not VICTOR HUGO's tragedy of *Lucrèce Borgia* turn on the defacement of a door plate? Mr Furlong must not be discouraged. Perhaps he will write poetry someday. If he does we would earnestly appeal to him to give up calling a cock 'proud chanticleer'.

❦ Between them HUGO and SHAKESPEARE have exhausted every subject. Originality is no longer possible – even in sin. So there are no real emotions left – only extraordinary adjectives.

❦ It was to his blindness, as an occasion, if not as a cause, that England's great poet owed much of the majestic movement and sonorous splendour of his later verse. When MILTON could no longer write he began to sing.

❧ WORDSWORTH went to the lakes, but he was never a lake poet. He found in stones the sermons he had already hidden there.

❧ It was his [JOHN RUSKIN's] prose I loved not his piety, his sympathy with the poor bored me.

❧ He [GEORGE MOORE] leads his readers to the latrine and locks them in.

❧ MATTHEW ARNOLD, a fine but very mistaken poet, was always trying to do the most impossible thing of all – to know himself. And that is why sometimes, in the middle of his most beautiful poems, he left off being the poet and became the school inspector.

❧ MR RUDYARD KIPLING – as one turns over the pages of his *Plain Tales from the Hills*, one feels as if one were seated under a palm tree reading life by superb flashes of vulgarity. The bright colours of the bazaars dazzle one's eyes. The jaded, second-rate Anglo-Indians are in exquisite incongruity with their surroundings. The mere lack of style of the storyteller gives an old journalistic realism to what he tells us. From the point of view of life, he is a reporter who knows vulgarity better than anyone has ever known it. DICKENS knew its clothes and its comedy. MR KIPLING knows its essence and its seriousness. He is our first authority on the second-rate and has seen marvellous things through keyholes, and his backgrounds are real works of art.

❧ One incomparable novelist we have now in England, MR GEORGE MEREDITH. There are better artists in France, but France has no one whose view of life is so large, so varied, so imaginatively true. There are tellers of stories in Russia who have a more vivid sense of what pain in fiction may be. But to him belongs philosophy in fiction. His people not merely live, but they live in thought. One can see them from myriad points of view. They are suggestive. There is a soul in them and around them. They are interpretative and symbolic. And he who made them, those wonderful, quickly moving figures, made them for his own pleasure, and never asked the public what they wanted, has never cared to know what they wanted, has never allowed the public to dictate to him or influence him in any way, but has gone on intensifying his own personality, and producing his own individual work. At first none came to him. That did not matter. Then the few came to him. That did not change him. The many have come now. He is still the same. He is an incomparable novelist.

❦ BALZAC was a most remarkable combination of the artistic temperament with the scientific spirit. A steady course of BALZAC reduces our living friends to shadows, and our acquaintances to the shadow of the shades. It is pleasanter to have the entrée to BALZAC's society than to receive cards from all the duchesses in Mayfair.

❦ MR HALL CAINE, it is true, aims at the grandiose, but then he writes at the top of his voice. He is so loud that one cannot hear what he says.

❦ MR ROBERT LOUIS STEVENSON, that delightful master of delicate and faithful prose. There is such a thing as robbing a story of its reality by trying to make it too true, and *The Black Arrow* is so inartistic as not to contain a single anachronism to boast of, while the transformation of Dr Jekyll reads dangerously like an experiment out of *The Lancet*.

❦ Shortly after Mr Stevenson published his curious psychological study of transformation, a friend of mine called Mr Hyde, who was in the north of London and, being anxious to get to a railway station, took what he thought would be a short cut, lost his way and found himself in a network of mean, evil-looking streets. Feeling rather nervous he began to walk extremely fast, when suddenly out of an archway ran a child right between his legs. It fell on the pavement, he tripped over it and trampled upon it. Being, of course, very much frightened and a little hurt, it began to scream, and in a few seconds the whole street was full of rough people who came pouring out of the houses like ants. They surrounded him and asked him his name. He was just about to give it when he remembered the opening incident in Mr Stevenson's story. He was so filled with horror at having realised in his own person that terrible and well-written scene, and at having done accidentally though in fact what the Mr Hyde of fiction had done with deliberate intent, that he ran away as hard as he could go. He was, however, very closely followed, and finally he took refuge in a surgery, the door of which happened to be open, where he explained to a young assistant who happened to be there exactly what had occurred. The humanitarian crowd were induced to go away on his giving them a small sum of money and as soon as the coast was clear he left; as he passed out, the name on the brass door-plate of the surgery caught his eye. It was 'Jekyll'. At least it should have been.

❧ Poets with the unfortunate exception of MR WORDSWORTH have been really faithful to their high mission and are universally recognised as being absolutely unreliable.

❧ MR HENRY JAMES writes fiction as if it were a painful duty, and wastes upon mean motives and imperceptible 'points of view' his neat literary style, his felicitous phrases, his swift and caustic satire.

❧ CHARLES READE, an artist, a scholar, a man with a true sense of beauty, raging and roaring over the abuses of contemporary life like a common pamphleteer or a sensational journalist, is really a sight for the angels to weep over.

❧ GEORGE MEREDITH. His style is chaos illuminated by flashes of lightning. As a writer he has mastered everything except language; as a novelist he can do everything except tell a story; as an artist he is everything except articulate.

❧ MR JAMES PAYN is an adept in the art of concealing what is not worth finding. He hunts down the obvious with the enthusiasm of a short-sighted detective.

❧ Yes, BROWNING was great. And as what will he be remembered? As a poet? Ah, not as a poet! He will be remembered as a writer of fiction, as the most supreme writer of fiction, it may be, that we have ever had. His sense of dramatic situation was unrivalled, and, if he could not answer his own problems, he could at least put problems forth, and what more should an artist do? Considered from the point of view of a creator of character he ranks next to him who made Hamlet. Had he been articulate, he might have sat beside him. The only man who can touch the hem of his garment is GEORGE MEREDITH. MEREDITH is a prose BROWNING, and so is BROWNING. He used poetry as a medium for writing in prose.

❧ ROBERT BROWNING has been called a thinker and was certainly a man who was always thinking and always thinking aloud. So much, indeed, did the subtle mechanism of mind fascinate him that he despised language, or looked upon it as an incomplete instrument of expression.

❧ Let any sensible man outside the Browning Society dip into the mysterious volume of literary hocus-pocus that has recently been solemnly reviewed and see whether he can find a single passage likely to stir the pulses of any man or woman, create a desire to lead a higher, a holier and a more useful life in the breast of the indifferent average citizen.

❧ As for the others, the scribblers and nibblers of literature, if they indeed reverence ROSSETTI's memory, let them pay him the one homage he would most have valued, the gracious homage of silence.

❧ As a general rule, his verse is full of pretty echoes of other writers, but in one sonnet he makes a distinct attempt to be original and the result is extremely depressing.

❦ How should one stop to listen to the lucubrations of a literary gamin, to the brawling and mouthing of a man whose praise would be as insolent as his slander is impotent, or the irresponsible and irrepressible chatter of the professionally unproductive?

On being asked by a prison warder if MARIE CORELLI *was a great writer*:

❦ Now don't think I've anything against her *moral* character, but from the way she writes she ought to be in here.

❦ To call an artist morbid because he deals with morbidity as his subject-matter is as silly as if one called SHAKESPEARE mad because he wrote *King Lear*.

❦ There are two ways of disliking poetry, one way is to dislike it, the other is to read POPE.

❦ The best play I ever slept through.

❦ *Andiatoroctè* is the title of a volume of poems by the Reverend Clarence Walworth of Albany, N.Y. It is a word borrowed from the Indians and should, we think, be returned to them as soon as possible.

❦ LONGFELLOW is a great poet only for those who never read poetry.

❦ LONGFELLOW has no imitators, for of echoes themselves there are no echoes.

❦ A true artist takes no notice whatever of the public. The public to him are non-existent. He leaves that to the popular novelist.

❦ In literature mere egotism is delightful. It is what fascinates us in the letters of personalities so different as CICERO and BALZAC, FLAUBERT and BERLIOZ, BYRON and MADAME DE SÉVIGNÉ. Whenever we come across it, and, strangely enough, it is rather rare, we cannot but welcome it.

❦ In his very rejection of art WALT WHITMAN is an artist . . . If poetry has passed him by, philosophy will take note of him.

❦ They lead us through a barren desert of verbiage to a mirage that they call life. However, one should not be too severe on English novels; they are the only relaxation of the intellectually unemployed.

❦ For our own part, we cannot help expressing our regret that such a shallow and superficial biography as this should ever have been published. It is but a sorry task to rip the twisted ravel from the worn garment of life and to turn the grout into a drained cup. Better after all that we only know a painter through his vision and a poet through his song, than that the image of a great man should be marred and made mean by the clumsy geniality of good intentions.

❦ FRANK HARRIS tells that he was once asked to write a book of one hundred thousand words for some $5,000 – in advance – by the American publishers Harper's. He wrote to them that as there were not one hundred thousand words in English he could not undertake the work.

❦ The nineteenth century may be a prosaic age, but we fear that, if we are to judge by the general run of novels, it is not an age of prose.

On [SIR HERBERT BEERBOHM] TREE's *Hamlet*:

❦ . . . funny without being vulgar.

❦ The brilliant phrase like good wine, needs no bush. But just as the orator marks his good things by a dramatic pause, or by raising or lowering his voice, or by gesture, so the writer marks his epigrams with italics, setting the gems, as it were, like a jeweller – an excusable love of one's art, not all mere vanity, I like to think.

❦ We fear that he will never produce any really good work till he has made up his mind whether destiny intends him for a poet or an advertising agent.

❦ A great poet, a really great poet, is the most unpoetical of creatures. But inferior poets are absolutely fascinating. The worse their rhymes the more picturesque they look. The mere fact of having published a book of second-rate sonnets makes a man quite irresistible. He lives the poetry he cannot write. The others write the poetry that they dare not realise.

❦ I write because it gives me the greatest possible artistic pleasure to write. If my work pleases the few I am gratified. As for the mob, I have no desire to be a popular novelist. It is far too easy.

❦ All fine imaginative work is self-conscious and deliberate. No poet sings because he must sing. At least no great poet does. A great poet sings because he chooses to sing.

❦ [This novel] can be read without any trouble and was probably written without any trouble also!

❦ The author has written, as he says, 'a tale without a murder', but having put a pistol-ball through his hero's chest and left him alive and hearty notwithstanding, he cannot be said to have produced a tale without a miracle.

❦ Medieval art is charming, but medieval emotions are out of date. One can use them in fiction, of course. But then the only things that one can use in fiction are the things that one has ceased to use in fact.

❦ . . . a form of poetry which cannot possibly hurt anybody, even if translated into French.

❦ The nineteenth-century dislike of Realism is the rage of Caliban seeing his own face in a glass. The nineteenth-century dislike of Romanticism is the rage of Caliban not seeing his own face in a glass.

❦ If one cannot enjoy reading a book over and over again, there is no use in reading it at all.

❦ 'And now I must bid goodbye to your excellent aunt. I am due at the Athenaeum. It is the hour when we sleep there.'

'All of you, Mr Erskine?'

'Forty of us, in forty armchairs. We are practising for an English Academy of Letters.'

❦ Literature always anticipates life. It does not copy it, but moulds it to its purpose. The nineteenth century, as we know it, is largely an invention of BALZAC.

❦ I quite admit that modern novels have many good points. All I insist on is that, as a class, they are quite unreadable.

❦ Romantic surroundings are the worst surroundings possible for a romantic writer.

❦ We have been able to have fine poetry in England because the public do not read it, and consequently do not influence it.

❦ The books that the world calls immoral books are books that show the world its own shame.

On CHARLES DICKENS*'s The Old Curiosity Shop*:
❦ One must have a heart of stone to read the death of Little Nell without laughing.

❦ For in some respects DICKENS might be likened to those old sculptors of our Gothic cathedrals . . . whose art lacking sanity was therefore incomplete. Yet they at least knew the limitations of their art, while Dickens never knew the limitations of his. When he tries to be serious, he only succeeds in being dull, when he aims at truth, he merely reaches platitude.

❦ Every good storyteller nowadays starts with the end and then goes on to the beginning and concludes with the middle. That is the new method.

❦ On a lazy June evening no more delightful companion could be found than a poet who has the sweetest of voices and absolutely nothing to say.

❦ He has always been a great poet. But he has his limitations, the chief of which is, curiously enough, an entire lack of any sense of limit. His song is nearly always too loud for his subject.

❦ Our second-rate *litterateurs* are the mere body-snatchers of literature. The dust is given to one, and the ashes to another, and the soul is out of their reach.

❦ As one turns over the pages the suspense of the author becomes almost unbearable.

❦ The good ended happily and the bad unhappily. That is what fiction means.

❦ As for that great and daily increasing school of novelists for whom the sun always rises in the East End, the only thing that can be said about them is that they find life crude and leave it raw.

❦ As a rule, the critics – I speak, of course, of the higher class, of those in fact who write for the sixpenny papers – are far more cultured than the people whose work they are called upon to review.

❦ Mr Marion Crawford has immolated himself upon the altar of local colour . . . he has fallen into a bad habit of uttering moral platitudes. He is always telling us that to be good is to be good, and that to be bad is to be wicked. At times he is almost edifying.

❦ We fear that Mr Routledge's edition will not do. It is well printed, and nicely bound; but his translators do not understand French.

❦ Eloquence is a beautiful thing, but rhetoric ruins many a critic; and MR SYMONDS is essentially rhetorical.

❦ What right has a man to the title of poet when he fails to produce music in his lines and cannot express his thoughts in a simple language that the people can understand; but, on the contrary, has so imperfect a command of his mother tongue that all the efforts of a society of intellectual pickaxes cannot discover what his words really mean?

❦ In modern days the fashion of writing poetry has become far too common, and should, if possible, be discouraged.

❦ Anybody can be reasonable, but to be sane is not common; and sane poets are as rare as blue lilies, though they may not be quite so delightful.

❦ Old fashions in literature are not as pleasant as old fashions in dress. I like the costume of the age of powder better than the poetry of the age of Pope.

❦ *En Route* is most overrated. It is sheer journalism. It never makes one hear a note of the music it describes. The subject is delightful, but the style is of course worthless, slipshod, flaccid. It is worse French than OHNET's. OHNET tries to be commonplace and succeeds. HUYSMANS tries not to be, and is.

❦ I dislike modern memoirs. They are generally written by people who have entirely lost their memories, or have never done anything worth remembering; which, however, is, no doubt, the true explanation of their popularity, as the English public always feels perfectly at its ease when a mediocrity is talking to it.

❦ Anybody can write a three-volumed novel. It merely requires a complete ignorance of both life and literature.

To know the vintage and quality of a wine one need not drink the whole cask. It must be perfectly easy in half an hour to say whether a book is worth anything or worth nothing. Ten minutes are really sufficient, if one has the instinct for form. Who wants to wade through a dull volume? One tastes it, and that is quite enough.

But there is no literary public in England for anything except newspapers, primers and encyclopaedias. Of all the people in the world the English have the least sense of the beauty of literature.

The popular novel that the public call healthy is always a thoroughly unhealthy production; and what the public call an unhealthy novel is always a beautiful and healthy work of art.

I hate vulgar realism in literature. The man who could call a spade a spade should be compelled to use one. It is the only thing he is fit for.

There is not a single real poet or prose writer of this century on whom the British public have not solemnly conferred diplomas of immorality, and these diplomas practically take the place, with us, of what in France is the formal recognition of an Academy of Letters and fortunately make the establishment of such an institution quite unnecessary in England.

Astray: A Tale of a Country Town is a very serious volume. It has taken four people to write it and even to read it requires assistance. It is a book that one can with perfect safety recommend to other people.

The aim of most of our modern novelists seems to be not to write good novels but to write novels that will do good.

Russian writers are extraordinary. What makes their books so great is the pity they put into them.

When the public say a work is grossly unintelligible, they mean that the artist has said or made a beautiful thing that is new; when they describe a work as grossly immoral, they mean that the artist has said or made a beautiful thing that is true.

It is a curious fact that the worst work is always done with the best intentions, and that people are never so trivial as when they take themselves very seriously.

We sincerely hope that a few more novels like these will be published as the public will then find out that a bad book is very dear at a shilling.

I appropriate what is already mine, for once a thing is published it becomes public property.

'Dry-goods! What are American dry-goods?' asked the duchess, raising her large hands in wonder, and accentuating the verb.
    'American novels,' answered Lord Henry, helping himself to some quail.

Poets know how useful passion is for publication. Nowadays a broken heart will run to many editions.

On his play The Importance of Being Earnest:
The first act is ingenious, the second beautiful, the third abominably clever.

I am sure you must have a great future in literature before you because you seem to be such a very bad interviewer. I feel sure that you must write poetry. I certainly like the colour of your necktie very much. Goodbye.

No modern literary work of any worth has been produced in the English language by an English writer – except of course Bradshaw.

The basis of literary friendship is mixing the poisoned bowl.

❧ There is a great deal to be said in favour of reading a novel backwards. The last page is, as a rule, the most interesting and when one begins with the catastrophe or the denouement one feels on pleasant terms of equality with the author. It is like going behind the scenes of a theatre. One is no longer taken in, and the hairbreadth escapes of the hero and the wild agonies of the heroine leave one absolutely unmoved.

❧ Details are the only things that interest.

❧ K. E. V.'s little volume is a series of poems on the saints. Each poem is preceded by a brief biography of the saint it celebrates – which is a very necessary precaution, as few of them ever existed. It does not display much poetic power and such lines as these on St Stephen . . . may be said to add another horror to martyrdom. Still it is a thoroughly well-intentioned book and eminently suitable for invalids.

❧ If your pistol is as harmless as your pen, this young tyrant will have a long life.

❧ The difficulty under which the novelists of our day labour seems to me to be this: if they do not go into society, their books are unreadable; and if they do go into society, they have no time left for writing.

❧ The impulse of the Irish literature of their time came from a class that did not – mainly for political reasons – take the populace seriously, and imagined the country as a humorist's Arcadia. What they did was not wholly false, they merely magnified an irresponsible type, found oftenest among boatmen, carmen and gentlemen's servants, into the type of a whole nation and created the stage-Irishman.

❧ Every great man nowadays has his disciples and it is always Judas who writes the biography.

A Sense of Sorrows

❦ After playing CHOPIN, I feel as if I had been weeping over sins that I had never committed and mourning over tragedies that were not my own. Music always seems to me to produce that effect. It creates for one a past of which one has been ignorant and fills one with a sense of sorrows that have been hidden from one's tears. I can fancy a man who has led a perfectly commonplace life, hearing by chance some curious piece of music and suddenly discovering that his soul, without his being conscious of it, had passed through terrible experiences and known fearful joys or wild romantic loves or great renunciations.

❦ If one plays good music people don't listen and if one plays bad music people don't talk.

❦ The typewriting machine, when played with expression, is not more annoying than the piano when played by a sister or near relation. Indeed, many among those most devoted to domesticity prefer it.

❦ LORD HENRY: You must play Chopin to me. The man with whom my wife ran away played Chopin exquisitely.

❦ Musical people are so absurdly unreasonable. They always want one to be perfectly dumb at the very moment when one is longing to be absolutely deaf.

❦ I don't play accurately – anyone can play accurately – but I play with wonderful expression. As far as the piano is concerned, sentiment is my *forte*. I keep science for life.

❦ I like Wagner's music better than anybody's. It is so loud that one can talk the whole time without people hearing what one says.

❦ Music is the art which most completely realises the artistic idea and is the condition to which all the other arts are constantly aspiring.

❦ Music is the art most nigh to tears and memory.

❦ I never talk during music – at least good music. If one hears bad music, it is one's duty to drown it by conversation.

❦ LADY HUNSTANTON: Music makes one feel so romantic – at least it always gets on one's nerves.
MRS ALLONBY: It's the same thing, nowadays.

❦ No; I don't want music at present. It is far too indefinite. Besides, I took the Baroness Bernstein down to dinner last night, and, though absolutely charming in every other respect, she insisted on discussing music as if it were actually written in the German language.

❦ Whatever music sounds like, I am glad to say that it does not sound in the smallest degree like German.

Some Extraordinary Mistake
in Nature

❦ Why will parents always appear at the wrong time? Some extraordinary mistake in nature, I suppose.

❦ Few parents nowadays pay any regard to what their children say to them. The old-fashioned respect for the young is fast dying.

❦ Children begin by loving their parents. After a time they judge them. Rarely, if ever do they forgive them.

❦ All women become like their mothers. That is their tragedy. No man does. That's his.

❦ To lose one parent, Mr Worthing, may be regarded as a misfortune; to lose both looks like carelessness.

To a fellow undergraduate at Trinity College:
❦ Come home with me, I want to introduce you to my mother. We have founded a society for the suppression of virtue.

❦ Fathers should neither be seen nor heard. That is the only proper basis for family life.

❦ The American father is better, for he is never in London. He passes his life entirely in Wall Street, and communicates with his family once a month by means of a telegram in cipher. The mother, however, is always with us, and, lacking the quick imitative faculty of the younger generation, remains uninteresting and provincial to the last.

❦ The longer I live the more keenly I feel that whatever was good enough for our fathers is not good enough for us. In art, as in politics, 'les grand pères ont toujours tort'.

❦ A mother's love is very touching, of course, but it is often curiously selfish. I mean, there is a good deal of selfishness in it.

❦ A mother who doesn't part with a daughter every Season has no real affection.

❦ Her mother is perfectly unbearable. Never met such a Gorgon . . .

❦ I should imagine that most mothers don't quite understand their sons.

❦ I was influenced by my mother. Every man is when he is young.

❦ She was a wonderful woman, and such a feeling as vulgar jealousy could take no hold on her. She was well aware of my father's constant infidelities, but simply ignored them. Before my father died, in 1876, he lay ill in bed for many days. And every morning a woman dressed in black and closely veiled used to come to our house in Merrion Square, and unhindered either by my mother or anyone else used to walk straight upstairs to Sir William's bedroom and sit down at the head of his bed, and so sit there all day, without ever speaking a word or once raising her veil.

   She took no notice of anybody in the room, and nobody paid any attention to her. Not one woman in a thousand would have tolerated her presence, but my mother allowed it, because she knew that my father loved this woman and felt that it must be a joy and a comfort to have her there by his dying bed. And I am sure that she did right not to judge that last happiness of a man who was about to die, and I am sure that my father understood her apparent indifference, understood that it was not because she did not love him that she permitted her rival's presence, but because she loved him very much, and died with his heart full of gratitude and affection for her.

❦ There are so many sons who won't have anything to do with their fathers, and so many fathers who won't speak to their sons.

❦ There is always something about an heir to a crown unwholesome to his father.

❦ It is the duty of every father to write fairy-tales for his children, but the mind of a child is a great mystery. It is incalculable, and who shall divine it or bring to it its own peculiar delights? You humbly spread before it the treasures of your imagination, and they are as dross. For example, a day or two ago Cyril came to me with the question, 'Father, do you ever dream?' 'Why, of course, my darling. It is the first duty of a gentleman to dream.' 'And what do you dream of?' asked Cyril with a child's disgusting appetite for facts. Then I, believing of course that something picturesque would be expected of me, spoke of magnificent things. 'What do I dream of? Oh, I dream of dragons with gold and silver scales, and scarlet flames coming out of their mouths, of eagles with eyes made of diamonds that can see over the whole world at once, of lions with yellow manes and voices like thunder, of elephants with little houses on their backs and tigers and zebras with barred and spotted coats . . .' So I laboured on with my fancy, till observing that Cyril was entirely unimpressed, and indeed quite undisguisedly bored, I came to a humiliating stop, and, turning to him, I said: 'But tell me, what do you dream of, Cyril?' His answer was like a divine revelation. 'I dream of *pigs*,' he said.

As Demoralising as Cigarettes

❦ Good heavens! How marriage ruins a man! It's as demoralising as cigarettes, and far more expensive.

❦ Men marry because they are tired; women because they are curious. Both are disappointed.

❦ The one charm of marriage is that it makes a life of deception absolutely necessary for both parties.

❦ Because the husband is vile – should the wife be vile also?

❦ Nowadays all the married men live like bachelors and all the bachelors like married men.

❦ You know I am not a champion of marriage. The real drawback to marriage is that it makes one unselfish, and unselfish people are colourless – they lack individuality. Still there are certain temperaments that marriage makes more complex. They retain their egotism, and add to it many other egos. They are forced to have more than one life. They become more highly organised, and to be highly organised is, I should fancy, the object of man's existence. Besides, every experience is of value, and whatever one may say against marriage it is certainly an experience.

❦ Of course married life is merely a habit, a bad habit. But then one regrets the loss of even one's worst habits. Perhaps one regrets them the most. They are such an essential part of one's personality.

❦ I have often observed that in married households the champagne is rarely of a first-rate brand.

❦ Loveless marriages are horrible. But there is one thing worse than an absolutely loveless marriage – a marriage in which there is love, but on one side only; faith, but on one side only; devotion, but on one side only, and in which of the two hearts one is sure to be broken.

❦ I am not in favour of long engagements. They give people the opportunity of finding out each other's character before marriage, which I think is never advisable.

❦ I always liked your taste in wine and wives extremely.

❦ The amount of women in London who flirt with their own husbands is perfectly scandalous. It looks so bad. It is simply washing one's clean linen in public.

❦ The happiness of a married man depends on the people he has not married.

❦ What nonsense people talk about happy marriages. A man can be happy with any woman so long as he does not love her.

❦ If we men married the women we deserve we should have a very bad time of it.

❦ It is most dangerous nowadays for a husband to pay any attention to his wife in public. It always makes people think that he beats her when they're alone. The world has grown so suspicious of anything that looks like a happy married life.

❦ Mrs Allonby: My husband is a sort of promissory note; I'm tired of meeting him.

❦ Marriage is hardly a thing that one can do now and then – except in America.

❦ For an artist to marry his model is as fatal as for a *gourmet* to marry his cook: the one gets no sittings, and the other no dinner.

❦ Polygamy – how much more poetic it is to marry one and love many.

❦ My dear general, your nephew must be a perfect Turk. He seems to get married three times a week regularly.

❦ A family is a terrible encumbrance, especially when one is not married.

❦ So much marriage is certainly not becoming. Twenty years of romance make a woman look like a ruin; but twenty years of marriage make her something like a public building.

❦ In married life affection comes when people thoroughly dislike each other.

❦ One can always know at once whether a man has home claims upon his life or not. I have noticed a very, very sad expression in the eyes of so many married men.

❦ LADY MARKBY: We might drive in the park at five. Everything looks so fresh in the park now!

MRS CHEVELEY: Except the people!

LADY MARKBY: Perhaps the people are a little jaded. I have often observed that the Season as it goes on produces a kind of softening of the brain. However, I think anything is better than high intellectual pressure. That is the most unbecoming thing there is. It makes the noses of the young girls so particularly large. And there is nothing so difficult to marry as a large nose.

❦ LORD AUGUSTUS: It is a great thing to come across a woman who thoroughly understands one.

DUMBY: It is an awfully dangerous thing. They always end by marrying one.

❦ LADY CAROLINE: Women have become so highly educated that nothing should surprise us nowadays, except happy marriages. They apparently are getting very rare.

MRS ALLONBY: Oh, they're quite out of date.

LADY STUTFIELD: Except amongst the middle classes, I have been told.

MRS ALLONBY: How like the middle classes!

❦ Englishwomen conceal their feelings till after they are married. They show them then.

❦ DUKE: I have noted how merry is that husband by whose hearth sits an uncomely wife.

❦ In married life three is company and two is none.

❦ I have always been of the opinion that a man who desires to get married should know either everything or nothing.

❦ The proper basis for marriage is mutual misunderstanding.

❦ LADY MARKBY: In my time we were taught not to understand anything. That was the old system, and wonderfully interesting it was. I assure you that the amount of things I and my poor sister were taught not to understand was quite extraordinary. But modern women understand everything, I am told.

MRS CHEVELEY: Except their husbands. That is the one thing the modern woman never understands.

LADY MARKBY: And a very good thing too, dear, I dare say. It might break up many a happy home if they did.

❦ To elope is cowardly. It's running away from danger. And danger has become so rare in modern life.

❦ As for domesticity, it ages one rapidly, and distracts one's mind from higher things.

❦ When a woman finds out about her husband she either becomes dreadfully dowdy, or wears very smart bonnets that some other woman's husband has to pay for.

❦ All men are married women's property. That is the only true definition of what married women's property really is.

❦ Her capacity for family affection is extraordinary. When her third husband died, her hair turned quite gold from grief.

❦ *On seeing* [SIR HERBERT BEERBOHM] TREE *in a play* (Once Upon a Time):
Since the appearance of TREE in pyjamas – there has been the greatest sympathy for Mrs Tree. It throws a lurid light on the difficulties of their married life.

❦ There is no pleasure in taking in a husband who never sees anything.

❦ When a woman marries again, it is because she detested her first husband. When a man marries again, it is because he adored his first wife. Women try their luck; men risk theirs.

❦ MRS ALLONBY: The Ideal Husband? There couldn't be such a thing. The institution is wrong.

❦ DUCHESS OF BERWICK: Our husbands would really forget our existence if we didn't nag at them from time to time, just to remind them that we have a perfect legal right to do so.

❦ It is a curious thing about the game of marriage – the wives hold all the honours and invariably lose the odd trick.

❦ Secrets from other people's wives are a necessary luxury in modern life. So, at least, I am always told at the club by people who are bald enough to know better.

❦ There's nothing in the world like the devotion of a married woman. It's a thing no married man knows anything about.

❦ Mrs Allonby: When Ernest and I were engaged, he swore to me positively on his knees that he never loved anyone before in the whole course of his life. I was very young at the time, so I didn't believe him, I needn't tell you. Unfortunately, however, I made no enquiries of any kind till after I had been actually married four or five months. I found out then that what he had told me was perfectly true. And that sort of thing makes a man so uninteresting.

❦ I am disgraced; he is not. That is all. It is the usual history of a man and a woman as it usually happens, as it always happens. And the ending is the ordinary ending. The woman suffers. The man goes free.

❦ I assure you women of that kind are most useful. They form the basis of other people's marriages.

❦ My wife was very plain, never had my ruffs properly starched, and knew nothing of cookery.

❦ Ah, nowadays people marry as often as they can, don't they? It is most fashionable.

❦ You talk as if you had a heart. Women like you have no hearts. Heart is not in you. You are bought and sold.

❦ Egad! I might be married to her; she treats me with such demmed indifference.

❦ I know it is the general lot of women; each miserably mated to some man wrecks her own life upon his selfishness: that it is general makes it not less bitter. I think I never heard a woman laugh for pure merriment, except one woman, and that was at night time, in the public streets. Poor soul, she walked with painted lips and wore the mask of pleasure: I would not laugh like her; no, death were better.

❦ The annoying thing is that the wretches can be perfectly happy without us. That is why I think it is every woman's duty never to leave them alone for a single moment, except during this short breathing space after dinner; without which, I believe, we poor women would be absolutely worn to shadows.

❦ LORD CAVERSHAM: What I say is that marriage is a matter for common sense.

LORD GORING: But women who have common sense are so curiously plain, father, aren't they? Of course I only speak from hearsay.

❦ More marriages are ruined nowadays by the common sense of the husband than by anything else. How can a woman be expected to be happy with a man who insists on treating her as if she were a perfectly rational being.

❦ Nothing ages a woman so rapidly as having married the general rule.

❦ London is full of women who trust their husbands. One can always recognise them. They look so thoroughly unhappy.

❦ LORD CAVERSHAM: If she did accept you she would be the prettiest fool in England.

LORD GORING: That is just what I should like to marry. A thoroughly sensible wife would reduce me to a condition of absolute idiocy in less than six months.

❦ MISS PRISM: No married man is ever attractive except
  to his wife.
  CHASUBLE: And often, I've been told, not even to her.

❦ Her sense of humour keeps her from the tragedy of a
  grande passion, and, as there is neither romance nor humility
  in her love, she makes an excellent wife.

❦ On the whole, the great success of marriage in the States is
  due partly to the fact that no American man is ever idle and
  partly to the fact that no American wife is considered
  responsible for the quality of her husband's dinners.

❦ He was eccentric, I admit. But only in later years. And that
  was the result of the Indian climate, and marriage, and
  indigestion, and other things of that kind.

❦ From childhood, the husband has been brought up on the
  most elaborate fetch-and-carry system, and his reverence
  for the sex has a touch of compulsory chivalry about it,
  while the wife exercises an absolute despotism, based upon
  female assertion, and tempered by womanly charm.

❦ It's perfectly scandalous the amount of bachelors who are
  going about society. There should be a law passed to
  compel them all to marry within twelve months.

❦ An engagement should come on a young girl as a surprise,
  pleasant or unpleasant, as the case may be.

❦ The American freedom of divorce has at least the merit
  of bringing into marriage a new element of romantic
  uncertainty. Where the bond can be easily broken, its very
  fragility makes its strength and reminds the husband that
  he should always try to please and the wife that she should
  never cease to be charming.

❦ Divorces are made in heaven.

❦ Nowadays everybody is jealous of everyone else, except, of course, husband and wife.

❦ Girls never marry the men they flirt with. Girls don't think it right. It accounts for the extraordinary number of bachelors that one sees all over the place.

The Sacrament of Life

- Love is the sacrament of life.

- It is difficult not to be unjust to what one loves.

- Love is an illusion.

- Love is easily killed.

- True romance is not killed by reality.

- You were the prettiest of playthings, the most fascinating of small romances.

- Shallow sorrows and shallow loves live on. The loves and sorrows that are great are destroyed by their own plenitude.

- The people who love only once in their lives are the really shallow people. What they call their loyalty and their fidelity I call either the lethargy of custom or their lack of imagination.

- LORD ILLINGWORTH: Women have become too brilliant. Nothing spoils a romance so much as a sense of humour in the woman.
  MRS ALLONBY: Or the want of it in the man.

- The worst of having a romance of any kind is that it leaves one so unromantic.

❦ You want a new excitement. Let me see – you have been married twice already; suppose you try falling in love for once.

❦ They do not sin at all who sin for love.

❦ I might mimic a passion that I do not feel, but I cannot mimic one that burns one like fire.

❦ Not love at first sight, but love at the end of the Season, which is so much more satisfactory.

❦ I am not quite sure that I quite know what pessimism really means. All I do know is that life cannot be understood without much charity, cannot be lived without much charity. It is love, and not German philosophy, that is the explanation of this world, whatever may be the explanation of the next.

❦ Oxford is the capital of Romance . . . in its own way as memorable as Athens and to me it was even more entrancing.

❦ Love can canonise people. The saints are those who have been most loved.

❦ There is always something ridiculous about the emotions of people whom one has ceased to love.

❦ It is strange that men who love and who teach their wives to love, should pass from the love that is given to the love that is bought.

❦ One should always be in love. That is the reason one should never marry.

❦ There is no such thing as a romantic experience; there are romantic memories and there is the desire for romance – that is all. Our most fiery moments of ecstasy are merely shadows of what somewhere else we have felt or of what we long someday to feel.

❦ MRS ALLONBY: There is a beautiful moon tonight.
LORD ILLINGWORTH: Let us go and look at it. To look at anything that is inconstant is charming nowadays.

❦ Keep love in your heart. A life without it is like a sunless garden when the flowers are dead. The consciousness of loving and being loved brings a warmth and richness to life that nothing else can bring.

❦ A really *grande passion* is comparatively rare nowadays. It is the privilege of people who have nothing to do. That is the one use of the idle classes in a country.

❦ The real Don Juan is not the vulgar person who goes about making love to all the women he meets, and what the novelists call 'seducing' them. The real Don Juan is the man who says to women, 'Go away! I don't want you. You interfere with my life. I can do without you.' SWIFT was the real Don Juan. Two women died for him!

❦ Any place you love is the world to you . . . but love is not fashionable any more, the poets have killed it. They wrote so much about it that nobody believed them, and I am not surprised. True love suffers, and is silent.

❦ Love and gluttony justify everything.

❦ To love oneself is the beginning of a lifelong romance.

❦ Faithfulness is to the emotional life what consistency is to the life of the intellect – simply a confession of failure.

❦ There is so much else to do in the world but love.

❦ Men always want to be a woman's first love. That is their clumsy vanity. Women have a more subtle instinct about things. What they like is to be a man's last romance.

❦ What a silly thing love is! It is not half as useful as logic, for it does not prove anything and it is always telling one things that are not going to happen and making one believe things that are not true.

❦ OUIDA loved LORD LYTTON with a love that made his life a burden.

❦ Nothing is serious except passion. The intellect is not a serious thing, and never has been. It is an instrument on which one plays, that is all. The only serious form of intellect I know is the British intellect. And on the British intellect the illiterates play the drum.

❦ It is said that passion makes one think in a circle.

❦ Chiromancy is a most dangerous science, and one that ought not to be encouraged, except in a tête-à-tête.

❦ Who on earth writes to him on pink paper? How silly to write on pink paper! It looks like the beginning of a middle-class romance. Romance should never begin with sentiment. It should begin with science and end with a settlement.

❦ I really don't see anything romantic about proposing. It is very romantic to be in love, but there is nothing romantic about a definite proposal. Why, one may be accepted. One usually is, I believe. Then the excitement is all over. The very essence of romance is uncertainty.

❦ Once a week is quite enough to propose to anyone, and it should always be done in a manner that attracts some attention.

❦ It is not the perfect but the imperfect who have need of love. It is when we are wounded by our own hands or by the hands of others that love should come to cure us – else what use is love at all.

❦ I am not at all romantic. I am not old enough. I leave romance to my seniors.

❦ A kiss may ruin a human life.

❦ If one really loves a woman, all other women in the world become absolutely meaningless to one.

❦ Who, being loved, is poor?

❦ Romance lives by repetition, and repetition converts an appetite into an art. Besides each tune one loves is the only tune one has loved. Difference of object does not alter singleness of passion. It merely intensifies it.

❦ DUCHESS OF MONMOUTH: We women, as someone says, love with our ears, just as you men love with your eyes, if you ever love at all.

❦ A man can be happy with any woman as long as he does not love her.

❦ When one is in love one begins by deceiving oneself. And ends by deceiving others. That is what the world calls a romance.

❦ Those who are faithful know only the trivial side of love: it is the faithless who know love's tragedies.

❦ What a fuss people make about fidelity. Why, even in love it is purely a question for physiology. It has nothing to do with our own will: young men want to be faithful and are not, old men want to be faithless and cannot – that is all one can say.

❦ Always! That is a dreadful word. It makes me shudder when I hear it. Women are so fond of using it. They spoil every romance by trying to make it last for ever. It is a meaningless word too. The only difference between a caprice and a lifelong passion is that the caprice lasts a little longer.

❦ The people who have adored me – there have not been very many, but there have been some – have always insisted on living on long after I have ceased to care for them, or they to care for me. They have become stout and tedious, and when I meet them they go in at once for reminiscences.

❦ Lovers are happiest when they are in doubt.

❦ The romance of life is that one can love so many people and marry but one.

❦ Every romance that one has in one's life is a romance lost to one's art.

❦ Romance is the privilege of the rich, not the profession of the unemployed. The poor should be practical and prosaic.

❦ All love is a tragedy.

❦ To be in love is to surpass oneself.

❦ I cannot live without the atmosphere of love: I must love and be loved, whatever price I pay for it.

❦ Love does not traffic in a marketplace, nor use a huckster's scales. Its joy, like the joy of the intellect, is to feel itself alive. The aim of love is love, and no less.

❦ Love makes people good.

❦ Love is merely passion with a holy name.

❦ Everyone is worthy of love, except he who thinks he is.

❦ Love can heal all wounds.

❦ Lust makes one love all that one loathes.

❧ Yet each man kills the thing he loves,
By each let this be heard,
Some do with a bitter look,
Some with a flattering word,
The coward does it with a kiss,
The brave man with a sword!

❧ No one can possibly shut the doors against love for ever.
There is no prison in the world into which love cannot
force an entrance.

Heaven in Its Infinite Mercy

🌰 Missionaries, my dear! Don't you realise that missionaries are the divinely provided food for destitute and underfed cannibals? Whenever they are on the brink of starvation, Heaven in its infinite mercy sends them a nice plump missionary.

🌰 There is a luxury in self-reproach. When we blame ourselves we feel that no one else has a right to blame us. It is the confession, not the priest, that gives us absolution.

🌰 Religion is the fashionable substitute for belief.

🌰 There is no thing more precious than a human soul, nor any earthly thing that can be weighed with it.

🌰 Prayer must never be answered: if it is, it ceases to be prayer and becomes correspondence.

🌰 Most religious teachers spend their time trying to prove the unproven by the unprovable.

🌰 I am sure the clergyman himself could not say such beautiful things as you do, though he does live in a three-storeyed house and wears a gold ring on his little finger.

🌰 Religions may be absorbed, but they are never disproved.

🌰 To die for one's theological beliefs is the worst use a man can make of his life.

❦ Believe me, sir, puritanism is never so offensive and destructive as when it deals with art matters.

❦ Through the streets of Jerusalem at the present day crawls one who is mad and carries a wooden cross on his shoulders. He is a symbol of the lives that are marred by imitation.

❦ A sermon is a sorry sauce when you have nothing to eat it with.

❦ LADY HUNSTANTON: There was, I remember, a clergyman who wanted to be a lunatic, or a lunatic who wanted to be a clergyman, I forget which, but I know the Court of Chancery investigated the matter, and decided he was quite sane. And I saw him afterwards at poor Lord Plumstead's with straws in his hair, or something very odd about him.

❦ I hope to be in Rome in about ten days – and this time I really must become a Catholic – though I fear that if I went before the Holy Father with a blossoming rod it would turn at once into an umbrella or something dreadful of that kind. It is absurd to say that the age of miracles is past. It has not yet begun.

❦ It is rarely in the world's history that its ideal has been one of joy and beauty. The worship of pain has far more often dominated the world. Medievalism, with its saints and martyrs, its love of self-torture, its wild passion for wounding itself, its gashing with knives, and its whipping with rods – Medievalism is real Christianity and the medieval Christ is the real Christ.

❦ People fashion their God after their own understanding. They make their God first and worship him afterwards. I should advise you however to postpone coming to any conclusion at present; and if you should happen to die in the meantime, you will stand a much better chance, should a future exist, than some of these braying parsons.

❦ 'Nay but God careth for the sparrows even, and feedeth them,' he answered.

'Do not the sparrows die of hunger in the winter?' she asked. 'And is it not winter now?'

❦ Scepticism is the beginning of faith.

❦ In a temple everyone should be serious, except the thing that is worshipped.

❦ Religions die when they are proved to be true. Science is the record of dead religions.

❦ To the wickedness of the Papacy humanity owes much. The goodness of the Papacy owes a terrible debt to humanity.

❦ We came to Rome on Holy Thursday – I appeared in the front rank of the pilgrims in the Vatican, and got the blessing of the Holy Father – a blessing they would have denied me.

He was wonderful as he was carried past me on his throne – not of flesh and blood, but a white soul robed in white – and an artist as well as a saint – the only instance in history, if the newspapers are to be believed.

I have seen nothing like the extraordinary grace of his gesture as he rose from moment to moment to bless – possibly the pilgrims but certainly me. [Sir Herbert Beerbohm] Tree should see him. It is his only chance.

I was deeply impressed, and my walking-stick showed signs of budding; would have budded indeed, only at the door of the chapel it was taken from me by the knave of spades. This strange prohibition is, of course, in honour of Tannhaüser.

How did I get a ticket? By a miracle, of course. I thought it was hopeless and made no effort of any kind. On Saturday afternoon at five o'clock Harold and I went to have tea at the Hôtel de l'Europe. Suddenly, as I was eating buttered toast, a man, or what seemed to be one, dressed like a hotel porter entered and asked me would I like to see the Pope on Easter Day. I bowed my head humbly and said, 'Non sum dignus,' or words to that effect. He at once produced a ticket!

When I tell you that his countenance was of supernatural ugliness, and that the price of the ticket was thirty pieces of silver, I need say no more.

An equally curious thing is that whenever I pass the hotel, which I do constantly, I see the same man. Scientists call that phenomenon an obsession of the visual nerve. You and I know better.

- The growth of common sense in the English Church is a thing very much to be regretted.

- The history of theology is the history of madness.

- Ordinary theology has long since converted its gold into lead, and words and phrases that once touched the heart of the world have become wearisome and meaningless through repetition.

- Martyrdom was to me merely a tragic form of scepticism, an attempt to realise by fire what one had failed to do by faith.

- Imaginative people will invariably be religious people for the simple reason that religion has sprung from the imagination.

- When I think about religion at all, I feel as if I would like to found an order for those who cannot believe.

- Everything to be true must become a religion. And agnosticism should have its ritual no less than faith. It has sown its martyrs, it should reap its saints, and praise God daily for having hidden Himself from man.

truth? In matters of religion it is simply the
on that has survived. In matters of science it is the
nate sensation. In matters of art it is one's last mood.

Religion consoles some. Its mysteries have all the charm of
a flirtation, a woman once told me.

❦ When I think of all the harm that book [the Bible] has
done, I despair of ever writing anything equal to it.

❦ The terror of society, which is the basis of morals, the
terror of God, which is the secret of religion – these are the
two things that govern us.

❦ The Catholic Church is for saints and sinners alone. For
respectable people the Anglican Church will do.

❦ Catholicism is the only religion to die in.

❦ I think half an hour's warping of the inner man daily is
greatly conducive to holiness.

❦ When you convert someone else to your own faith, you
cease to believe in it yourself.

❦ He who would lead a Christlike life is he who is perfectly
and absolutely himself.

❦ How else but through a broken heart may Lord Christ
enter in?

❦ Where there is sorrow there is holy ground.

❦ SIR ROBERT CHILTERN: But may I ask, at heart, are you an
optimist or a pessimist? Those seem to be the only two
fashionable religions left to us nowadays.

❦ Shallow speakers and shallow thinkers in pulpits and on
platforms often talk about the world's worship of pleasure,
and whine against it.

❦ In the English Church a man succeeds not through his capacity for belief but through his capacity for disbelief. Ours is the only Church where the sceptic stands at the altar, and where St Thomas is regarded as the ideal apostle.

❦ I can't understand this modern mania for curates. In my time we saw them, of course, running about the place like rabbits. But we never took any notice of them, I need hardly say. But I am told that nowadays country society is quite honeycombed with them. I think it most irreligious.

❦ 'How well you talk!' said the miller's wife, pouring herself out a large glass of warm ale; 'really I feel quite drowsy. It is just like being in church.'

❦ It is very difficult to keep awake, especially at church.

❦ As for the Church, I cannot conceive anything better for the culture of a country than the presence in it of a body of men whose duty it is to believe in the supernatural, to perform miracles, and to keep alive that mythopoeic faculty which is so essential for the imagination.

❦ A wet Sunday, an uncouth Christian in a mackintosh, a ring of sickly white faces under a broken roof of umbrellas, and wonderful phrases flung into the air by shrill, hysterical lips . . .

❦ All repetition is anti-spiritual.

The Shallow Mask of Manners

❦ CECILY: This is no time for wearing the shallow mask of manners. When I see a spade I call it a spade.
GWENDOLEN: I am glad to say that I have never seen a spade. It is obvious that our social spheres have been widely different.

❦ Men who are dandies and women who are darlings rule the world.

❦ To be born, or at any rate bred, in a handbag, whether it had handles or not, seems to me to display a contempt for the ordinary decencies of family life that reminds one of the worst excesses of the French Revolution.

❦ Any preoccupation with ideas of what is right or wrong in conduct shows an arrested intellectual development.

❦ To be natural is such a very difficult pose to keep up.

❦ To do nothing at all is the most difficult thing in the world, the most difficult and the most intellectual. To PLATO, with his passion for wisdom, this was the noblest form of energy. To ARISTOTLE, with his passion for knowledge, this was the noblest form of energy also. It was to this that the passion for holiness led the saint and the mystic of medieval days.

❦ A sensitive person is one who, because he has corns himself, always treads on other people's toes.

❦ Indiscretion is the better part of valour.

❦ What people call insincerity is simply a method by which we can multiply our personalities.

❦ All imitation in morals and in life is wrong.

❦ My duty is a thing I never do, on principle.

❦ The only thing that ever consoles man for the stupid things he does is the praise he always gives himself for doing them.

❦ If we lived long enough to see the results of our actions it may be that those who call themselves good would be sickened with a dull remorse, and those whom the world calls evil stirred by a noble joy.

❦ Conscience and cowardice are really the same things. Conscience is the trade-name of the firm.

❦ To be either a puritan, a prig or a preacher is a bad thing. To be all three at once reminds me of the worst excesses of the French Revolution.

❦ But then no artist expects grace from the vulgar mind or style from the suburban intellect.

❦ Duty is what one expects from others, it is not what one does oneself.

❦ It often happens that when we think we are experimenting on others we are really experimenting on ourselves.

❦ Early in life she had discovered the important truth that nothing looks so like innocence as an indiscretion; and by a series of escapades, half of them quite harmless, she had acquired all the privileges of a personality.

❦ All bad poetry springs from genuine feeling. To be natural is to be obvious, and to be obvious is to be inartistic.

❦ Moderation is a fatal thing. Nothing succeeds like excess.

❦ Nothing is good in moderation. You cannot know the good in anything till you have torn the heart out of it by excess.

❦ All excess, as well as all renunciation, brings its own punishment.

❦ The trivial in thought and action is charming.

❦ We should treat all trivial things of life very seriously, and all the serious things of life with sincere and studied triviality.

❦ Self-denial is simply a method by which man arrests his progress, and self-sacrifice a survival of the mutilation of the savage, part of that old worship of pain which is so terrible a factor in the history of the world, and which even now makes its victims day by day and has its altars in the land.

❦ What on earth you are serious about I haven't got the remotest idea. About everything, I should fancy. You have such an absolutely trivial nature.

❦ There is a great deal of good in Lord Augustus. Fortunately it is all on the surface. Just where good qualities should be.

❦ Now, Tuppy, you've lost your figure and you've lost your character. Don't lose your temper; you have only got one.

❦ Pure modernity of form is always somewhat vulgarising.

❦ To be modern is the only thing worth being nowadays.

❦ Nothing is so dangerous as being too modern. One is apt to grow old-fashioned quite suddenly.

❦ It is often said that force is no argument. That, however, entirely depends on what one wants to prove.

❦ Actions are the first tragedy in life, words are the second. Words are perhaps the worst. Words are merciless.

❦ Philanthropy seems to me to have become simply the refuge of people who wish to annoy their fellow creatures.

❦ Tact is an exquisite sense of the symmetry of things.

❦ Cynicism is merely the art of seeing things as they are instead of as they ought to be.

❦ The sentimentalist is always a cynic at heart. Indeed sentimentality is merely the bank holiday of cynicism.

❦ The basis of every scandal is an immoral certainty.

❦ The one advantage of playing with fire is that one never gets even singed. It is the people who don't know how to play with it who get burned up.

❦ When we are happy we are always good, but when we are good we are not always happy.

❦ There is no such thing as a good influence. All influence is immoral – immoral from the scientific point of view.

❦ To be good is to be in harmony with oneself. Discord is to be forced to be in harmony with others.

❦ Everyone should keep someone else's diary.

❦ Whenever a man does a thoroughly stupid thing, it is always from the noblest of motives.

❦ A little sincerity is a dangerous thing and a great deal of it is absolutely fatal.

❦ There is a fatality about good resolutions – they are always made too late.

❦ One should always play fairly – when one has the winning cards.

❦ Ambition is the last refuge of the failure.

❦ Being natural is simply a pose, and the most irritating pose I know.

❦ Your handwriting in your last was so dreadful that it looked as if you were writing a three-volume novel on the terrible spread of communistic ideas among the rich, or in some other way wasting a youth that has always been, and always will remain, quite full of promise.

❦ A good reputation is one of the many annoyances to which I have never been subjected.

❦ I don't like principles . . . I prefer prejudices.

❦ No crime is vulgar, but all vulgarity is crime. Vulgarity is the conduct of others.

❦ You never say a moral thing and you never do a wrong thing. Your cynicism is simply a pose.

❦ It is so easy to convert others. It is so difficult to convert oneself.

❦ It is only the superficial qualities that last. Man's deeper nature is soon found out.

❦ All influence is bad, but a good influence is the worst in the world.

❦ Optimism begins in a broad grin, and pessimism ends with blue spectacles. They are both of them merely poses.

❦ I have the greatest contempt for optimism.

❦ I rely on you to misrepresent me.

❦ I am but too conscious of the fact that we are born in an age when only the dull are treated seriously, and I live in terror of not being misunderstood.

❦ A temperament capable of receiving, through an imaginative medium, and under imaginative conditions, new and beautiful impressions is the only temperament that can be a work of art.

❦ What are the unreal things, but the passions that once burned like fire? What are the incredible things, but the things that one has faithfully believed? What are the improbable things? The things that one has done oneself.

❦ Moderation is a fatal thing. Enough is as bad as a meal. More than enough is as good as a feast.

❦ The prig is a very interesting psychological study, and though of all poses a moral pose is the most offensive, still to have a pose at all is something.

❦ I never put off till tomorrow what I can possibly do – the day after.

❦ They say a good lawyer can break the law as often as he likes, and no one can say him nay. If a man knows the law he knows his duty.

❦ To be premature is to be perfect.

❦ I think everyone should have their hands told once a month so as to know what not to do.

❦ It is always more difficult to destroy than to create, and when what one has to destroy is vulgarity and stupidity, the task of destruction needs not merely courage but also contempt.

❧ It is quite remarkable how one good action always breeds another.

❧ He would stab his best friend for the sake of writing an epigram on his tombstone.

❧ For a house lacking a host is but an empty thing and void of honour.

❧ The first duty in life is to be as artificial as possible. What the second duty is no one has yet discovered.

❧ Duty merely means doing what other people want because they want it.

❧ My duty to myself is to amuse myself terrifically.

❧ A sense of duty is like some horrible disease. It destroys the tissues of the mind, as certain complaints destroy the tissues of the body.

❧ People are afraid of themselves nowadays. They have forgotten the highest of all duties, the duty that one owes to oneself.

❧ A woman's first duty in life is to her dressmaker, isn't it? What the second duty is no one has as yet discovered.

❧ Dullness is the coming of age of seriousness.

❧ A publicist, nowadays, is a man who bores the community with the details of the illegalities of his private life.

❧ Every effect that one produces gives one an enemy. To be popular one must be a mediocrity.

❧ It is always nice to be expected and not to arrive.

❧ One should always be a little improbable.

❦ There *is* a good deal to be said for blushing, if one can do it at the proper moment.

❦ Perhaps one never seems so much at one's ease as when one has to play a part.

❦ One should never make one's début with a scandal. One should reserve that to give an interest to one's old age.

❦ If a man knows the law there is nothing he cannot do when he likes.

❦ All ways end at the same point . . . Disillusion.

❦ One must accept a personality as it is. One must never regret that a poet is drunk, but that drunkards are not always poets.

❦ Nothing is so fatal to a personality as the keeping of promises, unless it be telling the truth.

❦ When one comes in contact with the soul it makes one simple as a child, as Christ said one should be.

❦ When Jesus talks about the poor He simply means personalities, just as when He talks about the rich He simply means people who have not developed their personalities. An echo is often more beautiful than the voice it repeats. An eternal smile is much more wearisome than a perpetual frown. The one sweeps away all possibilities, the other suggests a thousand.

❦ To recognise that the soul of a man is unknowable is the ultimate achievement of wisdom. The final mystery is oneself. When one has weighed the sun in a balance, and measured the steps of the moon, and mapped out the seven heavens star by star, there still remains oneself. Who can calculate the orbit of his own soul?

❦ The soul itself, the soul of each one of us, is to each one of us a mystery. It hides in the dark and broods, and consciousness cannot tell us of its workings.

❦ Behind the perfection of a man's style, must lie the passion of a man's soul.

❦ To have a capacity for a passion, and not to realise it is to make oneself incomplete and limited.

❦ It is a very unimaginative nature that only cares for people on their pedestals.

❦ The only things worth doing are those that the world is surprised at.

❦ Nothing is worth doing except what the world says is impossible.

❦ There is a fatality about all physical and intellectual distinction. It is better not to be different from one's fellows.

❦ Secrecy seems to be the one thing that can make modern life mysterious or marvellous to us. The commonest thing is delightful if one only hides it.

❦ Besides the professional posers of the studio there are posers of the Row, the posers at afternoon teas, the posers in politics and the circus posers. All four classes are delightful, but only the last class is ever really decorative.

❦ 'Know thyself' was written over the portal of the antique world. Over the portal of the new world 'Be thyself' shall be written. And the message of Christ to man was simply: 'Be thyself.' That is the secret of Christ.

❦ I am a little too old now, myself, to trouble about setting a good example, but I always admire people who do.

Always in a Rage

❦ The English mind is always in a rage. The intellect of the race is wasted on the sordid and stupid quarrels of second-rate politicians and third-rate theologians. We are dominated by the fanatic, whose worst vice is his sincerity.

❦ I don't desire to change anything in England except the weather.

❦ England has done one thing; it has invented and established Public Opinion, which is an attempt to organise the ignorance of the community, and to elevate it to the dignity of physical force.

❦ The English have a miraculous power of turning wine into water.

❦ I can't stand your English house-parties. In England people actually try to be brilliant at breakfast. That is dreadful of them! Only dull people are brilliant at breakfast.

❦ I quite sympathise with the rage of the English democracy against what they call the vices of the upper orders. The masses feel that drunkenness, stupidity and immorality should be their own special property, and that if any one of us makes an ass of himself he is poaching on their preserves.

❦ Our countrymen never recognise a description. They are more cunning than practical. When they make up their ledger, they balance stupidity by wealth and vice by hypocrisy.

🐛 Tartuffe has emigrated to England and opened a shop.

🐛 I don't think England should be represented abroad by an unmarried man. It might lead to complications.

🐛 Mrs Cheveley: [He is] a typical Englishman, always dull and usually violent.

🐛 The *Peerage* is the one book a young man about town should know thoroughly and it is the best thing in fiction the English have ever done.

🐛 Bosie (Lord Alfred Douglas) has no real enjoyment of a joke unless he thinks there is a good chance of the other person being pained or annoyed. It is an entirely English trait. The English type and symbol of a joke being the jug on the half-opened door or the distribution of orange peel on the pavement of a crowded thoroughfare.

🐛 One of those characteristic British faces that once seen are never remembered.

🐛 West Kensington is a district to which you drive until the horse drops dead, when the cabman gets down to make enquiries.

🐛 Bayswater is a place where people always get lost, and where there are no guides.

🐛 London is too full of fogs – and serious people. Whether the fogs produce the serious people or the serious people produce the fogs, I don't know, but the whole thing rather gets on my nerves.

🐛 This grey, monstrous London of ours, with its myriads of people, its sordid sinners and its splendid sins.

🐛 The English people give intensely ugly names to places. One place had such an ugly name that I refused to lecture there. It was called Grigsville.

❦ To disagree with three-fourths of the British public on all points is one of the first elements of sanity, one of the deepest consolations in all moments of spiritual doubt.

❦ The first time that the absolute stupidity of the English people was ever revealed to me was one Sunday at the Oxford University Church when the preacher opened his sermon in something this way: 'When a young man says, not in polished banter but in sober earnestness, that he finds it difficult to live up to the level of his blue china, there has crept into the cloistered shades a form of heathenism which it is our bounden duty to fight against and crush out if possible.' I need hardly say that we were delighted and amused at the typical English way in which our ideas were misunderstood. They took our epigrams as earnest, and our parodies as prose.

❦ It is not so easy to be unpractical as the ignorant philistine imagines. It were well for England if it were so. There is no country in the world so much in need of unpractical people as this country of ours. With us, thought is degraded by its constant association with practice.

❦ The real weakness of England lies, not in incomplete armaments or unfortified coasts, not in the poverty that creeps through sunless lanes or the drunkenness that brawls in loathsome courts, but simply in the fact that her ideals are emotional and not intellectual.

❦ In this country it is enough for a man to have distinction and brains for every common tongue to wag against him. And what sort of lives do these people who pose as being moral lead themselves. We are in the native land of the hypocrite.

❦ Somehow I don't think I shall live to see the new century – if another century began and I was still alive, it would really be more than the English could stand.

On the British race:

🐛 It represents the survival of the pushing.

🐛 The English can't stand a man who is always saying he is in the right, but they are very fond of a man who admits he has been in the wrong. It is one of the best things in them.

🐛 There is an Italian cook – also the lad Eolo who waits at table. His father said that he was christened Eolo because he was born on a night on which there was a dreadful wind! I think it is rather nice to have thought of such a name. An English peasant would probably have said, 'We called him John, sir, because we were getting in the hay at the time.'

🐛 Beer, the Bible and the seven deadly virtues have made our England what she is.

🐛 The English public, as a mass, takes no interest in a work of art until it is told that the work in question is immoral.

🐛 There are only two forms of writers in England, the unread and the unreadable.

🐛 If the English had realised what a great poet he [SHELLEY] really was, they would have fallen on him with tooth and nail and made his life as unbearable to him as they possibly could.

🐛 England never appreciates a poet until he is dead.

🐛 The British public are really not equal to the mental strain of having more than one topic every three months.

🐛 The actual people who live in Japan are not unlike the general run of English people; that is to say, they are extremely commonplace and have nothing curious or extraordinary about them.

🐛 What a monstrous climate! I guess the old country is so overpopulated that they have not enough decent weather for everybody. I have always been of the opinion that emigration is the only thing for England.

Something in Their Climate

❦ All Americans lecture. I suppose it is something in their climate.

On arrival in America:
❦ I am not exactly pleased with the Atlantic, it is not so majestic as I expected.

On the return voyage:
❦ The Atlantic has been greatly misunderstood.

❦ We have really everything in common with America nowadays, except, of course, language.

❦ The discovery of America was the beginning of the death of art.

❦ Once in New York, you are sure to be a great success. I know lots of people there who would give a hundred thousand dollars to have a grandfather, and much more than that to have a family ghost.

On being asked by an American theatrical manager to make some changes in Vera, *then being considered for production*:
❦ 'Who am I to tamper with a masterpiece?'

❦ I am impelled for the first time to breathe a fervent prayer: Save me from my disciples.

❦ American youths are pale and precocious, or sallow and supercilious, but American girls are pretty and charming – little oases of pretty unreasonableness in a vast desert of practical common sense.

❦ It is a popular superstition that a visitor to the more distant parts of the United States is spoken to as 'Stranger'. But when I went to Texas I was called 'Captain'; when I got to the centre of the country I was addressed as 'Colonel'; and, on arriving at the borders of Mexico as 'General'.

❦ In America life is one long expectoration.

❦ 'I don't think I like American inventions, Arthur. I am quite sure I don't. I read some American novels lately, and they were quite nonsensical.

❦ The Americans are certainly great hero-worshippers, and always take heroes from the criminal classes.

❦ The Cantervilles have blue blood, for instance, the very bluest in England; but I know you Americans don't care for things of this kind.

❦ LADY CAROLINE: These American girls carry off all the good matches. Why can't they stay in their own country? They are always telling us it is the Paradise of Women.
    LORD ILLINGWORTH: It is, Lady Caroline. That is why, like Eve, they are so extremely anxious to get out of it.

❦ Warned by the example of her mother that American women do not grow old gracefully, she tries not to grow old at all, and often succeeds.

❦ With the exception of the United States Minister, always a welcome personage wherever he goes, and an occasional lion from Boston or the Far West, no American man has any social existence in London.

❦ Dreary as were the old Pilgrim Fathers, who left our shores more than two centuries ago to found a New England beyond seas, the Pilgrim Mothers, who have returned to us in the nineteenth century, are drearier still. Here and there, of course, there are exceptions, but as a class they are either dull, dowdy or dyspeptic.

❧ HESTER *(smiling)*: We have the largest country in the world, Lady Caroline. They used to tell us at school that some of our states are as big as France and England put together.

LADY CAROLINE: Ah! you must find it very draughty, I should fancy. Many American ladies on leaving their native land adopt an appearance of chronic ill-health, under the impression that it is a form of European refinement.

❧ It is true that when we meet him in Europe his conversation keeps us in fits of laughter; but this is merely because his ideas are so absolutely incongruous with European surroundings. Place him in his own environment and the very same observations will fail to excite a smile. They have sunk to the level of the commonplace truism, or the sensible remark; and what seemed a paradox when we listened to it in London, becomes a platitude when we hear it in Milwaukee.

❧ She behaves as if she was beautiful. Most American women do. It is the secret of their charm.

❧ Among the more elderly inhabitants of the South I found a melancholy tendency to date every event of importance on the late war. 'How beautiful the moon is tonight,' I once remarked to a gentleman standing near me. 'Yes,' was his reply, 'but you should have seen it before the war.'

❧ For him [the American man] art has no marvel, and beauty no meaning, and the past no message. He thinks that civilisation began with the introduction of steam, and looks with contempt upon all centuries that had no hot-water apparatuses in their houses.

❧ He is M. RENAN's *l'homme sensuel moyen*, MR ARNOLD's middle-class philistine. The telephone is his test of civilisation, and his wildest dreams of Utopia do not rise beyond elevated railways and electric bells.

❦ Real experience comes to them so much sooner than it does to us that they are never awkward, never shy, and never say foolish things except when they ask one how the Hudson River compares with the Rhine, or whether Brooklyn Bridge is not really more impressive than the dome of St Paul's.

❦ I can stand brute force but brute reason is quite unbearable. There is something unfair about its use. It is like hitting below the intellect.

❦ It is the noisiest country that ever existed. Such continual turmoil must ultimately be destruction of the musical faculty.

❦ I would rather have discovered MRS LANGTRY than have discovered America.

❦ The crude commercialism of America, its materialistic spirit, its indifference to the poetical side of things, and its lack of imagination and of high unattainable ideas, are entirely due to that country having adopted for its national hero a man who, according to his own confession, was incapable of telling a lie, and it is not too much to say that the story of George Washington and the cherry tree has done more harm and in a shorter space of time than any other moral tale in the whole of literature – and the amusing part of the whole thing is that the story of the cherry tree is an absolute myth.

❦ I believe a most serious problem for the American people to consider is the cultivation of better manners. It is the most noticeable, the most principal, defect in American civilisation.

❦ There are no trappings, no pageantry, and no gorgeous ceremonies. I saw only two processions: one was the fire brigade preceded by the police, the other was the police preceded by the fire brigade.

❦ Washington has too many bronze generals.

❧ The two most remarkable bits of scenery in the States are undoubtedly Delmonico's and the Yosemite Valley.

❧ A nation arrayed in stove-pipe hats and dress improvers might have built the Pantechnicon, possibly, but the Parthenon, never.

❧ Salt Lake City contains only two buildings of note, the chief being the Tabernacle, which is the shape of a soup-kettle.

❧ The cities of America are inexpressibly tedious. The Bostonians take their learning too sadly; culture with them is an accomplishment rather than an atmosphere, their 'Hub', as they call it, is the paradise of prigs. Chicago is a sort of monster-shop, full of bustle and bores. Political life at Washington is like political life in a suburban vestry. Baltimore is amusing for a week, but Philadelphia is dreadfully provincial; and though one can dine in New York, one could not dwell there.

❧ It is an odd thing, but everyone who disappears is said to be seen in San Francisco. It must be a delightful city and possess all the attractions of the next world.

❧ San Francisco has the most lovely surroundings of any city except Naples.

❧ California is an Italy without its art.

❧ In no place is society more free and cordial and ready to give a friendly reception to a stranger than in California. In no part of the world is the individual more free from restraint.

❧ America reminds me of one of EDGAR ALLAN POE'S exquisite poems, because it is full of belles.

❧ Let the Greek carve his lions and the Goth his dragons: buffalo and wild deer are the animals for you.

❦ In all my journeys through the country, the very well-dressed men that I saw were the Western miners. As I looked at them I could not help thinking with regret of the time when these picturesque miners would have made their fortunes and would go East to assume again all the abominations of modern fashionable attire. Indeed, so concerned was I that I made some of them promise that when they again appeared on the more crowded scenes of Eastern civilisation they would still continue to wear their lovely costume. But I do not believe they will.

❦ The youth of America is their oldest tradition. It has been going on now for three hundred years. To hear them talk we would imagine they were in their first childhood. As far as civilisation goes they are in their second.

❦ The gold is ready for you in unexhausted treasure, stored up in the mountain hollow or strewn on the river sand, and was not given to you merely for barren speculation. There should be some better record of it left in your history than the merchant's panic and the ruined home.

❦ LADY CAROLINE: There are a great many things you haven't got in America, I am told, Miss Worsley. They say you have no ruins, and no curiosities.
    MRS ALLONBY: What nonsense! They have their mothers and their manners.
    HESTER: The English aristocracy supply us with our curiosities.

❦ MRS ALLONBY: They say, Lady Hunstanton, that when good Americans die they go to Paris.
    LADY HUNSTANTON: Indeed? And when bad Americans die, where do they go to?
    LORD ILLINGWORTH: Oh, they go to America.

❦ English people are far more interested in American barbarism than they are in American civilisation.

❦ The Niagara Falls – simply a vast unnecessary amount of water going the wrong way and then falling over unnecessary rocks. The wonder would be if the water did not fall! Every American bride is taken there and the sight of the stupendous waterfall must be one of the earliest, if not the keenest, disappointments in American married life.

❦ America has never quite forgiven Europe for having been discovered somewhat earlier in history than itself.

❦ It is a vulgar error to suppose that America was ever discovered. It was merely detected.

❦ One is impressed in America, but not favourably impressed, by the inordinate size of everything. The country seems to try to bully one into a belief in its power by its impressive bigness.

❦ Bulk is their canon of beauty and size their standard of excellence.

❦ I am told that pork-packing is the most lucrative profession in America, after politics.

❦ The people of America understand money-making, but not how to spend it.

❦ In America the young are always ready to give those who are older than themselves the full benefits of their inexperience.

❦ The American child educates its father and mother.

❦ In America there is no opening for a fool. They expect brains, even from a bootblack, and get them.

❦ In going to America one learns that poverty is not a necessary accompaniment to civilisation.

❦ It is impossible not to think nobly of a country that has produced Patrick Henry, Thomas Jefferson, George Washington and Jefferson Davis.

❦ The Americans are the best politically educated people in the world. It is well worth one's while to go to a country which can teach us the beauty of the word FREEDOM and the value of the thing LIBERTY.

❦ On the whole, American girls have a wonderful charm, and, perhaps, the chief secret of their charm is that they never talk seriously, except to their dressmaker, and never think seriously, except about amusements.

❦ They have, however, one grave fault – their mothers.

❦ The American woman is the most decorated and decorative object I have seen in America.

❦ American women are bright, clever and wonderfully cosmopolitan. Their patriotic feelings are limited to an admiration for Niagara and a regret for the Elevated Railway; and, unlike the men, they never bore us with Bunker Hill.

❦ As for marriage, it is one of their most popular institutions. The American man marries early and the American woman marries often; and they get on extremely well together.

❦ In America, the horrors of domesticity are almost entirely unknown. There are no scenes over the soup, no quarrels over the entrées, and as, by a clause inserted in every marriage settlement, the husband solemnly binds himself to use studs and not buttons for his shirts, one of the chief sources of disagreement in ordinary middle-class life is absolutely removed.

❦ If the Americans are not the most well-dressed people in the world, they are the most comfortably dressed.

That Dreadful Vulgar Place

🐛 To Australia? Oh, don't mention that dreadful vulgar place.

🐛 Do you know, Mr Hopper, dear Agatha and I are so much interested in Australia. It must be so pretty with all the dear little kangaroos flying about. Agatha has found it on the map. What a curious shape it is! Just like a packing case.

🐛 I trust you will return from Australia in a position of affluence. I believe there is no society of any kind in the Colonies, nothing that I would call society.

🐛 When I look at the map and see what an ugly country Australia is, I feel that I want to go there and see if it cannot be changed into a more beautiful form!

The Criminal Calendar

❦ You give the criminal calendar of Europe to your children under the name of history.

❦ I don't like Switzerland: it has produced nothing but theologians and waiters.

❦ Freckles run in Scotch families just as gout does in English families.

❦ There are some who will welcome with delight the idea of solving the Irish problem by doing away with the Irish people.

❦ While in London one hides everything, in Paris one reveals everything.

❦ In Paris one can lose one's time most delightfully; but one can never lose one's way.

On the Eiffel Tower:
❦ Turn your back to that – you have all Paris before you. Look at it – Paris vanishes.

❦ La belle France is entirely ruined, through bad morals and worse cookery.

❦ The Rhine is of course tedious, the vineyards are formal and dull and, as far as I can judge, the inhabitants of Germany are American.

❦ The train that whirls an ordinary Englishman through Italy at the rate of forty miles an hour and finally sends him home without any memory of that lovely country but that he was cheated by a courier at Rome, or that he got a bad dinner at Verona, does not do him or civilisation much good.

❦ Ah! How I loathe the Romans! They are rough and common and they give themselves the airs of noble lords.

❦ He talks of Europe as being old; but it is he himself who has never been young.

❦ His one desire is to get the whole of Europe into thorough repair.

❦ I am not sure that foreigners should cultivate likes or dislikes about the people they are invited to meet.

A Kind of Ostentatious Obscurity

❧ Lying for the sake of a monthly salary is, of course, well known in Fleet Street, and the profession of a political leader-writer is not without advantages. But it is said to be a somewhat dull occupation, and it certainly does not lead to much beyond a kind of ostentatious obscurity.

❧ As for modern journalism, it is not my business to defend it. It justifies its own existence by the great Darwinian principle of the survival of the vulgarest.

❧ I am afraid that writing to newspapers has a deteriorating influence on style. People get violent, and abusive and lose all sense of proportion when they enter that curious journalistic arena in which the race is always to the noisiest.

❧ VICOMTE DE NANJAC: I read all your English newspapers. I find them so amusing.
   LORD GORING: Then, my dear Nanjac, you must certainly read between the lines.

❧ The newspapers chronicle with degrading avidity the sins of the second-rate, and with the conscientiousness of the illiterate give us accurate and prosaic details of the doings of people of absolutely no interest whatever.

❧ There is much to be said in favour of modern journalism. By giving us the opinions of the uneducated, it keeps us in touch with the ignorance of the community. By carefully chronicling the current events of contemporary life, it shows us what very little importance such events really have.

❦ With regard to modern journalists, they always apologise to one in private for what they have written against one in public.

❦ In the old days men had the rack, now they have the press.

❦ Journalism is unreadable, and literature is not read.

❦ I am very much pleased to see that you are beginning to call attention to the extremely slipshod and careless style of our ordinary magazine-writers.

❦ The public have an insatiable curiosity to know everything, except what is worth knowing. Journalism, conscious of this, and having tradesman-like habits, supplies their demands. In centuries before ours the public nailed the ears of journalists to the pump. That was quite hideous. In this century journalists have nailed their own ears to the keyhole. That is much worse.

❦ To have a style so gorgeous that it conceals the subject is one of the highest achievements of an important and much admired school of Fleet Street leader-writers.

❦ Instead of monopolising the seat of judgement, journalism should be apologising in the dock.

❦ Who are these scribes who, passing with purposeless alacrity from the *Police News* to the Parthenon, and from crime to criticism, sway with such serene incapacity the office which they have so lately swept?

❦ Somebody – was it BURKE? – called journalism the fourth estate. That was true at the time, no doubt. But at the present moment it really is the only estate. It has eaten up the other three. The Lords Temporal say nothing, the Lords Spiritual have nothing to say, and the House of Commons has nothing to say and says it. We are dominated by journalism. In America the president reigns for four years, and journalism goes on for ever and ever.

❦ What is behind the leading article but prejudice, stupidity, cant and twaddle?

❦ The journalist is always reminding the public of the existence of the artist. That is unnecessary of him. He is always reminding the artist of the existence of the public. That is indecent of him. Journalists record only what happens. What does it matter what happens? It is only the abiding things that are interesting, not the horrid incidents of everyday life. Creation for the joy of creation is the aim of the artist, and that is why the artist is a more divine type than the saint.

❦ Every time my name is mentioned in a paper I write at once to admit that I am the Messiah. Why is Pears' soap successful? Not because it is better or cheaper than any other soap, but because it is more strenuously puffed. The journalist is my John the Baptist.

❦ Newspapers even have degenerated. They may now be absolutely relied upon. One feels it as one wades through their columns. It is always the unreadable that occurs.

❦ MRS CHEVELEY: I am quite looking forward to meeting your clever husband, Lady Chiltern. They actually succeed in spelling his name right in the newspapers. That in itself is fame, on the Continent.

❦ In France, in fact, they limit the journalist and allow the artist almost perfect freedom. Here we allow absolute freedom to the journalist and entirely limit the artist.

❦ At present the newspapers are trying hard to induce the public to judge a sculptor, for instance, never by his statues but by the way he treats his wife; a painter by the amount of his income; and a poet by the colour of his necktie.

❦ Spies are of no use nowadays. The newspapers do their work instead.

❦ It was a fatal day when the public discovered that the pen is mightier than the paving stone, and can be made as offensive as the brickbat. They at once sought for the journalist, found him, developed him, and made him their industrious and well-paid servant.

❦ Bad manners make a journalist.

❦ The conscience of an editor is purely decorative.

The Mischievous Idea of Government

❦ In an evil moment the philanthropist made his appearance, and brought with him the mischievous idea of government.

❦ KELVIL: May I ask, Lord Illingworth, if you regard the House of Lords as a better institution than the House of Commons?

LORD ILLINGWORTH: A much better institution of course. We in the House of Lords are never in touch with public opinion. That makes us a civilised body.

❦ LADY BASILDON: I delight in talking politics. I talk them all day long. But I can't bear listening to them. I don't know how the unfortunate men in the House stand these long debates.

LORD GORING: By never listening.

❦ Really, this horrid House of Commons quite ruins our husbands for us. I think the Lower House by far the greatest blow to a happy married life that there has been since that terrible thing called the Higher Education of Women was invented.

❦ In England, a man who can't talk morality twice a week to a large, popular, immoral audience is quite over as a serious politician. There would be nothing left for him as a profession except Botany or the Church.

❦ He's sure to be a wonderful success. He thinks like a Tory, and talks like a Radical, and that's so important nowadays.

❧ There is hardly a single person in the House of Commons worth painting; though many of them would be better for a little whitewashing.

❧ Wherever there is a man who exercises authority there is a man who resists authority.

❧ MABEL CHILTERN: Oh! I hope you are not going to leave me all alone with Lord Goring? Especially at such an early hour in the day.

LORD CAVERSHAM: I am afraid I can't take him with me to Downing Street. It is not the Prime Minister's day for seeing the unemployed.

❧ If socialism is authoritarian; if there are governments armed with economic power as they are now with political power; if, in a word, we are to have industrial tyrannies, then the last state of man will be worse than the first.

❧ We are trying at the present time to stave off the coming crisis, the coming revolution as my friends the Fabianists call it, by means of doles and alms. Well when the revolution or crisis arrives, we shall be powerless because we shall know nothing.

❧ Believe me, in a good democracy, every man should be an aristocrat: but these people in Russia who seek to thrust us out are no better than the animals in one's preserves, and made to be shot at, most of them.

❧ What we want are unpractical people who see beyond the moment and think beyond the day. Those who try to lead the people can only do so by following the mob. It is through the voice crying in the wilderness that the ways of the gods must be prepared.

❧ Nothing is impossible in Russia but reform.

❦ What is a practical scheme? A practical scheme is either one that is already in existence, or a scheme that could be carried out under existing conditions. But it is exactly existing conditions that one objects to; and any scheme that could accept these conditions is wrong and foolish. The conditions will be done away with, and human nature will change. The only thing that one really knows about human nature is that it changes. The systems that fail are those that rely on the permanency of human nature, and not on its growth and development. The error of Louis XIV was that he thought human nature would always be the same. The result of his error was the French Revolution.

❦ Picturesqueness cannot survive the House of Commons.

❦ High hopes were once formed of democracy; but democracy means simply the bludgeoning of the people by the people for the people.

❦ There is this to be said in favour of the despot, that he, being an individual, may have culture, while the mob, being a monster, has none. One who is an emperor and king may stoop to pick up a brush for a painter, but when democracy stoops down it is merely to throw mud. And yet the democracy have not so far to stoop as the emperor. In fact, if they want to throw mud they have not to stoop at all. But there is no necessity to separate the monarch from the mob; all authority is equally bad. There are three kinds of despots. There is the despot who tyrannises over the body. There is the despot who tyrannises over the soul. There is the despot who tyrannises over the soul and body alike. The first is called the Prince. The second is called the Pope. The third is called the People.

❦ People sometimes enquire what form of government it is most suitable for an artist to live under. To this question there is only one answer. The form of government that is most suitable to the artist is no government at all.

❦ Patriotism is the virtue of the vicious.

❧ Agitators are a set of interfering meddling people, who come down to some perfectly contented class of the community and sow the seeds of discontent amongst them. That is the reason why agitators are so absolutely necessary.

❧ It is to be regretted that a portion of our community should be practically in slavery, but to propose to solve the problem by enslaving the entire community is childish.

❧ It is immoral to use private property in order to alleviate the horrible evils that result from the institution of private property. It is both immoral and unfair.

❧ Good kings are the only dangerous enemies that modern democracy has.

❧ Socialism annihilates family life, for instance. With the abolition of private property, marriage in its present form must disappear.

❧ A Russian who lives happily under the present system of government in Russia must either believe that man has no soul, or that, if he has, it is not worth developing.

❧ Only people who look dull ever get into the House of Commons, and only people who are dull ever succeed there.

❧ He pretends to be devoted to the people, and lives in a palace; preaches socialism, and draws a salary that would support a province.

❧ What a Communist he is! He would have an equal distribution of sin as well as property.

❧ While to the claims of charity a man may yield and yet be free, to the claims of conformity no man may yield and remain free at all.

❧ All authority is quite degrading. It degrades those who exercise it, and it degrades those over whom it is exercised.

❧ Whenever a community or a government of any kind attempts to dictate to the artist what he is to do, art either entirely vanishes, or becomes stereotyped, or degenerates into a low and ignoble form of craft!

❧ In a community like ours, where property confers immense distinction, social position, honour, respect, titles and other pleasant things of the kind, man being naturally ambitious, makes it his aim to accumulate this property, and goes on wearily and tediously accumulating it long after he has got more than he wants, or can use, or enjoy, or perhaps even know of. Man will kill himself by overwork in order to secure property, and really, considering the enormous advantages that property brings, one is hardly surprised.

❧ As long as war is regarded as wicked, it will always have its fascination. When it is looked upon as vulgar it will cease to be popular.

❧ All modes of government are failures.

❧ Life under a good government is rarely dramatic; life under a bad government is always so.

❧ Sir John's temper since he has taken seriously to politics has become quite unbearable. Really, now that the House of Commons is trying to become useful, it does a great deal of harm.

❧ I assure you my life will be quite ruined unless they send John at once to the Upper House. He won't take any interest in politics then, will he? The House of Lords is so sensible. An assembly of gentlemen.

❧ Were there no law there'd be no law-breakers, so all men would be virtuous.

❧ To be entirely free and at the same time entirely dominated by law is the eternal paradox of human life that we realise at every moment.

The First Serious Step in Life

❦ Sentiment is all very well for the buttonhole. But the essential thing for a necktie is style. A well-tied tie is the first serious step in life.

❦ In all unimportant matters, style, not sincerity, is the essential. In all important matters, style, not sincerity, is the essential.

❦ One's style is one's signature always.

❦ The best style is that which seems an unconscious result rather than a conscious aim.

❦ Style largely depends on the way the chin is worn.

❦ In the mode of the knotting of one's necktie or the conduct of onc's cane there is an entire creed of life.

❦ Beauty is the wonder of wonders. It is only the shallow people who do not judge by appearances.

❦ He atones for being occasionally somewhat over-dressed, by being always absolutely over-educated.

❦ I never saw anybody take so long to dress, and with such little result.

❦ With an evening coat and a white tie, anybody, even a stockbroker, can gain a reputation for being civilised.

❦ A really well-made buttonhole is the only link between art and nature.

❦ One should either be a work of art or wear a work of art.

❦ I once saw in a French journal, under a drawing of a bonnet, the words: 'With this style the mouth is worn slightly open.'

❦ He has nothing, but looks everything. What more can one desire?

❦ She wore far too much rouge last night and not quite enough clothes. That is always a sign of despair in a woman.

❦ Fashion is what one wears oneself. What is unfashionable is what other people wear.

❦ Knaves nowadays do look so honest that honest folk are forced to look like knaves so as to be different.

❦ In matters of grave importance, style, not sincerity, is the vital thing.

❦ A mask tells us more than a face.

❦ You're young and wouldn't be ill-favoured either, had God or thy mother given thee another face.

❦ Thy body is hideous. It is like the body of a leper. It is like a plastered wall where vipers have crawled.

❦ How can you see anything in a girl with coarse hands?

❦ There is nothing to my mind more coarse in conception and more vulgar in execution than modern jewellery.

❦ I am thoroughly sick of pearls. They make one look so plain, so good and so intellectual.

❦ LORD GORING: I should fancy Mrs Cheveley is one of those very modern women of our time who find a new scandal as becoming as a new bonnet, and air them both in the park every afternoon at five-thirty.

❦ Do you believe that the Athenian women were like the stately dignified figures of the Parthenon frieze, or like those marvellous goddesses who sat in the triangular pediments of the same building? If you judge from the art, they certainly were so. But read an authority like ARISTOPHANES, for instance. You will find that the Athenian ladies laced tightly, wore high-heeled shoes, dyed their hair yellow, painted and rouged their faces and were exactly like any silly fashionable or fallen creatures of our own day. The fact is that we look back on the ages entirely through the medium of art, and art, very fortunately, has never once told us the truth.

❦ One should never give a woman anything she can't wear in the evening.

❦ What a pity it is that LUTHER knew nothing of dress, had no sense of the becoming. He had courage but no fineness of perception. I'm afraid his neckties would always have been quite shocking.

❦ Cavaliers and Puritans are interesting for their costumes and not for their convictions.

❦ A man is called affected, nowadays, if he dresses as he likes to dress. But in doing that he is acting in a perfectly natural manner. Affectation, in such matters, consists in dressing according to the views of one's neighbour, whose views, as they are the views of the majority, will probably be extremely stupid.

❦ When she is in a very smart gown, she looks like an *édition de luxe* of a wicked French novel meant specially for the English market.

❧ To see the frock-coat of the drawing-room done in bronze or the double waistcoat perpetuated in marble adds a new horror to death.

❧ Greek dress was in its essence inartistic. Nothing should reveal the body but the body.

❧ Every right article of apparel belongs equally to both sexes and there is absolutely no such thing as a definitely feminine garment.

❧ All costumes are caricatures.

❧ Costume is a growth, an evolution, and a most important, perhaps the most important, sign of the manners, customs and mode of life of each century.

❧ Of SHAKESPEARE it may be said that he was the first to see the dramatic value of doublets and that a climax may depend on a crinoline.

❧ The artistic feeling of a nation should find expression in its costume quite as much as in its architecture.

❧ The imagination will concentrate itself on the waistcoat. Waistcoats will show whether a man can admire poetry or not.

❧ It is really only the idle classes who dress badly. Wherever physical labour of any kind is required, the costume used is, as a rule, absolutely right, for labour necessitates freedom, and without freedom there is no such thing as beauty in dress at all.

❧ Tails have no place in costume, except on some Darwinian theory of heredity.

❧ Fashion is merely a form of ugliness so unbearable that we are compelled to alter it every six months.

❦ From the sixteenth century to our own day there is hardly any form of torture that has not been inflicted on girls and endured by women in obedience to the dictates of an unreasonable and monstrous Fashion.

❦ Whatever limits, constrains and mutilates is essentially ugly, though the eyes of many are so blinded by custom that they do not notice the ugliness till it has become unfashionable.

❦ I saw the governess, Jane. She was far too good-looking to be in any respectable household.

❦ To be really medieval one should have no body. To be really modern one should have no soul. To be really Greek one should have no clothes.

The Only Proper Intoxication

❦ After all, the only proper intoxication is conversation.

❦ There is only one thing in the world worse than being talked about, and that is not being talked about.

❦ I may have said the same thing before . . . But my explanation, I am sure, will always be different.

❦ MRS ALLONBY: You should certainly know Ernest, Lady Stutfield. It is only fair to tell you beforehand he has got no conversation at all.
LADY STUTFIELD: I adore silent men.
MRS ALLONBY: Oh, Ernest isn't silent. He talks the whole time. But he has got no conversation.

❦ Murder is always a mistake. One should never do anything that one cannot talk about after dinner.

❦ I love scandals about other people, but scandals about myself don't interest me. They have not got the charm of novelty.

❦ Between me and life there is a mist of words always. I throw probability out of the window for the sake of a phrase, and the chance of an epigram makes me desert truth. Still I do aim at making a work of art.

❦ The value of the telephone is the value of what two people have to say.

❦ 'There is no good talking to him,' said a Dragonfly, who was sitting on the top of a large brown bulrush; 'no good at all, for he has gone away.'

'Well, that is his loss, not mine,' answered the Rocket. 'I am not going to stop talking to him merely because he pays no attention. I like hearing myself talk. It is one of my greatest pleasures. I often have long conversations all by myself, and I am so clever that sometimes I don't understand a single word of what I am saying.'

❦ LORD CAVERSHAM: Do you always really understand what you say, sir?
LORD GORING (*after some hesitation*): Yes, father, if I listen attentively.

❦ I dislike arguments of any kind. They are always vulgar, and often convincing.

❦ Nowadays to be intelligible is to be found out.

❦ PRINCE PAUL: I find these Cabinet Councils extremely tiring.
PRINCE PETROVITCH: Naturally, you are always speaking.
PRINCE PAUL: No; I think it must be that I have to listen sometimes. It is so exhausting not to talk.

❦ LORD GORING: I usually say what I really think. A great mistake nowadays. It makes one so liable to be misunderstood.

❦ I don't at all like knowing what people say of me behind my back. It makes one far too conceited.

❦ Everything you have said today seems to me excessively immoral. It has been most interesting, listening to you.

❦ What is the difference between scandal and gossip? Oh! gossip is charming! History is merely gossip, but scandal is gossip made tedious by morality.

❦ A man who can dominate a London dinner-table can dominate the world. The future belongs to the dandy. It is the exquisites who are going to rule.

❦ I like to do all the talking myself. It saves time and prevents arguments.

❦ That some change will take place before this century has drawn to its close we have no doubt whatsoever. Bored by the tedious and improving conversation of those who have neither the wit to exaggerate nor the genius to romance, tired of the intelligent person whose reminiscences are always based on memory, whose statements are invariably limited by probability and who is at any time liable to be corroborated by the merest philistine who happens to be present, society sooner or later must return to its lost leader, the cultured and fascinating liar.

❦ Lots of people act well but very few people talk well, which shows that talking is much more the difficult thing of the two, and much the finer thing also.

❦ I like talking to a brick wall, it's the only thing in the world that never contradicts me.

❦ There are things that are right to say, but that may be said at the wrong time and to the wrong people.

❦ I am afraid you have been listening to the conversation of someone older than yourself. That is always a dangerous thing to do, and if you allow it to degenerate into a habit you will find it absolutely fatal to any intellectual development.

❦ Conversation should touch everything but should concentrate itself on nothing.

❦ The simplicity of your character makes you exquisitely incomprehensible to me.

❧ Arguments are extremely vulgar, for everybody in good society holds exactly the same opinions.

❧ Learned conversation is either the affectation of the ignorant or the profession of the mentally unemployed. And as for what is called improving conversation, that is merely the foolish method by which the still more foolish philanthropist feebly tries to disarm the just rancour of the criminal classes.

❧ Questions are never indiscreet. Answers sometimes are.

❧ I hate people who talk about themselves, as you do, when one wants to talk about oneself, as I do.

❧ It is a very dangerous thing to listen. If one listens one may be convinced; and a man who allows himself to be convinced by an argument is a thoroughly unreasonable person.

❧ DORIAN GRAY: You would sacrifice anybody, Harry, for the sake of an epigram.

❧ HESTER: I dislike London dinner-parties.
MRS ALLONBY: I adore them. The clever people never listen, and the stupid people never talk.

❧ It is much more difficult to talk about a thing than to do it. In the sphere of actual life that is of course obvious. Anybody can make history. Only a great man can write it.

❧ I would much sooner talk scandal in the drawing-room than treason in a cellar. Besides, I hate the common mob, who smell of garlic, smoke bad tobacco, get up early and dine off one dish.

❧ She doesn't care much for eloquence in others. She thinks it a little loud.

❧ One dagger will do more than a hundred epigrams.

❧ It is always worth while asking a question, though it is not always worth while answering one.

❧ The only reason, indeed, that excuses one for asking any question is simple curiosity.

❧ He never said a brilliant or even an ill-natured thing in his life.

❧ It is only the intellectually lost who ever argue.

❧ I can't listen to anyone unless he attracts me by a charming style or by beauty of theme.

❧ The well-bred contradict other people. The wise contradict themselves.

❧ When people agree with me I always feel that I must be wrong.

❧ There is no mode of action, no form of emotion, that we do not share with the lower animals. It is only by language that we rise above them – by language, which is the parent not the child of thought.

❧ Conversation is one of the loveliest of the arts.

❧ Ultimately the bond of all companionship, whether in marriage or in friendship, is conversation.

❧ The state of the weather is always an excusable exordium, but it is convenient to have a paradox or heresy on the subject always ready, so as to direct the conversation into other channels.

❧ The art of conversation is really within the reach of almost everyone, except those who are morbidly truthful or whose high moral worth requires to be sustained by a permanent gravity of demeanor and a general dullness of mind.

❦ Recreation, not instruction, is the aim of conversation.

❦ The maxim 'If you find the company dull, blame yourself' seems to us somewhat optimistic.

❦ One wants something that will encourage conversation, particularly at the end of the Season when everyone has practically said whatever they had to say, which in most cases was probably not much.

❦ In the case of meeting a genius and a duke at dinner, the good talker will try to raise himself to the level of the former and to bring the latter down to his own level. To succeed among one's social superiors one must have no hesitation in contradicting them.

❦ One should never listen. To listen is a sign of indifference to one's hearers.

❦ Language is the noblest instrument we have, either for the revealing or the concealing of thought; talk itself is a sort of spiritualised action.

❦ It is much cleverer to talk nonsense than to listen to it . . . and a much rarer thing too, in spite of all the public may say.

One of the Necessary Elements

❦ To know nothing about our great men is one of the necessary elements of English education.

❦ Education is an admirable thing but it is well to remember from time to time that nothing that is worth knowing can be taught.

❦ I have forgotten about my schooldays. I have a vague impression that they were detestable.

❦ I do not approve of anything that tampers with natural ignorance. Ignorance is like a delicate exotic fruit: touch it, and the bloom is gone. The whole theory of modern education is radically unsound. Fortunately, in England at any rate, education produces no effect whatsoever. If it did it would prove a serious danger to the upper classes, and probably lead to acts of violence in Grosvenor Square.

❦ In examinations the foolish ask questions that the wise cannot answer.

❦ In the wild struggle for existence, we want to have something that endures, so we fill our minds with rubbish and facts. The mind of the thoroughly well-informed man is a dreadful thing. It is like a bric-à-brac shop, all monsters and dust, with everything priced above its proper value.

❦ Give children beauty, not the record of bloody slaughters and barbarous brawls, as they call history, or of the latitude and longitude of places nobody cares to visit, as they call geography.

❦ Too much care was taken with our education, I am afraid. To have been well brought up is a great drawback nowadays. It shuts one out from so much.

❦ Lying for the sake of the improvement of the young, which is the basis of home education, still lingers amongst us.

❦ A school should be the most beautiful place in every town and village – so beautiful that the punishment for undutiful children should be that they should be debarred from going to school the following day.

❦ To know everything about oneself one must know all about others.

❦ GILBERT: If you meet at dinner a man who has spent his life in educating himself – a rare type in our time, I admit, but still one occasionally to be met with – you rise from the table richer, and conscious that a high ideal has for a moment touched and sanctified your days. But oh! my dear Ernest, to sit next to a man who has spent his life in trying to educate others! What a dreadful experience that is! How appalling is that ignorance which is the inevitable result of imparting opinions!

❦ LADY BASILDON: Ah! I hate being educated!
MRS MARCHMONT: So do I. It puts one almost on a level with the commercial classes.

❦ I am afraid that we are beginning to be over-educated; at least everybody who is incapable of learning has taken to teaching – that is really what our enthusiasm for education has come to.

❦ It is always an advantage not to have received a sound commercial education, and what I learned on the playing fields at Eton has been quite as useful to me as anything I was taught at Cambridge.

❦ Just as the philanthropist is the nuisance of the ethical sphere, so the nuisance of the intellectual sphere is the man who is so occupied in trying to educate others that he has never had any time to educate himself.

❦ Examinations are pure humbug from beginning to end. If a man is a gentleman he knows quite enough, and if he is not a gentleman whatever he knows is bad for him.

❦ People say that the schoolmaster is abroad. I wish to goodness he were.

❦ Fortunately, in England at any rate, education produces no effect whatsoever.

❦ People never think of cultivating a young girl's imagination. It is the great defect of modern education.

❦ We teach people how to remember, we never teach them how to grow.

❦ In the summer term Oxford teaches the exquisite art of idleness, one of the most important things that any university can teach.

❦ Children have a natural antipathy to books – handicraft should be the basis of education.

❦ I would have a workshop attached to every school, and one hour a day given up to the teaching of simple decorative arts. It would be a golden hour to the children.

❦ Remember that the fool in the eyes of the gods and the fool in the eyes of man are very different.

❦ Nobody, even in the provinces, should ever be allowed to ask an intelligent question about pure mathematics across a dinner table.

❦ What a pity that in life we only get our lessons when they are of no use to us.

Never Any Use to Oneself

❦ I always pass on good advice. It is the only thing to do with it. It is never any use to oneself.

❦ Don't be conceited about your bad qualities. You may lose them as you grow old.

❦ Oh, I'm so glad you've come. There are a hundred things I want not to say to you.

❦ Never try to pull down public monuments such as the Albert Memorial and the Church. You are sure to be damaged by the falling masonry.

❦ It is very vulgar to talk like a dentist when one isn't a dentist. It produces a false impression.

❦ Never buy a thing you don't want merely because it is dear.

❦ What a mistake it is to be sincere!

❦ It is a dangerous thing to reform anyone.

❦ If you wish for reputation and fame in the world and success during your lifetime, you are right to take every opportunity of advertising yourself. You remember the Latin saying, 'Fame springs from one's own house.'

❦ Don't be led astray into the paths of virtue.

❦ One should never take sides in anything. Taking sides is the beginning of sincerity and earnestness follows shortly afterwards, and the human being becomes a bore.

❦ If you wish to understand others you must intensify your own individualism.

❦ It is always a silly thing to give advice, but to give good advice is absolutely fatal.

❦ Whenever one has anything unpleasant to say, one should always be quite candid.

❦ Create yourself. Be yourself your poem.

❦ People are very fond of giving away [advice] what they need most themselves. It is what I call the depths of generosity.

An Occupation of Some Kind

❦ LADY BRACKNELL: Do you smoke?

JACK: Well, yes, I must admit I smoke.

LADY BRACKNELL: I am glad to hear it. A man should always have an occupation of some kind. There are far too many idle men in London as it is.

❦ A cigarette is the perfect type of a perfect pleasure. It is exquisite and it leaves one unsatisfied.

❦ Gold-tipped cigarettes are awfully expensive. I can only afford them when I am in debt.

❦ Half the pretty women in London smoke cigarettes. Personally I prefer the other half.

❦ The only use of our attachés is that they supply their friends with excellent tobacco.

❦ On seeing a 'No Smoking' notice in the Academy of Design at Cincinnati, he remarked: 'Great Heaven! they speak of smoking as if it were a crime. I wonder they don't caution the students not to murder each other on the landings.'

❦ Oscar was once at a dinner-party where the ladies had sat too long and he wanted a chance to smoke. His hostess, seeing a lamp which was smouldering, asked him if he would, 'Please put it out, Mr Wilde, it's smoking.'
'Happy lamp,' said Wilde.

The Only Immortality I Desire

❦ For myself, the only immortality I desire is to invent a new sauce.

❦ When one is going to lead an entirely new life one requires regular and wholesome meals.

❦ He never touches water: it goes to his head at once.

❦ I have made an important discovery – that alcohol, taken in sufficient quantities, produces all the effects of intoxication.

❦ When I am in trouble, eating is the only thing that consoles me. Indeed, when I am in really great trouble, as anyone who knows me intimately will tell you, I refuse everything except food and drink.

❦ To make a good salad is to be a brilliant diplomatist – the problem is entirely the same in both cases. To know exactly how much oil one must put with one's vinegar.

❦ At dinner, once, a chicken was placed before Oscar. He took up the carvers and after a weary attempt to carve he turned to his wife, and said, 'Constance, why do you give me these . . . pedestrians . . . to eat?

❦ Oh, no doubt the cod is a splendid swimmer, admirable for swimming purposes, but not for eating.

❦ The British cook is a foolish woman – who should be turned for her iniquities into a pillar of salt which she never knows how to use.

❦ Society, civilised society at least, is never very ready to believe anything to the detriment of those who are both rich and fascinating. It instinctively feels that manners are of more importance than morals, and in its opinion the highest respectability is of much less value than the possession of a good chef. And, after all, it is a very poor consolation to be told that the man who has given one a bad dinner or poor wine is irreproachable in his private life. Even the cardinal virtues cannot atone for half-cold entrées.

❦ An egg is always an adventure: it may be different.

❦ Oh, he occasionally takes an alcoholiday.

❦ After the first glass of absinthe you see things as you wish they were. After the second you see them as they are not. Finally you see things as they really are, and that is the most horrible thing in the world. I mean disassociated. Take a top hat. You think you see it as it really is. But you don't because you associate it with other things and ideas. If you had never heard of one before, and suddenly saw it alone, you'd be frightened or you'd laugh. That is the effect absinthe has, and that is why it drives men mad. Three nights I sat up all night drinking absinthe, and thinking that I was singularly clear-headed and sane. The waiter came in and began watering the sawdust. The most wonderful flowers, tulips, lilies and roses, sprang up, and made a garden in the café 'Don't you see them?' I said to him. '*Mais non, monsieur, il n'y a rien.*'

❦ To partake of two luncheons in one day would not be liberty. It would be licence.

❦ There are twenty ways of cooking a potato, and three hundred and sixty-four ways of cooking an egg, yet the British cook up to the present moment knows only three methods of sending up either one or the other.

❦ The real difficulty, however, that we all have to face in life is not so much the science of cookery as the stupidity of cooks.

The Flight into Nothingness

❦ Wilde once explained the cause of his wearing mourning – 'This happens to be my birthday, and I am mourning, as I shall henceforth do on each of my anniversaries, the flight of one year of my youth into nothingness, the growing blight upon my summer.'

❦ No age borrows the slang of its predecessor.

❦ Lord Illingworth: There is nothing like youth. The middle-aged are mortgaged to life. The old are in life's lumber room. But youth is the lord of life. Youth has a kingdom waiting for it. Everyone is born a king, and most people die in exile, like most kings. To win back my youth there is nothing I wouldn't do – except take exercise, get up early or be a useful member of the community.

❦ The old believe everything; the middle-aged suspect everything; the young know everything.

❦ To get back one's youth, one has merely to repeat one's follies.

❦ Youth is the one thing worth having.

❦ The secret of remaining young is never to have an emotion that is unbecoming.

❦ The condition of perfection is idleness; the aim of perfection is youth.

❧ Youth smiles without any reason. It is one of its chiefest charms.

❧ The tragedy of old age is not that one is old, but that one is not young.

❧ We never get back our youth. The pulse of joy that beats in us at twenty, becomes sluggish. Our limbs fail, our senses rot. We degenerate into hideous puppets, haunted by the memory of the passions of which we were too much afraid, and the exquisite temptations that we had not the courage to yield to. Youth! Youth! There is absolutely nothing in the world but youth!

❧ Youth isn't an affectation. Youth is an art.

❧ It's absurd to talk of the ignorance of youth. The only people to whose opinions I listen now with any respect are persons much younger than myself. They seem in front of me. Life has revealed to them her latest wonder.

❧ LORD ILLINGWORTH: The soul is born old but grows young. That is the comedy of life.
MRS ALLONBY: And the body is born young and grows old. That is life's tragedy.

❧ The youth of the present day are quite monstrous. They have absolutely no respect for dyed hair.

❧ The old should neither be seen nor heard.

❧ I always contradict the aged; I do it on principle.

❧ As soon as people are old enough to know better, they don't know anything at all.

❧ Those whom the gods hate die old.

❦ Those whom the gods love grow young.

❦ I have never learned anything except from people younger than myself.

❦ He is old enough to know worse.

❦ To Lord Arthur it came early in life – before his nature had been spoiled by the calculating cynicism of middle-age.

❦ Hesitation of any kind is a sign of mental decay in the young, of physical weakness in the old.

An Essential Element of Progress

❦ What is termed sin is an essential element of progress. Without it the world would stagnate or grow old or become colourless. By its curiosity it increases the experience of the race. Through its intensified assertion of individualism it saves us from the commonplace. In its rejection of the current notions about morality it is one with the higher ethics.

❦ We cannot go back to the saint. There is far more to be learned from the sinner.

❦ One pays for one's sins, and then one pays again, and all one's life one pays. Suffering is an expiation.

❦ It has been said that the great events of the world take place in the brain. It is in the brain, and the brain only, that the great sins of the world take place.

❦ Nothing makes one so vain as being told that one is a sinner.

❦ Sin is a thing that writes itself across a man's face. It cannot be concealed. People talk sometimes of secret vices. There are no such things.

❦ I can resist everything except temptation.

❦ Wickedness is a myth invented by good people to account for the curious attractiveness of others.

❦ I hope you have not been leading a double life, pretending to be wicked and being really good all the time, that would be hypocrisy.

❦ 'Lord Henry, I am not at all surprised that the world says that you are extremely wicked.'

'But what world says that?' asked Lord Henry, elevating his eyebrows. 'It can only be the next world. This world and I are on excellent terms.'

❦ He hasn't a single redeeming vice.

❦ The sick do not ask if the hand that smoothes their pillow is pure, nor the dying care if the lips that touch their brow have known the kiss of sin.

❦ Every impulse that we strive to strangle broods in the mind and poisons us. The only way to get rid of a temptation is to yield to it. Resist it, and your soul grows sick with longing for the things it has forbidden to itself.

❦ There are terrible temptations that it requires strength, strength and courage, to yield to. To stake all one's life on one throw – whether the stakes be power or pleasure, I care not – there is no weakness in that. There is a horrible, a terrible courage.

❦ If your sins find you out, why worry! It is when they find you *in*, that trouble begins.

❦ Life's aim, if it has one, is simply to be always looking for temptations. There are not nearly enough. I sometimes pass a whole day without coming across a single one. It is quite dreadful. It makes one so nervous about the future.

❦ The only difference between the saint and sinner is that every saint has a past and every sinner has a future.

❦ The costume of the nineteenth century is detestable. It is so sombre, so depressing. Sin is the only real colour-element left in modern life.

❦ Surely Providence can resist temptation by this time.

❦   Anything approaching to the free play of the mind is practically unknown amongst us. People cry out against the sinner, yet is is not the sinful but the stupid who are our shame. There is no sin except stupidity.

❦   The body sins once and has done with its sin, for action is a mode of purification. Nothing remains then but the recollection of a pleasure, or the luxury of a regret.

❦   One can fancy an intense personality being created out of sin. The fact of a man being a poisoner is nothing against his prose. The domestic virtues are not the true basis of art.

❦   You will soon be going about like the converted, and the revivalist, warning people against all the sins of which you have grown tired.

❦   As a wicked man I am a complete failure. Why, there are lots of people who say I have never really done anything wrong in the whole course of my life. Of course, they only say it behind my back.

❦   One should believe evil of everyone, until, of course, people are found out to be good. But that requires a great deal of investigation nowadays.

❦   Sins of the flesh are nothing. They are maladies for physicians to cure, if they should be cured. Sins of the soul alone are shameful.

❦   There were sins whose fascination was more in the memory than in the doing of them; strange triumphs that gratified the pride more than the passions, and gave to the intellect a quickened sense of joy.

❦   The only horrible thing in the world is *ennui*. That is the one sin for which there is no forgiveness.

❦　Can it be that there is some immortality in sin which virtue has not?

❦　As for a spoiled life, no life is spoiled but one whose growth is arrested. If you want to mar a nature you have merely to reform it.

❦　It is a sign of a noble nature to refuse to be broken by force. Never attempt to reform a man. Men never repent.

❦　If one intends to be good one must take it up as a profession. It is quite the most engrossing one in the world.

❦　Nowadays so many conceited people go about society pretending to be good that I think it shows rather a sweet and modest disposition to pretend to be bad.

❦　One is not always happy when one is good; but one is always good when one is happy.

❦　The best way to make children good is to make them happy.

❦　Good people do a great deal of harm in the world. Certainly the greatest harm they do is that they make badness of such extraordinary importance.

❦　One is punished for the good as well as the evil that one does.

The Shrill Clamour of Criticism

❦ Why should the artist be troubled by the shrill clamour of criticism? Why should those who cannot create take upon themselves to estimate the value of creative work? What can they know about it? If a man's work is easy to understand an explanation is unnecessary.

❦ What one really wants is not to be either blamed or praised but to be understood.

❦ The praise of the man who can't understand me is quite as injurious as the abuse of any enemy can be.

❦ The critic is he who can translate into another manner of a new material his impression of beautiful things. The highest, as the lowest, form of criticism is a mode of autobiography.

❦ The moment criticism exercises any influence, it ceases to be criticism. The aim of the true critic is to try to chronicle his own moods, not to try to correct the masterpieces of others.

❦ They afterwards took me to a dancing saloon where I saw the only rational method of art criticism I have ever come across. Over the piano was printed a notice: 'Please do not shoot the pianist. He is doing his best.'

❦ The first duty of an art critic is to hold his tongue at all times and upon all subjects.

❦ I am always amused by the silly vanity of those writers and artists of our day who seem to imagine that the primary function of the critic is to chatter about their second-rate work.

❦ The sphere of art and the sphere of ethics are absolutely distinct and separate.

❦ It is exactly because a man cannot do a thing that he is the proper judge of it.

❦ Real critics? Ah, how perfectly charming they would be! I am always waiting for their arrival. An inaudible school would be nice.

❦ Then there were some arrows, barbed and brilliant, shot off, with all the speed and splendour of fireworks, at the archaeologists who spend their lives in verifying the birthplaces of nobodies and estimate the value of a work of art by its date or by its decay, at the art critics who always treat a picture as if it were a novel and try and find out the plot.

❦ Criticism demands infinitely more cultivation than creation does.

❦ The first step in aesthetic criticism is to realise one's own impressions.

❦ I never reply to my critics. I have far too much time. But I think someday I will give a general answer in the form of a lecture, which I shall call 'Straight Talks to Old Men'.

❦ That fine spirit of choice and delicate instinct of selection by which the artist realises life for us, and gives to it a momentary perfection . . . that spirit of choice, that subtle tact of omission, is really the critical faculty in one of its most characteristic moods, and no one who does not possess this critical faculty can create anything at all in art.

❦ When critics disagree the artist is in accord with himself.

❦ Yes, there is a terrible moral in *Dorian Gray* – a moral which the prurient will not be able to find in it, but it will be revealed to all whose minds are healthy. Is this an artistic error? I fear it is. It is the only error in the book.

❦ My story is an essay on decorative art. It reacts against the crude brutality of plain reason. It is poisonous if you like, but you cannot deny that it is also perfect, and perfection is what we artists aim at.

❦ Each of the arts has a critic, as it were, assigned to it. The actor is the critic of the drama.

❦ The one characteristic of a beautiful form is that one can put into it whatever one wishes, and see in it whatever one chooses to see; and the beauty that gives to creation its universal and aesthetic element makes the critic a creator in his turn, and whispers of a thousand different things which were not present in the mind of him who carved the statue or painted the panel or graved the gem.

❦ For a man to be a dramatic critic is as foolish and inartistic as it would be for a man to be a critic of epics or a pastoral critic or a critic of lyrics. All modes of art are one, and the modes of the art that employs words as its medium are quite indivisible. The result of the vulgar specialisation of criticism is an elaborate scientific knowledge of the stage – almost as elaborate as that of the stage carpenter and quite on a par with that of the call-boy – combined with an entire incapacity to realise that a play is a work of art or to receive any artistic impressions at all.

❦ There has never been a creative age that has not been critical also.

❦ The highest criticism, being the purest form of personal impression, is in its way more creative than creation.

❦ The censure of the puritan, whether real or affected, is always out of place in literary criticism, and shows a want of recognition of the essential distinction between art and life.

❦ The critic has to educate the public; the artist has to educate the critic.

❦ The true critic addresses not the artist ever but the public only.

❦ The true critic is he who bears within himself the dreams and ideas and feelings of myriad generations, and to whom no form of thought is alien, no emotional impulse obscure.

❦ Critics rarely know how to praise an artistic work. The fact is, it requires an artist to praise art; anyone can pick it to pieces.

❦ We are sorry too to find an English dramatic critic misquoting Shakespeare, as we had always been of the opinion that this was a privilege reserved specially for our English actors.

❦ Technique is really personality. That is the reason why the artist cannot teach it, why the pupil cannot learn it, and why the aesthetic critic can understand it.

❦ Just as it is only by contact with the art of foreign nations that the art of a country gains that individual and separate life that we call nationality, so, by curious inversion, it is only by intensifying his own personality that the critic can interpret the personality of others; and the more strongly this personality enters into the interpretation the more real the interpretation becomes – the more satisfying, the more convincing, and the more true.

❦ A critic should be taught to criticise a work of art without making any reference to the personality of the author. This, in fact, is the beginning of criticism.

❦ The primary aim of the critic is to see the object as it really is not.

❦ No publisher should ever express an opinion of the value of what he publishes. That is a matter entirely for the literary critic to decide. A publisher is simply a useful middle-man. It is not for him to anticipate the verdict of criticism.

❦ I don't believe there is a single dramatic critic in London who would deliberately set himself to misrepresent the work of any dramatist – unless, of course, he personally disliked the dramatist, or had some play of his own he wished to produce at the same theatre, or had an old friend among the actors.

❦ As for ROSSETTI's elaborate system of punctuation, MR KNIGHT pays no attention to it whatsoever. Indeed he shows quite a rollicking indifference to all the secrets and subtleties of style, and inserts and removes stops in a manner that is absolutely destructive to the logical beauty of the verse.

❦ MR MAHAFFY shows an amount of political bias and literary blindness that is quite extraordinary. He might have made his book a work of solid and enduring interest, but he has chosen to give it a merely ephemeral value, and to substitute for the scientific temper of the true historian the prejudice, the flippancy and the violence of the platform partisan.

❦ Your critic has cleared himself of the charge of personal malice – but he has only done so by a tacit admission that he has really no critical instinct about literature and literary work, which, in one who writes about literature, is, I need hardly say, a much graver fault than malice of any kind.

Others Might Pick Them Up

❧ There are many things that we would throw away, if we were not afraid that others might pick them up.

❧ A red rose is not selfish because it wants to be a red rose. It would be horribly selfish if it wanted all the other flowers in the garden to be both red and roses.

❧ Selfishness is not living as one wishes to live, it is asking others to live as one wishes to live.

❧ The most comfortable chair is the one I use myself when I have visitors.

❧ It is not selfish to think for oneself. A man who does not think for himself does not think at all. It is grossly selfish to require of one's neighbour that he should think in the same way and hold the same opinion.

A Sort of Aggravated Form of the Public

❦ Relations never lend one any money and won't give one credit, even for genius. They are a sort of aggravated form of the public.

❦ What is our son at present? An underpaid clerk in a small provincial bank in a third-rate English town.

❦ Relations are simply a tedious pack of people, who haven't got the remotest knowledge of how to live, nor the smallest instinct about when to die.

❦ I can't help detesting my relations. I suppose it comes from the fact that none of us can stand other people having the same faults as ourselves.

❦ After a good dinner one can forgive anybody, even one's own relations.

❦ No one cares about distant relations nowadays. They went out of fashion years ago.

❦ LORD GORING: Extraordinary thing about the lower classes in England – they are always losing their relations.
PHIPPS: Yes, my lord! They are extremely fortunate in that respect.

❦ Families are so mixed nowadays. Indeed, as a rule, everybody turns out to be somebody else.

❦ And now that I think of it I have never heard any man mention his brother. The subject seems distasteful to most men.

❦ Oh, brothers! I don't care for brothers. My elder brother won't die, and my younger brothers seem never to do anything else.

❦ It is a ridiculous attachment . . . she has no money, and far too many relations.

❦ I was in hopes he would have married Lady Kelso. But I believe he said her family was too large. Or was it her feet? I forget which.

❦ Good novelists are much rarer than good sons.

❦ I love hearing my relations abused. It is the only thing that makes me put up with them at all.

The Primary Duty of Life

❦ I do not approve of the modern sympathy with invalids. I consider it morbid. Illness of any kind is hardly a thing to be encouraged in others. Health is the primary duty of life.

❦ One knows so well the popular idea of health. The English country-gentleman galloping after a fox – the unspeakable in full pursuit of the uneatable.

On being asked if he was ill:
❦ No, not ill, but very weary. The fact is I picked a primrose in the wood yesterday, and it was so ill that I have been sitting up with it all night.

❦ I only care to see doctors when I am in perfect health; then they comfort one, but when one is ill they are most depressing.

❦ Why don't you ask me how I am? I like people to ask me how I am. It shows a widespread interest in my health.

❦ She has not touched the tambour frame for nine or ten years. But she has many other amusements. She is very much interested in her own health.

What Else is There to Live For?

❦ LORD GORING: I love talking about nothing, father. It is the only thing I know anything about.
LORD CAVERSHAM: You seem to me to be living entirely for pleasure.
LORD GORING: What else is there to live for, father?
Nothing ages like happiness.

❦ Pleasure is the only thing worth having a theory about. But I am afraid I cannot claim my theory as my own. It belongs to nature, not to me.

❦ An inordinate passion for pleasure is the secret of remaining young.

❦ I adore simple pleasures, they are the last refuge of the complex.

❦ My duty as a gentleman has never interfered with my pleasures in the smallest degree.

❦ Knowledge came to me through pleasure, as it always does, I imagine. I was nearly sixteen when the wonder and beauty of the old Greek life began to dawn on me. I began to read Greek eagerly for the love of it all, and the more I read the more I was enthralled.

❦ 'I have never searched for happiness. Who wants happiness? I have searched for pleasure.'
   'And found it, Mr Gray?'
   'Often. Too often.'

❦ No civilised man ever regrets a pleasure, and no uncivilised man ever knows what a pleasure is.

❦ It is better to take pleasure in a rose than to put its root under a microscope.

❦ When one has sinned, what consoles one nowadays is not repentance but pleasure. Repentance is quite out of date.

❦ I don't regret for a single moment having lived for pleasure. I did it to the full, as one should do everything that one does to the full. There was no pleasure I did not experience.

❦ Not happiness! Above all, not happiness. Pleasure!

Infinitely Precious Things

❦ Ordinary riches can be stolen from a man. Real riches cannot. In the treasury-house of your soul, there are infinitely precious things that may not be taken from you.

❦ Young people, nowadays, imagine that money is everything, and when they grow older they know it.

❦ Every man of ambition has to fight his century with its own weapons. What this century worships is wealth. The God of this century is wealth. To succeed one must have wealth. At all costs one must have wealth.

❦ There is always more brass than brains in an aristocracy.

❦ I don't want money. It is only people who pay their bills who want that, and I never pay mine.

❦ LORD ILLINGWORTH: A title is really rather a nuisance in these democratic days. As George Hartford I had everything I wanted. Now I have merely everything that other people want, which isn't nearly so pleasant.

❦ The typical spendthrift is always giving away what he needs most.

❦ The English think that a chequebook can solve every problem in life.

❦ It is better to have a permanent income than to be fascinating.

❦ When I was at Leadville and reflected that all the shining silver that I saw coming from the mines would be made into ugly dollars, it made me sad.

❦ Credit is the capital of a younger son, and he can live charmingly on it.

❦ One day a tax collector called at Wilde's house in Tite Street.
'Taxes! Why should I pay taxes?' said Wilde.
'But, sir, you are the householder here, are you not? You live here, you sleep here.'
'Ah, yes; but then I sleep so badly!'

❦ What between the duties expected of one during one's lifetime and the duties exacted from one after one's death land has ceased to be either a profit or a pleasure. It gives one position and prevents one from keeping it up.

❦ Some years ago people went about the country saying that property has duties. It is perfectly true. Property not merely has duties, but has so many duties that its possession to any large extent is a bore. If property had simply pleasures we could stand it, but its duties make it unbearable.

❦ Private property has really harmed individualism, and obscured it, by confusing a man with what he possesses.

❦ When one has learnt, however inadequately, what a lovely thing gratitude is, one's feet go lightly over sand or sea, and one finds a strange joy revealed to one, the joy of counting up, not what one possesses, but what one owes.

❦ God used poverty often as a means of bringing people to Him, and used riches never, or but rarely.

Blankets and Coal

❦ I am not at all in favour of amusements for the poor, Jane. Blankets and coal are sufficient.

❦ There is only one class in the community that thinks more about money than the rich, and that is the poor. The poor can think of nothing else.

❦ There are the poor, and amongst them there is no grace of manner, or charm of speech, or civilisation, or culture, or refinement in pleasures, or joy of life.

❦ The real tragedy of the poor is that they can afford nothing but self-denial. Beautiful sins, like beautiful things, are the privilege of the rich.

❦ It is a sad fact, but there is no doubt that the poor are completely unconscious of their own picturesqueness.

❦ 'Poor old chap!' said Hughie, 'how miserable he looks! But I suppose to you painters, his face is his fortune?'
'Certainly,' replied Trevor. 'You don't want a beggar to look happy, do you?'

❦ KELVIL: You cannot deny that the House of Commons has always shown great sympathy with the suffering of the poor.
LORD ILLINGWORTH: That is its special vice. That is the special vice of the age. One should sympathise with the joy, the beauty, the colour of life. The less said about life's sores the better.

❦ Sometimes the poor are praised for being thrifty. But to recommend thrift to the poor is both grotesque and insulting. It is like advising a man who is starving to eat less.

❦ As for the virtuous poor, one can pity them, of course, but one cannot possibly admire them.

❦ Nowadays we are all of us so hard up that the only pleasant things to pay are compliments. They're the only things we *can* pay.

❦ As for begging it is safer to beg than to take, but it is finer to take than to beg.

❦ If the poor only had profiles there would be no difficulty in solving the problem of poverty.

❦ And when scientific men are no longer called upon to go down to a depressing East End and distribute cocoa and blankets to starving people, they will have delightful leisure in which to devise wonderful and marvellous things for their own joy and the joy of everyone else.

❦ It is only by not paying one's bills that one can hope to live in the memory of the commercial classes.

❦ The only thing that can console one for being poor is extravagance. The only thing that can console one for being rich is economy.

❦ I am never in during the afternoon, except when I am confined to the house by a sharp attack of penury.

❦ If the lower orders don't set us a good example, what on earth is the use of them? They seem, as a class, to have absolutely no sense of moral responsibility.

❦ Extravagance is the luxury of the poor, penury the luxury of the rich.

❦ We are often told that the poor are grateful for charity. Some of them are, no doubt, but the best amongst the poor are never grateful. They are ungrateful, discontented, disobedient and rebellious. They are quite right to be so.

❦ Why should they [the poor] be grateful for the crumbs that fall from the rich man's table? They should be seated at the board, and are beginning to know it.

❦ The poor are wiser, more charitable, more kind, more sensitive than we are.

❦ Those who have much are often greedy. Those who have little always share.

34

Not at All a Bad Beginning

❦ Laughter is not at all a bad beginning for a friendship, and it is far the best ending for one.

❦ What is the good of friendship if one cannot say exactly what one means? Anybody can say charming things and try to please and to flatter, but a true friend always says unpleasant things and does not mind giving pain.

❦ Between men and women there is no friendship possible. There is passion, enmity, worship, love, but no friendship.

❦ An acquaintance that begins with a compliment is sure to develop into a real friendship. It starts in the right manner.

❦ One cannot extort affection with a knife. To awaken gratitude in the ungrateful were as vain as to try to waken the dead by cries.

❦ Anybody can sympathise with the sufferings of a friend, but it requires a very fine nature to sympathise with a friend's success.

❦ One has a right to judge a man by the effect he has over his friends.

❦ I always like to know everything about my new friends, and nothing about my old ones.

❦ I think that generosity is the essence of friendship.

❦   I dare say that if I knew him I should not be his friend at all. It is a very dangerous thing to know one's friends.

❦   I would sooner lose my best friend than my worst enemy. To have friends, you know, one need only be good-natured; but when a man has no enemy left there must be something mean about him.

❦   I choose my friends for their good looks, my acquaintances for their good characters and my enemies for their good intellects. I have not got one who is a fool. They are all men of some intellectual power and consequently they all appreciate me.

❦   She is without one good quality, she lacks the finest spark of decency and is quite the wickedest woman in London. I haven't a word to say in her favour . . . and she is one of my greatest friends.

❦   Robert gave Harry a terrible black eye, or Harry gave him one; I forget which, but I know they were great friends.

❦   It is always painful to part from people whom one has known for a very brief space of time. The absence of old friends one can endure with equanimity. But even a momentary separation from anyone to whom one has just been introduced is almost unbearable.

❦   I shall never make a new friend in my life, though perhaps a few after I die.

❦   Friendship is far more tragic than love. It lasts longer.

❦   He has no enemies, and none of his friends like him.

❦   At the holy season of Easter one is supposed to forgive all one's friends.

❦   Formal courtesies will strain a close friendship.

❦ Be careful to choose your enemies well. Friends don't much matter. But the choice of enemies is very important.

❦ Next to having a staunch friend is the pleasure of having a brilliant enemy.

35

The Cheap Severity of Abstract Ethics

❧ Oh, I hate the cheap severity of abstract ethics.

❧ Manners before morals!

❧ If you pretend to be good, the world takes you very seriously. If you pretend to be bad, it doesn't. Such is the astounding stupidity of optimism.

❧ The world divides actions into three classes: good actions, bad actions that you may do, and bad actions that you may not do. If you stick to the good actions you are respected by the good. If you stick to the bad actions that you may do you are respected by the bad. But if you perform the bad actions that no one may do then the good and the bad set upon you and you are lost indeed.

❧ Morality is simply the attitude we adopt to people whom we personally dislike.

❧ It is personalities, not principles, that move the age.

❧ Intellectual generalities are always interesting, but generalities in morals mean absolutely nothing.

❧ To be good, according to the vulgar standard of goodness, is obviously quite easy. It merely requires a certain amount of sordid terror, a certain lack of imaginative thought and a certain low passion for middle-class respectability.

❧ Good resolutions are useless attempts to interfere with scientific laws. Their origin is pure vanity. Their result is absolutely nil. They give us, now and then, some of those luxurious sterile emotions that have a certain charm for the weak. That is all that can be said of them. They are simply cheques that men draw on a bank where they have no account.

❧ Ideals are dangerous things. Realities are better.

❧ There is a fatality about all good resolutions. They are invariably made too soon.

❧ The majority of people spoil their lives by an unhealthy and exaggerated altruism.

❧ I never came across anyone in whom the moral sense was dominant who was not heartless, cruel, vindictive, log-stupid and entirely lacking in the smallest sense of humanity. Moral people, as they are termed, are simple beasts. I would sooner have fifty unnatural vices than one unnatural virtue.

❧ It is not good for one's morals to see bad acting.

❧ Modern morality consists in accepting the standard of one's age. I consider that for any man of culture to accept the standard of his age is a form of the grossest immorality.

❧ Several plays have been written lately that deal with the monstrous injustice of the social code of morality at the present time. It is indeed a burning shame that there should be one law for men and another law for women. I think there should be no law for anybody.

❧ Self-sacrifice is a thing that should be put down by law. It is so demoralising to the people for whom one sacrifices oneself. They always go to the bad.

❦ Conscience makes egotists of us all.

❦ You can't make people good by Act of Parliament – that is something.

❦ Nothing is more painful to me than to come across virtue in a person in whom I have never expected its existence. It is like finding a needle in a bundle of hay. It pricks you. If we have a virtue we should warn people of it.

❦ The reason we all like to think so well of others is that we are all afraid for ourselves. The basis of optimism is sheer terror. We think that we are generous because we credit our neighbour with the possession of those virtues that are likely to be a benefit to us. We praise the banker that we may overdraw our account, and find good qualities in the highwayman in the hope that he may spare our pockets.

❦ 'I am rather afraid that I have annoyed him,' answered the Linnet. 'The fact is that I have told him a story with a moral.'
  'Ah! that is always a very dangerous thing to do,' said the Duck. And I quite agree with her.

❦ The majority of men spoil their lives by an exaggerated and unhealthy altruism.

❦ The desire to do good to others produces a plentiful supply of prigs.

❦ Good intentions have been the ruin of the world. The only people who have achieved anything have been those who have had no intentions at all.

❦ People are so fond of giving away what they do not want themselves that charity is largely on the increase.

❦ Charity, as even those of whose religion it makes a formal part have been compelled to acknowledge, creates a multitude of evils.

❦ There is no such thing as morality, for there is no general rule of spiritual health; it is all personal, individual.

❦ Neither art nor science knows anything of moral approval or disapproval. Science is out of the reach of morals, for her eyes are fixed upon eternal truths. Art is out of the reach of morals, for her eyes are fixed upon things beautiful and immortal and ever-changing. To morals belong the lower and less intellectual spheres.

❦ Conscience is but the name which cowardice fleeing from battle scrawls upon its shield.

❦ When one is placed in the position of guardian one has to adopt a very high moral tone on all subjects. It's one's duty to do so. But a high moral tone can hardly be said to conduce very much to either one's health or one's happiness.

❦ The moral is too obvious.

❦ They were stupid enough to have principles, and unfortunate enough to act up to them.

❦ They all came to bad ends, and showed that universal altruism is as bad in its results as universal egotism.

❦ In the old days nobody pretended to be a bit better than his neighbour. In fact, to be a bit better than one's neighbour was considered excessively vulgar and middle class. Nowadays, with our modern mania for morality, everyone has to pose as a paragon of purity, incorruptibility and all the other seven deadly virtues. And what is the result? We all go over like ninepins – one after the other.

❦ LADY STUTFIELD: There is nothing, nothing like the beauty of home-life, is there?

KELVIL: It is the mainstay of our moral system in England, Lady Stutfield. Without it we would become like our neighbours.

❦ I was telling them [his two sons] stories last night of little boys who were naughty and made their mother cry, and what dreadful things would happen to them unless they became better; and what do you think one of them answered? He asked me what punishment could be reserved for naughty papas, who did not come home till the early morning, and made their mother cry far more!

❦ It is the growth of the moral sense in women that makes marriage such a hopeless one-sided institution.

36

All the Surprise of Candour

❧ I am prevented from coming in consequence of a subsequent engagement. I think that would be a rather nice excuse; it would have all the surprise of candour.

❧ The truth about the life of a man is not what he does, but the legend which he creates around himself.

❧ I think a man should invent his own myth.

❧ To know the truth one must imagine myriads of falsehoods. For what is truth?

❧ If one tells the truth, one is sure, sooner or later, to be found out.

❧ It is very painful for me to be forced to speak the truth. It is the first time in my life that I have ever been reduced to such a painful position, and I am really quite inexperienced in doing anything of the kind.

❧ It is a terrible thing for a man to find out suddenly that all his life he has been speaking nothing but the truth.

❧ The truth isn't quite the sort of thing that one tells to a nice, sweet, refined girl.

❧ People seldom tell the truths that are worth telling. We ought to choose our truths as carefully as we choose our lies, and to select our virtues with as much thought as we bestow upon the selection of our enemies.

❧ I could never have dealings with Truth. If Truth were to come unto me, to my room, he would say to me 'You are too wilful.' And I would say to him, 'You are too obvious.' And I should throw him out of the window! [And if Truth were a woman] then I could not throw her out of the window; I should bow her to the door.

❧ The truth is rarely pure and never simple. Modern life would be very tedious if it were either, and modern literature a complete impossibility.

❧ Many a young man starts in life with a natural gift for exaggeration which, if nurtured in congenial and sympathetic surroundings, or by the imitation of the best models, might grow into something really great and wonderful. But, as a rule, he comes to nothing. He either falls into careless habits of accuracy, or takes to frequenting the society of the aged and well informed. Both things are equally fatal to his imagination, as indeed they would be to the imagination of anybody, and in a short time he develops a morbid and unhealthy faculty of truth-telling, begins to verify all statements made in his presence, has no hesitation in contradicting people who are much younger than himself, and often ends by writing novels which are so life-like that no one can possibly believe in their probability.

❧ People have a careless way of talking about a 'born liar,' just as they talk about a born poet. Lying and poetry are arts – arts, as PLATO saw, not unconnected with each other – and they require the most careful study, the most interested devotion.

❧ In art there is no such thing as a universal truth. A truth in art is that whose contradictory is also true.

❧ A thing is not necessarily true because a man dies for it.

❧ Give him a mask, and he will tell you the truth.

❧ The truths of metaphysics are the truths of masks.

❧ No man dies for what he knows to be true. Men die for what they want to be true, for what some terror in their hearts tells them is not true.

❧ A truth ceases to be true when more than one person believes in it.

❧ As for believing things, I can believe anything, provided that it is quite incredible.

❧ He would be the best of fellows if he did not always speak the truth.

❧ It is enough that our fathers have believed. They have exhausted the faith-faculty of the species. Their legacy to us is the scepticism of which they were afraid.

On Patience *to a New York audience*:
❧ You have listened to the charming music of MR SULLIVAN and the clever satire of MR GILBERT for three hundred nights, and I am sure it is not too much to ask you, after having given so much time to satire, to listen to the truth for one evening.

❧ In modern life nothing produces such an effect as a good platitude. It makes the whole world kin.

❧ The truth is a thing I get rid of as soon as possible! Bad habit, by the way. Makes one very unpopular at the club with the older members. They call it being conceited.

❧ The things one feels absolutely certain about are never true. That is the fatality of faith and the lesson of romance.

❧ After all, what is a fine lie! Simply that which is its own evidence.

❦ Vulgarity is simply the conduct of other people and falsehoods the truths of other people.

❦ If something cannot be done to check, or at least to modify, our monstrous worship of facts, art will become sterile and beauty will pass away from the land.

❦ Facts are not merely finding a footing-place in history, but they are usurping the domain of fancy and have invaded the kingdom of romance. Their chilling touch is over everything. They are vulgarising mankind.

❦ The English are always degrading truths into facts. When a truth becomes a fact it loses all intellectual value.

❦ It is hard to have a good story interrupted by a fact.

❦ Truth is entirely and absolutely a matter of style.

❦ The way of paradoxes is the way of truth. To test reality we must see it on the tightrope. When the verities become acrobats we can judge them.

❦ If Truth has her revenge upon those who do not follow her, she is often pitiless to her worshippers.

❦ To lie finely is an art, to tell the truth is to act according to nature.

❦ The only form of lying that is absolutely beyond reproach is lying for its own sake.

❦ The aim of the liar is simply to charm, to delight, to give pleasure. He is the very basis of civilised society.

❦ If a man is sufficiently unimaginative to produce evidence in support of a lie, he might just as well speak the truth at once.

❦ There is no truth comparable to sorrow. There are times when sorrow seems to me to be the only truth.

The One Duty We Owe to History

❦ The one duty we owe to history is to rewrite it.

❦ He who stands most remote from his age is he who mirrors it best.

❦ To give an accurate description of what has never occurred is not merely the proper occupation of the historian, but the inalienable privilege of any man of parts and culture.

❦ The only form of fiction in which real characters do not seem out of place is history. In novels they are detestable.

❦ The ages live in history through their anachronisms.

❦ My *forte* is more in writing pamphlets than in taking shots. Still a regicide has always a place in history.

❦ Disobedience, in the eyes of anyone who has read history, is man's original virtue. It is through disobedience that progress has been made, through disobedience and through rebellion.

❦ The details of history are always wearisome and usually inaccurate.

❦ History never repeats itself. The historians repeat each other.

❦ There is no essential incongruity between crime and culture. We cannot rewrite the whole of history for the purpose of gratifying our moral sense of what should be.

Simply a Tragedy

- Society is wonderfully delightful. To be in it is merely a bore. But to be out of it is simply a tragedy.

- Nothing annoys people so much as not receiving invitations.

- The security of society lies in custom and unconscious instinct, and the basis of the stability of society, as a healthy organism, is the complete absence of any intelligence amongst its members.

- Never speak disrespectfully of society. Only people who can't get into it do that.

- I won't tell you that the world matters nothing, or the world's voice, or the voice of society. They matter a good deal. They matter far too much.

- Suicide is the greatest compliment that one can pay to society.

- There are always more books than brains in an aristocracy.

- I know myself that when I am coming back from the drawing-room I always feel as if I hadn't a shred on me, except a small shred of decent reputation, just enough to prevent the lower classes making painful observations through the windows of the carriage.

- Let me assure you that if I had not always had an entrée to the very best society, and the very worst conspiracies, I could never have been Prime Minister in Russia.

❦ The middle classes air their moral prejudices over their gross dinner tables, and whisper about what they call the profligacies of their betters in order to try and pretend that they are in smart society and on intimate terms with the people they slander.

❦ We don't want to be harrowed and disgusted with an account of the doings of the lower orders.

❦ Lord Caversham: Can't make out how you stand London society. The thing has gone to the dogs, a lot of damned nobodies talking about nothing.

❦ And now you must run away, for I am dining with some very dull people, who won't talk scandal, and I know that if I don't get my sleep now I shall never be able to keep awake during dinner.

❦ Oh, your English society seems to me shallow, selfish, foolish. It has blinded its eyes and stopped its ears. It lies like a leper in purple. It sits like a dead thing smeared with gold. It is all wrong, all wrong.

❦ Charming ball it has been! Quite reminds me of the old days. And I see that there are just as many fools in society as there used to be. So pleased to find that nothing has altered!

❦ We live in an age when unnecessary things are our only necessities.

❦ Lady Caroline: In my young days, Miss Worsley, one never met anyone in society who worked for their living. It was not considered the thing.
Hester: In America those are the people we respect most.
Lady Caroline: I have no doubt of it.

❦ I always like the last person who is introduced to me; but, as a rule, as soon as I know people I get tired of them.

❦ LADY HUNSTANTON: I hear you have such pleasant society in America. Quite like our own in places, my son wrote to me.

HESTER: There are cliques in America as elsewhere, Lady Hunstanton. But true American society consists simply of all the good women and good men we have in our country.

LADY HUNSTANTON: What a sensible system, and I dare say quite pleasant, too. I am afraid in England we have too many artificial social barriers. We don't see as much as we should of the middle and lower classes.

❦ Society, civilised society at least, is never very ready to believe anything to the detriment of those who are both rich and fascinating.

❦ To get into the best society nowadays one has either to feed people, amuse people or shock people – that is all.

❦ Society often forgives the criminal; it never forgives the dreamer.

❦ Everybody one meets is a paradox nowadays. It is a great bore. It makes society so obvious.

❦ What is interesting about people in good society is the mask that each one of them wears, not the reality that lies behind the mask.

❦ Our society is terribly over-populated. Really, someone should arrange a proper scheme of assisted emigration.

❦ I love London society! I think it has immensely improved. It is entirely composed now of beautiful idiots and brilliant lunatics. Just what society should be.

❦ I don't think that Lord Crediton cared very much for Cyril. He had never forgiven his daughter for marrying a man who had no title. He was an extraordinary old aristocrat, who swore like a costermonger and had the manners of a farmer.

❦ Each class preaches the importance of those virtues it need not exercise. The rich harp on the value of thrift, the idle grow eloquent over the dignity of labour.

❦ A child can understand a punishment inflicted by an individual, such as a parent or guardian, and bear it with a certain amount of acquiesence. What it cannot understand is a punishment inflicted by society.

❦ The canons of society are, or should be, the same as the canons of art. Form is absolutely essential to it. It should have the dignity of a ceremony as well as its unreality, and should combine the insincere character of a romantic play with the wit and beauty that make such plays delightful to us.

❦ Other people are quite dreadful. The only possible society is oneself.

❦ Half-past six! What an hour! It will be like having a meat-tea or reading an English novel. It must be seven. No gentleman dines before seven.

❦ Three addresses always inspire confidence, even in tradesmen.

❦ The man who possesses a permanent address, and whose name is to be found in the *Directory*, is necessarily limited and localised. Only the tramp has absolute liberty of living.

❦ Scandals used to lend charm, or at least interest, to a man – now they crush him.

❦ He knew the precise psychological moment when to say nothing.

❦ My own business always bores me to death. I prefer other people's.

❦ She tried to found a *salon*, and only succeeded in opening a restaurant.

Tears of Blood

❦ Don't talk to me about the hardships of the poor. The hardships of the poor are necessities; but talk to me about the hardships of the men of genius, and I could weep tears of blood.

❦ Geniuses are always talking about themselves, when I want them to be thinking about me.

❦ The public is wonderfully tolerant. It forgives everything except genius.

❦ I like looking at geniuses, and listening to beautiful people.

❦ Would you like to know the great drama of my life? It is that I have put my genius into my life – I have put only my talent into my works.

❦ Genius is born, not paid.

❦ I know so many men in London whose only talent is for washing. I suppose that is why men of genius so seldom wash, they are afraid of being mistaken for men of talent only!

❦ Not being a genius, he had no enemies.

❦ Indifference is the revenge the world takes on mediocrities.

❦ Caricature is the tribute mediocrity pays to genius.

❦ For a man to be both a genius and a Scotsman is the very stage for tragedy. Your Scotsman believes only in success. God saved the genius of ROBERT BURNS for poetry by driving him through drink to failure.

❦ Were men as intelligent as bees, all gifted individuals would be supported by the community, as the bees support the queen. We should be the first charge on the state. Just as SOCRATES declared that he should be kept in the Prytaneum at the public's expense.

❦ It is a sad thing to think about, but there is no doubt that genius lasts longer than beauty. That accounts for the fact that we all take such pains to over-educate ourselves.

❦ LORD GORING: I am delighted at what you tell me about Robert. It shows he has got pluck.
  LORD CAVERSHAM: He has got more than pluck, sir, he has got genius.
  LORD GORING: Ah! I prefer pluck. It is not so common, nowadays.

❦ The noblest character in the book is Lord Aubrey. As he is not a genius, he naturally behaves admirably on every occasion.

❦ The worst thing you can do for a person of genius is to help him: that way lies his destruction. I have had many devoted helpers – and you see the result.

❦ FRANK [HARRIS] insists on my being always at high intellectual pressure – it is most exhausting – but when we arrive at Napoule I am going to break the news to him – now an open secret – that I have softening of the brain and cannot always be a genius.

Enough for One Man's Life

🐦 Have I not stood face to face with beauty, that is enough for one man's life.

🐦 Beauty is a form of genius – is higher, indeed, than genius, as it needs no explanation. It is one of the great facts of the world, like sunlight, or springtime, or the reflection in dark water of that silver shell we call the moon. To me beauty is the wonder of wonders. It is only shallow people who do not judge by appearances. The true mystery of the world is the visible, not the invisible.

🐦 Beauty, real beauty, ends where an intellectual expression begins. Intellect is in itself a mode of exaggeration and destroys the harmony of any face. The moment one sits down to think, one becomes all nose, or all forehead, or something horrid. Look at the successful men in any of the learned professions. How perfectly hideous they are! Except, of course, in the Church. But then in the Church they don't think. A bishop keeps on saying at the age of eighty what he was told to say when he was eighteen, and as a natural consequence he always looks delightful.

🐦 To be perfectly proportioned is a rare thing in an age when so many women are either over life-size or insignificant.

🐦 I think that it is better to be beautiful than to be good. But on the other hand no one is more ready than I am to acknowledge that it is better to be good than to be ugly.

❦ To be pretty is the best fashion there is, and the only fashion that England succeeds in setting.

❦ Good looks are a snare that every sensible man would like to be caught in.

❦ There is nothing sane about the worship of beauty. It is too splendid to be sane. Those of whose lives it forms the dominant note will always seem to the world to be mere visionaries.

❦ People say sometimes that beauty is only superficial. That may be so, but at least it is not so superficial as thought is.

❦ Aesthetics are higher than ethics. They belong to a more spiritual sphere. To discern the beauty of a thing is the finest point to which we can arrive. Even a colour-sense is more important, in the development of the individual, than a sense of right and wrong.

❦ All beautiful things belong to the same age.

❦ Beauty has as many meanings as man has moods. Beauty is the symbol of symbols. Beauty reveals everything because it expresses nothing. When it shows us itself it shows us the whole fiery-coloured world.

❦ The worship of the senses has often, and with much justice, been decried, men feeling a natural instinct of terror about passions and sensations that seem stronger than themselves and which they are conscious of sharing with the less highly organised forms of existence. But it is probable the true nature of the senses has never been understood and that they have remained savage and animal merely because the world has sought to starve them into submission or to kill them by pain instead of aiming at making them elements of a new spirituality, of which a fine instinct for beauty will be the dominant characteristic.

❧ At twilight nature becomes a wonderfully suggestive effect, and is not without loveliness, though perhaps its chief use is to illustrate quotations from the poets.

❧ But even men of the noblest possible moral character are extremely susceptible to the influence of the physical charms of others. Modern no less than ancient history supplies us with many most painful examples of what I refer to. If it were not so, indeed, history would be quite unreadable.

❧ She has the remains of really remarkable ugliness.

❧ Those who find ugly meanings in beautiful things are corrupt without being charming. That is a fault.

❧ Those who find beautiful meanings in beautiful things are the cultivated. For these there is hope.

❧ Dandyism is the assertion of the absolute modernity of beauty.

❧ They are the elect to whom beautiful things mean only beauty.

❧ The desire for beauty is merely a heightened form of the desire for life.

❧ When the result is beautiful, the method is justified.

❧ The best service of God is found in the worship of all that is beautiful.

❧ Beauty, like wisdom, loves the lonely worshipper.

❧ Just as those who do not love PLATO more than truth cannot pass beyond the threshold of the Academe, so those who do not love beauty more than truth never know the inmost shrine of art.

❧ Love art for its own sake and then all things that you need will be added to you. This devotion to beauty and to the creation of beautiful things is the test of all great civilisations; it is what makes the life of each citizen a sacrament and not a speculation.

❧ Beauty is the only thing that time cannot harm. Philosophies fall away like sand, creeds follow one another, but what is beautiful is a joy for all seasons, a possession for all eternity.

❧ No object is so ugly that, under certain conditions of light and shade, or proximity to other things, it will not look beautiful; no object is so beautiful that, under certain conditions, it will not look ugly. I believe that in every twenty-four hours what is beautiful looks ugly, and what is ugly looks beautiful, once.

❧ I have found that all ugly things are made by those who strive to make something beautiful, and that all beautiful things are made by those who strive to make something useful.

❧ Utility will be always on the side of the beautiful things.

❧ The state is to make what is useful. The individual is to make what is beautiful.

❧ Good machinery is graceful, the line of strength and the line of beauty being one.

❧ The reason we love the lily and the sunflower, in spite of what Mr Gilbert may tell you, is not for any vegetable fashion at all. It is because these two lovely flowers are in England the two most perfect models of design.

❧ Aestheticism is a search after the signs of the beautiful. It is, to speak more exactly, the search after the secret of life.

❧ There is nothing more beautiful than to forget, except, perhaps, to be forgotten.

The Most Unhealthy Thing in the World

❦ Thinking is the most unhealthy thing in the world, and people die of it just as they die of any other disease. Fortunately, in England at any rate, thought is not catching. Our splendid physique as a people is entirely due to our national stupidity.

❦ All thought is immoral. Its very essence is destruction. If you think of anything, you kill it. Nothing survives being thought of.

❦ If one puts forward an idea to an Englishman – which is always a rash thing to do – he never dreams of considering whether the idea is right or wrong. The only thing he considers of any importance is whether one believes it oneself. The value of an idea has nothing whatever to do with the sincerity of the man who expresses it. Indeed, the more insincere the man is, the more purely intellectual will the idea be, and in that case it will not be coloured by either his wants, his desires or his prejudices.

❦ Yes: I am a dreamer. For a dreamer is one who can only find his way by moonlight, and his punishment is that he sees the dawn before the rest of the world.

❦ While, in the opinion of society, contemplation is the gravest thing of which any citizen can be guilty, in the opinion of the highest culture it is the proper occupation of man.

❦ The boy-burglar is simply the inevitable result of life's imitative instinct. He is fact, occupied, as fact usually is, with trying to reproduce fiction, and what we see in him is repeated on an extended scale throughout the whole of life. SCHOPENHAUER has analysed the pessimism that characterises modern thought, but Hamlet invented it. The world has become sad because a puppet was once melancholy.

❦ Consistency is the last refuge of the unimaginative.

❦ It is only the dull who like practical jokes.

❦ Whenever I think of my bad qualities at night, I go to sleep at once.

❦ Wisdom comes with winters.

❦ To the true cynic nothing is ever revealed.

❦ An idea that is not dangerous is unworthy of being called an idea at all.

❦ Nothing refines but the intellect.

❦ Conscience must be merged in instinct before we become fine.

❦ Only the shallow know themselves.

❦ The essence of thought, as the essence of life, is growth.

❦ Self-culture is the true ideal for man. The development of the race depends on the development of the individual, and where self-culture has ceased to be the ideal the intellectual standard is instantly lowered and often ultimately lost.

❦ Savages seem to have quite the same views as cultured people on almost all subjects. They are excessively advanced.

❧ You forget we are diplomatists. Men of thought should have nothing to do with action. Reforms in Russia are very tragic, but they always end in a farce.

❧ It is only about things that do not interest one that one can find a really unbiased opinion, which is no doubt the reason why an unbiased opinion is always absolutely valueless.

❧ 'What are you thinking?' is the only question that any civilised being should ever be allowed to whisper to another.

❧ The only thing which sustains one through life is the consciousness of the immense inferiority of everybody else, and this feeling I have always cultivated.

❧ Of what use is it to a man to travel sixty miles an hour? Is he any the better for it? Why, a fool can buy a railway ticket and travel sixty miles an hour. Is he any the less a fool!

❧ Those who see any difference between soul and body have neither.

❧ The dreams of the great middle classes of this country, as recorded in MR MYER's two bulky volumes on the subject and the *Transactions of the Psychical Society*, are the most depressing things I have ever read. There is not even a fine nightmare among them. They are commonplace, sordid and tedious.

❧ Action! What is action? It dies at the moment of its energy. It is a base concession to fact. The world is made by the singer for the dreamer!

❧ Action is limited and relative. Unlimited and absolute is the vision of him who sits at ease and watches, who walks in loneliness and dreams.

❧ We are never less free than when we try to act.

❦ I wonder who it was defined man as a rational animal. It was the most premature definition ever given. Man is many things, but he is not rational.

❦ The fatal errors of life are not due to man's being unreasonable: an unreasonable moment may be one's finest moment. They are due to man's being logical. There is a wide difference.

❦ It is not logic that makes men reasonable, nor the science of ethics that makes men good.

❦ It [action] is the last resource of those who know not how to dream.

❦ Nothing can cure the soul but the senses, just as nothing can cure the senses but the soul.

❦ To expect the unexpected shows a thoroughly modern intellect.

❦ Thought is wonderful, but adventure is more wonderful still.

❦ Do not be afraid of the past. The past, the present and the future are but one moment in the sight of God, in whose sight we should try to live. Time and space, succession and extension, are merely accidental conditions of thought. The imagination can transcend them and move in a free sphere of ideal existences. Things are, in their essence, what we choose to make them.

❦ I am glad that she has gone . . . she has a decidedly middle-class mind.

The Evil Remains

❦ It must be remembered that while sympathy with joy intensifies the sum of joy in the world, sympathy with pain does not really diminish the amount of pain. It may make man better able to endure evil, but the evil remains.

❦ All sympathy is fine, but sympathy with suffering is the least fine mode. There is in it a certain element of terror for our own safety.

❦ If there was less sympathy in the world there would be less trouble in the world.

❦ There is always something infinitely mean about other people's tragedies.

❦ In fact, you should be thinking about me. I am always thinking about myself, and I expect everybody else to do the same. That is what is called sympathy. It is a beautiful virtue, and I possess it in a high degree.

❦ I consider ugliness a kind of malady, and illness and suffering always inspire me with revulsion. A man with the toothache ought, I know, to have my sympathy, for it is a terrible pain, yet he fills me with nothing but aversion. He is tedious; he is a bore; I cannot stand him; I cannot look at him; I must get away from him.

❦ It is much more easy to have sympathy with suffering than it is to have sympathy with thought.

❦ I can sympathise with everything, except suffering. I cannot sympathise with that. It is too ugly, too horrible, too distressing. There is something terribly morbid in the modern sympathy with pain.

❦ I entered prison with a heart of stone, thinking only of my pleasure, but now my heart has been broken; pity has entered my heart; I now understand that pity is the greatest and the most beautiful thing that there is in the world. And that's why I can't be angry with those who condemned me, nor with anyone, because then I would not have known all that.

❦ Humanitarian sympathy wars against nature by securing the survival of the failure.

❦ The real harm that emotional sympathy does is that it limits knowledge and so prevents us from solving any single social problem.

I Have Sometimes Played Dominoes

❧ I am afraid I play no outdoor games at all. Except dominoes. I have sometimes played dominoes outside French cafés.

On being asked if he ever went in for games at school:
❧ No, I never liked to kick or be kicked.

❧ Football is all very well as a game for rough girls, but it is hardly suitable for delicate boys.

❧ The only possible form of exercise is to talk, not to walk.

❧ If it were not for the running-ground at Eton, the towing-path at Oxford, the Thames swimming baths and the yearly circuses, humanity would forget the plastic perfection of its own form and degenerate into a race of short-sighted professors and spectacled *precieuses*!

The Mystery of Moods

❦ Only one thing remains infinitely fascinating to me, the mystery of moods. To be master of these moods is exquisite, to be mastered by them more exquisite still.

❦ It is only shallow people who require years to get rid of an emotion. A man who is master of himself, can end a sorrow as easily as he can invent a pleasure.

❦ A woman's life revolves in curves of emotion. It is upon lines of intellect that a man's life progresses.

❦ A sentimentalist is simply one who desires to have the luxury of an emotion without paying for it.

❦ The advantage of the emotions is that they lead us astray, and the advantage of science is that it is not emotional.

❦ I cannot repeat an emotion. No one can, except sentimentalists.

❦ One could never pay too high a price for any sensation.

❦ Moods don't last. It is their chief charm.

❦ The tears that we shed at a play are a type of the exquisite sterile emotions that it is the function of art to awaken. We weep but we are not wounded. We grieve but our grief is not bitter.

❦ Where one laughs there is no immorality; immorality and seriousness begin together.

❧ One of the facts of physiology is the desire of any very intensified emotion to be relieved of some emotion that is its opposite. Nature's example of dramatic effect is the laughter of hysteria or the tears of joy.

❧ I never knew what terror was before; I know it now. It is as if a hand of ice were laid upon one's heart. It is as if one's heart were beating itself to death in some empty hollow.

❧ Even in acts of charity there should be some sense of humour.

❧ You can produce tragic effects by introducing comedy. A laugh in an audience does not destroy terror but by relieving it aids it. Never be afraid that by raising a laugh you destroy tragedy. On the contrary, you intensify it.

❧ The happy people of the world have their value, but only the negative value of foils. They throw up and emphasise the beauty and the fascination of the unhappy.

❧ What fire does not destroy, it hardens.

❧ Suffering is a terrible fire; it either purifies or destroys.

❧ Sorrow, being the supreme emotion of which man is capable, is at once the type and test of all great art.

❧ Behind joy and laughter there may be a temperament, coarse, hard and callous. But behind sorrow there is always sorrow. Pain, unlike pleasure, wears no mask.

❧ It is through joy that the individualism of the future will develop itself. Christ made no attempt to reconstruct society, and consequently the individualism that He preached to man could be realised only through pain or in solitude.

❧ It is the very passions about whose origin we deceive ourselves that tyrannise most strongly over us. Our weakest motives are those of whose nature we are conscious.

❦ You people who go in for being consistent have just as many moods as others have. The only difference is that your moods are rather meaningless.

❦ There must be no mood with which one cannot sympathise, no dead mode of life that one cannot make alive.

❦ To yield to all one's moods is really to live.

❦ There is no room for love and hate in the same soul. They cannot live together in that fair cavern house. Love is fed by the imagination, by which we become wiser than we know, better than we feel, nobler than we are: by which we can see life as a whole: by which, and by which alone, we can understand others in their real as in their ideal relations. Only what is fine, and finely conceived, can feed love. But anything will feed hate.

❦ She ultimately was so broken-hearted that she went into a convent or on to the operatic stage, I forget which. No; I think it was decorative art-needlework she took up. I know she had lost all sense of pleasure in life.

45

The Question of Return Tickets

- Everybody seems in a hurry to catch a train. This is a state of things which is not favourable to poetry or romance. Had Romeo or Juliet been in a constant state of anxiety about trains, or had their minds been agitated by the question of return tickets, SHAKESPEARE could not have given us those lovely balcony scenes.

- When one pays a visit it is for the purpose of wasting other people's time, not one's own.

- Time is waste of money.

- Punctuality is the thief of time – I am not punctual myself, but I do like punctuality in others.

- No one should make unpunctuality a formal rule, and degrade it to a virtue.

- I would sooner lose a train by the *ABC* than catch it by *Bradshaw*.

- I am due at the club. It is the hour when we sleep there.

So That Nothing May Be Lost

- Nature, which makes nothing durable, always repeats itself so that nothing which it makes may be lost.

- The things of nature do not really belong to us; we should leave them to our children as we have received them.

- In nature there is, for me at any rate, healing power.

- We all look at nature too much, and live with her too little.

- If nature had been comfortable, mankind would never have invented architecture, and I prefer houses to the open air.

- Nature is no great mother who has borne us. She is our creation. It is in our brain that she quickens to life.

- A thing in nature becomes much lovelier if it reminds us of a thing in art, but a thing in art gains no real beauty through reminding us of a thing in nature.

- Whenever we have returned to life and nature, our work has always become vulgar, common and uninteresting.

- I hate views – they are only made for bad painters.

- When I look at a landscape, I cannot help seeing all its defects.

❦ But birds and lizards have no sense of repose, and indeed birds have not even a permanent address. They are mere vagrants like the gypsies, and should be treated in exactly the same manner.

❦ It is not necessary to have great natural wonders at home to develop art. The landscapes of Italy are all-satisfying, and so the Italian artist does not reproduce them. You must go to the cloudy, the misty lands, for great landscape painters.

❦ Like most artificial people, he had a love of nature.

❦ We call ourselves a utilitarian age and we do not know the uses of any single thing. We have forgotten that water can cleanse and fire purify and that the earth is mother to us all. As a consequence our art is of the moon and plays with shadows. I feel sure that in elemental forces there is purification and I want to go back to them and live in their presence.

❦ Grass is hard and lumpy and damp, and full of dreadful black insects. Why, even [WILLIAM] MORRIS's poorest workman could make you a more comfortable seat than the whole of nature can.

Made for Something Better

- It is mentally and morally injurious to a man to do anything in which he does not find pleasure and many forms of labour are quite pleasureless activities and should be regarded as such. Man is made for something better than disturbing dirt. All work of that kind should be done by a machine.

- Cultivated idleness seems to me to be the proper occupation for man.

- Work is the curse of the drinking classes.

- It is always with the best intentions that the worst work is done.

- It is very vulgar to talk about one's business. Only people like stockbrokers do that, and then merely at dinner-parties.

- It is the philistine who seeks to estimate a personality by the vulgar test of production.

- One must have some occupation nowadays. If I hadn't my debts I shouldn't have anything to think about.

- I was working on the proof of one of my poems all the morning and took out a comma. In the afternoon I put it back again.

❦ We live in the age of the overworked and the under-educated; the age in which people are so industrious that they become absolutely stupid.

❦ Industry is the root of all ugliness.

❦ It is awfully hard work doing nothing. However, I don't mind hard work when there is no definite object of any kind.

❦ A cook and a diplomatist! an excellent parallel. If I had a son who was a fool I'd make him one or the other.

❦ Printing is so dull. There is nothing exquisite about it at present. In my next publication I am hoping to give examples of something more satisfying in this way. The letters shall be of a rare design; the commas will be sunflowers and the semicolons pomegranates.

❦ It is to do nothing that the elect exist.

❦ Nobody else's work gives me any suggestion. It is only by entire isolation from everything that one can do any work. Idleness gives one the mood in which to write, isolation the conditions. Concentration on oneself recalls the new and wonderful world that one presents in the colour and cadence of words in movement.

❦ Up to the present, man has been, to a certain extent, the slave of machinery, and there is something tragic in the fact that as soon as a man had invented a machine to do his work he began to starve.

❦ He rides in the Row at ten o'clock in the morning, goes to the opera three times a week, changes his clothes at least five times a day and dines out every night of the Season. You don't call that leading an idle life, do you?

❦ There is something tragic about the enormous number of young men there are in England at the present moment who start life with perfect profiles and end by adopting some useful profession.

❦ Every profession in which a man is in constant danger of losing his life has something fine about it.

❦ Action, indeed, is always easy, and when presented to us in its most aggravated, because most continuous, form, which I take to be that of real industry, becomes simply the refuge of people who have nothing whatever to do.

❦ A man whose desire is to be something separate from himself, to be a Member of Parliament, or a successful grocer, or a prominent solicitor, or a judge, or something equally tedious, invariably succeeds in being what he wants to be. That is his punishment.

❦ The salesman knows nothing of what he is selling save that he is charging too much for it.

❦ Each of the professions means a prejudice.

❦ He had gone on the Stock Exchange for six months; but what was a butterfly to do among bulls and bears?

❦ The fact is that civilisation requires slaves. The Greeks were quite right there. Unless there are slaves to do the ugly, horrible, uninteresting work, culture and contemplation become almost impossible.

❦ There is nothing necessarily dignified about manual l
at all, and most of it is absolutely degrading.

A Lie on the Lips of One's Own Life

- To reject one's own experiences is to arrest one's own development. To deny one's own experiences is to put a lie into the lips of one's own life. It is no less than a denial of the soul.

- Experience is the name everyone gives to their mistakes.

- Personal experience is a most vicious and limited circle.

- We always misunderstood ourselves and rarely understood others. Experience was of no ethical value.

- Experience is a question of instinct about life.

- Moralists have, as a rule, regarded it as a mode of warning, have claimed for it a certain ethical efficacy in the formation of charac___ have praised it as something that teaches ___ ___ ___ and shows us what to avoid. But ___ ___ ___ in experience. It is as little of an ___ ___ itself. All that it really ___ ___ ___ ture will be the same as our past ___ ___ one once, and with loathing, we ___ ___ ___ ith joy.

- ___ are often blessings in disguise.

Extraordinary Sensations

❦ Crime belongs exclusively to the lower orders. I should fancy that crime was to them what art is to us, simply a method of procuring extraordinary sensations.

❦ They drove me out to see the great prisons afterwards! Poor odd types of humanity in hideous striped dresses making bricks in the sun, and all mean-looking, which consoled me, for I should hate to see a criminal with a noble face.

❦ The English detectives are really our best friends, and I have always found that by relying on their stupidity, we can do exactly what we like.

❦ The more punishment is inflicted the more crime is produced.

❦ The criminal classes are so close to us that even the policeman can see them. They are so far away from us that only the poet can understand them.

❦ To turn an interesting thief into a tedious honest man was not His [Jesus'] aim. He would have thought little of the Prisoners' Aid Society and other modern movements of th kind.

❦ Reformation is a much more painful process tha punishment, is indeed punishment in its mos and moral form – a fact which accounts f failure as a community to reclaim that phenomenon who is called the con

❦ Society takes upon itself the right to inflict appalling punishments on the individual, but it also has the supreme vice of shallowness and fails to realise what it has done.

❦ Starvation, and not sin, is the parent of modern crime.

❦ Nobody ever commits a crime without doing something stupid.

❦ As one reads history one is absolutely sickened not by the crimes that the wicked have committed but by the punishments that the good have inflicted; and a community is infinitely more brutalised by the habitual employment of punishment than it is by the occasional occurrence of crime.

❦ Our criminals are, as a class, so absolutely uninteresting from any psychological point of view. They are not marvellous Macbeths and terrible Vautrins. They are merely what ordinary, respectable, commonplace people would be if they had not got enough to eat.

❦ There is only one thing worse than injustice, and that is justice without her sword in her hand. When right is not might it is evil.

aggravated
of our entire
most interesting
armed criminal.

One Can't Keep Going Abroad

❦ Advised to go abroad to avoid the trial, Wilde replied, 'Everyone wants me to go abroad. I have just been abroad, and now I have come home again. One can't keep going abroad, unless one is a missionary or, what comes to the same thing, a commercial traveller.'

❦ When Wilde was told that he would be cross-examined by Edward Carson (who had been a fellow-student at Trinity College, Dublin), he replied: 'No doubt he will perform his task with all the added bitterness of an old friend.'

❦ He tells me that he [Willie his brother] is defending me all over London. My poor dear brother could compromise a steam-engine.

This Loathsome Place

❦ Even if I get out of this loathsome place I know there is nothing for me but the life of a pariah, of disgrace and penury and contempt.

❦ I don't think I shall ever write again. Something is killed in me. I feel no desire to write – I am unconscious of power. Of course my first year in prison destroyed me body and soul. It could not be otherwise.

❦ I have the horror of death with the still greater horror of living.

❦ The refusal to commute my sentence has been like a blow from a leaden sword. I am dazed with a dull sense of pain. I had fed on hope and now anguish grown hungry feeds her fill on me as though she had been starved of her proper appetite. Th   however, kinder elements in this evil pris   were before; sympathies have been shown to me   onger feel entirely isolated from   which was before a source of terror and   DANTE and make excerpts and   ing a pen and ink . . . and I am   f German. Indeed this seems to   study.

                          e and things as they really
                         tone. It is the people
                          lusion of a life in constant

In Wandsworth Gaol:

❦ I could be patient, for patience is a virtue. It is not patience, it is apathy you want here, and apathy is a vice.

To a convict who thought the prison was haunted by ghosts:

❦ Not necessarily so. You see, prisons have no ancient tradition to keep up. You must go to some castle to see ghosts, where they are inherited along with the family jewels!

On the books he read in prison:

❦ I read DANTE every day, in Italian, and all through . . . It was his *Inferno* above all that I read; how could I help liking it? Cannot you guess? Hell, we were in it – Hell, that was prison.

Note to a warder in Reading Gaol:

❦ I hope to write about prison life and try to change it for others, but it is too terrible and ugly to make a work of art of. I have suffered too much in it to write plays about it.

Request to a warder in Reading Gaol:

❦ Please find out for me the name of A.2.11., also the names of the children who are in for the rabbits and the amount of the fine. Can I pay this and get them out? If so I will get them out tomorrow. Please, dear friend, do this for me. I must get them out! Think what a thing for me it would be to help three little children. I would be delighted beyond words. If I can do this by paying the fine tell the children they are to be released tomorrow by a friend and ask them to be happy and not tell anyone.

❦ When I was a boy my two favourite characters were Lucien de Rubempre and Julien Sorel. Lucien hanged himself, Julien died on the scaffold, and I died in prison.

❦ For romantic young people the world always looks best at a distance; and a prison where one's allowed to order one's own dinner is not at all a bad place.

❦ Prisoners are, as a class, extremely kind and sympathetic to each other. Suffering and the community of suffering makes people kind. In this, as in all other things, philanthropists and people of that kind are astray. It is not the prisoners who need reformation. It is the prisons.

❦ I know that when plays last too long, spectators tire. My tragedy has lasted far too long; its climax is over; its end is mean; and I am quite conscious of the fact that when the end does come I shall return as an unwelcome visitant to a world that does not want me.

❦ The only really humanising influence in prison is the influence of the prisoners.

❦ To those who are in prison, tears are a part of every day's experience. A day in prison on which one does not weep is a day on which one's heart is hard, not a day on which one's heart is happy.

❦ All trials are trials for one's life, just as all sentences are sentences of death.

❦ The most terrible thing about it [imprisonment] is not that it breaks one's heart – hearts are made to be broken – but that it turns one's heart to stone.

❦ I am not prepared to sit in the grotesque pillory they put me into for all time: for the simple reason that I inherited from my father and my mother a name of high distinction in literature and art . . . I don't defend my conduct, I explain it, also there are in the letter [*De Profundis*] certain passages which deal with my mental development in prison and the inevitable evolution of character and intellectual attitude toward life that has taken place, and I want you, and others who still stand by me and have affection for me, to know exactly in what mood and manner I hope to face the world. Of course, from one point of view I know that on the day of my release I shall be merely passing from one prison into another, and there are times when the whole world seems to me no larger than my cell and as full of terror for me. Still I believe that at the beginning God made a world for each separate man, and in that world, which is within us, one should seek to live.

This is an extract from a letter to Robert Ross from Reading Gaol, 1 April 1897, which Wilde intended to accompany the manuscript of De Profundis, *and in it he gave relevant instructions. The governor refused to hand over the manuscript and Wilde gave it to Ross on his release in May 1897.*

The Gate of Dullness

❦ I have blown my trumpet against the gate of dullness.

❦ My name has two Os, two Fs and two Ws. A name which is destined to be in everybody's mouth must not be too long. It comes so expensive in the advertisements. When one is unknown, a number of Christian names are useful, perhaps needful. As one becomes famous, one sheds some of them, just as a balloonist, when rising higher, sheds unnecessary ballast. All but two of my five names have already been thrown overboard. Soon I shall discard another and be known simply as 'The Wilde' or 'The Oscar'.

❦ Nothing pains me except stupidity.

❦ When I had to fill in a census paper I gave my age as nineteen, my profession as genius, my infirmity as talent.

❦ I'll be a poet, a writer, a dramatist, somehow or other I'll be famous, and if not famous I'll be notorious. Or perhaps I'll rest and do nothing. These things are on the knees of the gods. What will be, will be.

❦ They love me very much – simple, loyal people; give them a new saint, it costs nothing.

❦ We Irish are too poetical to be poets; we are a nation of brilliant failures, but we are the greatest talkers since the Greeks.

❧ We watch ourselves, and the mere wonder of the spectacle enthralls us, and I am the only person in the world I should like to know thoroughly, but I don't see any chance of it just at present.

❧ I do not write to please cliques. I write to please myself.

❧ The only writers who have influenced me are KEATS, FLAUBERT and WALTER PATER, and before I came across them I had already gone more than halfway to meet them.

❧ Accusations of plagiarism proceed either from the thin colourless lips of impotence or from the grotesque mouths of those who, possessing nothing of their own, fancy that they can gain a reputation for wealth by crying out that they have been robbed.

❧ I can hardly imagine that the public are in the very smallest degree interested in the shrill shrieks of 'Plagiarism' that proceed from time to time out of the lips of silly vanity or incompetent mediocrity.

❧ Of course I plagiarise. It is the privilege of the appreciative man.

❧ Never say you have 'adapted' anything from anyone. Appropriate what is already yours – for to publish anything is to make it public property.

❧ True originality is to be found rather in the use made of a model than in the rejection of all models – we should not quarrel with the reed if it whispers to us the music of the lyre.

❧ I never write plays for anyone. I write plays to amuse myself. After, if people want to act in them, I sometimes allow them to do so.

❦ Praise makes me humble, but when I am abused I know I have touched the stars.

❦ I have the simplest tastes. I am always satisfied with the best.

❦ I thought I had no heart. I find I have, and a heart doesn't suit me. Somehow it doesn't go with modern dress. It makes one look old and it spoils one's career at critical moments.

❦ It is sad. One half of the world does not believe in God, and the other half does not believe in me.

❦ French by sympathy, I am Irish by race, and the English have condemned me to speak the language of Shakespeare.

❦ By nature and by choice, I am extremely indolent.

❦ I did not sell myself for money. I bought success at a great price.

❦ Morality did not help me. I was one of those who were made for exceptions, not for laws.

❦ While the first editions of most classical authors are those coveted by bibliophiles, it is the second editions of my books that are the true rarities.

❦ If I were all alone, marooned on some desert island and had my things with me, I should dress for dinner every evening.

❦ If life be, as it surely is, a problem to me, I am no less a problem to life.

❦ I filled my life to the very brim with pleasure, as one might fill a cup to the very brim with wine.

❦ Whatever my life may have been ethically, it has always been *romantic*.

- My record of perversities of passion and distorted romances would fill many scarlet volumes.

- God would grow weary if I told my sins.

- I must say . . . that I ruined myself – and that nobody, great or small, can be ruined except by his own hand.

- A patriot put in prison for loving his country loves his country, and a poet in prison for loving boys loves boys. To have altered my life would have been to have admitted that Uranian love is ignoble. I hold it to be noble, more noble than other forms.

- I am not a scrap ashamed of having been in prison. I am horribly ashamed of the materialism of the life that brought me there. It was quite unworthy of an artist.

- I was a man who stood in symbolic relations to the art and culture of my age. I realised this for myself at the very dawn of my manhood, and forced my age to realise it afterwards. Few men hold such a position in their lifetime and have it so acknowledged. It is usually discerned, if it is discerned at all, by the historian or the critic, long after both the man and his age have passed away. With me it was different. I felt it myself and made others feel it.

- I made art a philosophy, and philosophy an art; I altered the minds of men, and the colour of things; I awoke the imagination of my century so that it created myth and legend around me; I summed up all things in a phrase, all existence in an epigram; whatever I touched I made beautiful.

- How could I have written to you during the last three months considering that I have been in bed since last Monday? I am very ill and the doctor is making all kinds of experiments. My throat is a limekiln, my brain a furnace and my nerves a coil of angry adders.

I am apparently in much the same state as yourself.

Maurice – you remember Maurice – has kindly come to see me and I've shared all my medicines with him and shown him what little hospitality I can. We are both horrified to hear that Bosie's suspicions of you are quite justified. That and your being a Protestant make you terribly *unique* (I have told Maurice how to spell the last word as I am afraid that he might have used a word which often occurs in the Protestant Bible).

Alec lunched with Bosie and me one day and I lunched alone with him another. He was most friendly and pleasant and gave me a depressing account of you. I see that you like myself have become a *neurasthenic*. I have been so for four months quite unable to get out of bed till the afternoon, quite unable to write letters of any kind. My doctor has been trying to cure me with arsenic and strychnine but without much success as I became poisoned through mussels. So you see what an exacting and tragic life I have been leading. Poisoning by mussels is very painful and when one has one's bath one looks like a leopard. Pray never eat mussels.

AVE ATQVE VALE

As soon as I get well I'll write you a long letter.

> *The last letter (to Robert Ross) from Hôtel d'Alsace,*
> *Rue des Beaux Arts, Paris.*
> *Wednesday (November 1900)*

❦ I am dying, as I have lived, beyond my means.

CONTENTS

Clockwise from top: Catedral de la Almudena and Palacio Real; Museo del Prado; Ana La Santa;
Cupola of San Francisco el Grande

MADRID

The sunniest, highest and liveliest capital city in Europe, Madrid has a lot to take pride in. Indeed, its inhabitants, the madrileños, are so proud of their city that they modestly declare "desde Madrid al Cielo": that after Madrid there is only one remaining destination – Heaven. While their claim may be open to dispute, this compact, frenetic and fascinating city certainly has bags of appeal and its range of attractions has made it a deservedly popular short-break destination.

Palacio Real

King Felipe II plucked Madrid from provincial oblivion when he made it capital of the Spanish empire in 1561. The former garrison town enjoyed an initial Golden Age when literature and the arts flourished, but centuries of decline and political turmoil followed. However, with the death of the dictator Franco in 1975 and the return to democracy the city had a second burst of creativity, *La Movida madrileña*, an outpouring of hedonistic, highly innovative and creative forces embodied by film director Pedro Almodóvar. In recent years Madrid has undergone a major facelift, with the completion of state-of-the-art extensions to the leading museums, the redevelopment of the river area and the regeneration of some of the historic parts of the centre.

Flamenco

The vast majority of the millions of visitors make a beeline for the Prado, the Reina Sofía and the Thyssen-Bornemisza, three magnificent galleries that give the city a weighty claim to being the "European capital of art". Of equal appeal to football fans is the presence of one of the world's most glamorous and successful clubs, Real Madrid. Aside from these heavy hitters, there's also a host of smaller museums, palaces and parks, not to mention some of the best tapas, bars and nightlife in Spain.

Madrid's short but eventful history has left behind a mosaic of traditions, cultures and cuisines, and you soon realize it's the inhabitants who play a big part in the city's appeal. Despite the morale-sapping economic crisis, *madrileños* still retain an almost insatiable appetite for enjoying themselves, whether it be hanging out in the cafés or on the summer terrazas, packing the lanes of the Rastro flea market, filling the restaurants or playing hard and late in the bars and clubs. The nightlife for which Madrid is

When to visit

Traditionally, Madrid has a typical **continental climate**, cold and dry in winter, and hot and dry in summer. There are usually two rainy periods, in October/November and any time from late March to early May. With temperatures soaring to over 40ºC in July and August, the best times to visit are generally **spring** and **autumn**, when the city is pleasantly warm. The short, sharp winter takes many visitors by surprise, but crisp, sunny days with clear blue skies compensate for the drop in temperature.

Although Madrid is increasingly falling into line with other European capitals, many places still shut down in **August** as its inhabitants head for the coast or countryside. Luckily for visitors, and those *madrileños* who choose to remain, sights and museums remain open and nightlife takes on a momentum of its own.

La Chata

Best places for tapas

There is a vast array of bars in Madrid, serving up tasty tapas: take a stroll around Huertas, La Latina, Chueca and Malasaña and you will stumble on some of the best. A few of our favourites are: *Casa González* (p.60), *La Chata* (p.34), *El Tempranillo* (p.35), *Cervecería Cervantes* (p.77), *Txirimiri* (p.35), *Casa del Abuelo* (p.60) and *El Bocaíto* (p.87).

renowned is merely an extension of the *madrileño* character and the capital's inhabitants consider other European cities positively dull by comparison with their own. The city centre is a mix of bustling, labyrinthine streets and peaceful squares, punctuated by historic architectural reminders of the past. As with many of its international counterparts, an influx of fast-food franchises and chain stores has challenged the once dominant local bars and shops, but in making the transition from provincial backwater to major European capital, Madrid has managed to preserve many key elements of its own stylish and quirky identity.

The Retiro

Where to...

Shop

Head for Gran Vía and Calle Preciados if you're looking for department and chain stores and for the streets around Plaza Mayor if you're on the hunt for traditional establishments. For fashion and designer labels, the smartest addresses are in Salamanca, but more alternative designers are in Malasaña and Chueca. Fans of street fashion will like the shops on C/Fuencarral. Most areas of the city have their own *mercados* (indoor food markets), many of which have been given a makeover, but for the classic *madrileño* shopping experience make your way to the flea market in the Rastro on a Sunday.

OUR FAVOURITES: Casa de Diego p.56. **Cacao Sampaka** p.83. **Agatha Ruiz de la Prada** p.96.

Eat

Eating out in Madrid is one of the highlights of any visit to the city. There's plenty to suit every pocket, from budget backstreet bars to high-class designer restaurants, and a bewildering range of cuisines encompassing tapas, traditional *madrileño* and Spanish regional dishes. Lunch is taken late, with few *madrileños* starting before 2pm, while dinner begins around 9pm. Opening hours can be flexible, with many bars and restaurants closing on Sunday evenings or Monday and for all or part of August. You should spend at least one evening sampling the tapas bars around Santa Ana/Huertas and La Latina. Chueca and Malasaña have some superb traditional bars and bright new restaurants, serving some of the most creative food in the city. The smarter district of Salamanca contains fewer bars of note, but some extremely good (and expensive) restaurants.

OUR FAVOURITES: Posada de la Villa p.33. **La Barraca** p.84. **Txirimiri** p.35.

Drink

Madrid is packed with a variety of bars, cafés and *terrazas*. In fact, they are a central feature of *madrileño* life and hanging out in bars is one of the best, and most pleasant, ways to get the feel of the city and its people. The areas bordering Puerta del Sol, in and around Cava Baja and Plaza Chueca are some of the liveliest, but you can stumble across a great bar in almost every street in the city centre.

OUR FAVOURITES: Almendro 13 p.33. **Café el Espejo** p.96. **Taberna Àngel Sierra** p.89.

Party

As you'd expect with a city whose inhabitants are known as the "gatos" (the cats), there's a huge variety of nightlife on offer in the Spanish capital. The mainstays of the Madrid scene are the *bares de copas*, which get going around 11pm and stay open till 2am. The flashier *discotecas* are rarely worth investigating until around 1 or 2am, although queues often build up quickly after this time. Alonso Martínez, Argüelles and Moncloa are student hangouts, Salamanca is for the wealthy and chic, while head for Malasaña and Chueca if you want to be at the cutting edge of trendiness. You'll find a more eclectic mix on offer in the streets around Sol and Santa Ana.

OUR FAVOURITES: Joy Madrid p.43. **Kapital** p.77. **Las Carboneras** p.35.

Madrid at a glance

UNIVERSIDAD

Plaza de España and beyond p.100. Swathes of parkland in Casa de Campo and Parque del Oeste provide respite from the bustling streets of the city centre and are home to landmarks of their own such as the zoo and the Parque de Atracciones.

Ministerio del Aire

Palacio Real and Ópera p.36. Centred around the monumental triangle of the Royal Palace, Almudena cathedral and opera house, this is one of the most elegant and alluring quarters of the city.

Centro Cultural Conde Duque

MALASAÑA

Museo de Historia de Madrid

Parque del Oeste

Edificio España

PLAZA DE ESPAÑA

Intercambiador de Príncipe Pío

Senado

Edificio Capitol

GRAN VÍA

Teatro Real

Palacio Real

ÓPERA

SOL

Campo del Moro

Catedral de la Almudena

Casa de Correos

SAN AN

Plaza Mayor

HUERT

MADRID DE LOS AUSTRIAS

Iglesia Colegiata de San Isidro

San Francisco el Grande

LA LATINA

Madrid de los Austrias p.26. The historic core of Madrid and the most atmospheric part of the city, Madrid de los Austrias is the first stop to head for in the Spanish capital.

LAVAPIÉS

RASTRO

Mercado Puerta de Toledo

EMBAJADORES

Museo de
Ciencias
Naturales

Salamanca and Paseo de la Castellana
p.90. Smart restaurants, corporate office blocks
and designer stores line the streets of this elegant,
upmarket district that borders the traffic-choked
Paseo de la Castellana.

Gran Vía, Chueca and Malasaña p.78.
North of the monumental buildings and shopping
outlets that line the Gran Vía lie the characterful
barrios of Chueca and Malasaña.

Sol, Santa Ana and Huertas p.50. The bustling
heart of is Madrid centred around the tourist
magnet of Plaza de Santa Ana and Calle Huertas.

SALAMANCA

Biblioteca
Nacional &
Museo
del Libro

Las Salesas
Reales

Museo
Arqueológico
Nacional

CHUECA

RETIRO

Palacio de
Buenavista

Palacio
de Cibeles

Paseo del Arte and Retiro p.64. Three
world-class art galleries – the Prado, the
Thyssen-Bornemisza and the Reina Sofía –
all lie within a stone's throw of each other in
this chic district that is also bordered by the
delightful urban green space of the Retiro
Park and the adjoining botanical gardens.

Museo
del Prado

Parque del Retiro

LAS CORTES

Rastro, Lavapiés and Embajadores
p.44. Low on sights, but high on atmosphere
and full of lively bars and restaurants, this is
Madrid's most cosmopolitan neighbourhood.

Convento de
Santa Isabel

Museo
Reina Sofía

Antigua
Estación
de Atocha

ATOCHA

17

Things not to miss

It's not possible to see everything that Madrid has to offer in one trip – and we don't suggest you try. What follows is a selective taste of the city's highlights, from museums to best places to eat.

> **Museo Thyssen-Bornemisza**
> **p.70**
> A superb collection of art put together by the Thyssen family and which acts as a marvellous complement to the Prado.

> **Tapas**
> **p.59 & p.33**
> For an authentic night out eating tapas, copy the locals and go bar-hopping in Huertas or La Latina.

< **Museo del Prado**
> **p.64**
> Quite simply one of the greatest art museums in the world.

∨ **Estadio Santiago Bernabéu**
> **p.94**
> The Galácticos may have gone, but this magnificent cathedral of football merits a visit, especially if you can enjoy a game.

< **Museo Reina Sofía**
p.68
An essential stop on the Madrid art circuit, the Reina Sofía is home to Picasso's iconic masterpiece *Guernica*.

∨ **Clubbing**
p.7
Madrid has a massive range of clubs, from unpretentious *bares de copas* to serious cutting-edge dance venues.

< Palacio Real
p.36
A sumptuous royal palace reflecting the past glories of the Spanish monarchy.

∨ Plaza Mayor
p.26
Tucked in behind Calle Mayor, this stunning arcaded plaza is the beating heart of the old city with its cafés, bars, restaurants, buskers, caricaturists and mime artists.

∧ The Retiro
p.70
This city-centre park has become *madrileños*' favourite playground with a boating lake, bandstands and a crystal palace housing regular exhibitions.

> Café culture
p.91
Watch the world go by and get a proper cup of coffee at one of the city's traditional cafés.

< Madrid specialities
p.48
The meat and chickpea stew *cocido* is one of Madrid's traditional dishes. Try it out at bars and restaurants all over the city, including *Malacatín*.

> Segovia
p.118
The breathtaking Roman aqueduct is just one of a host of attractions in this stunning Castilian city.

< Flamenco
p.49
Andalucía may be the home of flamenco, but Madrid has some top venues and acts. *Casa Patas* is a favourite.

< **Eating alfresco**
p.32, p.51, p.57 & p.101
When you start to feel the heat, head outside to the terrace bars and restaurants that litter the city. Head for Plaza Santa Ana, Plaza de las Comendadoras, La Latina or the Castellana.

∨ **Jardines Botánicos**
p.71
Dating back to the eighteenth century, the botanical gardens form an amazingly tranquil oasis in the heart of the city.

Day one

The Prado p.64. The Prado contains a fabulous array of masterpieces by artistic greats such as Bosch, El Greco, Titian, Rubens Velázquez and Goya.

The Retiro p.70. Ward off any museum fatigue by freshening up with a stroll around beautiful Retiro park.

Lunch p.33. For a taste of some classic Castilian cuisine served up in elegant surroundings, try the well-regarded *Posada de la Villa* on C/Cava Baja.

The Palacio Real p.36. Marvel at the magnificent, over-the-top decor in this one-time royal residence now used only for ceremonial purposes.

Coffee p.42. Looking out over the plaza towards the royal palace, the elegant *Café de Oriente* makes a great place for a relaxing drink.

Plaza Mayor p.26. Built when the city became Spain's capital in the sixteenth century, Madrid's atmospheric main square retains an aura of traditional elegance.

Madrid de los Austrias p.26. Take a step back in time and explore the twisting streets of ancient Madrid around La Latina.

Dinner p.60 Hit the tapas trail around Huertas. Hop from bar to bar, sampling local specialities. *Casa Alberto*, *Casa González* and *Casa del Abuelo II* are good places to make a start.

Flamenco p.49. Finish the night off with some authentic flamenco at *Casa Patas*.

The Retiro

Plaza Mayor

Tapas

Day two

The Thyssen p.70. An outstanding art collection assembled by the Thyssen-Bornemisza dynasty and providing an unprecedented excursion through Western art.

The Santiago Bernabéu p.94. Home to the all-star Real Madrid, a tour of this awesome stadium is a must for any football fan. Better still, take in a game.

🍽 **Lunch** p.87. Prepare yourself for a spot of shopping in Chueca and Malasaña after sampling a mouth-watering range of tapas at *El Bocaíto*.

Shopping p.83. Chueca and Malasaña are home to some of the city's hippest fashion outlets and most interesting independent stores.

Museo Reina Sofía p.68. An impressive home for Spain's collection of contemporary art, worth the visit if only to see Picasso's *Guernica*.

Gourmet Experience p.87. Take in some of the best views in Madrid from the terrace bars on the ninth floor of El Corte Inglés in Callao.

🍽 **Dinner** p.32. *El Botín* is reputedly the oldest *meson* in the city and serves up superb, traditional Castilian food.

Club p.43. Work off some calories with a dance at one of Madrid's clubs. *Joy Madrid* has an eclectic mix of music, a fun atmosphere and is a fantastic setting for a late-night drink.

Museo Thyssen-Bornemisza

Shopping on Calle Fuencarral

Views of the Gran Vía from El Corte Inglés

Budget Madrid

Many of Madrid's biggest sights are free at certain times of the week, while others charge no entry fee at all. Here are some suggestions on how to spend a great day without spending a penny on anything, apart from food and drink.

Museo de San Isidro p.31.
Housed in a sixteenth-century mansion that was supposedly once home to the city's patron saint, this museum traces the early history of the Spanish capital.

Museo de Historia de Madrid p.82.
Now fully reopened after a lengthy refurbishment, you can get a rundown of the history of the city at this free museum.

Lunch p.48. With a great three-course set lunch menu at around €11, *La Sanabresa* is one of the best-value local restaurants.

Palacio Real p.36.
The sumptuous royal palace allows free access for a couple of hours during the afternoon from Monday to Thursday – be prepared to queue.

Templo de Debod p.105.
Shipped stone by stone from the banks of the River Nile, this ancient Egyptian temple is an incongruous sight in the city. The little exhibition inside is free.

The Prado p.64.
Head here between 6 and 8pm on weekdays (Sun 5–7pm) and you'll see a rare collection of art for nothing.

The Retiro p.70.
Take a stroll by the lake in the Retiro park to relax and unwind.

Dinner p.49. Spoil yourself with the great-value *raciones* and toasted sandwiches at *Melo's* in Lavapiés.

Río Manzanares
Finish off the evening with a stroll by the redeveloped river area by the Puente de Segovia.

Museo de Historia de Madrid

Palacio Real

Toledo Bridge, Río Manzanares

Off-the-beaten-track Madrid

If you've got the time and have done the big sights, then why not take a break from the crowds and seek out some of Madrid's lesser-known, but highly rewarding attractions. Here are some of our suggestions.

Monasterio de las Descalzas Reales p.41. Hidden behind an innocuous-looking door, this sixteenth-century convent is brimming full of artistic treasures.

San Francisco el Grande p.31. Limited opening hours mean that this magnificent church and its frescoes are often overlooked.

Campo del Moro p.39. Surprisingly under-visited, this English-style park below the Palacio Real provides a verdant retreat away from the bustle of the nearby streets.

Museo de Cerralbo p.101. A charming museum housed in a beautifully restored mansion, home to the eclectic treasures of the nineteenth-century aristocrat, Marqués de Cerralbo.

🍽 **Lunch p.88.** Tucked away in the backstreets north of Gran Vía, *Pez Gordo* serves a fabulous range of tapas and beer at reasonable prices.

Museo Nacional del Romanticismo p.82. This delightful museum recreates bourgeois life in nineteenth-century Madrid.

Museo Sorolla p.91 The artist's elegant former home provides the perfect setting for his luminescent paintings.

Museo Lázaro Galdiano p.94. Well off the tourist trail, this former private collection gets less than its fair share of attention and yet it houses an amazing cornucopia of art treasures.

San Francisco el Grande

Museo Lázaro Galdiano

🍸 **Drink p.101.** Try out the little-known Plaza de las Comendadoras and its terrazas for a pre-meal *aperitivo*.

🍽 **Dinner p.110.** Try out some delicious home cooking at the popular *Gabriel* restaurant on Calle Conde Duque.

Kids' Madrid

Although it may not be able to boast the major child-oriented sights of some big cities, there is plenty to keep the kids entertained for a short stay in the Spanish capital. Children are welcome in nearly all cafés and restaurants.

The Teleférico p.106. For a bird's-eye view of the city, take the cable car across the Manzanares river to Casa de Campo.

Madrid's zoo p.107. The Casa de Campo is home to an engaging zoo, complete with lions, bears, pandas, sharks and an extensive collection of reptiles.

Parque de Atracciones p.107. If the zoo doesn't appeal, there is a popular theme park alongside with a vast range of dizzying rides catering for all ages.

🍽 **Lunch p.110.** Next to the lake in Casa de Campo *El Urogallo* has great views and is a good bet after a zoo or Attraction Park trip.

The Retiro p.70. The Retiro park has plenty of child-friendly attractions including play areas, puppet shows, duck ponds and a boating lake.

Museo de Ferrocarril p.47. With its model railways and array of full-size locomotives, this museum will be a hit with most children – and their parents too.

Museo de Cera p.91. Less parochial that it once was, there are now enough international figures and sports stars in the city's wax museum to interest most children, though some only bear a passing resemblance to the real thing.

🍽 **Dinner p.97.** With its burgers, rock memorabilia and outdoor patio, *Hard Rock Café* is a favourite with the kids.

The Teleférico

Madrid's Zoo

Parque de Atracciones

Green Madrid

Despite the hustle and bustle of the city centre, Madrid is home to some appealing green spaces that provide visitors with a chance to relax, unwind and recharge their batteries.

Campo del Moro p.39. For the best views of the Royal Palace head for an early morning stroll along the shady paths of one of Madrid's most beautiful and underused parks.

Casa de Campo p.106. Once part of the royal hunting estate, Casa de Campo is the biggest and wildest of the city's parks.

 Lunch p.110. Nothing better than a spot of roast chicken and cider after a morning stroll at *Casa Mingo* – a spit-and-sawdust – close to Parque del Oeste.

Parque del Oeste p.105. This lovely park contains assorted statues, a fragrant rose garden and even a genuine Egyptian temple. Offers some great views over Casa de Campo and out towards the mountains too.

CaixaForum Vertical Garden p.72. A stunning vertical garden, designed by French botanist Patrick Blanc, adorns the wall outside this innovative exhibition space.

Jardines Botánicos p.71. Dating back to the eighteenth century, the botanical gardens form an amazingly tranquil oasis in the city.

The Retiro p.70. The city-centre park has become the madrileños favourite playground with plenty of routes for runners, a boating lake, and a crystal palace hosting regular exhibitions.

Dinner p.76. *Taberna Laredo* is the perfect place to sample some high-quality tapas after an evening stroll in the Retiro.

Campo del Moro

Casa de Campo

Parque del Oeste

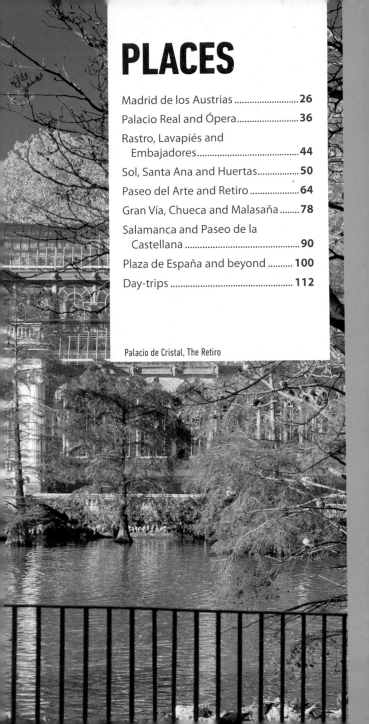

PLACES

Palacio de Cristal, The Retiro

Madrid de los Austrias

Named after the royal family and their original homeland, the district known as Madrid de los Austrias, or Habsburg Madrid, is made up of some of the oldest and most atmospheric parts of the city. Centred around extravagant Plaza Mayor, the area is a twisting grid of streets, filled with Flemish-inspired architecture of red brick and grey stone. Most visitors only make it to the Plaza Mayor and its over-priced cafés and restaurants, but there are appealing sights scattered throughout the area, especially in the barrio (district) of La Latina, which stretches south of the square. This region is also home to some of the city's best restaurants, tapas bars and flamenco tablaos, especially around calles Almendro, Cava Baja and Cava Alta.

Plaza Mayor

MAP p.28, POCKET MAP C12
Ⓜ **Sol.**

The splendidly theatrical Plaza Mayor was originally the brainchild of Felipe II who, in the late sixteenth century, wished to construct a more prestigious focus for his new capital. The Casa de la Panadería on the north side of the square is the oldest building, dating from 1590, but, like much of the plaza, it was rebuilt after fires in the seventeenth and eighteenth centuries. The gaudy frescoes that adorn the facade were only added in 1992. It now houses the municipal tourist office (daily 9.30am–9.30pm).

Capable of holding up to fifty thousand people, the square was used for state occasions, *autos-de-fé* (public trials of heretics followed, usually, by burning of the victims), plays and bullfights. The large bronze equestrian statue

Buildings near Plaza Mayor

in the middle is of Felipe III and dates from 1616.

Today, Plaza Mayor is primarily a tourist haunt, full of expensive outdoor cafés and restaurants. However, an air of grandeur clings to the plaza and it still hosts public functions, from outdoor theatre and music to Christmas fairs and a Sunday stamp and coin market.

Calle Mayor

MAP p.28, POCKET MAP A12–D12
Ⓜ Sol.

One of the oldest thoroughfares in the city, Calle Mayor was for centuries the route for religious processions from the Palacio Real to the Monastery of Los Jerónimos. The street is now home to souvenir shops and bars and is flanked by the facades of some of the most evocative buildings in the city. Set back from the road, near the entrance to the Plaza Mayor, is the splendid decorative ironwork of the **Mercado de San Miguel** (Sun–Wed 10am–midnight, Thurs–Sat 10am–2am; Ⓦ www.mercadodesanmiguel .es; see p.34). Built in 1916, it was formerly one of the old-style food markets scattered throughout the city, but it has now been refurbished and converted into a stylish tourist-oriented emporium complete with oyster and champagne bar.

San Nicolás de los Servitas

MAP p.28, POCKET MAP A12
Plaza de San Nicolás 1 Ⓜ Ópera. Mon 8.30am–1pm & 5.30–8.30pm, Tues–Sat 8.30–9.30am & 6.30–8.30pm, Sun 10am–1.45pm & 6.30–8.45pm.

Largely rebuilt between the fifteenth and seventeenth centuries, Madrid's oldest church still includes a twelfth-century Mudéjar tower featuring traditional Arabic horseshoe arches. Juan de Herrera, architect of El Escorial (see p.120), is buried in the crypt.

Statue of Alvaro de Bazán, Plaza de la Villa

Plaza de la Villa

MAP p.28, POCKET MAP A12
Ⓜ Sol.

This charming plaza, just off Calle Mayor, showcases three centuries of Spanish architectural development. The oldest buildings are the simple but eye-catching fifteenth-century **Torre y Casa de Los Lujanes**, where Francis I of France is said to have been imprisoned by Emperor Charles V after the Battle of Pavia in 1525. On the south side of the square is the **Casa de Cisneros**, constructed for the nephew of Cardinal Cisneros (early sixteenth-century Inquisitor-General and Regent of Spain) in the intricate Plateresque style.

The **Casa de la Villa** occupies the remaining side. An emblem of Habsburg Madrid, it was constructed in fits and starts from the mid-seventeenth century to house the offices and records of the council, who recently moved on to more grandiloquent headquarters in the Palacio de Cibeles. The initial design by Juan Gómez de Mora wasn't completed until 1693, 45 years after his death, and was mellowed by the addition of Baroque details in the eighteenth century.

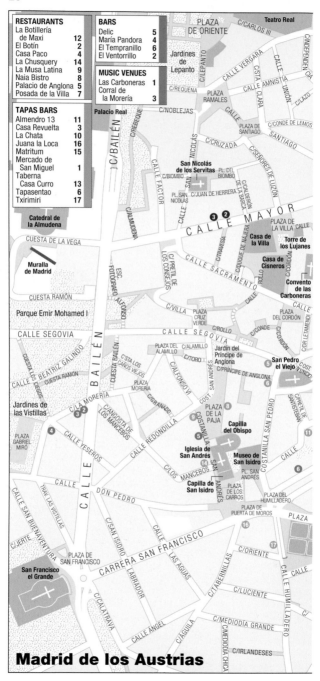

RESTAURANTS
La Botillería de Maxi	12
El Botín	2
Casa Paco	4
La Chusquery	14
La Musa Latina	9
Naia Bistro	8
Palacio de Anglona	5
Posada de la Villa	7

TAPAS BARS
Almendro 13	11
Casa Revuelta	3
La Chata	10
Juana la Loca	16
Matritum	15
Mercado de San Miguel	1
Taberna Casa Curro	13
Tapasentao	6
Txirimiri	17

BARS
Delic	5
María Pandora	4
El Tempranillo	6
El Ventorrillo	2

MUSIC VENUES
Las Carboneras	1
Corral de la Morería	3

Madrid de los Austrias

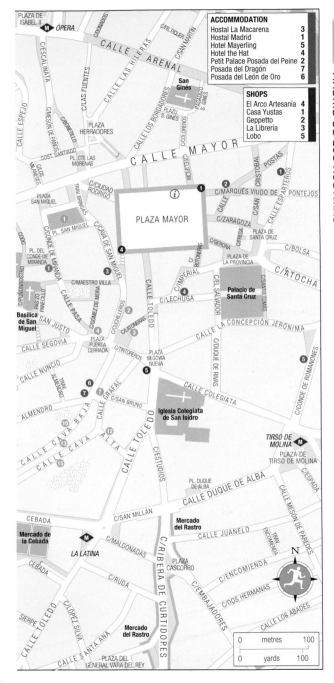

ACCOMMODATION

Hostal La Macarena	3
Hostal Madrid	1
Hotel Mayerling	5
Hotel the Hat	4
Petit Palace Posada del Peine	2
Posada del Dragón	7
Posada del León de Oro	6

SHOPS

El Arco Artesanía	4
Casa Yustas	1
Geppetto	2
La Librería	3
Lobo	5

Parque Emir Mohamed I

MAP p.28, POCKET MAP B6
Ⓜ Ópera.

It is easy to miss this small, enclosed park opposite the crypt of the Almudena cathedral, but it is notable for the fragments of the city walls that date back to the ninth and twelfth centuries. The park lies on the Cuesta de la Vega, former site of one of the main entrances to Muslim Madrid, while nearby, the narrow, labyrinthine streets of the former Moorish quarter, La Morería, are still clearly laid out on medieval lines.

Convento de las Carboneras

MAP p.28, POCKET MAP B13
Plaza Conde de Miranda 3 Ⓜ Sol.

Founded in the early seventeenth century, this convent belongs to the closed Hieronymite Order. It's famous for its home-made biscuits and cakes – a tradition in Spanish convents since the time of St Teresa of Ávila, who gave out sweetened egg yolks to the poor – which can be purchased every day (9.30am–1pm & 4–6.30pm). Ring the bell above the sign reading *venta de dulces* to be let in, then follow the signs to the *torno*; the business takes place by means of a revolving drum to preserve the closed nature of the order.

Basílica de San Miguel

MAP p.28, POCKET MAP B13
C/San Justo 4 Ⓜ La Latina or Sol. July to mid-Sept Mon–Sat 10am–1.15pm & 6–9.15pm, Sun 9.45am–1.30pm & 6.30–9.15pm; mid-Sept to June Mon–Sat 9.45am–1.30pm & 5.30–9pm, Sun 9.45am–2.15pm & 6–9.15pm.

Standing among a host of other graceful buildings – most of which house local government offices – San Miguel stands out as one of the few examples of a full-blown Baroque church in Madrid. Designed at the end of the seventeenth century for Don Luis, the precocious 5-year-old Archbishop of Toledo and youngest son of Felipe V, its features include an unconventional convex facade with four recesses, each containing a statue, variously representing Charity, Strength, Faith and Hope.

San Pedro el Viejo

MAP p.28, POCKET MAP B13
Costanilla de San Pedro Ⓜ La Latina. Mon–Thurs & Sat 9am–12.30pm & 5–8pm, Fri 7am–9pm, Sun 8am–12.30pm.

At the heart of busy La Latina is the Mudéjar tower of San Pedro El Viejo. The second-oldest church in Madrid, it's said to have been founded in the fourteenth century by Alfonso XI, and stands on the site of an old mosque, though most of the church was rebuilt in the seventeenth century.

Plaza de la Paja

MAP p.28, POCKET MAP A14
Ⓜ La Latina.

One of the real gems of old Madrid, this ancient sloping plaza was the commercial and civic hub of the city before the construction of the Plaza Mayor, and was once surrounded by a series of mansions owned by local dignitaries. With the restored houses beaming down on the former market square, this is a rare peaceful and traffic-free spot

Plaza de la Paja

in the city. At the bottom is the pretty little Jardin del Príncipe de Anglona (daily: winter 10am–6pm; summer 10am–10pm), a survivor of the gardens that used to be attached to the nearby mansions.

Iglesia de San Andrés, Capilla del Obispo and Capilla de San Isidro

MAP p.28, POCKET MAP A14
Plaza de San Andrés Ⓜ La Latina. Mon–Thurs & Sat 9am–1pm & 6–8pm, Fri 6–8pm, Sun 10am–1pm.

The Iglesia de San Andrés was badly damaged by an anarchist attack in 1936, and the adjoining Gothic Capilla del Obispo (guided tours Tues 10am, 10.45am & 11.30am. Thurs 4 & 4.45pm, closed July & Aug; reservation only on ☎ 915 592 874 or through the cathedral museum; €3), with its polychromed altarpiece and alabaster tombs, was only recently reopened following a forty-year restoration. The main church and the Baroque Capilla de San Isidro are reached by walking round the building into Plaza de San Andrés. The chapel was built in the mid-seventeenth century to hold the remains of Madrid's patron saint, San Isidro (since moved to the Iglesia de San Isidro), and the interior features a beautifully sculpted dome.

Museo de San Isidro

MAP p.28, POCKET MAP B7
Plaza de San Andrés 2 Ⓜ La Latina Ⓦ www.madrid.es/museosanisidro. Tues–Sun 9.30am–8pm; Aug Tues–Fri 9.30am–2pm, Sat & Sun 9.30am–8pm. Free.

Housed in a reconstructed sixteenth-century mansion – supposedly home to San Isidro – this museum includes an exhibition on the history of Madrid. The city's archeological collection is in the basement, while the rest of the building is given over to the saint himself, with displays relating to his life and miraculous activities. The house also contains a well, site

Iglesia de San Andrés

of one of Isidro's most famous exploits: he rescued his young son from the murky depths, by praying until the waters rose to the surface. The seventeenth-century chapel contained within the museum is built on the spot where the saint was said to have died in 1172.

San Francisco el Grande

MAP p.28, POCKET MAP B7
Plaza de San Francisco 11 Ⓜ La Latina. Tues–Fri 10.30am–12.30pm & 4–6pm, Sat 10.30am–1.30pm & 4–6pm, July & Aug Tues–Sun 10.30am–12.30pm & 5–7pm. €3 with guided tour.

Following a twenty-year restoration programme, you can appreciate this magnificent eighteenth-century domed church in something close to its original glory. Inside, each of the six chapels is designed in a distinct style ranging from Mozarabic and Renaissance to Baroque and Neoclassical. Look out for the early Goya, *The Sermon of San Bernadino of Siena*, in the chapel on your immediate left as you enter, which contains a self-portrait of the 37-year-old artist (in the yellow suit on the right).

Even if your Spanish is not that good, follow the guided tour to get a glimpse of the church's other art treasures, including paintings by José de Ribera and Zurbarán.

Shops

El Arco Artesanía

MAP p.28, POCKET MAP B13
Plaza Mayor 9 Ⓜ Sol Ⓦ artesaniaelarco
.com. Mon–Thurs & Sun 11am–9pm, Fri &
Sat 11am–11pm

Though at the heart of tourist
Madrid, the goods for sale here
are a far cry from the swords,
lace and castanets that fill most
shops in the area. Handmade
craft items and objets d'art
including ceramics, leather,
wood, jewellery and textiles are
all available in this delightful
little shop.

Casa Yustas

MAP p.28, POCKET MAP C12
Plaza Mayor 30 Ⓜ Sol Ⓦ casayustas
.com. Mon–Sat 9.30am–9.30pm, Sun
11am–9.30pm.

Established back in 1886,
Madrid's oldest hat shop sells
every conceivable model from
pith helmets and commando
berets to panamas and bowlers.
There's also a large range of
souvenir-style goods, including
Lladró porcelain figurines.

Geppetto

MAP p.28, POCKET MAP A12
C/Mayor 78 Ⓜ Sol Ⓦ geppettoitalia.com.
Daily 10.30am–8.30pm.

Surrounded by a host of garish
souvenir shops, this little place
offers something quite different:
handmade wooden toys and
trinkets from Italy. Perfect if
you're buying for a small child.

La Librería

MAP p.28, POCKET MAP A12
C/Mayor 80 Ⓜ Sol Ⓦ edicioneslalibreria.es.
Mon–Fri 10am–2pm & 5–8pm, Sat
11am–2pm. Closed Aug afternoons.

Tiny place full of books just about
Madrid. Most are in Spanish, but
many would serve as coffee-table
souvenirs. Also good for old prints
of the city.

Lobo

MAP p.28, POCKET MAP C13
C/Toledo 30 Ⓜ La Latina Ⓦ calzadoslobo
.com. Mon–Fri 9.45am–1.45pm &
4.30–8pm (mid-June–mid-Sept
5–8.30pm), Sat 9.45am–1.45pm.

Great old-fashioned shoe shop,
with anything from espadrilles to
Menorcan sandals (€25) in every
conceivable colour. Excellent for
kids' shoes.

Restaurants

La Botillería de Maxi

MAP p.28, POCKET MAP B14
C/Cava Alta 4 Ⓜ La Latina ☎ 913 651 249,
Ⓦ labotilleriademaxi.com. Tues–Sat
12.30–4pm & 8.30pm–12.30am, Sun
12.30–6pm. Closed 2 weeks in Aug.

A mix of fine traditional staples
and interesting new dishes.
Specialities include the Madrid
classic *callos* (tripe in tomato
sauce) and *rabo de toro* (oxtail),
but they also have international
dishes such as Greek salad and
Moroccan kebabs. A good-
value €12 lunchtime set menu is
available too.

El Botín

MAP p.28, POCKET MAP B13
C/Cuchilleros 17 Ⓜ Sol ☎ 913 664 217,
Ⓦ botin.es. Daily 1–4pm & 8pm–midnight.

Established in 1725, the
atmospheric *El Botín* is cited in
the *Guinness Book of Records*
as Europe's oldest restaurant.
Favoured by Hemingway, it's
inevitably a tourist haunt, but not
such a bad one. Highlights are
the Castilian roasts – especially
cochinillo (suckling pig) and
cordero lechal (lamb). Around
€40 a head.

Casa Paco

MAP p.28, POCKET MAP B13
Plaza Puerta Cerrada 11 Ⓜ La Latina
☎ 913 663 166, Ⓦ casapaco1933.es.
Tues–Sat 1–4pm & 8pm–midnght,
Sun 1–4pm.

This classic, traditional *comedor*, with no-nonsense service, dishes out some of the best meat dishes in town. Specializes in sirloin steak (*solomillo*), and another delicious cut known as *cebón de buey*. About €35 a head.

La Chusquery

MAP p.28, POCKET MAP A14
C/Mancebos 2 Ⓜ La Latina ☎ 910 703 215, Ⓦ la-chusquery.es. Tues–Sat 1.30–4pm & 8.30pm–midnight, Sun 1.30–4pm.

One of the newer arrivals on the La Latina scene, which serves up carefully selected dishes combining new Spanish cuisine and Asian influences. Specialities include Tataki butterfish, home-made *croquetas* and a delicious chocolate brownie dessert. Very reasonably priced (around €30 a head).

La Musa Latina

MAP p.28, POCKET MAP A14
Costanilla San Andrés 12 Ⓜ La Latina ☎ 913 540 255, Ⓦ grupolamusa.com. Mon–Wed 10am–1am, Thurs 10am–1.30am, Fri & Sat 10am–2am, Sun 10am–1am (food served from 1pm to an hour before closing).

Stylish place serving a great-value €12 *menú del día* (check the website for what's on offer each day), and a small selection of modern tapas such as langoustine and avocado tempura, roast sea bass and wok dishes. It has a cool brick-walled bar downstairs with DJ sessions.

Naia Bistro

MAP p.28, POCKET MAP A14
Plaza de la Paja 3 Ⓜ La Latina ☎ 913 662 783, Ⓦ naiabistro.com. Daily 1.30–4.30pm & 8.30–11pm (Fri & Sat till 11.30pm).

Relaxed restaurant with light, airy decor serving up well presented creative cuisine in a fine setting on an ancient plaza. Starters include pumpkin ravioli with sage butter; mains such as marinated tuna with wasabi and lime are also tempting. À la carte around €30 a head; group menus are also available.

Posada de la Villa

Palacio de Anglona

MAP p.28, POCKET MAP A13
C/Segovia 13 Ⓜ La Latina ☎ 913 653 153, Ⓦ palaciodeanglona.com. Mon–Sat 1–5pm & 8pm–1am, Sun 1–5pm.

Minimalist black and white decor in this good-value restaurant housed in the cellars of an old La Latina mansion. Mains (around €8–12) include black spaghetti with prawns, mini hamburgers and marinated langoustines. Cocktails are served in the lounge bar.

Posada de la Villa

MAP p.28, POCKET MAP B14
C/Cava Baja 9 Ⓜ La Latina ☎ 913 661 860, Ⓦ posadadelavilla.com. Mon–Sat 1–4pm & 8pm–midnight, Sun 1–4pm. Closed Aug.

La Latina's most attractive restaurant, spread over three floors of a seventeenth-century inn. Cooking is *madrileño*, including superb roast lamb. Reckon on €50 per person.

Tapas bars

Almendro 13

MAP p.28, POCKET MAP B14
C/Almendro 13 Ⓜ La Latina, Ⓦ almendro13 .com. Mon–Fri 1–4pm & 7.30pm–midnight, Sat, Sun & hols 1–5pm & 8pm–1am.

Packed at weekends, this fashion-able wood-panelled bar serves great *fino* sherry and house specials of *huevos rotos* (fried eggs on a bed of crisps) and *roscas rellenas* (bread rings stuffed with various meats).

Casa Revuelta

– *tortilla* with caramelized onion, grilled artichokes with parmesan – and a great selection of very tasty, but fairly pricey, canapés. Most dishes are in the €10–15 bracket.

Matritum

MAP p.28, POCKET MAP B14
C/Cava Alta 17 Ⓜ La Latina Ⓦ taberna matritum.es. Tues 8pm–midnight, Wed–Sun 1–4.30pm & 8pm–midnight. Closed Aug.
Delicious designer-style tapas, from marinated salmon with sea urchin to fresh couscous with razor shells. There's a collection of carefully selected wines too.

Mercado de San Miguel

MAP p.28, POCKET MAP B12
Plaza de San Miguel Ⓜ Sol Ⓦ mercadode sanmiguel.es. Sun–Wed 10am–midnight, Thurs–Sat 10am–2am.
Transformed from a neighbour-hood market into a hip location for an *aperitivo*, this beautiful wrought-iron *mercado* is worth exploring at almost any time of day. There's something for everyone, from vermouth and champagne to salt cod, oysters and sushi.

Casa Revuelta

MAP p.28, POCKET MAP C13
C/Latoneros 3 Ⓜ Sol or La Latina. Tues–Sat 10.30am–4pm & 7–11pm, Sun 10.30am–4pm. Closed Aug.
A timeless, tiny, down-to-earth bar located in an alleyway just south of Plaza Mayor. It serves a melt-in-the-mouth tapa of *bacalao frito* (battered cod).

La Chata

MAP p.28, POCKET MAP B14
C/Cava Baja 24 Ⓜ La Latina Ⓦ lachata cavabaja.com. Daily 1.30–4.30pm & 8.30pm–12.30am. Closed Tues & Wed lunchtime & Sun eve.
One of the city's most traditional and popular tapas bars, with hams hanging from the ceiling and taurine memorabilia on the walls. Serves a variety of dishes, including excellent *rabo de toro* (oxtail) and *pimientos del piquillo rellenos* (stuffed onions and peppers).

Juana la Loca

MAP p.28, POCKET MAP C7
Plaza Puerta de Moros 4 Ⓜ La Latina Ⓦ juanalalocamadrid.com. Mon 7/8pm–midnight, Tues–Fri 1–5pm & 7/8pm–midnight, Sat & Sun 1pm–midnight or 1am. Closed Aug.
Fashionable hangout on the edge of the square serving inventive tapas

Taberna Casa Curro

MAP p.28, POCKET MAP B14
C/Cava Baja 23 Ⓜ La Latina Ⓦ tabernacasa curro.com. Tues 7pm–1.30am, Wed & Thurs noon–4.30pm & 7pm–1.30am, Fri, Sat & Sun noon–1.30am.
An Andalucian bar in this most traditional of Madrid streets, *Casa Curro* promises to cure you of your ills with its mouthwatering fried prawns from Huelva, slices of *jamón* and *fino* all served up to the accompaniment of flamenco music which is sometimes played live.

Tapasentao

MAP p.28, POCKET MAP A14
C/Príncipe Anglona Ⓜ La Latina. Tues–Sun 12.30–11.30pm. Closed 2 weeks Aug.
Just opposite the church of San Pedro el Viejo, this popular bar serves up a wide range of interesting and original tapas, many of which are suitable for vegetarians. Favourites include

crunchy, fried aubergines, vegetable tempura and battered mushrooms.

Txirimiri

MAP p.28, POCKET MAP C7
C/Humilladero 6 Ⓜ La Latina Ⓦ txirimiri.es. Daily noon–midnight.

Fantastic range of tapas and *pintxos* in this ever-popular bar beside the Mercado de la Cebada. Mouth-watering combinations include cuttlefish and langoustine risotto and their speciality, Unai hamburger with porchini sauce.

Bars

Delic

MAP p.28, POCKET MAP A14
Costanilla San Andrés 14 Ⓜ La Latina Ⓦ delic.es. Tues–Sun 11am–2am. Closed first half of Aug.

Serving home-made cakes, fruit juices and coffee, this is a pleasant café by day, transforming into a crowded but friendly cocktail bar by night.

María Pandora

MAP p.28, POCKET MAP B7
Plaza Gabriel Miró 1 Ⓜ La Latina Ⓦ mariapandora.com. Mon–Sat 7pm–2am, Sun 4pm–2am. Closed second half of Aug.

An incongruous mix of *champagnería* (champagne bar) and library, where quality *cava* can be enjoyed with the perfect accompaniment of chocolates and mellow jazz.

El Tempranillo

MAP p.28, POCKET MAP B14
C/Cava Baja 38 Ⓜ La Latina. Daily 1–4pm & 8.30pm–midnight. Closed 2 weeks in Aug.

Popular little wine bar serving a vast range of domestic wines by the glass. A great place to discover your favourite Spanish *vino* – and the tapas are excellent too.

El Ventorrillo

MAP p.28, POCKET MAP C7
C/Bailén 14 Ⓜ La Latina or Ópera. Daily 11am–1am, Fri & Sat till 2am, Sun till midnight.

This popular terraza is great for a relaxing drink while enjoying the *vistillas* (little views) over the cathedral and mountains, but avoid the overpriced tapas.

Music venues

Las Carboneras

MAP p.28, POCKET MAP B13
Plaza Conde de Miranda Ⓜ Sol ☎ 915 428 677, Ⓦ tablaolascarboneras.com. Mon–Sat: shows 8.30pm & 10.30pm; Fri & Sat also 11pm.

Geared up for the tourist market, this *tablao* has gained a decent reputation on the flamenco scene with a good range of guest artists. At around €70 with dinner, or €36 with a drink, it remains slightly cheaper than its rivals.

Corral de la Morería

MAP p.28, POCKET MAP C7
C/Morería 17 Ⓜ La Latina or Ópera ☎ 913 658 446, Ⓦ corraldelamoreria.com. Daily 7pm–2am; shows at 8.30pm & 10.30pm.

A renowned and atmospheric, if expensive, venue for serious flamenco acts. Around €40 to see the show and double that if you want to dine in the restaurant as well.

Corral de la Morería

Palacio Real and Ópera

Although the barrio only became fashionable in the mid-nineteenth century, the attractions found in the compact area around Ópera metro station date back as far as the 1500s. The imposing and suitably lavish Palacio Real (Royal Palace) dominates this part of the city, bordered by the somewhat disappointing Catedral de la Almudena and the tranquil gardens of the Campo del Moro. The restored Teatro Real and Plaza de Oriente bring some nineteenth-century sophistication to the area, while the two monastery complexes of la Encarnación and las Descalzas Reales conceal an astounding selection of artistic delights. For after-dark attractions, the area is home to one of the city's leading clubs as well as a handful of pleasant cafés and restaurants.

Palacio Real

MAP p.38, POCKET MAP B5–C5
C/Bailén Ⓜ Ópera Ⓦ patrimonionacional.es. Daily: April–Sept 10am–8pm; Oct–March 10am–6pm. Closed for state occasions and on Jan 1 & 6, May 1 & 15, Oct 12, Nov 9, Dec 24, 25 & 31. €11; free for EU citizens Mon–Thurs: Oct–March 4–6pm; April–Sept 6–8pm.

The present Palacio Real (Royal Palace) was built by Felipe V after the ninth-century Arab-built Alcázar was destroyed by fire in 1734. The Bourbon monarch, who had been brought up in the more luxurious surroundings of Versailles, took the opportunity to replace it with an altogether grander affair. He did not, however, live to see its completion and the palace only became habitable in 1764 during the reign of Carlos III. Nowadays it's used only for ceremonial purposes, with the present royal family preferring the more modest Zarzuela Palace, 15km northwest of the city.

The ostentation lacking in the palace's exterior is more than compensated for inside, with swirling marble floors, celestial frescoes and gold furnishings. It's a flamboyant display of wealth and power that was firmly at

The Palacio Real

Catedral de la Almudena

odds with Spain's declining status at the time. Look out for the grandiose **Salón del Trono** (Throne Room), the incredible oriental-style **Salón de Gasparini** (the Gasparini Room) and the marvellous **Sala de Porcelana** (Porcelain Room), decorated with one thousand gold, green and white interlocking pieces.

The palace outbuildings and annexes include the **Armería Real** (Royal Armoury), with its fascinating collection of guns, swords and armour. There's also a laboratory-like eighteenth-century **farmacia** (pharmacy) and a **Galería de Pinturas** which displays works by Caravaggio, Velázquez and Goya and also hosts temporary exhibitions.

Jardines de Sabatini

MAP p.38, POCKET MAP B4–C4
Ⓜ Ópera. Daily: May–Sept 9am–10pm; Oct–April 9am–9pm.

The Jardines de Sabatini (Sabatini Gardens) make an ideal place from which to view the northern facade of the palace or to watch the sun go down. They contain a small ornamental lake, some fragrant magnolia trees and manicured hedges, while, in summer, they're often used as a concert venue.

Catedral de la Almudena

MAP p.38, POCKET MAP B6
Ⓜ Ópera. Daily: 9am–8.30pm; July & Aug 10am–9pm. Not open for visits during Mass: Mon–Sat noon, 6pm & 7pm, Sun & hols 10.30am, noon, 1.30pm, 6pm & 7pm; July & Aug noon & 8pm.

Planned centuries ago, Madrid's cathedral, Nuestra Señora de la Almudena, was plagued by lack of funds, bombed in the Civil War and finally opened in 1993. More recently, it was the venue for the wedding of the then heir to the throne, Prince Felipe, and his former newsreader bride, Letizia Ortiz.

The cathedral's cold Gothic interior housed within its stark Neoclassical shell is not particularly inspiring, though the garish ceiling designs and the sixteenth-century altarpiece in the Almudena chapel are exceptions. To one side of the main facade is a small **museum** (Mon–Sat 10am–2.30pm; €6, €4 for Madrid residents, students and pensioners) containing some of the cathedral's treasures, though the main reason to visit is to gain access to the dome from where you can enjoy some fantastic views over the city. The entrance to the **crypt** (guided visits Mon–Sat noon; €3) with its forest of columns and dimly lit chapels is on C/Mayor.

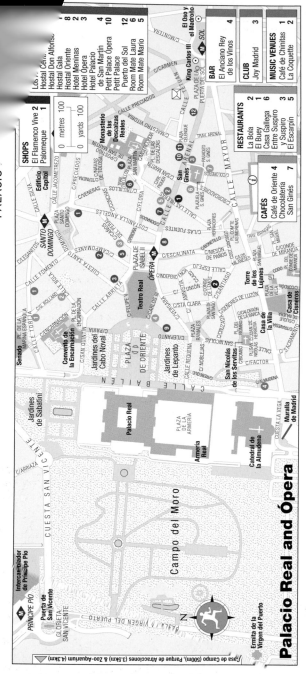

Palacio Real and Ópera

Campo del Moro

MAP p.38, POCKET MAP A4–B6
Entrance on Paseo de la Virgen del Puerto
Ⓜ Príncipe Pío. Daily: April–Sept 10am–
8pm; Oct–March 10am–6pm. Closed
occasionally for state occasions.

One of the most underused –
largely because of its inconvenient
entrance down by the river – and
beautiful of Madrid's parks, the
Campo del Moro gets its name
from being the site of the Moors'
encampment, from where, in 1109,
they mounted their unsuccessful
attempt to reconquer Madrid. It
later became a venue for medieval
tournaments and celebrations.
After the building of the Palacio
Real several schemes to landscape
the area were put forward, but
it wasn't until 1842 that things
got under way. Based around
two monumental fountains, *Las
Conchas* and *Los Tritones*, the
grassy gardens are very English in
style, featuring shady paths and
ornamental pools, and provide an
excellent refuge from the summer
heat, as well as a splendid view of
the palace.

Plaza de Oriente

MAP p.38, POCKET MAP A11
Ⓜ Ópera.

The aristocratic, pedestrianized
Plaza de Oriente is one of the
most attractive open spaces in
Madrid. The days when Franco
used to address crowds here from
the balcony of the royal palace
now seem a distant memory,
although a small number of
neo-Fascists still gather here
on the anniversary of his death,
November 21.

The fountain in the centre
was designed by Narciso
Pascual y Colomer, who also
transferred the bronze equestrian
statue of Felipe IV here from the
garden of the Buen Retiro Palace,
near the Prado. Dating from
1640, this statue is reputedly
the first-ever bronze featuring
a rearing horse – Galileo is
said to have helped with the
calculations to make it balance.
Other statues depict Spanish
kings and queens, and were
originally designed to adorn
the palace facade, but were
too heavy or, according to one
version, too ugly, and were
removed on the orders of Queen
Isabel Farnese.

There's a very French feel to
the buildings overlooking the
square, with their glass-fronted
balconies, underlined by the
elegant neo-Baroque *Café de
Oriente*, a favourite with the
opera crowd.

Plaza de Oriente

Monasterio de las Descalzas Reales

Teatro Real

MAP p.38, POCKET MAP A11–B11
Plaza de Isabel II ⓦ Ópera ☎ 915 160 660,
ticket line ☎ 902 244 848, ⓦ teatro-real.
com. Open for visits daily 10am–1pm.
Closed mid-July to mid-Sept; reservations
☎ 915 160 696. €8; tickets on sale
9.15am–1pm at the box office.

When it opened in 1850, the
hulking grey hexagonal opera
house became the hub of
fashionable Madrid and staged
highly successful works by Verdi
and Wagner. It fell into decay in
the late twentieth century and
after a ten-year refurbishment
– that should have lasted four –
and a staggering US$150 million
in costs, it finally reopened in
October 1997. With its lavish
red and gold decor, crystal
chandeliers, state-of-the-art
lighting and superb acoustics it
makes a truly magnificent setting
for opera, ballet and classical
concerts. Tickets range from €10
to €400, but you'll need to book
well in advance for the best seats.

Convento de la Encarnación

MAP p.38, POCKET MAP A10
Plaza de la Encarnación 1 ⓦ Ópera
ⓦ patrimonionacional.es. Tours only (some
in English) Tues–Sat 10am–2pm &
4–6.30pm, Sun & hols 10am–3pm. €6; joint
ticket with Monasterio de las Descalzas
Reales €8, valid for 48 hours; Wed & Thurs
4–6.30pm free for EU citizens.

Founded in 1611 by Felipe III
and his wife Margarita de
Austria, this convent was
intended as a retreat for titled
women and merits a visit for
its reliquary alone – one of the
most important in the Catholic
world. The solemn granite facade
is the hallmark of architect Juan
Gómez de Mora, also responsible
for the Plaza Mayor. Much of
the painting contained within is
uninspiring, but there are some
interesting items, including an
extensive collection of royal
portraits and a highly prized
collection of sculptures of
Christ. The library-like **reliquary**
contains more than 1500
saintly relics from around the
world: skulls, arms encased in
beautifully ornate hand-shaped
containers and bones from every
conceivable part of the body.
The most famous of the lot is a
small glass bulb said to contain
the blood of St Pantaleón – a
fourth-century doctor martyr –
which supposedly liquefies at
midnight every July 26 (the eve

of his feast day). Great tragedies are supposed to occur if the blood fails to liquefy. The tour ends with a visit to the Baroque-style church which features a beautifully frescoed ceiling and a marble-columned altarpiece.

Monasterio de las Descalzas Reales

MAP p.38, POCKET MAP C10–C11
Plaza de las Descalzas 3 Ⓜ Callao, Sol or Ópera Ⓦ patrimonionacional.es. Tours only (some in English) Tues–Sat 10am–2pm & 4–6.30pm, Sun & hols 10am–3pm. €6; joint ticket with Convento de la Encarnación €8, valid for 48 hours; Wed & Thurs 4–6.30pm free for EU citizens.

One of the less well-known treasures of Madrid, the "Monastery of the Barefoot Royal Ladies" was originally the site of a medieval palace. The building was transformed by Juana de Austria into a convent in 1564, and the architect of El Escorial, Juan Bautista de Toledo, was entrusted with its design. Juana was the youngest daughter of the Emperor Charles V and, at the age of 19, already the widow of Prince Don Juan of Portugal. Royal approval meant that it soon became home to a succession of titled ladies who brought with them an array of artistic treasures, helping the convent acc[...] fabulous collection of pa[...] sculptures and tapestries. [...] place is still unbelievably o[...] and remains in use as a relig[...] institution, housing 23 shoel[...] nuns of the Franciscan order.

The magnificent main staircase connects a two-levelled cloister, lined with small but richly embellished chapels, while the Tapestry Room contains an outstanding collection of early seventeenth-century Flemish tapestries based on designs by Rubens. The other highlight of the tour is the Joyería (Treasury), piled high with jewels and relics of uncertain provenance. Royal portraits and beautiful, wooden sculptures, most of unknown origin, decorate other rooms.

San Ginés

MAP p.38, POCKET MAP C11
C/Arenal 13 Ⓜ Ópera/Sol. Mon–Sat 8.45am–1pm & 6–9pm, Sun 9.45am–2pm & 6–9pm. Free.

Of Mozarabic origin (built by Christians under Moorish rule), this ancient church was completely reconstructed in the seventeenth century. There is an El Greco canvas of the moneychangers being chased from the temple in the Capilla del Cristo (on show Mon 12.30pm).

Shops

El Flamenco Vive

MAP p.38, POCKET MAP B12
C/Conde de Lemos 7 Ⓜ Ópera or Sol Ⓦ elflamencovive.com. Mon–Fri 10am–2pm & 5–8.30pm, Sat 10am–2pm.
A fascinating little slice of Andalucía in Madrid, specializing in all things flamenco, from guitars and CDs to dresses and books.

Palomeque

MAP p.38, POCKET MAP C11
C/Arenal 17 Ⓜ Ópera or Sol Ⓦ palomequearte.com. Mon–Fri 9.30am–1.30pm & 4.30–8pm, Sat 9.30am–1.30pm.
Founded back in 1873, this somewhat incongruous religious superstore has kept its place among the fashion outlets, hotels and restaurants that line this busy shopping street. Inside you'll find all manner of spiritual paraphernalia from elaborate alabaster altarpieces and sculptures of angels to rosary beads and postcard collections of Spanish saints and virgins.

e Oriente

8, POCKET MAP A11
de Oriente 2 Ⓜ Ópera. Mon–Thurs
8.30am–1.30am, Fri & Sat till
am.

legant but pricey Parisian-
style café with a popular terraza
looking across the plaza to the
palace. The café was opened
in the 1980s by a priest, Padre
Lezama, who ploughs his profits
into various charitable schemes.
There's an equally smart bar,
La Botillería (open noon–1am,
an hour later on Fri & Sat),
next door.

Chocolatería San Ginés

MAP p.38, POCKET MAP C12
Pasadizo de San Ginés 11 Ⓜ Sol or
Ópera Ⓦ chocolateriasangines.com.
Daily 24hrs.

A Madrid institution, this café,
established in 1894, serves
chocolate con churros (thick hot
chocolate with deep-fried hoops
of batter) to perfection – just
the thing to finish off a night of
excess. It's an almost compulsory
madrileño custom to end up
here after the clubs close, before
heading home for a shower and
then off to work.

Restaurants

La Bola

MAP p.38, POCKET MAP A10
C/Bola 5 Ⓜ Santo Domingo or Ópera ☎ 915
476 930, Ⓦ labola.es. Mon–Sat 1–4.30pm
& 8.30–11pm, Sun 1–4.30pm.

Opened back in 1870, *La Bola*
is renowned for its *cocido
madrileño* (soup followed by
chickpeas and a selection of
meats; €21), cooked in the
traditional way over a wood fire.
Don't plan on doing anything
energetic afterwards. They don't
accept cards, and service can be a
little brusque.

Chocolatería San Ginés

El Buey

MAP p.38, POCKET MAP C4
Plaza de la Marina Española 1 Ⓜ Santo
Domingo or Ópera ☎ 915 413 041,
Ⓦ restauranteelbuey.com. Mon–Sat 1–4pm
& 9pm–midnight, Sun 1–4pm.

A meat-eaters' paradise,
specializing in superb steak that
you fry yourself on a hotplate.
Great side dishes and home-
made desserts, with a highly
drinkable house red, all for
around €35 per head.

Casa Gallega

MAP p.38, POCKET MAP B12, C11
C/Bordadores 11 Ⓜ Ópera or Sol ☎ 915
419 055, Ⓦ lacasagallega.com. Daily
noon–midnight.

An airy and welcoming
marisquería that has been
importing seafood on overnight
trains from Galicia since opening
in 1915. Costs vary according to
the market price of the fish or
shellfish that you order. *Pulpo*
(octopus) and *pimientos de Padrón*
(small peppers, spiced up by the
odd fiery one) are brilliantly done
and relatively inexpensive. There
are set menus for €45–65 a head.

Entre Suspiro y Suspiro

MAP p.38, POCKET MAP B10
C/Caños de Peral 3 Ⓜ Ópera ☎ 915 420
644, Ⓦ entresuspiroysuspiro.com. Mon–Fri
2–4pm & 9pm–1am, Sat 9pm–1am.

Given Madrid's links with Latin America, this is one of surprisingly few decent Mexican restaurants in the city. Quesadillas, tacos and some imaginative takes on traditional dishes are served up in pleasant surroundings, although it is rather cramped. Around the €20 mark for main courses.

El Escarpín

MAP p.38, POCKET MAP C11
C/Hileras 17 Ⓜ Ópera ☎ 915 599 957, Ⓦ elescarpinsidreria.com. Mon–Thurs 9am–12.30am, Fri 9am–2am, Sat 10am–2am, Sun 10am–12.30am.

Reasonably-priced Asturian bar-restaurant offering regional specialities including *chorizo a la sidra* (chorizo with cider), *fabes con almejas* (beans with clams) and, of course, cider. Eat tapas at the bar or try the brick-lined dining room.

Bar

El Anciano Rey de los Vinos

MAP p.38, POCKET MAP C6
C/Bailén 19 Ⓜ Ópera Ⓦ elancianorey delosvinos.es. Mon & Wed–Sun 9.30am–11.30pm.

Traditional bar whose layout, furniture and decorative tiles have changed little since its foundation back in 1909. Well-poured beer, *vermút*, a decent selection of wine and some good tapas add further to the appeal.

Club

Joy Madrid

MAP p.38, POCKET MAP C11
C/Arenal 11 Ⓜ Sol or Ópera Ⓦ www .joy-eslava.com. Daily midnight–6am. €10–15 including first drink.

This long-standing club is one of the staples of the Madrid night scene. It has a busy schedule of sessions every day of the week, catering for everything from house to seventies disco. If you arrive early, there are discounts on the entry fee.

Music venues

Café de Chinitas

MAP p.38, POCKET MAP C4
C/Torija 7 Ⓜ Santo Domingo ☎ 915 595 135, Ⓦ chinitas.com. Mon–Sat 7pm–midnight; shows at 8.15pm & 10.30pm. Drink and show €36; dinner and show €67.

One of the oldest flamenco clubs in Madrid, hosting a dinner-dance spectacular. The music is authentic but keep an eye on how much you order as the bill can mount up very quickly indeed. Be sure to make an advance reservation.

La Coquette

MAP p.38, POCKET MAP C11
C/Hileras 14 Ⓜ Ópera. Daily 8pm–3am. Closed Aug.

A small, crowded basement jazz and blues bar, where people sit around watching the band perform on a tiny stage. Live acts Tuesday–Saturday and a jam session on Sunday.

Café de Chinitas

astro, Lavapiés and Embajadores

Lavapiés and Embajadores were originally tough, working-class districts built to accommodate the huge population growth of Madrid in the eighteenth and nineteenth centuries. Traditional sights are thin on the ground, but some original tenement blocks survive and the area is now famous for the Rastro street market. These barrios are also home to the castizos – authentic madrileños – who can be seen decked out in traditional costume during local festivals. The character of these areas has changed, however, in recent years. Young Spaniards and large numbers of immigrants have arrived, meaning that Lavapiés and Embajadores are now Madrid's most racially mixed barrios, with teahouses, kebab joints and textile shops sitting alongside some of the most original bars and restaurants in the city. Petty crime can be a problem round here but the reality is not as dramatic as newspapers suggest.

Iglesia Colegiata de San Isidro

MAP p.46, POCKET MAP C14
C/Toledo 37 Ⓜ Tirso de Molina or La Latina. Daily 7.30am–1pm & 6–9pm. Tours Sat 11.30am.

Built from 1622 to 1633, this enormous twin-towered church was originally the centre of the Jesuit Order in Spain. After Carlos III fell out with the Order in 1767, he redesigned the interior and dedicated it to the city's patron, San Isidro. Isidro's remains – and those of his equally saintly wife – were brought here in 1769 from the nearby **Iglesia de San Andrés** (see p.31). The church was the city's cathedral from 1886 until 1993 when the **Catedral de la Almudena** (see p.37) was completed. It has a single nave with ornate lateral chapels and an impressive altarpiece.

San Cayetano

Plants on sale at El Rastro

Mercado del Rastro

MAP p.46, POCKET MAP D8
Ⓜ La Latina.

Every Sunday morning, the
heaving mass of El Rastro
fleamarket takes over Calle Ribera
de Curtidores. On offer is just
about anything you might – or
more likely might not – need,
from old clothes and military
surplus to caged birds and fine
antiques. Real bargains are rare,
but the atmosphere is enjoyable
and the nearby bars are as good
as any in the city. Petty theft is
common, so keep a close eye
on your belongings. If you're
looking for something more
upmarket, try the antiques shops
in **Galerías Piquer** at C/Ribera
de Curtidores 29, which are also
open Sunday mornings.

La Corrala

MAP p.46, POCKET MAP E8
C/Tribulete 12 Ⓜ Lavapiés.

Built in 1839 and restored in
the 1980s, this is one of many
traditional *corrales* (tenement
blocks) in Lavapiés, with balconied
apartments opening onto a central
patio. Plays, especially farces
and *zarzuelas* (a mix of classical

opera and music hall), used to be
performed regularly in *corrales*;
this one usually hosts summer
performances.

San Cayetano

MAP p.46, POCKET MAP E8
C/Embajadores 15 Ⓜ Tirso de Molina or La
Latina. Variable hours, usually Mon–Sat
9.30am–noon & 6–8pm, Sun 9.30am–2pm.

José de Churriguera and Pedro de
Ribera, both renowned for their
extravagant designs, were involved
in the design of the elaborate
facade, which dates from 1761.
Most of the rest of the church was
destroyed in the Civil War and has
since been rebuilt.

Plaza Lavapiés

MAP p.46, POCKET MAP F8
Ⓜ Lavapiés.

In the Middle Ages, bustling Plaza
Lavapiés was the core of Jewish
Madrid, with the synagogue
situated on the site now occupied
by the Teatro Valle-Inclán. Today,
with its Chinese, Arabic and
African inhabitants, it remains
a cosmopolitan place, and the
plaza, along with Calle Argumosa
running off from its southeastern
corner, is an animated spot, with a
variety of bars and cafés.

Cine Doré

Calle Atocha

MAP p.46, POCKET MAP E6–H8
Ⓜ **Atocha or Antón Martín.**

Calle Atocha, one of the old ceremonial routes from Plaza Mayor to the basilica at Atocha, forms the northeastern border of Lavapiés. At its southern end it's a mishmash of fast-food and touristy restaurants, developing, as you move north up the hill, into a strange mixture of cheap hostels, fading shops, bars, lottery kiosks and sex emporia. With its brash neon lighting and shiny black facade, the huge sex shop at no. 80, El Mundo Fantástico, stands unashamedly opposite a convent and the site of an old printing house that produced the first edition of the first part of *Don Quixote*.

Cine Doré

MAP p.46, POCKET MAP F14
C/Santa Isabel 3 Ⓜ **Antón Martín** ☎ 913 691 125. Closed Mon. Films €2.50.

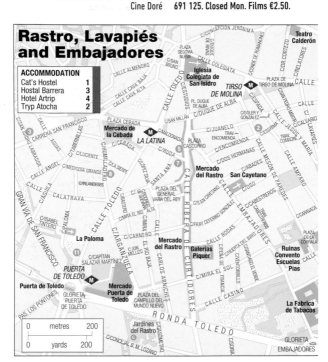

At the end of the narrow Pasaje Doré alley is the Cine Doré, the **oldest cinema** in Madrid. Dating from 1922 with a later Modernista/Art Nouveau facade, it's now the **Filmoteca Nacional**, an art-house cinema with bargain prices and a pleasant, inexpensive café/restaurant (Tues–Sun 4–11pm).

La Casa Encendida

MAP p.46, POCKET MAP F9
Ronda Valencia 2 Ⓜ **Embajadores** Ⓦ lacasaencendida.es. Tues–Sun 10am–10pm. Exhibitions free admission.

At the southern end of Lavapiés is La Casa Encendida, an alternative cultural centre with an internationalist and slightly avant-garde streak. Hosting everything from groundbreaking art exhibitions and concerts to films and workshops, the centre has an open and welcoming atmosphere, a decent café and is worth investigating if you happen to be in the area.

Museo del Ferrocarril

MAP p.46, POCKET MAP H9
Paseo de las Delicias 61 Ⓜ **Delicias** Ⓣ 902 228 822, Ⓦ museodelferrocarril .org. Mon–Thurs 9.30am–3pm, Fri–Sun 10am–8pm; June–Sept daily 10am–3pm; €6, 4–12 yr olds €4; €2.5 Fri after 2pm, Sat & Sun.

The Museo del Ferrocarril (Railway Museum) is one of the largest historic railroad collections in Europe and contains an impressive assortment of engines, carriages and wagons that once graced the train lines of Spain. The museum, which is housed in the handsome old station of Delicias, also has a fascinating collection of **model railways** and there's an atmospheric little café in one of the more elegant carriages. The museum also offers the possibility of travelling between Madrid and Aranjuez in a historic train, the Tren de la Fresa, every spring and autumn.

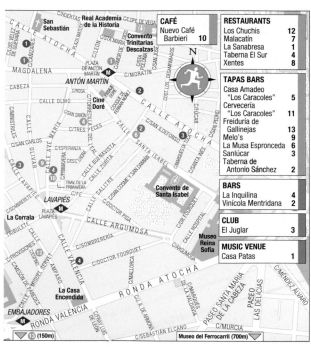

afé

Nuevo Café Barbieri

MAP p.46, POCKET MAP F8
C/Ave María 45 Ⓜ Lavapiés Ⓦ cafebarbieri
.es. Mon–Thurs 8am–1am, Fri 8am–2am,
Sat 9am–2am, Sun 9am–1am.

A relaxed, slightly dilapidated, fin
de siècle bar-café, with marbled
tables, a wide selection of coffees
and occasional live music.

Restaurants

Los Chuchis

MAP p.46, POCKET MAP F8
C/Amparo 82 Ⓜ Lavapiés ☎ 911 276 606,
Ⓦ facebook.com/LosChuchisBar. Tues–
Thurs 11am–midnight, Fri 11am–12.30am,
Sat noon–12.30am, Sun noon–8pm.

Run by Brit Scott Preston, this
gastro bar is a welcoming place
serving some great food. The *menú
del día* is a great-value €11.50 and
features options such as hake with
pesto and a selection of tasty soups.

Malacatín

MAP p.46, POCKET MAP D8
C/Ruda 5 Ⓜ La Latina ☎ 913 655 241,
Ⓦ malacatin.com. Mon–Sat 11am–5.30pm,
Wed–Sat also open 8pm–12.30am. Closed
mid-July–mid-Aug.

Established in 1895 to serve wine
to local workmen, this authentic
castizo restaurant serves generous
helpings of arguably the best *cocido*
(stew) in the city for a reasonable
€20. Sample it at the bar for €5 too.

La Sanabresa

MAP p.46, POCKET MAP G14
C/Amor de Diós 12 Ⓜ Antón Martín ☎ 914
290 338. Mon–Sat 1–4.30pm & 8.30–
11.30pm, Fri & Sat till midnight. Closed Aug.

Unpretentious local *comedor* with
reasonably priced dishes. There
is a *menú del día* for around €11.
Don't miss the grilled aubergines.

Taberna El Sur

MAP p.46, POCKET MAP F7
C/Torrecilla del Leal 12 Ⓜ Antón Martín.

Tues–Thurs 8pm–midnight, Fri & Sat
noon–2am, Sun 1.30–5pm.

Friendly bar/restaurant with an
interesting array of good-value
raciones including *ropa vieja*
(Cuban-style beef) and curried
chicken. A good wine selection
and a welcoming atmosphere.

Xentes

MAP p.46, POCKET MAP C8
C/Humilladero 13 Ⓜ La Latina/Puerta de
Toledo ☎ 913 664 266, Ⓦ xentes.es. Tues–
Sat 1.30–4.30pm & 8.30pm–midnight, Mon
& Sun 1.30–4.30pm.

Deservedly popular Galician
restaurant with a wide-ranging
menu, including excellent *arroz
caldoso* (rice dishes) accompanied
by a range of seafood ingredients.
The meat dishes are also good and
there is a very tasty selection of
steaks. Mains come in at between
€15–20, while there is a taster menu
for €35. You can also eat at the bar.

Tapas bars

Casa Amadeo "Los Caracoles"

MAP p.46, POCKET MAP D7
Plaza Cascorro 18 Ⓜ La Latina. Tues–Sun
11am–4pm & 7–11pm.

A favourite since the 1940s,
with tapas from the eponymous
caracoles (snails) to *callos* and
oreja. It's heaving on Sundays, and
keep an eye on the bill.

Cervecería "Los Caracoles"

MAP p.46, POCKET MAP C8
C/Toledo 106 Ⓜ Puerta de Toledo. Tues–Sat
9am–10.30pm, Sun 9am–4pm. Closed July.

Rough-and-ready bar
specializing in snails, washed
down with local *vermút del grifo*
(draught vermouth).

Freiduría de Gallinejas

MAP p.46, POCKET MAP F9
C/Embajadores 84 Ⓜ Embajadores
Ⓦ gallinejasembajadores.com. Mon–Sat
11am–11pm & Sun noon–10pm. Closed Aug.

This traditional tiled, family-run bar is famed for serving the best fried lambs' intestines in the city. A variety of different cuts are available as well as straightforward fried lamb.

Melo's

MAP p.46, POCKET MAP F8
C/Ave María 44 Ⓜ Lavapiés. Tues–Sat 8pm–1am. Closed Aug.

Standing room only at this very popular Galician bar serving *zapatillas* (huge toasted sandwiches filled with *lacón* – shoulder of pork – and cheese) plus delicious *pimientos de padrón* (hot-fried green peppers).

La Musa Espronceda

MAP p.46, POCKET MAP G7
C/Santa Isabel 17 Ⓜ Atocha or Antón Martín. Tues–Sun 12.30–4pm & 7pm–midnight.

Great-value tapas – classics such as *tortilla* and *croquetas* and creative bites such as brie wrapped in bacon – served in this friendly Lavapiés local. Lunchtime menu €10.50.

Sanlúcar

MAP p.46, POCKET MAP C7
C/San Isidro Labrador 14 Ⓜ La Latina Tues–Sat 1–5pm & 8.30pm–midnight, Sun 1–5pm.

Authentic Andalucian bar with a fine selection of tapas, including a great *salmorejo* (a variety of fried fish), prawns from Huelva and a decent glass of the cold, white Barbadillo wine from Sanlúcar.

Taberna de Antonio Sánchez

MAP p.46, POCKET MAP E7
C/Mesón de Paredes 13 Ⓜ Tirso de Molina Ⓦ tabernaantoniosanchez.com. Mon–Sat noon–4pm & 8pm–midnight, Sun noon–4.30pm.

Said to be Madrid's oldest *taberna*, this seventeenth-century bar has a stuffed bull's head (in honour of the founder's son, who was killed by one) and a wooden interior. Lots of *finos*, plus *jamón* tapas or *tortilla de san isidro* (salt cod omelette).

Bars

La Inquilina

MAP p.46, POCKET MAP F8
C/Ave María 39 Ⓜ Lavapiés Ⓦ facebook .com/la.inquilina. Daily 11am–1am (Fri & Sat till 2am).

Once an old furniture shop, now a mainstay on the Lavapiés bar scene, *La Inquilina* is a deceptively large, bohemian bar that hosts regular art exhibitions and acoustic concerts. It serves an interesting range of beers, ecological ciders and vermouth as well as some Portuguese and French-influenced tapas, too.

Vinícola Mentridana

MAP p.46, POCKET MAP G7
C/San Eugenio 9 Ⓜ Antón Martín. Mon–Thurs & Sun 1pm–1am, Fri & Sat 1pm–2am. Closed Aug.

Atmospheric traditional wine bar lined with dusty old bottles, a favourite with the Lavapiés crowd. A great selection of wine and beer, plus appetising canapés and tapas.

Club

El Juglar

MAP p.46, POCKET MAP F8
C/Lavapiés 37 Ⓜ Lavapiés Ⓦ salajuglar.com. Wed–Sun 9.30pm–3am, Fri & Sat till 3.30am.

Down-to-earth club with DJs playing funk and soul. There are also regular concerts with an entry fee of €7-15 depending on the act.

Music venue

Casa Patas

MAP p.46, POCKET MAP E14
C/Cañizares 10 Ⓜ Antón Martín or Tirso Molina ☎ 913 690 496 Ⓦ casapatas.com. Shows: Mon–Thurs 10.30pm, Fri & Sat 9pm & midnight. €38, including drink.

Authentic flamenco club with a bar and restaurant that gets its share of big names. The best nights are Thursday and Friday – check website for schedules.

Sol, Santa Ana and Huertas

The busy streets around Puerta del Sol, Plaza Santa Ana and Huertas are the bustling heart of Madrid and the reference point for most visitors to the capital. The city began to expand here during the sixteenth century and the area subsequently became known as Barrio de las Letras (literary neighbourhood) because of the many authors and playwrights – including Cervantes – who made it their home. Today, the literary theme continues, with theatres, bookshops and cafés proliferating alongside the Círculo de Bellas Artes (Fine Arts Institute), the Teatro Español (historic theatre specializing in classic works) and the Congreso de Los Diputados (Parliament). For art lovers, there's the Real Academia de Bellas Artes de San Fernando museum, but for most visitors the main attraction is the vast array of traditional bars, particularly concentrated around the picturesque Plaza Santa Ana.

Puerta del Sol

MAP p.52, POCKET MAP D11
Ⓜ Sol.

This half-moon-shaped plaza, thronged with people at almost any hour of the day, marks the epicentre of Madrid and, indeed, of Spain – **Kilometre Zero**, an inconspicuous stone slab on the south side of the square, is the spot from which all distances in the country are measured. Opposite is an equestrian bronze of King Carlos III, and to the east a statue of Madrid's emblem, *el oso y el madroño* (bear and strawberry tree).

The square has been a popular meeting place since the mid-sixteenth century, when it was

Puerta del Sol

the site of one of the main gates into the city. Its most important building is the Casa de Correos, built in 1766 and originally the city's post office. Under Franco it became the headquarters of the much-feared security police and it now houses the main offices of the Madrid regional government. The Neoclassical facade is crowned by the nation's most famous clock which officially ushers in the New Year: on December 31, *madrileños* pack Puerta del Sol and attempt to scoff twelve grapes – one on each of the chimes of midnight – to bring themselves good luck for the next twelve months.

The square has also witnessed several incidents of national importance, including the slaughter of a rioting crowd by Napoleon's marshal, Murat, aided by the infamous Egyptian cavalry, on May 2, 1808. The massacre is depicted in Goya's canvas, *Dos de Mayo*, now hanging in the Prado (see p.65).

Plaza Santa Ana

MAP p.52, POCKET MAP F13
Ⓜ Sol or Antón Martín.

The main reason for visiting vibrant Plaza Santa Ana is the mass of bars, restaurants and cafés on the square itself and in the nearby streets that bring the area alive in the evenings.

The square was one of a series created by Joseph Bonaparte, whose passion for open spaces led to a remarkable remodelling of Madrid in the six short years of his reign. It's dominated by two distinguished buildings at either end: to the west, the *ME Madrid Reina Victoria*, a giant white confection of a hotel; to the east, the nineteenth-century Neoclassical Teatro Español. There has been a playhouse on this site since 1583, and the current theatre is the oldest in Madrid, its facade decorated with busts of famous Spanish playwrights.

Plaza Santa Ana

Casa Museo Lope de Vega

MAP p.52, POCKET MAP G13
C/Cervantes 11 Ⓜ Antón Martín
Ⓦ casamuseolopedevega.org. Tues–Sun 10am–6pm. Closed mid-July to mid-Aug. Guided tours every 30 mins. Ring ☎ 914 299 216 to reserve a tour in English.

Situated in the heart of the Huertas district, the reconstructed home of the great Golden Age Spanish dramatist offers a fascinating glimpse of life in seventeenth-century Madrid. Lope de Vega, a prolific writer with a tangled private life, lived here for 25 years until his death in 1635 at the age of 72. The house itself has been furnished in authentic fashion using the inventory left at the writer's death and highlights include a chapel containing some of his relics, his study with a selection of contemporary books, an Arabic-style drawing room and a delightful courtyard garden.

Cervantes lived and died at no. 2 on the same street and though the original building has long gone, a plaque above a shop marks the site.

Sol, Santa Ana and Huertas

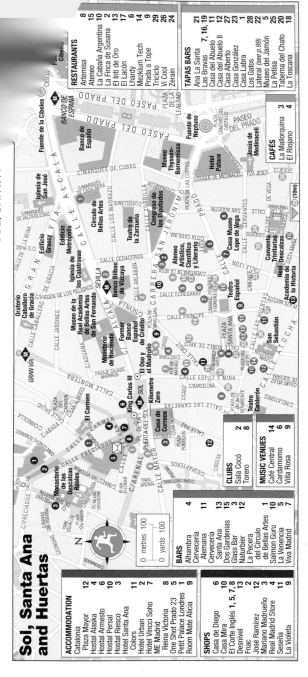

ACCOMMODATION	
Catalonia	12
Plaza Mayor	
Hostal Alaska	4
Hostal Armesto	6
Hostal Persal	10
Hostal Riesco	3
Hotel Santa Ana	
Colors	11
Hotel Urban	2
Hotel Vincci Soho	7
ME Madrid	
Reina Victoria	8
One Shot Prado 23	5
Petit Palace Londres	
Room Mate Alicia	9

SHOPS	
Casa de Diego	6
Casa Mira	10
El Corte Inglés	1, 5, 7, 8
Desnivel	13
Fnac	2
La Pecera	
José Ramírez	12
Mariano Madrueño	3
Real Madrid Store	4
Sesña	11
La Violeta	9

BARS	
Alhambra	4
Cervecería	
Alemana	11
Cervecería	
Santa Ana	13
Dos Gardenias	15
Glass Bar	3
Naturbier	12
La Pecera	
del Círculo	
de Bellas Artes	1
Salmon Guru	10
La Venencia	5
Viva Madrid	7

CLUBS	
Sala Cocó	2
Torero	8

MUSIC VENUES	
Café Central	14
Cardamomo	6
Villa Rosa	9

RESTAURANTS	
Artemisa	8
Ateneo	15
La Cabaña Argentina	10
La Finca de Susana	2
El Inti de Oro	13
El Lacón	17
Lhardy	6
Mezklum Tech	14
Prada a Tope	9
Tricicló	29
Vi Cool	26
Zerain	24

TAPAS BARS	
Ana La Santa	21
Las Bravas	7, 16, 19
Casa del Abuelo	11
Casa del Abuelo II	12
Casa Alberto	27
Casa González	23
Casa Labra	1
Los Gatos	28
Lateral (see p.99)	22
Museo del Jamón	5
La Petisa	25
Taberna del Chato	20
La Toscana	18

CAFÉS	
La Mallorquina	3
El Riojano	4

Banco Español de Crédito

Ateneo Artístico, Científico y Literario

MAP p.52, POCKET MAP G12
C/Prado 2 Ⓜ Antón Martín or Sevilla
Ⓦ ateneodemadrid.com. Tours Mon–Fri
10am–1pm; €3; booking necessary
via website.

The Ateneo (literary, scientific and political club) was founded after the 1820 Revolution and provided a focus for the new liberal political ideas circulating at that time. The exterior is neo-Plateresque in style, while the inside features a Neoclassical lecture theatre, a wooden panelled corridor with portraits of past presidents of the club and a splendid reading room. It also has a café and hosts occasional exhibitions.

Congreso de los Diputados

MAP p.52, POCKET MAP G12
Plaza de las Cortes Ⓜ Sevilla Ⓦ www
.congreso.es. Sat 10.30am–12.30pm (bring
passport). Closed Aug & hols.

The lower house of the **Spanish parliament** meets in a rather unprepossessing nineteenth-century building; its most distinguished feature is the two bronze lions that guard the entrance, made from a melted-down cannon captured during the African War of 1859–60. Sessions can be visited by appointment only, though you can turn up and queue for a free tour on Saturday mornings. This takes in several important rooms and the chamber with the bullet holes left by mad Colonel Tejero and his Guardia Civil associates in the abortive coup of 1981.

Calle Alcalá

MAP p.52, POCKET MAP E11–J10
Ⓜ Sol or Sevilla.

An imposing catalogue of Spanish architecture lines Calle Alcalá, an ancient thoroughfare that originally led to the university town of Alcalá de Henares. It starts at Puerta del Sol; in this first stretch, look out particularly for the splendid early twentieth-century wedge-shaped Banco Español de Crédito adorned with **elephant heads** and plaques listing all the branches of the bank in Spain, soon to be turned into a luxury hotel, shopping centre and apartment block. The Banco de Bilbao Vizcaya, with its Neoclassical facade complete with charioteers on top, and the Baroque Ministerio de Hacienda (Inland Revenue) are similarly impressive.

San José

...Ⓜ Banco de España. Daily 7am–
... 6–8.30pm, Sun open from 9am.

...-brick Iglesia de San José,
...ne junction with Gran Vía,
... back to the 1730s and was the
... building designed by the prolific
...dro de Ribera. The interior holds
...ne ornate Santa Teresa de Ávila
chapel and an impressive collection
of colourful images of Christ and
the Virgin Mary.

Iglesia de las Calatravas

MAP p.52, POCKET MAP F11
C/Alcalá 25 Ⓜ Sevilla Ⓦ iglesiacalatravas
.com. Mon 8am–1pm, Tues–Fri 8am–1pm &
6.30–8pm, Sat 6.30–8pm, Sun 11.30am–
1pm & 6.30–8pm.

The pastel-pink Baroque Iglesia
de las Calatravas was built in
the seventeenth century for the
nuns of the Calatrava, one of the
four Spanish military orders.
Inside, it contains a fantastically
elaborate gold altarpiece by
José Churriguera.

Museo de la Real Academia de Bellas Artes de San Fernando

MAP p.52, POCKET MAP F11
C/Alcalá 13 Ⓜ Sevilla ☏ 915 240 864
Ⓦ realacademiabellasartessanfernando
.com. Tues–Sun 10am–3pm. €8, free Wed.

Established by Felipe V in 1744
and housed in its present location
since 1773, the Museo de la Real
Academia de Bellas Artes de
San Fernando is one of the most
important art galleries in Spain.
Its displays include sections on
sculpture, architecture and music,
some interesting French and
Italian work and an extraordinary
– but chaotically displayed –
collection of Spanish paintings,
including El Greco, Velázquez,
Murillo and Picasso.

The Goya section has two
revealing self-portraits, several
depictions of the despised royal
favourite *Don Manuel Godoy*,
the desolate representation of *The
Madhouse* and *The Burial of the
Sardine* (a popular procession that
continues to this day in Madrid).

The gallery also holds the national
copper engraving collection (Mon–
Thurs 9am–5pm, Fri 9am–3pm,
July & Sept Mon–Fri 9am–3pm,
closed Aug; free), which includes
Goya etchings and several of the
copper plates used for his *Capricho*
series on show in the Prado.

Círculo de Bellas Artes

MAP p.52, POCKET MAP G11
C/Marqués de Casa Riera 2 Ⓜ Banco de
España Ⓦ circulobellasartes.com.
Exhibitions Tues–Sun 11am–2pm &
5–9pm. €5.

Museo de la Real Academia de Bellas Artes de San Fernando

This striking 1920s Art Deco building, crowned by a statue of Pallas Athene, is home to one of Madrid's best arts centres. Inside, there's a theatre, music hall, galleries, cinema and café bar (see p.62). For many years a stronghold of Spain's intelligentsia, it attracts the city's arts and media crowd but is not exclusive, nor expensive. As the Círculo is theoretically a members-only club, it issues day membership on the door.

Plaza de Cibeles

MAP p.52, POCKET MAP J10
Ⓜ Banco de España.

Encircled by four of the most monumental buildings in Madrid, Plaza de Cibeles is one of the city's most famous landmarks. At its centre, and marooned in a sea of never-ending traffic, is the late eighteenth-century fountain and statue of the goddess Cybele riding in a lion-drawn chariot. Built to celebrate the city's first public water supply, today the fountain is the post-victory congregation point for Real Madrid fans (Atlético supporters bathe in the fountain of Neptune just down the road).

Palacio de Cibeles

MAP p.52, POCKET MAP J10
Ⓜ Banco de España Ⓦ centrocentro.org.
Exhibitions Tues–Sun 10am–8pm.

This grandiose wedding-cake of a building on the eastern side of Paseo del Prado, constructed between 1904 and 1917 by the prolific architect partnership of Antonio Palacios and Joaquín Otamendi, was once Madrid's main post office, but has recently been usurped by the Madrid City Council. It is now home to a smart exhibition space, a viewing gallery (Tues–Sun 10.30am–1.30pm & 4–7pm; €2, under-12s €0.50), a café (daily 10am–midnight), an expensive restaurant run by Toledan restaurateur Adolfo Muñoz, and

Plaza de Cibeles

an overpriced and rather *pijo* terrace bar (daily 1pm–2am), which does offer some great views over the Paseo del Prado.

Palacio de Linares

MAP p.52, POCKET MAP J10
Plaza de Cibeles 2 Ⓜ Banco de España
Ⓦ www.casamerica.es. Exhibitions usually Mon–Sat 11am–8pm, Sun 11am–3pm; guided tours Sat & Sun 11am, noon, 1pm. €8, students and over-65s €5, under-8s free.

This palatial eighteenth-century mansion, built by the Marqués de Linares, is now home to the Casa de América, a cultural organization that promotes Latin American art through concerts, films and exhibitions. At weekends, there are guided tours through the sumptuous mansion decorated with some marvellous frescoes, crystal chandeliers and elaborate tapestries from the Real Fábrica (see p.74). The *palacio* also has an expensive designer restaurant and an excellent summer garden terrace.

hops

asa de Diego

MAP p.52, POCKET MAP E11
Puerta del Sol 12 Ⓜ Sol Ⓦ casadiego.info.
Mon–Sat 9.30am–8pm.

Old-time shop with helpful staff
selling a fabulous array of Spanish
fans (*abanicos*) ranging from cheap
offerings at under €12 to beautifully
hand-crafted works of art costing
up to €1500. Sells umbrellas,
walking sticks and shawls too.

Casa Mira

MAP p.52, POCKET MAP F12
C/San Jerónimo 30 Ⓜ Sevilla Ⓦ casamira.
es. Daily 10am–2pm & 5–9pm. Closed
mid-July to Sept.

The place to go for *turrón*
(flavoured nougat, eaten by
Spaniards at Christmas) and
marzipan. The family business has
been open for over 150 years since
the founder, Luis Mira, arrived
from Asturias and set up a stall in
Puerta del Sol.

El Corte Inglés

MAP p.52, POCKET MAP D10 & D11
C/Preciados 1–4 Ⓜ Sol & Plaza Callao 2
Ⓜ Callao Ⓦ elcorteingles.com. Mon–Sat
10am–10pm, Sun 11am–9pm.

The Spanish department store *par
excellence*. It's not cheap, but the
quality is very good, the staff are

Casa de Diego

highly professional (the majority
speak English) and there's a
gourmet section on the ninth floor
of the Callao branch with fantastic
views over the city (see p.87).

Desnivel

MAP p.52, POCKET MAP F14
Plaza Matute 6 Ⓜ Antón Martín
Ⓦ libreriadesnivel.com. Mon–Fri
10am–8.30pm, Sat 11am–8.30.

A great selection of maps and
guides if you fancy a hike in the
nearby Sierra Guadarrama.

Fnac

MAP p.52, POCKET MAP D10
C/Preciados 28 Ⓜ Callao Ⓦ fnac.es. Mon–
Sat 10am–9.30pm, Sun 11.30am–9.30pm.

Department store with sections
for books, videos, CDs and
electrical equipment. Also sells
concert tickets.

José Ramírez

MAP p.52, POCKET MAP D12
C/Paz 8 Ⓜ Sol Ⓦ guitarrasramirez.com.
Mon–Fri 10am–2pm & 4.30–8pm, Sat
10.30am–2pm.

The Ramírez family have been
making handcrafted guitars since
1882 and, even if you are not a
budding flamenco artist, this
beautiful old shop is still worth a
visit to appreciate these works of
art used by some of the world's
leading musicians.

Seseña

La Violeta

MAP p.52, POCKET MAP F12
Plaza de Canalejas 6 Ⓜ Sol/Sevilla
Ⓦ lavioletaonline.es. Mon–Sat 10am–8p
Closed Aug.

Old-style confectionary store
founded in 1915 and famous for its
violetas, delicate sweets made from
the essence of the violet flower. They
also sell violet marmalade, honey
and tea as well as more traditional
delights for the sweet-toothed.

Cafés

La Mallorquina

MAP p.52, POCKET MAP D12
Puerta del Sol 2 Ⓜ Sol Ⓦ pasteleria
lamallorquina.es. Daily 8.30am–9.15pm.

Classic Madrid café, great for
breakfast or sweet snacks. Try
one of their *napolitanas* (cream
slices) in the upstairs salon that
overlooks Puerta del Sol.

El Riojano

MAP p.52, POCKET MAP D12
C/Mayor 10 Ⓜ Sol Ⓦ confiteriaelriojano
.com. Daily 10am–2am & 5–9pm.

Traditional patisserie shop
founded back in 1885 and café
selling a wonderful range of
Spanish-style sweets and cakes,
such as *buñuelos de viento* (balls
of chocolate, custard or cream
covered in batter) and *torrijas*
(bread cooked in milk, egg, sugar,
cinnamon and lemon).

Restaurants

Artemisa

MAP p.52, POCKET MAP F12
C/Ventura de la Vega 4 Ⓜ Sevilla ☎ 914
295 092, Ⓦ restaurantesvegetarianos
artemisa.com. Daily 1.30–4pm &
9pm–midnight.

Long-standing vegetarian
restaurant, serving a wide range of
dishes including courgettes with
curry and raisins. There is a good-
value set lunch for €12.90.

Mariano Madrueño

MAP p.52, POCKET MAP C10
C/Postigo San Martín 3 Ⓜ Callao
Ⓦ marianomadrueno.es. Mon–Fri
9.30am–2pm & 5–8pm, Sat 9.30am–2pm.

Traditional wine seller's,
established in 1895, where there's
an overpowering smell of grapes
as you peruse its vintage-crammed
shelves. Intriguing tipples include
potent Licor de Hierbas from
Galicia and home-made Pacharán
(aniseed liqueur with sloe berries).

Real Madrid Store

MAP p.52, POCKET MAP D11
C/Carmen 3 Ⓜ Sol. Mon–Sat 10am–9pm,
Sun 11am–8pm.

Club store where you can pick up
replica shirts and all manner of –
expensive – souvenirs related to
the club's history. There is another
branch in the shopping centre
on the corner of Real's Bernabéu
stadium (see p.94) at C/Padre
Damian Puerta 55.

Seseña

MAP p.52, POCKET MAP E12
C/Cruz 23 Ⓜ Sol Ⓦ sesena.com. Mon–Fri
10am–2pm & 5–8pm, Sat 11am–2.30pm.

Open since 1901, this shop
specializes in traditional
madrileño capes for royalty and
celebrities. Clients have included
Luis Buñuel, Gary Cooper and
Hillary Clinton.

...o

MAP ..., POCKET MAP G12
...a Catalina 10 Ⓜ Sol/Sevilla ☎ 914
...32, Ⓦ restauranteateneo.es. Mon–Sat
...–1am, Sun 9am–10pm.

...nartly decorated café/restaurant
...naring its name with the literary
club to which it is connected
(see p.53). It specializes in well
prepared traditional Spanish
dishes with an international
twist served up in pleasant
surroundings. There is a very
decent €15 set lunch on weekdays.

La Cabaña Argentina

MAP p.52, POCKET MAP F12
C/Ventura de la Vega 10 Ⓜ Sevilla ☎ 913
697 202, Ⓦ lacabanaargentina.es. Mon–
Thurs & Sun 1.15pm–midnight, Fri & Sat
1.30pm–12.30am.

One of the best Argentine eateries
in the city. Excellent-quality meat
(*el bife de lomo alto* is a house
favourite) and classic desserts
including *panqueques*. Friendly
service and only around €35 a head.

La Finca de Susana

MAP p.52, POCKET MAP F11
C/Arlabán 4 Ⓜ Sevilla. Daily 1–3.45pm &
8.30–11.45pm.

One of three good-value
restaurants set up by a group of
Catalan friends (another, *La Gloria
de Montera*, is just off Gran Vía).

Lhardy

Food isn't out of this world and
service is impersonal, but if you
want a varied *menú del día* at a
decent price (around €11) this is a
good bet. You can't book, so arrive
early to avoid queueing.

El Inti de Oro

MAP p.52, POCKET MAP F12
C/Ventura de la Vega 12 Ⓜ Antón Martín
☎ 914 296 703, Ⓦ intideoro.com. Daily 1.30–
4pm & 8.30pm–midnight. Also at C/Amor de
Dios 9 Ⓜ Antón Martín ☎ 914 291 958.

The friendly staff at this good-value
Peruvian restaurant are more
than ready to provide suggestions
for those new to the cuisine. The
pisco sour, a cocktail of Peruvian
liquor, lemon juice, egg white and
sugar is a recommended starter,
while the *ceviche de merluza* (raw
fish marinated in lemon juice) is a
wonderful dish. A full meal costs
around €30.

El Lacón

MAP p.52, POCKET MAP F12
C/Manuel Fernández y González 8 Ⓜ Sol
☎ 914 296 042, Ⓦ mesonellacon.com.
Daily 1–4pm & 8pm–midnight. Closed Aug.

A large Galician bar-restaurant
with plenty of seats upstairs. Great
pulpo, caldo gallego (meat and
vegetable broth) and *empanadas*.
They also do a neat *menú exprés*
at lunchtime consisting of a single
course and a drink for just €4.

Lhardy

MAP p.52, POCKET MAP E12
C/San Jerónimo 8 Ⓜ Sol ☎ 915 213 385,
Ⓦ lhardy.com. Restaurant: Mon–Sat
1–3.30pm & 8.30–11pm, Sun 1–3.30pm.
Shop: Mon–Sat 9am–10pm, Sun
10am–3pm. Closed Aug.

Once the haunt of royalty, this is
one of Madrid's most beautiful
and famous restaurants. It's greatly
overpriced – expect to pay over
€70 per head for a three-course
meal – but on the ground floor,
there's a wonderful bar/shop where
you can have breakfast or snack
on canapés, *fino* and consommé,
without breaking the bank.

Mezklum Tech

MAP p.52, POCKET MAP F12
C/Príncipe 16 Ⓜ Sevilla ☎ 915 218 911,
Ⓦ mezklum.com. Mon–Thurs 1–4pm &
9–11.45pm, Fri & Sat 1–4pm & 9pm–1am,
Sun 1–4pm.

Newly decked out with wooden
floors and brick walls, this casual
but chic eatery serves a fine array
of Mediterranean and fusion-
influence dishes with good pasta
and rice dishes. It has a lunchtime
set menu at €11.35 and two
evening menus at €20 and €25.

Prada a Tope

MAP p.52, POCKET MAP F12
C/Príncipe 11 Ⓜ Sol ☎ 914 295 921. Tues–
Sun 12.30–5pm & 8pm–midnight.

Quality produce from the El Bierzo
region of León. The *morcilla* (black
pudding), *empanada* (pasty) and
tortilla are extremely tasty, while
the smooth house wines provide
the ideal accompaniment.

Triciclo

MAP p.52, POCKET MAP G14
C/Santa María 28 Ⓜ Antón Martín
☎ 910 244 798, Ⓦ eltriciclo.es. Mon–Sat
1.30–4pm & 8.30pm–midnight.

Set up by a trio of young chefs in
2013 with the aim of creating a
restaurant where they themselves
would like to eat. The results are
impressive and *Triciclo* serves
up a wide range of innovative
dishes, from seafood lasagne to
grilled artichokes with prawns and
almonds. Prices range from €7
to €25 a dish. If you can't book a
table try the more informal sister
restaurant *Tandem* at nº 39 in the
same street (closed Mon).

Vi Cool

MAP p.52, POCKET MAP F13
C/Huertas 12 Ⓜ Antón Martín ☎ 914 294
913, Ⓦ vi-cool.com. Daily 1–4pm &
8pm–midnight.

Originally established by Catalan
celebrity chef Sergi Arola as a
more affordable outlet for his
renowned food. The low-key,
minimalist interior is the setting

Ana La Santa

for some simple but classy and
creative offerings including meat
and spinach cannelloni, fried
langoustines in a curry and mint
sauce, and gourmet hamburgers
and pizzas. There are tapas
selections at €22 and €35.

Zeraín

MAP p.52, POCKET MAP G13
C/Quevedo 3 Ⓜ Antón Martín ☎ 914 297
909, Ⓦ restaurante-vasco-zerain-sidreria
.es. Mon–Sat 1.30–4pm & 7.30pm–midnight,
Sun 1.30–4pm. Closed Aug.

Basque cider house serving excellent
meat and fish dishes. The *chuletón*
(T-bone steak) is the speciality, but
it also does a very good *tortilla de
bacalao* and grilled *rape* (monkfish).
Set menus for between €32–37 and
one for under-12s at €15.

Tapas bars

Ana La Santa

MAP p.52, POCKET MAP E13
Plaza Santa Ana 14 Ⓜ Sol/Antón Martín
☎ 917 016 013, Ⓦ encompaniadelobos
.com. Daily 7am–midnight.

A stylish bar/restaurant housed in
smart surroundings in the lobby
of the *ME Victoria* hotel at one
end of Plaza Santa Ana. On offer is
a mixture of classic *raciones* with a
modern touch – mussels with lime
and coriander, roast asparagus
with rosemary and fried baby
squid, all at between €4–15 a dish.

MAP E12 & E13
Ⓜ Sol. Other branches at
. 13 Ⓜ Sol; & Pasaje Mathéu
sbravas.com. Mon–Thurs
pm & 7–11.30pm, Fri & Sat
n & 7pm–12.30am, Sun
pm & 7–11.30pm.

ding room only at these three
s, where, as the name suggests,
tatas bravas are the thing – they
patented their own version of the
spicy sauce.

Casa del Abuelo

MAP p.52, POCKET MAP E12
C/Victoria 12 Ⓜ Sol Ⓦ lacasadelabuelo.es.
Daily noon–midnight (Fri & Sat until 1am).

A tiny, atmospheric bar serving
just their own cloyingly sweet
red wine (stick with a beer
instead) and delicious cooked
prawns – try them *al ajillo* (in
garlic) or *a la plancha* (grilled) –
which are fried up in the tiny
corner kitchen.

Casa del Abuelo II

MAP p.52, POCKET MAP E12
C/Núñez de Arce 5 Ⓜ Sol
Ⓦ lacasadelabuelo.es. Daily noon–
midnight (Fri & Sat until 1am).

There's a *comedor* (dining room)
at the back of this classic Madrid
bar, with a selection of traditional
raciones – the *croquetas* are great –
and a jug of house wine.

Casa Alberto

MAP p.52, POCKET MAP F13
C/Huertas 18 Ⓜ Antón Martín ☎ 914 299 356,
Ⓦ casaalberto.es. Bar: Tues–Sat noon–
1.30am, Sun noon–4pm. Restaurant: Tues–Sat
1.30–4pm & 8pm–midnight, Sun 1.30–4pm.

Traditional *tasca* that has
resisted the passage of time since
it was founded back in 1827.
Good *caracoles* (snails), *gambas*
(prawns) and great *croquetas*,
ideally accompanied by a glass of
house vermouth.

Casa González

MAP p.52, POCKET MAP F13
C/León 12 Ⓜ Antón Martín Ⓦ casagonzalez
.es. Mon–Thurs 9.30am–midnight, Fri & Sat
9.30am–1am, Sun 11am–6pm.

Friendly delicatessen/tapas bar
with an extensive range of wines
and cheese and serving up some
great tapas including a fantastic
salmorejo, speciality sausage from
around Spain and some imaginative
tostas covered in a variety of patés.

Casa Labra

MAP p.52, POCKET MAP D11
C/Tetuán 12 Ⓜ Sol ☎ 915 310 081,
Ⓦ casalabra.es. Bar daily: 9.30am–3.30pm
& 5.30–11pm. Restaurant: Mon–Sat
1.15–3.30pm & 8.15–10pm.

Dating from 1869 – and where the
Spanish Socialist Party was founded
ten years later – this traditional
and highly popular place retains

Casa Alberto

much of its original interior. Order a drink at the bar and a *ración* of *bacalao* (cod fried in batter) or some of the best *croquetas* in town. There's also a restaurant at the back serving classic *madrileño* food. Be prepared to queue.

Los Gatos

MAP p.52, POCKET MAP H13
C/Jesús 2, Ⓜ Antón Martín. Mon–Thurs & Sun 11am–1am, Fri & Sat 11am–2am.

Decorated with a multifarious collection of curiosities including a model of a choirboy with sunglasses, a jazz musician and a horned gramophone, this old-style bar serves up an excellent selection of canapés and beer for its loyal clientele.

Museo del Jamón

MAP p.52, POCKET MAP E12
C/San Jerónimo 6 Ⓜ Sol Ⓦ museo deljamon.com. Mon–Thurs 9am–12.30am, Fri & Sat 9am–1am, Sun 10am–12.30am.

This is the largest branch of this unpretentious Madrid chain, from whose ceilings are suspended hundreds of *jamones* (hams). The best – and they're not cheap – are the *jabugos* from the Sierra Morena, though a filling ham sandwich is only around €2.

La Petisa

MAP p.52, POCKET MAP G13
C/Lope de Vega 15 Ⓜ Antón Martín Ⓦ lapetisabar.com. Tues–Thurs 1–4.30pm & 7pm–midnight, Fri & Sat 1pm–1.30am, Sun 1–6pm.

Carving out a niche for itself in the highly competitive tapas market is this friendly little bar, which serves some delicious Argentine-influenced dishes such as *empanadillas*, plus gourmet hamburgers, very good salads and a delicious carrot cake for dessert.

Taberna del Chato

MAP p.52, POCKET MAP E13
C/Cruz 35 Ⓜ Sol/Antón Martín ☎ 915 231 629, Ⓦ tabernadelchato.com. Mon–Thurs 7pm–1am, Fri 7pm–2.30am, Sat & Sun 12.30–4pm & 7pm–1am.

Museo del Jamón

Reasonable prices, friendly service and some very good tapas on offer in this increasingly popular bar sandwiched between Sol and Santa Ana. There is a selection of appetisers featuring tiny dishes of chicken curry, *morcilla*, *paté de perdiz* (partridge paté), tuna tartare and so on, while there are more substantial offerings of *sardinas*, *chistorra* and teriyaki salmon.

La Toscana

MAP p.52, POCKET MAP F12
C/Manuel Fernández y González 10 Ⓜ Antón Martín or Sevilla. Tues–Sat 1–4pm & 8pm–midnight. Closed Aug.

This popular and friendly Huertas classic serves up some delicious home-made tapas. The *morcillo* (beef shank) is excellent, while the *croquetas*, *chistorra* and tuna salads are also very tasty.

Bars

Alhambra

MAP p.52, POCKET MAP E12
C/Victoria 9 Ⓜ Sol. Daily 11am–1.30am (2am at weekends).

Friendly tapas bar by day, fun disco bar by night, with the crowds spilling over into the *El Buscón* bar next door.

...ecería Alemana

...52, POCKET MAP F13
...de Santa Ana 6 ⓂSol or Antón
...ín Ⓦcerveceriaalemana.com. Mon &
...d–Sun 10.30am–12.30am, Fri & Sat till
...m. Closed Aug.

...raditional old beer house, once
frequented by Hemingway. Order
a *caña* (draught beer) and go
easy on the tapas, as the bill can
mount up fast.

Cervecería Santa Ana

MAP p.52, POCKET MAP F13
Plaza de Santa Ana 10 ⓂSol or Antón
Martín Ⓦcerveceriasantaana.com. Daily
11am–1.30am, Fri & Sat till 2.30am.
Has tables outside, and offers
quality beer, friendly service and
a good selection of tapas. Always
packed at night.

Dos Gardenias

MAP p.52, POCKET MAP G14
C/Santa María 13 ⓂAntón Martín. Tues–Sat
9.30pm–2am.
Intimate and relaxed little bar in
the Huertas area where you can
chill out in their comfy chairs, sip
on a mojito, and escape from the
hubbub of the city outside.

Glass Bar

MAP p.52, POCKET MAP F12
C/San Jerónimo 34 ⓂSevilla. Daily
10.30am–2am (Thurs–Sat till 3am).

Glass Bar

Housed in the ultra-chic *Hotel
Urban* (see p.129), this glamorous
cocktail bar has become a favourite
with the well-heeled in-crowd.
Designer tapas such as sushi, wild
salmon and oysters accompany
drinks. In summer, a terrace bar
opens on the sixth floor.

Naturbier

MAP p.52, POCKET MAP F13
Plaza de Santa Ana 9 ⓂSol or Antón
Martín Ⓦnaturbier.com. Daily 10am–1am
(Fri & Sat till 2.30am).
Try this place's own tasty beer
with a variety of German sausages
to accompany it. There's usually
room to sit in the cellar if the
top bar is too crowded, although
service is often slow.

La Pecera del Círculo de Bellas Artes

MAP p.52, POCKET MAP G11
C/Alcalá 42 ⓂBanco de España
Ⓦlapeceradelcirculo.com. Daily 8am–2am,
Fri & Sat till 3am.
Stylish bar in this classy arts
centre (€1 entry fee), complete
with reclining nude sculpture,
chandeliers and sofas and a
pleasant lack of pretensions.
Service can be slow though.
Also serves up breakfasts and
a €15 set lunch. From May to
October, there's a comfortable
terraza outside.

Salmon Guru

MAP p.52, POCKET MAP F13
C/Echegaray 21 ⓂSevilla/Antón Martín
Ⓦfacebook.com/SalmonGuru. Tues–Sun
5pm–2am.
Excellent cocktails in this fun
gastrobar run by Diego Cabrera
in a characterful street to the
east of Plaza Santa Ana. Mirrors,
neon lights and comic book
heroes adorn the walls, while
behind the bar the cocktails menu
includes classics like Tom Collins
or Long Island Ice Tea as well as
nonalcoholic "mocktails". There
is a small selection of tapas on
offer too.

La Pecera del Círculo de Bellas Artes

Torero

MAP p.52, POCKET MAP E13
C/Cruz 26 Ⓜ Sol Ⓦ discotecatorero.es
Thurs–Sat 11pm–5.30am. Entrance €10
including first drink.

Popular two-floored club right in
the heart of the Santa Ana area.
The bouncers are pretty strict,
but once inside a fun place to be.
Music ranges from salsa to disco.

Music venues

Café Central

MAP p.52, POCKET MAP E13
Plaza del Ángel 10 Ⓜ Tirso de Molina
Ⓣ 913 694 143, Ⓦ cafecentralmadrid.com.
Mon–Thurs 12.30pm–2.30am, Fri
12.30pm–3.30am, Sat 11.30pm–3.30am,
Sun 11.30pm–2.30am. €12–15 for gigs.

Small jazz club that gets the odd
big name, plus strong local talent.
The Art Deco café (lunchtime
menu €13; €16 at weekends) is
worth a visit in its own right.

Cardamomo

MAP p.52, POCKET MAP F12
C/Echegaray 15 Ⓜ Antón Martín or Sevilla
Ⓣ 913 690 757, Ⓦ cardamomo.com. Mon &
Wed–Sun 8pm–4am. Shows at 9pm.

This flamenco bar has evolved
into a respected fully blown
tablao. The show with a drink
is €39, while dinner will set you
back an extra €20–33. Check the
website for the schedule.

Villa Rosa

MAP p.52, POCKET MAP E13
Plaza Santa Ana 15 Ⓜ Sevilla/Antón Martín
Ⓦ tablaoflamencovillarosa.com. Daily
shows at 8.30 & 10.30pm. €35 inc drink,
€65–78 inc meal.

One of the prime reasons to
visit this flamenco *tablao* is the
stupendous painted tiles that
adorn the façade and the Mudéjar
decor within which once featured
in Almodóvar's 1991 classic
Tacones Lejanos (High Heels). *Villa
Rosa* now puts on two enjoyable,
tourist-oriented shows a night.

La Venencia

MAP p.52, POCKET MAP F12
C/Echegaray 7 Ⓜ Sevilla Ⓦ restaurante
vivamadrid.com. Daily 1–3.30pm &
7.30pm–1.30am. Closed Aug.

Rather dilapidated, wood-
panelled bar that's great for sherry
sampling. The whole range is here,
served from wooden barrels, and
accompanied by delicious olives
and *mojama* (dry salted tuna).

Viva Madrid

MAP p.52, POCKET MAP F12
C/Manuel Fernández y González 7 Ⓜ Antón
Martín or Sevilla. Daily noon–2am, Fri &
Sat till 3am.

A fabulous tiled bar with a
popular terrace that is a longtime
stalwart of the Madrid night
scene. Refurbished and now
offering a wide selection of food
and tapas, but still best for a drink.

Clubs

Sala Cocó

MAP p.52, POCKET MAP F11
C/Alcalá 20 Ⓜ Sevilla. Thurs–Sat
midnight–6am.

Über-modern decor in a slick
club, one of the most fashionable
stops of the night on the Madrid
scene. Electronic sounds in
the Mondo Disko sessions on
Thursday and Saturday nights
from midnight, popular house
sessions on Fridays. Entry from
€15 (includes one drink).

Paseo del Arte and Retiro

Madrid's three world-class art galleries are all located within a kilometre of each other along what is known as the Paseo del Arte. The Prado, the most renowned of the three, houses an unequalled display of Spanish art, an outstanding Flemish collection and some impressive Italian work. The Thyssen-Bornemisza, based on one of the world's greatest private art collections, provides a dazzling excursion through Western art from the fourteenth to the late twentieth centuries. Finally, the Centro de Arte Reina Sofía displays contemporary art, including Picasso's iconic masterpiece Guernica. The area around the Paseo del Prado has two beautiful green spaces: the Jardines Botánicos and the Parque del Retiro, as well as lesser-known sights including the fascinating Real Fábrica de Tapices (Royal Tapestry Workshop) and the Museo Naval. It isn't an area renowned for its bars, restaurants and nightlife, but there are plenty of decent places for a drink or lunch.

Museo del Prado

MAP p.66, POCKET MAP J13–14
Ⓜ Atocha or Banco de España Ⓦ www
.museodelprado.es. Mon–Sat 10am–8pm,
Sun & hols 10am–7pm. €15, free Mon–Sat
6–8pm, Sun & hols 5–7pm and for
under-18s.

The Prado is Madrid's premier tourist attraction and one of the oldest and greatest collections of art in the world, largely amassed by the Spanish royal family over the last two hundred years.

Bosch's Garden of Earthly Delights, Museo del Prado

Tickets are purchased at the Puerta de Goya opposite the *Hotel Ritz* on C/Felipe IV and the entrance is round the back at the Puerta de los Jerónimos, which leads into the new extension. To avoid the large ticket queues, buy them from the museum website.

The museum, which was given a new lease of life following the addition of the controversial €152 million Rafael Moneo-designed extension, is set out according to national schools. To follow the route proposed by the museum, bear right upon entering and head into the central hallway, the Sala de las Musas; from here you are guided through the collections on the ground floor before being directed upstairs.

The coverage of Spanish paintings begins with some striking twelfth-century Romanesque frescoes. Beyond is a stunning anthology that includes just about every significant Spanish painter, from the adopted Cretan-born artist El Greco (Domenikos Theotokopoulos), who worked in Toledo in the 1570s, to Francisco de Goya, the outstanding painter of eighteenth-century Bourbon Spain. Don't miss the breathtaking collection of work by Diego Velázquez, including his masterpiece, *Las Meninas* (room 12).

No visit is complete without taking in Goya's deeply evocative works, *Dos de Mayo* and *Tres de Mayo* (rooms 64–65), and his disturbing series of murals known as the *Pinturas Negras* (*Black Paintings*; room 67) with their mix of witches, fights to the death and child-eating gods. The artist's remarkable versatility is clear when these are compared with his voluptuous portraits of the *Maja Vestida* (*Clothed Belle*) and *Maja Desnuda* (*Naked Belle*; room 36).

The Italian paintings include the most complete collection of painters from the Venice School in any single museum, among them

Museo del Prado

Titian's magnificent equestrian portrait, *Emperor Carlos V at Mühlberg* (room 27). There are also major works by Raphael and epic masterpieces from Tintoretto, Veronese and Caravaggio.

The early Flemish works are even more impressive and contain one of Hieronymus Bosch's greatest triptychs, the hallucinogenic *Garden of Earthly Delights* (room 56A). Look out, too, for the works of Pieter Bruegel the Elder, whose *Triumph of Death* must be one of the most frightening canvases ever painted, Rogier van der Weyden's magnificent *Descent from the Cross* (room 58) and the extensive Rubens collection.

German and French painting is less well represented but still worth seeking out – especially the pieces by Dürer, Cranach and Poussin – while downstairs in the basement is a glittering display of the jewels that belonged to the Grand Dauphin Louis, son of Louis XIV and father of Felipe V, Spain's first Bourbon king.

The new wing houses temporary exhibition spaces, restoration workshops and a sculpture gallery as well as a restaurant, café and shops.

Paseo del Arte and Retiro

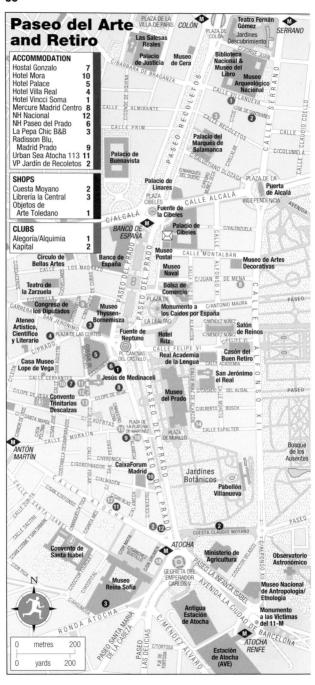

ACCOMMODATION

Hostal Gonzalo	7
Hotel Mora	10
Hotel Palace	5
Hotel Villa Real	4
Hotel Vincci Soma	1
Mercure Madrid Centro	8
NH Nacional	12
NH Paseo del Prado	6
La Pepa Chic B&B	3
Radisson Blu, Madrid Prado	9
Urban Sea Atocha 113	11
VP Jardín de Recoletos	2

SHOPS

Cuesta Moyano	2
Librería la Central	3
Objetos de Arte Toledano	1

CLUBS

Alegoría/Alquimia	1
Kapital	2

PLAZA DE LA VILLA DE PARIS
COLÓN
Teatro Fernán Gómez
SERRANO

Las Salesas Reales
PLAZA DE COLÓN
Jardines Descubrimiento

Palacio de Justicia
C/BARBARA DE BRAGANZA
Museo de Cera
Biblioteca Nacional & Museo del Libro
C/JORGE JUAN
Museo Arqueológico Nacional

CALLE VILLANUEVA

C/GIL DE SANTIVAÑES

CALLE RECOLETOS

Palacio de Buenavista

CALLE PRIM

Palacio del Marqués de Salamanca

C/MARQUES DEL DUERO
C/SALUSTIANO OLOZAGA
PLAZA DE LA INDEPENDENCIA

Palacio de Linares
PLAZA CIBELES
Puerta de Alcalá

CALLE ALCALÁ
Fuente de la Cibeles
AVENIDA

C/CALCALÁ
BANCO DE ESPAÑA

Palacio de Cibeles
C/VALENZUELA

Círculo de Bellas Artes
Banco de España
Museo Postal
CALLE MONTALBÁN
Museo de Artes Decorativas

Teatro de la Zarzuela
Museo Naval

Congreso de los Diputados
Museo Thyssen-Bornemisza
Bolsa de Comercio
C/JUAN DE MENA
PASEO

Ateneo Artístico, Científico y Literario
PLAZA DE LAS CORTES
Monumento a los Caídos por España
C/ANTONIO MAURA
Salón de Reinos

Casa Museo Lope de Vega
Fuente de Neptuno
LA LEALTAD
Casón del Buen Retiro

PL. CANOVAS DEL CASTILLO
Hotel Ritz
CALLE FELIPE IV
San Jerónimo el Real

Jesús de Medinaceli
Real Academia de la Lengua
CALLE ACADEMIA

Convento Trinitarias Descalzas
CALLE CERVANTES
Museo del Prado

ANTÓN MARTÍN
C/LOPE DE VEGA
PLAZA DE LA PLATERÍA DE MARTÍNEZ
PLAZA DE MURILLO

Bosque de los Ausentes

CaixaForum Madrid
Jardines Botánicos
Pabellón Villanueva

CALLE ATOCHA
CUESTA CLAUDIO MOYANO

Convento de Santa Isabel
ATOCHA
Ministerio de Agricultura
Observatorio Astronómico

Museo Reina Sofía
GLORIETA DEL EMPERADOR CARLOS V
AVENIDA LA CIUDAD DE BARCELONA
Museo Nacional de Antropología/Etnología

N

RONDA ATOCHA
Antigua Estación de Atocha
Monumento a las Víctimas del 11-M

ATOCHA RENFE
Estación de Atocha (AVE)

0	metres	200
0	yards	200

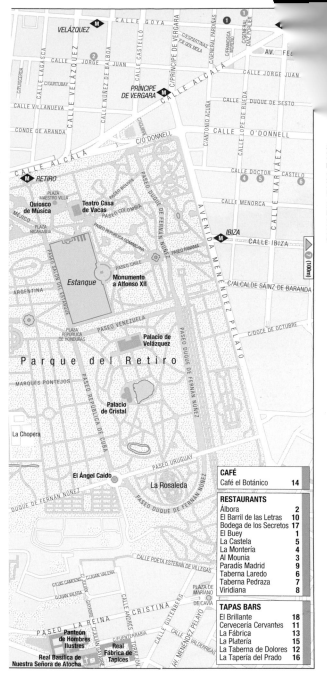

CALLE GOYA

VELÁZQUEZ

C/GENERAL PARDIÑAS
C/FRANCISCA MORENO

AV. FE

CALLE LAGASCA
CALLE VELÁZQUEZ
CALLE CASTELLO
C/ESPARTINAS
C/DE GEN. MOLA
C/GENERAL DÍAZ PORLIER

CALLE JORGE JUAN
C/GURTUBAY
C/PUIGCERDA

PRÍNCIPE DE VERGARA

CALLE NÚÑEZ DE BALBOA
PRÍNCIPE DE VERGARA
CALLE ALCALÁ

CALLE VILLANUEVA

CONDE DE ARANDA

C/O'DONNELL

C/ANTONIO ACUÑA
CALLE LOPE DE RUEDA
CALLE DUQUE DE SESTO
CALLE JORGE JUAN
CALLE O'DONNELL

CALLE ALCALÁ

RETIRO

PLAZA MAESTRO VILLA

Quiosco de Música

MÉJICO

PLAZA NICARAGUA

Teatro Casa de Vacas

PASEO BOLIVIA
PASEO DUQUE DE FERNAN NÚÑEZ
PASEO COLOMBIA
PASEO REPÚBLICA DOMINICANA

CALLE DOCTOR
CALLE NARVÁEZ
CALLE CASTELO

CALLE MENORCA

IBIZA
CALLE IBIZA

PASEO PANAMÁ

PASEO CHILE

Estanque

Monumento a Alfonso XII

AVENIDA MENÉNDEZ PELAYO

C/ALCALDE SÁINZ DE BARANDA

ARGENTINA

PLAZA REPÚBLICA DE HONDURAS

PASEO VENEZUELA

Palacio de Velázquez

PASEO DUQUE DE FERNAN NÚÑEZ

C/DOCE DE OCTUBRE

Parque del Retiro

MARQUÉS PONTEJOS

PASEO REPÚBLICA DE CUBA

Palacio de Cristal

La Chopera

PASEO URUGUAY

El Ángel Caído

La Rosaleda

PASEO DUQUE DE FERNAN NÚÑEZ

DUQUE DE FERNAN NÚÑEZ

CALLE POETA ESTEBAN DE VILLEGAS

C/LUIS CAMOENS
C/JUAN VALERA

C/JUAN VALERA

PLAZA DE MARIANO DE CAVIA

CALLE ANDRÉS
CRISTINA

CALLE GUTENBERG
CALLE GAZTAMBIDE
CALLE JULIÁN GAYARRE
CALLE FUENTERRABÍA
CALLE TORREÓN
CALLE VALDERRIBAS
AV. MENÉNDEZ PELAYO

PASEO LA REINA

Panteón de Hombres Ilustres

Real Fábrica de Tapices

Real Basílica de Nuestra Señora de Atocha

CAFÉ	
Café el Botánico	14

RESTAURANTS	
Álbora	2
El Barril de las Letras	10
Bodega de los Secretos	17
El Buey	1
La Castela	5
La Montería	4
Al Mounia	3
Paradís Madrid	9
Taberna Laredo	6
Taberna Pedraza	7
Viridiana	8

TAPAS BARS	
El Brillante	18
Cervecería Cervantes	11
La Fábrica	13
La Platería	15
La Taberna de Dolores	12
La Tapería del Prado	16

(100m)

Reina Sofía

POCKET MAP G8

ⓦ museoreinasofia.es. Mon &
t 10am–9pm, Sun 10am–7pm.
e Mon, Wed–Sat 7–9pm, Sun
1.30pm and for under-18s and
r-65s.

n essential stop on the Madrid art circuit is the Museo Reina Sofía, an immense exhibition space providing a permanent home for the Spanish collection of modern and contemporary art, including the Miró and Picasso legacies.

If the queues at the main entrance are too long, try the alternative one in the extension on the Ronda de Atocha.

As well as its collection of twentieth-century art, the museum has a theatre, cinema, excellent bookshops, a print, music and photographic library, a restaurant, bar and café in the basement and a peaceful inner courtyard garden. A guidebook examining some of the key works is available from the shops, priced €13. At the entrance, there are audio-guides in English (€4.50), which provide informative commentaries for the first-time visitor.

The **permanent collection** begins on the second floor with a section examining the origins of modern Spanish art, largely through the two artistic nuclei that developed in Catalunya and the Basque Country at the end of the nineteenth century.

Midway round Collection 1 is the Reina Sofía's main draw – Picasso's *Guernica* (see box below), an emblematic piece that has always evoked strong reactions. Strong sections on Cubism – in the first of which Picasso is again well represented – and the Paris School follow. Dalí and Miró make heavyweight contributions too in the Surrealism section. The development of Dalí's work and his variety of techniques are clearly displayed, with pieces ranging from the classic *Muchacha en la Ventana* to famous Surrealist works such as *El Enigma de Hitler*. Impressive works from the Cubist Juan Gris are intermingled with a fascinating collection of Spanish sculpture to complete the circuit on this floor.

Collection 2 continues on the fourth floor, although here it's no match for the attractions of the previous exhibits. This section

PASEO DEL AR

Guernica

Superbly displayed and no longer protected by the bulletproof glass and steel girders that once imprisoned it, Picasso's *Guernica* is a monumental icon of twentieth-century Spanish art and politics which, despite its familiarity, still has the ability to shock. Picasso painted it in response to the bombing of the Basque town of Gernika in April 1937 by the German Luftwaffe, acting in concert with Franco, during the Spanish Civil War. In the preliminary studies, displayed around the room, you can see how he developed its symbols – the dying horse, the woman mourning, the bull and so on – and then return to the painting to marvel at how he made it all work. Picasso determined that the work be "loaned" to the Museum of Modern Art in New York while Franco remained in power, meaning that the artist never lived to see it displayed in his home country – it only returned to Spain in 1981, eight years after Picasso's death and six after the demise of Franco.

Museo Reina Sofía

covers Spain's postwar years up to 1968 and includes Spanish and international examples of abstract and avant-garde movements such as Pop Art, Constructivism and Minimalism, one of the highlights being Francis Bacon's *Figura Tumbada* (*Reclining Figure*). Worth hunting out is the section on photography during the years of Franco's dictatorship, and the work by British artists Henry Moore and Graham Sutherland. There are also some striking pieces by the Basque abstract sculptor Chillida and Catalan Surrealist painter Antoni Tàpies.

Jean Nouvel's 79 million-euro state-of-the-art extension, known as the **Area Nouvel**, is built around an open courtyard topped by a striking delta-shaped, metallic, crimson-coloured roof. It now houses the third part of the collection covering the period 1962–82, with a focus on experimental, revolutionary and feminist art, dealing with themes from the final years of the Franco dictatorship to the present day. The new wing is also home to temporary exhibition spaces, an auditorium, library, bookshop and café/restaurant.

If you plan to visit all three art museums on the Paseo del Prado during your stay, it's well worth buying the **Paseo del Arte ticket** (€28), which is valid for a year and allows one visit to each museum at a substantial saving although it does not include the temporary exhibitions. It's available at any of the three museums.

o Thyssen-
emisza

.66, POCKET MAP H12

.nco de España ⓦ museothyssen.org.
 noon–4pm, Tues–Sun 10am–7pm. €12
 permanent collection and temporary
 xhibitions, combined ticket €13–17,
permanent collection free Mon.

This fabulous private collection, assembled by Baron Heinrich Thyssen-Bornemisza, his son Hans Heinrich and his former beauty-queen wife Carmen was first displayed here in 1993 and contains pieces by almost every major Western artist since the fourteenth century.

An extension, built on the site of an adjoining mansion and cleverly integrated into the original format of the museum, houses temporary exhibitions and Carmen's collection, which is particularly strong on nineteenth-century landscape, North American, Impressionist and Post-Impressionist work.

To follow the collection chronologically, begin on the second floor with pre-Renaissance work from the fourteenth century. This is followed by a wonderful

Museo Thyssen-Bornemisza

array of Renaissance portraits by, among others, Ghirlandaio, Raphael and Holbein, including the latter's commanding *Henry VIII*. Beyond are some equally impressive pieces by Titian, Tintoretto, El Greco, Caravaggio and Canaletto, while a superb collection of landscapes and some soothing Impressionist works by Pissarro, Monet, Renoir, Degas and Sisley are housed in the new galleries.

The first floor continues with an outstanding selection of work by Gauguin and the Post-Impressionists. There's excellent coverage, too, of the vivid Expressionist work of Kandinsky, Nolde and Kirchner.

Beyond, the displays include a comprehensive round of seventeenth-century Dutch painting of various genres and some splendid nineteenth-century American landscapes. There are strong contributions from Van Gogh – most notably one of his last and most gorgeous works, *Les Vessenots* – and more from the Expressionists, including the apocalyptic *Metropolis* by George Grosz.

The ground floor covers the period from the beginning of the twentieth century with some outstanding Cubist work from Picasso, Braque and Mondrian to be found within the "experimental avant-garde" section. There are also some marvellous pieces by Miró, Pollock and Chagall. Surrealism is, not surprisingly, represented by Dalí, while the final galleries include some eye-catching work by Bacon, Lichtenstein and Freud.

Parque del Retiro

MAP p.66, POCKET MAP J4–K7
ⓜ Retiro, Ibiza, Atocha Renfe, Atocha or Banco de España. Winter daily 6am–10pm, summer 6am–midnight.

The origins of the wonderful Parque del Retiro (Retiro Park) go back to the early seventeenth

Parque del Retiro

century when Felipe IV produced a plan for a new palace and French-style gardens, the Buen Retiro. Of the buildings, only the ballroom (Casón del Buen Retiro) and the Hall of Realms (Salón de Reinos) remain.

The park's 330-acre expanse offers the chance to jog, rollerblade, cycle, picnic, row on the lake, have your fortune told, and – above all – **promenade**. The busiest day is Sunday, when half of Madrid turns out for the *paseo*.

Promenading aside, there's almost always something going on in the park, including concerts in the Quiosco de Música, performances by groups of South American pan-piping musicians by the lake and, on summer weekends, puppet shows by the Puerta de Alcalá entrance.

Travelling art exhibitions are frequently housed in the graceful **Palacio de Velázquez** (daily: April–Sept 10am–10pm; Oct–March 10am–6pm; free) and the splendid **Palacio de Cristal** (same hours during exhibitions, but closed when raining; free), while the

Teatro Casa de Vacas (usually daily 10am–9pm; closed Aug) hosts shows, concerts and plays. Look out, too, for the magnificently ostentatious statue to Alfonso XII by the lake and the Ángel Caído, supposedly the world's only public statue to Lucifer, in the south of the park. The Bosque de los Ausentes, 192 olive trees and cypresses planted by the Paseo de la Chopera in memory of the victims who died in the train bombings at the nearby Atocha station on March 11, 2004, is close by.

Puerta de Alcalá

MAP p.66, POCKET MAP J4
Ⓜ Retiro or Banco de España.

The Puerta de Alcalá is one of Madrid's most emblematic landmarks. Built in Neoclassical style in 1769 by Francesco Sabatini to commemorate Carlos III's first twenty years on the throne, it was the biggest city gate in Europe at the time. Once on the site of the city's easternmost boundary, it's now marooned on a small island on the traffic-choked Plaza de la Independencia.

Jardines botánicos

MAP p.66, POCKET MAP H7
Plaza de Murillo 2 Ⓜ Atocha Ⓦ www .rjb.csic.es. Daily 10am–dusk. €4, under-10s free.

The delightful botanical gardens were opened in 1781 by Carlos III. The king's aim was to collect and grow species from all over his Spanish Empire, develop a research centre, and supply medicinal herbs and plants to Madrid's hospitals. Abandoned for much of the last century, they were restored in the 1980s and are now home to some 30,000 species from around the globe. Don't miss the hothouse with its amazing cacti or the bonsai collection of former prime minister Felipe González. Temporary exhibitions take place in the Pabellón Villanueva within the grounds.

CaixaForum Madrid

MAP p.66, POCKET MAP H7

Paseo del Prado 36 Ⓜ Atocha Ⓦ obrasocialla caixa.org. Daily 10am–8pm. €4.

An innovative exhibition space, opened in 2008 by the Catalan savings bank, which complements the existing attractions on the Paseo del Arte. The centre, which hosts a variety of high-quality art shows, is flanked by an eye-catching **vertical garden** designed by French botanist Patrick Blanc in which some 15,000 plants form an organic carpet extending across the wall. There is a decent art bookshop and a restaurant inside, as well.

Museo de Artes Decorativas

MAP p.66, POCKET MAP J5

C/Montalbán 12 Ⓜ Banco de España Ⓦ mecd.gob.es/mnartesdecorativas. Tues–Sat 9.30am–3pm, Sun 10am–3pm, plus Thurs 5–8pm Sept–June. €3, free Sat 2–3pm, Sun and Thurs eve.

The national collection of decorative arts is housed in an elegant nineteenth-century mansion. The highlight is its collection of *azulejos* (tiles) and other ceramics with a magnificent eighteenth-century tiled Valencian kitchen on the top floor. The rest of the exhibits include an interesting but unspectacular

collection of furniture, a series of reconstructed rooms and objets d'art from all over Spain.

Museo Naval

MAP p.66, POCKET MAP J5

Paseo del Prado 5 Ⓜ Banco de España Ⓦ armada.mde.es. Tues–Sun 10am–7pm, Aug 10am–3pm. Closed public hols. Free (bring ID; voluntary €3 donation requested).

As you might expect, the Naval Museum is strong on models, charts and navigational aids relating to Spanish voyages of discovery. Exhibits include the first map to show the New World, drawn in 1500 by Juan de la Cosa, cannons from the Spanish Armada and part of Cortés' standard used during the conquest of Mexico. The room dedicated to the *Nao San Diego*, sunk during a conflict with the Dutch off the Philippines in 1600, contains fascinating items recovered during the salvage operation in the early 1990s.

San Jerónimo el Real

MAP p.66, POCKET MAP H6

C/Ruiz de Alarcón 19 Ⓜ Atocha or Banco de España. Sept–June: Mon–Sat 10am–1pm & 5–8pm, Sun & hols 9.30am–2.30pm & 5.30–8pm; July–mid-Sept daily 10am–1.30pm & 6–8.30pm.

Madrid's high-society church was built on the site of a monastery

Museo de Artes Decorativas

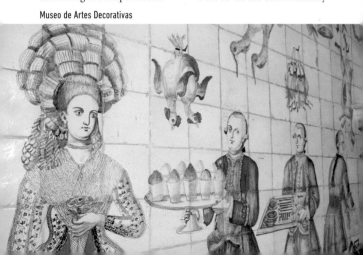

founded in the early sixteenth century by the Catholic monarchs, Fernando and Isabel. It later became the venue for the swearing-in of the heirs to the throne and setting for many royal marriages and coronations (including the former king, Juan Carlos, in 1975). Despite remodelling and the addition of two Gothic towers, the old form of the church is still visible; but the seventeenth-century cloisters have fallen victim to the Prado extension.

Plaza de la Lealtad (Monumento a los Caídos por España)

MAP p.66, POCKET MAP H6
Ⓜ Banco de España.

This aristocratic plaza contains the **Monument to Spain's Fallen**. Originally a memorial to the *madrileños* who died in the 1808 anti-French rebellion (the urn at the base contains their ashes), it was later changed to commemorate all those who have died fighting for Spain, and an eternal flame now burns here. On one side of the plaza stands the opulent *Ritz Hotel*, work of Charles Mewès, architect of the *Ritz* hotels in Paris and London, while opposite is the Madrid stock exchange.

Estación de Atocha

MAP p.66, POCKET MAP J9
Ⓜ Atocha or Atocha Renfe.

The grand Estación de Atocha is now sadly infamous as the scene of the horrific train bombings that killed 191 people and injured close to two thousand in March 2004. A glass memorial to the victims stands just outside one of the entrances on Paseo de la Infanta Isabel. The tower channels light into an underground chamber (access via the station) lined with an inner membrane on which are written messages of condolence. The old station alongside was revamped in 1992 and is a glorious 1880s glasshouse,

Monumento a los Caídos por España

resembling a tropical garden. It's a wonderful sight from the walkways above, as a constant spray of water rains down on the jungle of vegetation. At the platforms beyond sit the gleaming AVE trains.

Museo Nacional de Antropología/Etnología

MAP p.66, POCKET MAP J8
C/Alfonso XII 68 Ⓜ Atocha or Atocha Renfe
Ⓦ mnantropologia.mcu.es. Tues–Sat 9.30am–8pm, Sun 10am–3pm. €3, free Sat after 2pm & Sun.

The National Anthropology and Ethnography Museum was founded by the eccentric Dr Pedro González Velasco to house his private collection. The displays give an overview of different cultures, particularly those linked to Spanish history. The most interesting exhibits include a macabre collection of deformed skulls, a Guanche mummy (the original inhabitants of the Canary Islands), some shrivelled embryos and the skeleton of a 2.35m tall circus giant, which Velasco had agreed to buy from the owner after his death – payment in advance of course.

Real Fábrica de Tapices

Real Fábrica de Tapices

MAP p.66, POCKET MAP K9
C/Fuentarrabía 2 Ⓜ Atocha Renfe or
Menéndez Pelayo Ⓦ realfabricadetapices
.com. Mon–Fri 10am–2pm. Closed Aug &
Dec 24–Jan 2. €5. Tours on the hour (noon
in English).

The Royal Tapestry Workshop
makes for a fascinating visit.
Founded in 1721 and moved to
its present site in the nineteenth
century, the factory uses processes
and machines unchanged for
hundreds of years. The handful of
workers that remain can be seen
coolly looping handfuls of bobbins
around myriad strings and sewing
up worn-out masterpieces with
exactly matching silk. With
progress painfully slow – one
worker produces a square metre
of tapestry every three and a half
months – the astronomical prices
soon seem easily understandable.

Shops

Cuesta Moyano

MAP p.66, POCKET MAP H8
Cuesta de Claudio Moyano Ⓜ Atocha.

A row of little wooden kiosks on
a hill close to the Retiro selling
just about every book you could
think of, from secondhand copies
of Captain Marvel to Cervantes.
Other items include old prints
of Madrid and relics from the
Franco era.

Librería la Central

MAP p.66, POCKET MAP G8
Ronda de Atocha 2 Ⓜ Atocha Ⓦ lacentral
.com/museoreinasofia.com. Mon & Wed–
Sat 10am–8.45pm, Sun 10am–3pm.

Nestled in the interior courtyard
of the Reina Sofía extension, *La
Central* is the best of the art gallery
bookshops with an extensive
range of posters, coffee-table art
books and more academic tomes.

Objetos de Arte Toledano

MAP p.66, POCKET MAP H8
Paseo del Prado 10 Ⓜ Atocha or Banco de
España. Mon–Sat 10am–8pm.

Souvenir shop stocking "typical
Spanish"-style goods including
fans, Lladró porcelain, T-shirts
and tacky flamenco accessories,
as well as more unlikely gifts like
armour and Toledan swords.

Café

Café el Botánico

MAP p.66, POCKET MAP H7
C/Ruiz de Alarcón 27 Ⓜ Atocha or Banco
de España Ⓦ restaurantebotanico.com.
Daily 8am–2am.

Ideal for a refreshing drink after visiting the Prado; this well-established café/bar sits in a quiet street by the botanical gardens and serves good beer and a small selection of tapas. Service can be slow.

Restaurants

Álbora

MAP p.66, POCKET MAP K3
C/Jorge Juan 33 Ⓜ Velázquez or Príncipe de Vergara ☎ 917 816 197, Ⓦ restaurantealbora.com. Restaurant: Mon–Sat 1.30–4pm & 8.30pm–midnight. Bar: Mon–Sat noon–midnight, Sun noon–5pm.

A slick, modern Michelin-star restaurant serving exquisite contemporary Spanish cuisine based on seasonal products. There are taster menus at €58 and €78 per head, but you can also sample some more reasonably priced offerings such as ham croquettes and prawns with sweetmeats at the bar.

El Barril de las Letras

MAP p.66, POCKET MAP G13
C/Cervantes 28 Ⓜ Antón Martín ☎ 911 863 632 798, Ⓦ barrildelasletras.com. Daily 12.30pm–12.30am.

Smart, modern-looking bar-restaurant specialising in Galician seafood products so it isn't cheap but the *raciones* are delicious and if you stick to the bar you can sample a few dishes rather than going for a whole meal. The seafood rice dishes are a very good bet at €17 a head.

Bodega de los Secretos

MAP p.66, POCKET MAP G7
C/San Blas 4 Ⓜ Atocha ☎ 914 290 396, Ⓦ bodegadelossecretos.com. Mon–Sat 1.30–5pm & 8.30pm–midnight, Sun 1.30–5pm. Closed one week in second half of Aug.

Located in an atmospheric brick-lined wine cellar (access is difficult) just behind the

CaixaForum exhibition space, this restaurant offers a range of stylishly-presented Spanish dishes with a modern twist and has an excellent wine list too. Mains such as duck with apple gnocchi or mushroom and asparagus risotto around €15–17.

El Buey

MAP p.66, POCKET MAP K3
C/General Diaz Porlier 9 Ⓜ Goya ☎ 915 758 066, Ⓦ restauranteelbuey .com. Mon–Sat 1–4pm & 9pm–midnight, Sun 1–4pm.

Top-quality meat accompanied by an excellent array of starters, side dishes and salads in this friendly little restaurant near the Retiro. Prices – €35 a head – are reasonable considering the quality, and there is a very good three-course set menu with a decent house red for under €40.

La Castela

MAP p.66, POCKET MAP K4
C/Dr Castelo 22 Ⓜ Ibiza ☎ 915 735 590, Ⓦ restaurantelacastela.com. Bar: noon–4.30pm & 7.30pm–12.30am; Restaurant: 2–4pm & 9pm–midnight.

Mouthwateringly good *raciones* in this very popular bar-restaurant in the up-market area to the east of the Retiro. The fried fish, *almejas* (clams) and seafood *croquetas* are superb. Prices are pretty reasonable too given the quality (around €13 per dish). Get there early if you want a seat.

La Montería

MAP p.66, POCKET MAP K4
C/Lope de Rueda 35 Ⓜ Ibiza ☎ 915 741 812, Ⓦ lamonteria.es. Mon–Sat 2–4pm & 8.30–11pm, Sun 1.30–4pm.

This inconspicuous little restaurant on the Retiro's eastern edge was recently revamped, and serves some of the tastiest food in the area. Excellent fish dishes include sardines and tuna and a mouth-watering mushroom risotto. Around €40 a head for a three-course meal.

El Brillante

Delicious salads, risottos and fish dishes served up with style at this acclaimed bar/restaurant close to the Retiro. You are looking at around €50 a head for a meal. Reservations essential.

Taberna Pedraza

MAP p.66, POCKET MAP K4
C/Ibiza 38 Ⓜ Ibiza ☎ 910 327 200, Ⓦ tabernapedraza.com. Tues–Sun 1–4.30pm & 8–11.30pm.

Well-regarded gastrobar just to the east of the Retiro, run by a married couple. Excellent *tortilla* and *croquetas*, as well as a seasonal selection of dishes from around Spain. Expect to pay around €35 per head for an evening meal.

Viridiana

MAP p.66, POCKET MAP J5
C/Juan de Mena 14 Ⓜ Banco de España ☎ 915 311 039, Ⓦ restauranteviridiana .com. Daily 1.30–4pm & 8.30pm–midnight. Closed Easter & Aug.

A bizarre temple of Madrid *nueva cocina* (new cuisine), decorated with photos from Luis Buñuel's film of the same name and offering mouth-watering creations, plus a superb selection of wines. The bill for a three-course meal is likely to come close to €100 a head but it's an unforgettable experience.

Tapas bars

El Brillante

MAP p.66, POCKET MAP H8
Glorieta de Emperador Carlos V 8 Ⓜ Atocha Ⓦ barelbrillante.es. Daily 6.30am–12.30am.

Down-to-earth, open-all-hours, brightly-lit bar next to the Reina Sofía. Claims to serve the best *calamares bocadillo* (filled baguette) in Madrid. Perfect for a quick snack between museum visits, but not the place for a meal.

Al Mounia

MAP p.66, POCKET MAP H4
C/Recoletos 5 Ⓜ Banco de España ☎ 914 350 828, Ⓦ restaurantealmounia.es. Mon–Sat 1.30–4pm & 9–11.30pm, Sun 1.30–4pm. Closed Aug.

Moroccan cooking at its best in the most established Arabic restaurant in town. The couscous, lamb and desserts are a must. There is a taster menu at €49 and a more affordable lunchtime option at €29 (both with wine included).

Paradís Madrid

MAP p.66, POCKET MAP H12
C/Marqués de Cubas 14 Ⓜ Banco de España ☎ 914 297 303, Ⓦ restaurante paradismadrid.es. Mon–Sat 1.30–4pm & 9pm–midnight, Sun 9pm–midnight.

Upmarket Catalan restaurant frequented by politicians from the nearby parliament. High-quality Mediterranean food with superb starters, fish and rice dishes; the *fideuà* (sort of a paella) with duck's liver and boletus mushrooms is a stand out. Substantial lunchtime set menus at €35.

Taberna Laredo

MAP p.66, POCKET MAP K4
C/Dr Castelo 30 Ⓜ Ibiza ☎ 915 733 061, Ⓦ tabernalaredo.com. Mon–Sat noon–midnight. Closed Aug.

Cervecería Cervantes

MAP p.66, POCKET MAP H13
Plaza de Jesús 7 Ⓜ Antón Martín or Banco
de España. Mon–Sat 12.30–5pm &
7.30–11.45pm, Sun noon–4pm.

Great beer and excellent fresh
seafood tapas in this busy little
bar just behind the *Palace Hotel*.
The *gambas* (prawns) go down a
treat with a cool glass of the beer,
while the *tosta de gambas* (a sort
of prawn toast) is a must.

La Fábrica

MAP p.66, POCKET MAP H13
Plaza de Jesús 2 Ⓜ Antón Martín or Banco
de España. Mon–Thurs 9.30am–12.30am,
Fri & Sat 11am–2am, Sun 10am–5pm.

Bustling, friendly bar serving
a delicious range of canapés –
the smoked cod is one of the
favourites – plus chilled beer and
good vermouth.

La Platería

MAP p.66, POCKET MAP H14
C/Moratín 49 Ⓜ Antón Martín or Atocha.
Mon–Fri 7.30am–1am, Sat & Sun
9.30am–1am.

This bar has a popular summer
terraza geared to a tourist
clientele and a good selection of
reasonably priced tapas available
all day. Service can be a little
brusque though.

La Taberna de Dolores

MAP p.66, POCKET MAP H13
Plaza de Jesús 4 Ⓜ Antón Martín or Banco
de España. Daily 11am–midnight.

A standing-room-only tiled bar,
decorated with beer bottles from
around the world. The beer is great
and the splendid food specialities
include roquefort and anchovy and
smoked-salmon canapés.

La Tapería del Prado

MAP p.66, POCKET MAP J14
Plaza Platerías de Martínez 1 Ⓜ Antón
Martín or Banco de España ☏ 914 294 094,
Ⓦ lataperia.es. Mon–Thurs 8am–1am,
Fri–Sun 10am–2am.

Modern bar serving up a range
of tapas and *raciones*, as well as
breakfasts and afternoon snacks.
Portions are on the small side.

Clubs

Alegoría/Alquimia

MAP p.66, POCKET MAP J3
C/Villanueva 2 (entrance on C/Cid) Ⓜ Colón
☏ 915 772 785, Ⓦ alegoriamadrid.com.
Thurs 7pm–4am, Fri 9pm–5am, Sat
9pm–6am, Sun 6pm–12.30am. Entrance
€12, free Thurs & Sun.

Modelled on an English
gentleman's club, this restaurant,
bar and disco comes complete
with leather sofas, a wood-
panelled library, Gothic statuary
and models of old sailing ships
hanging from the ceiling.

Kapital

MAP p.66, POCKET MAP H8
C/Atocha 125 Ⓜ Atocha Ⓦ grupo-kapital
.com/kapital. Thurs–Sat midnight–6am.
€17 with two drinks.

A seven-floor club catering for
practically every taste, with three
dancefloors, lasers, go-go dancers,
a cinema and a terraza. The
eclectic musical menu features
disco, house, merengue, salsa,
sevillanas and even the occasional
session of karaoke.

Alegoría

Gran Vía, Chueca and Malasaña

The Gran Vía, one of Madrid's main thoroughfares, effectively divides the old city to the south from the newer parts in the north. Heaving with traffic, shoppers and sightseers, it's the commercial heart of the city, and a monument in its own right, with its turn-of-the-twentieth-century, palace-like banks and offices. North of here, and bursting with bars, restaurants and nightlife, are two of the city's most vibrant barrios: Chueca, focal point of Madrid's gay scene, and Malasaña, former centre of the Movida madrileña, the happening scene of the late 1970s and early 1980s, and still a somewhat alternative area, focusing on lively Plaza Dos de Mayo. As well as the bustling atmosphere, a couple of museums and a number of beautiful churches in the area provide even more reasons for a visit.

Gran Vía

MAP p.80, POCKET MAP D10–G10
Ⓜ Gran Vía.

The Gran Vía (Great Way), built in three stages at the start of the twentieth century, became a symbol of Spain's arrival in the modern world. Financed on the back of an economic boom, experienced as a result of the country's neutrality in World War I, the Gran Vía is a showcase for a whole gamut of architectural styles, from Modernist to Neo-Rococo.

The finest section is the earliest, constructed between 1910 and 1924 and stretching from C/Alcalá to the Telefónica skyscraper. Particularly noteworthy are the Edificio Metrópolis (1905–11), complete with cylindrical facade, white stone sculptures, zinc-tiled

Gran Vía

roof and gold garlands, and the nearby Grassy building (1916–17). The vast 81m-high slab of the Telefónica building was Spain's first skyscraper. During the Civil War it was used as a reference point by Franco's forces to bomb the area. The stretch down to Plaza de Callao is dominated by shops, cafés and cinemas, while the plaza itself is now the gateway to the shoppers' haven of C/Preciados. On the corner is the classic Art Deco Capitol building (1930–33), its curved facade embellished with lurid neon signs. Cast your eyes skywards on the final stretch downhill towards Plaza de España to catch sight of an assortment of statues and decorations that top many of the buildings.

Plaza de Chueca

MAP p.80, POCKET MAP G3
Ⓜ **Chueca.**

The smaller streets north of Gran Vía are home to some of the city's more go-ahead businesses and shops, while in and around Plaza de Chueca, there's a strong neighbourhood feel and a lively gay scene at night. The area has been rejuvenated in recent years and now holds some enticing streets lined with offbeat restaurants, small private art galleries and unusual corner shops. Calle Almirante has some of the city's most fashionable clothes shops and Calle Augusto Figueroa is the place to go for shoes.

Las Salesas Reales

MAP p.80, POCKET MAP H3
Plaza de las Salesas Ⓜ Colon. Mon–Fri 9am–1pm & 6–9pm, Sat 10am–1pm & 6–9pm, Sun 10am–2pm & 6–9pm.

The Santa Bárbara church was originally part of the convent complex of Las Salesas Reales, founded in 1747. The church is set behind a fine forecourt, while inside, there's a grotto-like chapel, delightful frescoes and stained-glass windows, and some striking

Plaza de Chueca

green marble altar decoration. The tombs of Fernando VI, his wife Bárbara de Bragança and military hero General O'Donnell lie within.

Sociedad de Autores

MAP p.80, POCKET MAP G3
C/Fernando VI 4 Ⓜ Alonso Martinez.

Home to the Society of Authors, this is the most significant Modernista building in Madrid. Designed in 1902 by the Catalan architect José Grases Riera, its facade features a dripping decoration of flowers, faces and balconies.

Plaza del Dos de Mayo

MAP p.80, POCKET MAP E2
Ⓜ Tribunal or Bilbao.

Plaza del Dos de Mayo is the centre of a lively bar scene, with people spilling onto the streets that converge on the square. The plaza commemorates the rebellion against occupying French troops in 1808, while the neighbourhood gets its name from a young seamstress, Manuela Malasaña, who became one of the rebellion's heroines.

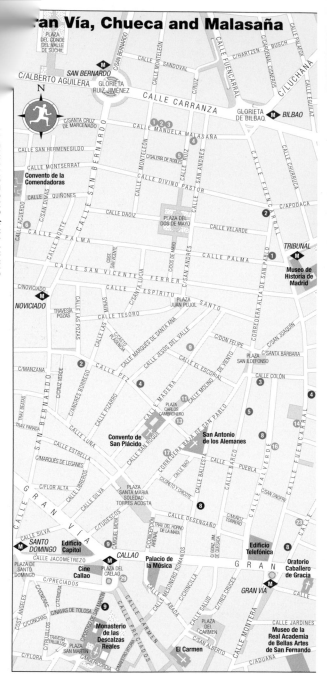

ran Vía, Chueca and Malasaña

PLAZA DEL CONDE DEL VALLE DE SUCHIL

C/ALBERTO AGUILERA

SAN BERNARDO M

GLORIETA RUIZ-JIMÉNEZ

CALLE MONTELEÓN

C/SAN BERNARDO

CALLE SANDOVAL

CALLE FUENCARRAL

C/CARDENAL CISNEROS

C/HARTZEN.

BUSCH

CALLE PALAFOX

C/LUCHANA

CALLE EGUILAZ

CALLE CARRANZA

C/RUIZ

GLORIETA DE BILBAO

BILBAO M

C/SANTA CRUZ DE MARCENADO

CALLE MANUELA MALASAÑA

CALLE SAN HERMENEGILDO

C/GALERÍA DE ROBLES

CALLE MONTELEÓN

C/SAN BERNARDO

CALLE RUIZ

CALLE SAN ANDRÉS

CALLE FUENCARRAL

C/CHURRUCA

CALLE MONTSERRAT

Convento de la Comendadoras

CALLE DIVINO PASTOR

CALLE DIMAS

C/SAN

CALLE ACUERDO

CALLE NORTE

CALLE PALMA

QUIÑONES

CALLE DAOIZ

PLAZA DEL DOS DE MAYO

CALLE VELARDE

CALLE PALMA

C/APODACA

TRIBUNAL M

CALLE SAN VICENTE FERRER

COST. SAN VICENTE

DOS DE MAYO

C/SAN ANDRÉS

Museo de Historia de Madrid

C/NOVICIADO

CALLE SANTA LUCÍA

CALLE ESPÍRITU

PLAZA JUAN PUJOL

SANTO

CORREDERA ALTA DE SAN PABLO

NOVICIADO M

CALLE LAS MINAS

CALLE TESORO

C/DON FELIPE

C/SAN JOAQUÍN

TRAVESÍA POZAS

C/CASTO PLASENCIA

CALLE MARQUÉS DE SANTA ANA

CALLE JESÚS DEL VALLE

PLAZA SAN ILDEFONSO

C/SANTA BÁRBARA

C/MANZANA

CALLE PEZ

CALLE EL ESCORIAL

CALLE COLÓN

C/CRUZ VERDE

CALLE PIZARRO

CALLE MADERA

PLAZA CARLOS CAMBRONERO

C/ANDRÉS BORREGO

CALLE MOLINO

CALLE DEL VIENTO

C/MUÑOZ TORRERO

C/SAN

BERNARDO

CALLE LUNA

Convento de San Plácido

CALLE SAN ROQUE

CORREDERA BAJA DE SAN PABLO

San Antonio de los Alemanes

CALLE NIÑO

CALLE BALLESTA

CALLE BARCO

PUEBLA

C/SAN ONOFRE

CALLE FUENCARRAL

TRAV. BEXTAS

CALLE ESTRELLA

C/MARQUÉS DE LEGANÉS

CALLE LIBREROS

CALLE SILVA

C/CONCEPCIÓN ARENAL

C/LORETO Y CHICOTE

TRAV. PARADA

G R A N

CALLE SILVA

Edificio Capitol

PLAZA SANTA MARÍA SOLEDAD TORRES ACOSTA

CALLE DESENGAÑO

Edificio Telefónica

V Í A

C/FLOR ALTA

C/MIGUEL MOYA

C/TUDESCOS

TRAV. DEL HORNO DE LA MATA

SANTO DOMINGO M

CALLAO M

CALLAO

PLAZA DEL CALLAO

Palacio de la Música

C/IGNACIO JIM. DE QUESADA

G R A N

Oratorio Caballero de Gracia

CALLE JACOMETREZO

PLAZA DE SANTO DOMINGO

Cine Callao

C/PRECIADOS

C/MESONERO ROMANOS

C/CHINCHILLA

V Í A

GRAN VÍA M

CALLE MONTERA

COST. ANGELES

C/CONCHAS

CALLENAVAS DE TOLOSA

C/CARMEN

C/SALUD

C/TRES CRUCES

CALLE JARDINES

C/PRECIADOS

C/NAVAS DE TOLOSA

Monasterio de las Descalzas Reales

C/SAN CRISTÓBAL

CALLE CARMEN

CALLE PREGIADOS

CALLE ABADA

PLAZA DEL CARMEN

C/SAN ALBERTO

CALLE MONTERA

Museo de la Real Academia de Bellas Artes de San Fernando

TRAVESÍA TRUJILLOS

PLAZA SAN MARTÍN

C/MISERICORDIA

El Carmen

CALLE

C/FLORA

C/ABADA

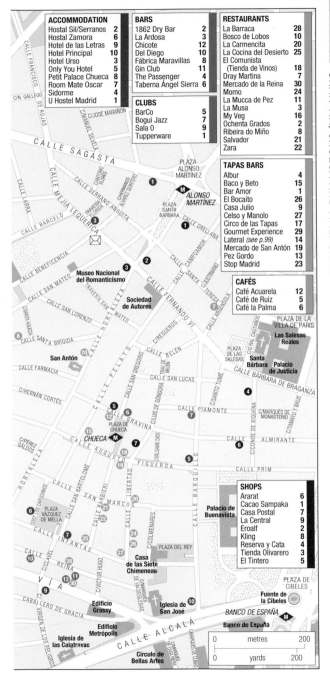

ACCOMMODATION

Hostal Sil/Serranos	2
Hostal Zamora	6
Hotel de las Letras	9
Hotel Principal	10
Hotel Urso	3
Only You Hotel	5
Petit Palace Chueca	8
Room Mate Oscar	7
Sidorme	4
U Hostel Madrid	1

BARS

1862 Dry Bar	2
La Ardosa	3
Chicote	12
Del Diego	10
Fábrica Maravillas	8
Gin Club	11
The Passenger	4
Taberna Ángel Sierra	6

CLUBS

BarCo	5
Bogui Jazz	7
Sala 0	9
Tupperware	1

RESTAURANTS

La Barraca	28
Bosco de Lobos	10
La Carmencita	20
La Cocina del Desierto	25
El Comunista	
(Tienda de Vinos)	18
Dray Martina	7
Mercado de la Reina	30
Momo	24
La Mucca de Pez	11
La Musa	3
My Veg	16
Ochenta Grados	2
Ribeira do Miño	8
Salvador	21
Zara	22

TAPAS BARS

Albur	4
Baco y Beto	15
Bar Amor	1
El Bocaíto	26
Casa Julio	9
Celso y Manolo	27
Circo de las Tapas	17
Gourmet Experience	29
Lateral (see p.99)	14
Mercado de San Antón	19
Pez Gordo	13
Stop Madrid	23

CAFÉS

Café Acuarela	12
Café de Ruiz	5
Café la Palma	6

SHOPS

Ararat	6
Cacao Sampaka	1
Casa Postal	7
La Central	9
Eroalf	2
Kling	8
Reserva y Cata	4
Tienda Olivarero	3
El Tintero	5

GRAN VÍA, CHUECA AND MALASAÑA

Museo Nacional del Romanticismo

MAP p.80, POCKET MAP F2
C/San Mateo 13 Ⓜ Tribunal Ⓦ museo
romanticismo.mcu.es. May–Oct Tues–Sat
9.30am–8.30pm (closes 6.30pm Nov–
April), Sun 10am–3pm. €3, free on Sat
after 2pm, Sun.

The Museo del Romanticismo aims to show the lifestyle and outlook of the late-Romantic era through the recreation of a typical bourgeois residence in the turbulent reign of Isabel II (1833–68), and this it does brilliantly. Overflowing with a marvellously eclectic and often kitsch hoard of memorabilia, the mansion is decorated with some stunning period furniture and ceiling frescoes, together with more bizarre exhibits such as the pistol which the satirist Mariano José de Larra used to shoot himself in 1837 after being spurned by his lover.

Museo de Historia de Madrid

MAP p.80, POCKET MAP F2
C/Fuencarral 78 Ⓜ Tribunal Ⓦ www
.madrid.es/museodehistoria. Tues–Sun
10am–8pm. Free.

Just around the corner from the Museo del Romanticismo, the Museo de Historia de Madrid has now been fully reopened after a lengthy restoration programme. The former city almshouse was remodelled in the early eighteenth century by Pedro de Ribera and features one of his trademark elaborately decorated Baroque doorways superimposed on a striking red-brick facade. Inside, the museum contains an intriguing collection of paintings, photos, models, sculptures and porcelain, all relating to the history and urban development of Madrid since 1561 (the date it was designated imperial capital by Felipe II). One of the star exhibits is a fascinating 3-D model of the city made in 1830 by military engineer León Gil de Palacio.

San Antonio de los Alemanes

MAP p.80, POCKET MAP E3
Corredera de San Pablo 16 Ⓜ Chueca or
Callao. Mon–Sat 10.30am–2pm. Closed
Aug. €2.

Opening hours are limited, coinciding with Mass, but this little church – designed in 1624 by the Jesuit architect Pedro Sánchez and Juan Gómez de Mora – is one of the city's hidden treasures. The elliptical interior is lined with dizzying floor-to-ceiling pastel-coloured frescoes by Neapolitan artist Luca Giordano which depict scenes from the life of St Anthony.

San Antonio de los Alemanes

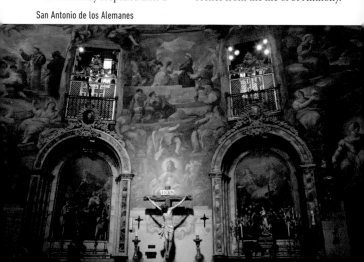

La Central

Shops

Ararat

MAP p.80, POCKET MAP G3
C/Almirante 10 Ⓜ Chueca. Mon–Sat
11am–2pm & 5–8.30pm.

Spanish and foreign designers for
women, often at reduced prices.
You can find formal and party
wear, as well as younger styles in
this elegant and original shop with
attentive service.

Cacao Sampaka

MAP p.80, POCKET MAP G3
C/Orellana 4 Ⓜ Alonso Martinez
Ⓦ cacaosampaka.com. Mon–Sat
10am–9pm. Closed Aug.

There's every conceivable shape,
colour and flavour of chocolate here,
ranging from rose and strawberry
to gin and tonic. The only surprise is
that their restaurant menu has some
non-chocolate options.

Casa Postal

MAP p.80, POCKET MAP G3
C/Libertad 37 Ⓜ Chueca Ⓦ casapostal.net.
Mon–Fri 10am–2pm & 5–7.45pm, Sat
11am–2pm. Closed July & Aug.

Marvellous old-fashioned shop
for lovers of nostalgia, packed
with postcards, posters and other
original mementos of the city. A
good place for an unconventional
souvenir of Madrid.

La Central

MAP p.80, POCKET MAP C10
C/Postigo de San Martín 8 Ⓜ Callao
Ⓦ lacentral.com. Mon–Thurs
10am–9.30pm, Fri & Sat 10am–10pm,
Sun 11am–9pm.

Stunning bookshop over four
floors of a beautifully decorated
building just off Plaza Callao. As
well as thumbing through copies
of its comprehensive selection
of Spanish, Latin American and
English classics, you can admire
the frescoed ceilings, check out
the basement cocktail bar or have
a drink in the café.

Eroalf

MAP p.80, POCKET MAP G2
C/Hortaleza 116 Ⓜ Alonso Martínez
Ⓦ eroalf.com. Mon–Sat 10.30am–8pm.

High-quality fashion for
men and women but with a
difference; everything is made
from recycled material. Founded
by Javier Goyeneche in 2012
with the aim of creating a truly
sustainable business, this sleek-
looking store is the showcase for
his knitwear, jackets, accessories
and sneakers.

Kling

MAP p.80, POCKET MAP E4
C/Ballesta 6 Ⓜ Gran Vía Ⓦ kling.es.
Mon–Thurs 9.30am–2pm & 3.30–6pm, Fri
9am–2.30pm.

Fun, young fashion for women at
good prices in this popular store,
located in an up-and-coming area
north of Gran Vía that is trying to
throw off its reputation as a red
light area.

Reserva y Cata

MAP p.80, POCKET MAP G3
C/Conde de Xiquena 13 Ⓜ Chueca
Ⓦ reservaycata.com. Mon 5–9pm, Tues–Fri
11am–3pm & 5–9pm, Sat 11am–3pm.

Staff at this friendly shop help you
select from some of the best new
wines in the Iberian peninsula,
and run tastings too. There is a
wide selection of Spanish liqueurs
also available.

…da Olivarero

MAP p.80, POCKET MAP G2
…ejia Lequerica 1 Ⓜ Alonso Martinez.
…pt–June Mon–Fri 10am–2pm & 5–8pm,
…at 10am–2pm; July 10am–3pm. Closed Aug.

This olive-growers' co-operative outlet has useful information sheets to help you buy the best olive oils from around Spain.

El Tintero

MAP p.80, POCKET MAP G3
C/Gravina 5 Ⓜ Chueca Ⓦ eltintero.es. Mon–Sat 11am–3pm & 5–9pm, Sun noon–8pm.

A cut above your usual souvenir T-shirt shop, *El Tintero* sells subtly ironic images and Spanish slogans with designs for babies, children and adults. Prices are around the €25 mark.

Cafés

Café Acuarela

MAP p.80, POCKET MAP G3
C/Gravina 10 Ⓜ Chueca. Daily 2pm–2am.

Comfy café with over-the-top kitsch Baroque decor, cocktails and chocolate cake. Popular with a mostly LGBT crowd.

Café de Ruiz

MAP p.80, POCKET MAP E2
C/Ruiz 11 Ⓜ Bilbao Ⓦ cafederuiz.com. Mon–Thurs 4pm–2am, Fri & Sat 3.30pm–2.30am, Sun 3.30–11.30pm.

Classic Malasaña café and a great place to while away an afternoon.

La Barraca

Discreet background music and good cakes are followed by cocktails and sets by local jazz, swing and folk artists in the evening.

Café la Palma

MAP p.80, POCKET MAP D2
C/Palma 62 Ⓜ Noviciado Ⓦ cafelapalma.com. Daily 4pm–3am.

Part traditional café, part arts and music venue, *Café la Palma* acts as a stage for a myriad of local artists ranging from singer-songwriters to storytellers. It also has popular DJ sessions on many evenings, as well as holding regular open mic nights.

Restaurants

La Barraca

MAP p.80, POCKET MAP F10
C/Reina 29 Ⓜ Bilbao ☎ 915 327 154,
Ⓦ labarraca.es. Daily 1.30–4.15pm & 8–11.45pm.

Step off the dingy street into this little piece of Valencia for some of the best paella in town. The starters are excellent and there's a great lemon sorbet for dessert too. A three-course meal with wine costs around €35 a head.

Bosco de Lobos

MAP p.80, POCKET MAP F3
C/Hortaleza 63 Ⓜ Chueca/Tribunal ☎ 915 249 464, Ⓦ encompaniadelobos.com. Daily noon–midnight.

The location is half the attraction of this delightful Italian restaurant

tucked away in a garden courtyard, off the main street in the Colegio de Arquitectos (School of Architects). On offer are the usual Italian staples of pizza, pasta and risottos combined with some more original starters. Expect to pay between €10–15 for a main course.

La Carmencita

MAP p.80, POCKET MAP G4
C/Libertad 16 Ⓜ Chueca ☎ 915 310 911,
Ⓦ tabernalacarmencita.es. Daily 9am–1am.

This traditional *taberna*, whose roots date back to 1854, has undergone a recent refurbishment but remains faithful to its origins serving up an authentic range of classic dishes with carefully sourced ingredients including traditional stews, *pollo en pepitoria* (chicken in an almond sauce) and stuffed peppers. Mains range from €13–20. It is also open for breakfast, weekend brunches and serves up a excellent range of *vermút* for a pre-lunch *aperitivo*.

La Cocina del Desierto

MAP p.80, POCKET MAP F4
C/Barbieri 1 Ⓜ Chueca ☎ 915 231 142.
Daily 1.30–4pm & 9pm–12.30am.

Authentic Moroccan food in this cluttered little restaurant with its multicoloured tiled bar, alcoves and cushions strewn across the floor. The couscous and lamb dishes are excellent, as you would expect, while portions are generous and prices competitive.

El Comunista (Tienda de Vinos)

MAP p.80, POCKET MAP G4
C/Augusto Figueroa 35 Ⓜ Chueca ☎ 915 217 012. Daily noon–4pm & 8pm–midnight. Closed mid-Aug to mid-Sept.

Step back in time at this long-established *comedor* that has changed little since it was given its unofficial name as a student haunt under Franco. Home-cooking at its best; the *sopa de ajo* (garlic soup) and the *lentejas* (lentils) are delicious.

Dray Martina

MAP p.80. POCKET MAP G3
C/Argensola 7 Ⓜ Alonso Martínez ☎ 910 810 056, Ⓦ draymartina.com. Mon–Fri 8.30am–2am, Sat & Sun 10am–2am.

This popular new gastrobar is a café, restaurant and *bar de copas* all rolled into one. Trendy vintage-style decor provides the backdrop, and they serve up a decent, though light, set lunch for around €12 and good coffee and cake.

Momo

MAP p.80, POCKET MAP G4
C/Libertad 8 Ⓜ Chueca ☎ 915 327 348.
Daily 1–4pm & 9.30pm–midnight.

A good-value *menú del día* in this Chueca stalwart features some inventive twists such as meatballs in a red berry sauce and grilled beef marinated in soya and honey, all for €11.50 (€18 on weekends).

La Mucca de Pez

MAP p.80, POCKET MAP E3
C/Plaza de Carlos Cambronero 4 Ⓜ Tribunal/Callao ☎ 915 210 000, Ⓦ lamuccacompany .com. Mon–Wed & Sun 1pm–1.30am, Thurs 1pm–2am, Fri & Sat 1pm–2.30am.

Popular restaurant with its own terrace that sits at the top of this plaza in Malasaña. Food ranges from Tex-Mex and Italian to Spanish staples like *pimientos de Padrón* and *salmorejo* though it is the atmosphere that brings most people here. There is a varied *menú del día*, though you need to get here early if you want a table. Expect to pay around €20 a head.

La Musa

MAP p.80, POCKET MAP E1
C/Manuela Malasaña 18 Ⓜ Bilbao ☎ 914 487 558, Ⓦ grupolamusa.com. Mon–Thurs 9am–1am, Fri 9am–2am, Sat 1pm–2am, Sun 1pm–1am.

A firm favourite on the Malasaña scene. A decent-value set lunch (€10), good tapas, generous helpings, a strong wine list and chic decor are all part of *La Musa*'s recipe for success – the only real problem is the crowds.

My Veg

MAP p.80, POCKET MAP F3
C/Valverde 28 ⓜ Chueca/Gran Vía ☎ 915 311
702, ⓦ myveg.es. Mon & Sun 1.30–4pm,
Tues–Sat 1.30–4pm & 8.30pm–midnight.

Not a vegetarian restaurant, but vegetables are, nevertheless, given pride of place at this new arrival in Chueca. The menu is seasonal but delights such as cream of asparagus with peppers, lemon and parmesan or fried squid with avocado and tomato sauce are on offer. Set lunch for €16, while there are evening options for €25–27.

Ochenta Grados

MAP p.80, POCKET MP E1
C/Manuela Malasaña 10 ⓜ Bilbao ☎ 914
458 351, ⓦ ochentagrados.com. Mon–Thurs
& Sun 1.30–4pm & 8.30pm–midnight, Fri
& Sat 1.30–4.30pm & 8.30pm–2am.

The idea behind *Ochenta Grados* is to serve traditional main course dishes in miniature, and it works wonderfully. Forget the idea of a starter and a main; just order a few dishes to share from the menu, maybe steak tartare with mustard or parmesan ice cream and prawn risotto. Each dish is around €5.

Ribeira do Miño

MAP p.80, POCKET MAP F3
C/Santa Brígida 1 ⓜ Tribunal ☎ 915 219 854,
ⓦ marisqueriaribeiradomino.com. Tues–Sun
1–4pm & 8pm–midnight. Closed Aug.

Great-value *marisquería*, serving fabulous seafood platters and Galician specialities at great prices; try the slightly more expensive Galician white wine, Albariño. Reservations essential. The full works will set you back around €40.

Salvador

MAP p.80, POCKET MAP G4
C/Barbieri 12 ⓜ Chueca ☎ 915 214 524,
ⓦ casasalvadormadrid.com. Mon–Sat
1.30–4pm & 8.30pm–midnight. Closed Aug.

Chueca mainstay with bullfighting decor and dishes such as *rabo de toro* (bull's tail), stuffed peppers and *arroz con leche* (rice pudding). Lunch around €25.

Zara

MAP p.80, POCKET MAP F4
C/Barbieri 8 ⓜ Chueca/Gran Vía ☎ 915
322 074, ⓦ restaurantezara.com. Tues–
Sat 1–4pm & 8.30pm–midnight. Closed
public hols.

Excellent food for very good prices at this Cuban restaurant. *Ropa vieja* (strips of beef), fried yucca, minced beef with fried bananas and other specialities; the daiquiris are very good, too. Prices are moderate (under €30).

Tapas bars

Albur

MAP p.80, POCKET MAP E1
C/Manuela Malasaña 15 ⓜ Bilbao
ⓦ restaurantealbur.com. Mon–Thurs
12.30–5pm & 7.30pm–midnight, Fri
12.30–5pm & 7.30pm–1.30am, Sat
1pm–1.30am, Sun 1pm–midnight.

The decor is rustic, the atmosphere is good and the food excellent here. The salads and rice dishes are particularly tasty and the lunchtime menu good value at €11.50.

Baco y Beto

MAP p.80, POCKET MAP F3
C/Pelayo 24 ⓜ Chueca ⓦ baco-beto.com.
Mon–Fri 8pm–1am, Sat 2–4.30pm &
8pm–1am.

Creative, delicious-tasting tapas in this small bar in the heart of Chueca. The constantly changing menu features a selection of wonderful flavours and fresh ingredients.

Bar Amor

MAP p.80, POCKET MAP E1
C/Manuela Malsaña 22 ⓜ San Bernardo or
Bilbao ☎ 915 944 829, ⓦ baramor.es.
Tues–Sat 1.30–4pm & 8pm–midnight.

A relatively new arrival on the Malasaña scene, this compact little corner restaurant has a carefully selected menu of appetising and appealingly presented *raciones* – think quail in teriyaki sauce or mango ravioli in sweet wine. There is a good wine list, too.

El Bocaíto

MAP p.80, POCKET MAP G4
C/Libertad 6 Ⓜ Chueca Ⓦ bocaito.com.
Mon–Sat 12.30–4pm & 8pm–midnight, Sun
12.30–4pm. Closed 2 weeks in Aug.

Watch the busy staff preparing
the food in the kitchen as you
munch on delicious tapas. Try the
Luisito (chilli, squid and a secret
sauce all topped with a prawn), the
hottest canapé you're ever likely to
encounter. If you prefer to sit down,
there is a restaurant at the back.

Casa Julio

MAP p.80, POCKET MAP E3
C/Madera 37 Ⓜ Tribunal. Mon 1–3.30pm &
6.30–11.30pm.

Famed for its *croquetas*, this old-
style Madrid bar is nearly always
full, and rightly so. The *croquetas*
come in a range of flavours from
the traditional ham to spinach, leek
and mushroom and blue cheese, the
rest of the dishes are very good too.

Celso y Manolo

MAP p.80, POCKET MAP G10
C/Libertad 1 Ⓜ Chueca ☎ 915 318 079,
Ⓦ celsoymanolo.es. Daily 1–5pm &
7.30pm–2am.

Named in honour of the original
owners of an old *taberna* that used
to occupy the site, entrepreneur
Carlos Zamora has refurbished the
bar while retaining the traditional
fare, albeit with a contemporary.
He has certainly succeeded and
the wide-ranging menu offers
delicious *raciones* such as *croquetas
de bacalao* (cod croquettes), great
rice dishes and a fantastic selection
of tomato salad dishes.

Circo de las Tapas

MAP p.80, POCKET MAP E4
C/Corredera Baja de San Pablo 21
Ⓜ Callao/Tribunal ☎ 911 886 014,
Ⓦ circodelastapas.com. Daily noon–2am.

This cosy bar-restaurant has
a comprehensive offering of
interesting tapas at competitive
prices. Salads, home-made
croquetas, mussels and stuffed
peppers are all popular while the
tortilla is outstanding. There is a
good-value set lunch at €10.50 and
paellas on Saturdays too.

Gourmet Experience

MAP p.80, POCKET MAP D10
El Corte Inglés, Plaza Callao 2 Ⓜ Callao.
Mon–Sat 10am–midnight.

Head for the ninth floor of this
branch of the classic Spanish
department store to enjoy some
breathtaking views of Madrid.
Gaze out over the Capitol building
on the Gran Vía, the Palacio
Real, and out towards the distant
mountains as you sample a tapa,
some oysters, a drink or an ice
cream from one of the bars and
food stalls set up on the top floor.

Mercado de San Antón

MAP p.80, POCKET MAP G4
C/Augusto Figueroa 24 Ⓜ Chueca
Ⓦ mercadosananton.com. Mon–Sat
10am–10pm, terrace & restaurant Mon–
Thurs & Sun 10am–midnight, Fri & Sat
10am–1.30am.

Like the *Mercado San Miguel*
near Plaza Mayor, this local
market has become a trendy
meeting place on the Chueca
scene with gourmet foodstands,
a wine bar, a café, a sushi stall
and a stylish terrace restaurant
La Cocina de San Antón.

Mercado de San Antón

Pez Gordo

MAP p.80, POCKET MAP E3

C/Pez 6 Ⓜ Santo Domingo/Callao ☎ 915 223 208, Ⓦ elpezgordo.es. Daily 6.30pm–2am.

A fabulous array of tapas at this popular bar in this up and coming street north of Gran Vía. The aubergines in honey and tuna with caramelised onions and grapes are great options, but all the dishes are excellent. There is a good range of wines and beers on offer, the service is friendly and the prices are reasonable too.

Stop Madrid

MAP p.80, POCKET MAP F4

C/Hortaleza 11 Ⓜ Gran Vía Ⓦ stopmadrid.es. Daily 12.30pm–2am.

Dating back to 1929, this corner bar has hams hanging from the windows and wine bottles lining the walls. Tapas consist largely of *jamón* and chorizo, and the "Canapé Stop" of ham and tomato doused in olive oil is an excellent option.

Bars

1862 Dry Bar

MAP p.80, POCKET MAP D3

C/Pez 27 Ⓜ Noviciado Ⓦ facebook.com /1862DryBar. Mon–Fri 3.30pm–1am, Fri– Sat 12.30pm–2am.

1862 Dry Bar

Expertly mixed and poured cocktails at this chic and compact two-floored watering hole in this bar-packed street north of Gran Vía. On the menu are the usual classics but also some signature cocktails developed by owner Alberto, all at very reasonable prices.

La Ardosa

MAP p.80, POCKET MAP F3

C/Colón 13 Ⓜ Tribunal Ⓦ www.laardosa .com. Mon–Fri 8.30am–2am, Sat & Sun 11.45am–2.30am.

One of the city's classic *tabernas*, serving limited but delicious tapas including great *croquetas*, *salmorejo* and an excellent home-made *tortilla*. Also *vermút*, draught beer and Guinness.

Chicote

MAP p.80, POCKET MAP F10

Gran Vía 12 Ⓜ Gran Vía Ⓦ grupomercado delareina.com. Mon–Thurs 7pm–3am, Fri & Sat 7pm–3.30am, Sun 4pm–midnight.

Opened back in 1931 by Perico Chicote, ex-barman at the *Ritz*. Sophia Loren, Frank Sinatra, Ava Gardner, Luis Buñuel, Orson Welles and Hemingway have all passed through the doors of this cocktail bar. It's lost much of its old-style charm as it has tried to keep up to date, though it's still worth a visit for nostalgia's sake.

Del Diego

MAP p.80, POCKET, MAP F10

C/Reina 12 Ⓜ Gran Vía Ⓦ deldiego.com. Mon–Thurs 7pm–3am, Fri & Sat 7pm–3.30am. Closed Aug.

New York-style cocktail bar set up by former *Chicote* waiter Fernando del Diego and now better than the original place. The expertly mixed cocktails are served up in a friendly, unhurried atmosphere. Margaritas, mojitos and manhattans; the eponymously named vodka-based house special is a must.

Fábrica Maravillas

MAP p.80, POCKET MAP F3

C/Valverde 29 Ⓜ Gran Vía or Tribunal Ⓦ fabricamaravillas.com. Mon–Wed 6pm–

midnight, Thurs 6pm–1am, Fri 6pm–2am, Sat 12.30pm–2am, Sun 12.30pm–midnight.

Opened in 2012 in this fashionable, rejuvenated street running parallel to C/Fuencarral, Fábrica has helped promote the trend for craft beers in Madrid. An excellent collection of ales, including the fruity Malasaña, stout and an excellent IPA.

Gin Club/Mercado de la Reina

MAP p.80, POCKET MAP G10 & F10
Gran Vía 12 Ⓜ Gran Vía Ⓦ grupomercado delareina.com. Gin Club 1.30pm–2am, bar & tapas: Mon–Thurs 9am–2am, Fri 9am–2.30am, Sat 10am–2.30am, Sun 10am–2am, restaurant: Mon–Thurs & Sun 10am–2am, Fri & Sat 10am–2.30am.

A tapas bar, restaurant and *bar de copas*. The bar serves a wide range of *pinchos* and *raciones* as well as a house special (upmarket) hamburger meal at €10.50. The restaurant is rather more pricey, with main courses around €15. At the back, with its mirrored ceilings and black leather chairs, is the *Gin Club* cocktail bar, offering over twenty different brands.

The Passenger

MAP p.80, POCKET MAP E3
C/Pez 16 Ⓜ Noviciado. Mon–Thurs 8pm–3am, Fri–Sun 4pm–3am.

Original and fun, this long, narrow coffee shop/cocktail bar is designed to look like the interior of a luxurious old train carriage, while landscapes are projected onto the "windows" to create the sensation of movement. There is an extensive cocktail menu in the evenings and occasional live music too.

Taberna Ángel Sierra

MAP p.80, POCKET MAP G3
C/Gravina 11 Ⓜ Chueca. Daily noon–2am.

Perched on the edge of the plaza, this is one of the great bars in Madrid, where everyone drinks *vermút* accompanied by free, exquisite pickled anchovy tapas. *Raciones* are also available in the seated area, though they are a little pricey.

Clubs

BarCo

MAP p.80, POCKET MAP E4
C/Barco 24 Ⓜ Tribunal Ⓦ barcobar.com. Mon–Thurs & Sun 10pm–5.30am, Fri & Sat 10pm–6am.

Popular venue in the midst of the increasingly fashionable Triball district, *BarCo* hosts regular concerts and jam sessions, while the DJs take over late night at weekends with an eclectic selection of music – anything from the latest funk and hip hop to 80s classics.

Bogui Jazz

MAP p.80, POCKET MAP G3
C/Barquillo 29 Ⓜ Chueca Ⓦ bogui.es. Club Thurs–Sat 1pm–6am, concerts 8 or 9pm.

Two-for-one at this long-standing club in Chueca. On one hand Bogui stages regular jazz concerts by a range of Spanish and international artists, on the other it plays host to a dance club from Thursday to Saturday, with guest DJs playing everything from funk and hip-hop to reggae and R&B. Gigs €12–18, club €8–15 with two drinks.

Sala 0

MAP p.80, POCKET MAP E4
Plaza Callao 4 Ⓜ Callao Ⓦ independance club.com. Fri & Sat 11.30pm–6am. €10–15.

Previously known as *Sala Bash* and a mainstay of Madrid nightlife, this venue has been taken over by the *Independance Dance Club* with guest DJs on Fridays and Saturdays.

Tupperware

MAP p.80, POCKET MAP F2
C/Corredera Alta de San Pablo 26 Ⓜ Tribunal. Daily 8pm–3am.

A Malasaña legend with retro decor and reasonably priced drinks, this is the place to go for indie tunes, with grunge and punk-era classics. Always packed downstairs, but a more relaxed atmosphere upstairs.

Salamanca and Paseo de la Castellana

Exclusive Barrio de Salamanca was developed in the second half of the nineteenth century as an upmarket residential zone under the patronage of the Marquis of Salamanca. Today, it's still home to Madrid's smartest apartments and designer emporiums, while the streets are populated by the chic clothes and sunglasses brigade, decked out in fur coats, Gucci and gold. Shopping aside, there's a scattering of sights here, including the pick of the city's smaller museums and Real Madrid's imposing Santiago Bernabéu stadium. Bordering Salamanca to the west is the multi-lane Paseo de la Castellana, peppered with corporate office blocks, where, in summer, the section north of Plaza de Colón is littered with trendy terrazas.

Plaza de Colón

MAP p.92, POCKET MAP H3
Ⓜ Colón.

Overlooking a busy crossroads and dominating the square in which they stand are a Neo-Gothic monument to Christopher Columbus (Cristóbal Colón), given as a wedding gift to Alfonso XII, and an enormous Spanish flag. Directly behind are the Jardines del Descubrimiento (Discovery Gardens), a small park containing three huge stone blocks representing Columbus's ships, the *Niña*, *Pinta* and *Santa María*. Below the plaza, underneath a cascading wall of water, is the **Teatro Fernán Gómez**, a venue for theatre, film, dance, music and occasional exhibitions.

Biblioteca Nacional and Museo del Libro

MAP p.92, POCKET MAP J3
Paseo de Recoletos 20 Ⓜ Colón Ⓦ bne.es.
Tues–Sat 10am–8pm, Sun & hols 10am–2pm. Free.

The National Library contains over six million volumes, including every work published in Spain since 1716. The museum within displays a selection of the library's treasures, including Arab, Hebrew and Greek manuscripts, and hosts regular temporary exhibitions related to the world of art and literature.

Museo Arqueológico Nacional

MAP p.92, POCKET MAP J3
C/Serrano 13 Ⓜ Serrano or Colón Ⓦ man.
es. Tues–Sat 9.30am–8pm, Sun 9.30am–3pm. €3, free Sat after 2pm & Sun.

Revitalised after a lengthy refurbishment, the archeological museum's collections have been given a new lease of life with their arrangement around a naturally lit central atrium, while the labelling and video explanations (in English and Spanish) put the exhibits in context. The museum holds some very impressive pieces, among them the celebrated Celto-Iberian busts known as *La Dama de Elche* and *La Dama de Baza*, and a wonderfully rich hoard of Visigothic treasures found at Toledo. The museum also contains

La Dama de Elche, Museo Arqueológico Nacional

outstanding Roman, Egyptian, Greek and Islamic finds.

Museo de Cera

MAP p.92, POCKET MAP H3
Paseo de Recoletos 41 Ⓜ **Colón** Ⓦ **museo
ceramadrid.com. Mon–Fri 10am–2.30pm
& 4.30–8.30pm, Sat, Sun & hols 10am–
8.30pm. €19, €12 for 4–12 year olds;
discounts on website.**

Over 450 different personalities – including a host of VIPs, heads of state and, of course, Real Madrid football stars – are displayed in this expensive and tacky museum, which is nevertheless popular with children. There's also a chamber of horrors and a 3-D film history of Spain.

Museo de Arte Público

MAP p.92, POCKET MAP J1
Paseo de la Castellana 41 Ⓜ **Rubén Darío.**

An innovative use of the space underneath the Juan Bravo flyover, this open-air art museum is made up of a haphazard collection of sculptures, cubes, walls and fountains, including work by Eduardo Chillida, Joan Miró and Julio González.

Museo Sorolla

MAP p.92, POCKET MAP J1
Paseo del General Martínez Campos 37
Ⓜ **Rubén Darío, Gregorio Marañón or
Iglesia** Ⓦ **mecd.gob.es/msorolla. Tues–Sat
9.30am–8pm, Sun 10am–3pm. €3,
under-18s free, free Sat 2–8pm & Sun.**

Part museum and part art gallery, this tribute to an artist's life and work is one of Madrid's most underrated treasures. Situated in Joaquín Sorolla's former home, it's a delightful oasis of peace and tranquillity, its cool and shady Andalucian-style courtyard and gardens decked out with statues, fountains, assorted plants and fruit trees. The ground floor has been kept largely intact, recreating the authentic atmosphere of the artist's living and working areas. The upstairs rooms, originally the sleeping quarters, have been turned into a gallery, where sunlight, sea, intense colours, women and children dominate Sorolla's impressionistic paintings. On your way out in the Patio Andaluz, there's a collection of his sketches and gouaches.

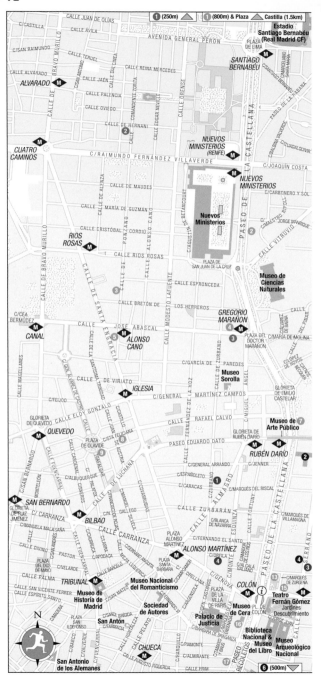

Salamanca and Paseo de la Castellana

SHOPS	
ABC Serrano	2
Adolfo Domínguez	1, 6
Agatha Ruiz de la Prada	4
Ekseptión	5
Lavinia	3

ACCOMMODATION	
Hostal Residencia Don Diego	5
Hotel Orfila	4
Hotel Santo Mauro	1
Hotel Único	2
Petit Palace Embassy Serrano	3

CAFÉS	
Café el Espejo	16
Café Gijón	17

RESTAURANTS	
DiverXO	1
Estay	14
Gaudium	8
Hard Rock Café	13
Mama Campo	9
La Máquina	3
El Pescador	10
Poncelet Cheese Bar	4
Ramón Freixa Madrid	12
Sala de Despiece	5

TAPAS BARS	
Hevia	6
Lateral	2, 7, 11
Platea	15

BAR	
El Quinto Vino	2

CLUBS	
Moby Dick	1
Opium	3

| 0 | metres | 250 |
| 0 | yards | 250 |

Plaza de Toros de las Ventas (500m)

Museo Lázaro Galdiano

MAP p.92, POCKET MAP J1
C/Serrano 122 Ⓜ Gregorio Marañón
Ⓦ flg.es. Tues–Sat 10am–4.30pm, Sun
10am–3pm. €6, under-12s free, free
3.30–4.30pm & Sun 2–3pm.

When businessman and publisher
José Lázaro Galdiano died in 1947,
he left his private collection – a
vast treasure trove of paintings and
objets d'art – to the state. Spread
over the four floors of his former
home, the collection contains
jewellery, outstanding Spanish
archeological pieces and some
beautifully decorated thirteenth-
century Limoges enamels. There's
also an excellent selection of
European paintings with works
by Bosch, Rembrandt, Reynolds
and Constable, plus Spanish artists
including Zurbarán, Velázquez, El
Greco and Goya. Other exhibits
include several clocks and watches,
many of them once owned by
Emperor Charles V.

Museo de Ciencias Naturales

MAP p.92, POCKET MAP J1
C/José Gutiérrez Abascal 2 Ⓜ Gregorio
Marañón Ⓦ mncn.csic.es. Tues–Fri
10am–5pm, Sat & Sun 10am–8pm (July &
Aug 10am–3pm). €7, 4–16 year-olds €3.50
The Natural History Museum's
displays are split between two
buildings. One contains a fairly
predictable collection of stuffed
animals, skeletons and audio-
visual displays on the evolution
of life on earth, the other is home
to some rather dull fossil and
geological exhibits.

Estadio Santiago Bernabéu

MAP p.92, POCKET MAP J1
C/Concha Espina 1 Ⓜ Santiago Bernabéu
Ⓣ 913 984 300, tickets Ⓣ 902 324 324,
Ⓦ realmadrid.com. Ticket office daily
10am–7pm (match days from 9am). Tickets
from €30. Tour and trophy exhibition: Mon–
Sat 10am–7pm, Sun 10.30am–6.30pm
(closes five hours before games on match
days); €24, under-14s €18.

The magnificent 80,000-seater
Bernabéu stadium provides a
suitably imposing home for one
of the most glamorous teams in
football, Real Madrid. Venue of the
1982 World Cup final, the stadium
has witnessed countless triumphs
of "Los blancos", who have notched
up 33 Spanish league titles and
eleven European Cup triumphs
in their 115-year history. Real
have broken the world transfer
record three times in the last
seventeen years, and their latest
star is Portugal forward Cristiano
Ronaldo. Tickets for big games
can be tricky to get hold of, but the
club runs a telephone and internet
booking service (see above).

You can catch a glimpse of the
hallowed turf on the exorbitantly-
priced stadium tour during which
you visit the changing rooms, walk
around the edge of the pitch and
sit in the VIP box before heading
to the trophy room with its endless
cabinets of gleaming silverware.
The tour ends with the obligatory
visit to the club shop – where
you soon come to realize why
Real is one of the richest football
clubs in the world. The stadium
also has a surprisingly affordable
café (*Realcafé*) and three more
expensive restaurants (*Puerta 57,
El Asador* and *Zen Market*), all
affording views over the pitch.

Trophies at Estadio Santiago Bernabéu

Plaza Castilla

MAP p.92, POCKET MAP J1
Ⓜ Plaza de la Castilla.

The Paseo de la Castellana ends with a flourish at Plaza Castilla with the dramatic leaning towers of the Puerta de Europa and four giant skyscrapers constructed on Real Madrid's former training ground, the result of a controversial deal that allowed the club to solve many of its financial problems. The two tallest towers – one by Norman Foster – soar some 250 metres skywards.

Plaza de Toros de Las Ventas

Plaza de Toros de Las Ventas

MAP p.92, POCKET MAP K3
C/Alcalá 237 Ⓜ Ventas ☎ 913 562 200,
Ⓦ las-ventas.info. Box office March–Oct Thurs–Sun 10am–2pm & 4–7pm; ☎ 912 352 343. €4–150.

On the easternmost tip of the Barrio de Salamanca, Madrid's 23,000-capacity, Neo-Mudéjar bullring, Las Ventas, is the most illustrious in the world. The season lasts from March to October and *corridas* (bullfights) are held every Sunday at 7pm and every day during the three main *ferias* (fairs): La Comunidad (early May), San Isidro (mid-May to June) and Otoño (late Sept to Oct). Tickets go on sale at the ring a couple of days in advance, though many are already allocated to season-ticket holders. The cheapest seats are *andanadas* and *gradas*, the highest rows at the back; the front rows are known as the *tendidos bajos* or *barreras*. Seats are also divided into *sol* (sun), *sombra* (shade) and *sol y sombra* (shaded after a while), with *sombra* the most expensive.

There's a refurbished taurine **museum** attached to the bullring (daily 10am–5.30pm; closes four hours before the start of the *corrida* on days of bullfights; €9.90 with audioguide, under-12s €5.90) with an intriguing collection of memorabilia including stunning *trajes de luces*, the beautifully decorated suits worn by the *toreros*. As well as stepping out onto the sand yourself you can visit the medical room where injured *toreros* are treated and the chapel where they pray beforehand.

Bullfighting

The bullfight is a classic image of Spain, but the ethical arguments against it are well-known – the governments of Catalunya and the Canary Islands have gone so far as to ban it. Spain's main opposition to bullfighting is organised by ADDA (Ⓦ addaong.org), whose website has information about international campaigns and current actions. To aficionados, the bulls are a ritual part of Spanish culture, with the emphasis on the way man and bull "perform" together. Fighting bulls are, they will tell you, bred for the industry; they live a reasonable life before they are killed, and if the bullfight went, so, too, would the bulls. If you decide to attend a *corrida*, try to see a big, prestigious event, where star performers are likely to despatch the bulls with "art" and a "clean" kill; there are few sights worse than a matador making a prolonged, messy kill.

Shops

SALAMANCA AND PASEO DE LA CASTELLANA

ABC Serrano

MAP p.92, POCKET MAP J1
Paseo de la Castellana 34 and C/Serrano
61, both Ⓜ Rubén Darío Ⓦ abcserrano.com.
Mon–Sat 9am–9pm.

Upmarket shopping mall
housed in the beautiful former
headquarters of the ABC
newspaper. There are fashion
and household outlets, as well as
a couple of bars and restaurants,
and a popular rooftop terrace.

Adolfo Domínguez

MAP p.92, POCKET MAP J4
C/Serrano 5 Ⓜ Retiro Ⓦ adolfodominguez
.com. Mon–Sat 10am–9pm, Sun noon–8pm.

Domínguez has opened a massive
five-storey flagship store for his
slightly sober but elegant modern
Spanish designs – a wide range of
natural colours and free lines for
both men and women. There is
another branch at C/Serrano 96.

Agatha Ruiz de la Prada

MAP p.92, POCKET MAP J2
C/Serrano 27 Ⓜ Serrano Ⓦ agatharuizdela
prada.com. Mon–Sat 10am–8.30pm.

Movida-era designer who shows and
sells her gaudily coloured clothes
and accessories at this dazzling
outlet. There's a children's line,
stationery and household goods too.

ABC Serrano

Ekseptión

MAP p.92, POCKET MAP K3
C/Velázquez 28 Ⓜ Velázquez Ⓦ ekseption.es.
Mon–Sat 10.30am–8.30pm.

A dramatic catwalk bathed in
spotlights leads into this shop
selling some of the most expensive
women's clothes in Madrid. Next
door is the EKS concept store selling
designer clothes from top names
around the world. There is also a
branch selling discounted lines at
C/Marqués de la Ensenada 2.

Lavinia

MAP p.92, POCKET MAP K1
C/José Ortega y Gasset 16 Ⓜ Nuñez de
Balboa Ⓦ lavinia.es. Mon–Sat 10am–9pm,
first Sun in month noon–8pm.

A massive wine shop with a great
selection from Spain and the rest
of the world. The perfect place
to get that Ribera del Duero,
Albariño or Rueda that you
wanted to take home.

Cafés

Café el Espejo

MAP p.92, POCKET MAP H3
Paseo de Recoletos 31 Ⓜ Colón
Ⓦ restauranteelespejo.com. Daily 9am–1am.

Opened in 1978, but you wouldn't
guess it from the antiquated
decor – think mirrors, gilt and
a wonderful, extravagant glass
pavilion. The leafy terraza is an
ideal spot to enjoy a coffee and
watch the world go by.

Café Gijón

MAP p.92, POCKET MAP H4
Paseo de Recoletos 21 Ⓜ Colón
Ⓦ cafegijon.com. Daily 8am–1.30am.

A famous literary café dating
from 1888, decked out in Cuban
mahogany and mirrors. A centre
of the *Movida* in the 1980s, it
still hosts regular artistic *tertulias*
(discussion groups). There is a
restaurant, but you're best off
sticking to drinks in the bar or on
the pleasant summer terraza.

Café el Espejo

Restaurants

DiverXO

MAP p.92, POCKET MAP J1
C/Padre Damián 23 Ⓜ Cuzco ☎ 915 700
766, Ⓦ diverxo.com. Tues–Sat 2–3.30pm
& 9–11.30pm.

Madrid's only three-Michelin-
star restaurant, located in the
NH Eurobuilding hotel, is run
by chef David Muñoz and has a
deserved reputation for stunning
presentation, mouth-watering food
and unpretentious service. Prices
are sky-high – taster menus are
€185 and €225 – and the waiting list
is long. You have to book months in
advance, paying a €60 charge which
is discounted from the final bill.

Estay

MAP p.92, POCKET MAP K2
C/Hermosilla 46 Ⓜ Velázquez ☎ 915 780
470, Ⓦ estayrestaurante.com. Restaurant:
Mon–Thurs 1–4.30pm & 8pm–12.30am, Fri
& Sat 1–4.30pm & 8pm–1.30am; bar:
Mon–Thurs 8am–12.30am, Fri
8am–1.30am, Sat 9am–1.30am.

Basque-style cuisine in miniature
(canapés and mini casseroles) in
this pleasant, roomy restaurant. A
great range of *pintxos*, including

jamón with roquefort cheese,
langoustine vol-au-vents and a
fine wine list too. A meal will cost
around €30.

Gaudium

MAP p.92, POCKET MAP G1
C/Santa Feliciana 14 Ⓜ Quevedo/Rubén
Darío ☎ 915 943 037, Ⓦ gaudiumchamberi
.com. Mon–Wed 1.30–4.30pm Thurs–Sat
1.30–4.30pm & 8.30–11.30pm.

Quality ingredients, good service
and a selection of simple dishes
with a creative twist served
up in this intimate restaurant
close to the popular Plaza de
Olavide. Offerings include grilled
vegetables, oxtail with grapes and
cod with garlic, basil and dried
tomato. The lunchtime set menu is
around €20.

Hard Rock Café

MAP p.92, POCKET MAP J2
Paseo de la Castellana 2 Ⓜ Colón ☎ 914
364 340, Ⓦ hardrock.com/cafes/madrid.
Daily 12.30pm–2am.

A children's favourite, with its
tried-and-tested formula of
rock memorabilia, Tex-Mex and
burgers at under €20 a head. The
best part is the summer terraza
overlooking Plaza de Colón.

Mama Campo

MAP p.92, POCKET MAP F1

Plaza Olavide Ⓜ Quevedo/Iglesia ☎ 914 474 138, Ⓦ mamacampo.es. Tues–Sat 1.30–4pm & 8.30pm–midnight, Sun 1.30–4pm

Organic food for vegetarian and non-vegetarians alike in this cool and airy restaurant/bar perched on the edge of this popular tree-lined plaza. There are two spaces, one for meals, the other (*La Cantina*) for tapas and snacks. There is always something interesting on offer in the seasonal menu.

La Máquina

MAP p.92, POCKET MAP G1

C/Ponzano 39–41 Ⓜ Ríos Rosas ☎ 918 263 774, Ⓦ lamaquinachamberi.es. Bar: Sun–Wed noon–1am, Thurs noon–2am, Fri, Sat & Sun 1–5pm & 8pm–1am; restaurant: daily 1–5pm & 8pm–1am.

Three different spaces in this sleek eatery: the bar and terrace areas serve up a great range of *pinchos*, tapas and *raciones* including excellent fried fish, while the restaurant at the back is for more formal meals with rice dishes, stews and quality meat and fish. *Raciones* from €13–18, mains €15–25.

El Pescador

MAP p.92, POCKET MAP K1

C/José Ortega y Gasset 75 Ⓜ Lista ☎ 914 021 290. Mon–Sat 12.30–4.30pm & 8pm–12.30am. Closed Aug.

One of the city's top seafood restaurants, with specials flown in daily from the Atlantic. Prices are high (around €60 per head), but you'll rarely experience better-quality seafood than this. If funds don't stretch to a full meal, you can try a *ración* in the bar instead.

Poncelet Cheese Bar

MAP p.92, POCKET MAP J1

C/José Abascal 61 Ⓜ Ríos Rosas/Rubén Darío ☎ 913 992 550, Ⓦ ponceletcheese bar.es. Tues–Fri noon–midnight, Sat 11am–midnight, Sun 11am–4pm.

A cheese-lover's paradise with a mission to educate customers on the wealth of artisan cheeses available in Spain. Huge whole cheeses are laid out in the centre of this stylish eatery while a beautiful vertical garden covers one of the walls. As you would expect, cheese-based dishes such as fondues and raclettes are to the fore, but more subtle options such as mushroom risotto, caramelised cod and meatballs are also available. Mains cost between €15–20.

Ramón Freixa Madrid

MAP p.92, POCKET MAP J2

C/Claudio Coello 67 Ⓜ Serrano ☎ 917 818 262, Ⓦ ramonfreixamadrid.com. Tues–Sat 1–3.30pm & 9–11pm. Closed Easter, Aug & Christmas.

Catalan chef Ramón Freixa's flagship Michelin-star restaurant in Madrid, situated in the luxury surroundings of the *Hotel Único* (see p.132) in the heart of Salamanca. Creative and impeccably presented dishes from an ever-changing menu featuring superb game, fish and new twists on Spanish classics. À la carte dishes are €25–65, while there is a "short" taster menu at €53 and the works for an eye-watering €140 or €165 (wine extra). Only has space for 35 diners, so book well in advance, especially if you want a table on the summer terrace.

Sala de Despiece

MAP p.92, POCKET MAP G1

C/Ponzano 11 Ⓜ Ríos Rosas ☎ 917 526 106, Ⓦ academiadeldespiece.com. Mon–Thurs 1–5pm & 7.30pm–12.30am, Fri till 1am, Sat & Sun 1–5.30pm & 8pm–1am.

Despiece means cutting up into pieces and the concept behind this bar is that high quality raw material is king. Inside, there is just one long, white bar lined with stools and eating feels more like a tasting session rather than a meal. On offer is a selection of supremely tasty hand-picked ingredients pared down to the essentials and delivered on plastic or metal trays. Arrive unfashionably early or be prepared for a long wait for a slot at the bar. Expect to pay around €30 a head.

Platea

run by renowned chefs, scattered over several floors in a former theatre by Plaza de Colón. Spanish, Mexican, Peruvian and Japanese specialities are all on offer, and there's a patisserie, a cocktail bar and a restaurant run by Ramón Freixa all under the same roof.

Tapas bars

Hevia

MAP p.92, POCKET MAP J1
C/Serrano 118 Ⓜ Rubén Darío or Gregorio Marañón Ⓦ heviamadrid.com. Mon–Sat 9am–1am.

Plush venue for plush clientele feasting on pricey but excellent tapas and canapés – the guacamole with anchovies is delicious, as is the selection of smoked fish.

Lateral

MAP p.92, p.52 & p.80, POCKET MAP J1
Paseo de la Castellana 42 Ⓜ Rubén Darío Ⓦ lateral.com. Mon–Wed 9am–midnight, Thurs & Fri 9am–1am, Sat noon–1am, Sun noon–midnight.

A swish tapas bar serving classic dishes such as *croquetas* and *pimientos rellenos* (stuffed peppers) with a modern twist. There are other branches at C/Velázquez 57, C/Fuencarral 43, Paseo de la Castellana 89 and Plaza Santa Ana 12.

Platea

MAP p.92, POCKET MAP J2
C/Goya 5–7 Ⓜ Colón or Serrano Ⓦ platea madrid.com. Mon–Wed & Sun noon–12.30am, Thurs–Sat noon–2.30am.

A gastronome's paradise: a host of upmarket tapas bars and food stalls

Bar

El Quinto Vino

MAP p.92, POCKET MAP G1
C/Hernani 48 Ⓜ Nuevos Ministerios/Cuatro Caminos Ⓦ elquintovino.com. Mon–Fri 10.30am–11.30pm, Sat 1–4pm & 9pm–midnight, Sun 11am–4pm.

Superb home-made *croquetas*, *huevos estrellados* and *rabo de toro* with a great selection of wines in this very popular bar just behind Nuevos Ministerios. They also do a decent traditional set lunch for €12.

Clubs

Moby Dick

MAP p.92, POCKET MAP J1
Avda Brasil 5 Ⓜ Cuzco or Santiago Bernabéu Ⓦ mobydickclub.com. Wed 10pm–3am, Thurs 10pm–5am, Fri & Sat 10pm–6am.

Intimate club/music venue with a friendly atmosphere. Plays host to a variety of Spanish groups and the odd international star – Roddy Frame was a recent visitor. The music ranges from indie to pop-rock and jazz.

Opium

MAP p.92, POCKET MAP J1
C/José Abascal 56 Ⓜ Gregorio Marañón Ⓦ opiummadrid.com. Daily midnight–6am. €15–20 including first drink; often free entry before 1.30am.

Electronic/house music from resident DJs in this reopened club (its predecessor was closed for exceeding maximum capacity). Popular with *pijos* – fashion-conscious rich kids – and the upmarket glamour crowd.

Plaza de España and beyond

Largely constructed in the Franco era and dominated by two early Spanish skyscrapers, the Plaza de España provides an imposing full stop to Gran Vía and a breathing space from the densely packed streets to the east. Beyond the square lies a mixture of aristocratic suburbia, university campus and parkland, distinguished by the green swathes of Parque del Oeste and Casa de Campo. Sights include the eclectic collections of the Museo Cerralbo, the fascinating Museo de América, the Ermita de San Antonio de la Florida, with its stunning Goya frescoes and, further out, the pleasant royal residence of El Pardo. Meanwhile, the spacious terrazas along Paseo del Pintor Rosales provide ample opportunity for refreshment.

Plaza de España

MAP p.102, POCKET MAP C3
Ⓜ **Plaza de España.**

The Plaza de España was the Spanish dictator Franco's attempt to portray Spain as a dynamic, modern country. The gargantuan apartment complex of the **Edificio de España**, which heads the square, looks like it was transplanted from 1920s New York, but was in fact completed in 1953. It is now set to be turned into a 600-room hotel. Four years later, the 32-storey **Torre de Madrid** took over for some time as the tallest building in Spain. Together they tower over an elaborate monument to Cervantes in the middle of the square, set by an uninspiring pool. The plaza itself can be a little seedy at night, although there are plans to remodel the area and convert it into a more open and pleasant park space.

Plaza de España

Centro Cultural Conde Duque

Museo de Cerralbo

MAP p.102, POCKET MAP B3
C/Ventura Rodríguez 17 Ⓜ Plaza de
España Ⓦ museocerralbo.mcu.es. Tues,
Wed, Fri & Sat 9.30am–3pm, Thurs
9.30am–3pm & 5–8pm, Sun & hols
10am–3pm. €3, free Thurs 5–8pm, Sat
after 2pm & Sun.

Reactionary politician, poet,
traveller and archeologist, the
seventeenth Marqués de Cerralbo
endowed his elegant nineteenth-
century mansion with a
substantial collection of paintings,
furniture and armour. Bequeathed
to the state on his death, the
house opened as a museum in
1962 and the cluttered nature of
the exhibits is partly explained
by the fact that the marqués's will
stipulated that objects should
be displayed exactly as he had
arranged them. The highlight is
a fabulous over-the-top mirrored
ballroom with a Tiepolo-inspired
fresco, golden stuccowork and
marbled decoration.

Centro Cultural Conde Duque

MAP p.102, POCKET MAP C2
C/Conde Duque 9–11 Ⓜ Ventura Rodríguez
Ⓦ condeduquemadrid.es.

Constructed in the early
eighteenth century, this former
royal guard barracks has been
converted into a dynamic
cultural centre, housing the city's
contemporary art collection
(Tues–Sat 10am–2pm &
5.30–9pm, Sun 10.30am–2pm;
free), a recreation of the study of
early twentieth-century writer
Ramón Gómez de la Serna and
hosting a variety of exhibitions
and concerts.

Plaza de las Comendadoras

MAP p.102, POCKET MAP D2
Ⓜ Noviciado.

Bordered by a variety of
interesting craft shops, bars
and cafés, this tranquil square
is named after the convent that
occupies one side of it. The
convent is run by nuns from the
military order of Santiago and the
attached church is decked out with
banners celebrating the victories
of the Order's knights. A large
painting of their patron, St James
the Moor-slayer, hangs over the
high altar. The plaza itself comes
alive in the summer months when
the terrazas open and locals gather
for a chat and a drink.

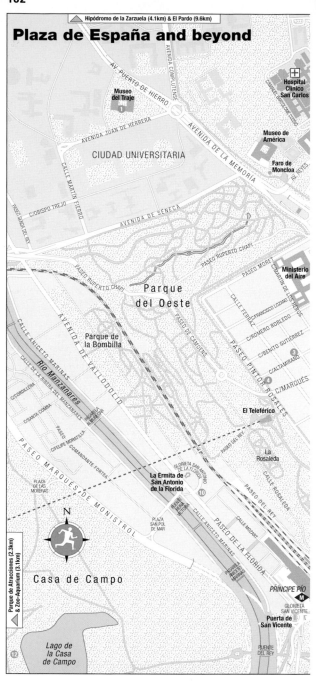

Plaza de España and beyond

Hipódromo de la Zarzuela (4.1km) & El Pardo (9.6km)

AV. PUERTO DE HIERRO

AVENIDA COMPLUTENSE

CAMINO DE CASTILLA A COSLADA

Hospital Clínico San Carlos

Museo del Traje

AVENIDA JUAN DE HERRERA

AVENIDA DE LA MEMORIA

Museo de América

CALLE MARTÍN FIERRO

CIUDAD UNIVERSITARIA

Faro de Moncloa

AV. REYES

PASEO SEÑOR DEL REY

C/OBISPO TREJO

AVENIDA DE SENECA

PASEO RUPERTO CHAPI

Ministerio del Aire

PASEO MORET

PASEO RUPERTO CHAPI

Parque del Oeste

C/MARTÍN DE LOS HEROS

CALLE FERRAZ

C/FRANCISCO LOZANO

C/ROMERO ROBLEDO

AVENIDA DE VALLODOLID

Parque de la Bombilla

PASEO DE CAMOENS

PASEO PINTOR ROSALES

C/BENITO GUTIÉRREZ

C/ALTAMIRANO

CALLE ANICETO MARINAS

Río Manzanares

C/MARQUÉS

CALLE DE LA RIBERA DEL MANZANARES

El Teleférico

C/CORDILLERA

C/SANTA COMBA

PASEO MORATILLA

C/FELIPE COMANDANTE FORTEA

PASEO DEL REY

La Rosaleda

CALLE ROSALEGA

PASEO MARQUÉS DE MONISTROL

GLORIETA SAN ANTONIO DE LA FLORIDA

PLAZA DE LAS MORERAS

La Ermita de San Antonio de la Florida

PASEO DEL REY

N

PLAZA SAN POL DE MAR

CALLE ANICETO MARINAS

CALLE MOZART

PASEO DE LA FLORIDA

Casa de Campo

PRÍNCIPE PÍO M

GLORIETA SAN VICENTE

Parque de Atracciones (2.3km) & Zoo-Aquarium (3.1km)

Puerta de San Vicente

PUENTE DEL REY

Lago de la Casa de Campo

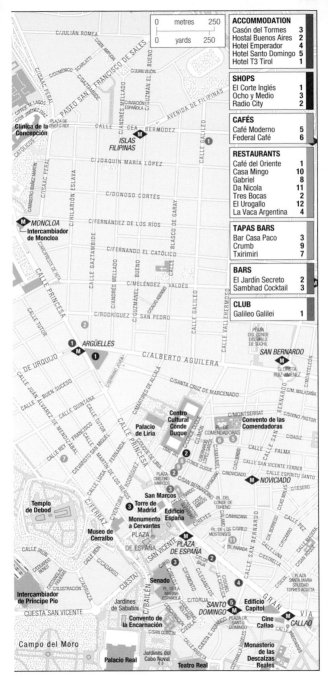

ACCOMMODATION

Casón del Tormes	3
Hostal Buenos Aires	2
Hotel Emperador	4
Hotel Santo Domingo	5
Hotel T3 Tirol	1

SHOPS

El Corte Inglés	1
Ocho y Medio	3
Radio City	2

CAFÉS

Café Moderno	5
Federal Café	6

RESTAURANTS

Café del Oriente	1
Casa Mingo	10
Gabriel	8
Da Nicola	11
Tres Bocas	2
El Urogallo	12
La Vaca Argentina	4

TAPAS BARS

Bar Casa Paco	3
Crumb	9
Txirimiri	7

BARS

El Jardín Secreto	2
Sambhad Cocktail	3

CLUB

Galileo Galilei	1

PLAZA DE ESPAÑA AND BEYOND

Ministerio del Aire

MAP p.102, POCKET MAP B1
Ⓜ Moncloa.

The Air Ministry is a product of the post-Civil War Francoist building boom. Work on the mammoth edifice began in 1942, and even the Third Reich's architect, Albert Speer, was consulted. However, with the defeat of the Nazis, plans were soon changed and a Habsburg-style structure was built instead – nicknamed the "Monasterio" del Aire because of its similarity to El Escorial. The neighbouring Arco de la Victoria was constructed in 1956 to commemorate the Nationalist military triumph in the Civil War.

Museo de América

MAP p.102, POCKET MAP B1
Avda de los Reyes Católicos 6 Ⓜ Moncloa
Ⓦ www.mecd.gob.es/museoamerica.
Tues, Wed, Fri & Sat 9.30am–3pm, Thurs
9.30am–7pm, Sun 10am–3pm. €3, free on
Sun and for under-18s.

This fabulous collection of pre-Columbian American art

Museo de América

and artefacts includes objects brought back at the time of the Spanish Conquest, as well as more recent acquisitions and donations. The layout is thematic, with sections on geography, history, social organization, religion and communication. The Aztec, Maya and Inca civilizations are well represented and exhibits include: the Madrid Codex, one of only three surviving hieroglyphic manuscripts depicting everyday Maya life; the Tudela Codex, with indigenous paintings describing the events of the Spanish Conquest; and the Quimbayas Treasure, a breathtaking collection of gold objects from a funeral treasure of the Colombian Quimbaya culture, dated 900–600 BC.

Museo del Traje

MAP p.102, POCKET MAP B1
Avda de Juan de Herrera 2 Ⓜ Moncloa
Ⓦ museodeltraje.mcu.es. Tues–Sat
9.30am–7pm, Sun & hols 10am–3pm (July
& Aug open late from 9.30am–10.30pm on
Thurs). €3, free for under-18s, Sat after
2.30pm and all day Sun.

A fascinating excursion through the history of clothes and costume. Exhibits include garments from a royal tomb dating back to the thirteenth century, some stunning eighteenth-century ballgowns and a selection of Spanish regional costumes as well as shoes, jewellery and underwear. Modern Spanish and international designers are also featured, with a Paco Rabane mini-skirt and elegant shoes from Pedro del Hierro. There is an upmarket restaurant in the grounds, which has a cool garden terrace in the summer (see p.109).

Parque del Oeste

MAP p.102, POCKET MAP A2–B3
Ⓜ Moncloa. Daily 10am–9pm.

Featuring a pleasant stream, assorted statues and shady walks, this delightful park offers a welcome respite from the busy streets of the capital. In summer, there are numerous terrazas overlooking it on Paseo del Pintor Rosales. The beautiful rose garden – in C/Rosaleda – is at its most fragrant in May and June, while further down the hill is a small cemetery where the 43 Spaniards executed by occupying French troops on May 3, 1808 – and immortalized by Goya in his famous painting in the Prado (see p.65) – lie buried.

Templo de Debod

MAP p.102, POCKET MAP B3
C/Ferraz 1 ⓜ Plaza de España ⓦ madrid .es/templodebod. April–Sept Tues–Fri 10am–2pm & 6–8pm, Sat & Sun 9.30am–8.30pm; Oct–March Tues–Fri 9.45am–1.45pm & 4.15–6.15pm, Sat & Sun 9.30am–8pm. Free.

A fourth-century BC Egyptian temple in the middle of Madrid may seem an incongruous sight. It's here, however, as a thank-you from the Egyptian government for Spanish help in salvaging archeological sites threatened by the construction of the Aswan High Dam. Reconstructed here stone by stone in 1968, it has a

Museo del Traje

multimedia exhibition on the culture of Ancient Egypt inside. Archeologists have called for it to be enclosed and insulated from the open air as pollution is taking a heavy toll on the stone.

Templo de Debod

Casa de Campo

El Teleférico

MAP p.102, POCKET MAP A2
Paseo del Pintor Rosales Ⓦ Argüelles
Ⓦ teleferico.com. April–Sept Mon–Fri
noon–dusk (exact times vary), Sat & Sun
noon–around 8pm; Oct–March Sat, Sun &
hols noon–dusk. €4.20 single, €5.90 return.

The Teleférico **cable car** shuttles
passengers from the edge of the
Parque del Oeste high over the
Manzanares river to a restaurant/
bar in the middle of Casa de
Campo (see below). The round trip
offers some fine views of the park,
the Palacio Real, the Almudena
cathedral and the city skyline.

La Ermita de San Antonio de la Florida

MAP p.102, POCKET MAP A4
Paseo de la Florida 5 Ⓦ Príncipe Pío
Ⓦ madrid.es/ermita. Tues–Sun
9.30am–8pm. Free. Guided tours on Sat at
noon in English, 1pm in Spanish.

Built on a Greek-cross plan
between 1792 and 1798, this little
church is the burial site of Goya
and also features some outstanding
frescoes by him. Those in the
dome depict St Anthony of Padua
resurrecting a dead man to give
evidence in favour of a prisoner
(the saint's father) unjustly accused
of murder. The *ermita* also houses
the artist's mausoleum, although his
head was stolen by phrenologists
for examination in the nineteenth
century. The mirror-image chapel
on the other side of the road was
built in 1925 for parish services
so that the original could become
a museum. On St Anthony's Day
(June 13), girls queue at the church
to ask the saint for a boyfriend; if
pins dropped into the holy water
then stick to their hands, their wish
will be granted.

Casa de Campo

MAP p.102, POCKET MAP A4
Ⓦ Lago.

The Casa de Campo, an enormous
expanse of heath and scrub, is
in parts surprisingly wild for a
place so easily accessible from the
city. Founded by Felipe II in the
mid-sixteenth century as a royal
hunting estate, it was only opened
to the public in 1931 and soon after
acted as a base for Franco's forces
to shell the city. Large sections
have been tamed for conventional
pastimes and there are picnic tables
and café/bars throughout the park,
the ones by the lake providing fine
views of the city. There are also
mountain-bike trails, a jogging
track, an open-air swimming pool
(June–Sept daily 11am–8.30pm;
€4.50), tennis courts and rowing
boats for rent on the lake, all
near Metro Lago. The park is best
avoided after dark as many of its
roads are frequented by prostitutes.

Zoo-Aquarium

MAP p.102, POCKET MAP A4
Casa de Campo Ⓜ Batán Ⓦ zoomadrid.com.
Daily 10.30/11am–dusk. €23.30, 3–7 year
olds €18.90, under-3s free; discounts via
website.

Laid out in sections corresponding
to the five continents, Madrid's
zoo, on the southwestern edge of
Casa de Campo, provides decent
enclosures and plenty of space for
over two thousand different species
– though of course all of the usual
animal welfare concerns about
zoos apply here, too. When you've
had your fill of big cats, pandas,
koalas and venomous snakes,
you can check out the aquarium,
dolphinarium, children's zoo or
bird show. Boats can be rented and
there are mini-train tours too.

Parque de Atracciones

MAP p.102, POCKET MAP A4
Casa de Campo Ⓜ Batán Ⓦ parquede
atracciones.es. April–Sept most days
noon–8/9pm (midnight on Sat & in July &
Aug); Oct–March weekends and hols
noon–7pm. €31.90, children between
100–140cm €24.90, children under 1m tall
free. Significant discounts via website.

This is Madrid's most popular
theme park, where highlights for

Parque de Atracciones

adults and teenagers include the
100km/hr Abismo rollercoaster,
the swirling Tarantula ride,
the 63-metre vertical drop La
Lanzadera, the stomach-churning
La Máquina and the whitewater
raft ride Los Rápidos. El Viejo
Caserón is a pretty terrifying
haunted house, but there are some
more sedate attractions too, as well
as an area for younger children.
Spanish acts perform in the open-
air auditorium in the summer and
there are frequent parades too,
plus plenty of burger/pizza places
to replace lost stomach contents.

Hipódromo de la Zarzuela

MAP p.102, POCKET MAP A4
Carretera La Coruña km 8 Ⓦ hipodromodela
zarzuela.es. From €5, under-14s free. There
is a free bus that goes from Paseo de Moret
next to the Intercambiador in Moncloa.

The **horseracing** track just out
of the city on the A Coruña
road holds races every Sunday
in the spring and autumn and
on Thursday evenings in July. If
you enjoy horseracing (bearing
in mind the usual ethical issues
involved), you'll find that the
unstuffy atmosphere and beautiful
setting can make this a fun day
out for all the family.

PLAZA DE ESPAÑA AND BEYOND

Palacio del Pardo

El Pardo

MAP p.102, POCKET MAP A4
C/Manuel Alonso Ⓦ www.patrimonio
nacional.es. Daily: April–Sept 10am–8pm;
Oct–March 10am–6pm. Closed for official
visits. Guided tours €9, 5–16 year-olds €4,
free Wed & Thurs 5–8pm (April–Sept),
3–6pm (Oct–March). Buses (#601) from
Moncloa (daily 6.30am–midnight; every
10–15min; 25min).

Nine kilometres northwest of
central Madrid lies Franco's
former principal residence at El
Pardo. A garrison still remains
at the town, where most of the
Generalíssimo's staff were based,
but the place is now a popular
excursion for *madrileños*, who
come here for long lunches at the
excellent terraza restaurants. The
tourist focus is the **Palacio del
Pardo**, rebuilt by the Bourbons
on the site of the hunting lodge
of Carlos I and still used by
visiting heads of state. Behind the
imposing but blandly symmetrical
facade, the interior houses the
chapel where Franco prayed,
and the theatre where he used
to censor films. On display are
a number of mementos of the

dictator, including his desk, a
portrait of Isabel la Católica
and an excellent collection of
tapestries. With its highly ornate
interior, the country house retreat
known as the Casita del Príncipe,
designed by Prado architect
Juan de Villanueva for Carlos IV
and his wife María Luisa de
Parma, is also open for visits by
appointment only (Ⓣ 913 761
500; €3).

Faro de Moncloa

MAP P.102, POCKET MAP B1
Avenida de los Reyes Católicos 6
Ⓜ Moncloa, take the Plaza de Moncloa exit
Ⓦ https://faro-de-moncloa.shop.secutix
.com. Tues–Sun 10am–8pm. €3, 7–14
year-olds €1.50, under-7s free.

Next to the Museo de América
is Faro de Moncloa, a futuristic
110-metre-high viewing tower
which has reopened after eleven
years. Originally built in 1992
by architect Salvador Pérez
Arroyo, when Madrid was named
European City of Culture, the
tower offers fantastic views over
the city, Casa de Campo and out
towards the mountains.

Shops

El Corte Inglés

MAP p.102, POCKET MAP B1

C/Princesa 41 & 56 Ⓜ Argüelles. Mon–Sat 10am–10pm, Sun 11am–9pm.

One of many branches of Spain's biggest and most popular department store. It stocks everything from souvenirs and gift items to clothes and electrical goods. Prices are on the high side, but quality is usually very good.

Ocho y Medio

MAP p.102, POCKET MAP C3

C/Martín de los Heros 11 Ⓜ Plaza de España. Mon–Sat 10am–2pm & 5–10pm, Sun 4–10pm.

Fascinating cinema bookshop with a pleasantly anarchic collection of books and film star-backed products, as well as a great terrace and small café. Perfect for a stop before watching one of the original-version films in the nearby cinemas.

Radio City

MAP p.102, POCKET MAP C2

C/Conde Duque 14 Ⓜ Plaza de España/ Ventura Rodríguez Ⓦ radiocitydiscos.com. Mon–Sat noon–8pm.

One for vinyl collectors, this cluttered old-style record shop has an excellent assortment of new and secondhand LPs from rock 'n' roll and jazz to indy and world music. Worth browsing even if you don't own a turntable. Be aware that the opening hours are not always reliable, though there are plenty of other interesting shops and bars on the same street.

Cafés

Café Moderno

MAP p.102, POCKET MAP D2

Plaza de las Comendadoras 1 Ⓜ Noviciado Ⓦ cafemodernomadrid.com. Daily 1pm–2.30am.

Relaxing café-bar serving good-value drinks, snacks and evening cocktails with a busy summer terraza, situated on one of the city's nicest squares. There are two other decent café-bars alongside if this one is too crowded.

Federal Café

MAP p.102, POCKET MAP D2

Plaza de las Comendadoras 9 Ⓜ Plaza España Ⓦ federalcafe.es. Mon–Thurs 9am–midnight, Fri & Sat 9am–1am, Sun 9am–5pm.

Relaxing and spacious café with large windows looking out onto a pleasant plaza. *Federal* serves up good coffee, breakfasts and snacks, although service can be a bit hit and miss. With its free wi-fi and large tables, it's just the place to catch up on your emails, do some work or read the paper.

Restaurants

Café del Oriente

MAP p.102, POCKET MAP B1

Avda. Juan de Herrera 2 Ⓜ Ciudad Universitaria ☏ 915 502 055. Café daily 9am–7pm, restaurant Fri 9pm–midnight, Sat 1.30–4.30pm & 9pm–1am.

Situated in the delightful pine-fringed grounds of the Museo del Traje, this Basque-influenced restaurant run by chef Delia Bautista serves two set menus at around €50, with offerings such as suckling pig or seabass.

Discounts for restaurants

The website El Tenedor (Ⓦ eltenedor.es) provides discounts of up to 40% on the food at many restaurants in Madrid. Just make your booking through the website and quote the reference when you arrive at the restaurant to make sure they apply any discounts.

Casa Mingo

Casa Mingo

MAP p.102, POCKET MAP A4
Paseo de la Florida 34 Ⓜ Príncipe Pío
☎ 915 477 918, Ⓦ casamingo.es. Daily
11am–midnight. Closed Aug.
Crowded and reasonably priced
Asturian chicken-and-cider
house. The spit-roast chicken is
practically compulsory, though
the chorizo cooked in cider and
cabrales (blue cheese) is also very
good. Around €15 a head.

Gabriel

MAP p.102, POCKET MAP C2
C/Conde Duque 10 Ⓜ Plaza España
☎ 915 428 019, Ⓦ restaurantegabriel.com.
Mon 10am–4pm, Tues–Sat 10am–2am.
Serving up an excellent home-
made lunchtime menu for around
€14 and some carefully selected à
la carte dishes in the evenings, this
is a deservedly popular restaurant
on one of the most pleasant
streets in this part of the city. The
croquetas de bacalao (cod) are
recommended, and to finish off
they do a mean mojito.

Da Nicola

MAP p.102, POCKET MAP D3
Plaza Mostenses 11 Ⓜ Plaza de España
☎ 915 422 574, Ⓦ danicola.es. Daily
1.30–4pm & 8.30pm–midnight.
Popular Italian restaurant with an
extensive range of pizzas, pastas
and meat dishes all at reasonable
prices; the gnocchi filled with
cheese and pesto are particularly
good. A good option for families.

Tres Bocas

MAP p.102, POCKET MAP B1
C/Gaztambide 11 Ⓜ Argüelles ☎ 917 525
564. Tues–Sun 1.30–4.15pm &
8.30pm–midnight.
Fusion-style food in this friendly
restaurant in the Argüelles area.
Starters include baby squid with
couscous, but the duck with
pak choi and rice is a house
favourite. There are some excellent
desserts such as white chocolate
cheesecake with coconut. Expect
to pay around €25–30 a head.

El Urogallo

MAP p.102, POCKET MAP A4
Lago de la Casa del Campo Ⓜ Lago
☎ 915 262 369, Ⓦ elurogallo.net. Tues–
Sun 8.30am–midnight.
On the shores of the artificial
lake in Casa de Campo, this
bar-restaurant has superb views
of the Palacio Real and cathedral –
perfect for a lazy lunch. Eating à la
carte is expensive but there's a €15
lunchtime menu.

La Vaca Argentina

MAP p.102, POCKET MAP A1
Paseo del Pintor Rosales 52 Ⓜ Argüelles
☎ 915 596 605, Ⓦ lavaca.es. Daily 1–5pm
& 9pm–midnight.

One of a chain of restaurants serving Argentine-style grilled steaks (*churrasco*). This branch has good views of the Parque del Oeste from its summer terrace, but service can be slow. Average cost is around €35.

Tapas bars

Bar Casa Paco

MAP p.102, POCKET MAP A1
C/Altamirano 38 Ⓜ Argüelles ☏ 915 432 821. Mon–Sat 9am–11.30pm.
Old-style bar close to Parque del Oeste that's been around since the mid-fifties and serves up some of the best *tortillas* in town, including tasty variations with prawns, goats' cheese, spinach, and steak.

Crumb

MAP p.102, POCKET MAP C2
C/Conde Duque 8 Ⓜ Plaza de España Ⓦ crumb.es. Tues–Sat 1.30–4pm & 8.30pm–midnight, Sun 1.30–4.30pm.
If you are fed up with production-line sandwich joints try this place which prides itself on its selection of home-made breads and fillings. The gourmet sandwiches include varieties like free-range chicken and guacamole, tuna with red onion and spinach and a sandwich of the day. They also offer a set lunch with soups, salads and home-made desserts.

Txirimiri

MAP p.102, POCKET MAP C7
C/Ferraz 38 Ⓦ txirimiri.es Ⓜ Argüelles/ Ventura Rodríguez. Daily noon–midnight.
Branch of an excellent small chain of tapas bars specialising in Basque-style *pintxos* and *raciones*. Apart from the house speciality Unai hamburger, the marvellous hot *pintxos* include steak, caramelised onion and pepper, cod in tempura and paté with fig marmalade. If you want something more substantial the risottos are a good bet.

Bars

El Jardín Secreto

MAP p.102, POCKET MAP C2
C/Conde Duque 2 Ⓜ Ventura Rodríguez or Plaza de España Ⓦ eljardinsecretomadrid .com. Mon, Tues & Wed 5.30pm–12.30am, Thurs 6.30pm–1.30am, Fri & Sat 6.30pm–2.30am, Sun 5.30pm–12.30am.
Cosy, dimly-lit bar on the corner of a tiny plaza close to Plaza de España serving reasonably priced drinks and cocktails. Service is friendly and the atmosphere unhurried.

Sambhad Cocktail

MAP p.102, POCKET MAP C3
C/Duque de Osuna 4 Ⓜ Plaza de España. Tues–Sun 5pm–2.30am.
Friendly, unpretentious cocktail bar with a little terrace perched on a small plaza above C/Princesa. The cocktail menu is extensive: over a dozen different types of mojito and twenty different gins. The prices are reasonable at around €7–8.

Club

Galileo Galilei

MAP p.102, POCKET MAP C1
C/Galileo 100 Ⓜ Islas Filipinas Ⓦ salagalileo galilei.com. Daily 9pm–4.30am. €6–25.
Bar, concert venue and disco rolled into one. Latin music is regularly on offer, along with cabaret and flamenco.

El Jardín Secreto

Day-trips

If you want to take a break from the frenetic activity of the city centre, there are some fascinating day-trips all within easy reach of the Spanish capital.

If you only have time for one day-trip, make it Toledo. The city preceded Madrid as the Spanish capital and is today a monument to the many cultures – Visigothic, Moorish, Jewish and Christian – which have shaped the destiny of Spain. Immortalized by El Greco, who lived and worked here for most of his later career, the city is packed with memorable sights. A close second is stunning Segovia, with its spectacular Roman aqueduct, fantasy castle and mountain backdrop. Third on the list is El Escorial, home to Felipe II's vast monastery-palace complex, a monument to out-monument all others, although the adjacent Valle de los Caídos, built under the orders of Franco, is even more megalomaniacal and far more chilling. And not forgetting Aranjuez, an oasis in the parched Castilian plain famed for its strawberries, lavish Baroque palace and gardens, and the plaza at nearby Chinchón, which provides a fabulous setting for a long, lazy lunch.

Segovia

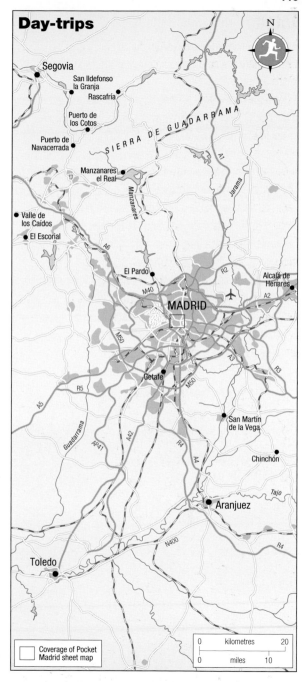

DAY-TRIPS

Toledo

El Alcázar and Museo del Ejército

C/Unión s/n Ⓦ www.museo.ejercito.es.
Thurs–Tues 10am–5pm. €5, under-18 &
EU pensioners free, free Sun.

If one building dominates Toledo, it's the imposing fortress of the **Alcázar.** Originally the site of a Roman palace, Emperor Charles V ordered the construction of the current fortress in the sixteenth century, though it has been burned and bombarded so often that little remains of the original building. The monument enjoyed iconic status during the Franco era after the Nationalist forces inside, under siege by the Republican town, were eventually relieved by an army heading for Madrid which took severe retribution on the local inhabitants. After a tortuous relocation and refurbishment programme, the Alcázar is now home to an impressive new army museum. Encompassing a new building constructed over the archeological remains of the original fortress, the museum provides two fascinating routes – one historic and one thematic – through which the role of the Spanish military is examined in exhaustive detail. Exhibits include everything from medieval swords and suits of armour to toy soldiers and Civil War uniforms.

Hospital y Museo de Santa Cruz

C/Cervantes 3. Mon–Sat 10am–7pm,
Sun 10am–2.30pm. €5, free for
under-18s & EU pensioners, free after
6pm Tues–Sat.

A superlative Renaissance building with a magnificent

Toledo

Visiting Toledo

There are **buses** to Toledo from the bus station in Plaza Elíptica (Ⓜ Plaza Elíptica) in Madrid every thirty minutes, taking about 1hr. The city's bus station is in the modern part of the city; bus #5 runs from it to central Plaza de Zocódover. A high-speed train service from Atocha takes just 30min; it's around €20 for a day return ticket, but purchase this in advance on Ⓦ renfe.com. Toledo's train station is a 20min walk or a bus ride (#5 or #6) from the heart of town. The main **tourist office** (daily 10am–6pm; ☎ 925 254 030, Ⓦ www.toledo-turismo.com) is opposite the cathedral in the Plaza del Consistorio. There's another office (Mon–Fri 8am–6pm, Sat 10am–6pm & Sun 10am–3pm) at the top of the escalators leading into the city from the Glorieta de La Reconquista, and one outside the city walls opposite the Puerta Nueva de Bisagra (Mon–Sat 10am–6pm, Sun 10am–2pm). You can save on the entry fees to some of the sights if you invest in the €9 *pulsera turística* which is available at many of the key sights (Ⓦ toledomonumental.com) or the Toledo Card (€23–73; Ⓦ toledocard.com).

Plateresque main doorway, this refurbished museum houses some of the greatest El Grecos in Toledo, including *The Immaculate Conception* and *The Holy Family*. As well as outstanding works by Luca Giordano and Ribera, there's an impressive collection of exhibits dating from prehistory through to the twentieth century, including archeological finds, ceramics and sculpture.

La Catedral

C/Cardenal Cisneros Ⓦ catedralprimada.es. Mon–Sat 10am–6pm, Sun 2–6pm. Coro closed Sun mornings. €10–12.50, free Sun evenings for Spanish citizens.

Toledo's stunning cathedral reflects the importance of the city that for so long outshone its neighbour, Madrid. A robust Gothic construction, which took over 250 years (1227–1493) to complete, it's richly decorated in Gothic, Renaissance and Baroque styles. The cavernous interior is home to some magnificent stained glass, an outstanding **Coro** (Choir), a wonderful **Gothic Capilla Mayor** (Main Chapel) and an extravagant high altar. The cathedral **museums** are worth a look for their impressive collections including paintings by El Greco, Goya and Velázquez, as well as one of El Greco's few surviving pieces of sculpture.

Santo Tomé and the Burial of the Count of Orgaz

Plaza del Conde Ⓦ www.santotome.org. Daily: mid-March–mid-Oct 10am–6.45pm; mid-Oct to mid-March 10am–5.45pm. €2.50.

Housed alone, in a small annexe of the church of Santo Tomé, one of the most celebrated attractions of Toledo is El Greco's masterpiece, *The Burial of the Count of Orgaz*. The painting depicts the count's funeral, at which St Stephen and St Augustine appeared in order to lower him into the tomb. Combining El Greco's genius for the mystic with his great powers as a portrait painter and master of colour, the work includes a depiction of the artist himself – he can be spotted seventh from the left, looking out at the viewer with his son in the foreground.

There are plenty of bars and restaurants scattered around the old town, although inevitably most of the options are pretty touristy. For a budget option try *Casa Ludeña* at Plaza Magdalena 13, close to the Alcázar, while *Casa Aurelio* at C/Sinagoga 1 & 6, near the cathedral, offers regional specialities at reasonable prices. For a more sophisticated option try *Los Cuatro Tiempos* at C/Sixto Ramón Parro 5.

Museo del Greco

C/Samuel Levi Ⓦ mecd.gob.es/mgreco. March–Oct Tues–Sat 9.30am–7.30pm, Sun 10am–3pm; Nov–Feb Tues–Sat 9.30am–6pm, Sun 10am–3pm. €3, €5 entry with Museo Sefardi, free Sat after 2pm & Sun.

This museum in the former Jewish quarter close to Santo Tomé is devoted to the life and work of the ground-breaking sixteenth-century artist so closely associated with Toledo. A refurbished exhibition space houses his famous **View and Map of Toledo**, a series of the Twelve Apostles, completed later than the set in the cathedral, and other outstanding works.

Museo de Victorio Macho

Plaza de Victorio Macho Ⓦ realfundaciontoledo.es. Mon–Sat 10am–7pm, Sun 10am–3pm. €3.

Splendidly situated on a spur overlooking the Tajo, this museum contains the sculptures, paintings and sketches of Spanish artist Victorio Macho (1887–1966). The museum is set in a delightfully tranquil garden with the auditorium on the ground floor showing a documentary film (available in English) about the city and its history.

Museo Sefardí/Sinagoga del Tránsito

C/Samuel Levi Ⓦ museosefardi.mcu.es. Tues–Sat 9.30am–6pm (summer until 7.30pm), Sun 10am–3pm. €3, €5 with entry to Museo del Greco, free Sat after 2pm & Sun.

Built along Moorish lines by Samuel Levi in 1366, the Sinagoga del Tránsito became a church after the fifteenth-century expulsion of the Jews and was restored to its original form only in the last century. The interior is a simple galleried hall, brilliantly decorated with polychromed stuccowork and superb filigree windows, while Hebrew inscriptions praising God, King Pedro and Samuel Levi adorn the walls. It also houses a small but engaging Sephardic Museum (same hours) tracing the distinct traditions and development of Jewish culture in Spain.

Sinagoga Santa María la Blanca

C/Reyes Católicos 4. Daily: March–mid-Oct 10am–6.45pm; mid-Oct–Feb 10am–5.45pm. €2.80, free under-10s.

The second of Toledo's two surviving synagogues, the tranquil Santa María la Blanca pre-dates the Sinagoga del Tránsito by over a century. Despite having been both a church and synagogue, the horseshoe arches and the fact that it was built by Mudéjar craftsmen give it the look of a mosque. The arches are decorated with elaborate plaster designs of pine cones and palm trees, while its Baroque *retablo* (altarpiece) dates from the time it was a church. The whole effect is stunning, all set off against a deep-red floor that contains some of the original decorative tiles.

Monasterio de San Juan de los Reyes

C/San Juan de los Reyes 2. Daily: March–mid-Oct 10am–6.45pm; mid-Oct–Feb 10am–5.45pm; €2.80, free under-10s.

The exterior of this beautiful church is bizarrely festooned with the chains worn by Christian prisoners from Granada, who were released on the reconquest of the city in 1492. It was originally a **Franciscan convent** founded by the Reyes Católicos (Catholic Monarchs) Fernando and Isabel – who completed the Christian reconquest of Spain – and in which, until the fall of Granada, they had planned to be buried. Its double-storeyed cloister is outstanding, with an elaborate Mudéjar ceiling in the upper floor.

Convento de Santo Domingo Antiguo

Plaza Santo Domingo Antiguo. Summer: Mon–Sat 11am–1.30pm & 4–7pm, Sun 4–7pm. €2.

The Convento de Santo Domingo Antiguo's chief claim to fame is as the resting place of El Greco, whose remains lie in the crypt that can be glimpsed through a peephole in the floor. The convent's religious treasures are displayed in the old choir, but more interesting is the high altarpiece of the church – El Greco's first major commission in Toledo. Unfortunately, most of the canvases have gone to museums and are here replaced by copies.

Mezquita del Cristo de la Luz

Cuesta de los Carmelitas Descalzos 10. Daily: March–mid-Oct 10am–6.45pm; mid-Oct–Feb 10am–5.45pm. €2.80.

Although this is one of the oldest Moorish monuments in Spain (the mosque was built by Musa Ibn Ali in the tenth century on the foundations of a Visigothic church), only the nave, with its nine different cupolas, is the original Arab construction. The apse was added when the building was converted into a church, and is claimed to be the first product of the Mudéjar style. The mosque itself, set in a tiny patio-like park and open on all sides to the elements, is so small that it seems more like a miniature summer pavilion, but it has an elegant simplicity of design that few of the town's great monuments can match.

La Catedral, Toledo

Segovia

The Aqueduct

Plaza del Azoguejo.

Over 700m long and almost 30m high, Segovia's aqueduct is an impressive sight. Built without a drop of mortar or cement, it has been here since around the end of the first century AD – no one knows exactly when – though it no longer carries water to the city. For an excellent view of both the aqueduct and the city, climb the stairs beside it up to a surviving fragment of the city walls.

La Catedral

Plaza Mayor. Daily: April–Oct Mon–Sat 9am–9.30pm; Nov–March Mon–Sat 9.30am–6pm, Sun 1–6pm. €3, under-10s free. Open for mass Sun morning; free. Museum same hours.

Segovia's cathedral was the last major Gothic building constructed in Spain. Pinnacles and flying buttresses are tacked on at every conceivable point, although the interior is surprisingly bare and its space is cramped by a great green marble choir in the very centre. The cathedral's treasures are almost all confined to the museum.

The Alcázar

Plaza Reina Victoria Eugenia ⓦ www .alcazardesegovia.com. Daily: April–Sept 10am–7pm; Oct–March 10am–6pm. €5.50, free for EU citizens Tues 2–4pm.

At the edge of town and overlooking the valley of the Eresma river is the Alcázar, an extraordinary fantasy of a castle with its narrow towers and flurry of turrets. Although it dates from the fourteenth and fifteenth centuries, it was almost completely destroyed by a fire in 1862 and rebuilt as a deliberately exaggerated version of the original. Inside, the rooms are decked out with armour, weapons and tapestries, but the major attractions are the splendid wooden sculptured ceilings and the magnificent panoramas.

Vera Cruz

Carretera Zamarramala. Tues 4–6pm, Wed–Sun 10.30am–1.30pm & 4–6pm. Closed Nov. €2, free Tues pm.

This remarkable twelve-sided church stands in the valley facing the Alcázar. Built by the Knights Templar in the early thirteenth century on the pattern of the Church of the Holy Sepulchre in Jerusalem, it once housed part of the supposed True Cross (hence its name). Today, you can climb the

Visiting Segovia

Segovia is an easy day-trip from Madrid, with up to ten high-speed trains daily (28min; €25 return) from Atocha and Chamartín stations, plus **buses** operated by La Sepulvedana leaving from Moncloa bus station (Metro Príncipe Pío; every 30min; 1hr 15min). The high-speed train station is out of town – take bus #11 (every 15min) to the aqueduct. There's a local **tourist office** in the Plaza Mayor at no. 10 (Mon–Sat 10am–2pm & 4–7/8pm, Sun 9.30am–5pm; ⓦ turismocastillayleon.com). A visitor reception centre is situated in the Plaza del Azoguejo (daily 10am–6.30pm; ⓦ turismodesegovia. com) by the aqueduct and an information point at the high-speed train station (Mon–Fri 8.15am–3.15pm, Sat & Sun 10am–1.30pm & 4–6.30pm). A regular bus service from Segovia to La Granja is operated by La Sepulvedana, leaving from the station at Paseo Ezequiel González 12.

The Aqueduct, Segovia

tower for a highly photogenic view of the city, while nearby is a very pleasant riverside walk along the banks of the tranquil Eresma river.

Convento de San Antonio el Real

C/San Antonio el Real ⓦ sanantonioelreal .es. Tues 4–6pm, Wed–Sat 10am–2pm & 4–6.30pm, Sun 10.45am–2pm. €2.

If you follow the line of the aqueduct away from the old city for about ten minutes, you will come to a little gem of a palace originally founded by Enrique IV in 1455 and containing an intriguing collection of Mudéjar and Hispano-Flemish art. The convent, part of which now serves as a luxury hotel, has some of the most beautiful **artesonado** (wooden sculptured) ceilings in the city and there's a wonderfully detailed fifteenth-century wooden Calvary in the main church.

La Granja

ⓦ patrimonionacional.es. Palace open daily: April–Sept 10am–8pm; Oct–March 10am–6pm. €9, under-16s and EU pensioners €4, free Wed & Thurs: April–Sept 5–8pm; Oct–March 3–6pm. Gardens daily: 10am–dusk.

The summer palace of La Granja was built by the first Bourbon king of Spain, Felipe V, no doubt in another attempt to alleviate his homesickness for Versailles. Its chief appeal lies in its mountain setting and extravagant wooded grounds and gardens, but it's also worth casting an eye over the plush furnishings and fabulous tapestries of the palace which, though damaged by a fire in 1918, has been successfully restored.

Outside, the highlight of the eighteenth-century gardens is a series of majestic fountains. They're a fantastic spectacle, with some of the jets rising forty metres, but they usually only operate between Easter and July – at 1pm on Sundays and 5.30pm on Wednesdays and Saturdays – with special displays on May 30, July 25 and August 25 (€4).

Segovia is renowned for its delicious Castilian roasts; some of the best places to sample the local specialities are the *Mesón José María* at C/Cronista Lecea 11, just off the Plaza Mayor, *Mesón de Cándido* below the aqueduct at Plaza del Azoguejo 5 and *Casa Duque* at nearby C/Cervantes 12.

El Escorial and Valle de los Caídos

El Escorial

Ⓦ patrimonionacional.es. Tues–Sun: April–Sept 10am–8pm; Oct–March 10am–6pm. €10, under-16s and EU pensioners €4; free Wed & Thurs: April–Sept 5–8pm; Oct–March 3–6pm.

El Escorial was the largest Spanish building of the Renaissance, built to celebrate a victory over the French in 1557 and divided into different sections for secular and religious use. Linking the two zones is the Biblioteca (Library), a splendid hall with vivid, multicoloured frescoes by Tibaldi, and containing some gorgeously executed Arabic manuscripts.

The enormous, cold, dark interior of the Basílica contains over forty altars, designed to allow simultaneous Masses to be held. Behind the main altar lies some of Felipe II's mammoth collection of saintly relics, including six whole bodies, over sixty heads and hundreds of bone fragments set in fabulously expensive caskets.

Many of the monastery's religious treasures are contained in the Sacristía and Salas Capitulares and include paintings by Titian, Velázquez and José Ribera. Below these rooms is the Panteón Real, where past Spanish monarchs lie in their gilded marble tombs. The royal children are laid in the Panteón de los Infantes and there's also a babies' tomb with room for sixty infants.

What remains of El Escorial's art collection – works by Bosch, Dürer, Titian, Zurbarán, among others that escaped transfer to the Prado – is kept in the elegant Museos Nuevos. Don't miss the Sala de Batallas, a long gallery lined with an epic series of paintings depicting important

El Escorial

imperial battles. Finally, there are the treasure-crammed Salones Reales (Royal Apartments), containing the austere quarters of Felipe II, with the chair that supported his gouty leg and the deathbed from which he was able to contemplate the high altar of the Basílica.

La Silla de Felipe

Around 3km out of town is the Silla de Felipe – "Felipe's Seat" – a chair carved into a rocky outcrop with a great view of the palace, and from where the king is supposed to have watched the building's construction. You can reach it on foot by following the path which starts by the arches beyond the main entrance to the Biblioteca; keep to the left as you go down the hill and then cross the main road and follow the signs. If you have a car, take the M-505 Ávila road and turn off at the sign after about 3km.

Valle de los Caídos

Tues–Sun: April–Sept 10am–7pm; Oct–March 10am–6pm. €9, under-16s and EU pensioners €4; free Wed & Thurs 4–7pm (3–6pm Oct–March) for EU citizens.

Almost at first glance, this basilica complex, constructed by Franco after his Civil War victory, belies its claim to be a memorial to the dead of both sides. The grim, pompous architectural forms employed, the constant inscriptions "Fallen for God and for Spain" and the proximity to El Escorial clue you in to its true function – the glorification of General Franco and his regime. The dictator himself lies buried behind the high altar, while the only other named tomb is that of his guru, the Falangist leader, José Antonio Primo de Rivera. The "other side" is present only in the fact that the whole thing was built by the Republican army's survivors.

Above the basilica is a vast 150m-high cross, reputedly the largest in the world and visible for miles around. The socialist government of José Luis Rodríguez Zapatero tried to depoliticize the site, and it was mooted that Franco's remains might be removed from the basilica, but this was rejected when the right-of-centre Popular Party returned to power in the 2011 general election.

> Good restaurants in El Escorial include *La Fonda Genara* at Plaza de San Lorenzo 2 (Mon–Sat 1–4pm & 9–11pm, Sun 1–4pm; ☎ 918 901 636), a relaxed place filled with theatrical mementos and offering a wide range of delicious Castilian cuisine. Set menus available for around €16, otherwise around €30 per person.

Visiting El Escorial

There are around 25 **trains** a day to El Escorial from Madrid (5.45am–11.30pm from Atocha, calling at Chamartín), or **buses** (#661 and #664 from the intercambiador at Moncloa) run every fifteen minutes on weekdays and hourly at weekends. To visit the Valle de los Caídos from El Escorial, take a local bus run by Herranz (#660), which starts from the bus station at C/Juan de Toledo 3, just north of the visitors' entrance to the monastery. It departs at 3.15pm and returns at 5.30pm, giving you more than enough time to look around the complex.

Aranjuez and Chinchón

The Palacio Real

ⓦ patrimonionacional.es. Tues–Sun: April–Sept 10am–8pm; Oct–March 10am–6pm. €9, under-16s and EU pensioners €4; free for EU citizens Wed & Thurs: April–Sept 5–8pm; Oct–March 3–6pm.

The centrepiece of Aranjuez is the Palacio Real and its gardens. The present building dates from the 1700s and was an attempt by Spain's Bourbon monarchs to create a Spanish Versailles. The palace is noted for its exotic decor highlighted in the fabulously elaborate Porcelain and Smoking rooms.

Jardín de la Isla and Jardín del Príncipe

Daily: 8am–dusk. Free.

Two palace gardens worthy of a visit are the Jardín de la Isla with its fountains and neatly tended gardens, and the more attractive Jardín del Príncipe, which inspired Rodrigo's famous *Concierto de*

The Smoking Room at Palacio Real, Aranjuez

El Rana Verde close to the palace and on the banks of the river at Plaza Santiago Rusiñol is probably Aranjuez's best-known restaurant and serves a selection of set menus from €17.

Aranjuez, offering shaded walks along the river and plenty of spots for a siesta.

Casa del Labrador

Jardín del Príncipe. Daily: April–Sept 10am–8pm; Oct–March 10am–6pm; €5.

At the far end of the Jardín del Príncipe is the Casa del Labrador (Peasant's House), which is anything but what its name implies. The house contains more silk, marble, crystal and gold than would seem possible to cram into so small a place, as well as a huge collection of fancy clocks. Although the hotchpotch of styles will offend purists, this miniature palace still provides a fascinating insight into the tastes of the Bourbon dynasty.

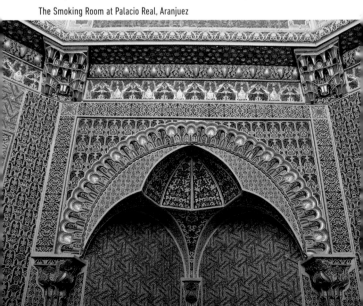

Visiting Aranjuez and Chinchón

From the end of April to July and September to mid-October, a weekend service on an old wooden steam train, the **Tren de la Fresa**, runs between Madrid and Aranjuez. It leaves the Museo del Ferrocarril around 10am and departs from Aranjuez at 7pm (information ☎ 902 228 822). The €26-30 fare (under-12s €14–15) includes a guided bus tour in Aranjuez, entry to the monuments and *fresas con nata* (strawberries and cream) on the train. Standard trains leave every 15–30min from Atocha, with the last train returning from Aranjuez at about 11.30pm. **Buses** run every half-hour during the week and every hour at weekends from Estación Sur. You'll find a helpful **tourist office** in the Casa de Infantes (daily 10am–6pm; ☎ 918 910 427, ⓦ aranjuez.es & ⓦ aranjuez.com).There are hourly buses (#337) from Madrid **to Chinchón** from the bus station at Avda Mediterráneo 49 near the Plaza Conde Casal, or you can reach the town from Aranjuez on the service from Avenida de las Infantas (Mon–Fri hourly, Sat & Sun 8 daily; #430). There's a small **tourist office** in the Plaza Mayor (July–Sept Mon–Fri 10am–3pm & 5–8pm, Sat & Sun 10am–3pm; Oct–June daily 10am–7pm ☎ 918 935 323, ⓦ ciudad-chinchon.com).

Casa de los Marinos (Falúas Reales)

Daily: April–Sept 10am–8pm; Oct–March 10am–6pm. Included with entrance to Palacio Real. April–Sept 5–8pm; Oct–March 3–5pm.

The small Casa de los Marinos museum contains the brightly coloured launches in which royalty would take to the river – try the modern equivalent with a 45-minute boat trip through the royal parks from the jetty by the bridge next to the palace (Sat & Sun 12.30 & 5.30pm; ⓦ elcuriosity.com; €6–15).

Plaza de Toros

Guided tours: Mon 11.15am, 12.15pm, 1.15pm, Sat & Sun 11.15am, 12.15pm, 1.15pm, 4.15pm; €5.

Aranjuez's beautiful eighteenth-century Plaza de Toros houses an exhibition space, part of which is made up of a **bullfighting museum**, while the rest traces the town's history and royal heritage. Nearby, on C/Naranja and C/Rosa, there are a number of *corrales*, traditional-style wooden-balconied tenement blocks.

Chinchón

A stroll around the elegant little town of Chinchón, followed by lunch at one of its restaurants, is a popular pastime for *madrileños*. Noteworthy monuments include a fifteenth-century castle (not open to visitors), a picture-postcard medieval Plaza Mayor and the Iglesia de la Asunción, with a panel by Goya of *The Assumption of the Virgin*, but it is as the home of *anís* that the town is best known. To sample the local aniseed spirit, try one of the local bars or the Alcoholera de Chinchón, a shop on the Plaza Mayor – most visitors come for a tasting before eating at one of the town's traditional *mesones* (see box below).

For a classic Castilian lunch in Chinchón, try the *Mesón el Comendador, La Casa del Pregonero* or *La Balconada* overlooking the main plaza or the nearby *Mesón Cuevas del Vino*.

ACCOMMODATION

Stained-glass dome, Hotel Palace

Accommodation

Madrid has a plentiful supply of accommodation and most of it is very central. With increasing competition in the sector, many hotels have been busy upgrading facilities in recent years and there is now a much wider range of stylish, medium-priced hotels, including a number of design-conscious boutique hotels. The city has a sprinkling of exclusive top-range hotels too, while if you're after a budget place to stay, go for one of the hostales – small, frequently family-run establishments housed in large, centrally located apartment blocks.

The main factor to consider in choosing a place is location. To be at the heart of the old town, choose the areas around Puerta del Sol, Plaza de Santa Ana or Plaza Mayor; for nightlife, Malasaña or Chueca will appeal; if you are looking for a quieter location and a bit more luxury, consider the Paseo del Prado, Recoletos or Salamanca areas; and if you are with children the areas by the main parks are good options. Another thing to bear in mind is noise. Madrid is a high-decibel city so avoid rooms on lower floors or choose a place away from the action. As for facilities, air conditioning is usual and a welcome extra in summer.

Prices given in our reviews are for the average cost of a double room.

Madrid de los Austrias

HOSTAL LA MACARENA MAP P.28, POCKET MAP B13. C/Cava de San Miguel 8, 2° Ⓜ Sol ☎ 913 659 221, Ⓦ www .silserranos.com. Family-run *hostal* in a back street just beside Plaza Mayor. The neat, well-kept rooms are on the small side, but all have bathroom, satellite TV and a/c. It can be a little noisy, but the location is perfect. **Doubles from €79.**

HOSTAL MADRID MAP p.28, POCKET MAP D12. C/Esparteros 6 Ⓜ Sol ☎ 915 220 060, Ⓦ hostal-madrid.info. In a fantastic setting between Sol and Plaza Mayor, this no frills *hostal* is renowned for its clean, en-suite, a/c rooms and friendly service. Rooms are small and can be a little noisy, but this is more than compensated for by the location. **Doubles from €50.**

HOTEL MAYERLING MAP p.28, POCKET MAP D13. C/Conde de Romanones 6 Ⓜ Tirso de Molina ☎ 914 201 580, Ⓦ mayerlinghotel.com. This stylish, designer hotel is housed in a former textile warehouse close to C/Atocha. Clean lines and black and white decor predominate in the simple, neat rooms. There's free internet and wi-fi as well as a sun terrace. **Doubles from €90.**

HOTEL THE HAT MAP p.28, POCKET MAP C13. C/Imperial 9 Ⓜ La Latina ☎ 917 728 572, Ⓦ thehatmadrid.com. Modern, centrally located hostel with hotel-like services and a wonderful roof-top bar. A range of accommodation available from dormitories and family rooms to female-only, doubles and suites. All the pine-furnished rooms are bright

Booking accommodation

Madrid's increasing popularity as a weekend-break destination means that it's best to book accommodation in advance if possible. Nearly all hotels will have website reservation facilities but for smaller places you may have to email or phone; nearly all will understand English.

Hotels in the more expensive categories run special weekend offers, so it's always worth checking their websites for details. Good deals and the lowest prices are usually available in the summer months, but it is best to avoid Spanish national holidays, when prices peak.

If you do arrive without a reservation, the tourist information service at the airport, train and bus stations can usually help (branches and contact details are under Tourist Information in the Directory section; see p.143).

and airy, some have private bathrooms. There is a good buffet breakfast and free wi-fi. **Dormitory beds from €25, double from €75.**

PETIT PALACE POSADA DEL PEINE MAP p.28, POCKET MAP C12. C/Postas 17 Ⓜ Sol ☎ 915 238 151, Ⓦ petitpalace posadadelpeine.com. This upmarket branch of the *Petit Palace* hotel chain is situated in a refurbished building right next to the Plaza Mayor and was once the site of a seventeenth-century inn. Sleek rooms with minimalist decor and stylish fittings. Family rooms also available. Buffet and free use of bicycles to tour the city centre. **Doubles from €95.**

POSADA DEL DRAGÓN MAP p.28, POCKET MAP B14. C/Cava Baja 14 Ⓜ La Latina ☎ 911 191 424, Ⓦ posadadeldragon.com. Slap back in the middle of one of the best streets for tapas in Madrid, this historic inn has been refurbished and turned into a boutique hotel. Compact, brightly-coloured rooms with comfortable beds, a/c and flat-screen TVs. Very popular bar-restaurant downstairs, serving up tasty *raciones*. **Doubles from €100.**

POSADA DEL LEÓN DE ORO MAP p.28, POCKET MAP B14. C/Cava Baja 12 Ⓜ La Latina ☎ 911 191 494, Ⓦ posadadelleondeoro.com. This former inn has been converted into a chic, designer hotel with large, individually decorated rooms complete with walk-in showers, flat-screen TVs and free wi-fi.

Three-night minimum stay at some times of year. Good breakfasts and a very popular bar-restaurant. **Doubles from €100.**

Ópera

LOS AMIGOS HOSTEL MAP p.38, POCKET MAP B11. C/Arenal 26, 4° Ⓜ Ópera ☎ 915 592 472, Ⓦ losamigoshostel.com. Great backpacking option just a few minutes from Sol. Dormitories (€20 per bed) cater for four to six people, and there are a couple of communal rooms, plus free wi-fi. The staff speak English, and bed linen and use of kitchen are included. **Doubles with bathroom from €50.**

HOSTAL CENTRAL PALACE MAP p.38, POCKET MAP A11. Plaza de Oriente 2, 3° Ⓜ Ópera ☎ 915 482 018, Ⓦ centralpalacemadrid.com. Refurbished and very friendly *hostal* with a fabulous location on the plaza. All of the airy rooms are en-suite with good facilities, a/c and flat-screen TVs, and some have views over the plaza towards the Palacio Real. Price includes breakfast. **Doubles from €90.**

HOSTAL DON ALFONSO MAP p.38, POCKET MAP C11. Plaza Celenque 1, 2° Ⓜ Sol ☎ 915 319 840, Ⓦ hostaldonalfonso.es. Just off the pedestrianized shopping street C/Arenal and a stone's throw from Sol, this clean, recently refurbished *hostal* has fourteen doubles, two triples and some singles, all with bathrooms, a/c, free wi-fi and TV. **Doubles from €50.**

HOSTAL GALA MAP p.38, POCKET MAP B10. C/Costanilla de los Ángeles 15 Ⓜ Callao ☏ 915 419 692, Ⓦ hostalgala .com. An upmarket, very tasteful *hostal* close to the shopping areas of C/Preciados and Gran Vía. All rooms have a/c, power showers and free wi-fi. Some have small balconies and there are family rooms available. **Doubles from €70.**

HOSTAL ORIENTE MAP p.38, POCKET MAP B11. C/Arenal 23 Ⓜ Ópera ☏ 915 480 314, Ⓦ hostaloriente.es. Well-appointed *hostal* close to the Opera house. The nineteen classically decorated rooms are comfortable and have recently refitted bathrooms. **Doubles from €45.**

HOTEL MENINAS MAP p.38, POCKET MAP B10. C/Campomanes 7 Ⓜ Ópera ☏ 915 412 805, Ⓦ hotelmeninas.es. A stylish 37-room hotel in a quiet street near the Teatro Real. Professional staff, fantastic attic rooms and flat-screen TVs. Guests can use the gym and sauna at the nearby *Hotel Ópera* (see below). Breakfast included for web reservations. Prices vary according to availability but usually **doubles from €85.**

HOTEL ÓPERA MAP p.38, POCKET MAP B10. C/Cuesta de Santo Domingo 2 Ⓜ Ópera ☏ 915 412 800, Ⓦ hotelopera .com. In a pleasant location near the Plaza de Oriente, this slick hotel has smallish, but smart rooms (some with terraces) at reasonable rates. In keeping with the name, at weekends the waiters in the restaurant entertain diners with arias from operas and *zarzuelas*. **Doubles from €85.**

HOTEL PALACIO DE SAN MARTÍN MAP p.38, POCKET MAP C10. Plaza de San Martín 5 Ⓜ Ópera ☏ 917 015 000, Ⓦ hotelpalaciosanmartin.es. Situated in an attractive square by the Descalzas Reales monastery, this elegant, old-school hotel offers spacious rooms, a small gym and sauna, plus a fine rooftop restaurant. **Doubles from €90.**

PETIT PALACE ÓPERA MAP p.38, POCKET MAP C11. C/Arenal 16 Ⓜ Sol ☏ 915 644 355, Ⓦ petitipalaceopera.com. A member of a popular hotel chain with 64 sleek, snug, modern rooms. All have a/c and there are special family and multi-bed rooms too, though the location can be a little noisy. Another member of the chain, the *Puerta del Sol*, is close by at C/Arenal 4. **Doubles from €75.**

ROOM MATE MARIO MAP p.38, POCKET MAP B10. C/Campomanes 4 Ⓜ Ópera ☏ 915 488 548, Ⓦ room-matehotels.com /mario. Hip designer hotel close to the Teatro Real. Staff are friendly and the ultra-cool rooms, though compact, are well equipped with neat bathrooms, flat-screen TVs and DVD. Buffet breakfast included in price. There is a similarly trendy member of the chain, the *Laura*, at Travesía de Trujillos 3 (☏ 917 011 670) in the plaza by the Descalzas monastery. **Doubles from €90.**

Rastro, Lavapíes and Embajadores

CAT'S HOSTEL MAP p.46, POCKET MAP E14. C/Canizares 6 Ⓜ Antón Martín ☏ 913 692 807, Ⓦ catshostel.com. Certainly not your run-of-the-mill hostel, *Cat's* has an Andalusian patio and subterranean bar, though be aware that it markets itself as a 'party hostel'. Doubles are available on request, otherwise accommodation is in clean, a/c four- to twelve-bed dorms. Price includes breakfast. **Dorm bed from €14.**

HOSTAL BARRERA MAP p.46, POCKET MAP G7. C/Atocha 96, 2° Ⓜ Antón Martín ☏ 915 275 381, Ⓦ hostalbarrera.com. Upmarket fourteen-room *hostal* a short distance from Atocha station and with an English-speaking owner. The smart a/c rooms are a cut above most found in this category and the bathrooms are modern. One of the best in this part of town. **Doubles from €70.**

HOTEL ARTRIP MAP p.46, POCKET MAP F9. C/Valencia 11 Ⓜ Lavapiés ☏ 915 393 282, Ⓦ artriphotel.com. This self-styled "Art Hotel" is conveniently located close to the Reina Sofia and other art galleries. It has seventeen sleek, design-conscious rooms, including family options, that combine the modern with the traditional. Buffet breakfast included in website bookings. **Doubles from €95.**

TRYP ATOCHA MAP p.46, POCKET MAP G14. C/Atocha 83 Ⓜ Antón Martín ☏ 913 300 500, Ⓦ melia.com. This large, business-style hotel, which is not far from Huertas, has modern rooms with all the facilities you'd expect, though some are a little small. Family rooms with bunks for children start at €160. **Doubles from €85.**

Sol, Santa Ana and Huertas

CATALONIA PLAZA MAYOR MAP p.52, POCKET MAP E13. C/Atocha 35 Ⓜ Antón Martín ☎ 913 694 409, Ⓦ hoteles-catalonia.com. Close to Plaza Santa Ana and the Huertas area, this modern business-style hotel has spacious, functional rooms with slick modern decor and comfortable beds. There's a small fitness area and jacuzzi as well as free wi-fi. **Doubles from €90.**

HOSTAL ALASKA MAP p.52, POCKET MAP E12. C/Espoz y Mina 7, 4° dcha Ⓜ Sol ☎ 915 211 845, Ⓦ hostalalaska.es. Doubles, triples and a single in this modest, but friendly *hostal*. All seven of the basic, brightly decorated rooms have bathrooms, a/c and TV. There's an apartment available on the fifth floor with a bedroom, sofa-bed and kitchen (from €150 for six). **Doubles from €50.**

HOSTAL ARMESTO MAP p.52, POCKET MAP G13. C/San Agustín 6, 1° dcha Ⓜ Antón Martín ☎ 914 299 031, Ⓦ hostalarmesto .com. Charming *hostal* in the centre of the city, with some nicely decorated rooms, all with small bathrooms, a/c and TV. The best ones overlook the delightful little garden in the Casa de Lope de Vega next door. Very well positioned for the Huertas/Santa Ana area. **Doubles from €42.**

HOSTAL PERSAL MAP p.52, POCKET MAP E13. Plaza del Angel 12 Ⓜ Sol ☎ 913 694 643, Ⓦ hostalpersal.com. Eighty-room *hostal* that's closer to a hotel in terms of services and facilities. The simple, clean rooms all have a/c, bathrooms, TV and free wi-fi. Triples and quadruples available from €85 and €105 respectively. **Doubles from €70.**

HOSTAL RIESCO MAP p.52, POCKET MAP D12. C/Correo 2, 3° Ⓜ Sol ☎ 915 222 692, Ⓦ hostalriesco.es. Neat and simple rooms in this old-school, friendly family-run *hostal* located in a street just off Sol. All rooms (some of which are triples) are en suite and have a/c. **Doubles from €65.**

Our picks

Friendly – *Hostal Gonzalo* see p.130
Good value – *Hostal Gala* see opposite
Boutique – *Room Mate Mario* see opposite
Designer chic – *Hotel Urban* see below
Location – *Hostal Central Palace* see p.127
Exclusive – *Hotel Orfila* see p.132
Family – *Hotel T3 Tirol* see p.133

HOTEL SANTA ANA COLORS MAP p.52, POCKET MAP F13. C/Huertas 14, 2° izda Ⓜ Antón Martín ☎ 914 296 935, Ⓦ santaanacolors.com. Smart *hostal* in the heart of Huertas with simple but modern en-suite rooms, all complete with a/c and plasma TVs. There is a self-service breakfast and a common room where you can read the paper. **Doubles from €50.**

HOTEL URBAN MAP p.52, POCKET MAP G12. C/San Jerónimo 34 Ⓜ Sevilla ☎ 917 877 770, Ⓦ hotelurban.com. Über cool, fashion-conscious, five-star hotel in the heart of town. The designer rooms come with all mod cons, a rooftop pool, a summer terrace and two "pijo" cocktail bars. It even has its own small museum consisting of items from owner Jordi Clos's collection of Egyptian and Chinese art. Look out for special deals on the website. **Doubles from €218.**

HOTEL VINCCI SOHO MAP p.52, POCKET MAP G13. C/Prado 18 Ⓜ Antón Martín ☎ 911 414 100, Ⓦ vinccisoho.com. A great location in the heart of Huertas for this new, four-star 170-room hotel. Smart wooden decor and furnishings and modern facilities, though bathrooms are rather small. Worth it only if you can get one of the cheaper offers on the website. **Doubles from €120.**

ME MADRID REINA VICTORIA MAP p.52, POCKET MAP E13. Plaza de Santa Ana 14 Ⓜ Sol ☎ 917 016 000, Ⓦ meila.com. Once a favourite haunt of bullfighters, this giant white wedding cake of a hotel that dominates the plaza is now part of the exclusive *ME* chain. It comes complete with the de rigueur minimalist decor, designer furnishings, high-tech fittings, a super cool penthouse bar and a very good tapas bar in the foyer. **Doubles from €170.**

ONE SHOT PRADO 23 MAP p.52, POCKET MAP G12. C/Prado 23 Ⓜ Sevilla/ Antón Martín ☎ 914 204 001, Ⓦ hoteloneshotprado23.com. Smart, minimalist, new arrival situated in the thick of things in Huertas. A range of room options available from the basic "Económica" to the more spacious "Ejecutiva", but all are bright with sleek furnishings and excellent walk-in showers. **Doubles from €85.**

PETIT PALACE LONDRES MAP p.52, POCKET MAP D11. C/Galdo 2 Ⓜ Sol ☎ 915 314 105, Ⓦ petitpalacelondresmadrid .com. One of a chain of hotels that offer good rates and decent services. This one is in a refurbished mansion close to Sol and has the trademark smart, well-appointed rooms with a range of facilities. **Doubles from €75.**

ROOM MATE ALICIA MAP p.52, POCKET MAP F13. C/Prado 2 Ⓜ Sol ☎ 913 896 095, Ⓦ room-matehotels.com. Perched on the corner of Plaza Santa Ana, *Alicia* is in a great location, if a little noisy. Seriously cool decor by interior designer Pascua Ortega, stylish rooms and unbeatable value. There are suites from €145 with great views over the plaza and they have nearby apartments sleeping up to six people from €219. **Doubles from €114.**

Paseo del Arte and Retiro

HOSTAL GONZALO MAP p.66, POCKET MAP H13. C/Cervantes 34, 3° Ⓜ Antón Martín ☎ 914 292 714, Ⓦ hostalgonzalo.com. One of the most welcoming *hostales* in the city, tucked away close to Paseo del Prado. Fifteen simple, bright, en-suite rooms, all of which have a/c, TV and recently refurbished bathrooms as well as free wi-fi. It's a very good-value, smart place run by charming owner Antonio and his brother Javier. **Doubles from €50.**

HOTEL MORA MAP p.66, POCKET MAP H7. Paseo del Prado 32 Ⓜ Atocha ☎ 914 201 569, Ⓦ hotelmora.com. A simple, slightly dated hotel perfectly positioned for the galleries on the Paseo del Prado. All of the refurbished rooms have a/c and some have pleasant views across the street (double glazing blocks out the worst of the traffic noise). **Doubles from €86.**

HOTEL PALACE MAP p.66, POCKET MAP H12–13. Plaza de las Cortes 7 Ⓜ Sol ☎ 913 608 000, Ⓦ westinpalacemadrid .com. Colossal, sumptuous hotel with every imaginable facility but none of the snootiness you might expect from its aristocratic appearance. A spectacular, glass-covered central patio and luxurious rooms are part of its charm. **Doubles from €220.**

HOTEL VILLA REAL MAP p.66, POCKET MAP G12. Plaza de las Cortes 10 Ⓜ Sol ☎ 914 203 767, Ⓦ hotelvillareal.com. Aristocratic and highly original, the *Villa Real* comes complete with its own art collection owned by Catalan entrepreneur Jordi Clos. Each of the elegant double rooms has a spacious sitting area (there are several suites too) and many have a balcony overlooking the plaza. The rooftop restaurant, which has some Andy Warhol originals on the wall, affords splendid views down towards the Paseo del Prado. **Doubles from €114.**

HOTEL VINCCI SOMA MAP p.66, POCKET MAP K3. C/Goya 79 Ⓜ Goya ☎ 914 357 545, Ⓦ vinccisoma.com. This modern hotel, which is close to the Salamanca shops and Plaza Colón, has a sophisticated feel to it with its tasteful rooms and good service. **Doubles from €110.**

MERCURE MADRID CENTRO MAP p.66, POCKET MAP H13. C/Lope de Vega 49 Ⓜ Atocha ☎ 913 600 011, Ⓦ hotellopedevega.com. With a great location close to the main art galleries, this hotel is a good mid-priced option. Each of the seven floors is dedicated to a theme relating to playwright Lope de Vega, while the business-style rooms are neat and comfortable. **Doubles from €98.**

NH PASEO DEL PRADO MAP p.66, POCKET MAP H13. Plaza Cánovas del Castillo 4 Ⓜ Banco de España ☎ 914 292 887,

nh-hotels.com. This large, plush member of the *NH Collection* chain is attractively situated in front of the Neptune fountain on the Paseo del Prado. Excellent facilities and a perfect location for the nearby art galleries. The hotel's restaurant serves some high-class tapas too. There is a slightly cheaper sister hotel, the *NH Nacional*, just up the road at Paseo del Prado 48. **Doubles from €144.**

LA PEPA CHIC B&B MAP p.66, POCKET MAP H12. Plaza de los Cortes 4, 7° dcha Ⓜ Banco de España ☎ 648 474 742, Ⓦ lapepa-bnb.com. Boutique accommodation in this neat B&B in the heart of the art museum quarter. The rooms have a brilliant white and red colour scheme, clean lines and functional furnishings. **Doubles from €65.**

RADISSON BLU, MADRID PRADO MAP p.66, POCKET MAP J14. C/Moratín 52, Plaza de Platería Martínez Ⓜ Atocha ☎ 915 242 626, Ⓦ radissonblu.com /pradohotel-madrid. Designer hotel located along the Paseo del Prado featuring sleek rooms in black, brown and white, photos of the Madrid skyline adorning the walls, black slate bathrooms and coffee machines. There is a small spa area and indoor pool, a whisky bar and a restaurant too. **Doubles from €130.**

URBAN SEA ATOCHA 113 MAP p.66, POCKET MAP G7. C/Atocha 113, 3° Ⓜ Atocha ☎ 913 692 895, Ⓦ blueseahotels.com. Just across the roundabout from Atocha station, this member of the *Blue Sea* chain contains sleek but simple rooms at a very competitive price. A sun terrace on the sixth floor and the location make this a good option. **Doubles from €59.**

VP JARDÍN DE RECOLETOS MAP p.66, POCKET MAP J4. C/Gil de Santivañes 6 Ⓜ Retiro/Serrano ☎ 917 811 640, Ⓦ recoletos-hotel.com. If you are looking for a little peace and quiet this elegant hotel close to the Retiro is a very good option. The recently refurbished rooms are spacious and well furnished, while the real attraction is the lovely shady garden terrace. The price is very competitive too. **Doubles from €127.**

Gran Vía, Chueca and Malasaña

HOSTAL SIL/SERRANOS MAP p.80, POCKET MAP F2. C/Fuencarral 95, 2° & 3° Ⓜ Tribunal ☎ 914 488 972, Ⓦ silserranos.com. Two friendly *hostales* located at the quieter end of C/Fuencarral in Malasaña. A variety of simple but comfortable rooms all with a/c, modern bathrooms and TV. Triples and quadruples available. **Doubles from €64.**

HOSTAL ZAMORA MAP p.80, POCKET MAP F4. Plaza Vázquez de Mella 1, 4° izqda Ⓜ Gran Vía ☎ 915 217 031, Ⓦ hostalzamora.com. Seventeen simple rooms in an agreeable family-run place, most of which overlook the plaza. All rooms have a/c, modern bathrooms and TV. There are good-value family rooms too. Closed Aug. **Doubles from €50.**

HOTEL DE LAS LETRAS MAP p.80, POCKET MAP F10. Gran Vía 11 Ⓜ Gran Vía ☎ 915 237 980, Ⓦ hoteldelasletras.com. An elegant design-conscious hotel housed in a lovely early nineteenth-century building at the smarter end of Gran Vía. The stylish, high-ceilinged rooms decorated with literary quotations come complete with plasma TVs. Downstairs, there's a smooth bar and lounge area and a high-quality restaurant with reasonably priced dishes. **Doubles from €125.**

HOTEL PRINCIPAL MAP p.80, POCKET MAP H10. C/Marqués de Valdeiglesias 1 Ⓜ Banco de España ☎ 915 218 743, Ⓦ theprincipalmadridhotel.com. Luxury five-star hotel with large, modern rooms with walk-in showers, a seventh-floor roof-top cocktail bar with wonderful views across Gran Vía and an attic restaurant run by Michelin-star chef Ramón Freixa. **Doubles from €227.**

HOTEL URSO MAP p.80, POCKET MAP F2. C/Mejía Lequerica 8 Ⓜ Alonso Martínez ☎ 914 444 458, Ⓦ hotelurso.com. A new, upmarket hotel sandwiched between Chamberí and Chueca. Rooms are spacious – most have a small sitting area – well equipped and comfortable. There is a small spa area and a pleasant bar and bamboo-fringed indoor terrace. **Doubles from €160.**

ONLY YOU HOTEL MAP p.80, POCKET MAP G4. C/Barquillo 21 Ⓜ Chueca ☎ 910 052 222, Ⓦ onlyyouhotels.com. A new arrival on the scene, this boutique-style hotel, housed in a refurbished nineteenth-century building, is in a great location between Chueca and Recoletos. There are seventy chic, individually decorated rooms, plus a gastrobar and cocktail bar and a small gym. **Doubles from €165.**

PETIT PALACE CHUECA MAP p.80, POCKET MAP F4. C/Hortaleza 3 Ⓜ Gran Vía ☎ 915 211 043, Ⓦ petitpalacechueca.com. A former *hostal* upgraded and refurbished to become one of the *Petit Palace* chain of hotels. Situated in the heart of Chueca, it has 58 sleek rooms (including larger family rooms for around €145) with all manner of mod cons. **Doubles from €90.**

ROOM MATE OSCAR MAP p.80, POCKET MAP F4. Plaza Vázquez de Mella 12 Ⓜ Gran Vía ☎ 917 011 173, Ⓦ room-matehotels.com. Part of the hip *Room Mate* chain, this hotel is in the heart of Chueca and popular with the gay community. It has a garish psychedelic lobby, super cool sparkling white bar area, as well as space age, design-conscious rooms and a rooftop splash pool (additional charge) popular for evening cocktails. **Doubles from €125 (minimum two-night stay at certain times of the year).**

SIDORME MAP p.80, POCKET MAP F3. C/Fuencarral 52 Ⓜ Chueca/Tribunal ☎ 912 787 962, Ⓦ sidorme.com. Sleek, minimalist rooms with large, comfortable beds and walk-in showers in this well-situated and very competitively priced budget hotel that punches above its weight in this category. **Doubles start at €84.**

U HOSTEL MADRID MAP p.80, POCKET MAP G2. C/Sagasta 22 Ⓜ Alonso Martínez ☎ 914 450 300, Ⓦ uhostels.com. Spacious, comfortable and smart rooms in this sparkling new hostel which sprawls its way over five floors of a renovated building close to the pleasant Plaza Santa Bárbara. Options include en-suite doubles, family suites, quadruples, female dormitories and six-, eight- and twelve-bed dormitories. Other extras include a/c, free wi-fi, a chill-out zone and a €3 breakfast. **Dorm beds from €21, doubles from €65.**

Salamanca and Paseo de la Castellana

HOSTAL RESIDENCIA DON DIEGO MAP p.92, POCKET MAP K2. C/Velázquez 45, 5° Ⓜ Velázquez ☎ 914 350 760, Ⓦ hostaldondiego.com. Although officially a *hostal*, this comfortable, friendly place situated in an upmarket area of town is more like a hotel. The rooms, though a little dated have a/c and wi-fi though the walls are a little thin. Reasonably priced for the area. **Doubles from €75.**

HOTEL ORFILA MAP p.92, POCKET MAP H2. C/Orfila 6 Ⓜ Alonso Martínez ☎ 917 027 770, Ⓦ www.hotelorfila.com. Transport yourself back in time at this exclusive boutique hotel housed in a beautiful nineteenth-century mansion on a quiet street north of Alonso Martínez. Twelve of the exquisite rooms are suites, there is an elegant terrace for tea and drinks and an upmarket restaurant (run by Michelin-star chef Mario Sandoval), too. **Doubles from €250.**

HOTEL SANTO MAURO MAP p.92, POCKET MAP H1. C/Zurbano 36 Ⓜ Rubén Darío ☎ 913 196 900, Ⓦ acsantomauro.com. This is where the Beckhams first installed themselves when David signed for Real Madrid in 2003 and this former aristocrat's residence has all the luxury and exclusivity you'd expect. Palatial rooms, a restaurant that looks like a gentleman's club, a delightful outdoor terrace and an indoor pool are all part of the package. **Doubles from €245.**

HOTEL ÚNICO MAP p.92, POCKET MAP J2. C/Claudio Cuello 67 Ⓜ Serrano ☎ 917 810 173, Ⓦ unicohotelmadrid.com. Luxury 44-room boutique-style hotel in a renovated nineteenth-century mansion. Large rooms, bathrooms with power showers, elegant communal areas and a garden terrace. The restaurant (see p.98) is run by distinguished Catalan chef Ramón Freixa. **Doubles from €220.**

PETIT PALACE EMBASSY SERRANO MAP p.92, POCKET MAP J2. C/Serrano 46 Ⓜ Serrano ☎ 914 313 060, Ⓦ petit palaceembassyserrano.com. A four-star member of the sleek *Petit Palace* chain of hotels, close to Plaza Colón and in the middle of the upmarket Salamanca shopping district. The *Embassy* has

75 rooms, including ten family ones for up to four people. Free internet access and flat-screen TVs. **Doubles from €130.**

Plaza de España

CASÓN DEL TORMES MAP p.102, POCKET MAP C4. C/Río 7 Ⓜ Plaza de España ☎ 915 419 746, Ⓦ hotelcasondeltormes .com. Welcoming three-star place in a quiet street next to Plaza de España. The 63 a/c, en-suite rooms are functional but very comfortable and hotel facilities include a bar and breakfast room, and helpful, English-speaking staff. **Doubles from €87.**

HOSTAL BUENOS AIRES MAP p.102, POCKET MAP D4. Gran Vía 61, 2° Ⓜ Plaza de España ☎ 915 420 102, Ⓦ hostalbuenosaires-madrid.com. Twenty-five pleasantly decorated but small rooms with a/c, satellite TV, free wi-fi, modern bathrooms, plus double glazing to keep out much of the noise. **Doubles from €61.**

HOTEL EMPERADOR MAP p.102, POCKET MAP D4. Gran Vía 53 Ⓜ Santo Domingo ☎ 915 472 800, Ⓦ emperadorhotel .com. The main reason to come here is the stunning rooftop swimming pool with its magnificent views. The hotel itself is geared up for the organized tour market and is rather impersonal, but the rooms are large and well decorated. **Doubles from €108.**

HOTEL SANTO DOMINGO MAP p.102, POCKET MAP D4. C/San Bernardo 1 Ⓜ Santo Domingo ☎ 915 479 800, Ⓦ hotelsantodomingo.es. What with the jungle paintings adorning the car park, the private art collection, the hanging garden and the rooftop swimming pool with views over the city, this hotel is full of surprises. Rooms have tasteful individual decor, large beds and walk-in shower rooms. **Standard doubles from €95.**

HOTEL T3 TIROL MAP p.102, POCKET MAP B1. C/Marqués de Urquijo 4 Ⓜ Argüelles ☎ 915 481 900, Ⓦ t3tirol.com. A good option if you are travelling with young children, the *Tirol* provides family rooms with a double bed and bunks or an adjoining kids' room. There is a play area too and the hotel is close to the Parque del Oeste and the teleférico into Casa de Campo. €160–180 for a family of four. **Doubles from €99.**

ESSENTIALS

The Teleférico

Arrival

Whatever your point of arrival, it's an easy business getting into the centre of Madrid. The airport is connected by metro, shuttle buses and taxis, while the city's main train and bus stations are all linked to the metro system.

By plane

The **Aeropuerto Adolfo Suárez Madrid-Barajas** (☎ 913 211 000, ⓦ aena.es) is 16km east of the city. It has four terminals, including the vast T4 building designed by Richard Rogers and Carlos Lamela. All Iberia's domestic and international flights, as well as airlines that belong to the Oneworld group, such as British Airways and American Airlines, use T4 (a 10min shuttle bus ride from the other terminals); other international flights and budget airlines, including Aer Lingus, Easyjet and Ryanair, go from T1, while Air France, KLM, Alitalia and Lufthansa use T2.

From the airport, the **metro link** (Line 8) takes you from T4 and T2 to the city's Nuevos Ministerios station in just twelve minutes (daily 6am–2am; €4.50–5). From there, connecting metro lines take you to city-centre locations in about fifteen minutes. The new Cercanías train line takes you directly from T4 to Chamartín in the north of the city in twenty minutes (daily 6am–1.30pm; €2.60).

The route by road to central Madrid is more variable, depending on rush-hour traffic, and can take anything from twenty minutes to an hour. Airport express buses run round the clock from each terminal to Cibeles and Atocha (stops only at Cibeles from 11.30pm–6am; every 15–35min; €5) with a journey time of around forty minutes. Taxis are always available outside, too, and cost €30 to the centre (fixed tariff; includes a €5.50 airport supplement).

By train

Trains from France and northern Spain (including the high-speed links to Segovia, Valladolid and Leon) arrive at the **Estación de Chamartín**, in the north of the city, connected by metro with the centre, and by regular commuter trains (*trenes de cercanías*) to the more central **Estación de Atocha**. Atocha has two interconnected terminals: one for local services; the other for all points in southern and eastern Spain, including the high-speed services to Barcelona, Seville, Toledo, Malaga, Valencia, Alicante, Albacete and Zaragoza. For train information and **reservations**, call ☎ 902 320 320 or go to ⓦ renfe.com.

By bus

Bus terminals are scattered throughout the city, but the largest – used by all of the international bus services – is the **Estación Sur de Autobuses** at C/Méndez Álvaro 83, 1.5km south of Atocha train station (☎ 914 684 200, ⓦ estaciondeautobuses.com; Ⓜ Méndez Álvaro).

By car

All main roads into Madrid bring you right into the city centre, although eccentric signposting and even more eccentric driving can be unnerving. The two main ring roads – the M40 and the M30 – and the Paseo de la Castellana, the main north–south artery, are all notorious bottlenecks, although virtually the whole city centre can be close to gridlock during **rush-hour periods** (Mon–Fri 7.30–9.30am & 6–8.30pm). Be prepared for a long trawl around the streets to find **parking** and even when you find somewhere, in most central areas you'll have to buy a ticket at one of the complex roadside meters (€8.40 for a maximum stay of four hours in the blue-coloured bays; €4.70 for a maximum stay of two hours in the green-coloured bays. Charges apply Sept–July Mon–Fri 9am–9pm, Sat 9am–3pm; Aug Mon–Sat 9am–3pm). Another option is to put your car in one of the many signposted parkings (up to €2.50 for an hour and around €31 for a day). The city council plans to ban diesel cars from the centre in the near future. Once in the city, and with public transport being both efficient and good value, your own vehicle is really only of use for out-of-town excursions.

Getting around

Madrid is an easy city to get around. The central areas are walkable and going on foot is certainly the best way to appreciate and get to know the city. The metro is clean, modern and efficient; buses are also generally very good and serve some of the more out-of-the-way districts, while taxis are always available.

The metro

The **metro** (Ⓦ www.metromadrid.es) is by far the quickest way of getting around Madrid, serving most places you're likely to want to get to. It runs from 6am until 2am and the fare is €1.50–2 for the central zone stations

or €12.20 for a ten-trip ticket (*bono de diez viajes*) which can be used on buses too. The network has undergone massive expansion in recent years and some of the outlying commuter districts are now connected by light railways which link with the existing metro stations (supplement fares for some of these). Lines are numbered and colour-coded, and the direction of travel is indicated by the name of the terminus station. You can pick up a free colour map of the system (*plano del metro*) at any station.

Local trains

The **local train** network, or Cercanías, is the most efficient way of connecting between the main train stations and also provides the best route out to many of the suburbs and nearby towns. Most trains are air conditioned, fares are cheap and there are good connections with the metro. Services generally run every fifteen to thirty minutes from 6am to around midnight. For more information, go to the RENFE website (Ⓦ renfe.com) and click on the Cercanías section for Madrid.

Buses

The comprehensive **bus network** (Ⓦ emtmadrid.es) is a good way to get around and see the sights. There

The tourist travel pass

If you're using public transport extensively, it's worth thinking about getting a **tourist pass** (*abono turístico*) covering the metro, train and bus. These are non-transferable and you'll need to show your passport or identity card at the time of purchase. Zone A cards cover the city of Madrid, Zone T cards cover the whole region including Toledo and Guadalajara but not the airport buses. They are available for a duration of one to seven days and range in cost from €8.40 for a Zone A daily card to €70.80 for a weekly one for Zone T (under-11s are half price, under-4s are free) and can be purchased at all metro stations, the airport and tourist offices. If you are staying longer, passes (*abonos*) covering the metro, train and bus are available for a calendar month.

are information booths at Plaza de Cibeles and Puerta del Sol, which dispense a huge route map (*plano de los transportes de Madrid*) and also sell bus passes. Fares are similar to the metro, at €1.50 a journey, or €12.20 for a ten-trip ticket (*bono de diez viajes*) which can be used on both forms of transport. When you get on the bus, punch your ticket in a machine by the driver. You can also buy tickets from the driver, but try and have the right money.

Services run from 6am to midnight, with *búho* (owl) buses operating through the night on twenty routes around the central area and out to the suburbs: departures are half-hourly 11.15pm–5.30am from Plaza de Cibeles.

Taxis

Madrid has thousands of reasonably priced taxis that you can wave down on the street – look for white cars with a diagonal red stripe on the side. Seven or eight euros will get you to most places within the centre and, although it's common to round up the fare, you're not expected to tip. The minimum fare is €2.40 (€2.90 on Sat, Sun and hols) and supplements (€3–5.50) are charged for baggage, going to the airport, train and bus stations or outside the city limits. To phone for a taxi, call 915 478 600 (also for wheelchair-friendly cabs), 914 051 213, 913 712 131 or 914 473 232.

Bicycles

Traditionally a nightmare for cyclists, Madrid has become a more bike-friendly city with the introduction of a new bike hire scheme and the extension of cycle paths and lanes in the centre. The scheme, known as BiciMAD (bicimad.com), allows you to pick up and return an electric-assisted bike at stations scattered all over the city centre (€4 for 2 hours and €4 for each subsequent hour, with a €150 returnable deposit paid by bank card; minimum age 14).

Be aware that it is compulsory for under-16s to wear helmets and that the cycle lanes are also used by cars, though they are supposed to adjust their speed to that of the bicycles.

For bike tours in and around Madrid, get in touch with bravobike.com at Juan Alvarez Mendizábal 19 (917 582 945 or 607 448 440;

Useful bus routes

#2 From west to east: from Argüelles metro station running along C/Princesa, past Plaza de España, along Gran Vía, past Cibeles and out past the Retiro.

#3 From south to north: Puerta de Toledo, through Sol, up towards Gran Vía and then Alonso Martínez and northwards.

#5 From Sol via Cibeles, Colón and the Paseo de la Castellana to Chamartín.

#27 From Embajadores, via Atocha, up the length of the Castellana to Plaza de Castilla.

#33 From Príncipe Pío out via the Puente de Segovia to the Parque de Atracciones and Zoo in Casa de Campo.

#C1 and C2 The Circular bus route takes a broad circuit round the city from Atocha, via Puerta de Toledo, Príncipe Pío, Plaza de España, Moncloa, Cuatro Caminos, Avenida de América and Goya.

City tours

The *oficina de turismo* in Plaza Mayor (see p.26) can supply details of guided **English-language walking tours**. Additionally their website ⓦ esmadrid.com/visitas-guiadas-por-madrid has a list of the companies that run tours around the city, which usually cost around €10. For a **bus tour** of all the major sights, hop on at the stop between the Prado and the *Ritz* hotel; tickets cost €21 (children €10, under-6s free; ⓦ madridcitytour.es) and allow you to jump on and off at various points throughout the city. Pick-up points include Puerta del Sol, Plaza de Colón, Plaza de España and the Palacio Real. For the more adventurous, a number of companies offer **segway tours** of the city with prices starting at €25 for an hour-long tour (ⓦ madsegs.com; ⓦ madrid-segway.es; ⓦ madrid.segwaytour.com; ⓦ segwayfun.es; ⓦ segwaytrip.com), while GoCar (C/Ferraz 26, near Plaza de España; prices start at €35/hr for a two-person car, all day €99; ☎ 915 594 535, ⓦ gocartours.es/madrid) offers tours in little yellow computer-guided storytelling vehicles. Foodies should try the Madrid Food Tour to explore the city's culinary highlights (from €75; ☎ 695 111 832, ⓦ madridfoodtour.com).

ⓦ Ventura Rodríguez) or ⓦ bikespain.info at Plaza de la Villa 1 (☎ 917 590 653; ⓜ Ópera).

Car rental

See p.136 for more information on driving in Madrid. Major operators have branches at the airport and train stations. Central offices include: Avis, Gran Vía 60 (ⓜ Santo Domingo) ☎ 915 484 204, reservations ☎ 902 103 739, ⓦ www.avisworld.com; Enterprise, Atocha ☎ 915 061 846, ⓦ enterprise.es; Europcar, C/San Leonardo 8 (ⓜ Plaza España) ☎ 915 418 892, ⓦ europcar.com; Hertz, Atocha station ☎ 902 023 932, ⓦ hertz.com; EasyCar, ⓦ easycar.com; Pepecar, near to Atocha and Chamartín stations ☎ 916 350 317, ⓦ pepecar.com.

Directory A-Z

Addresses

Calle (street) is abbreviated to C/ in addresses, followed by the number on the street, then another number that indicates the floor, eg C/Arenal 23, 5˚ means fifth floor of no. 23 Arenal Street. You may also see *izquierda* and *derecha*, meaning (apartment or office) left or right of the staircase.

Cinema

Madrileños love going to the cinema (*cine*) and, though most foreign films are dubbed into Spanish, a number of cinemas have original-language screenings, listed in a separate *subtitulada/versión original* (v.o.) section in the newspapers. Tickets cost around €8–9 but most cinemas have a *día del espectador* (usually Mon or Wed) with a reduced admission charge. Be warned that on Sunday night what seems like half of Madrid goes to the movies and queues can be long. The most central cinemas showing v.o. films include the two Renoirs at C/Martín de los Heros 12 and C/Princesa 5, and Golem at C/Martín de los Heros 14, all next to Plaza de España, and the nine-screen Ideal Yelmo Complex, C/Doctor Cortezo 6, south off C/Atocha and near Plaza Santa Ana (ⓜ Sol).

For the police, medical services and the fire brigade, call ☎ 112.

Crime

Central Madrid is so densely populated – and so busy at just about every hour of the day and night – that it seems to carry very little "big city" threat. However, that's not to say that crime is not a problem, nor that there aren't any sleazy areas to be avoided. Tourists in Madrid, as everywhere, are prime targets for pickpockets and petty thieves so take care of belongings in crowded areas, on buses, in the metro, burger bars and in the Rastro. Be aware also that although the city council has taken steps to combat the problem, the main routes through Casa de Campo and the Parque del Oeste are still frequented by prostitutes and are best steered clear of at night. Calle Montera, near Sol, and some streets just north of Gran Vía are also affected. To report a crime go to the nearest police station or ring ☎ 901 102 112 or ☎ 915 488 537

Electricity

220 volts. Plugs are two round pins.

Embassies and consulates

Australia, Torre Espacio, Paseo de la Castellana 259D (☎ 913 536 600, ⓦ spain.embassy.gov.au; Ⓜ Begoña); Britain, Torre Espacio, Paseo de la Castellana 259D (☎ 917 146 300 or ☎ 902 109 356, ⓦ www.gov.uk /government/world/spain; Ⓜ Begoña); Canada, Torre Espacio, Paseo de la Castellana 259D (☎ 913 828 400, ⓦ canadainternational.gc.ca); Ⓜ Begoña); Ireland, Paseo de la Castellana 46, 4° (☎ 914 364 093, ⓦ dfa.ie/irish-embassy/spain; Ⓜ Rubén Darío); New Zealand, C/Pinar 7, 3° (☎ 915 230 226, ⓦ nzembassy

.com/spain; Ⓜ Gregorio Marañón); US, C/Serrano 75 (☎ 915 872 200, ⓦ madrid.usembassy.gov; Ⓜ Rubén Darío); South Africa, C/Claudio Coello 91 (☎ 914 363 780, ⓦ www.dirco.gov.za /madrid; Ⓜ Rubén Darío).

Gay and lesbian travellers

The main gay organization in Madrid is Coordinadora Gay de Madrid, C/Puebla 9 (Mon–Fri 10am–2pm & 5–8pm; ☎ 915 230 070, ⓦ www.cogam.org; Ⓜ Gran Vía), which can give information on health, leisure and gay rights. The national LGTB group can be found nearby at C/Infantas 40, 4° izqda (Mon–Thurs 8am–8pm & Fri 8am–3.30pm, ☎ 913 604 605, ⓦ felgtb.org; Ⓜ Banco de España/ Chueca). For a good one-stop shop with lots of info on the gay scene, try Berkana Bookshop, C/Hortaleza 62 (Mon–Sat 10.30am–9pm, Sun noon–2pm & 5–9pm; ⓦ libreriaberkana.com; Ⓜ Chueca). The website ⓦ shangay.com has listings and information about upcoming events.

Health

EU citizens are entitled to health care free of charge, but ensure you have a European Health Insurance Card. If you are a non-EU citizen ensure you have health insurance as you may be liable for the costs of any treatment. Health centres are scattered throughout the city and open 24 hours: one of the most central is at Carrera San Jerónimo 32 (☎ 913 690 491; Ⓜ Sol). Central hospitals include El Clínico San Carlos, C/Profesor Martín Lagos s/n (☎ 913 303 000; Ⓜ Islas Filipinas); Hospital Gregorio Marañón, C/Dr Esquerdo 46 (☎ 915 868 000; Ⓜ O'Donnell); Ciudad Sanitaria La Paz, Paseo de la Castellana 261 (☎ 917 277 000, Ⓜ Begoña). Many doctors speak English but there is a private English-speaking clinic, the Anglo-American Medical Unit at C/Conde de Aranda 1 (☎ 914 351 823; Mon–Fri 9am–8pm,

Sat 10am–1pm; Ⓜ Retiro). The Clínica Dental Plaza Prosperidad at Plaza Prosperidad 3, 2°B (☎ 914 158 197, Ⓦ clinicadentalplazaprosperidad.com; Ⓜ Prosperidad) has some English-speaking dentists as does the Clínica Dental Cisne at C/Magallanes 18 (☎ 914 463 221, Ⓦ cisnedental.com; Ⓜ Quevedo). The following **pharmacies** (distinguished by a green cross) are open 24 hours: C/Mayor 13 (☎ 913 664 616); Ⓜ Sol); C/Toledo 46 (☎ 913 653 458; Ⓜ La Latina); C/Atocha 46 (☎ 913 692 000; Ⓜ Antón Martín); C/Goya 12 (☎ 915 754 924; Ⓜ Serrano).

Internet

There are free wi-fi hotspots at many newspaper stands in the city and on buses, while the city centre is peppered with *locutorios* that provide internet, and most hotels have free wi-fi. The tourist offices in Plaza Mayor and below Plaza Colón offer free internet while there are free wi-fi hotspots in Plaza Mayor, Plaza Olavide and Plaza Santo Domingo.

Left luggage

There are left-luggage facilities (*consignas*) at Barajas Airport in terminals 1, 2 and 4 (open 24hr; €10/day); the Estación Sur bus station; and lockers at Atocha (Mon–Fri 5.30am–10.20pm, Sat 6.15am–10.20pm, Sun 6.30am–10.20pm; €3.10–5.20 /day) and Chamartín (open 7am–11pm; €3.10–5.20/day) train stations.

Lost property

For lost property, ring the municipal depot on ☎ 915 279 590 at Paseo del Molino 7 (open Mon–Fri 8.30am–2pm; Ⓜ Legazpi); bring ID. For property left in a taxi, call ☎ 914 804 613; on a bus, call ☎ 902 507 850; on the metro, call ☎ 917 212 957.

Money

Banks are plentiful throughout the city and are the best places to change money. Opening hours are normally Mon–Fri 8.30am–2pm and Thurs 4.30–6.30pm. Branches of El Corte Inglés have exchange offices with long hours and reasonably competitive rates; the most central is on C/Preciados, close to Puerta del Sol. Barajas Airport also has a 24-hour currency exchange office. The rates at the exchange bureaux scattered around the city are often very poor, though they don't usually charge commission. ATM cash machines (*cajeros automáticos*) are widespread and accept most credit and debit cards. Credit cards are widely accepted in hotels, restaurants and shops.

Opening hours

Smaller shops generally open 10am–2pm and 5–8pm Mon–Fri, but only open in the mornings on Sat. Department stores and chains tend not to close for lunch and open all day Sat and Sun. Larger ones open on the first Sun of the month too (except in Aug). Stores in the tourist zones in the

Madrid apps

There are a number of apps for phones and tablets which visitors may find useful. The Prado, Thyssen and Reina Sofía all produce guide apps, while the local authority markets the Essential Art Walk Guide app and a 5-D guide to the city. The Metro de Madrid, the city transport agency, the EMT and the BiciMAD bike hire scheme all have their own apps that are available on the Apple Store or Google Play and can be quite helpful in getting around the city.

centre also open on Sun. Restaurants generally serve from 1.30–4pm and 8.30pm–11.30pm, with many closing for a rest day on Mon. Bars stay open till the early hours – usually around 2am – while clubs close around 5am, depending on the licence they hold. Museums close on Jan 1, Jan 6, May 1, Dec 24, Dec 25 and Dec 31.

Phones

With phone boxes disappearing, the best way to make an international call is from a *locutorio* (call centre) via the internet. The latter are plentiful in the centre. Calling Madrid from abroad, dial your international access code, then 34, followed by the subscriber's number which will nearly always start with 91. Mobile phone users from the UK should be able to use their phones in Spain – check with your service provider before leaving about costs. Many American cellphones do not work with the Spanish mobile network. For national directory enquiries, ring ☏ 11818; for international enquiries, call ☏ 11825.

Post offices

Centrally located post offices are at Paseo del Prado 1 and in El Corte Inglés, C/Preciados 3 (Ⓜ Sol) and there's another with extended hours at C/Mejía Lequerica 7 (Ⓜ Alonso Martínez). Buy stamps (*sellos*) at *estancos*.

Public holidays

The main national holidays are: Jan 1 (Año Nuevo); Jan 6 (Reyes); Easter Thursday (Jueves Santo); Good Friday (Viernes Santo); May 1 (Fiesta del Trabajo); May 2 (Día de la Comunidad); May 15 (San Isidro); Aug 15 (Virgen de la Paloma); Oct 12 (Día de la Hispanidad); Nov 1 (Todos Los Santos); Nov 9 (Virgen de la Almudena); Dec 6 (Día de la Constitución); Dec 8 (La Inmaculada); Dec 25 (Navidad).

Smoking

Smoking is banned in all bars, restaurants and clubs, though it is common on outdoor terrazas.

Swimming pools and aquaparks

The Piscina Canal Isabel II, Avda de Filipinas 54 (daily 10am–8.30pm; Ⓜ Ríos Rosas), is a large outdoor swimming pool, and the best central option. Alternatively, try the open-air *piscinas* at Casa de Campo (daily 10am–8.30pm; Ⓜ Lago) or the Centro Municipal Vicente del Bosque at Avda Monforte de Lemos 13 (10am–8.30pm; Ⓜ Begoña). There are also a number of aquaparks around the city, the closest being Aquópolis de San Fernando (Ⓦ san-fernando.aquopolis.es), 16km out on the N-II Barcelona road (buses #281, #282 and #284 from the intercambiador at Arda de América). Outside May–Sept, most outdoor pools are closed.

Ticket agencies

For theatre and concert tickets, try: Atrapalo ☏ 902 200 808, Ⓦ atrapalo. com; Ⓦ entradas.com; El Corte Inglés ☏ 902 400 222, Ⓦ elcorteingles.es /entradas; FNAC ☏ 915 956 100, Ⓦ fnac.es; and Ticketmaster Ⓦ ticketmaster.es.

Time

Madrid is one hour ahead of Greenwich Mean Time during winter and two hours ahead from March–Oct. Clocks go forward in late March and back an hour in late Oct.

Tipping

When tipping, adding around five to ten percent to a restaurant bill is acceptable but rarely more than €5, while in bars and taxis, rounding up to the nearest euro is the norm.

Tourist information

The chief tourist offices are at the following locations: Barajas International Airport T1, T2 & T4; T1 (Mon–Sat 8am–8pm, Sun 9am–2pm; ☎ 913 058 656); T2 (daily 9am–8pm; ☎ 914 544 410); T4 (daily 9am–8pm; ☎ 913 338 248); Colón (daily 11am–8pm; ☎ 915 881 636; Ⓜ Colón), in the underground passageway accessed at the corner of C/Goya; Palacio de Cibeles (Tues–Sun 10am–8pm; Ⓜ Banco de España); Estación de Atocha (Mon–Fri 9am–8pm, Sat & Sun 9am–1pm; ☎ 915 284 630; Ⓜ Atocha Renfe); Estación de Chamartín (Mon–Fri 8am–8pm, Sat 9am–2pm; ☎ 913 159 976; Ⓜ Chamartín); Plaza Mayor 27 (daily 9.30am–8.30pm; ☎ 915 881 636; Ⓜ Sol). These are supplemented by booths near the Prado, the Reina Sofia and in Plaza del Callao off Gran Vía (daily 9.30am–8.30pm). The Madrid tourist board has a comprehensive website at ⓦ esmadrid.com, while the regional one has one covering the whole of the province at ⓦ turismomadrid.es. You can phone for tourist information in English on ☎ 902 100 007, a premium-rate number that links all the regional tourist offices mentioned below, and on ☎ 915 881 636.

Listings information is in plentiful supply in Madrid. The newspapers *El País* (ⓦ elpais.es) and *El Mundo* (ⓦ metropoli.com) have excellent daily listings (in Spanish), and on Friday both publish magazine sections devoted to events, bars and restaurants. The *ayuntamiento* (city council) also publishes a monthly what's-on magazine, *esMadrid* (in English and Spanish), free from any of the tourist offices. Finally, ⓦ nakedmadrid.com is an English-language website that features useful reviews of bars and restaurants.

Theatre

Madrid has a vibrant theatre scene which, if you speak the language, is worth sampling. You can catch anything from Lope de Vega to contemporary productions, and there's a good range on offer during the annual Festival de Otoño a Primavera (Nov–June). For current productions, check the listings sources above.

Travellers with disabilities

Madrid is slowly getting geared up for disabled visitors (*minusválidos*). The local authority has produced a guide with some practical advice at ⓦ esmadrid.com/en/accessible-madrid. The Organizacíon Nacional de Ciegos de España (ONCE; National Organization for the Blind, C/Prim 3 (☎ 915 325 000, ⓦ www.once.es; Ⓜ Chueca) provides specialist advice, as does the Federación de Asociaciones de Minusválidos Físicos de la Comunidad de Madrid (FAMMA) at C/Galileo 69 (☎ 915 933 550, ⓦ famma.org; Ⓜ Islas Filipinas). ⓦ discapnet.es is a useful source of information (Spanish only). Wheelchair-accessible taxis can be ordered from Eurotaxi (☎ 630 026 478 or ☎ 687 924 027) and Radio Taxi (☎ 915 478 200 or 915 478 600).

Travelling with children

Although many of Madrid's main sights may lack children-specific activities, there's still plenty to keep kids occupied during a short stay, from various parks – including the Retiro (see p.70) – to swimming pools (see opposite) and the zoo (see p.107). There is also an ecological theme park/zoo on the outskirts of the city (ⓦ faunia.es). Children are doted on in Spain and welcome in nearly all cafés and restaurants.

Festivals and events

As well as these festivals, check out the **cultural events** organized by the city council, in particular the Veranos de la Villa (July–Sept) and Festival de Otoño a Primavera (Nov–June), which include music concerts, theatre and cinema. There are annual festivals for flamenco (June), books (end of May), dance (Nov–Dec), photography (mid-July to Aug) and jazz (Nov). See ⓦ esmadrid.com.

Cabalgata de los Reyes

January 5
To celebrate the arrival of the gift-bearing Three Kings, there is a gigantic, hugely popular evening procession through the city centre in which children are showered with sweets. It's held on the evening before presents are traditionally exchanged in Spain.

Carnaval

The week before Lent
Partying and fancy-dress parades, especially in the gay zone around Chueca. The end of Carnaval is marked by the bizarre parade, El Entierro de la Sardina (The Burial of the Sardine), on Paseo de la Florida.

Semana Santa

Easter week is celebrated with a series of solemn processions around Madrid, with Jueves Santo (Maundy Thursday) and Viernes Santo (Good Friday) both public holidays in the city.

Fiesta del Dos de Mayo

May 2
Celebrations are held around Madrid to commemorate the city's uprising against the French in 1808.

Fiestas de San Isidro

May 15, for a week.
Evenings start out with traditional *chotis*, music and dancing, and bands play each night in the Jardines de las Vistillas (south of the Palacio Real). The fiestas mark the start of the bullfighting season.

La Feria del Libro

End of May
Madrid's great book fair takes place with stands set up in the Retiro Park.

WorldPride Madrid

End of June or beginning of July
WorldPride Madrid (LGTB Pride Week) is a week-long party in Chueca culminating in a parade that brings the city centre to a standstill.

Castizo fiestas

August 6 to 15
Madrileños put on traditional fiestas to celebrate the saints' days of San Cayetano, San Lorenzo and La Virgen de la Paloma. Much of the activity centres around C/Toledo, Plaza de la Paja and the Jardines de las Vistillas.

Navidad

The Christmas period in Madrid sees Plaza Mayor taken over by a model of a Nativity crib and a large seasonal market with stalls selling all manner of festive decorations.

Noche Vieja

Dec 31
Puerta del Sol is the customary place to gather for midnight, waiting for the strokes of the clock and then attempting to swallow a grape on each strike to bring good luck in the coming year.

Chronology

800s Muslims establish a defensive outpost on the escarpment above the Manzanares river. It becomes known as "mayrit" – the place of many springs – successively modified to Magerit and then Madrid.

1086 Madrid taken by the Christians under Alfonso VI, but it remains a relatively insignificant backwater.

1561 Felipe II chooses Madrid as a permanent home for the court because of its position in the centre of the recently unified Spain. The population surges with the arrival of the royal entourage, and there is a boom in the building industry.

1700–46 With the emergence of the Bourbon dynasty under Felipe V, a touch of French style, including the sumptuous Palacio Real, is introduced into the capital.

1759–88 Carlos III tries to make the city into a home worthy of the monarchy. Streets are cleaned up, sewers and street lighting installed, and work begins on the Museo del Prado.

1795–1808 Spain falls under the influence of Napoleonic France, with their troops entering the capital in 1808. The heavily out-gunned *madrileños* are defeated in a rising on May 2 and Napoleon installs his brother Joseph on the throne.

1812–14 The French are removed by a combined Spanish and British army and the monarchy makes a return under the reactionary Fernando VII.

1833–75 Spanish society is riven with divisions which explode into a series of conflicts known as the Carlist Wars and lead to chronic political instability, including a brief period as a republic.

1875–1900 Madrid undergoes significant social changes prompted by a rapid growth in population and the emergence of a working class. The socialist party, the PSOE, is founded in the city in 1879.

1923–31 A hard-line military regime under Miguel Primo de Rivera takes control, with King Alfonso XIII relegated to the background. The king eventually decides to abdicate in 1931, and the Second Republic is ushered in.

1936–39 The Right grows increasingly restless and a group of army generals organize an uprising in July 1936 which ignites the Spanish Civil War. Madrid resists and becomes a Republican stronghold.

1939 Franco and his victorious Nationalists enter the city. Mass reprisals take place and Franco installs himself in the country residence of El Pardo.

1939–53 Spain endures yet more suffering during the post-war years until a turnaround in American policy. The Pact of Madrid is signed to rehabilitate Franco, as the US searches for anti-Communist Cold War allies.

1970s Franco eventually dies in November 1975. He is succeeded by King Juan Carlos who presides over the transition to democracy.

1981 In a last-gasp attempt to re-establish itself, the military under Colonel Tejero storms the parliament in Madrid, but a lack of support from the king and army causes its collapse. The Socialists led by Felipe González win the 1982 elections.

1980s Freedom from the shackles of dictatorship and the release of long-pent-up creative forces help create *La Movida*, with Madrid becoming the epicentre of the movement.

1990s The Socialists become increasingly discredited as they are entangled in a web of scandal and corruption, losing control of Madrid in 1991 and the country in 1996 to the conservative Partido Popular (PP).

1992 Madrid is named European Capital of Culture.

2004 The March 11 bombings carried out by Muslim extremists at Atocha train station kill 191 and injure close to 2000. The Socialists return to power in the general elections which follow, although the PP remain firmly in control of the local government.

2004–08 Madrid fails in its bids for the 2012 and 2016 Olympics, losing out to London and then Rio de Janeiro. High-profile building projects such as the Richard Rogers' airport terminal, Norman Foster's Torre Caja Madrid skyscraper, Rafael Moneo's Prado extension and the M30 ring road 6-km long mega-tunnel are all completed before the onset of the recession and the end of the property boom.

2008–13 The effects of the global economic crisis combined with the endemic problems of property speculation, profligate spending on showcase projects and corruption mean the crisis hits Spain even harder. The centre-right Popular Party is returned to power in the 2011 general election. Unemployment reaches record highs, the economy flatlines in terms of growth and corruption scandals continue to plague the country.

2014 Juan Carlos abdicates after nearly forty years on the throne. His son Felipe succeeds as King of Spain.

2015 Support for the Popular Party plummets and the left-of-centre citzen-based Ahora Madrid group, led by mayor Manuela Carmena, come to power. They pick up the pieces and try to get to grips with the problems of corruption and debt bequeathed by the PP.

Spanish

Once you get into it, Spanish is one of the easiest languages around, and people are eager to try and understand even the most faltering attempt. English is spoken at the main tourist attractions, but you'll get a far better reception if you try communicating with *madrileños* in their own tongue.

Pronunciation

The rules of pronunciation are pretty straightforward and strictly observed.

A somewhere between the A sound of back and that of father.

E as in get.

I as in police.

O as in hot.

U as in rule.

C is spoken like a TH before E and I, hard otherwise: *cerca* is pronounced "thairka".

G is a guttural H sound (like the ch in loch) before E or I, a hard G elsewhere – *gigante* becomes "higante".

H is always silent.

J is the same as a guttural G: *jamón* is "hamon".

LL sounds like an English Y: *tortilla* is pronounced "torteeya".

N is as in English unless it has a tilde (accent) over it, when it becomes NY: *mañana* sounds like "manyana".

QU is pronounced like an English K.

R is rolled when it is at the start of a word, RR doubly so.

V sounds more like B, *vino* becoming "beano".

X has an S sound before consonants, normal X before vowels.

Z is the same as a soft C, so *cerveza* becomes "thairbaytha".

Words and phrases

Basics

yes, no, ok	sí, no, vale
please, thank you	por favor, gracias
where?, when?	¿dónde?, ¿cuándo?
what?, how much?	¿qué?, ¿cuánto?
Help!	¡socorru!
here, there	aquí, allí
this, that	esto, eso
now, later	ahora, más tarde
open, closed	abierto/a, cerrado/a
with, without	con, sin
good, bad	buen(o)/a, mal(o)/a
big, small	gran(de), pequeño/a
cheap, expensive	barato, caro
hot, cold	caliente, frío
more, less	más, menos
today, tomorrow	hoy, mañana
yesterday	ayer
the bill	la cuenta
price	precio
free	gratis
doctor	un médico
police	la policía

Greetings and responses

hello, goodbye	hola, adiós
good morning	buenos días
good afternoon/ night	buenas tardes/ noches
see you later	hasta luego
sorry	lo siento/disculpe
excuse me	con permiso/perdón
How are you?	¿Cómo está (usted)?
I (don't) understand	(no) entiendo
not at all/you're welcome	de nada
Do you speak english?	¿Habla (usted) inglés?
I (don't) speak Spanish	(no) hablo español
My name is...	Me llamo...
What's your name?	¿Cómo se llama usted?
I am English/ Scottish/ Welsh/ Australian/ Canadian/ American/ Irish/ New Zealander	Soy inglés(a)/ escocés(a)/ galés(a)/ australiano(a)/ canadiense/ americano(a)/ irlandés(a)/ neozelandés(a)

Hotels, transport and directions

I want	Quiero
I'd like	Quisiera
Do you know...?	¿Sabe....?
I don't know	No sé
Give me (one like that)	Deme (uno así)

Do you have...?	¿Tiene...?
the time	la hora
single room	habitación individual
double room	habitación doble
two beds/	dos camas/cama de
double bed	matrimonio
with shower/bath	con ducha/baño
it's for one person	es para una persona
for one night	para una noche
for one week	para una semana
How do I get to...?	¿Por dónde se va a...?
left, right,	izquierda, derecha,
straight on	todo recto
opposite	frente a..
behind	detrás de...
in front of	enfrente de...
next to	al lado de...
Where is the bus	¿Dónde está la
station/post	estación de
office/toilet?	autobuses/la
	oficina de correos/
	el baño?
What´s this in	¿Cómo se dice
Spanish?	en español?
Where does the bus	¿De dónde sale el
to... leave from?	autobús para...?
I'd like a (return)	Quisiera un billete
ticket to...	(de ida y vuelta)
	para...
What time does it	¿A qué hora sale?
leave?	
platform	el andén
ticket office	la taquilla
timetable	el horario

Money

How much?	¿Cuánto es?
I would like to change	Me gustaría
some money	cambiar dinero
ATM cash machine	cajero automático
foreign exchange	la oficina de cambio
bureau	
credit card	tarjeta de crédito
travellers' cheques	cheques de viaje

Numbers/days/months/seasons

1	un/uno/una
2	dos
3	tres
4	cuatro
5	cinco
6	seis
7	siete
8	ocho
9	nueve
10	diez
11	once
12	doce
13	trece
14	catorce
15	quince
16	dieciséis
17	diecisiete
18	dieciocho
19	diecinueve
20	veinte
21	veintiuno
30	treinta
40	cuarenta
50	cincuenta
60	sesenta
70	setenta
80	ochenta
90	noventa
100	cien(to)
101	ciento uno
200	doscientos
500	quinientos
1000	mil
Monday	lunes
Tuesday	martes
Wednesday	miércoles
Thursday	jueves
Friday	viernes
Saturday	sábado
Sunday	domingo
today	hoy
yesterday	ayer
tomorrow	mañana
January	enero
February	febrero
March	marzo
April	abril
May	mayo
June	junio
July	julio
August	agosto
September	septiembre
October	octubre
November	noviembre
December	diciembre
spring	primavera
summer	verano

autumn	otoño
winter	invierno

Food and drink

Basics

aceite	oil
agua	water
ajo	garlic
arroz	rice
azúcar	sugar
huevos	eggs
mantequilla	butter
miel	honey
pan	bread
pimienta	pepper
pinchos/pintxos	a small bite-sized tapa
queso	cheese
sal	salt
sopa	soup
tapa	small serving of food
vinagre	vinegar

Meals

almuerzo/comida	lunch
botella	bottle
carta	menu
cena	dinner
comedor	dining room
cuchara	spoon
cuchillo	knife
desayuno	breakfast
menú (del día)	daily set-lunch
menú de degustación	set menu offering a taste of several house specialities
mesa	table
platos combinados	mixed plate
ración	a plateful of food
tenedor	fork
vaso	glass

Meat

albóndigas	meatballs
callos	tripe
caracoles	snails
chorizo	spicy sausage
conejo	rabbit
cochinillo	roast suckling pig
hígado	liver
jamón serrano	cured ham
jamón de york	regular ham
morcilla	black pudding
pollo	chicken
salchicha	sausage

Seafood

ahumados	smoked fish
almejas	clams
anchoas	anchovies
atún	tuna
a la marinera	seafood cooked with garlic, onions and white wine
bacalao	cod
bonito	premium-quality tuna
boquerones	small, anchovy-like fish, usually served in vinegar
calamares	squid
cangrejo	crab
champiñones	mushrooms
gambas	prawns
langostinos	langoustines
mejillones	mussels
ostras	oysters
pulpo	octopus

Fruit and vegetables

aceitunas	olives
alcachofas	artichokes
berenjena	aubergine/eggplant
cebolla	onion
cerezas	cherries
coliflor	cauliflower
ensalada	salad
fresa	strawberry
garbanzos	chickpeas
granada	pomegranate
habas	broad/fava beans
higos	figs
lechuga	lettuce
lentejas	lentils
limón	lemon
manzana	apple
melocotones	peaches
nabos	turnips
naranja	orange
pepino	cucumber
pimientos	peppers

...ientos de padrón	small peppers, with the odd hot one thrown in
piña	pineapple
pisto	assortment of cooked vegetables (like ratatouille)
plátano	banana
pomelo	grapefruit
puerros	leeks
puré	thick soup
repollo	cabbage
sandía	watermelon
setas	oyster mushrooms
sopa	soup
tomate	tomato
uvas	grapes
zanahoria	carrot

specialities

bocadillo	French-loaf sandwich
cocido	meat and chickpea stew
croquetas	croquettes, with bits of ham in
empanada	slices of fish/meat pie
ensaladilla	Russian salad (diced vegetables in mayonnaise, often with tuna)
patatas alioli	potatoes in garlic mayonnaise
patatas bravas	fried potatoes in spicy tomato sauce
tortilla (española)	potato omelette
tortilla francesa	plain omelette
tostas	toasted bread with a topping

Cooking methods

al ajillo	with olive oil and garlic
a la parilla	charcoal-grilled
a la plancha	grilled on a hot plate
a la romana	fried in batter
al horno	baked in the oven
asado	roast
frito	fried

Desserts

arroz con leche	rice pudding
crema catalana	Catalan crème brûlée
cuajada	cream-based dessert often served with honey
flan	crème caramel
helado	ice cream
melocotón en almíbar	peaches in syrup
membrillo	quince paste
nata	whipped cream
natillas	custard
yogur	yoghurt

Drinks

anís	aniseed liqueur
café (con leche)	(white) coffee
cerveza	beer
té	tea
vino	wine
...blanco	white
...rosado	rosé
...tinto	red
vermút	vermouth
zumo	juice

Glossary

alameda park or grassy promenade
alcázar Moorish fortified palace
asador restaurant specialising in roast meats such as lamb
avenida avenue (usually abbreviated to avda)
ayuntamiento town hall or council
azulejo glazed ceramic tilework
barrio suburb or neighbourhood
bodega cellar or wine bar
calle (usually abbreviated to C/) street or road
capilla mayor chapel containing the high altar
capilla real royal chapel
carretera highway
castillo castle
cervecería bar specializing in beer
chotis Madrid's traditional dance
correos post office
corrida bullfight
cuadrilla a bullfighter's team of assistants
edificio building
ermita hermitage
estanco small shop selling stamps and tobacco, recognizable by the brown and yellow signs bearing the word *tabacos*
farmacia pharmacy/chemist
gasolina petrol
iglesia church
judería Jewish quarter
lavabo washbasin, toilet
lonja market
marisquería seafood restaurant

mercado market
mesón an old-style restaurant
mirador viewing point
Movida late Seventies/early Eighties creative explosion in Madrid, viewed as Spain's Swinging Sixties
Mudéjar Muslim Spaniard subject to medieval Christian rule, but retaining Islamic worship; most commonly a term applied to architecture which includes buildings built by Moorish craftsmen for the Christian rulers and later designs influenced by Moors. The 1890s to 1930s saw a Mudéjar revival, blended with Art Nouveau and Art Deco forms
museo museum
oficina de turismo tourist office
palacio aristocratic mansion
parador state-run hotel, usually housed in a building of historic interest
patio inner courtyard
Plateresco/Plateresque an elaborately decorative Renaissance style, the sixteenth-century successor of Isabelline forms. Named for its resemblance to silversmiths' work (*platería*)
plaza square
plaza de toros bullring
posada old name for an inn
puerta gateway
puerto port
servicio toilet
sidrería bar specializing in cider
taberna tavern
tasca old-style bar
terraza summer outdoor bar/terrace
zarzuela light opera

SMALL PR...

Publishing information

This fourth edition published January 2018 by **Rough Guides Ltd**
80 Strand, London WC2R 0RL
11, Community Centre, Panchsheel Park, New Delhi 110017, India
Distributed by Penguin Random House
Penguin Books Ltd, 80 Strand, London WC2R 0RL
Penguin Group (USA) 345 Hudson Street, NY 10014, USA
Penguin Group (Australia) 250 Camberwell Road, Camberwell, Victoria 3124, Australia
Penguin Group (NZ) 67 Apollo Drive, Mairangi Bay, Auckland 1310, New Zealand
Penguin Group (South Africa) Block D, Rosebank Office Park, 181 Jan Smuts Avenue,
Parktown North, Gauteng, South Africa 2193
Rough Guides is represented in Canada by
DK Canada 320 Front Street West, Suite 1400, Toronto, Ontario M5V 3B6
Typeset in Minion and Din to an original design by Henry Iles and Dan May.
Printed and bound in China © Simon Baskett 2018
Maps © Rough Guides except Madrid Metro map © Metro de Madrid S.A. 2017

160pp includes index
A catalogue record for this book is available from the British Library
ISBN 978-0-24130-627-7

The publishers and authors have done their best to ensure the accuracy and
currency of all the information in **Pocket Rough Guide Madrid**, however, they
can accept no responsibility for any loss, injury, or inconvenience sustained by
any traveller as a result of information or advice contained in the guide.
1 3 5 7 9 8 6 4 2

MIX
Paper from
responsible sources
FSC® C018179
www.fsc.org

Rough Guides credits

Editor: Payal Sharotri
Layout: Nikhil Agarwal
Cartography: Ed Wright
Picture editor: Phoebe Lowndes
Photographers: Lydia Evans,
Tim Draper
Proofreader: Stewart Wild

Managing editor: Keith Drew
Production: Jimmy Lao
Cover photo research: Sarah Stewart-Richardson
Editorial assistant: Aimee White
Senior DTP coordinator: Dan May
Publishing director: Georgina Dee

Author: Simon Baskett lives and
works in Madrid with his wife, Trini,
and two children Patrick and Laura.
He is a long-suffering Atlético Madrid
fan, and has not yet given up hope
that he might live long enough to
see them win the Champions League.
His ambition is to win El Gordo (the
huge Christmas lottery) and retire to
a local bar.

Acknowledgements

Special thanks to Trini once again for all her hard work and patience. Thanks, too, go to Antonio and Javier of the *Hostal Gonzalo*, to Itziar Herrán and to the Metro de Madrid.

Help us update

We've gone to a lot of effort to ensure that the fourth edition of the **Pocket Rough Guide Madrid** is accurate and up-to-date. However, things change – places get "discovered", opening hours are notoriously fickle, restaurants and rooms raise prices or lower standards. If you feel we've got it wrong or left something out, we'd like to know, and if you can remember the address, the price, the hours, the phone number, so much the better.

Please send your comments with the subject line "**Pocket Rough Guide Madrid Update**" to mail@roughguides.com. We'll credit all contributions and send a copy of the next edition (or any other Rough Guide if you prefer) for the very best emails.

Find more travel information, connect with fellow travellers and book your trip on ⓦroughguides.com

Readers' updates

Thanks to all the readers who have taken the time to write in with comments and suggestions (and apologies if we've inadvertently omitted or misspelt anyone's name):

Natalia Ageitos; Michael Blatchford; Marta Carballal Broome; Terry Craven; Jade Devey; Tim Godfray; Chris Lorenzen; Rosa Martín; Carol O'Gorman; Claudia Roca; John Yanez

Photo credits

SMALL PRI...

Cover: Gran Via **Alamy Stock Photo**: Beatrice Prev
1 SuperStock: age fotostock/Lucas Vallecillos
2 Alamy Stock Photo: Jozef Sedmak (bl). **Ana La Santa**: Olga Planas (br). **AWL Images**: Hemis (cr). **SuperStock**: age fotostock/Ivan Pendjakov (t)
11 Museo Thyssen Bornemisza: Pablo Casares (t)
13 Getty Images: Matias Nieto (b). **Picfair.com**: Artur Bogacki (c)
14 Sorolla Museum: (b)
15 Getty Images: Ellen van Bodegom (t). Matteo Colombo (b)
16 Alamy Stock Photo: ZUMA Press, Inc. (b). **Dreamstime.com**: Alexander Mychko (c). **Getty Images**: Peter Adams (t)
17 Alamy Stock Photo: Invictus Sarl/Irène Alastruey (bl)
18 Dreamstime.com: Mariusz Prusaczyk (tr)
19 Alamy Stock Photo: Patrick Forget (c). **Corbis**: Maurizio Borgese (b)
20 Alamy Stock Photo: Sergio Azenha (cr); Lucas Vallecillos (br)
22 Corbis: Reuters/Sergio Perez (tr)
24-25 SuperStock: age footstock/Luis Domingo
27 Corbis: Design Pics
34 Getty Images: Lonely Planet Images
37 Getty Images: Krivinis
39 Getty Images: Daniel Hernanz Ramos
42 Picfair.com: John Greim
43 Cafe de Chinitas: Nacho Casares

45 Corbis: Eric G. Madroal
50 Alamy Stock Photo: Lucas Vallecillos
51 Alamy Stock Photo: Peter Eastland
55 Alamy Stock Photo: Artur Bogacki
58 Alamy Stock Photo: age fotostock/Alvaro Leiva
59 Ana La Santa: Olga Planas
62 Alamy Stock Photo: Tim E White
63 Alamy Stock Photo: Hemis
76 Alamy Stock Photo: Lucas Vallecillos
79 Alamy Stock Photo: Peter Eastland
83 Alamy Stock Photo: SBMR
87 Alamy Stock Photo: Lucas Vallecillos
88 Dry Bar 1862
91 Getty Images: UniversalImagesGroup
94 Alamy Stock Photo: Travstock
95 Dreamstime.com: Nacroba
96 Getty Images: Cristina Arias
99 Platea Madrid (br)
101 Alamy Stock Photo: Paco Gómez García
104 Alamy Stock Photo: PRISMA ARCHIVO
105 Alamy Stock Photo: WENN Ltd (t). **Alamy Stock Photo**: Alex Segre (b)
106 Alamy Stock Photo: imagebroker
108 SuperStock: robertharding
117 Corbis: Jose Fuste Raga
124-125 Alamy Stock Photo: Douglas Lander
134-135 Alamy Stock Photo: Alex Segre

Index

Maps are marked in **bold**.

ESCAPE THE EVERYDAY

ADVENTURE BECKONS
YOU JUST NEED TO KNOW WHERE TO LOOK

roughguides.com

KAREN ROBARDS

The Last Kiss Goodbye

HODDER

First published in the USA in 2013 by Ballantine Books
An imprint of The Random House Publishing Group
A division of Random House, Inc.

First published in Great Britain in 2014 by Hodder & Stoughton
An Hachette UK company

This paperback edition published 2014

1

A CIP catalogue record for this title is available from the British Library

ISBN 978 1 444 78621 7

Printed and bound by CPI Group (UK) Ltd, Croydon, CR0 4YY

Hodder & Stoughton policy is to use papers that are natural, renewable
and recyclable products and made from wood grown in sustainable forests.
The logging and manufacturing processes are expected to conform to the
environmental regulations of the country of origin.

Hodder & Stoughton Ltd
338 Euston Road
London NW1 3BH

www.hodder.co.uk

The Last Kiss Goodbye *is dedicated to*
my wonderful editor, Linda Marrow.
It is also dedicated, as always, with love to
my three sons, Peter, Christopher, and Jack,
and to my husband, Doug.

ACKNOWLEDGMENTS

Writing is a lonely profession until it's not. That's when the fantastic team at my publishing house steps in and starts to work their magic. My thanks to Linda Marrow, Gina Centrello, Anne Speyer, Ania Markiewicz, and the entire team at Ballantine Books.

The Last Kiss Goodbye

CHAPTER ONE

The sight of the dead man stretched out on her couch stopped Dr. Charlotte Stone in her tracks.

Except for the flickering glow of the TV, the house was dark, but his big body sprawled across the pale natural linen upholstery was impossible to miss. Freezing in place just inside the threshold of her living room, Charlie fought desperately to get a grip. Lying on his back with his head resting on one of the couch's thickly padded arms, eyes closed and arms folded across his wide chest, he could almost have been asleep. But she knew better: he was beyond sleep now. The sudden tightness in her chest as she looked at him made it difficult to breathe. Her heart pounded. Her pulse raced.

She was swallowing hard, working on corralling her runaway emotions and whipping them into some kind of acceptable shape, when he opened his eyes and looked at her.

Even seen by TV light, those sky blue eyes of his were enough to make an unsuspecting woman go weak at the knees. Luckily, she had experienced their power before. Plus, she knew what he was, what he was capable of. But the sad fact was, she was a sucker for him anyway.

He smiled at her. It wasn't a particularly nice smile. Didn't matter: her stomach still fluttered.

Idiot.

"So how's that whole moving on thing working out for you, Doc?" he drawled.

The hint of acidity in Michael Garland's honey-dipped voice didn't stop the warm rush of—let's call it relief—that had started flooding her veins the second she'd laid eyes on him. She absolutely should not have been so glad to see him. In fact, she should not have been glad to see him at all. But where he and she were concerned, "should" had flown out the window a while back.

"Fine." Charlie's answer was as cool and untroubled as she *wasn't* feeling. Regaining her power of movement, she hit the wall switch that turned on the lamps on either side of the couch. Then she walked across the polished wood floor to the bleached oak coffee table, picked up the remote, and turned the TV off, ending the deafening blast of the sports channel he had been watching. Cranked to an almost painful loudness, the sound was what had brought Charlie rushing in from the porch a couple of moments before—and what had broken up the more than friendly good-night that she'd been exchanging at her front door with Tony Bartoli, the handsome FBI agent whom Garland thought she was moving on to. Garland had clearly seen her kissing Tony, and he just as clearly hadn't liked it. What his jibe meant was that he thought that she was moving on to Tony from *him*. Not that she and Garland had the kind of relationship that she could move on from, exactly, but—well, it was complicated.

The short version was, she was a psychiatrist who studied serial killers. Garland was a convicted serial killer, and, as an inmate at Wallens Ridge State Prison, where she was conducting her latest government-sponsored study, her former research subject. That association had ended with his death.

This was the part that bore repeating: Michael Garland was absolutely, positively, no-coming-back-from-it dead. As in, what she was looking at and talking to was his ghost.

See, she had the unfortunate ability to see ghosts. Oh, not all ghosts. Only the recently, violently departed, who, confused about what had happened to them, sometimes lingered for a short period on earth after their passing. Garland had been murdered eleven days before, shanked by one of his fellow inmates. Charlie had tried to save his life, to no avail. In classic no-good-deed-goes-unpunished style, his ghost had attached itself to her at the moment of his passing, to torment and harass (among other things) her until he should finally pass on to the Great Beyond.

Which, in typically irritating fashion, he was resisting.

Usually the ghosts she could see lingered for no more than a week. By that yardstick, Garland was already well past his sell-by date.

Which was one reason she had been so glad—strike that—so surprised to see him. She had last set eyes on him some four days before, when he had saved her life. Since then, she had been afraid—strike that, too—increasingly convinced that she would never see him again.

Much as she hated to admit it even to herself, the thought had made her heart bleed.

But here he was, all six-foot-three hunky inches of him. Thirty-six years old at the time of his death. Chippendales-worthy body in a snug white T-shirt and faded jeans. A thick mane of tawny hair that didn't quite reach his wide shoulders. Square jaw, broad cheekbones and forehead, straight nose and well-cut mouth. Absurdly tan and healthy-looking for a ghost—or a man who had spent the last four years of his life in federal prison, which he had done. Outrageously handsome. Certifiably dangerous. The proverbial bad penny.

Who could make her heart pound and her blood heat and her good sense fly out the window. He was the very last thing she needed—or wanted—in her life.

Dead or alive.

Not that she had any choice in the matter.

She could no more control his presence in her life than she could control the sun, the moon, and the stars. He had just shown up, and one day—probably sooner rather than later—he would disappear. The universe was in charge here, not her.

The thought steadied her.

"Where have you been?" If there was a snap in her tone, he had earned it, simply because he had somehow managed to make her care about the answer. Still, afraid her question might reveal how stupidly involved with him she had become, she would have taken it back if she could have.

"Missed me bad, hmm?" Garland swung his long legs off the couch and sat up. Under other circumstances, Charlie would have given a dirty look to the scuffed cowboy boots that he hadn't seemed to have any qualms about planting on her pristine couch. But ghost boots—she was pretty sure that they didn't leave marks.

Anyway, the smirk in the grin he directed at her was way more annoying than the boots on the linen, so she directed her dirty look right into his twinkling baby blues before turning on her heel and walking away.

"Nope." She hadn't missed him one bit, she told herself. She threw the reply over her shoulder as she reached the hall and headed toward the kitchen, past the old-fashioned staircase that led to the second floor. Standing up, he followed her. She was wearing nothing more exciting than a silky white sleeveless blouse and a pair of well-tailored black slacks with heels, a little dressier than her usual attire because Tony had been taking her out to dinner but nothing special. Still, she could feel Garland's eyes on her, and strongly suspected that he was watching her trim backside with appreciation as she walked. Casting a quick, suspicious glance over her shoulder, she tried to catch him at it, but he was (a) too quick, (b) too wily, or (c) just too damned lucky to get caught. As their eyes met, he grinned at her.

"Liar," he said.

She snorted, shaking her head in firm denial. Terrifying to think that having a ghost following her made her feel more fully alive than she had in days. Even more terrifying to realize that what she really wanted to do was turn around and walk right into his arms.

Which she couldn't do, because he had no more substance than air. And which she wouldn't do even if she could.

Because she truly wasn't that self-destructive. She didn't think.

Moonlight pouring through the kitchen windows—a tall, wide one that took up almost all the back wall behind the eating area, and a smaller one set into the top of the kitchen door—illuminated the white cabinets and stainless steel appliances and hardwood floor. She'd left the curtains in the front of the house closed, so no one could see in from the street. The kitchen blinds were raised all the way to the top of the windows, because there was no one living behind her to see in, and because she liked the view. As she stepped from the hall's gloom into the silvery light, Charlie saw her reflection in the big window's dark glass. Her chestnut brown hair hung in loose waves around her shoulders. Her fair skin was, as usual, pale, but her denim blue eyes looked kind of sultry because she had deliberately played them up with liner and shadow, which she almost never wore, and an extra coat or two of mascara. Her wide mouth looked full and soft, but more vulnerable than it should have, given that right after dinner she had freshly applied deep red (vampy) lipstick. That softly smudged look would be because, she realized belatedly, Tony had subsequently kissed all her lipstick off, so her lips were now both slightly swollen and bare. She was five-six, slender and fit at age thirty-two, and over the years a lot of guys had told her that she was beautiful. If she remained skeptical, it was because most of the time those same guys had been trying to talk her into the sack. Tonight, the makeup plus the three-inch heels made her look, um, sexier. Ordinarily she wore low-heeled, sensible shoes because the last thing she wanted to do was give off any kind of look-at-me-I'm-hot vibe. This almost daily exercise in discretion owed a lot to the fact that her usual work was carried out in a prison full of incarcerated men. Which was also why she customarily wore her hair up and minimal makeup. But tonight, for Tony, she'd made an effort. With, yes, the thought that she might allow their relationship to progress to the next level, as in, sleep with him. Because Tony was way handsome and because she really liked him and because she badly needed a normal, uncomplicated man-woman relationship in her life.

And because she'd feared—thought—that Garland was gone for good and she was determined to eradicate any lingering memories of him. Of *them*.

In the end, she hadn't been able to bring herself to invite Tony in.

She'd already been sending him on his way when the blasting of her should-have-been-silent TV had reached her ears and caused her heart to swell with hope and hurried things along. Sex with Tony, she had decided somewhere between dinner and her front door, was something that just wasn't going to happen. At least, not yet.

But Garland didn't have to know that.

In fact, she wasn't about to let Garland know that.

He was way too full of himself already.

Charlie suddenly realized that hers was the only reflection that she saw in the window, although Garland was right behind her. A lightning glance over her shoulder confirmed it: he was still there.

But to judge by what she could see in the window, she was alone. His reflection didn't show up. And that would be because, in the physical world in which she and every other living creature existed, he did not.

Only she could see him.

"Admit it, Doc: you were worried about me."

Charlie closed her eyes.

Worried about him. That vastly understated the case. Truth was, when he had not shown back up after materializing for just long enough to take the killing blow meant for her, she had been sick with fear over him. Afraid that he had been sucked up into Eternity, and that she would never see him again.

The pain that had accompanied that fear had shown her how very vulnerable she had become where he was concerned. Now that he was back, she was determined to better guard her clearly way-too-susceptible heart.

Falling in love with him was not an option. In life he'd been the baddest of bad men, the convicted murderer of seven women, sentenced to death for horrible, brutal crimes.

And as sexy and charming as he might be, he was the exact same person in death.

That's what she had to keep reminding herself of, even if some too-stupid-to-live part of her refused to accept it.

He claimed he was innocent. All the evidence said otherwise.

Even if, for the sake of argument, she allowed herself to believe in his innocence, believe that the exhaustive police investigation and all the evidence and the courts and the entire criminal justice system were plain wrong in his case, she still wasn't about to let herself go where she feared their association was headed.

She wasn't about to commit the ultimate folly of letting herself fall in love with him. No way, no how.

Bottom line was, he was dead, she was alive.

Whatever their relationship was or wasn't, the hard truth was, there was absolutely no future in it.

If she let herself forget that, she deserved every bit of heartbreak that would be hurtling her way.

So get over being so ridiculously glad to see him already.

Charlie opened her eyes. There she still was, looking at her own reflection in the kitchen window, with not so much as a glimmer to indicate that a gorgeous (dead) guy was standing right behind her.

"I was actually very comfortable with the idea that nature had finally taken its course with you." She spoke over her shoulder, admirably cool, as she crossed to the light switch beside the back door and flipped on the kitchen light. A round oak table with four slat-back chairs stood in the eating area in front of the window. Because she had been away, the table was piled high with mail. Beyond it, out the window, she could see the tall, nodding shadows of the sunflowers that grew in a patch along her back fence. Backlit by moonlight, they were striping the grass with shifting lines of black. Beyond that, a thickly wooded mountainside formed an impenetrable wall of darkness as it rose to meet the night sky.

This old-fashioned, two-story white clapboard farmhouse with its gingerbread trim and wide front porch was the first real home she had ever had, and she loved it. Located on a quiet street at the edge of Big Stone Gap, Virginia, a coal mining town deep in the heart of Appalachia that was still reeling from the recession, it provided her with a much-needed respite from the daily grimness of her work at the prison, which perched like a vulture at the top of the mountain, overlooking the town. Decorating and furnishing the house had been a project that she had enjoyed.

Until right this minute, when Garland's presence suddenly seemed to fill it to bursting, she had never recognized that with only her in it, the house had sometimes felt empty. No, strike that: lonely.

"Bullshit," he said without heat, and the inescapable fact that he'd hit the nail on the head there made her lips tighten. Ignoring him, she crossed to the table with the intention of checking out her mail. He stopped in the kitchen doorway and, folding his arms over his chest, propped a broad shoulder against the jamb. *"Thank you for saving my life, Michael."*

His mocking falsetto earned him a narrow-eyed glance. But truth was, he *had* saved her life, and she was grateful.

"Thank you." She turned her attention to the mail. Nothing like a fat stack of bills to provide a distraction.

"Michael," he prompted. She could feel his eyes on her.

Ostensibly busy flipping through the pile of envelopes, she said nothing. The last time she had called him Michael—well, she wasn't going there. She was going to forget that whole mind-blowingly sexy episode.

Yeah, right. Never gonna happen as long as you live.

Well, she was going to try.

"So, you shack up with FBI guy while I was gone?"

The question annoyed her. Actually, he annoyed her. Greatly.

In the process of tearing open an envelope, she flicked him a look. And lied. "Yes."

"Your nose just grew, Pinocchio."

"If you're not going to believe me, why ask?"

"Good question." He shrugged. "So why *aren't* you shacking up with FBI guy?"

"Because, believe it or not, I don't sleep with everything in pants," she snapped before she thought. As a slow smile spread across his face, she felt like biting her tongue. Because, of course, she had slept with Garland. Sort of. As in, ghost sex. Again, it was complicated.

But whether or not it had been, in the strictest sense, real or not, it had definitely been the hottest sex of her life.

And she was not going there. Not again. Not even in her thoughts.

"I do believe it." He crossed the kitchen to stand across the table from her. His big hands curled around a chair back. His steady gaze made her uncomfortable. She concentrated on the mail. "Thing is, I think I'm starting to know you pretty well. I think you're a one-man woman, Doc."

Her eyes snapped up to meet his. At what she saw for her there, she felt a wave of heat.

God, don't let it show.

"You might be right," she said with a false cordiality of which she was justifiably proud. "And if ever I find that man, I'll be sure to let you know."

His answering look made her foolish, reckless heart pick up its pace. Afraid of what he might read in her eyes, she let them drop to the square brown packing box that had been the next item of mail to come within reach of her hands. Damned tape—the box was swaddled in it. Clear and shiny, it was stubbornly resistant to all her attempts to breach it. Reaching for the small pair of scissors she kept along with items like pushpins and paper clips in a basket on the sideboard behind her, she cast another glance at him. She was just in time to watch him fade into translucence. Eyes widening, hand tightening convulsively around the scissors, she registered with a tingle of shock that she could absolutely see the rest of the kitchen through him. Even as she stared, he wavered, then started to solidify once more.

She was still struggling to wrap her mind around what she was seeing when he did it again.

"Might want to close your mouth, Doc. Damned if you don't look like you've seen a ghost."

That at least had the virtue of snapping her out of total immobility. Her lips met and firmed. Her eyes collided with his. "Funny."

He seemed to look at her more closely. Of course, it was hard to tell when he was once again as diaphanous as smoke. "So what's up?"

"You—you're flickering." Her mouth had gone dry. Wetting her lips, she tried to swallow.

He was returning to being almost—*almost*—solid-looking. *Oh, God.*

"Flickering?" He glanced down at himself. Seeming to notice nothing amiss—okay, he looked solid again, so why would he?—he lifted his eyebrows at her.

"Fading in and out. Like—like Tinker Bell at the end of *Peter Pan*. You know, the Disney movie. When Tink was dying, and the children had to clap to bring her back." The comparison made Charlie feel cold all over. She was so rattled that she was hardly making sense, she knew. Her eyes stayed glued to him: he'd started fading again as she spoke, and was now as insubstantial as a layer of chiffon, and rippling like one, too, if said chiffon had been caught in a breeze. It wasn't the first time she'd seen an apparition flicker, but it was definitely the first time that the sight had made her heart lurch and her blood drain toward her toes.

The other times—she'd been relieved. And she'd been relieved because the flickering was a sign that the ghost she was looking at would soon cease to be a problem to the living. And that would be because that flicker meant the apparition was minutes away from fading into nothingness, and she was comfortable in the knowledge that it was leaving this earthly plane and never coming back.

But now, with him, she felt her composure shattering into a million lacerating shards as she faced what that flickering probably meant: either he was getting to the stage where she wasn't going to be able to see him anymore, or he was being drawn permanently into the Hereafter. One way or the other, it didn't matter. If what she'd seen happen in the past was a prologue to the present, he was going.

It wouldn't be long before she was free of him. For good.

Which she had known all along was going to happen.

He was a ghost, and ghosts couldn't stay.

So why did that make her feel so utterly devastated?

"Must've missed that one," he replied drily.

Her eyes stayed fixed on him with a kind of horrified desperation. The glowing green numbers of the digital clock over the microwave were perfectly visible through his wide and muscular chest. She could read the time: 11:22.

"How—how do you feel?"

"To tell the truth, like I died about a week back."

"Would you stop joking?" Her tone was fierce. "I'm serious."

He shrugged. "Thing is, I had a hell of a fight getting back here this time. Way harder than I've ever had before. Them Spookville walls—they didn't want to let me out. If I hadn't been so worried about you, I don't think I could have made it through. Ever since I did, I've been feeling the damned place pulling at me, like it's doing its best to reel me back in. Right now, it's pulling pretty strong." His eyes narrowed at her. "You got a particular reason for asking?"

"Oh, God." Her chest felt tight. Drawing a breath required real work. "I think—it might be time. I think—you might be getting ready to leave."

His brows snapped together. "What? Hell, no. I'm not going anywhere."

"I don't think you have a choice."

"So do something. Ju-ju me." His relatively unalarmed tone told her that he did not perceive the immediacy of the danger.

Charlie shook her head, speechless because he was now pulsing like a lightbulb getting ready to burn out and was clearly unaware of it. Something that felt like a giant fist closed around her heart. She gripped the scissors so hard the metal hurt her fingers.

She already knew how this story had to end. But she wasn't ready. There was so much still unresolved between them, so much to say . . .

"Please don't take him yet." The words were scarcely louder than a breath. Emerging of their own volition, they weren't addressed to him: she was speaking to the universe, to the vast, unknowable forces of Eternity, to God himself. Then, realizing what she had said—and what it revealed—she shifted her grip on the scissors and looked down and started cutting through the tape on the box. Savagely.

Anything to keep from watching him disappear.

Because there was nothing she could do to stop it. Because this was the way it had to be.

"Whoa, hold on there. What was that?" Even in this moment of what felt to Charlie like extremis, there was humor in his voice. "Sounded to me like that was you admitting you're not ready to see the last of me."

"Oh, go—soak your head." Her fingers stilled as she looked back at him. She'd been about to tell him to go to hell, before it had hit her like a baseball bat between the eyes that that was in all likelihood exactly where he was going.

"Quit fighting it." He was all but transparent now, as see-through as delicately colored cellophane, coming in and out of focus faster than she could blink. Grief and dread combined to turn her blood to ice. "Would it kill you to give up and admit that you're crazy about me?"

His eyes teased her. Her heart felt as if it would crack in half.

Okay, so she'd known this moment was coming. Known it from the beginning, from her first horrified realization that this scariest of ghosts had attached himself to her: the affliction was temporary.

At first, she'd reminded herself of that as a source of comfort.

Then she had simply tried not to think about it.

But now, she discovered, she couldn't bear the knowledge that he was actually about to be gone from her world.

That she would never see him again.

That he would be caught up in the horrible purple fog of the place he called Spookville, forever.

Or at least until he was dragged off to someplace even worse.

Abandoning the box, she put the scissors down on the table. Her movements were careful. Precise. Otherwise, she feared her hands would shake. Then, because her eyes were glued to him, she accidentally knocked the box over. All kinds of white packing peanuts came tumbling out, spilling across the table, onto the floor, everywhere.

She scarcely noticed. She didn't care.

He was barely there at all now, with no more substance than a heat shimmer. Her fists clenched so hard that her nails dug into her palms. It was all she could do to breathe. Her heart wept.

In consequence, her tone was angry. "You think this is a joke? Look at yourself *now*."

He looked down at himself. It was instantly plain that he saw what was happening. Charlie could feel the sudden tension emanating from him, a new and electric sense of urgency in the air.

His jaw was tight as he looked back at her. "You might want to get cracking with that ju-ju, Doc."

"There's nothing I can do." At his behest and against her better judgment, she'd already used every scrap of spirit lore she'd ever learned that might keep him grounded to earth. There wasn't anything left, or at least nothing that she knew. If running to him and throwing her arms around him would have done any good, she would have been racing around the table to his side, but she already knew it would be easier to try to hold on to mist. *This is how it has to be.* She knew that, accepted it. And still her next words were nothing she had ever imagined she would say to him: "Concentrate. Try to hang on."

"Ain't working." He was fading so fast now, she was afraid he'd be gone in the next instant. "Better start clapping, Doc."

She sucked in air. "Garland—"

He was gone. Just like that. Her stomach dropped to her toes. Her knees went weak.

"Shit." She could still hear him. "I don't make it back, don't worry about me. Charlie . . ."

The rest of what he said was indistinct.

"Michael!" Forget keeping her distance, keeping her cool. Despite what she knew was the absolute futility of it, she rushed around the table to where he had been standing anyway, reaching for him, plowing her hands through the now-empty air. Nothing. Not even the slightest hint of an electric tingle—the telltale sign of contact with an invisible spirit—to mark where he had been. Defeated, she gripped a chair back hard. God, what had she expected? The universe always reclaimed its own. She knew that, knew it had to happen, knew this was no more than the natural order of things, but still she felt as if her heart was being ripped out of her chest. She wanted to cry. She wanted to scream.

"There has to be a white light," she called urgently through the pain, because helping him navigate Eternity was the only thing she could do for him now. "Michael, do you hear? You have to look for the light."

She thought he said something typical like, "Fuck that," and then, "Charlie," with something else after, but she couldn't be sure: his voice was too faint.

"Michael!"

This time there was nothing. No response. No voice. No sign of him. She took a deep, shuddering breath. Her throat closed up. The pain she was experiencing was acute. *This is what grief feels like.* Then she realized, *No, this is what* heartbreak *feels like.*

Her eyes stung: it was from welling tears. Second time in the last eleven days that she, who never cried, had found herself doing just that. Both times had been over him.

Cursing herself for her idiocy, she dashed her knuckles across her eyes.

Bam! Bam! Bam!

A frantic pounding on the kitchen door tore Charlie's eyes away from the spot where he had last been, made her jump and gasp and shoot a startled glance toward the sound.

Pale and big-eyed and terrified-looking in the darkness, a woman's face peered in at her through the diamond-paned window in the top of the door.

"Help me," the woman screamed, pounding the door again. *"Please, you have to let me in!"*

CHAPTER TWO

In an instant Charlie saw that the woman was young, with long, dark hair, pale skin—and a scarlet river of blood running down the side of her face.

"Hurry!" the stranger cried, rattling the doorknob now even as she continued to pound on the door. "Please let me in! Please!"

Her eyes locked with Charlie's. They begged. Charlie knew that look—it was mortal fear. She recognized it instantly because she had experienced it more than once herself. She knew what it felt like, processed it viscerally, and her pulse leaped and her gut clenched in response. Thrusting her own pain aside, reacting automatically to this new emergency, to this fellow creature in such obvious distress, she dashed her knuckles across her burning eyes one more time and flew to open the door.

"Goddamn it, Charlie, no!" It wasn't a roar, although she could tell that was what it was meant to be. It had more the quality of an echo, faint in volume but furious in tone: Michael. Glancing frantically around for him at the same time as she yanked the door wide, she saw nothing of him.

"Michael?" His name was wrenched from her. A warm wind, thick with humidity, ruffled her hair. The scent of the mountain in late August—mossy and damp, laced with honeysuckle—filled her nostrils.

There was no answer from him. No sign.

The woman spilled headlong through the door—*"Thank you, oh, thank you!"*—instantly reclaiming Charlie's attention. Bursting past her into the house, moving so fast that her wet, muddy shoes slipped and skidded on the hardwood, she was breathing in great, gasping sobs. Outside, fat drops of rain were just starting to fall. The steady plop as they splattered on the stoop and the concrete pavers leading up to it made Charlie think of fast-approaching footsteps, and the tiny hairs on the back of her neck stood on end.

"He's got a gun! He's coming! He's going to kill me!" Choking out the warning over her shoulder, the woman stopped and bent double, then dropped to a crouch as if her knees had suddenly given out. Coughing and gagging, she huddled near the table while Charlie stood stupidly gaping at her while even more stupidly holding the door wide.

"Who?" Hand tightening convulsively on the doorknob, Charlie cast a frightened look outside, searching the darkness for a sign of anyone who might be giving chase. Although she could see nothing out of place, the soft summer's night with its starry sky had changed dramatically in the brief time since she had stood outside on her front porch saying good-night to Tony. A gathering storm had blown in, transforming the sky into something dark and menacing. The light from the kitchen spilled over the small back stoop, turning the quickening raindrops to a mercurial silver, but beyond that Charlie could see nothing.

"Shut the door! Lock it! Oh, my God, he's right behind me!"

Charlie's heart jumped. Her pulse leaped into overdrive. Already slamming the door as the girl's nerve-jangling screech reached its apex, Charlie shot a jittery glance at the shivering figure crouched on her floor.

The woman—a girl, really, no more than twenty, was Charlie's guess—was soaking wet, far wetter than the newly falling rain would account for. She was also muddy, with a swampy scent that spoke of stagnant rather than fresh water. Slender and pretty, she wore shorts that had once been white, a red T-shirt with some kind of logo on it, and sandals. Visibly shaking, breathing like she had run for miles, she streamed water and blood. Charlie registered all that in the blink of an eye. Then, with a last apprehensive glance out the window into the night—she saw nothing that shouldn't have been there, but the sense that someone *was* there was strong—she shot the deadbolt closed.

"*Who's* right behind you?" Skin crawling as the probable inadequacy of the door as a source of protection from a determined intruder occurred to her, Charlie rushed forward to crouch down herself and wrap a steadying arm around the girl's heaving back. The slender body felt wet, cold, frail. A puddle of muddy water swirled with blood was forming around her feet. At Charlie's touch, the girl threw up her head and looked at her. Cold drops of water flung from the long strands of her hair spattered Charlie's cheek. Even as she automatically swiped the droplets away, Charlie registered that the blood came from an ugly, inch-long gash in the girl's forehead. "You're hurt."

"It doesn't matter. Don't you understand? *He's going to kill me.*" The shrill, unsteady cry sent a cold chill running down Charlie's spine. Every nerve ending she possessed quivered in sympathetic reaction to the sheer terror that was impossible to mistake. Fear was suddenly as tangible in the air as the smell of swampy water. Beneath her sheltering arm, Charlie could feel the girl's tremors. Her eyes—they were golden brown—were huge and dark with fright. "He was—I can't believe I got away! He made us—he made me—" Her hysterical voice deteriorated into a series of shuddering gasps. Wild-eyed, she looked around the kitchen. "We've got to call the police. Quick, quick, quick! Before he gets here! He'll kill me! He's got a *gun!*"

"Damn it to hell, woman, do you have a fucking death wish? You think whoever's after her won't kill you, too?" That was Michael again, closer, louder, still sounding as if his voice should have been a furious roar although it wasn't: it had a muffled sound as though it was reaching her through some sort of interference. Charlie's heart lurched. Then she could see him: a shimmer a few feet away.

She tensed, instantly riveted on that shimmer. *Michael*—even though every cell in her body yearned toward him, she retained just enough presence of mind not to call out to him aloud.

"Where's your phone?" the girl cried.

"On the wall." Charlie gestured toward it as Michael started to solidify, and then for a second there she forgot about everything but him. About the girl, and any possible looming threat, and her own burgeoning sense of danger.

"In the kitchen?" The girl followed Charlie's gesture with her eyes, then pulled away from her, scrambling forward, pitching upright, wet shoes noisily slapping the floor as she stumbled past the foggy shape that was Michael toward the far end of the kitchen, where the slim, beige landline phone hung near the microwave. Charlie registered her progress distractedly. She couldn't help it: in that heartbeat of time, her focus was almost exclusively on Michael.

She could see his face. His features. His eyes.

He was scowling at her.

"Jesus Christ, what part of 'man with a gun' did you miss? Run! Get the hell out of here! Get away from her!"

Relief at his reappearance was tempered by a stabbing fear that it might be very brief. In all likelihood, this was just another flicker.

Her throat tightened. Her eyes locked with his.

"I can see you. Can you hold on?" Her voice was low and hoarse, the words meant only for him.

"Who the hell knows?" He was almost completely solid now. Striding toward her, he made an urgent gesture toward the hall. "Go! That way! Run! If she's got some guy after her trying to kill her, the last thing you want to do is get caught up in the middle of it."

"I can't." The urgency of the present reasserted itself like a thunderclap. Even for her own safety, she knew that abandoning her traumatized and endangered guest was beyond her, and knew, too, that the hard truth was that agonizing over him—over something she couldn't control—was useless. Even as her heart was being put through what felt like a meat grinder, she had to leave him to the mercy (or not) of the universe and deal with the reality of the emergency in her kitchen.

"What do you mean you"—this time his response actually started as a roar, only to fade as he grew fainter again—"can't?"

A knot formed in her chest. He was once again barely there.

"Michael. If you get sucked back in, you need to ask for forgiveness. You need to pray." The words were wrenched out of her even as she tore her eyes away from him, got a grip, and launched herself after the girl. She might not be able to stop what was happening to him, but maybe she could make a difference here, tonight, this minute, in the real world, for this endangered girl. And maybe, if he followed her advice, she could help him avoid the ultimate horror, after all. It might be the only thing she was able to do for him. Because the sad truth was, even if he did deserve eternal damnation, she couldn't bear to think of him suffering it.

Fool.

He snorted. "Kinda late for that. Damn it, what the hell are you *doing*?"

As she raced past him she saw that he was little more than a shimmer again now, and her heart sank.

"What I can." Instead of running into the hall as he'd clearly expected, she darted around the breakfast bar into the food preparation area, which was basically a narrow galley kitchen that looked across the open counter of the breakfast bar at the table and the back door beyond. The girl was there, in the process of snatching the phone from the kitchen wall. She threw a wide-eyed look over her shoulder at Charlie.

"Who are you *talking* to? Oh, no, are you *nuts*?" The girl squeezed closer to the wall as though to put as much distance between them as possible. Of course, the girl could neither see nor hear Michael. Looking at things from her point of view, having the person she was counting on for help conduct a frantic, one-sided conversation with an unseen entity must be unnerving. Charlie sympathized, but there were more urgent matters to deal with. Like where the girl's attacker was now.

"How close behind you is he?" Casting another lightning glance out the windows—nothing to see but a whole lot of dark, plus silvery streaks as rain ran down the glass—Charlie felt her stomach cramp.

"Close. I don't know. It was dark." As she gasped out the words, the girl looked at Charlie as if she was afraid of her now, too.

"I'm a doctor, okay? You can trust me." Usually, when she was where anyone could overhear, Charlie was way careful not to talk back to the spirits who afflicted her, but this moment—Michael—was the stress-induced exception. God, he was gone again! Looking desperately around, she wanted to scream his name but did not. Not only to keep from freaking the girl out, or to save herself from looking, um, nuts, but also because she knew that it would do absolutely no good. Taking a deep breath, she did her best to focus on the girl. "Who's chasing you? Is it your boyfriend, or—"

"*No.* You don't get it, do you? He's a *killer.*" The girl kept throwing quick, terrified glances at the door. "Oh, my God, is it 911 here?" Shaking visibly, breathing as if she might hyperventilate at any second, she was already frantically stabbing an unsteady finger at the number pad. With her inky black hair streaming water and blood pouring down the right quarter of her face, she looked like something out of a nightmare—or a horror movie. The mere sight of her was enough to send goose bumps racing over Charlie's skin—and convince her that whatever the details might prove to be, the girl definitely had been the victim of something horrific.

"Yes." Shooting more increasingly spooked glances out first the window in the door and then the big window behind the table—as dark as it was outside, with the light on in the kitchen anyone out there could see everything that was going on inside, she realized with a stab of dread. Then Charlie had an epiphany: there was a better way to get help fast. But first things first. Working hard to maintain the outward appearance of calm, she grabbed a handful of paper towels from the dispenser and thrust them at the girl.

"Press that against the cut on your forehead," she ordered. "Hold it firmly. *Do it.*"

That last was in response to the girl's hesitation, which manifested itself in a suspicious look from the paper towels to Charlie. As the girl did as she was told, Charlie left her to run for the cell phone in her purse, which she had dropped on the console table in the front hall when she'd rushed inside earlier. She knew from experience that here the response to 911 could sometimes be slow, and every instinct she possessed screamed at her that they needed help *now.*

"This chick ain't your problem," Michael growled from behind her.

Looking around, Charlie saw the shimmer that was him at the top of the hallway, and drew a ragged breath.

"Did you do it? Did you pray?" she demanded fiercely.

"Hell, no."

"Where are you going? Don't leave me!" the girl shrieked after her. The echoing shrillness of it practically curled Charlie's hair.

"I'm not leaving you." Charlie snatched up her purse. "I'm coming right back." Then, at Michael, she snapped, "Pray, damn it," and bolted past him.

"Leave her," Michael said furiously. "Run the fuck upstairs and lock yourself in your bedroom. You hear me? This whole savior complex you got going on is gonna get you killed."

"Savior complex?" Charlie was outraged.

"Oh, yeah." The shimmer appeared in front of her, blocking her path.

"Go *away*," Charlie snapped before she thought. Fumbling around in her purse in an effort to find her phone, a process that was slightly hampered by the fact that she was running and glaring at him at the same time, she dodged around him because that seemed more appropriate than running right through him, which she easily could have done, and immediately took it back. "I mean, *stay*. Only out of the way."

"Damn it, Charlie—"

"Who are you *talking* to?" Sounding terrified, the girl hugged the phone to her ear. Holding the clump of rapidly reddening paper towels clamped to her forehead, she jiggled from foot to foot in nervous agitation as she watched Charlie dart toward her while conducting a running argument with something she couldn't see.

"Don't worry about it," Charlie snapped, her façade of composure on the verge of coming dangerously unglued. Sliding to a halt feet from the girl, Charlie found her phone at last and snatched it out of her purse.

"A cell phone? Hell, I thought you were rooting around in there for a gun." Michael was right behind her. "You do have a gun around here somewhere, right? Now would be the time to grab it."

Unable to reply, both because she didn't want to be caught supposedly talking to herself again and because, in actual fact, she didn't possess a gun at all and didn't want to listen to him bitch about it, Charlie ignored that. Instead she fumbled to call up her contact list and listened as the girl gasped into the landline, "I need the police! Now! A man's chasing me! He has a gun and he wants to kill me!"

Then, to Charlie, who had just hit the button to call her across-the-street neighbor Ken Ewell, the (armed) sheriff's deputy, she cried, "They need the address! What's the address?"

"A death wish *and* a savior complex." Despite the savagery of his tone, Michael's voice in her ear would have been welcome if what he was saying hadn't been so maddening. "Looks like the real question is, how many ways can you come up with to get yourself killed before somebody actually wins the prize?"

Shut up, Charlie almost snarled, but managed to swallow the words in time so that the girl wouldn't go totally ape. Heart racing, working hard to focus on the here and now and at the same time disregard the furious vibrations Michael was sending her way, she listened to the Ewells' phone beginning to ring in her ear as she answered the girl in a carefully controlled voice, "23 Laurel Way."

"Take it from me, babe, being dead ain't that fun."

A quick glare over her shoulder in the direction of that velvety drawl found Michael in heat vapor mode right behind her.

Her gut twisted as she realized one more time how tenuous his hold on this world was.

The girl repeated the address into the phone then moaned to the dispatcher, "Hurry! Oh, please, please, hurry!" while giving Charlie another mistrustful look. Taking a shuddering breath, she added to the dispatcher in a wobbly, barely there voice, "There are two other girls—they're up there—they're dead!"

"*What?*" Charlie and Michael exclaimed in suddenly riveted unison.

Instinctively shooting Michael a did-you-hear-that-too look, Charlie encountered nothing but barely there shimmer. Was he fainter than before? Oh, God, he definitely was. Panic made her feel cold all over. Remembering something he'd once said to her—about running water drawing him back from wherever he had been at that time—she hastily leaned over the sink and turned the faucet on full blast. Cold water gushed out, splashing into the sink, the *whoosh* of it adding just one more jarring note to the discordant background symphony of drumming rain and shuffling feet and gasping breaths, plus the rhythmic drone of a distant telephone ringing away in her ear.

"Good thinking," said Michael, and Charlie felt a rush of relief as the shimmer seemed to grow brighter and denser.

"There were three of us." The girl's eyes were wide and haunted. She was talking into the phone but looking at Charlie, and besides the rampant wariness that Charlie knew was absolutely aimed at her, there was such fear in the girl's expression that Charlie felt sweat start to dampen her palms. In response to something the dispatcher must have asked, the girl repeated her words, then added unsteadily, "I'm the only one left. He made me—he made us—"

Tears filled her eyes, and she broke off with a shaky indrawn breath that turned into a sob. She trembled so violently that Charlie could hear her teeth chattering. Beneath the streaks of blood, her skin had gone beyond paper white to almost gray. If the girl hadn't been wedged in the corner formed by the wall and the counter, Charlie thought that there was a good chance she would have collapsed.

"You're safe now." Charlie felt a fresh well of fellow feeling: this kind of terror she knew. *Safe* might not be exactly accurate, but it was close enough: as long as there was breath in Charlie's body, nobody was getting to that girl again. She would have put a comforting arm around her guest, but the girl shrank away from her—clearly, doctor or not, she wasn't coming across as all that reassuring, for which she knew she had Michael to thank—and with some chagrin Charlie let her arm drop. She was doing her best to project steady strength, to ignore the rushing adrenaline that caused her nerves to jump and her heart to jackhammer. But the situation—Michael, the girl, the possibility that some kind of murderous lunatic was right outside—was making it difficult. Way difficult. As she processed the possibility that whoever was out there had killed two other girls, she felt a wave of fear threaten. What she had first thought was likely a case of domestic violence was starting to sound like something even worse.

Something horrifyingly familiar.

"At least get the hell away from the windows." Michael's voice held a note of barely controlled ferocity that made her breath catch. He, too, was clearly afraid—for her. "Unless you like the idea of giving some loony tune the chance to put a bullet in your brain, that is."

Oh, God, he had a point. Darting another fearful look at the black blankness of the windows, Charlie touched the girl's arm, say-ing, "Probably we should try to get below the counter."

The girl jerked her arm away, and moved as far from Charlie as she could get, which wasn't very far.

"I don't know," she sobbed into the phone while fixing wary, tear-filled eyes on Charlie. "He was chasing me. Oh, I need them to *hurry.*"

"See, that's normal survival instinct. Teen-queen there spots trou-ble, at least she has the sense to try to get away from it," Michael said. Charlie's response was an aggravated thinning of her lips and a quick glare thrown his way. That's when Charlie realized that she could see him again. Although he was still a little foggy around the edges, she was getting enough detail to know that he was looking at the girl like she guessed he might have looked at a live bomb.

"We need to get down." As Charlie gestured at the windows then dropped into a crouch, the girl's eyes went even bigger than before. "He could shoot through the glass."

With one more terrified glance at the windows, the girl followed suit, letting her back slide down the wall, sinking down until she was folded in a soggy huddle with her chin almost touching her knees. A puddle was already forming around her as her eyes locked with Char-lie's. They were glassy with fright.

"I don't *know,*" she answered the operator. "They just need to get here. *Please.*"

"Look, I . . ." Charlie began, meaning to conclude with, *I'm on your side,* only to be interrupted by the sound of the Ewells' phone being picked up at last.

"Hello," Ken's wife, Debbie, said in her ear.

"It's Charlie Stone across the street." In the spirit of not wanting to further spook the girl, Charlie tried hard not to sound as panicky as she was starting to feel. "I need Ken over here right away. There's a girl in my kitchen, and she says"—explaining the whole thing was going to be too complicated and time-consuming, and anyway Char-lie still had no idea precisely what the whole thing was, so she cut to the chase—"there's a man with a gun after her. We need Ken *now.*"

"Cops going to get here any faster 'cause you're hanging out with The Black Dahlia here in the kitchen trying to get yourself killed? Run upstairs and lock yourself in your bedroom and stay put until the po-po show up." A solid-looking presence now, Michael planted himself between her and the girl. That was deliberate, Charlie knew, as was his aggressive stance. Whatever he was or wasn't, where she at least was concerned he seemed to have a marked protective streak. Of course, since she was all that was anchoring him to the world of the living that shouldn't come as a big surprise. "Damn it, Charlie, you're not doing her one bit of good by sitting here looking into her eyes. You've done your Mother Teresa thing: you let her in. Cops are coming. So leave her to it and *go*."

Shooting him a shut-up-or-die look, Charlie gave a quick, negative shake of her head.

"How far away are they?" the girl moaned to the dispatcher.

"He's in bed asleep," Debbie objected. Of course, it was nearing midnight. In Big Stone Gap, that was late for decent folks.

"Can you *wake him up*?" Charlie did her best not to yell on that last part, with indifferent success. At the same time she watched Michael disgustedly mime a gunshot to his own head with a thumb and forefinger. Charlie frowned. The frown was directed at Michael, of course, but the girl, whose eyes she had been holding until she had flicked that sharp *stop it* look up at Michael, shrank away. "I really, really need him. Like I said, there's a girl in my kitchen being chased by a *man with a gun*."

"Well, I guess." There was a sound that Charlie interpreted as Debbie laying the receiver down. Over the still-open line, she listened to her neighbor calling to her husband. Who as far as she could tell wasn't answering.

Damn it.

"I'm Jenna McDaniels," the girl said into the phone on a shuddering intake of breath, in obvious answer to a question posed by the dispatcher. "I was kidnapped three days ago. The other girls are—uh, w-were—Laura Peters and Raylene Witt. There has to be somebody looking for us. Are the police even *close*?"

Jenna McDaniels? Even caught up in the aftermath of a nightmare as she had been, Charlie had heard of the University of Richmond sorority girl who had vanished from a college-sponsored event just as preparations for the fall rush were getting under way: reports of the disappearance had been all over TV. But Charlie didn't have the chance to do more than look at her with widening eyes, because a sound—a faint rattle from the direction of the back door—froze both her and Jenna in place. Suddenly as still as rabbits with a dog nearby, united by fear, they shot simultaneous panicky looks in the direction of the sound, to no avail: the solid base of the breakfast bar was in the way, preventing them from seeing anything beyond it. But for Charlie at least, there was no doubting what they had heard: the doorknob rattling. Her heart thudded in her chest. Goose bumps chased themselves over her skin. As she strained every sense she possessed in an effort to divine what was happening beyond that door, she tried to swallow, only to discover that her mouth had gone desert dry.

This can't be happening.

"He's here," Jenna gasped on a note of purest horror, her hand around the receiver tightening until her knuckles showed white. The wad of paper towels she had been holding to her forehead dropped, forgotten, as her hand fell. Oblivious to the blood that still oozed from the cut, she shot Charlie a petrified look.

Charlie knew exactly how she felt.

"That's it," Michael barked at Charlie as his big, semi-solid-looking body surged right through the breakfast bar in a preemptive rush toward the back door and whoever was on the other side of it. "Move your ass. Upstairs. *Now.*"

CHAPTER THREE

"Don't go outside. You might get sucked in. You need to stay close to the running water," Charlie called urgently after him as, galvanized by fear, she shot into motion herself. If he heard her, she couldn't tell: he had disappeared from view. Physically formidable in life, in death Michael could provide her with about as much in the way of actual protection as a whisper of air, although he didn't seem to remember that most of the time and there were indeed occasional moments when he solidified and was once again the badass he had formerly been. Not that those moments were anything that he could control, or she could count on, so she didn't. Thrusting her cell phone into her pants pocket, careful to stay hunched over so that she couldn't be seen through the windows, Charlie lunged across the kitchen toward the only possible source of a weapon in the house: the silverware drawer.

Pathetic? Oh, yeah. But she had no gun, no burglar alarm, no real defensive system set up in the house, because after what felt like a lifetime of living in fear she had been sick to death of it.

"Who are you talking to? There's nobody there," Jenna wailed. Then, into the phone as Charlie threw her a startled, self-conscious look because she hadn't even realized that she had been talking to

Michael out loud, Jenna added in a voice that shook: *"He's here. He's trying to get in the door. Tell the police to hurry. Please, please tell them to hurry."*

Trotting out her standard line that she was talking to herself seemed pointless under the circumstances, so Charlie didn't bother. Pulse racing, eyes fixed on what she could see of the windows—she could make out nothing beyond the darkness and the rain, which was falling heavily now, but she knew, *knew* that someone malignant was out there—Charlie snatched a steak knife from the silverware drawer. Then cautiously raising her head above the level of the counter, she did a lightning scan of the kitchen. Despite the fact that she was focused on the whereabouts of the man with the gun, the thought that instantly struck her was, *No sign of Michael.* The panicked realization curled through her mind, threading through the more immediate issue of getting to safety like a worm through soft wood. Was Michael outside, or had he been sucked back into Spookville? Not that it made any real difference. In either case, there was nothing she could do.

And right then, living through the next few minutes was paramount.

Gesturing to Jenna to head for the hall, acutely conscious that the bad guy might be right outside and even, possibly, able to hear them, Charlie whispered, "Our best bet is to lock ourselves in my bedroom until help gets here. Upstairs, second door on the right."

Jenna nodded jerkily. Breathing *"Hurry"* one more time into the phone, Jenna dropped the receiver. Staying low, she darted toward the hall with Charlie right behind her. Without the sheltering breakfast bar to conceal them, they had to be perfectly visible to whoever was outside as they flew across those last few yards. Charlie imagined that she could feel eyes—evil eyes—trained on them the entire way, and a cold chill snaked down her spine.

"I'm scared." Along with that charged whisper, Jenna threw a hunted look back at Charlie as they gained the dubious security of the shadowy hall and raced down it toward the stairs. Blood and tears mixed on Jenna's face: she looked ghastly in the dim light. Drops of water splattered the floor in her wake, making it dangerously slippery beneath Charlie's unaccustomedly high heels. She would have kicked them off if it had been possible, but it wasn't: the elegant sandals had ankle straps. *Do not fall down.*

"He's going to kill me, I know it. Oh, please don't let him get me again."

At the terror in Jenna's expression, Charlie felt cold sweat break out on her own brow. "I won't. I promise. Head up the stairs."

A sudden loud *thud* from the kitchen—Oh, God, was that the sound of the door being kicked in?—sent Charlie's heart leaping into her throat. *This has to be a nightmare.* Only it wasn't. Jenna looked back at her, horror-stricken.

"What was that? Did he just break in?" Her eyes were wild.

Shaking her head—a silent *I don't know*—while her blood ran cold, Charlie mouthed, *"Go."*

The police—Ken Ewell—help—would be there at any second. Charlie hoped. No, she prayed. But would they be in time? If he was already in the house—she couldn't finish the thought. Strain her ears though she might, she could hear nothing else from the kitchen over the clatter of her own and Jenna's harried footsteps and the harsh pant of their combined breathing.

That very stillness made her stomach cramp. She couldn't stop herself from looking over her shoulder.

Where is he?

Jenna was on the stairs, clambering up them as if she expected to be grabbed from behind at any second. It was a noisy, clumsy progress that no one who was inside the house could possibly miss hearing. Clenching her teeth in an effort to keep a lid on her own fear, Charlie grabbed the newel post, meaning to fly up the stairs in Jenna's wake. The sudden loud buzz of the doorbell caught her by surprise before she could so much as plant a foot on the steps. Both she and Jenna squeaked and jumped like terrified mice.

"Oh, no, oh, no!" Jenna gasped, shooting a look at the door as, halfway up the stairs, she nearly lost her footing.

The killer wouldn't ring the doorbell. That was the near certainty that struck Charlie like a lifeline even as an instant, reactive terror exploded along her nerve endings and, heart in throat, she whirled to face the door.

"Are you kidding me? Is that a fucking *steak knife* in your hand?"

Michael demanded furiously. Charlie was so glad to know that he hadn't yet been trapped forever in the Great Beyond she didn't even mind the attitude. Along with a surge of profound thankfulness, she felt instantly safer simply because he was there, no matter how stupid that might be. "Well, that would sure scare the hell outta *me.*"

I don't care how relieved you are to see him: don't answer. The adrenaline she'd been mainlining made her shiver. Michael must have seen because he swore.

"It's got to be the police." Her pounding heart and jumping nerves notwithstanding, that doorbell had to be good news, she was almost sure. Charlie threw the reassurance up the staircase at Jenna just as the girl gained the second floor and scrambled from view. Certain that she was right—praying that she was right—even while her ears acutely sought any sounds of an intruder rushing at her from the kitchen and her eyes were busy trying to detect some glimmer of Michael, Charlie leaped for the door.

Enough doubt about who might be on the other side of it remained to prompt her to take a few nerve-racking seconds to peer through the peephole—"*She's* hiding and *you're* opening the door? You don't see anything wrong with that?" was Michael's incensed take on it, in reply to which she was goaded into hissing, "Shut up, you, it's my neighbor"—before fumbling with the lock and throwing the door wide.

"Oh, Ken, thank goodness!" The scent of wet earth rushed past her into the house. Outside, it was as dark as a dungeon now, with pouring rain that sounded like a waterfall and fell in silvery sheets. Across the street, she could see, pale and wavery, lights on in the Ewells' house. Hurtling toward her—thank God!—she could hear sirens, although from the sound of them they were still some little distance away. Right in front of her stood Ken, foursquare and solid, squinting questioningly at her. He wasn't tall, maybe five-nine or so, and wasn't particularly imposing, either, but as a sworn officer of the law he was exactly what she needed. Bathed in the porch light's yellow glow, fully dressed down to a clear plastic rain poncho with a hood that he had pulled on over jeans and a dark-colored shirt, he was the most welcome thing she'd set eyes on since finding Michael on her couch earlier. A solid family man, father of two young boys, he was around her own age, as was Debbie, but his stocky build coupled with thinning brown hair made him look older. Not that Charlie particularly noticed, or cared, beyond what interested her most about him right at that moment: his gun. The weapon was in his hand, covered protectively by a fold of the poncho.

"Would you look at that, it's Paul Blart, Mall Cop," Michael marveled, and Charlie's lips tightened. "I know *I* feel all safer now."

Okay, so maybe the physical comparison was apt. But Ken was still an armed deputy, damn it, which beat a sarcastic ghost hands-down in this situation.

"So what—" Ken began, his blunt, not unattractive features contracting in a frown, but Charlie didn't let him finish. Grabbing his arm through the wet layer of plastic, she pulled him into the hall. She didn't even need a sideways glance to spot Michael: he was right beside her, having progressed from a shimmer to being semi-transparent. Solid enough so that she could see the frown on his face.

"A man with a gun. He was in the kitchen." Talking fast, she pointed the way to Ken. "At least, I think he was. It sounded like he kicked the door in. I don't know if he actually came inside, though. A girl—Jenna McDaniels, she disappeared three days ago from the University of Richmond, you've probably heard about it on the news—banged on my kitchen door about five minutes ago. I let her in. She was hurt and frightened and said that a man with a gun was chasing her and was going to kill her. And then the back doorknob rattled and there was a huge thud that I thought might have been him kicking in the door and he may or may not be in the house now."

In her rush to get the most pertinent facts out as quickly as possible, Charlie realized she was probably being less than clear. Ken didn't seem to be paying a whole lot of attention to what she was saying anyway. He frowned in the direction of the kitchen. Then his eyes swept the hallway, missing nothing except, of course, Michael. Finally he looked at Charlie.

"Where's the girl?"

Charlie was about to tell him when two police cars hove into view at the far end of the street, their bubble lights pulsing brightly through the darkness and the rain.

"Thank God." She touched his arm and pointed. Turning, he saw them, too. "Now you'll have backup," Charlie added on a note of relief, because she really hadn't liked the idea of sending her mild-mannered neighbor into harm's way alone.

"You can stop worrying. The boogeyman's long gone." Michael was looking out through the rain at the cops. "I couldn't get outside—when I tried I got yanked into Spookville and had to work like hell to get out again—but after I finally broke through I ended up back in your kitchen. The door's open, but nobody's in there."

As Charlie absorbed the information, she felt some of the desperate energy leave her tense muscles. Thinking about what he must have gone through to return to her, she felt her heart quiver. What she wanted to say to him was, *I'm so glad you made it back*. But she didn't, and not simply because they had an audience.

"You say you've got Jenna McDaniels?" As he spoke, Ken was fishing for something in his pocket—his cell phone, she saw as he managed to free it from both his pocket and the protective plastic in which he was shrouded. He looked toward the kitchen again, but made no move to head in that direction. Probably, Charlie thought, he was more than happy to wait for the reinforcements. Hitting a button, Ken lifted the phone toward his ear.

"He wants to take credit for finding the girl before the real po-po arrive," Michael said. "You might want to think about losing the steak knife, by the way. Unless you've got some late supper plans I don't know about."

"She's upstairs," Charlie answered Ken, ignoring Michael—she would be damned if she was going to acknowledge him in front of anyone else again by even so much as a dirty look cast his way. At the same time, she unobtrusively sidled to her left and put the knife down on the console table. Not that she was doing so because Michael had suggested it. It was only, now that the danger was past, clutching it in her fist made her feel—okay, let's face it—foolish. "She said she was kidnapped three days ago. She said she was with two other girls, both of whom are now dead." Shivering again, she glanced up the stairs and caught a glimpse of Jenna lurking fearfully in the shadows at the top.

"It's safe now," Charlie called to her. "The police are here."

Ken looked up at Jenna, who shrank back out of sight. "That the girl?"

"Yes."

"Hey, Sheriff, you know that girl who's been missing for the last three days? The one who's been all over TV? Jenna McDaniels? I got her," Ken said into the phone on a note of excitement. "Yeah, she's alive."

"Made his day," Michael said. "Bet he gets a big ole attaboy for this."

"She says there are two other girls besides her, who are dead," Ken continued. "Dr. Stone's house. Right across the street from me. You know, Charlotte Stone, works up at the Ridge? Yeah, that's her."

The police cars pulled up in front of Charlie's house. As the sirens were cut and the lights died, Charlie took a deep breath and said to Ken, "I'll be right back," then went up the stairs to find Jenna—and, not incidentally, do what she could to help Michael.

The thought of him going to hell for all eternity was more than she could live with. Whether he deserved it or not.

She might be fresh out of ju-ju, but she'd just remembered someone she could possibly turn to for advice. The sudden rush of excitement that the tiny glimmer of hope brought with it was eye-opening.

You're getting way too involved here.

"You even got a gun in the house?" Michael growled. He was right behind her again, a semi-solid phantom whose presence would have been absolutely driving her around the bend by this time if the thought of him vanishing forever hadn't been so shattering. Since she was halfway up the stairs, equally far away from both Jenna and Ken and presumably out of earshot of both, Charlie whispered a short, "No."

"A burglar alarm?"

"No. Hush."

Michael replied to that with a snort and a disgusted, "Why am I even surprised?"

It was only as she reached the top of the stairs that Charlie realized her knees felt wobbly. Probably because the adrenaline rush that was part and parcel of all the stress she'd just been through was starting to subside.

"Jenna?" The second floor was dark except for a night-light sifting through the open bedroom doors, but because Jenna was crying Charlie had no trouble spotting the girl, who was huddled in a little ball in a shadowy corner slightly to the right of the top of the stairs. Behind Charlie, Michael was now so see-through that a shaft of light passing through him glimmered off dust motes where he stood, and with a shiver of fear Charlie was once again reminded of the small amount of time she probably had to work with before he was irretrievably gone. But then Jenna made an inarticulate sound by way of reply, and Charlie forced herself to focus on her.

The living have to take precedence over the dead. With that firmly in mind, Charlie switched on the light in the upstairs hall. It wasn't particularly bright but the instant illumination still felt shocking under the circumstances, and Jenna sucked in a ragged breath.

"It's okay," Charlie said again. Wet and bedraggled, visibly shivering, the girl was huddled in a ball with her dripping hair spilling around her like a curtain and her arms wrapped around her knees. Although more sluggishly than before, blood still slid down the right side of her face, which was white and pinched and suddenly very young-looking. Her eyes were huge as she stared up at Charlie.

"Is he"—Jenna's voice cracked—"gone?"

"Yes." As she spoke, Charlie took the two steps required to reach the linen closet and extracted a washcloth and a large green-and-white-striped beach towel from it. "The man in the hall is a deputy, and two police cars pulled up out front as I came upstairs. You don't have to be afraid anymore. You're absolutely safe, I promise. It's over."

"Oh, my God." Jenna dropped her head onto her knees and began to cry again, in great wrenching wails that had Michael grimacing and looking uncomfortable and backing off. Shooting him a *stay out of this* look, Charlie shook the towel out, draped it around the girl's heaving shoulders, then hunkered down beside her.

This kind of pain she knew.

"Jenna. It's all right. Here, let me hold this to your cut." Clutching the towel around her now, Jenna glanced up at that. Charlie smoothed the cold, wet strands of her hair back from her face, tucking them behind her ear before pressing the folded washcloth to the still-bleeding wound. The cut was jagged and the edges gaped, showing the layer of white tissue beneath through the oozing blood. It would need stitches, probably about a dozen.

For a second Charlie found herself speculating about what kind of weapon could cause such a wound.

"Can you c-call my mother?" Jenna asked between sobs.

"Yes. Of course. Here, keep this pressed to your head and give me her number." As Jenna's hand replaced hers on the washcloth, Charlie fumbled to pull her phone out of her pocket.

Jenna gasped out a number. Charlie tapped it in.

"Hello?" A woman answered on the first ring. From the desperate sound of her voice Charlie guessed that she somehow knew that this call was about her daughter. Maybe she had a special cell phone number that only certain people, like Jenna, knew. Charlie had no idea, but hope and dread were there in equal measures in the woman's voice. Charlie's heart went out to her even as she struggled to keep her own voice steady and calm.

"This is Dr. Charlie Stone. I have good news: Jenna's safe. She's here with me right now."

The woman let out a broken cry that it was apparent Jenna heard, because she reached a shaking hand out for the phone. "Mama?"

Charlie passed the phone to her without another word.

"Mama, I'm okay," Jenna said into the phone, then in response to whatever her mother replied once more broke down into noisy tears.

"Here come the cops," Michael said. Charlie became aware of the sound of heavy feet on the stairs seconds before Ken and two uniformed police officers stepped into the hall.

"Jenna McDaniels?" one of the cops asked. Weeping into the phone as if she was never going to stop this side of general anesthesia, Jenna nodded wordlessly.

"We need an ambulance," Charlie said, and one of the cops replied, "Already on the way."

"My mother's coming," Jenna told Charlie, tears rolling unchecked down her cheeks as she passed Charlie's phone back to her. "Can you tell her where we are?"

Charlie took the phone and complied.

The EMTs arrived just as she was ending the conversation by promising to call Mrs. McDaniels if Jenna should be taken anywhere other than Lonesome Pine Hospital, which Charlie was virtually certain would be the case. As they converged on Jenna, Charlie relinquished her patient to them. For a moment, because of a sense of duty toward Jenna, she watched critically: they seemed very competent. Satisfied, she stood up and moved out of the way to let them work. A wave of profound relief washed over her as she realized that her part in this was ending, that the cops and appropriate-for-the-situation medical professionals would take it from here. She had played her small role in rescuing Jenna McDaniels from whatever hell she had been caught up in, and now that role was played out.

By this time her house was filled with cops, upstairs and down, and from what she could glean from various conversations more were on the way. She knew how investigations worked: they would take Jenna to the hospital, take Charlie's own statement, take lots of pictures of anything that needed taking pictures of in her house, maybe check the back door, which the intruder had forced open, for fingerprints and the yard for footprints. Then they would be gone, to focus their investigation where it needed to be focused, which was on finding out what had happened to Jenna and the other girls.

Charlie would be left alone to get back to her life.

Which right at the moment included a maddening, not-much-longer-for-this-earthly-plane ghost who was dangerously close to becoming way too important to her. Him she needed to deal with immediately, if, indeed, she planned to deal with him at all. The easy route would be to do nothing. To simply let him go. Allowing him to fade out of her life would be the absolute smartest choice she could possibly make.

And Charlie already knew that she was not going to be able to do it.

"And there you see it again, folks: we have one more unfortunate victim rescued from the jaws of death by our heroic doctor, Charlie Stone." Michael accompanied that infuriating remark by making a show of ironically clapping applause.

Forget how drained and shaky she was feeling: Michael's sardonic pseudo-announcement had the effect of stiffening her spine and heating her temper. Still translucent as smoke, he was standing near the door to her bedroom, out of the way of the hive of activity surrounding Jenna. Charlie shot him a narrow-eyed look and managed not to snap *You know what you can do with that, right?* in reply. Instead she murmured to the nearest cop, "I'm just going to go wash my hands," which were, in fact, smeared with blood, and which did, in fact, need to be washed. The cop nodded, clearly uninterested. Charlie walked (stalked?) past Michael into her bedroom. As she knew he would, he followed her in, moving past her into the room. Clicking on the light, Charlie shut—and locked—the door.

Then she turned on him.

CHAPTER FOUR

"What is your problem?" Charlie demanded in a furious whisper.

Michael had stopped near the foot of her bed. Her big brass bed was dressed in layers of spotless white bedclothes that, fortunately, had been changed and made up yesterday in anticipation of her homecoming by the maid who cleaned her house once a week. The bed that she had last been in, less than a week ago, with him. Having the hottest, most mind-blowing sex of her life.

After a single comprehensive glance, Charlie jerked her gaze from the bed to Michael. Luckily, she wasn't prone to blushing. Luckily, too, he didn't seem to have been struck by the same memory that still had the power to curl her toes. Shrugging his broad shoulders, crossing his arms over his chest, looking as big and bad in death as he ever had in life except for the fact that she could see right through him, he looked her up and down.

"It's not my problem you should be worried about," said Michael. "It's yours."

"I don't have a problem." As she spoke, she stalked across the room to the first of the two long windows that overlooked her backyard and the mountain beyond it. Looking to her right, she was able to see part of the street. At least half a dozen cop cars were parked

where she could see them, which meant there w[...]
couldn't see parked right in front of the house. A[...]
screaming, was just turning the corner, heading[...]
the police cars were all dark and only the ambula[...]
lights were still flashing, she could see the vehicle[...]
darkness and rain, courtesy of the house and outd[...]
single dwelling within view: the sirens had clearly roused the neighborhood. Knowing the way the community worked, she had little
doubt that the neighbors who were not at this moment actively converging on her house were peering out their windows. Given everything that had happened, she hated the idea that anyone, good guy or
bad, could see in, which with the overhead light on was a given. Jerking the curtains closed, then stalking to the other window to close
those, too, she said, "My only problem is you."

"Hah." He had turned to watch her. Stopping in front of the fireplace, which was between the windows—it was a lovely room, big
and high-ceilinged, with white walls and dark hardwood floors and
an ornate fireplace below a painting of a waterfall splashing down in
a woody Blue Ridge Mountain glen, her own oasis of serenity—she
glared at him. He continued: "You really don't see it, do you? You
think I was kidding, downstairs? I wasn't. You've got a fucking death
wish. You need a shrink, shrink."

"What I need," she said, goaded "is an exorcist. Who specializes
in removing unwanted ghosts."

"Baby, if I was unwanted you wouldn't have turned the water on
in your kitchen."

Charlie's lips firmed: he had her there. And the fact that she was
still frightened silly by his see-through state—okay, truth was truth.
Dead serial killer or not, he had become (stupidly, dangerously) important to her. Not that she meant to admit it.

And he was right about the shrink. She was exhibiting classic
symptoms of what even she recognized as a real self-destructive streak.
But when she thought of trying to describe her current dilemma to one
of her esteemed, non-ghost-seeing colleagues, she went cold all over.
Nobody would believe her. They'd think she was delusional, possibly
schizophrenic or the victim of something organic such as temporal
lobe seizures. Whatever, the word would spread that she was a couple

. plugs short of an engine. Best case scenario, she would lose redibility. Worst case, her job and her medical license.

He added: "You've got blood on your face, by the way."

Without another word, Charlie turned and headed for the en suite bathroom, pulling her phone from her pocket with angry resignation on the way. If there was a chance to save him from whatever Eternity had in store for him, which from every indication was shaping up more along the lines of fire and brimstone than Pearly Gates, she was going to go for it.

Michael followed her into the white-tiled bathroom with its big, claw-foot tub and separate shower and pedestal sink and water-saving toilet: old-fashioned in style but completely modern, because she'd had it redone. "That's the second time I've been scared enough about what was happening with you to fight my way out of Spookville when I didn't think there was any chance I was going to be able to get out ever again. Second time since I *died,* which hasn't been all that long. You following me here? Twice in less than a week that you've scared me shitless because you've been that close"—he held his thumb and forefinger about a quarter of an inch apart—"to getting yourself killed. That I know of. Like I said, you've got a death wish."

"I do not." Charlie's back stiffened with indignation even as she went ahead and pushed the button on her contact list that would place the call she knew she would never forgive herself if she didn't make. "What difference does it make to you anyway if I get killed? Looking at it from your point of view, I think I'd be thinking we could be two little angels—or whatever—together."

He snorted. Mouth twisting, he met her eyes as she glanced around at him. The expression in his was impossible to read. After a second he said, "You're not me, and you don't know shit about my point of view. What I've learned from being dead is, your life is something that has more value than you realize. You did your best to save mine; I'm doing my best to save yours."

"Quid pro quo, hmm?"

"Whatever them fancy Latin words mean, Doc."

"If you know they're Latin, I'm guessing you know what they mean." She'd already discovered that his laid-back southern exterior concealed a keen intelligence.

"Yeah, well, take them fancy words you just threw at me and add in the fact that if you bite the big one, I'm toast. You ready to sentence me to an eternity in whatever the hell—and *hell* sounds about right—I'm looking at after Spookville?"

No, she wasn't. And he knew it as well as she did, so she didn't even have to tell him so. Instead, she sighed. "I don't have a death wish, okay? That's ridiculous. Didn't you ever simply have a bad week?"

"A bad week? That's what you're calling it?" As they'd been talking, Charlie had put the phone on speaker, laid it down on the narrow glass ledge above the sink, and begun to wash her hands and face. He continued, "You're a scientist. Look at the facts: you spend your workdays penned up in a little room with serial killers. Oh, I know you like to think you're protected because you're in a prison, and there are armed guards around, and the prisoners are locked in and shackled six ways to Sunday, but you're not. You think I couldn't have grabbed you if I'd wanted to? All I would have had to do was fake like I was choking or something, and you know as well as you know your name that you would have come on around that desk that stood between us to try to save me, and I would have had you. You think I didn't work that out about five minutes after we started our first session? You think I'm the only one who's thinking of trying something like that? Wake up, buttercup. The men you're working with have been sentenced to death. They got nothing to lose. Every single one of them who isn't crazy enough to want to die is thinking about how to break out of there. What's the best way? I can't speak for everybody, but I can tell you one of the possibilities I was considering: take the pretty doc hostage and use her as a ticket to the outside."

"You were thinking about taking me hostage?" Charlie looked around, blinking, from rinsing her face to ask indignantly. One shoulder propping the door frame, he was standing in the open bathroom doorway, his tall, muscular body oversized enough to fill most of the available space. He might even have looked scary if she hadn't progressed way past being afraid of him—and if he hadn't been as see-through as delicately tinted glass.

More see-through than when he had followed her into the bathroom? She wasn't even going to let herself answer that. Just asking herself the question was enough to make her stomach twist.

Damn it.

"Hell, yes, I was thinking about taking you hostage. I was thinking about trying anything that might have saved my damned life." The soft sounds of the phone ringing on the other end as the call finally went through caught his attention and he squinted at the distraction. As Charlie reached for a towel, he added on a note of disbelief, "You calling somebody? Right now? Really?"

"Yes." She ran a brush through her hair. Her cosmetics were kept in a small plastic case on the glass shelf. Her bare face was way too pale and tired-looking, so, after giving him a quick glare simply because he was in a position to watch, she picked up her blush, opened it, and brushed a little of the pink powder on her cheeks.

He *was* watching, critically. "Who?"

"What are you, my keeper?" she asked as she progressed to slicking a rosy lip gloss over her mouth.

He looked impatient. "Damn it, Charlie, I probably don't have a lot of time left, and there's a point I'm trying to—"

He was interrupted by the sound of the phone call being picked up.

"That you, cherie?"

The cheerful voice booming through the phone prompted Charlie to answer, "Hey, Tam. Yes, it's me. Listen, I have a problem and you are the only one I can think of who might be able to help me with it."

"I'm all ears," Tam said.

Mindful that Michael's time could very well be measured in minutes rather than hours, Charlie got right down to it. "I have a ghost who's getting ready to leave this plane. He doesn't want to go, and I need him to stay—and to stay visible to me. I've tried everything I know to do to fix him to earth, but I don't know all that much about it and nothing I do know seems to be working. If you can help, I'd owe you big-time."

"You want to keep a ghost? Why?" Charlie already had been rethinking the use of the speakerphone as Tam's incredulous voice came through loud and clear, but because time was at a premium and because she had needed to wash her face and hands and because she really hadn't wanted to appear among all the people converging on her house looking completely unkempt, she had made the choice to multitask and here was the result: an initially intent look on said ghost's face that was morphing into an irritating twinkle directed right into her eyes.

"Yes, I do. And never mind why." Giving Michael a sour look, Charlie snatched up her phone and turned the speaker function off. Feeling hope spreading inside her like kudzu as her friend talked, Charlie listened intently, had a whole multitude of second, third, and fourth thoughts, then said, "Thanks, Tam," as she finally accepted the inevitable and disconnected.

"Did I hear that right? You putting that savior complex of yours to work on trying to save me now?" The slow, mocking smile he gave her as she stuck the phone in her pocket, turned, and marched toward him would have infuriated her had it not been accompanied by an almost tender glint in his eyes. Rattled, she scowled at him.

"Shut up and move," she said, hating to find herself in the position of having to do something that she feared (a) was a terrible mistake and (b) revealed way too much about the muddled state of her heart where he was concerned. Unfortunately, the thought of the consequences should she fail to act was enough to keep her with the program. "So I made a call to a psychic friend and asked her how to keep you here. Don't go reading into it."

"I won't," he promised as he obligingly moved out of the bathroom doorway to let her pass, and she guessed that he wanted what he hoped she could do for him more than he wanted to tease her, at least for the moment. Still, that smart mouth of his was going to get him killed one day, she thought savagely before she remembered that, oops, that horse had already left the barn. "So does your friend *know* how to keep me here?"

"Her name's Tamsyn Green. And *maybe* she knows how to keep you here." Being careful to keep her voice low as muffled sounds from beyond the bedroom door reminded her of the activity in the hall, Charlie headed for her long, low mahogany dresser, where she kept a supply of jasmine candles in a drawer. The candles were a staple of her Miracle-Go kit, which was so named because the items in it were useful in dealing with the occasional ghost with evil intent that occasionally afflicted her. She'd already used a jasmine candle once in an attempt to banish Michael, with, as his continuing presence attested, less than stellar success. Now she would use one to do the exact opposite of what she had done to him the last time: instead of forcing him into the Hereafter, she would try to keep him in the Here on Earth.

"That word *maybe*? I'm not a fan." He was frowning, she saw with a quick glance at him.

"Tough. Maybe's the best I can do."

A sharp knock on the bedroom door made Charlie jump.

"Dr. Stone?" It was a man's voice, calling to her from the hall. She didn't recognize it.

"Shit," Michael said. "Take a number, buddy."

"I'll be with you in a minute." Charlie raised her voice in answer.

Michael made an impatient sound. "Forget about Snow White and the Seven Dwarfs out there. Let's get this thing done."

Charlie nodded: he had to be her first priority. Obviously tense now, Michael watched a little warily as she grabbed one of the smaller candles, fished out the cigarette lighter she kept on hand specifically to light them, should the need arise, from a delicate porcelain dish in the center of the dresser, and headed back toward the bathroom.

"So who's this Tamsyn Green?" He was following her.

"Your best hope for staying here," Charlie whispered sharply. Not that she thought anyone in the hall outside could actually hear her from the bathroom, which was where she was by then, but still. Her professional reputation wouldn't survive too many rumors that ran along the lines of *she talks to somebody who isn't there*. She could only hope that Jenna had sufficient traumatic memories to share with investigators to have forgotten about Charlie's seemingly one-sided chats with thin air. "She's from New Orleans. Her mother was some kind of voodoo priestess, apparently. I met her my freshman year of college, when I was still having trouble processing the whole I-see-dead-people thing. I went to this psychic fair, thinking maybe I'd find other people kind of going through the same thing, and she was one of the featured psychics. Since nobody was able to see the two or three spirits that I could see who were actually in the room, I had already more or less given up on getting any insight into what I was experiencing by the time I walked by Tam's table and she asked me why I didn't embrace what she called my gift and get over it. When she was able to describe the same spirits I could see, I knew she was legit. She's more than legit, actually: she's a full-spectrum psychic medium and clairvoyant who lives out in California now and makes her living giving readings for movie stars. She knows way more about this stuff than I ever want to or will." Mindful of the instructions Tam had given her, Charlie had been setting things up as she spoke.

Then she hesitated, looking at Michael.

"What?" he said.

"If I do this, you have to promise to abide by any rules I come up with," she said. "Chief of which is, do not be a pain in the ass."

"I promise," he said, way too promptly for her peace of mind.

She gave him a skeptical look.

The smile he gave her dazzled. "Cross my heart and hope to die."

Said the spider to the fly.

But she knew herself: charismatic psychopath or not, there was nothing else she could do.

"I mean it," she warned, and he laid his hand piously over his heart.

Fine. Get on with it.

Positioning the short, fat white candle on the edge of the sink, she dumped her toothbrush and toothpaste out in order to use the heavy, clear drinking glass they were kept in. With a couple of flicks of her thumb she got the lighter burning and, taking a deep breath, held the flame to the candle.

And tried to will away the nervous flutter in her stomach.

Please let this work.

"Whoa. Hold on a minute." Michael's expression was a study in alarm as the wick caught. Straightening to his full height, he shook his head at her. "We've been down this road before. You light that candle and I get vacuumed up by this big ole wind that spits me out right in the middle of Spookville. I don't think so. That hurt and—"

"Just trust me, will you please?" Charlie interrupted. The candle was burning strongly now, and the scent of jasmine was building.

Although she couldn't feel it, she could see the effect of the passage that was opening on Michael: his hair was beginning to ruffle, as if a breeze were blowing past him. Conscious of her quickening heartbeat, Charlie wet suddenly dry lips. Then she picked up the glass and waited.

Tam had warned her that timing was all.

If this doesn't work . . . She wasn't even going to let herself go there.

Michael was eyeing the candle uneasily. "Believe it or not, you I trust. This whole voodoo thing you're doing here? Not so much. Charlie—"

"You have any better ideas?"

"Goddamn it."

She took that as a *no*. His hair was really blowing now, and he seemed to be bracing himself against a force that she knew had to be substantial if he had to exert that much effort to resist it. The breeze had apparently turned into a strong wind, while on the other end she knew a steady suction was being created, although she couldn't feel a thing. Not that she was supposed to: only spirits were susceptible. The purpose of the burning candle was to open a portal to the Other Side while at the same time drawing the Light, that legendary white light that she thought of as the pathway to heaven, nearer, and from all indications at least the first part of it was happening. A vortex was being formed and it was growing stronger until, soon now, it would be strong enough to suck him up and whirl him away to where he was supposed to be. Even as she watched, the suction apparently increased. Michael instinctively tried to grab on to the door frame to resist its force, but of course that was useless: his hands went right through the wood. His widening eyes locked on hers as he was pulled, slowly and with a great deal of resistance, toward the candle.

"Charlie—" His voice was hoarse, with an unmistakable undernote of fear. To hear Michael sounding afraid—well, she didn't like it. "Can you hear it? The screaming?"

Oh, God. No, she couldn't hear a thing. But what he was hearing—in the purple twilight-y part of the Afterlife that he called Spookville there were, according to him, things called Hunters. They were called that because they hunted the screaming, terrified souls of recently deceased human beings who wound up there. Of which, if this didn't work, he would be one.

"It's okay. That just means it's working." *I think.* She didn't add that last out loud. Her throat had gone tight. Her heart knocked in her chest. If she didn't time this exactly right . . .

"Ahh!" His face contorted with pain as he was lifted off his feet and jerked toward her.

"Michael!" Heart in throat, Charlie snapped the glass down over the candle. As quick as that, the vortex dropped him like he was hot, as the suction pulling him in instantly ceased. Landing on his feet, he staggered, then dropped into a crouch inches away from her.

"Oh, my God," Charlie said, as, inside the glass, the flame flickered and went out.

"Jesus Christ." Michael flexed his shoulders as he looked at the still-smoking candle. "For the record, that hurt like a mother."

He had already solidified. Just like that: no more cellophane man. Did that mean it had worked? She thought it did. *Thank God.* Her racing heart started to slow. The tide of dread that had been building inside her began to ebb. Crouched at her feet, he now looked as vividly alive as she did. Probably more so, Charlie reflected with a touch of wryness, because she had never possessed his degree of magnetism—or good looks.

Okay. Deep breath.

"Don't be such a baby." Her tone was brisk because realizing how much the idea of him being in pain bothered her bothered her. Current crisis apparently averted, she had no intention of allowing herself to dwell on how frightened for him she had been—or to clue him in to it.

Bottom line remained: he might be here for the time being, but he was still dead—and still subject to the laws of the universe, which might decide to take him at any time. Whatever the (twisted?) relationship between them was, there was still absolutely no future in it. Not that she wanted a future that included him anyway.

But still, here they were.

What have I done? was the harrowing thought that occurred to her. It was almost immediately followed by its corollary: *Too late now.*

"Baby? Me?" Sounding mildly affronted, he looked up at her then. The shadow of pain still etched his eyes, and Charlie found the tightening of her stomach in response more than a little alarming.

Again she took refuge in flippancy. "No pain, no gain. The good news is, I think it worked."

"I sure hope so, 'cause I ain't doing that again. Next time you start ju-juing me, think you could go with something that doesn't feel like it's tearing me limb from limb?"

She smiled.

"Dr. Stone?" A brisk rapping on the bedroom door caused her to shift focus in a hurry. It sounded like the same male voice as before. "Could I please speak to you a minute? It's important."

She raised her voice. "I'll be right there."

Her eyes were already back on Michael before she had even finished speaking. She hated to so much as consider the possibility, but she discovered that she was terrified he was going to start fading out, or flickering, or something similar, again. If he did, she had no idea what she would do. That call to Tam had been the last card she had to play.

"Fuck." Michael slowly stood up, straightening to his full height, stretching and flexing and grimacing as if he actually had muscles and sinews and tendons that could actually hurt. "I feel like I got hit by a semi."

"You're dead," she reminded him in an astringent whisper. "You shouldn't be able to feel a thing."

"Like I think I may have told you before: you don't know shit about it."

For a moment they looked measuringly at each other. He was so close that she had to tilt her head back to meet his eyes. She could see the darkness in the sky blue depths, the tightness at the corners of his beautifully cut mouth, the tension in his square jaw. His hair, a sun-kissed dark blond that made her think of beaches and waves and sunny summer days, was tousled in the aftermath of the vortex. The fine texture of his skin, the slight stubble on his chin and jaw, the golden tan, all looked as real as her own slightly freckled, baby-smooth flesh. His broad shoulders and wide chest filled out the simple white cotton tee in a way that made her eyes want to linger. The brawny muscles of his arms, his flat abdomen and narrow hips and long, powerful legs, all proclaimed youth and strength and a healthy virility. Her breasts were millimeters from the muscled wall of his chest. If he had been alive, she would have been able to feel his body heat, feel the warmth of his breath on her face.

She would have been able to go up on tiptoe and kiss him.

For a second there, looking at the hard curve of his mouth, she wanted to so much that it made her dizzy.

But, she reminded herself savagely, *he is not alive. And if he were, he would still be locked up in that sad little six by eight cell in Wallens Ridge.*

And all you'd know about him is what you would know about any other death row prisoner who was your research subject.

She took a step back from him.

"Thank you, Charlie, for saving my life." She mimicked his mocking comment from earlier, then faltered as she remembered that it wasn't exactly his life that she had saved. "Or whatever."

"Thank you. For saving my whatever. Though I have to say, you're not looking any too happy about having snatched me off of the highway to hell."

"The thing is, I keep asking myself how evil you have to be to find yourself on the highway to hell to begin with."

The look he gave her was impossible to interpret. "I've got a question for you, buttercup: if you really think I'm so evil, then what the hell are you doing with me?"

His eyes bored into hers: she couldn't hold his gaze. With a small grimace she turned away from him, spotted the glass over the candle, and, glad for something to do, carefully lifted it off.

"Let's get this straight: I am *not* with you. At least, not on purpose." She replaced her toothbrush and toothpaste in the glass and carefully sat it back on the ledge above the sink. Then she placed the candle beside it. In case, she told herself, she ever needed to use it again. Although whether such a thing would work twice she had no idea. "Just because you happen to have barged into my life does not mean that I'm with you."

"I think it's the sex that means that." His voice was dry.

She threw him a quick, charged look.

"I—I—" Stuttering like that was idiotic. She was not the kind of woman who, when confronted with an awkward situation, stuttered. Her chin came up, and she turned to face him. "I'm not with you, okay? No way in hell am I *with* the ghost of a serial killer."

"I'll give you the ghost, but I'm no serial killer. Come on, Charlie, you know I didn't kill those women."

Surprised to find herself suddenly angry, she glared at him. "I do not know that."

"Yes, you do, if for no other reason than because I'm standing here telling you so."

A momentary lightness which she identified as hope fluttered inside her. "So I'm supposed to believe you in the face of all evidence?" Then she recalled said evidence and felt hope crash and burn. The case against him was overwhelming. Seven beautiful young women, brutally slashed to death. His DNA had been found on every victim and at every crime scene. Eyewitnesses had identified him. Security cameras had recorded him. He had no alibi for any of the crimes. The list went on and on. Even the fact that she was considering the possibility that he might be telling the truth concerned her. The stock-in-trade of a charismatic psychopath, which had been her diagnosis of him, was the ability to convince everyone around him that he was charming and likable and trustworthy. It was camouflage, similar to a chameleon's ability to change its coloring to match its surroundings. She *knew* that. *Unless I'm wrong. Unless the cops and the FBI and the judge and the jury and the evidence and the whole damned legal system is wrong.* Listening to that tiny voice of dissent inside her head, Charlie gritted her teeth. If her emotions started trumping her intellect, there would be no place left for her that was safe and true. "In your dreams."

His eyes hardened as they slid over her face. "You wouldn't believe me if I swore it on a stack of Bibles, would you? I know you: when it comes to everything except your damned ghosts, you believe in the infallibility of authority, of evidence, of the man. If some damned court says it's so then it must be. But here's the best part: I don't care what you think you believe, somewhere deep inside you know I didn't kill those women. You wouldn't be giving me the time of day otherwise, much less sleeping with me."

"I am not—" Charlie began hotly, about to deny that she was sleeping with him. The word was *slept,* as in past tense. Singular.

"You did," he interrupted ruthlessly. "Have a little faith in your instincts for a change."

A sharp knock on the bedroom door made Michael swear.

"Dr. Stone?" Same man. Same summons. It was all Charlie could do not to groan.

"I'm coming," Charlie called back, and, with a narrow-eyed look at Michael, started to suit the action to her words.

He didn't move.

"Do you mind?" If she sounded a little cranky, well, she had reason: *mess* did not begin to describe the situation she had gotten herself into with him. And reminding herself that none of it, not one teeny tiny bit (well, okay, except for maybe the sex part), was her fault didn't help at all. When he still didn't move in response to that very pointed hint, she edged around him, because walking right through him was beyond her for the moment. "*I* have better things to do than stand around and argue with you. Like go talk to the man who keeps banging on the fricking door."

"You're determined not to believe me, aren't you? Fine. If it gives you a thrill to imagine that you're fucking a murderous psychopath, so be it. Seems a little sick, but probably that's just me."

Which was infuriating on so many levels, Charlie didn't even know where to begin.

"You know what? I'm not talking to you anymore. I have a houseful of other problems to deal with."

"Before you give me the silent treatment, think you could explain what you did with the whole glass and candle thing? So I know what to expect if anything should come up." He was following her through the bedroom. Of course he was following her through the bedroom. After what she had done, for all she knew, he would be following her everywhere she went for the rest of her life. The only thing more horrifying than that thought was the one that he would not be. Who knew for how long the action she had taken would tether him to her? Days, weeks, years?

All she could be sure of was that he was here now. The future was up in the air.

In an effort to shake off the impossible-to-sort-out combination of anger and doubt and regret and relief that she was experiencing, her reply was coolly brisk.

"When you die, you're supposed to move on, you know. That's how it works. Sometimes spirits will stay for a few days, until they can accept that they're dead, but then they go on to where they're supposed to be. Since you weren't leaving voluntarily, a portal was opening to transport you to"—in his case, she didn't even want to try to put a name to his probable final destination—"the next place. That's why you were flickering. What lighting the candle did was go ahead and open the portal all the way, and then when the resulting vortex got strong enough to pull you in I slammed the portal shut again by dropping the glass over the candle before it could actually take you. Slamming the portal closed like that makes the vortex collapse. It can't open again, at least not in the same general area. In theory."

"In theory?"

"Tam said that's how it works. I've never done it myself, so I'm taking her word for it." Stopping at her closet, keeping her voice down because if she could hear the hubbub in the hall—which she could—then it was pretty obvious that she could be overheard, too, she shoved the folding, shutter-style doors apart.

"Close your eyes," she ordered.

"What?"

"Close your eyes." Her hands were already at her buttons as she looked around at him. "I need to change my blouse. I don't need you to watch."

"Oh, for God's sake." But when she glared at him, he obediently closed his eyes. Stripping off her damp and bloodstained shirt while casting him a suspicious glance—as far as she could tell his eyes were staying shut—she dropped the soiled garment into the laundry basket on the floor of her closet.

"Nice bra," he said. "Sexy."

It was, pale pink and lacy and low cut, carefully chosen along with a pair of matching panties because when she'd gotten dressed she had thought Tony might be seeing her in her undies later. That hadn't happened, thanks in large part to the infuriating creature behind her. As she snatched a leaf green replacement blouse from its hanger, the look she shot him should have fried his eyeballs. If his eyes had been open to encounter it, that is. But they weren't, and—

She couldn't be sure they ever had been. In fact, she suspected that they had stayed closed, that he was merely teasing her. For all his faults, which were many and varied, he had never actually gone the creepy Peeping Tom route on her. Which, given what he was, would have been ridiculously easy.

"You're not funny," she said crossly, shrugging into her shirt. At that he opened his eyes and grinned at her. And got a look at her bra after all, between the parted edges of her shirt. "Hey, I didn't say you could open your eyes yet."

Knock, knock.

"Dr. Stone?" It was the same man again, sounding as if he knew she was standing right there on the other side of the door, a mere few feet away from him. Damn it, had she forgotten to lower her voice on that last exchange with Michael?

"Coming," she called back. Finishing up with her buttons, she remembered something and gave Michael a quick, admonishing frown as she whispered, "By the way, you need to stay close. Collapsing a portal only works for a certain amount of space around it, apparently. Tam said, to be safe, we should consider that space about fifty feet."

"Let me get this straight: now I have to stay within fifty feet of you?" His slow grin made her want to throw something at him. She knew how his mind worked: dirty thoughts abounded. "Works for me."

"Yes, well, I'm not so sure it works for me. This is only temporary. Just until I can come up with something else," she warned in an impatient whisper, and opened the door before he could reply.

"Dr. Stone." A bullet-headed bald guy in a police uniform greeted her. Maybe five-eleven, fortyish, relatively fit-looking, he stood right outside the door with his fist raised, obviously having been about to knock again. If he was surprised that the door had opened so opportunely, he recovered fast. "I'm Detective Todd Sager." He held out his hand. Stepping into the hall, Charlie shook it with a polite murmur. Sager continued, "If you could come downstairs with me, there's something I'd like you to take a look at."

"Sexy shoes, too," the curse she was afflicted with said. "Oh, right, you had a hot date with FBI guy tonight. I get it. Wow, Doc, you were pulling out all the stops. Things had played out different, right now you might have been wrapping up your evening right over there in your bed."

Since snapping *Shove it* was not an option, she didn't.

"Certainly," she answered Sager. Having slipped back into her professional persona with the ease of long habit, Charlie managed a tight nod, and in response to Sager's gesture preceded him toward the stairs. Her knees felt a little wobbly, and she had the beginnings of a killer headache: a reaction, no doubt, to the crisis-filled last half hour. A police photographer was busy taking pictures of the corner by the stairs where she had last seen Jenna. A record was being made of the wet spot on the floor where Jenna had crouched, plus the droplets of blood surrounding it. Charlie was busy processing the rise and fall of voices, the clicking of the camera and the rattle of metal and shuffle of footsteps, the swirl of activity around her and on the stairs and in the hall below when, just as she reached the top of the stairs, a woman's piercing scream stopped her in her tracks. A startled glance at Sager was all that it took to tell her that the scream causing the hair to rise on the back of her neck was unheard by him. No one else seemed to hear it, either. Looking down, she could see that Jenna, eyes closed, swathed in blankets, was lying on a stretcher in the hall below. Surrounded by paramedics in a hallway filled to overflowing with cops, she looked as if she was either asleep or unconscious. A square of white gauze covered the wound on her forehead. An IV drip had been inserted into her arm.

The scream was coming from a second dark-haired, wet, and bloody young woman. Flying across the hall toward the oblivious Jenna, the woman held a jagged rock in her upraised hand. Even as Charlie's heart jumped, even as she started to call out and alert Jenna, alert the people around her, stop the terrible thing that was obviously getting ready to happen, she realized that what she was seeing wasn't a living attacker at all, but a phantom.

A phantom who, even as Charlie watched, went through the motions of bashing Jenna's head in with the rock, slamming the jagged edge down into the pale forehead again and again and again. Without making a mark or disturbing so much as a hair on Jenna's head. Since it had no corporeal existence, the phantom rock passed right through the living would-be victim's flesh.

Even as the girl wielding it screamed over and over again, "You murdered me, you bitch! You murdered me!"

CHAPTER FIVE

Charlie's mind was spinning. What the phantom was saying—accusing Jenna of murdering her—was so off the wall that it couldn't possibly be true. Could it?

A low whistle from behind her told Charlie that Michael was witnessing the same thing. She almost turned to say something to him before she caught herself. As far as everyone else in the whole world was concerned, he—and the bloody, screaming phantom in the hallway below—was not there. If she wanted to retain any credibility at all, she could not let herself forget that.

"Now that's what you call a whole 'nother can of worms." Michael sounded more entertained than taken aback. Taken aback would be how *she* felt, Charlie realized.

"Dr. Stone? Is something wrong?" Sager asked. Since she had frozen at the top of the stairs, he had been forced to stop, too.

"No." Okay, she'd had lots of practice at keeping her cool in the presence of ghosts. She sounded perfectly normal, and was able to continue on down the stairs as if nothing out of the ordinary had occurred. The phantom girl had vanished, which helped. "Except for the fact that I've got a girl who apparently barely escaped being murdered in my house, of course."

"I hear you. Not the kind of thing that usually happens around here." Sager made a sound that almost could have been a grim chuckle. Charlie couldn't be sure, because right as he finished speaking the spine-tingling scream was repeated. It was all Charlie could do to control her impulse to fly to Jenna's aid as the phantom girl reappeared. Instead, she could do nothing more than watch as the phantom rushed across the hall toward Jenna, who still lay, eyes closed and unmoving, on the stretcher while the paramedics rigged up some kind of waterproof shield above her to protect her from the rain that was still falling outside, in apparent preparation for moving her to the waiting ambulance.

"How's she doing?" Charlie asked the closest paramedic with careful control as she stepped down into the hall. The paramedic, a young Asian woman in a blue uniform, looked around at her just as the phantom reached the side of the stretcher and brought the rock crashing down.

Charlie felt her pulse jump.

It can't hurt her, she reminded herself. Looking at Jenna's colorless face, Charlie tried turning the scenario she'd been picturing on its head and envisioning Jenna inflicting the hideous wounds that the phantom girl exhibited.

Her mind boggled.

"Her vital signs are stable. We've sedated her because of the degree of emotional upset she was experiencing. We'll know more once we get her to the hospital."

Had Jenna killed that girl? What was the alternative, a lying—or mistaken—ghost?

Grappling with the need to warn him to keep Jenna in custody until the investigation could determine the facts—and how could she do that, without revealing what she had seen?—Charlie looked at Sager. "Did she say anything? Did you get her statement?"

Sager shook his head. "We're waiting on the FBI for that. We've already been informed that they're on the way."

Of course the FBI would be involved in such a high-profile disappearance.

"You'll keep her in some kind of protective custody, won't you? Because whoever did this is still out there." Asking for a guard to be kept on Jenna was the best Charlie could do under the circumstances.

"She won't get out of our guys' sight," Sager promised.

"You murdered me, you bitch! You murdered me!" The shriek echoed off the walls. Charlie couldn't help it: what felt like a cold finger slid down her spine, and her notoriously sensitive stomach clenched.

I'll never get used to this.

Watching the rock slash through Jenna's forehead again, Charlie felt nausea building.

Oh, no.

"Hellfire, you been seeing this kind of thing your whole life?" Michael's question reminded her that, for what was practically the first time in her existence, someone else was seeing the same thing she was. It was unsettling, but kind of comforting, too.

I'm not alone in this anymore.

Since that thought was almost more disconcerting than the screaming phantom, Charlie was still trying to come to terms with it when the phantom girl suddenly looked her way. Their eyes met. Charlie felt the jolt of connection, and knew instantly that the girl could see her, which, with phantoms, wasn't always the case. Just like most people can't see ghosts, most ghosts can't see the living, but this traumatized spirit was clearly one of the exceptions—and she obviously knew that Charlie could see her as well.

"Look at me—I'm bleeding! There's so much blood! It hurts—oh, it hurts! She stabbed me! That bitch stabbed me! You have to help me—please!" The girl rushed toward Charlie, the rock still clutched in her hand. Her feet didn't touch the floor; her soaked, seal-black hair flew behind her. A gaping wound in her neck spouted a waterfall of bright crimson blood that gushed down the front of her body, staining her clothes, her legs, splashing around her feet. More blood ran down her face from a slash in her cheek, and there was another heavily bleeding gash in her upper arm. Like Jenna, she was dressed in shorts and a T-shirt, denim and pink respectively, both now saturated with blood, and she was wet and muddy and wild-eyed. Having learned already that (in every case she knew of, although it was possible there were exceptions) spirits couldn't harm the living, Charlie was horrified and filled with pity, but not afraid as a wave of freezing cold air engulfed her in advance of the spirit's arrival. Michael, however, hadn't been dead long enough to know the rules that covered ghosts on the ground, as she called them. Charlie realized that when he jumped in front of her, interposing his big body between her and the phantom before the girl could reach her. His intervention was effective: the phantom stopped dead, shifting her attention from Charlie to Michael.

"The bitch stabbed me!" she wailed again, lifting the hand that wasn't holding the rock to clutch at her bleeding throat. Blood instantly coated her hand, spurted through the spread fingers, and she pulled her hand back and looked at it in horror. Her eyes shot to Michael's face. "Oh, oh, I'm bleeding! What do I do?"

"It's over. You're dead. There's nothing to do," Michael said brutally, employing way less than the degree of tact Charlie would have used, if she had chosen to convey the same message. Hamstrung as she was by being surrounded by the living, however, Charlie couldn't say a word.

The girl screamed as if she was being stabbed again. Then she vanished.

Charlie couldn't help it. Gathering herself, moving on toward the kitchen, she shot Michael a condemning look.

"What? She needed to know," he said.

"If you wouldn't mind, I'd like to get this cleared up before the FBI gets here." Sager took her arm, discreetly urging her along toward the kitchen in an obvious indication that he thought her progress was too slow. Charlie nodded and picked up the pace, moving past the knot of people in her entryway with only a few blind nods to those of them she thought she might know: neighbors, she was pretty certain because of their civilian clothes, but she was so distracted by this sudden shocking revelation about Jenna that she couldn't concentrate enough to even start putting names and faces together. Plus, she had another pressing concern. She had taken only a few steps down the hall when the nausea that had been building inside her hit full bore. Swallowing, she pulled her arm free.

"Excuse me," she managed, before bolting into the small half bath beneath the stairs.

She barely had time to hit the light switch, lock the door, and stumble to the toilet before she vomited.

"Jesus H. Christ," Michael said.

He was in the bathroom with her, leaning against the locked door, Charlie saw as she straightened.

"Go away." Feeling weak but definitely better, Charlie glared at him as she flushed the toilet and went to the sink. Turning the cold water on full blast, she washed her hands and rinsed her mouth. The blush and gloss had been a waste of time; she looked as white as a sheet, she saw with disgust. "Do you have no understanding whatsoever of the concept of privacy?"

"I was worried about you." It was a small bathroom, and he took up way too much space in it.

For just a second or two, the idea that he had been worried about her made her feel all warm and fuzzy inside. And that annoyed her.

"Seeing ghosts makes me sick, remember?" she reminded him tartly. Although apparently she was now immune to him. Repeated exposure to the same stomach-churning stimuli obviously mitigated the effect. "And I don't *want* you worrying about me. I don't want you trying to protect me, either. I don't need you jumping between me and other ghosts."

He shrugged. "Get used to it. It's part of the deal."

"What deal?" She was drying her hands. "We don't have a deal. There is no deal."

He snorted, looked at her. "You need to find a new line of work."

"Wouldn't help. Ghosts are everywhere." Taking a deep breath, she turned toward the door. He was blocking her way.

"Screaming, bleeding murder victims aren't. They're kind of like psycho murderers: you don't go poking around in their business, you're probably not ever going to encounter one."

"Would you move?" She reached for the knob, prepared to thrust her hand right through him if she had to. She didn't have to: he stepped aside.

"It ain't healthy, what you do. Mentally or physically."

"Quit talking to me. We're not speaking, remember?" Opening the door, she stepped back into the hall. Detective Sager was waiting for her.

"You were the one who said you weren't speaking to me. I never said a thing about not speaking to you."

Charlie swallowed a growl.

"Are you all right, Dr. Stone?" Sager, frowning in concern, asked as she rejoined him. "You've been through quite an ordeal, I realize. The paramedics—"

Charlie shook her head. "I'm fine."

Behind her, Michael made a rude sound. "You got low standards for 'fine.' I'm just sayin'."

With Sager looking at her, she couldn't even shoot a glare Michael's way.

Taking a cleansing breath, she focused on her surroundings instead. A glance told her that Jenna was no longer in the entry hall. The paramedics had apparently taken her away. The population of cops had thinned out, too. Two stood on either side of the front door as if stationed there, but the rest had gone. The neighbors—had she actually seen some neighbors mixed in with the cops? If so, they were gone now, too. As Charlie continued on down the hall toward the kitchen, she wondered how the spirit of the murdered girl had found Jenna. If someone suffered a violent death, it wasn't uncommon for the shocked spirit to stick around, attaching to something or someone (as Michael had attached to her) that had been nearby at the moment the soul exited the body. But if the phantom had been attached to Jenna, it would have been with her from the first.

Where, then, had the spirit come from?

Charlie had no answer for that.

Her kitchen was full of cops. The partially open back door was being dusted for fingerprints. Tape blocked off a path from the door to the kitchen table. A police photographer was taking pictures while something was being sprayed on the wood floor inside that path: Luminol, to check for blood? Charlie couldn't be sure.

The sense of violation that she felt because the peaceful sanctuary that was her house had been invaded by horror was suddenly immense.

"Did he actually come inside?" she asked Sager over her shoulder. Michael was back there, too, looking grim, but Charlie didn't have any trouble ignoring him.

"Looks like it," Sager replied. "Unless you left your back door standing open. Because it was open when we got in here."

Charlie shook her head. A breeze blew in through the open door-way, carrying the smell of rain on it. She could see that the downpour had eased off, hear the gentler splatter of droplets hitting the ground. Beyond the spill of light from the kitchen, the night was black as pitch.

"You keep your curtains closed at night, you wouldn't have to worry about some whack job seeing in," Michael pointed out tren-chantly. Irritating as the remark might be, their thinking once again seemed to be on pretty much the same page. Charlie was already re-pressing a shiver at the idea that an armed killer might be up on the mountainside watching them through the windows at that very mo-ment.

Only maybe there wasn't an armed killer. Maybe Jenna was the killer. Maybe Jenna's frantic advent into her kitchen had been part of some elaborate cover-up and . . .

No way. Jenna's terror had been real. And *someone* had opened the back door.

Sager continued, "I want you to look at something on your kitchen table for me."

Charlie nodded.

" . . . called my wife . . ." Ken stood right inside the entrance to the kitchen talking earnestly to a cop, who was writing down what he said. His eyes tracked Charlie until she met them, when they slid away. "When I got here Dr. Stone let me in and . . ."

Charlie overheard those snippets as she walked past him. By then his arms were crossed over his chest, his head was down, and he seemed to be trying very hard not to look at her.

"Can you tell me if there's anything on the table there that wasn't on it before?" Sager asked.

Charlie looked at the table. There was the mail she'd been open-ing, the overturned box, the spill of foam peanuts—

And a white, business-sized envelope with a knife resting on top of it.

The knife was about five inches long, with a wooden handle, and looked old. The handle was damp, and the blade appeared clean and razor sharp. Just looking at it made Charlie feel cold all over.

"That settles it. Looks like Teen Queen was telling the truth." An involuntary glance his way told Charlie that Michael was looking at the same thing.

Although she couldn't say so, that was Charlie's conclusion, too. Because Jenna had never gotten out of her sight from the time she had entered the kitchen, and the door had been forced open, and the knife and envelope, which had definitely not been on the table when they had fled the kitchen together, were now there. Ergo, someone else had to have put them on her table—such as the man with the gun Jenna had insisted was chasing her.

It was a relief to definitively conclude that he was real. That whatever had prompted the phantom girl's accusation, Jenna's terror had not been faked.

"The knife—and the envelope," Charlie said to Sager. "They aren't mine. They weren't on the table."

"That's what I thought." Sager nodded with satisfaction. He waved a hand at the photographer, who was busy snapping pictures of the door. "Hey, Torres, you get a picture of that table?"

"Yeah. The whole thing, plus close-ups of everything on it."

"The knife and envelope?"

"Oh, yeah. At least a dozen."

"Okay." Sager looked at Charlie. She was close enough to the table now that she could see the wet splotch the knife had left on the envelope. She could see something else, too, that made her eyes widen. Her name was written on the envelope: Dr. Charlotte Stone. In what looked like black Sharpie, unsmudged despite the damp spot in the middle of it. The writing was large enough so that her name was easily readable. The script itself was delicate, flowing.

A shiver slid over her skin as she looked at it.

"Envelope's addressed to you. Would you mind opening it?" As Charlie nodded assent Sager added, "I'll need you to put on some gloves first."

Michael was frowning at the table. He cast a sharp look at Charlie. "You get that your name on that envelope means the sick bastard thinks he's got some kind of connection going on with *you*."

Charlie got it, all right. Her pulse picked up the pace as, briefly, she held Michael's gaze. Once again she was burningly conscious of the open curtains. The sudden sense of vulnerability she felt at the thought that whoever had left that envelope on the table might be watching through the window was only slightly mitigated by reminding herself that her house was full of cops.

"Dr. Stone." A cop handed Charlie a pair of latex gloves. As she pulled them on, another similarly gloved cop picked up the knife and dropped it in a plastic bag.

"Tag that for the FBI," Sager told him, then added to Charlie, "Be real careful with that, please. I'll get my butt handed to me if there's damage to the evidence."

Charlie nodded, and picked up the envelope. It wasn't sealed, she saw as she turned it over. Of course, whoever had left it had wanted her to open it.

Taking a deep breath, conscious of the weight of many eyes on her, she lifted the flap and pulled out the single sheet of paper that was inside.

On plain white typing paper, in black Sharpie, in the same flowing script that was on the envelope, were written the words:

You can't catch me.

Looking at them, Charlie felt her heart start to slam in her chest. Her breath caught. She looked up quickly, her eyes going instinctively to Michael, who like Sager was watching her with frowning attention.

"I know who did this." There was a sudden tightness in her chest. Then, remembering that to Sager and anyone else who was watching it would look like she was directing her words to thin air, she transferred her gaze from Michael to Sager.

"I know who did this," she repeated urgently.

CHAPTER SIX

"Who?" Michael and Sager demanded almost in unison, as every eye in the kitchen that hadn't already been watching her turned her way.

Charlie took a deep, steadying breath as all the pieces suddenly started fitting together in her mind. The truth was terrifying: this was a case she had recently consulted on and she recognized the killer's signature MO right off the bat. She felt her blood drain toward her toes as she faced it. "I'm almost positive that we're dealing with a serial killer. He's known as the Gingerbread Man."

"You know what, you need to rethink this whole serial killer gig you got going on," Michael said. "And I'm being completely serious here."

"The Gingerbread Man?" Sager frowned doubtfully at her.

"He's been operating up and down the East Coast for at least the last two years." Talking around the sudden tightness in her throat, Charlie directed her remarks to Sager and ignored the grim stare Michael was giving her. She took one last look at the piece of paper—the words *You can't catch me* leaped out at her like the taunt they were meant to be—then carefully refolded it, slid it back inside the envelope, and started to put the envelope on the table.

It took every bit of self-control she had to keep her hands steady.

"You can get another job," Michael told her. "Most shrinks write prescriptions for kids with ADHD. They talk fat cats off the ledge when the economy tanks. They listen to middle-aged women cry about their empty nests. They don't put their lives at risk every single day. That's crazy."

"Uh, would you mind dropping that in here?" The same cop who had bagged the knife held open another plastic bag to receive the letter. Doing her best to keep a clear head, Charlie obediently dropped it in. The idea that yet another serial killer had her in his sights was stirring up nightmare memories that she'd thought, hoped, and prayed she'd put to rest.

"Well, now, I never heard of anyone called that," Sager said. "A serial killer, you say. Here in town?"

"Yes. At least, tonight he was." Serial killers had always existed. They always would. That she had become enmeshed in their darkness was her bad luck. As she accepted the harsh truth of that, Charlie forgot all about her wobbly legs, the lingering remnants of nausea, the exhaustion that had been creeping over her, her very mixed emotions about what she had done with Michael. What she had been hoping to return to—her peaceful existence, her safe little house, the distance she had carefully crafted between herself and the serial killers she analyzed in hopes of learning what made them tick so that others of their ilk could be identified and stopped before they hurt anyone else—had just been blasted to hell. Once again, she was being plunged into the horror she had spent most of her life trying to avoid.

The Gingerbread Man had been in her house less than an hour before. What she wanted to do—turn back the clock, erase the last hour, go on like Jenna McDaniels had never come banging on her door—was impossible. That being the case, she had no choice but to deal. And dealing meant taking up the Gingerbread Man's challenge, doing her best to make sure that he got caught. If she did not succeed, he would kill again, and soon. Even if she turned her back on the challenge, left the investigation up to Sager and the FBI agents who were supposedly on the way, she still would not be able to simply go on with her life. A vicious, conscienceless serial killer had entered her house and left her a message. He knew who she was, where she lived, and what she did. He was interested in her. What were the chances that he would just forget all about her, go away and leave her alone if she refused to play? None. Zero. Zip.

She had always been good at grasping the reality of a situation, and as she recognized the reality of that she pushed the fear and dread that were her first reactions aside. They would do her no good at all. For whatever reason, this was the hand she had been dealt.

If she had no choice but to play, then she was damned well going to play to win.

You have to outthink him, she told herself, and squared her shoulders in preparation.

Okay. He had to have left trace evidence behind. For one thing, it was raining: there should be footprints in the muddy yard. Jenna had run to her house from somewhere presumably nearby. If investigators were very, very lucky, it would be the crime scene, where two bodies could possibly still be found. A fresh, intact crime scene.

Plus, in Jenna, they had a living witness. A living witness with the crime still vivid in her mind.

Maybe, this time, this particular monster had cut it too close. Maybe this was the mistake that would cause him to be caught. Maybe she could help put one more dangerous predator away where he could never hurt anyone again.

The thought strengthened her. It cleared her head, fired her determination.

I can do this.

The local PD and sheriff's department were great. She was sure the FBI agents who were coming, the ones who had been spearheading the search for Jenna, were competent. But they didn't have the expertise or experience necessary to even begin to handle a monster like this one.

Fortunately, she knew people who did. In fact, earlier that very night she had regretfully kissed one goodbye. If she was lucky, he might still be within reach.

"Heads up, folks. We're going to be turning out the lights for a minute to see if our spray illuminates any footprints on the floor," a technician called.

So apparently the chemical they'd been using wasn't Luminol, after all.

As the lights went out, as darkness descended, Charlie felt a shiver run down her spine. Ignoring it, *resolutely* ignoring it, she pulled her phone out of her pocket, called up her contact list, and hit the number she was looking for.

"You phoning somebody?" Having moved closer to her in the darkness, Sager eyed her glowing cell phone askance. Unable to help herself—being too close to a stranger in the darkness didn't feel comfortable now—Charlie took a step away from him even as she replied.

"This is something that local law enforcement, no matter how good they are, isn't equipped for," Charlie told him as the phone rang in her ear. "If you've got men outside searching for evidence or for those other two girls or the crime scene or whatever, they need to stop where they are. I—"

"Charlie?" The warmly masculine voice answering the phone was music to her ears. "What's up?"

"Tony," she greeted him with relief, then felt even more relief as the lights came back on.

"Fuck," Michael said. "That guy?"

"Dr. Stone, I don't think—" Sager sounded unhappy.

"Stop everything," Charlie interrupted Sager, pinning him with what she hoped was a commanding look. "Stop. Now."

"I would." On the other end of the phone, Tony was sounding amused. "But I'm really not doing much. Napping in a chair. Looks like I'm going to be spending the next few hours right here in Lonesome Pine Airport. Plane can't take off because of the storm."

"With all due respect, Dr. Stone," Sager said, "we have an investigation to conduct. Stopping it isn't an option."

"When's the last time your department handled any kind of murder investigation at all? How many years ago? This is a serial killer. The case needs to be overseen by experts in catching them," Charlie answered Sager fiercely, while at the same time, except for shooting him a dirty look, doing her best to ignore Michael, who had just finished telling her, "You know you've got a major screw loose, right?" To Tony, whom she considered the only one really worth talking to at the moment, Charlie responded, "Thank God for the storm. Have you ever heard of the Gingerbread Man?"

"Yeah, sure. He's on the Active List"—meaning the FBI's list of serial killers who were known to be active in the country at any given time—"but—"

"He's here." Simply saying it made her palms go damp. "He's been in my house. Tonight."

"What?" From the sound of his voice, Tony had sat bolt upright in his chair. He responded to a sudden burst of chatter on his end of the call with an impatient, "Quiet, you two. I need to hear this."

As he was obviously not talking to her, Charlie had to ask. "Who's there with you?"

"Kaminsky and Crane. Their plane didn't get out of here, either." In the background Charlie could hear the other members of the team— FBI Special Agents Lena Kaminsky and Buzz Crane—demanding to know what was up. They were quickly silenced, and Charlie imagined Tony, who was their boss, gesturing at them to be quiet.

Charlie gave Tony a quick, condensed version of events, finishing with "The trail's still fresh. We've got a real chance to catch this guy if you can get here fast. We—"

"We?" Michael erupted. He was giving her the kind of hard, intimidating, *you will bend to my will* look that she hoped she had just turned on Sager. Once upon a time, coming from the big, scary convict in the orange jumpsuit who she was pretty sure had lied to her about her inkblots, she might actually have found that look alarming. Now, though, she found herself battling the impulse to stick her tongue out at him. "If you mean you and him, there is no *we* in this, buttercup. Your boyfriend there's a federal agent who gets paid to lay his life on the line. You're a shrink. You get paid to listen to people talk. Damn it, Charlie, I'm going to say this one more time: messing with serial killers is stupid. It's fucking *dangerous*. Didn't anybody ever teach you that if you poke a sleeping bear enough times sooner or later it's going to wake up and eat you?"

Charlie shot Michael a narrow-eyed *mind your own business* look. Replying to him was, of course, out of the question.

So she continued talking to Tony instead.

"—have a survivor, we have an envelope with handwriting on it as well as other possible trace evidence, we have a knife that may or may not be a murder weapon, we have—"

"We're out the door," Tony interrupted her to say. "Thirty minutes, max."

That was exactly the response Charlie had hoped for. Tony and his team were as invested in the apprehension of serial killers as she was in the studying of them. She knew how good they were at their jobs because she had watched them work: on the very day that Michael had been killed, Tony and his team had come to her and asked for her help in finding the Boardwalk Killer, the serial killer who had murdered her best friend, Holly, and Holly's family when she and Holly were only seventeen. Charlie had been staying the night with Holly at the time, and had hidden from the killer and survived. When the Boardwalk Killer had resurfaced after fifteen years, she had been reluctant (okay, afraid) to get involved—but she had done it anyway. As a result, the Boardwalk Killer had been captured, and, not incidentally, Charlie had been freed of the secret terror she had lived with ever since she'd survived the attacker who had killed Holly: that the Boardwalk Killer would sooner or later come back and kill her, too. And in the process, she had been enormously impressed with Tony and his team.

Now there was another madman, more victims, fresh horror. Another serial killer who had turned his eyes toward her. Simply thinking about it made Charlie imagine that she could feel the darkness closing in. *Her* darkness, her own private one, the one that came from looking evil in the face and barely surviving. The darkness of her own mortal fear.

She could feel a tightening in her chest.

I don't know if I can go through this again.

Tony was saying, "Did you say the local police are there now? Could you let me speak to whoever's in charge?"

Stay in the moment. "That would be Detective Todd Sager."

Passing her phone to Sager, Charlie told him, "This is FBI Special Agent Tony Bartoli, from the Special Circumstances Division out of Quantico. They're an elite team whose sole purpose is to track and catch serial killers. They're on their way here right now."

"Well, hell, there goes the neighborhood," Michael said with disgust, leaning back against the breakfast bar and folding his arms over his chest. Charlie shot him an angry look. Serial killers were evil by definition, and no matter how much he proclaimed his innocence, Michael was a convicted serial killer. She ought to hate him. She ought to fear him. She definitely ought to have let him go to his just reward when she'd had the chance. *He* was one of *them*.

You know I'm innocent. Oh, God, she didn't. The sad truth almost certainly was, he had said the words she needed to hear, and she just wanted to believe.

"Oh, so now you're mad at *me*?" Michael said. "Nice."

"I don't think—" were the first words Sager said into the phone. Then he was silent, listening, finally nodding. "I'll pass the word." He looked at Charlie. "Special Agent Bartoli wants to speak to you," he said, and handed the phone back to her.

"Sit tight. We'll be with you shortly," Tony told her, while Sager barked at the other cops in the room, "Everybody, change of plan. We're going to wait until Special Agent Bartoli's team gets here to go forward." He pointed to two cops near the back door. "Get out there and tell those guys outside to hold up. If we've got a crime scene, the last thing we want to do is contaminate it."

"You want I should finish up with the door?" The technician who was dusting for fingerprints asked. Kneeling on the floor below him, another cop was measuring the distance from the edge of the door to an area of damage in the door's lower third that hadn't been there previously and that Charlie assumed was the result of something like a hard kick. Looking at it and realizing how ridiculously easy it had been for a killer to gain access to her house made her skin crawl. What had she been thinking, to imagine that she could live in a world where there was no need to keep a gun for protection, or to have a burglar alarm or something more than an ordinary, run-of-the-mill lock on her doors? When had wishful thinking become her modus operandi? "In this rain, I wouldn't want to wait."

Sager hesitated. Then he nodded. "Go ahead."

When this guy's caught, I'll be safe again. And there will be one less monster in the world.

That was the thought that steadied Charlie's nerves, calmed her down, helped her pull herself together. Mentally, she took a deep breath and stood tall.

I'm not a scared teenager anymore. I'm an expert on serial killers. So this time the Gingerbread Man has messed with the wrong expert.

"Did Jenna tell you where she had come from?" Charlie asked Sager as, Tony having disconnected, she slid her phone into her pocket again. If she didn't have her emotions totally under control yet, well, she was working on it. Under the circumstances, there was no shame in taking a few moments to adjust.

Sager shook his head. "No. At least, she wasn't real specific. She was crying too hard to get anything of much value out of her, but she did say she ran down the mountain. Since she wound up at your back door, I figure she must have come down Big Rock Trail. Muddy as it's bound to be, she must have left some tracks. I figure we can follow them back."

Charlie nodded. Big Rock Trail was the dirt path that she favored for her almost daily runs. Starting only a few yards beyond her back fence, it wound up through the thick piney woods of Smoke Mountain all the way to the top of the ridge. She would have worried about the downpour washing away any tracks Jenna might have left, except for the fact that at this time of year the canopy was so dense she couldn't imagine much rainfall got through. Sager was apparently aware of that, too.

"The screamer said Teen Queen killed her," said Michael. "You say the killer is somebody called the Gingerbread Man. Want to explain to me what's up with that?"

Charlie caught herself just as she was about to answer, and almost had to bite her tongue to hold the words back. The glare she gave him this time was downright threatening. Fortunately Sager was talking to the fingerprint technician who apparently—from the fact that he was closing the back door—had finished, as had the cop who had been measuring the damage on the door and was now on his feet writing something on a clipboard. Point was, Sager wasn't watching her; otherwise, no telling what he would have made of her fierce scowl at nothing.

"Ooo," Michael said. "There's that *you're really pissing me off now* look of yours. You were always giving me that one back at the Ridge. Turned me on then. Turns me on now."

Bite me, her eyes said, but having a one-sided argument, she was discovering, only actually worked for the side who could talk. She might be seething inside, but Charlie was proud of her own self-control: she fell back on the one weapon she had that she knew from experience actually kind of bugged him, and ignored him. Pointedly.

"So what can you tell me about this Gingerbread Man?" Sager asked her as two of the cops he'd been talking to headed across the kitchen for the hall, signaling to a couple of others who fell in behind them. In response to her look questioning this mini exodus, Sager said, "They're going to be putting together some equipment so we can head up the mountain." He added hastily, in response to what she could only assume was a change in her facial expression: "We won't actually go until Special Agent Bartoli's team gets here."

"Did I hear you say there's a serial killer in town?" Freed from the cop who'd been questioning him, Ken came over to join Sager. Both of them looked at Charlie expectantly. At the breakfast bar, Michael lifted his eyebrows at her. The silent message she took from that was: *So, see, I'm not talking. You want me to keep it up, you talk.*

"Fine. Um, yes." After that first snapped-out slip of the tongue, she was careful to moderate her tone and direct her reply to Ken and Sager rather than Michael: "The Gingerbread Man is fairly unique in the annals of serial killers in that he doesn't actually kill the majority of his victims himself. What he has done historically is kidnap three people at a time and force them to kill one another. He appears to try to match them in terms of gender, with a lesser correlation in age and body size, although there seems to be a degree of correlation with those factors, too. Sometimes the victims know one another, sometimes they don't. In both of the last two years, he has kidnapped three disparate groups of three people within a period of about a month. Then he goes dormant for another year. As far as I know, the group in which Jenna McDaniels was a part is the first group for this, the third year. There have been five survivors if you include Jenna McDaniels tonight, which I do, and much of what we know we've learned from them. The survivors consistently tell us that they were put into

some kind of confined area together, given weapons, and told they
would all be killed unless they started killing one another. They were
promised that the last one standing would be released alive provided
that whoever survived had participated in the killing of at least one of
the other victims. The Gingerbread Man appears to keep his promise,
although it's difficult to tell because only two of the survivors have
admitted to investigators that they actually killed anyone. But they
were released by the Gingerbread Man, which indicates that they ful-
filled the conditions he set for them."

"So if Teen Queen was let go because she was the winner in a
cage fight to the death, why was she screaming her head off about a
man with a gun who was chasing her?" Michael asked.

So much for him not talking. Well, she hadn't expected it to last.
Charlie looked at him, put her nose in the air, and deliberately transferred her attention to Sager, who said slowly, as if her words were just
starting to compute for him: "Are you saying that Jenna McDaniels
herself might have killed those other two girls she was telling us about?"

Bingo, Charlie thought, but that was one more answer she
couldn't give.

"If she did, it was because she had no choice," she ended up saying. Revealing what she knew through the phantom girl wasn't possible, so she couldn't definitively say yes. "In the environment in
which the victims find themselves, it's strictly kill or be killed."

"Come on, Charlie, talk to me," Michael said impatiently. "You
really think you're going to be able to treat me like a potted plant?"

Since she caught herself shooting him a dirty look in response, the
inescapable answer was, obviously not. She gave up: because he'd
asked a legitimate question as opposed to being annoying, she would
try to answer. To all appearances, she hoped, she was simply providing additional information to Sager and Ken.

"The first two survivors were let go. The last two, not counting
Jenna, were apparently chased by the Gingerbread Man after he released them. All three, and I'm including Jenna in this, reported that
he was armed with a gun. All three reported that when he let them go,
he told them to run, then came after them. They were sure he was
going to kill them, too."

Ken said, "Since there are eyewitnesses, I'm assuming law enforcement has a description of—what did you call him, the Ginger-bread Man?—on file somewhere?"

"He wears a mask," Charlie answered. "We have eyewitness descriptions of that."

Michael said, "Don't serial killers usually have butch names like the Boardwalk Killer and the Bind, Torture, Kill Killer? I mean, when I was on trial the news channels were calling me the Southern Slasher, for cripe's sake. What is this guy, the sissy serial killer? Where'd anybody come up with a name like the Gingerbread Man?"

"It's from the nursery rhyme," Charlie answered, and immediately gave herself a mental smack—she would save the glare at Michael for a time when it wouldn't simply serve to underline the fact that as far as anyone watching was concerned she was conversing with thin air—and transferred her gaze to Sager and Ken. "The reason he's called the Gingerbread Man is from the nursery rhyme. You know, 'Run! Run! As fast as you can! You can't catch me, I'm the Gingerbread Man!' Because he told several of his surviving victims to run, and because four times that I am aware of he has sent or left a letter addressed to someone in authority or an expert he wants to match wits with, saying 'You can't catch me.'" She finished a little lamely, "I just thought you'd want to know."

"Debbie reads that nursery rhyme to the kids." Ken sounded appalled.

Michael said, "So what you're telling me is that now the sick bastard wants to match wits with you?"

Charlie gave a truncated nod. The icy little prickle that snaked down her spine as she acknowledged the truth of that was something she couldn't do anything about.

Soldier through the fear. She had done it before. She could do it now. No, she *would* do it now.

Sager was saying, "Yeah, go ahead, I guarantee you we'll be doing the grunt work anyway" in a low voice to the fingerprint technician, who apparently wanted next to begin work on the table and chairs. While the technician nodded and turned away to start scooping up the foam peanuts, which he dropped into a plastic Ziploc bag, Charlie said, "It's like a game to him. A challenge. As soon as I saw the words *you can't catch me,* I knew who it was."

"This guy knows who you are, too." Michael's voice was flat. "And that ain't good."

A commotion from the front hall distracted all of them. Hoping it was Tony and crew, Charlie started forward, only to fall back with disappointment when three strangers walked into her kitchen. The tall, burly, gray-haired man in uniform she had seen before: Wise County Sheriff Hyram Peel. The two men in dark suits were, of course, FBI, although not the agents she was anxiously awaiting. Introducing themselves as Agents Greg Flynn and Dean Burger, they were part of the team that had been involved in what apparently had been a massive search for Jenna McDaniels. While other agents had gone to the hospital to secure her, they said, they had been detailed to talk to Charlie.

She was just beginning to tell them her part of what had happened when Michael exclaimed, "Damn, that's my watch."

Distracted from her recital of events, Charlie quit talking to frown at him. He had been leaning against the breakfast counter looking grim. Now he was standing upright, staring at the table as if there was something on it that was getting ready to leap at him. Automatically she followed his gaze to find that, now that the technician had finished scooping up the last of the foam peanuts—he was shaking them in a plastic bag with fingerprint powder—it was possible to see a man's matte silver watch still resting inside the overturned package she had received.

"I told those damned clowns that it wasn't my watch they found next to that dead woman." Michael's charged gaze shifted to Charlie. "Did they believe me? Hell, no. But look at that: there it is. That's my watch."

CHAPTER SEVEN

"Pick it up. Look at it." Because Michael was talking to her, because of the intensity of his tone, because of the emotion she could feel rolling off him, Charlie completely forgot about Agents Flynn and Burger. "It's got *Semper Fi* engraved on the back of the case. Go ahead, check it out. It's my damned watch."

Semper Fi, Charlie recalled, was the Marine Corps motto. She was familiar enough with his file to know that Michael had spent eight years as a marine.

"Uh, Dr. Stone, you were saying?" Flynn prompted.

Realizing that she had broken off in mid-sentence, Charlie dragged her eyes away from Michael and sought desperately to recall where she had stopped. Flynn was frowning at her. He was a stocky, muscular man of about forty, with short brown hair and average looks. There was impatience in his narrowed brown eyes.

"Jenna was obviously traumatized," Charlie picked up the thread, and with that launched back into her story.

Even with Flynn and Burger both looking at her, even as she talked, it was impossible for Charlie not to watch, out of the corner of her eye, as Michael moved over to the table. His big hands wrapping around a chair back, his powerful shoulders bunching so that the muscles strained against his shirt, he stared down at the watch. Of course, it was impossible for him to touch it, much less pick it up. His hands would pass right through.

"How in hell is that thing turning up now?" Michael looked and sounded angry, and more as if he was talking to himself than her. "All this fucking time, and it turns up *now*?"

"Thank you," Flynn said, and Charlie realized that she had stopped talking again. Fortunately it was in a place where Flynn could conclude that she had finished with what she had to say. He nodded toward the galley part of the kitchen, where Ken and Sheriff Peel were quietly conversing. Charlie noted in passing that the kitchen faucet was no longer running: someone had obviously turned it off. She was only glad that Michael no longer seemed to need whatever strengthening effect it had on him. "Is that Deputy Ewell? Didn't you say that he was the first person on the scene here?"

"Yes."

"Excuse us. We have a few questions for him." With a nod at her, Flynn and Burger headed toward Ken.

A quick glance around told Charlie that everybody was now busy doing something else. She moved over to the table and frowned at Michael questioningly.

"Look at it." He nodded at the watch. "Tell me if it doesn't say *Semper Fi* on the back of the case."

Although as far as she could tell none of the other roughly half-dozen people in the room were paying the least bit of attention to her, Charlie knew that all it would take would be for her to start talking aloud, supposedly to herself, for that to instantly change.

Picking up the watch—it was cool and heavy, with all kinds of fancy little dials on the face and an expandable wristband—she turned it so she could see the back of the watch face. Engraved on the smooth metal surface was the Marine Corps motto.

"Semper Fi?" There was tension in Michael's face.

Charlie nodded. His gaze returned to the watch.

"Goddamn it. Of course the thing would show up now, when it's too fucking late." He sounded almost savage.

Charlie picked up the box the watch had arrived in. Fortunately, cutting through the layers of tape that had been wrapped around it had left the return address intact. It read *Mariposa Police Department.*

Her fingers tightened on the box.

I wrote to them. Of course.

Tiny Mariposa, North Carolina, was where Michael first had been arrested, for the last of the seven murders with which he had subsequently been charged. As part of her research into the backgrounds of the men she was studying, Charlie had sent the department an official request for access to any materials/information/files they still had concerning him.

This was their reply. In addition to the watch, at the bottom of the box was a DVD, and tucked to the side was a tri-folded sheet of letter-sized paper.

Charlie pulled it out.

"What the hell *is* this?" Michael growled as she unfolded the single, typewritten sheet. The letter was brief and she read it quickly. "Some kind of cosmic joke?"

"Ma'am, I'm going to have to ask you not to touch anything on the table until I'm done here." This interruption by the fingerprint technician, who had been standing a little distance away while his gloved hands busily rifled through the now powder-coated foam peanuts, almost made Charlie jump. "Could you put that back, please?"

"I'm sorry." She managed a smile for him. Then, with Michael in mind, she added, "Um, I just got this material from the Mariposa Police Department and I needed to look at it. I wrote to them, you know, about a month ago, concerning a research subject I was studying." She put the letter down on the table, open and positioned for Michael to read. He flicked her a glance.

"Don't let go of that damned watch."

She barely managed not to nod. Mouth tight, he leaned forward to read the letter.

The technician said in an apologetic tone, "That box was out on the table, wasn't it? It's possible that the perp touched it. I need to test it for fingerprints."

"I understand."

Charlie set the box back down on the table. The watch she slipped onto her own wrist. She was fine-boned, with long, slender limbs, and the watch, sized for a big man's solid forearm, was way too large for her. The expandable metal band was not adjustable, so there was nothing to do but wear it as it was. As it slid up her arm, as she felt the weight of it and the glide of the cool metal against her skin, a prickle rippled along her nerve endings. It felt weird to have something real and solid that belonged to Michael touching her.

It was almost like having him touch her himself.

"Sorry," she told the technician again. He nodded. It was clear that he was waiting for her to step away from the table, but she wasn't ready to do that until she saw Michael's reaction to what he was reading.

Having read it herself, she already knew what the letter said:

Dear Dr. Stone,

In response to your inquiry about County Inmate #876091, Michael Alan Garland, I am sending you a copy of what we have retained in our files. In addition, I am enclosing our department's video records concerning him, as well as a man's wristwatch that was tagged with his name and was found during the course of our recent move. As far as I can tell, this is the only personal effect of his still in our custody. Because of misfiling by a clerical worker, it was inadvertently left out of the bag containing his personal effects that was passed on to the FBI some years ago. We apologize for any inconvenience this may have caused, and hope that you will now pass it on to whoever should have possession of it.

Thank you.

If you have any additional questions, please feel free to contact me.

Sincerely,
Betty Culver
Executive Assistant to the Chief
Mariposa County Police Department

"Son of a bitch," Michael said. Charlie didn't say anything, but he must have felt the weight of her eyes on him, or else she must have made some small sound. Because his head came up, and he looked at her then, his eyes blazing.

"They found a damned watch exactly like this next to the body of the last chick I'm supposed to have sliced to ribbons. It was broken, had her blood on it. They said it was mine, ripped from my wrist in the struggle. I told the stupid bastards it wasn't."

Charlie's heart lurched. What he was telling her was that this watch was evidence of his innocence. Weighed against all the evidence of his guilt, it was a small thing, but still—it was something tangible.

If he was telling the truth. If he wasn't somehow playing her.

Charismatic psychopaths had a genius for playing people, she knew. They were so good at it that it wasn't even embarrassing to the people who studied them when they, too, fell victim to their lies.

The Mariposa Police Department had identified the watch as belonging to Michael right there in the letter. Plus, he'd known that *Semper Fi* was engraved on its back.

How could he have manipulated something like that?

She didn't think he could have. She didn't see how it was possible.

How important a part a watch such as the one she was wearing had played in his case was something she would have to check into.

For now—it wasn't nearly enough to persuade her.

Sway her a little, maybe, but not persuade her.

Still, it was something.

"Fuck." The blaze in Michael's eyes had hardened and cooled. "What the hell difference does it make now, right? It's done."

Shaken by the glimpse she had just gotten into what lay beneath the tough guy exterior, Charlie felt as if the earth were shifting beneath her feet, as if she were no longer standing on solid ground. Before she could formulate a response, the sound of new arrivals, coupled a moment later with a familiar voice behind her, distracted her, causing her to glance around.

"I'm Special Agent Tony Bartoli. This is Special Agent Lena Kaminsky. Special Agent Buzz Crane."

Bringing a whiff of fresh air with him into a room that was now overwarm and smelled faintly metallic, from either the aerosol spray or the fingerprint powder, Tony was there, in her kitchen, at last. *Thank God.* Raindrops gleaming on his hair and the shoulders of his jacket, he was shaking hands, first with Sager and then with Sheriff Peel, Ken, and Agents Flynn and Burger, as he introduced himself, Kaminsky, and Crane. As apparently all of the law enforcement types in the house converged on the newcomers, the room felt suddenly small and crowded. Relief welled up inside her, and Charlie cast one more worried glance at Michael. Still tense with anger and whatever other clearly negative emotions he was experiencing, he looked at the new arrivals, too, with a less than welcoming expression. But at least the raw pain she thought she had glimpsed in his eyes was gone, and he seemed more or less his usual badass self. In any case, there was nothing she could do for him at the moment, Charlie concluded. That being the case, her focus had to be on what was most important: catching a serial killer.

With that firmly fixed in the forefront of her mind, she hurried toward Tony, Kaminsky, and Crane.

"Hey," Tony said when he saw her, taking the hand she held out for him to shake—anything more intimate, like, say, a quick hug or a kiss on the cheek, would be unprofessional, and anyway she wasn't a huggie/kissie kind of person—and giving her a slow smile in which the memory of the very sexy good-night kiss they had so recently shared lingered. His coffee brown eyes crinkled around the edges when he smiled, she noted in passing, and his long mouth stretched and quirked up at the corners to reveal even white teeth. He had black hair, cut short and brushed back, and a lean, mobile face that, while not as flat-out gorgeous as Michael's, was nonetheless handsome enough to merit a second look. At the moment he was faintly red-eyed, with more than a hint of five o'clock shadow darkening his jaw, which wasn't surprising considering that it was now well after one in the morning and he had been going since seven a.m. She knew that for sure because seven a.m. (yesterday now) was when the four of them had risen to meet for breakfast before going over some files for what she had thought would be the last time; later, they'd driven to the airport to catch the private plane that had brought her back to Big Stone Gap.

Tony was six-one, about a hundred eighty pounds, lean compared to Michael's ripped body but still nicely muscled. Anyway, all that leanness looked particularly good in the well-tailored dark suits that were the Bureau's de facto uniform. He was still wearing the one he'd taken her to dinner in, as a matter of fact. His white shirt still looked fresh. His red tie was snugly in place.

Michael was right, Charlie decided as she smiled back at Tony: she did have a serious screw loose. This was the guy who should be making her heart go pitter-pat. This was the guy whose arms she should be wanting to walk into, whose mouth she should be wanting to kiss, who she should be wanting to fall into bed with. This guy liked her, more than liked her, wanted to sleep with her, wanted to have a relationship. This decent, gainfully employed, law-abiding, honorable, kind, very handsome, and *alive* man had happily ever after written all over him.

He had been clasping her hand just a couple of beats too long. Still smiling at him, she gently disengaged.

"I'm glad you're here," she said, and his smile widened.

Charlie was suddenly burningly conscious of the weight of Michael's gaze.

Sliding a sideways glance his way, she encountered blue eyes gone stony gray, a hard mouth, a granite jawline. His expression—no, his whole body—radiated frustrated, barely controlled tension. He made her think of a wild animal, a big one, a predator, that had suddenly been made aware of its situation, aware that it was trapped hopelessly and forever in an impossible-to-escape cage.

Charlie's heart unexpectedly stuttered. Her mouth went dry. She felt as if she was falling, the sensation as unmistakable as if she'd stepped into an elevator and dead-dropped three floors. The feeling wasn't good, and it certainly wasn't welcome, but there it was.

How Michael felt mattered to her.

As epiphanies went, that one kind of blew.

Talk about smart women, foolish choices, she thought, mentally aiming a swift kick at her own posterior. Lately she was practically its poster child.

"Long time no see, Dr. Stone," Kaminsky greeted her. Twenty-nine-year-old Kaminsky was small and curvy, with shiny, chin-length black hair that turned under on the ends and an olive complexion.

Pretty in an exotic kind of way, she favored snug, above-the-knee skirt suits like the pale gray one she was currently wearing and, because she was only five-two and sensitive about it, sky-high stilettos. Since Charlie had last seen Kaminsky only a few hours before, when their plane had touched down at the Lonesome Pine Airport to drop Charlie off in Big Stone Gap, and Kaminsky and Crane had been left behind to take a commercial flight to their home base of Quantico while Tony had gone with Charlie to take her to what he had described to them as a "thank-you" dinner, Kaminsky's sarcasm was not really a surprise. "Bartoli says you've managed to attract *another* serial killer. How is that even possible?"

"The Gingerbread Man, no less," Crane added on a note of what almost sounded like glee. In the classic combination known to any woman who frequented bars or other places where men tended to hang out, he was, at thirty-two, the geek to Tony's hottie. Five-ten and slightly built, with black-framed glasses dominating a thin, sharp-featured face topped by a halo of short brown curls, he was more clumsy-puppy cute than handsome. His bright blue eyes were alive with interest as he looked at Charlie. "He's somebody we sure would like to catch. In a little more than two years he's taken out fourteen people."

"I think that as of tonight the number is probably sixteen," Charlie said. "Jenna McDaniels said there were two other girls with her and they are dead. She told me their names were Raylene—" She stopped, frowned. "Oh, God, I'm drawing a blank here. I can't remember that girl's last name."

"Raylene Witt and Laura Peters," Agent Flynn finished for her. "I just got a call from our agents at the hospital who've been talking to Ms. McDaniels. She gave us the names. That's who we're looking for now."

"Is Jenna's mother with her yet?" Whatever Jenna had or had not done, Charlie hated to think of her being alone. She knew what the girl was going through: the sense of being caught up in a nightmare, the ever-present fear, the grief. She knew, because she had lived it herself. "Do you know?"

"I don't." Flynn shook his head. "Next time I talk to our guys I'll check."

Charlie nodded thanks.

"The McDaniels girl has been all over the news the last couple days, but I haven't seen anything about the other two," Sager said. "I didn't even realize there were two more young women gone missing."

"I'm not sure the other two have even been reported," Flynn said. "We haven't found anything on them. At this point, we're not even one hundred percent certain that they exist, to tell you the truth, or if they do that they're victims. They may be Ms. McDaniels' hallucinations, for example. Or her lies. I don't necessarily think that's the case, but I've learned to keep an open mind."

"So has Ms. McDaniels given a statement?" Tony asked, and Flynn shook his head.

"We've got guys at the hospital waiting to take it as soon as she's up to talking to them. As of right now, though, it hasn't happened."

"Kaminsky, when there's a statement from Ms. McDaniels, I want you to get on it. Flynn, if you'd make sure Kaminsky gets a copy as soon as it's available, I'd appreciate it. Anything that can help us locate those two girls, we need to know as soon as possible. The rest can wait for tomorrow." Tony looked at the assembled group. "Right now, our top priority has to be to find those other girls. Until we have proof that they're dead or don't exist, we can't just assume it. For all we know, one or both of them could still be at this guy's mercy, or lying out in the rain somewhere dying."

There were nods of agreement all around. Charlie didn't mention that she already had been furnished with proof positive that at least one of the girls was real, but also dead. From the background check he had done on her when he had first wanted her to come work with his team in their race to find the Boardwalk Killer, Tony knew that she had what he called "some psychic ability." She had even admitted to him that sometimes she saw the spirits of the dead, and he had used information that she had gleaned from her ghostly encounters to help solve the previous case.

Not that he knew anything like the full extent of what she routinely experienced. And he certainly didn't know a thing about Michael. No one did, and however the whole mess worked out, no one was ever going to.

She had her career to think about. Her personal life, too.

No real worries there, though: even if she flat-out told everyone she met about Michael, about the things she saw, nobody was going to believe her. Oh, they might pretend to, they might even kinda, sorta, halfway buy into it like Tony sometimes seemed to, but in the end they couldn't know, not for certain, and what they would carry away with them when they thought about her was something on the order of "headcase." That she knew from painful experience.

"Even if they're up the mountain, finding them in the dark and rain isn't going to be easy. That trail back there has dozens of branches, and the girls might not even be on any kind of trail." Sager looked at Sheriff Peel. "You get ahold of Jerry Ferrell?"

"I did," Sheriff Peel said. "He's on the way, him and the dogs."

"If they're up there, Jerry and his dogs'll find them." Sager addressed that remark to Tony. "Ferrell has the best damned tracking dogs in the state. We've got equipment coming to help us recover any bodies we might find, too."

"Let's hope we don't need it, but it's best to be prepared in case we do." Tony looked at Charlie. "So while we wait, why don't you tell us what happened, from the beginning?"

Charlie once again recounted the whole story (judiciously edited to leave out the phantom girl and, of course, Michael) from the time Jenna had banged on her kitchen door. Tony and the other newcomers examined the dent in the back door, as well as the knife and the *You can't catch me* message the Gingerbread Man had left, and Tony had Crane make arrangements to have the latter two sent on to the FBI lab for analysis on an expedited basis. After that, everybody in the room talked logistics as they discussed (argued about) the best way to mount a search and rescue or retrieval operation up a muddy, treacherous mountainside in the middle of the night in the pouring rain.

Leaving them to it, Charlie ran upstairs to change into a tee, jeans, and sneakers for the trek up the mountain. That's where she was when the dogs came. Although their arrival was almost certainly announced by some other method downstairs, Charlie was clued in by the sudden onset of a dolorous howling right outside her house.

"Your boyfriend had a lick of sense, he wouldn't let you go with them," Michael said sourly. Since she had forbidden him to enter the bathroom, where she was changing, his voice came to her through the closed bathroom door.

"I have to go with them." Charlie discovered that she almost welcomed the heretofore annoying boyfriend reference because it meant that Michael was starting to get back to normal. The silent and brooding presence who had followed her upstairs had been slightly unnerving. She was still pulling her hair back into a low ponytail as she emerged from the bathroom to find him stretched full length on her bed. His head was planted on one of her lace-trimmed pillows, his arms were folded behind it, and his booted feet were crossed at the ankle and resting on her snowy white coverlet.

Ghost boots, Charlie reminded herself, and limited her response to a disapproving glance along the length of his powerful body. The thing was, she had decorated her house to suit the needs of a single, childless woman whose workaday life was generally spent within the dull gray walls of a prison. It was light, airy, and, yes, feminine, with delicate, expensive fabrics and lots of pale colors and white.

He was entirely too masculine for it.

His eyes followed her as she walked across the bedroom, toward the door. "That's just plain stupid. You know that? You're not a cop. You're a tracker. You're not part of a search and rescue team. It's pitch black out there and it's raining and muddy and it's a damned mountain and there's a psycho killer on the loose who's made himself your new pen pal. What part of that makes it smart for you to go with them?"

"If you say something about me having a death wish again I'll murder you." She said it lightly, deliberately, hoping to provoke a smile in return. He hadn't smiled, not once, since setting eyes on the watch.

He still didn't smile, exactly, but the quick upward quirk of one side of his lips was a start. "Too late."

Finishing with her ponytail, Charlie paused at the foot of the bed to look at him. It was a queen-sized bed, and she had always thought that it was huge. Now, with his big body taking up one whole side, it looked surprisingly small. Her hands curled around the cool smooth brass of the footboard as she tried to make him understand. "The one thing I can bring to this investigation that nobody else can is that I can sometimes see the dead. If the second girl is dead, and her spirit is still hanging around up there somewhere, I might be able to talk to her. And she might be able to tell me something we can't get any other way. Something that will help us catch this monster."

"Catching this monster isn't your job."

"I have to help if I can."

"No, you don't. Not if helping puts you at risk. And it does."

So much for trying to get Michael to see things from her point of view. Although why she cared if he did she didn't know. He was the intrusion into *her* life. Intrusions did not get to call the shots. They didn't even get a vote.

Enough already.

"I'm going. End of discussion." She headed for the door.

"You think I don't know that?" There was disgust in his voice as he swung his feet to the floor, stood up, and came after her. She had opened the door and was stepping out into the hall when he added, "Nice ass in those jeans, by the way."

CHAPTER EIGHT

Thanks to Jerry Ferrell's hounds, it took the search party not quite an hour to locate the bodies. There were two of them, floating in a water-filled, abandoned mine shaft some three quarters of the way up the mountain, about a mile and a half off the path where Charlie ran every day. Fortunately, by the time they got there the rain had slowed to little more than intermittent sprinkles. But the cloud cover remained, obscuring the moon, making the night almost as black when they stepped out into the open area around the mine shaft as it had been under the thick canopy of trees. So black that, without flashlights, they wouldn't have been able to see the ground beneath their feet.

"That's something you hate to see," Sheriff Peel said as half a dozen klieg lights that had been hooked to a generator powered on at once, illuminating the site so that there was no longer any hope of a mistake. The pale objects that could be glimpsed just beneath the shining black surface of the water were not the white bellies of dead fish, or quartz-laced rocks, or any of the dozens of other faintly luminescent things that they could have been. They were the bare and swollen arms and legs of the corpses that drifted facedown in a lazy rotation of death.

The dead bodies of two girls in shorts and T-shirts, with long dark hair floating around them, looking like grotesque lily pads in some horrible inky pond.

The sight of the bodies made Charlie feel sick at heart. It made her want to weep.

Poor girls, went the refrain that kept running through her mind. She wondered if, when the sun had risen that morning, they had guessed this would be their last day alive.

"Life's a bitch," Michael said from behind her. "No point in getting all teary-eyed about it."

A little annoyed because she was absolutely sure that she was *not* getting (outwardly anyway) all teary-eyed about it, she was startled by his apparent ability to read her mind. Charlie shot him a killing glare.

A corner of his mouth quirked up in response. Having apparently recovered from his earlier bout of the dismals—at least, if he was still upset, she couldn't tell—he was standing right beside her, his big body protectively close. Although nothing short of torture would have gotten her to admit it, Charlie was glad he was there. The hiss of the wind moving through the towering trees that crowded close around the clearing, the ageless quality of the absolute darkness beyond the reach of the klieg lights, the swampy scent of the place, which she had smelled before on Jenna, were combining to slightly creep her out.

Given what he was, Michael was an unlikely antidote for a developing case of the heebie-jeebies, but for her he was.

"Everybody keep to the edge of the clearing. Nontechnical personnel, stay out of the way. Let's try to preserve this crime scene as much as possible so we can get a good look at it when the sun comes up." Tony called instructions from the side of the pit. Like the rest of the agents, he had traded his sport coat for an FBI windbreaker, and the big white letters made him easier to keep track of in the confusion than he otherwise would have been. Charlie watched as he turned to speak to a body retrieval crew in blue jumpsuits who were standing by, presumably until the photographers were finished taking pictures. Off to one side, a police department sketch artist was looking at the pit as she drew. Charlie assumed she was making a rough drawing of the bodies and their position in the crime scene. Two cops were setting tall tent stakes and stringing yellow crime scene tape from them around the edge of the clearing, leaving only a narrow pathway between it and the trees.

"Boss, I think I've found our point of egress," Crane yelled, and Tony turned away from the pit to head toward him. Crane was on an upward slope at the right side of the clearing; since he was beyond the reach of the klieg lights Charlie could only locate him by his voice and the round glow of his flashlight. A moment later all she could see of Tony, too, was his flashlight. Several other flashlights converged on the spot, but it was too dark for Charlie to identify any of the people holding them.

"Being dead doesn't have a whole lot of good points, but one of them is not having to worry about mosquitoes," Michael said. "Just so you know, there's one on your arm. I'd smack it for you, but that ain't happening."

Charlie had already slapped at a good half a dozen. After a hasty glance down, she slapped again.

"Damned mosquitoes," Sheriff Peel said. "Perfect breeding conditions for them, though. All this standing water, and then it's been hot as Hades."

The rain should have cooled things off. It hadn't. The day—typical for late August—had been baking hot, and even in these, the small hours of the morning, the humidity made the air feel almost too thick to breathe. There were two water-filled pits on the site, although as far as anyone could tell only one held bodies. Steam rose up from the surface of the water in both pits, from the piled shale and mossy rocks around the edge of the clearing, from the thick mulch beneath the huge pines and oaks and beeches, from the flat grassy area where Charlie (and Michael) stood with Sheriff Peel and Ken, who were at the bottom of the law enforcement food chain on this investigation and thus had nothing to do at this point, and Jerry Ferrell and his dogs, whose part was played out. The dogs, big, loose-limbed, floppy-eared bloodhounds, lay panting on the ground at Ferrell's feet. They cast occasional suspicious looks at Michael, whom Charlie was almost certain they could see, but having been ordered by their handler to lie down and be quiet that's what they did.

"You don't think I ought to be getting on home to Debbie and the kids, do you?" Ken asked the sheriff uneasily as he, too, slapped at a mosquito. "Half the time, she doesn't even lock the doors."

"I were you, I'd wait for the rest of us," Sheriff Peel said. "No telling if the guy who did this is still on the mountain. And starting tomorrow, you make sure Debbie locks them doors."

"If you've finished with your pictures, I'd like to start getting the bodies out of the water now," Frank Cramer, the medical examiner, called to the police photographers. He was an older guy to whom Charlie had been introduced shortly after he'd arrived on the scene.

Tony and Crane were once again back within the glare of the klieg lights, Charlie saw. Tony was standing next to the ME looking down into the pit with the bodies, while Crane was now videotaping everything, with the purpose, Charlie knew, of allowing the team to play the footage over and over again in an exhaustive search for clues. Even as she looked at him, Crane panned the camera over her and the men she was standing with, then moved on to the cops and firefighters and coroner's assistants and the rest of what seemed like a cast of thousands currently milling around on the sidelines. Charlie knew what he was doing: watch the watchers was one of Tony's maxims. Sometimes it yielded surprisingly fruitful results.

Because a lot of times a killer would show up at a crime scene to drink in the efforts of law enforcement to find him. This killer in particular was likely to still be somewhere in the vicinity, Charlie knew. He would take pleasure in observing everything that went on in the aftermath of what he had done.

It was part of the power trip he was on.

One of the hounds—Mabel, Charlie thought her name was; the other one was Max—picked up her head and stared intently at the far side of the pit. Charlie followed her gaze curiously. What she saw when she did had her drawing in a sharp breath.

"You okay?" Ken asked.

"Damned mosquitoes," Charlie echoed Sheriff Peel, and gave her arm another slap.

But mosquitoes weren't what had caused her reaction. On the other side of the pit, just beyond the bright circle cast by the klieg lights, a girl sat with her knees drawn up to her chin, her arms wrapped around her legs, and her head bent and resting on her knees. A girl with long, curly dark hair that spilled around her body to almost brush the flat shelf of rock she was sitting on. A girl with bare feet, and bare legs beneath mid-thigh-length shorts and slender bare arms emerging from a dark-colored T-shirt. A girl who looked to be soaking wet, with water streaming from her body.

A girl who hadn't been there the last time Charlie had glanced that way.

A dead girl. The spirit of one of the two girls whose bodies were still floating in the pit.

Charlie felt her heartbeat speed up.

She looked fixedly at the girl, saw her shoulders heave, and guessed that the spirit was crying.

Every muscle in Charlie's body tensed.

I hate this.

But finding out what she could from the newly deceased victims was the primary reason she had come. If she had only wanted to look over the crime scene, she could have waited until daylight. Or she could have looked at pictures. There had been no guarantee that the remaining girl's spirit would be here, of course, but if she was still anywhere on earth at all, the place where she had been killed was the most likely for her to be found.

And here she was.

For a moment there, the small victory almost made Charlie feel good. Then the tragedy of what she was seeing reasserted itself, and her throat tightened.

All I can do for her is help find who did this.

"Excuse me, I'm going to go have a word with Agent Kaminsky." Charlie chose that excuse because Kaminsky, heels and skirt suit ditched in favor of an FBI windbreaker along with black pants and sneakers, which she had retrieved from her luggage when she'd changed at Charlie's house before tackling the mountain, had just walked briskly past. Small as Kaminsky was in flat shoes, she still looked formidable with a shovel in her hands and not so much as a sideways glance to spare for anyone. Speculating on what Kaminsky might do with that shovel was a waste of effort, so Charlie gave up on it almost at once. Instead she followed in Kaminsky's wake without the least intention of catching up, skirting the dogs, dodging the fluid clusters of law enforcement types who were presumably engaged in one evidence-gathering activity or another, keeping to the shadowy edges of the clearing as she headed toward the crying girl.

"You see her, too, huh?" Michael was right behind her. His voice had a resigned quality to it. "I figured."

Where they were, the darkness was obscuring enough that a quick nod in reply wasn't going to work. Cops, deputies, FBI agents, rescue workers, coroner's assistants, technicians—the clearing was swarming with official types. A steady stream of foot traffic moved continuously around the periphery as people went where they needed to go while trying to follow Tony's directive to stay out of the crime scene as much as possible. But most of them were busy, doing their jobs, bustling from place to place. As far as she could tell, no one was paying any particular attention to her.

So she took a chance.

"I see her," Charlie admitted, keeping her voice low. "I'm going to try to talk to her."

"You know, I kind of guessed that when you started heading this way. Got your barf bag with you?"

That bit of sarcasm earned him a glower. "Shut up, okay? I'm talking to her, and that's the end of the discussion."

"Go for it. Knock yourself out."

"Stay out of it," Charlie warned, his blunt treatment of the other girl's spirit still fresh in her mind. Then she had a corollary thought: "Unless I need you."

"Try not to need me. Weeping women ain't exactly my thing."

"So get over it already. Weren't you the one who just said life's a bitch?"

"Then I guess it's a good thing I don't have to worry about it anymore, right?"

At that, Charlie made an exasperated sound under her breath and abandoned the conversation. Cool and heavy, his too-big watch had slid down her arm to lodge against her hand, and with exasperation she shoved it back up almost to her elbow, reflecting that of course any possession of his would be as annoying as he was. Then it hit her: *Maybe he really* isn't *a serial killer. Maybe he actually* is *innocent, and this watch is proof.* Before she could even start to get all excited about that, a cool sprinkle of water distracted her as she passed too close beneath an overhanging evergreen branch and dislodged a shower of droplets that ran down her neck, making her flinch. In front of her, the long shadows cast by the trees seemed to twist in upon themselves like crooked, arthritic fingers. The smell of the woods—pine and moss and wet earth—was strong enough to sup-plant what was now the background note of the swampy scent of the water in the pit. Snatches of conversation rose and fell around her, their individual threads more discernible than before. The steady hum of the generator, the clank of metal on rock as a boat hook attached to a chain was readied for the removal of the bodies, the rustle of bright blue body bags being laid out by the side of the pit, filled her ears. The dead girl now looked almost more vivid than the living people on the scene. Charlie's senses had heightened. It sometimes happened when she was in the close vicinity of the newly dead. She cast a quick, consuming look all around to try to make certain she wasn't being observed. As far as she could tell, no one was paying the least attention to her. Still, the sensation she had of being watched could have come from anywhere, or nowhere, like her imagination. It could be the Gingerbread Man, who might be somewhere keeping an eye on the kill site. But she saw no one looking in her direction, and at the moment that's all she had to go by. Concentrating on the spirit, who was only a few yards away now, Charlie did her best to block everything else out.

As she approached she could hear the girl crying. The sound tore at Charlie's heart.

"I'm here to help you," Charlie told her, positioning herself so that her back was turned to most of the people in the clearing as she stopped a few steps from the edge of the rock shelf the girl was sitting on. She ignored the sudden queasiness that attacked her stomach like clockwork. She had no intention of letting anyone—read Michael—know about it unless and until it got to the point where she couldn't hide it anymore. Until then, she would power through and hope for the best. Thanks to the klieg lights, it wasn't entirely dark where she stood, but the tangled shadows were thick enough to obscure a lot of detail. Another uneasy glance around found tiny pairs of glowing orbs shining among the trees: animal eyes, Charlie identified them even as she shivered. At least they accounted for the eerie feeling she had that she was being intently watched. Without looking up, the girl continued to sob pitifully. The sound made Charlie feel sick at heart. "Are you Laura? Or Raylene?"

The girl cried on as if she hadn't heard.

Michael made a rough sound under his breath. He was no longer behind Charlie. Instead, he had moved to her left and slightly in front of her, not blocking her view of the girl but clearly positioning himself to step in between them if the need should arise. Noticing that with impatience, Charlie made a mental note to give him, the first chance she got, a quick overview of the rules covering ghosts on the ground.

"Hell, somebody's beat her to death," Michael said. His face had tightened. His position allowed him to view the girl from a different angle, and it was apparent that what he was seeing was bad. Even as Charlie instinctively craned her neck to look, Michael shook his head at her. "You don't want to see this."

Charlie shot him a look. This whole Protective-R-Us thing he had going on was actually kind of cute, but it was also annoying and, given who and what he was, ridiculous.

"Believe me, I've seen worse." Her response was tart. Charlie then got an eyeful of what he was trying to keep her from seeing and immediately wished she hadn't.

The back of the girl's head was bashed in. Crushed like an egg. Dark clots of blood matted her hair to the wound. More blood made the strands around the wound clump together. Shattered remnants of her skull were embedded in gelatinous brain matter. Part of the brain itself hung out of the hole, looking like a slimy lump of congealed oatmeal, dripping blood mixed with a milky liquid Charlie could only surmise was brain fluid.

It was, in a word, gruesome.

Charlie's stomach, which had been fighting the good fight against nausea so that she had been registering only mild gastric distress, started to churn.

"Told you not to look," Michael said, and Charlie guessed that she must have blanched.

"Hello?" The girl looked up suddenly, hopefully, her eyes going straight to Michael. Blinking, she peered at him as if trying to get him into focus. The light hit the tears rolling down her face so that they made glistening tracks along her cheeks. She was a pretty girl, twenty-ish, small and slender, with big dark eyes currently welling with tears and delicate features framed by masses of wet black curls. As she blinked at Michael, her breath caught on a shuddering sob. From her expression it was clear that, if she hadn't been able to see him before, she could see him now. Her voice took on an urgent note. "Who are you? Do you know what's happened?"

She scrambled to her feet as she spoke: she was maybe five foot two. More tears spilled from her eyes. Taking first one and then another hesitant step toward Michael, as if she wasn't quite sure she was actually seeing him, she then whispered, "Oh, thank goodness!" and broke into a run. An instant later she threw herself against him, wrapping her arms around his waist as she started to cry again in earnest. Michael looked down at her with as much alarm as if he had just been grabbed by a ghost—and he wasn't one himself.

Well, the ins and outs of finding himself among the dead were new to him. He was still adjusting.

"Yo," he said, his eyes sliding Charlie's way. Sobbing loudly, the girl buried her face in the front of his white T-shirt and clung. His hard, handsome face turned grim as he looked down at her shattered head. Seeing how small the girl looked in comparison to him— the top of her head didn't even begin to reach his broad shoulders, and a whole lot of wide chest was visible on either side of her— Charlie registered again in passing how tall and muscular he truly was. Add his surfer God good looks to the mix and, in life, he must have had women hanging off him like Christmas tree ornaments. Except as part of appraising his qualities as a predator, it wasn't something she'd really thought about before, but . . . now she did. She also registered something else: a tiny niggle of—what? Awareness, that was it. Seeing Michael with a woman was new, and what she was feeling was simply herself becoming aware of the newness of it.

It was different, that was all. And that's why she was feeling the niggle.

"So do something already," he said, glancing at Charlie again.

"Don't talk to me. She doesn't know I'm here," Charlie instructed. "I want you to talk to *her*. Tell her you're here to help."

Lips tightening, he transferred his attention back to the weeping girl and gave her a couple of clumsy-looking pats on the back.

"Don't worry, I'm here to help," he said.

"Good job," Charlie encouraged him, and in return received a look that she roughly interpreted as meaning something on the order of *eat dirt*. The niggle that was her awareness of him with a woman in his arms subsided—he couldn't have looked more uncomfortable if a python were twining itself around him—and Charlie was glad to dismiss it as the nothing it had been. She would have found his obvious unease with his situation almost amusing if the girl's distress hadn't been so heartrending. "You're doing great."

"Please." The girl's voice trembled as she looked up at him. "I don't know where I am. I—I think I'm lost. Can you help me?"

It was obvious to Charlie that, as was the case with many new spirits, she had no idea she was dead. She also was no longer able to experience the world of the living. The girl could see only Michael. The people around her—Charlie, law enforcement, rescue workers, everyone on the scene—were invisible to her, as were the details of her surroundings. Why? Because she was dead and they were not: each existed in a different plane. Here in this moment, in this place, for this dead girl, only Michael existed.

"Don't come right out and tell her she's dead," Charlie said quickly to Michael as he looked like he was getting ready to do just that. She had a lively fear that he was about to be as forthright with this girl as he had been with the one in her house. "Ask her her name."

Michael sent Charlie another of those narrow-eyed *this sucks* flickers before looking down at the girl again.

"Everything's okay," he told her, rather gingerly putting an arm around her shoulders as, with both arms still wrapped around his waist, she looked beseechingly up into his face. Charlie had to admit that she was impressed by how reassuring he was actually being. "My name's Michael. What's your name?"

"L-Laura. Laura Peters." The girl looked wildly all around. "Where are we? What's happened?"

"Ask her what she remembers," Charlie instructed, and Michael did.

"Oh. Oh, oh." Laura's expression changed dramatically. Pushing away from him, looking all around, she suddenly started gasping. "I'm drowning. The water—the water's pouring in. I can't—they said kick your feet, and move your arms like this." She mimed trying to breaststroke. "They're trying to help me. But I'm sinking—" She started to cough violently. "I can't swim! I can't swim!"

"You don't have to be afraid. You're safe now," Michael told her. Shaking her head, Laura looked up at him with blind terror, then sank down on her haunches and covered her face with her hands as she burst into tears again. With a glinting look at Charlie, Michael crouched beside her.

"Ask her who tried to help her swim," Charlie directed.

"Laura. Can you tell me who tried to help you swim?" In contrast to his face, which could have been carved from stone, Michael's voice was soft and steady.

Her hands dropped away from her face. Her expression was agitated as she looked at him. "The other girls. They can swim. They tried to help me, but I can't. I can't swim! My head keeps going under and—" She broke off, gasping and gagging as if she was choking. "There's a man. I'm afraid of him. He's drowning us. He wants us to—he wants us to— The water's pouring in. Oh, no! Oh! Oh!"

"You're all right," Michael told her swiftly, and when she dropped her head and burst into tears again his arm went around her once more.

"Ask her about the man. Can she describe him?"

Encountering his gaze, Charlie was surprised at the anger in his eyes.

"Did you see the man, Laura? What did he look like?" Michael's tone as he shifted his attention back to the girl was, in contrast, very gentle.

Laura shivered violently. "Death. He looks like death. All in black—his face, it's white. Horrible white. Oh, no, *please*. He's going to kill me—*why?* I was in the bar and then . . ." Closing her eyes, she gave a piteous-sounding whimper.

"What bar?" Charlie prompted. Michael, face taut, repeated the question.

Laura's eyes were still closed. "Omar's. I didn't win. I—I left, and then—there was a van." She moaned, and Michael's arm tightened around her.

Charlie knew the signs. The spirit was growing increasingly distressed. They needed to get as much information out of her as they could as quickly as they could. Charlie prompted Michael: "What did the van look like? Color, make, model?"

He said, "What did the van look like, Laura? What color was it? Do you remember the make or model?"

"I don't know. I don't know! It was blue, I think. Or maybe gray. Old. It—it smelled bad. Like fish."

Charlie said, "Does she remember anything else about the van? Or the driver?"

Michael asked.

"I heard—a phone call. Ben. *I can't talk right now, Ben,* is what he said. I tried to scream but I couldn't. That's all I remember. Oh, won't you please help me? Please! I just want to go home! Can't you please take me home?" Laura started to sob again, while Michael shot Charlie a seething look and rubbed the girl's shoulder comfortingly.

"Ask her: where is Omar's?" Charlie said, but before he could, Laura shook free of Michael's arm and jumped to her feet, glancing behind her in shock as she clutched the sides of her head with both hands. "No! That hurts! Oh! Jen—Raylene—something hit me in the head! Stop! It hurts! It hurts!" By the end, she had whirled around to bat at an unseen assailant even as Michael, having straightened to his full height beside her, put his hands on her shoulders to try to calm her down.

"Laura . . ."

"No, no, no!" She looked at him with abject fear in her eyes. *"They're killing me."*

Her voice rose to a screech on that last. Then, abruptly, her face turned up toward the lightless night sky as if she heard or saw something there that Charlie at least could not. Laura's eyes widened. She shook from head to toe.

"Laura. It's okay." Michael's voice sounded strained.

"There's Kylie," Laura moaned. "And Sara. Oh, my God, where am I?"

CHAPTER NINE

In the next instant Laura dissolved into nothingness beneath Michael's hands.

"Holy fucking hell," Michael said.

"What?" Charlie demanded. It was obvious that Michael was seeing—had seen—something that she had not.

"Two little girls came down out of the fucking sky. Two little girls who were covered with blood."

"Laura must have known them. Something bad must have happened to them."

"Yeah, I gathered that." The look he turned on Charlie was grim. "Jesus Christ, don't you ever see any happy dead people? You know, old folks who were ready to go or somebody who was so sick death was a release? Somebody like that?"

"No." Charlie's response was flat. Her stomach continued to churn, but her senses were getting back to normal. The hypersensitivity was going, and that meant the spirit(s) were gone, too. Well, present company excepted. She fought to get the nausea under control.

I will not throw up.

"No wonder you're twisted," Michael said.

"Twisted?" Charlie began indignantly, only to jump sky-high as someone behind her asked, "What's twisted?"

Tony. Charlie recognized his voice even before Michael had finished with his sardonic, "Oh, yay, it's Dudley Do-Right," even before she had finished whirling around to confront the newcomer. The sight of Tony was instantly steadying: he looked so normal, so *real.* So totally nice and uncomplicated: a genuine good guy. Exactly what she needed in her life, in fact.

Instantly she vowed to try harder where he was concerned.

"Uh—what was done to these poor victims," she said. Luckily, thinking fast on her feet was something she was getting really good at. "It's twisted, is all."

"It is that," Tony agreed, while Michael said, "Just so you know, every time you tell a lie you stick out that pretty pink tongue of yours. Only a little bit, like you're getting ready to wet your lips. I caught on to it while you were still doing the starched-up-shrink thing back at the Ridge. It's sexy as all get-out, but it's a dead tell."

Charlie's reaction to that was to clamp her lips together. Realizing what she had done, she barely managed to not shoot the thorn in her side a dirty look. Instead, with what she considered commendable control, she ignored him in favor of saying to Tony: "So how's it going?"

Okay, the question was inane. It was the best she could do with Michael mock-sexily wetting his lips at her.

Tony appeared to notice nothing amiss. "We've got the bodies, which should give us time and cause of death. Including the knife that was left in your kitchen, we've got a variety of possible murder weapons. The rain's made everything else problematic. It's going to be hard to tell what we have that's usable until the sun comes up and everything dries out."

"Try telling him about Laura," Michael said. "Go on, I want to hear this."

It took effort, but Charlie managed to keep her expression neutral. Curling a hand around Tony's arm, which felt strong and firm through the slick windbreaker, she tugged, towing him with her as she walked determinedly away from the font of perpetual annoyance.

Mindful of the possibility that her stomach might disgrace her at any second, she headed for a relatively secluded section of the site, away from the klieg lights. But the increasing darkness made her skin crawl, and she was suddenly thankful for Tony's solid presence. Unlike Michael—who was, of course, dogging her every footstep—Tony could actually offer something in the way of physical protection. Plus, he had a gun.

Charlie said, "I—uh—actually have some information that might help the investigation."

Tony lifted his eyebrows at her. "Oh, yeah?"

"Laura Peters was at a bar called Omar's right before the Gingerbread Man got hold of her. She was put into an old blue or gray van that smelled like fish. The man who took her spoke to someone named Ben on the phone." Even as Charlie recited the details that Laura had passed on to Michael, her stomach roiled. Taking a deep breath, she swallowed hard in an effort to make the sudden upsurge of nausea go away.

Michael said, "You left out the part where he looked like Skeletor. You know, all in black with a white face."

Swallowing hard, Charlie stopped walking as she willed her stomach to settle. Tony stopped, too, to look down at her with a frown.

She said, "The man who took Laura Peters—the Gingerbread Man, unless he has an accomplice, which I don't think he does—was dressed all in black. His face appeared very white. Like death."

"There you go," Michael said. "That's what she said."

"How do you know all that?" Tony's eyes were intent on her face. Then they flickered, and he frowned. "You have one of your psychic experiences back there?"

"A psychic experience? Is that what he calls them?" Michael stopped on her other side.

"Yes," Charlie said to both of them. Defiantly.

Michael grimaced. "From what I've seen, what you go through is more like full-on *American Horror Story*. You planning on keeping Dudley around, you probably ought to tell him how bad it gets."

"Okay," Tony said at the same time. He had pulled out his cell phone, and was busy pecking at its virtual keyboard. She assumed he was making a note of what she had told him, or perhaps texting or e-mailing it, although whether or not there was cell service up here on the mountain was questionable. Finishing, he looked at her. "You sure of your information?"

Charlie nodded, smiling at Tony gratefully because dealing with him was just so damned easy. Then, since she really was feeling sick as a dog, she turned her back on both of them to head for a nearby rock, where she abruptly sat down.

"Here we go again," Michael said grimly. "For God's sake, put your head between your knees. You look like you're about ready to pass out."

Tony, having also followed her, stopped on her other side to say, "You've gone a little pale. Are you all right?"

Michael snorted. "A little pale? You're white as a fucking ghost—no, whiter, if the ones I've seen are anything to judge by. If you need to barf, do it. Maybe your boyfriend will start getting a clue."

It took a moment's worth of deep breathing before Charlie could say anything at all. When she did, she ignored the irate-looking ghost looming over her in favor of smiling at Tony, who stood a few feet away watching her with concern. "It's nothing. I . . . well, get a little nauseated sometimes when I have these psychic experiences. If I sit here for a minute, it'll pass."

Michael said, "That's right, babe. Sugarcoat it," while Tony said, "Take all the time you need."

Charlie fought for control, both of her stomach and her temper. She was starting to feel like a Ping-Pong ball bouncing between the two of them, which, given the state of her stomach, was not good. The look she wanted to direct at Michael would be a waste of a good glare—glaring at him didn't seem to abash him one iota—and might be misinterpreted by Tony. Likewise, snapping something on the order of *stick it where the sun don't shine* was subject to misinterpretation by the only other living human being within earshot, who was not its intended target. Glancing around in hopes of a distraction, Charlie spotted the body that was at that moment being dragged from the pit by a boat hook and then, when it was close enough, by two of the coroner's assistants, who grabbed it under the armpits with their gloved hands and hauled it, streaming water, up on the rocks.

Having so recently seen Laura Peters, she was able to identify this body as belonging to Raylene Witt: the phantom girl with the rock from her house.

Funnily enough, the sight of an actual corpse didn't make her sick. It was only the close proximity of spirits that did that. What seeing that poor, limp corpse did was fill her with sorrow. And grief. And a deep and corrosive fear.

What was it about her and violent death anyway? Was it drawn to her, in some sort of hideous karma? Secretly, almost shamefully, Charlie realized that what bothered her most about the spirits she saw was her near conviction that one day, she, too, would come to just such a horrible, violent end.

The prospect made her shiver.

"You okay?" Michael frowned down at her.

"Better?" Tony asked at almost the same time.

Clearly Michael at least had seen that unmistakable sign of her distress.

Get it together.

"Yes," she said firmly.

Out of the corner of her eye, she saw Raylene Witt's corpse being zipped into a body bag. This time she did not shiver.

Instead she focused on staying strong.

Deep breath.

"What I can't understand is how the Gingerbread Man managed to get all three of the victims up here," she said, and was proud of how coolly professional she sounded. Her stomach still churned, but she was determined not to give in to it—or to the abiding fear that she had discovered curling like a parasite deep in her psyche. "Even if he brought them one at a time, it's a long way up the mountain. I don't think he can have carried them, and if he made them walk—" She considered Laura's failure to relate anything about what was sure to have been a harrowing journey. "Well, I don't think he did that."

"He didn't walk 'em. Too hard to control them over that kind of distance," Michael said, which earned him a sharp glance as Charlie instantly wondered how he would know something like that. Clearly (and correctly) interpreting that look to mean that she was once again picturing him as the serial killer she'd actually begun harboring doubts that he was, his mouth twisted.

"I was a *marine*," Michael said. "Sometimes we took prisoners."

Considering that, she decided it made sense. Anyway, if she remembered the details correctly, at least the last woman he was supposed to have murdered had been killed in her bed. No death march required.

Okay, then.

"As a matter of fact, we just located an old mining road that passes to within about a quarter of a mile south of here," Tony said. "I'm betting that's what he used to get the victims in place. The ME has a truck coming up it right now to transport the bodies back down, which is why I came looking for you: I think you ought to ride down with his team, then grab a few hours' sleep. I'm depending on your expertise to help us tomorrow. I'll send Kaminsky with you, of course."

Although she couldn't argue about the value of sleep, Charlie looked at him with a gathering frown. "I don't need Kaminsky to babysit me."

"Oh, yes, you do," Michael said. "Sugar Buns kicks butt and takes names. She also carries a gun."

That nickname for Kaminsky earned him a glinting look. *Sugar Buns* was demeaning and disrespectful, and she didn't like it. He knew how she felt about it, which was probably exactly why he had used it. In fact, the quick quirk of his lips with which he responded to her look confirmed it: Michael was being deliberately annoying again.

"Given that the perp knows who you are and is specifically reaching out to you, I feel it's best that you have protection." Clearly recognizing the resistance in her face, Tony smiled coaxingly at her as he spoke. She really did like the way his eyes crinkled when he smiled like that. Unlike the mocking glint in the sky blue eyes currently sliding over her face, the expression in Tony's eyes was actually kind of sweet. "Come on, Charlie, don't give me a hard time about this. You know as well as I do that you need protection. And I need to be able to do my job without worrying about you."

"So bring on Kaminsky," Charlie capitulated with a sigh. Physically, she was starting to feel exhausted as well as sick to her stomach, and the thought of going home held increasing appeal. "She's not going to be happy about it, though. And what about you? And Crane? Aren't you coming? You need sleep to function, too."

She had already offered, and they had already agreed, that he, Kaminsky, and Crane would be spending what was left of the night at her house.

"Crane and I will be down as soon as I'm sure everything that can be processed or preserved here is being processed or preserved," Tony said. "I'll crawl into bed sometime before dawn, I hope."

Michael folded his arms over his chest. "You get that he's weighing his chances of topping off his night by crawling into your bed, right? And just for the record, it ain't happening. Not while I have to stay within fifty feet of you. I'm not big on watching."

Charlie's lips tightened, and she battled the urge to flip Mr. Infuriating the bird.

"I hope so, too," she answered Tony, and smiled at him way more flirtatiously than she would have if the ghost from hell hadn't been watching her with hawk eyes.

Which promptly narrowed.

Tony, on the other hand, smiled back.

"I've got your house key." Tony patted his pocket where the key presumably was located. "So no worries. You feel up to moving yet?"

The truthful answer was no, but Charlie nodded gamely. Tony reached out to help her up. Only when she felt the warmth of his hand closing on hers did she realize that, despite the clammy heat of the night, she was bone cold.

Tony said, "Let's go give Kaminsky the good news," as he hauled her upright, then released her hand, only to slide his fingers supportively around her upper arm. Conscious of Michael's gaze on her arm where Tony was holding it, Charlie straightened her spine and lifted her chin. Silent message: her real, live relationships were none of Casper's business.

"You know she's not going to like it," Charlie said to Tony. As they headed toward Kaminsky, who was directing a technician to store something in what looked like a black plastic garbage bag, what Charlie saw out of the corner of her eye made her chest tighten: Laura was back, standing beside the pit, watching as her corpse was hauled from the water.

Crying as if her heart would break.

"Oh, hell," Michael said, and Charlie knew that he saw Laura, too.

There was only one thing to do. The problem was getting the chance to do it.

It was while Tony was briefing Kaminsky that Charlie had a chance to step a little away and whisper to Michael, "You need to go tell her to look for the light and, when she sees it, walk into it."

He knew that she was talking about Laura: both of them had been watching her—Charlie covertly—as the spirit had hovered over her corpse while it was examined, photographed, and then put into the body bag. Now Laura was sitting cross-legged beside the zipped blue plastic shroud, rocking back and forth as she watched the other body bag, the one holding the remains of Raylene Witt, being loaded onto a stretcher to be carried the short distance to the waiting truck.

"What? No," Michael said.

"I would do it, but she can't hear me. It would be cruel to leave her like this."

"It would be cruel to tell her to look for a white light when there damned well isn't one."

"Just because you haven't seen it doesn't mean that there isn't one."

"How about we let nature take its course here?"

"Are you really willing to simply abandon her?"

"Hell, yeah."

Charlie made an exasperated sound. "Michael—"

Tony came up behind her. "Everything's all set. Come on, I'll walk you to the truck."

Trying not to appear as ruffled as she was feeling, swallowing the rest of what she had been going to say to Michael with an effort, Charlie managed a slightly strained, "You don't have to do that," for Tony. He smiled at her, a quick, intimate smile that probably would have made her feel all toasty inside if she hadn't been so aggravated at the blue-eyed devil on her other side, and said, "I want to," and slid his hand around her elbow, where it rested, warm and strong and unmistakably possessive. Seeing that, Michael shot Charlie a hard-eyed look. An instant later, over Tony's shoulder, Charlie encountered Kaminsky's frosty stare.

Okay, well, there are clearly no fans of Tony and me as a couple in the vicinity.

"*Really* glad to be working with you again, Dr. Stone," Kaminsky said as they all started walking toward the far side of the clearing. Having no trouble recognizing sarcasm when she heard it, Charlie made a face.

"The pleasure's all mine," she replied with false cordiality. Then, because Kaminsky was looking so miffed, Charlie's smile turned genuine. It lasted until she glanced toward where Laura's spirit had been, only to find that the girl was on her feet and moving now, forlornly following the body bag that held her corpse as it was carried to the waiting stretcher.

Charlie's gaze flew to Michael. Face tight, he was watching the same thing. He must have felt the weight of Charlie's eyes on him, because he looked at her then.

Please, Charlie begged him silently. He knew what she was asking him: the knowledge was there in the tightening of his lips and the narrowing of his eyes. There was only a small window of time in which he could act. Since he had to stay in Charlie's close proximity, he just had until she—they—reached the edge of the clearing. Of course, she could delay things—by, say, throwing up, which she absolutely felt like doing—but not for long. Once they were gone, it might be days before she could get back to the clearing. And she hated the idea of leaving Laura's poor confused spirit up here all alone.

"It's not like something's going to happen to her. She's already dead," Michael groused. Then in response to whatever it was he could read in Charlie's face, his mouth twisted. "You want me to try that bad? Fine. I'll try."

CHAPTER TEN

"So why is *this* serial killer such a threat to you?" Kaminsky asked Charlie. Having been occupied with watching Michael as he approached Laura, Charlie jerked her gaze to Kaminsky. Taking a second to process what she had just been asked, she frowned at the other woman even as Tony ordered, "Play nice, Kaminsky." If Charlie hadn't known how much Kaminsky hated being pulled off an active investigation to babysit, as she called it, as well as how much she disapproved of Charlie and Tony's developing relationship, she might have been taken aback by the other woman's attitude. But she did know both those things, and so she chalked it up to Kaminsky being Kaminsky.

"He's not a threat to me," Charlie answered, slowing her step as her gaze slid back toward Michael. Where he was standing, the night was dark and shadowy, but she could see that Laura, whose awareness of her situation was obviously expanding because she had been able to see enough of what was going on in the real world to identify and follow her corpse, had her face buried in his chest again. He was patting her back a little awkwardly, and his tawny head was bent as he talked to her. Charlie could only surmise that as soon as the spirit had seen him she had thrown herself into his arms. Charlie was too far away to overhear any of their conversation, but she could hear the sounds of Laura's steady weeping.

Seeing Michael with the girl wrapped around him bothered her *again,* Charlie realized. And she realized something else, too—the unpleasant niggle she was experiencing had nothing to do with the fact that seeing Michael with a woman in his arms was *new.* It had everything to do with seeing Michael with a woman in his arms, period.

Not good.

"I'd say that having the Gingerbread Man break in to your house and send you a personal message means he's a threat to you," Tony said dryly, pulling Charlie's attention back to the conversation.

Forcing herself to focus, Charlie replied, "The last person he sent his *You can't catch me* message to is still alive, I know for certain, and so are the other three, I'm pretty sure. Now that I've had a chance to think about it, I don't feel I'm in any physical danger from him."

"I'm not prepared to chance it." Tony's voice held a note of finality. Kaminsky grimaced, but didn't argue. Charlie didn't, either. Still watching Michael and Laura out of the corner of her eye, Charlie saw Laura lift her head sharply and look into the darkness on the opposite side of the clearing, as if she heard or saw something there. When Michael appeared to follow her gaze, Charlie was positive that those two were seeing something that she could not.

The white light?

Then the thought occurred: if Michael was with Laura when Laura saw the white light, would he be able to see it, too? If so, could he not walk into it along with Laura? *Would* he walk into it along with Laura?

Charlie's heart beat faster. She wanted to call out to him—to suggest that, if he saw the light, he should grab the opportunity to go into it, too? or to beg him not to go into it even if he got the chance? she wasn't sure, and really didn't want to know—but she could not say a word, of course.

All she could do was watch and wait.

Kaminsky said to her, "What, do you have, like, this photographic memory of how all the serial killers at large right now operate? Because knowing how many others were sent the same message you got tonight, and whether or not those recipients are still alive, seems pretty specific."

Michael's arms dropped away from Laura. The spirit looked up at him once, then started walking slowly away.

Toward what? On pins and needles now, Charlie had no way of knowing.

"Dr. Stone?" Kaminsky's voice pulled Charlie back into the conversation. It took her a beat to recall what she had been asked.

"No, of course not." She took a breath. Whatever was happening with Laura, Michael was simply standing there watching. He was *not* going with her, and Charlie was a little bit ashamed to find herself fiercely glad about that. "I know a lot about this particular serial killer because last year I was asked to consult on an investigation involving him. I turned them down."

Charlie's step faltered as Laura disappeared: the spirit was there one minute and gone the next. Tony's hand tightened on her arm as if to steady her, and she immediately got a grip and resumed walking.

Michael's still here.

"Who asked you to consult?" Tony wanted to know. Michael was heading back toward them, his long stride eating up the distance.

"Dr. David Myers. After the Gingerbread Man attacked a previous group of victims, he was sent one of the *You can't catch me* notes," Charlie answered. Michael reached her side, said, "Happy now?" to her in a way that told her he was not. Since the truthful answer was *yes*—both because Laura was gone and equally because he was still there—it was, she reflected, just as well that she couldn't reply. Without answering Michael by anything more than a quick flicker of her eyelashes in his direction, Charlie continued, "He's a professor at the University of South Carolina. He wrote the definitive textbook on criminal psychology. He's one of the most widely respected experts in the field."

A hooded look—because it was filled with guilty knowledge?—from Tony reminded her that he undoubtedly knew the rest of the story. And he knew the rest of the story because he had done a thorough background check on her before he'd approached her for help in the beginning. She hadn't liked it then, didn't like it now, but there it was.

"And, yes, Dr. Myers and I were once in a relationship," Charlie added tartly. The look she gave Tony was cold with rebuke. "Which is why he contacted me to consult when he was pulled into the Gingerbread Man case. He went over the facts with me, asked for my input. I gave him what insight I could, but beyond that I declined to get involved."

"Didn't want to work with an old boyfriend, hmm?" Kaminsky sent a snarky glance her way.

"Didn't want to work on an investigation with an active serial killer slaughtering real-time victims," Charlie retorted. "What I do is strictly research based. Or, at least, it was until your team came along."

"We appreciate your help," Tony broke in smoothly before Kaminsky could reply. "We got the Boardwalk Killer off the streets, and we'll get this guy, too, believe me."

The sound of metal clanking loudly ahead of them caused Charlie to jump a little: despite her brave words, and the indisputable fact that the other recipients of the Gingerbread Man's message hadn't been harmed, she was still scared. It was, she decided, something visceral inside her that had been awakened by the Boardwalk Killer years ago and would probably stick with her for as long as she lived. Not that anyone was ever going to know it. Glancing through the woods, she saw the truck, which looked like a modified ambulance. Pointing the opposite direction, its headlights cut through the darkness, revealing a stockade's worth of sturdy tree trunks and a rutted gravel road that disappeared into the night. Two blue-garbed assistants had just loaded the last of the bodies inside and appeared to be getting ready to close the back doors.

"Hold up," Tony called to them, urging Charlie to a faster pace. "You've got passengers."

"We weren't leaving without your agents," a cheery voice answered, and the ME walked into view from behind the other side of the truck. Apparently having seen so much death had not affected a naturally sunny disposition, because Frank Cramer—short, stout, white-haired, a former pediatrician who'd been coroner for the past twenty years—was positively jolly as he assisted Charlie and Kaminsky onto the front bench seat, beside the driver, while he and one of his assistants got into the back with the corpses. Jolting down the muddy mountain road to the accompaniment of the running series of jokes with which Dr. Cramer chose to entertain the company, Charlie forced her lips into a smile when appropriate and kept a wary eye on the back, in case Laura, who seemed to have a strong affinity for her corporeal body, should reappear. But she didn't, and except for Michael, who sat silently in the back with Dr. Cramer et al, the journey was thankfully spirit-free.

"So did she go to the light?" Charlie hissed impatiently at Michael the first chance she got. Along with Kaminsky, they had just walked through the front door of her house, having been dropped off curbside by the ME's truck. Since everything that needed to be processed in her house had been processed and it was not officially designated a crime scene, all the law enforcement types had gone. Likewise, there was no sign of Raylene Witt. But there were plenty of reminders of what had happened. Starting with only what Charlie could see, the floors were streaked with dried mud and there were dirty footprints on the stairs. As she had been leaving with Tony's team to go up the mountain, she had heard Sheriff Peel order a couple of his deputies to fix the back door so that it would close and lock. Hopefully that had been done, although for the moment Charlie had no way of knowing for sure; she was confined to the front hall. With a peremptory, "Wait here," Kaminsky had gone off, gun in hand, to do a quick search of the premises. Since Michael had stayed with Charlie, that meant the two of them were briefly alone in the hall.

Michael said, "Nope."

"What?" Charlie was aghast. "What happened?"

"Remember those two little girls I told you about? They came back, only this time they looked like they were wearing their Sunday-go-to-meeting clothes. No blood on 'em anywhere. They called to Laura, told her to come with them. She went."

That was so unexpected that Charlie was nonplussed. "But—what about the white light?"

"Like I keep telling you, buttercup: there is no white light."

"There is!" An instant reflection that she had never seen it tempered Charlie's indignation. "There has to be. Oh, my God, where do you suppose Laura went?"

He shrugged.

She glared at him.

"You got me to do what you wanted, it turned out wrong, and now you're blaming me," Michael said with disgust. "Women."

"No sign of the boogeyman, Dr. Stone." Kaminsky's voice dripped sarcasm as, holstering her gun, she rejoined them. Without her customary high heels, she was surprisingly small: the top of her head reached the middle of Charlie's nose. Napoleon Complex, Charlie knew, was a real issue for some height-challenged men. Kaminsky, she decided, must suffer from the female version.

Whatever, Charlie was not in the mood. "Can you give the snark a rest, please? You're stuck with me, I'm stuck with you, and the only thing to do is make the best of it." She walked past Kaminsky toward the stairs.

"I'm fine with that," Kaminsky said. "Just so long as we're clear that I am a highly trained federal agent and not your personal bodyguard."

With one hand on the newel post, Charlie stopped to skewer Kaminsky with a look. "And I am a highly educated expert who already helped your team catch one serial killer, and may very well help you catch a second. Which is why I'm worth protecting." For a moment they stared measuringly at each other, while Michael, clearly having found a fresh source of enjoyment, added his two cents with, "Catfight! You know I've got your back, babe, but I gotta warn you that nowadays that don't count for much."

Ignoring him except for a slight contraction of her eyebrows, Charlie said, "I'm going to bed," to Kaminsky, who had already been given the room across the hall from Charlie's and, search completed, was free to go to bed herself at any time. "If you need towels or anything, you know where the linen closet is."

Then she turned and walked on up the stairs.

By the time Charlie reached her bedroom, it was a quarter to five in the morning. Exhaustion was blunting the horrors of the night and even tempering the aggravation that she was feeling toward every other being (both dead and living) in her house. The fact that she was drooping with fatigue wasn't even her most pressing problem. As soon as she (and her shadow) was inside with the door closed, she made a beeline for the bathroom.

"You. The bathroom is off-limits," she told Michael over her shoulder. Then, shutting the door firmly behind her—locking it was a waste of time, considering that the creature she most wanted to keep out could walk right through it if he wanted to—she hurried to the medicine cabinet, shook two Pepto-Bismol tablets into her hand, and chewed desperately, hoping they would quell the nausea that the ride down the mountain had done little to ease. While she waited for the medicine to (hopefully) work she managed to brush her teeth and, after a single regretful glance at the waiting tub, take a quick shower that was steamy hot enough to chase away the terrible chill that still afflicted her. After that, she was so tired she felt boneless, but she was warmer and the nausea was better. Michael hadn't put in an appearance—actually, she had trusted him not to—and she felt comfortable enough that he wouldn't to drop her towel and rub lotion into her skin before pulling on her nightgown. Then she covered the flimsy, mid-thigh-length thing with her blue terry bathrobe, which she tied firmly at the waist, shook her hair out of the knot she'd twisted it into for the shower, and even ran a brush through it (vanity, thy name is woman) before heading back out into the bedroom.

Where she knew Michael would be waiting.

Having taken his watch off before she showered, she was carefully carrying it.

"So, you upchuck in there?" was how he greeted her.

"No, I did not," she answered, nettled that he knew so much about her, before she regrouped enough to remember the watch and hold it up for him to see. "Is there somebody I can send this to for you? Someone you'd like to give it to?"

Because after all the watch was no good to him now: he couldn't wear it, would never wear it again, and there might be someone to whom he'd like to leave a memento. The matter could have waited for morning, but she was addressing it now as a way of sliding past any awkwardness that might result from him hanging out in her bedroom while she went (alone) to bed. She'd known that having him tethered to her would come with its share of drawbacks, but the reality of it was proving downright unnerving: if she didn't find some way to change the terms of his continued earthly existence, he might very well be dogging every step she took for as long as she lived. Then she realized that he was shirtless, and that the soft glow of the bedside lamp was playing over a magnificent display of rippling muscles and tanned skin, and she forgot what she'd been thinking. Despite being so weary that her legs felt shaky, as her eyes slid over his powerful shoulders and wide, sculpted chest and as much of his sinewy abdomen as she could see above the low-slung waistband of his jeans, her heart sped up and she felt an electric tingle that started deep inside and shivered across every nerve ending she possessed. He was standing sideways to her, on the far side of the bed, holding his T-shirt out at arm's length in front of him as if he'd been examining it. The tattoo on his bulging biceps caught her eye: like the rest of him, it looked totally badass and she was embarrassed to realize that the sight of it excited her. With a quick, comprehensive glance, she took in the smooth planes of his shoulder blades and his long, strong back, his brawny arms and square-palmed, long-fingered hands and felt a rush of heat. The instant quickening of her body was immediately followed by a sense of profound helplessness. Like practically everything else where he was concerned, she had no control over her body's instinctive reaction to him. The one saving grace in the face of what she could only consider her really stupid weakness for him was that there wasn't any way she could act on it. He might look as solid and substantial as any living, breathing man, but he was not. She could fantasize about running her hands over all that hard-bodied splendor, about kissing that chiseled mouth, about falling into bed and having mind-blowing sex with him all she wanted to, and it still wasn't going to happen.

Which, she told herself sternly, was a good thing.

His eyes met hers across the not-as-wide-as-she-might-have-wished-it-was expanse of her spotless white bed. Charlie felt as if the temperature in the bedroom had suddenly warmed by about a hundred degrees.

"You wearing something pretty under that robe?"

He knew her affinity for beautiful, feminine lingerie. It resulted, Charlie was sure, from the no-nonsense, practically androgynous clothes she chose to wear professionally. The answer was yes: her simple summer nightgown was cream silk with lashings of lace, and it was, indeed, very pretty. Not that she had any intention whatsoever of telling him so.

"None of your business," she answered. "What's up with your shirt?"

He smiled slowly back at her. His eyes had gone all heavy-lidded and hot. "Thought I'd try turning you on."

Her eyes narrowed. Her lips firmed. His smile kicked it up a notch.

"It's wet, okay?" he said. "Unless you have access to a ghost Laundromat, I'm just going to have to wait and see if it dries."

The sizzle that was suddenly there in the air between them made her body throb. It made her burn. Instantly she started doing everything she could to shut that down. There was no point in even taking so much as the first step down the path this thing with him was heading.

Hot, mindless sex was *not* going to happen. What *was* going to happen was that they would have the conversation about the watch, and then she would get some much-needed sleep.

"I asked you who you'd like me to send your watch to," she persisted, resolutely ignoring the shivery little tendrils of wanting she could feel coursing around inside her.

His mouth twisted. "Don't waste your time." His eyes slid over her again, lingering on the deep vee of the robe she had belted around her waist, openly assessing the scrap of creamy lace visible in the opening. "For future reference, I like lace."

There was a huskiness to his voice that made butterflies take flight in her stomach. Against the hardwood floor, her toes curled.

Do not let him see you react.

"For future reference, I don't care."

"There you go with that pretty pink tongue of yours again."

She was *not* wetting her lips. She didn't think. It was all she could do not to glare at him, but that would be a dead tell—giveaway—that he was getting under her skin.

"So are you going to give me the name of your next of kin or not?" Charlie snapped, attempting to battle her body's shameless response by trying to call to mind what she knew about him. For one thing, at the time of his arrest he'd had a girlfriend. Charlie even remembered her name: Jasmine. She liked the idea that she remembered his girlfriend's name only slightly less than she liked the idea of sending his watch to her.

"I got no next of kin." He was looking her in the eye again now, instead of staring at her chest. The sad thing was, that didn't help what ailed her a bit. The steamy glint at the backs of those sky blue eyes had the unfortunate effect of making her go all gooey inside. "You're it, babe: you're the closest thing I've got to anybody who gives a damn about me. You keep it."

There was no self-pity in his face, no chagrin that she could see, no sadness or sorrow. He looked perfectly fine, his usual drop-dead sexy self in fact, but Charlie felt a pang in the region of her heart.

It was wrong that he had no one.

Something of what she was feeling must have shown on her face, because his gaze sharpened.

"Are you standing over there feeling sorry for me?" he demanded.

"No," she replied guiltily.

"Yes, you are. I can tell." Wadding up the T-shirt, he threw it into the elegantly upholstered armchair in the corner. "There goes that soft heart of yours again."

Charlie raised her chin. "You say that like having a soft heart is a bad thing."

"Believe me, most of the time it is. But that's why you get the watch, Doc: because you have a heart as soft and squishy as a big ole giant marshmallow. And because you—how was it you put that once?—oh, yeah: you *care* about me."

About to deny it, Charlie realized that she couldn't. And the fact that she couldn't scared her enough to make her cross. Enough to make her brows snap together and her arms fold over her chest.

"Go to hell," she said, not caring much at the moment if he actually did. He laughed.

"You gonna show me that pretty thing you're wearing?"

"No." She was still scowling at him. A yawn caught her by surprise, and she clapped a hand to her mouth a split second too late.

His expression changed to something she couldn't read.

"You're out on your feet," he said in a totally different tone than before. "Go on to bed."

She almost said no just to be contrary. But she really was exhausted, and the thought of climbing into bed and closing her eyes was all but irresistible.

Of course, before she did that, she was going to have to lose the robe.

Giving him a peep show was *not* on the evening's agenda.

She could tell from the hooded way he was watching her that he was waiting for it. Lips curving in secret triumph, she set his watch down on the bedside table, pulled back the covers, positioned her pillows—and turned off the lamp, which was on her side of the bed. When he said *"Shit,"* she smiled. With the room plunged into almost complete darkness, she took off her robe, crawled into bed, and curled up with her back to him.

Then she lay there sightlessly listening to the too-rapid beating of her heart, so conscious of him standing there on the other side of the bed looking down at her that she couldn't even close her eyes, that she had to remind herself to breathe. He didn't move, or make a sound, and she knew that the most he could possibly see of her was a shadow-enshrouded shape beneath the covers. But simply knowing that he was there made her supremely conscious of the cool slide of her silk nightgown against her skin, of the tautness of her nipples against the slight abrasion of the lace covering them, of the dampness between her legs. The body lotion she used was scented with lavender: she could smell it on her own skin.

"Just for the record"—his voice was low and thick enough to send a shiver down her spine—"I want to fuck you. Bad."

Her breath caught. Her hands fisted in the sheets. Her bones turned to water. Her body caught fire.

Oh, God, I want you to.

But she didn't say it. Wild horses couldn't have dragged those words out of her mouth.

What she did say, very firmly, was "Good-night."

Then she closed her eyes.

So aroused it felt as if flames were licking over every inch of her skin, she practically prayed for sleep.

CHAPTER ELEVEN

Of course she had bad dreams. Who wouldn't, under the circumstances? But when Charlie woke up in the morning, she couldn't remember them. All she remembered was crying out once, and hearing Michael say, "Don't worry, babe, I'm right here." Which had made her feel absurdly safe and protected, and so she had fallen back to sleep until sunlight filtering through the curtains—and her shrilling alarm—announced the arrival of another day.

Michael was nowhere to be found. That worried her. At least until she got downstairs, followed the smell of coffee to the kitchen, and discovered him with his back to the room, looking out through the big kitchen window while Crane hovered over the coffeemaker and Tony and Kaminsky sat at her breakfast bar discussing something that Charlie surmised had to do with the laptop that was open in front of Kaminsky. A sweeping glance told her that the back door was indeed, to all outward appearances anyway, repaired, and the mail was still piled as she had left it in the center of the table, which was probably why no one was using it. The gang was dressed in their usual FBI-agent suits, and Michael was once again wearing his T-shirt. Charlie presumed it had dried. Although how he had gotten down to the kitchen while still staying within the prescribed fifty-foot limit mystified her, until it dawned on her that Michael could go through the floor. As the ghost traveled, she calculated swiftly, her bedroom was only about thirty feet away.

"Morning," Tony greeted her as she walked into the kitchen. "Hope you don't mind us making ourselves at home."

"Not at all," she said, as Crane waved a spoon at her, Kaminsky favored her with a sour look, and Michael turned to face her. He was unsmiling, and the sunlight pouring in through the window spilled over his tall, powerfully built body as if he were as solid as the house itself. It picked up golden threads in his tawny hair and emphasized the hard planes and sculpted angles of his face. If she hadn't known for sure that what she was looking at was his ghost, she wouldn't have believed it: that's how alive he looked. Even across the distance separating them she could see the beautiful sky blue of his eyes. *God, he's gorgeous,* was the thought that ricocheted through her idiot brain, only to be squashed like an annoying little bug with the reality slap of, *And dead.* She pulled her eyes away from him to concentrate on the living, breathing good guy she was talking to. "Only I didn't think I had any coffee in the house."

"You didn't." Tony smiled at her. Obviously not long out of the shower, he was looking very handsome himself with his well-groomed black hair brushed back from his face and his brown eyes crinkling at her. "Crane ran to the store. Got some doughnuts, too."

For people who she knew were operating on only a few hours' sleep, everybody looked good, Charlie thought. Bright-eyed and ready to go. The men clean-shaven. Kaminsky in one of her snug skirt suits—this one had pinstripes—and, God help her, her usual towering heels. Knowing that they would be going after the Gingerbread Man full bore, Charlie, too, had put on a work-appropriate outfit, consisting of black flats, slim black pants, and a sleeveless peach silk blouse. She had twisted her hair up in a loose knot in deference to the heat, and when they left would take her black blazer with her, to be carried until she needed to put it on.

She wore jewelry, too—small, tasteful silver hoops in her ears, and Michael's big silver watch pushed halfway up her arm.

Leaving it behind on her nightstand just hadn't felt right. If what he had told her was the truth, it was too important as evidence—and

clearly too important to him personally as well. Now, as Michael's
eyes touched on the watch then rose to meet hers, she returned his
gaze a tad defensively: *don't read anything into it.*

He smiled at her. She refused to even allow herself to speculate on
the meaning behind that smile. But a shiver passed through her at the
sheer seductive charm of it, and she realized with a thrill of alarm that
she was in even bigger trouble where he was concerned than she had
thought.

Do not fall in love with him.

She was horribly afraid that was like warning herself not to
breathe.

"Coffee?" Crane asked her, and she nodded. Glancing at the
clock over the microwave, Charlie saw that it was a couple of minutes
after nine a.m. It was Saturday, which was a good thing because it
meant that she didn't have to worry about going in to work, and already so bright with sunshine that simply looking out the window
made Charlie want to wince.

It was hard to reconcile a world that looked as if it belonged in a
happy Disney movie with the terrible things that she had seen last
night.

Michael said, "You've got chickens in your backyard. And a big
ole orange tabby looking like he's thinking about having McNuggets
for breakfast."

"Oh, no." Charlie was already charging out the back door into
what felt like a wall of steamy heat before it occurred to her that she
had spoken aloud. Well, she would just have to hope that everyone
thought she had seen the impending carnage through the window for
herself. Mrs. Norman, the elderly widow who lived next door on one
side, raised prize-winning Leghorn chickens of which she was fiercely
proud; the Powells, a high school teacher, his K-Mart assistant manager wife, and their twelve-year-old daughter, Glory, who lived on
Charlie's other side, adored Pumpkin, their cat. Unfortunately the cat
and the chickens were the animal world equivalents of the Hatfields
and the McCoys. Both warring parties frequently breached Charlie's
fence, the chickens because of a partiality for her sunflowers and the
cat because of a partiality for the chickens. Her backyard had become
the battleground on which the two species waged their deadliest bat-

tles. So far, the toll was one badly mauled chicken and a frequently pecked bloody cat.

"Shoo!" Making the appropriate shooing motions with her hands, Charlie stomped toward the chickens. The big white birds were actually surprisingly aggressive, particularly toward Pumpkin, so the sides were not as unevenly matched as she had, upon moving into the house and discovering the ongoing war, at first supposed. At that moment the chickens were scratching around in the grass beneath the sunflowers, oblivious to Pumpkin, who crouched, tail twitching and eyes fixed on his putative prey, behind a nearby rock. "Go home, Pumpkin!"

Squawking, the chickens scattered at her approach, making for the fence and then launching themselves over it into their own yard with all the grace of boulders trying to fly.

Charlie turned back to see Pumpkin, his fun ruined, sitting up and eyeing her with an unblinking golden gaze. As if to allay her suspicions about his intentions, he lifted a paw and proceeded to wash his face.

"Yeah, right. I know what you were up to," Charlie told him. Scooping him into her arms, she turned to restore him to his own yard and found herself looking at the mountain behind her. Unnerving as it was to think about, last night a killer who had committed unspeakable crimes had been on that mountainside, peering into her windows through the foliage. The thickly wooded slope stretched upward against the background of cerulean sky until it was lost in a froth of low-hanging, misty white clouds. Despite the bright sunshine, the variegated green of the treetops struck her as dark and forbidding, and the entrance to the path where she always began her run to the ridge seemed filled with sinister shadows. Tamping down a shudder, Charlie reflected that it would be a long time before she ran that particular path again. Always before, she had thought of the mountain as a place of renewal, of peace and tranquillity.

Now just looking at it made her feel as if a clammy hand had gripped the back of her neck.

"Charlie?" At the sound of her name, uttered on a note of uncertainty, Charlie turned to see Melissa Powell waving at her from her own backyard on the other side of the fence. Since Charlie had lived there for only a few months, she was still getting to know her neighbors, most of whom had lived in the area all of their lives. They were a close-knit group who were friendly and welcoming but a little slow to fully accept a stranger. Having never had a settled existence, much less a hometown full of family and friends and neighbors, Charlie found their easy connection to one another enviable. It was something, she had decided when she had moved in, she would like to try to be a part of. A year or so previously, it had occurred to her that she didn't really know how to have friends. After her unstable childhood, and especially after the trauma of what had happened to Holly, she simply hadn't wanted or perhaps she'd been unable to form many lasting bonds. Cautiously, like a swimmer putting a toe into a pool she feared might be icy, she was working to remedy that now. Here in Big Stone Gap, she was trying small town life on for size. That kind of happy normalcy was something she badly wanted for herself, even though she wasn't quite sure if it was going to fit.

"Hi, Melissa." Pumpkin was wriggling in Charlie's arms now that he saw his owner, and Charlie carried him to the fence and handed him over. Probably no older than Charlie's own age, attractive rather than pretty, Melissa had short brown hair and a thin, boyish figure. Having apparently seen Charlie with Pumpkin from her kitchen, she had stepped outside in a knee-length, zip-up pink robe. Except for the length of her hair, which reached halfway down her back, Glory, who was standing on the back porch watching Charlie, too, looked exactly like her mother, while Brett, the husband and father, whom she could just glimpse inside the open back door, was a big guy, with a bluff laugh and a beer belly. Charlie smiled a little apologetically at Melissa. "He was after Mrs. Norman's chickens."

"Oh, dear." Melissa looked dismayed. Glancing down at the cat in her arms, she said, "No, Pumpkin. Bad kitty." Shaking her head at Charlie, she added, "We're trying to keep him in, but—" She shrugged, then gave Charlie an almost shamefaced look. "I heard—everybody's saying—I wouldn't pry, but with Glory, you know, I have to be so careful—did a *serial killer* murder two girls up on the mountain last night, and did a third one escape by running to your house?"

So Melissa hadn't been one of the neighbors who had flocked to her house in the aftermath—but still she knew what had happened.

Well, of course she did. That was part of the reality of small town life. It was part—Charlie thought—of what she wanted for her own life.

Charlie gave her neighbor the bare bones of the story in a few quick sentences. Eyes rounding in horror, Melissa listened, exclaimed, "Oh, my goodness, I'm never letting Glory out of my sight again," and "The police department needs to release a city-wide alert!"

"Did you hear or see anything unusual out here last night? Say, between 11:30 and midnight?" Charlie asked.

Melissa shook her head. "We were in bed by eleven. All of us." She made a little face. "Everybody says there were police cars and ambulances and all kinds of commotion going on, but we didn't hear that, either. We didn't know a thing in the world was wrong until Sally Bennett called me this morning."

"If you can think of anything, will you call and let me know?"

Melissa nodded. Then, with a quick "'Bye" and Pumpkin still clasped in her arms, she rounded up Glory and hurried inside her house, where Charlie had little doubt that she would soon be burning up the phone and Internet.

Suddenly conscious of the humidity wrapping around her like a blanket, sure she was already rosy with the heat, Charlie turned toward the house to discover Michael standing not ten feet away.

His eyes twinkled at her. "Anybody ever tell you you look cute chasing chickens?"

Her eyes swept him. "It's nice to see you with all your clothes on."

He grinned. "The shirt dried. That silky nightgown you were wearing last night? Real pretty."

She was not about to ask *How do you know?* But her face must have said it for her, because after a single comprehensive look at it his grin widened and he continued, "You kicked all the covers off. About the same time you started letting out panicky little cries like something was after you."

Remembering how comforting she had found his presence in the middle of the night, she scowled at him. "What did you do, spend the entire night hovering over me?"

"Nah, I spent most of it in Sugar Buns' bedroom. I just checked on you occasionally."

Now, that would have been infuriating if she had believed it. The thing was, she didn't. He might (or might not) be a charismatic psychopath/serial killer, but she'd already figured out that he wasn't a creep. Flicking him a look that said *Aren't you funny,* she walked on past him through the door into the blessedly cool air-conditioning. She was impatiently waiting on Michael to follow her so that she could close the door on the heat that billowed in behind her—she hadn't yet quite totally internalized the fact that he could walk right through a closed door anytime he wanted to—when Kaminsky, half turning on the bar stool to look at her, said, "So what did your gossipy neighbor have to say?"

"She wanted to know what had happened," Charlie replied, closing the door after Michael did, indeed, walk through it—and while she was still holding it open, too. "She'd heard things, and she wanted to check."

"We need to canvass the neighbors, see if they saw or heard anything," Tony said.

Skirting the table, Charlie headed for the breakfast bar. "I already asked Melissa. She said the entire family went to bed at eleven and they didn't know a thing about it until this morning, when a friend called and told her."

"I bet the whole town's running scared," Crane said. He looked at Charlie. "You want a cup of coffee?"

"Thanks." Charlie slid up onto the bar stool beside Tony, who smiled at her. "The horrible thing about it is, this wouldn't have happened here if I didn't live here."

"Tell me you're not gonna start feeling guilty about it." Michael leaned against the bar on her other side. Having his big body close enough to where she could have shifted an inch or so sideways and brushed him with her arm if she'd wanted to was vaguely unsettling. The thing was, every single bit of him from the faintest suggestion of stubble on his square jaw to the rock-hard abs inches from her elbow looked as real and solid as Tony did on her other side. It was difficult to keep her eyes off him, difficult to keep from letting his nearness kick her pulse rate up a notch. "The whole world ain't your problem, babe."

"It would have happened somewhere," Tony told her. "This

guy's a killer, and whether you're involved or he's pulling in some other expert he feels like challenging, he'll kill until we catch him. Simple as that."

"The locals shouldn't be in danger anyway. I've plotted out the location of the kill zones, which in this case are always the same as the disposal zones, and he never goes back to the same place," Kaminsky said. "Right now, as far as this unsub is concerned, this town is probably the safest place on the planet."

"Oh, yay, I'll tell my neighbors." Charlie's response was wry. "I'm sure that'll make up for everything."

Tony's eyes touched hers, dropped.

"Just so you know, from where I'm standing, right above that first button you've got done up on your blouse, I can see this really mouthwatering little bit of cleavage. What do you want to bet Dudley can see it, too?" Michael drawled.

Charlie couldn't help it. Even as she shot him a fierce *Stop talking to me* look, she laid a protective hand across the bottom of the vee formed by the open collar of her blouse. It was all she could do to keep from doing up another button, simply to make sure that there was no cleavage to be seen. But that, she knew, would provide Michael with way too much entertainment. And would be a dead giveaway to how easily he could get under her skin, too.

"After we go over some things, I'd like you to come with me to the hospital to talk to Jenna McDaniels," Tony said to Charlie, who (a little jerkily) nodded agreement. Very subtly (she hoped) she adjusted her position so that she was sitting straight enough that presumably neither of the men on either side of her could see down her shirt. Not that she had any evidence except Michael's suggestion that *Tony* had been looking. "Crane, when we're through here you and Kaminsky can get busy talking to the neighbors. Plus, we need to pull all the surveillance video from every ATM, every convenience store, every traffic cam in the area. If the police cruisers have video, pull that, too. Everything. We know this guy was here in town yesterday and last night. It's possible that he, or his vehicle, were caught on tape."

"Sure thing, boss," Crane said as he handed Charlie a cup of coffee. Charlie dosed it liberally with Sweet'N Low from the sugar bowl on the counter, pointed Crane to a cabinet when he bemoaned the lack of real sugar, declined a doughnut (despite Michael telling her, "Take it. You need to eat."), discreetly did up another blouse button when she judged that everyone (read Michael) was looking elsewhere, and allowed her attention to be directed to the laptop screen as Tony gestured at it and said, "Kaminsky, bring us up to speed, would you please?"

Kaminsky put down her coffee cup.

"First, there are seven separate groups of three victims each, for twenty-one known total victims of the Gingerbread Man." Kaminsky tapped the screen, which displayed what looked like a bulletin board with small photos grouped together by threes. "Of that number, there have been sixteen fatalities. Five survived the attacks, including Jenna McDaniels." She pointed to a line-up of five photos at the far side of the screen: the top one was of Jenna. "Three attacks occurred in each of the last two years and one attack—that would be Jenna McDaniels' group—has occurred so far this year. The time frame for all of them is August/September. If the Gingerbread Man stays true to pattern, the attack on the McDaniels' group is only the first this year. We can expect three more victims to be kidnapped approximately ten to fourteen days from now. The next kill date should be two weekends away, on either Friday or Saturday. That's the pattern."

"So we've got about ten days to find this guy before he starts up again," Crane said, and Kaminsky nodded. "Always supposing he stays true to the pattern."

"Any idea how he chooses his victims?" Tony took a bite of a doughnut. From the corner of her eye, Charlie saw that Michael was watching Tony almost broodingly, and frowned. Surely he wasn't looking like that because he thought the other man had been ogling her cleavage. After all, he had been doing the same thing. Then she had another thought: she was thinking of her pesky ghost strictly as Michael now. Calling him "Garland" no longer entered her head. And what that said about the changing state of their relationship she didn't even want to contemplate.

Kaminsky shook her head. "I've listed the victims' names, ages, genders, races, marital status, occupations, and hometowns, and any other known identifying characteristics. I can't find a pattern in the criteria he uses to select them—yet."

Charlie said, "If I'm remembering correctly"—she scanned the identifying information for each group to confirm it—"each group is roughly similar in composition. For example, the first group was made up of boys aged twelve, thirteen, and fourteen."

Kaminsky nodded. "That's right. Group Two was three fifteen-year-old girls. Group Three was teenage boys again—two fourteen-year-olds and a sixteen-year-old. Group Four was a departure in that two of the victims were adults and one was markedly dissimilar to the other two—two women in their forties and a fifteen-year-old boy. Group Five was a sixteen-year-old girl, a seventeen-year-old girl, and seventeen-year-old boy. Group Six was a fourteen-year-old boy, a fifteen-year-old boy, and an eighteen-year-old girl. Group Seven— well, that was the group last night. Raylene Witt and Laura Peters were both twenty-one. Jenna McDaniels is twenty."

"Who are the survivors?" Tony asked, polishing off his doughnut with a last, super-sized bite then wiping his fingers on a napkin. Michael was still watching him as he chewed and swallowed, Charlie saw. But when she took another sip of coffee, Michael's eyes, glinting with some emotion she still couldn't quite pinpoint, flickered to the cup she had just set down, where they lingered. It took a second, but then Charlie had an epiphany: she realized that Michael wasn't ticked off at Tony at all. He was envying them their breakfast.

Of course, he missed eating.

She hated the idea of that.

Michael must have felt her gaze on him, because he looked up then, saw her expression, and frowned at her.

"So what's up with the big sad eyes you're giving me?" he demanded suspiciously.

Charlie altered her expression in a hurry. *No idea what you're talking about,* was the first part of what she hoped her expression conveyed. The second, which she already knew he was about as likely to pay attention to as he was to suddenly sprout an angelic halo, was *Hush.* Then, as Kaminsky started talking, Charlie wrenched her gaze away.

"Ariane Spencer, fifteen at the time, from Group Two." Not quite touching the screen, Kaminsky pointed to what looked like a year-book photo of a pretty blond teen. "Matthew Hayes, sixteen, from Group Three." The kid was wiry, with spiky black hair and a small silver ring piercing a nostril. "Andrew Russell, seventeen, from Group Five." This boy had very short brown hair and thick black glasses. "Saul Tunney, fifteen, from Group Six." He had a round, earnest-looking face and blond waves. "And, last but not least, Jenna Mc-Daniels from Group Seven."

"So what we've got are sixteen teenagers ranging in age from fourteen to eighteen and five adult women, if you count Jenna Mc-Daniels at twenty as an adult," Tony said.

"Did any of the victims know one another?" Having polished off his meal, Crane had come around the breakfast bar so he could look at the computer screen, too. Leaning toward it, he started to rest a hand on the counter. It passed right through Michael, who grimaced. Snatching his hand back, Crane straightened with a sharp *"Ah!"* and started rubbing his fingers.

"Counter shocked me," he said defensively in response to the surprised looks he got from the others. "Damned static electricity."

"Boo," Michael growled after him as Crane moved on down to stand on the other side of Kaminsky.

Involuntarily, Charlie smiled.

Michael was smiling, too, as he met her gaze. After a second his eyes darkened. Then they moved down to her lips.

"When you smile like that, all I want to do is kiss you," he told her. "Damned shame I can't. But I'm working on it."

He was trying to get a reaction out of her, Charlie told herself. She knew he took a great deal of pleasure from teasing her, rattling her composure, provoking her, turning her on. The only defense she had against him was to not respond. So she didn't. At least, not outwardly.

But there wasn't a thing in the world she could do about the instant mental image she had of his mouth covering hers. Just like there wasn't a thing in the world she could do about the way her body suffused with heat.

"I think some of them did know the others in their group." Looking away from Michael, who, having clearly seen something that interested him in her face, was now watching her like a cat at a mouse hole, Charlie concentrated on Crane instead as she picked up the thread of the (important, real-world) conversation. "Which ones and what the relationships were exactly I don't recall right off the top of my head."

"We need to find that out." As Tony spoke he looked at Kaminsky, who nodded.

"What strikes me is that all the males are kids. I'm betting that seventeen-year-old boy was undersized. This guy's afraid to tangle with a grown man. Which makes me think he's not a real big guy himself, and probably doesn't have any military or police background. No combat training or anything like that," Crane said.

Tony made a face. "I don't think we can rule out a military or police background on the basis of that. A grown man is harder for anyone to deal with than a woman or a child. And it may be that grown men aren't this guy's thing."

Crane shrugged. "Good point."

"Forget the damned victims. You're the key," Michael told Charlie. His face had hardened, and the look he gave her was suddenly grim. "You want to figure out who this guy is, figure out how he knows *you*."

CHAPTER TWELVE

Charlie cast a surprised look at Michael: she hadn't expected him to have tuned out the conversation, exactly—knowing him, that would have been expecting too much—but she equally hadn't realized that he had been following it to such an extent. Certainly she hadn't expected him to make such an astute observation. As soon as the words came out of his mouth, she realized that he was right.

"Faster this guy's caught, faster I quit having to worry about you getting yourself killed. And the faster Dudley there goes back to where he came from," Michael replied to the look she gave him.

Remembering in the nick of time that she had an audience, Charlie didn't respond to that by so much as the flicker of an eyelash. Instead, she looked at Tony as she repeated Michael's suggestion aloud. Only she expanded it to include figuring out how the Gingerbread Man knew all the experts to whom he had sent his message.

"That's a really good idea. Four's a much more manageable number to start an investigation with than twenty-one," Tony said thoughtfully. "Who're the experts?"

"Dr. David Myers, who as I told you last night wrote the definitive text on criminal psychology. Dr. Jeffrey Underwood, research geneticist and professor at Wake Forest School of Medicine. And Eric

Riva, a reporter who wrote a series of articles about the case for the *Charlotte Observer*. That would be the primary newspaper in Charlotte, North Carolina," Charlie said.

"And you," Kaminsky added, giving Charlie an inscrutable look. "Dr. Charlotte Stone, certified forensic psychiatrist, one of the top serial killer experts in the country."

"Who needs to find a new specialty," Michael said, while Charlie, ignoring him, said to Tony, "I think what we need to ask ourselves is how the Gingerbread Man came to know about each of the experts. For example, I don't think anybody outside of academia or the forensic psychiatric community has ever heard of *me*. So that should narrow the list of possible suspects right there."

"Are you kidding? You've been all over TV," Kaminsky shot Charlie an incredulous glance. "For a few days there, practically every news channel and talk show host in the country was covering the Boardwalk Killer case twenty-four seven. You included."

"The girl who lived," Michael told her on a satiric note. "Think about it: as a theme, it's classic."

Considering the source, this clear reference to Harry Potter came as a shock. Michael had told her before that there wasn't much to do in prison besides read and work out, but at the time they'd been talking about Shakespeare. Charlie decided that her mind had just officially been blown by the eclecticism of his literary choices.

"Prison library," Michael explained, clearly able to correctly interpret the look on her face. "If they had it, I read it."

"You *were* all over TV," Crane was saying to her when she forced her attention to return to the living. "Including CNN. Anybody in the whole world practically could know who you are and what you do."

Charlie hadn't realized. Or, rather, she hadn't let herself realize. Probably, she decided, because she hadn't wanted to know.

"I forgot about that." Okay, that sounded lame.

"You've been busy," Michael said excusingly.

"So let's consider the other three," Tony said. "How could this guy know them?" He looked at Charlie. "How did you know who they were?"

She said, "I knew their identities from looking over the case for Dr. Myers. I knew him, of course, and I had heard of Dr. Underwood, but I had never heard of Eric Riva before Dr. Myers sent me the case files."

"Eric Riva was the first person to receive the Gingerbread Man's *You can't catch me* message, right?" Tony asked. When Charlie nodded, he said, "Let's start with him." He looked at Kaminsky. "Find out how widely read those columns he wrote were. And how he came to write them in the first place."

Kaminsky nodded. "I'm on it."

"I would say the first group of victims is the most important, too," Charlie said slowly. "Something caused the Gingerbread Man to start with that group. I would posit that either he knew one of the victims in some way, or that he saw himself in one of the victims. Something traumatic may have happened to him at that age."

"Check them out, too," Tony directed, and Kaminsky nodded again.

Then, remembering Raylene Witt's appearance in her front hall—to be there, the spirit almost had to have been attached to someone or something nearby—Charlie added, "One more thing. We know the Gingerbread Man chased Jenna down the mountain. He—or a confederate, although I am almost one hundred percent certain we'll find he works alone—kicked open my back door and entered my kitchen to leave the note and the knife for me to find. He may very well have walked around to the front of the house after that, and may even have come inside with the rescuers. We should check for video or photos of the front of my house—maybe one of the neighbors whipped out his phone and took pictures of the ambulance crew, or of Jenna on the stretcher, for example. We should compare fingerprints from the front door and hall with fingerprints on the back door. Also, we should probably get as complete a list as we can of who was on the scene."

Tony looked at Kaminsky and Crane. "Got it covered, boss," Crane said.

"Anybody up for grisly details?" Kaminsky cast an inquiring glance around.

"No," Michael said. As Charlie glanced at him in some surprise it struck her that, for a supposed serial killer, he didn't seem to have a real high tolerance for gore. In her experience of him, every time he'd been exposed to it—take Laura Peters' bashed-in head, for example—he had seemed more bothered than she would have expected the typical serial killer to be, because serial killers have no ability to empathize with anyone. Had he been faking an empathetic response? Maybe, but she didn't think so: the reactions were too consistent. Then she remembered his descriptions of her inkblots: they had been gory enough. Of course, she had suspected at the time that he was messing with her, and even if he hadn't been, that had been before he was killed. Maybe death had changed that part of him. Maybe death had changed everything about him. Maybe, in death, he was not the same bad-to-the-bone person that he had been before.

"A heads-up, babe. You're staring at me with your eyes wide and your pretty lips parted. Now, me, I think it's because you're fantasizing about jumping my bones. But your friends might wonder." The slow half-smile Michael gave her then really might have sent Charlie's thoughts running along the lines of jumping his bones if his words hadn't been so annoying. He was doing it on purpose, of course, just as he had been annoying her on purpose ever since, as a shackled and jumpsuited convict, he had first shuffled into her office. Snapping her mouth shut and dragging her eyes away from him even as she did a lightning mental review of every interaction she'd ever had with him, alive or dead, she came to an inescapable conclusion: in every way that mattered, he hadn't changed a bit.

For him at least, death was no magic elixir washing away his sins. He was still whatever he had been before.

How bad a thing that was Charlie couldn't quite decide. But annoying was definitely still there in the mix. So, unfortunately, was sexy as hell.

"Snakes," she heard Kaminsky say, and the word jerked her attention back to the real world conversation like very few others could have done. "The bastard locked those three girls in Group Two in a roomful of poisonous snakes." Charlie wasn't a fan of snakes. Merely thinking about it made her shudder. From reading the files, she had a vivid mental image of what Kaminsky was talking about— how the Gingerbread Man had coerced the girls in that group into killing one another by dropping snakes on them from a grating high above—but she needed a second to refresh her memory on what had been done to the previous group, the description of which she had obviously missed: oh, yes, Group One, the young boys, had died of thirst. No one knew whether or not the Gingerbread Man had offered to let one live if the others were killed, because no one in that group had survived. "Group Three was forced to choose who would be shot with an arrow. Group Four was menaced with a propeller; Group Five was locked in a trash compacter; Group Six faced suffocation; and Group Seven, as we know, was threatened with drowning."

"Where are the survivors now?" Tony asked. Kaminsky hit a button, and a new screen popped up.

"Pretty much everywhere: I've got their addresses." Kaminsky indicated a map of the United States on which five blue dots glowed. Two of them, Charlie saw, were clear across the country. Well, she couldn't blame the victims for wanting to get as far away from what had happened as possible. In the aftermath of Holly's murder, she had experienced that impulse herself. Only she had been afraid that no matter how far away she ran, it wouldn't be far enough, which in the end had meant that she hadn't run very far away at all.

Instead, she'd tried hiding in plain sight. And look how well that had worked out: she'd almost gotten herself killed, and had ended up all over CNN.

Tony was looking at the map with his brow creased. "So where are the experts?"

Kaminsky hit a button again, and four green dots showed up on the same map. They were all within the tri-state area of North and South Carolina and Virginia, which put them much closer at hand.

"Kill grounds?" Tony asked next. Kaminsky tapped another button, and seven red dots showed up. They, too, were all within the same tri-state area. Four of the red dots nearly overlapped the green dots that represented the experts.

"It's clear that the kill sights were chosen with proximity to the experts in mind," Charlie pointed out.

"Were all the *You can't catch me* messages hand-delivered to the intended recipient?" Tony looked at Charlie, who shook her head to indicate she didn't know.

"The first one, to Eric Riva, was snail-mailed to him at the *Observer*," Kaminsky answered. "The other three were hand-delivered."

"Okay." Tony nodded. "Maybe somebody saw something.

Maybe there's a description. Do we know the locations where the victims were last seen alive?"

"Not all of them," Kaminsky answered apologetically. "Crane and I are working on it."

"I found out where Omar's is," Crane volunteered. "The bar where you said Laura Peters was last seen, remember? It's in Hampton, Virginia."

"That's about seventy miles from Richmond," Tony responded with a frown. "We have information that Laura Peters was grabbed from right outside that bar. What about Raylene Witt and Jenna McDaniels? Do we know where he grabbed them?"

"Not yet," Kaminsky said. "But we will."

"Do we know why there wasn't more of an outcry over the disappearance of Laura Peters and Raylene Witt?" Charlie asked. "Or if they were even reported missing?"

"Laura was, by her mother yesterday morning," Michael said, surprising Charlie into looking at him again. "Google her name and a Facebook page listing her as missing comes up. Apparently the mother thought Laura was staying with her boyfriend. The boyfriend thought Laura had gone home to her mother. As for the other girl, I didn't get that far."

You were Googling? was the question that came rushing to the tip of Charlie's tongue, but she managed to swallow it just in time.

Michael's lips quirked. "I figured if I could learn to work the remote I could learn to work a computer. I spent part of last night playing with the one in the room across the hall from your bedroom. I'm getting pretty fair at it."

The room across the hall from her bedroom was the smallest of the three upstairs bedrooms, and Charlie had turned it into an office. She had a desk in there, along with a file cabinet and shelves of books. Her Mac Pro computer was on her desk, usually in sleep mode. Also in the room was a love seat that opened into a twin bed.

Last night, Crane had slept in there.

"You'll catch flies," Michael warned with a dawning smile.

Recollecting herself, Charlie pressed her lips together and dropped her gaze, which landed on her coffee cup. Automatically reaching for it, she remembered that Michael couldn't drink coffee, and stopped.

If you only do what he can do, you won't be doing much, she told herself severely. But then she thought, *By now, the coffee's probably cold.* So she didn't want to drink it anyway, and that had nothing to do with Michael at all. Having come to that conclusion, she glanced a little furtively around. If anyone else had replied to her question, she had missed the answer. With an effort, she tuned back in to the conversation.

"The kill methods require planning, and a fairly elaborate setup," Tony was saying. "He'd have to put some time into them. And some work, and some money. Which means he is either employed at something that pays fairly well, or he has access to money through family or some other means."

"The killings occur on weekends," Kaminsky pointed out. "That argues for someone who works, and works a fairly normal schedule, too."

Crane said, "But he grabs his victims several days earlier. And, while there is only one killing ground for each group, the groups are fairly far apart in terms of location. So we know he is able to travel, possibly through his job, and that he has someplace to keep his victims until he is ready to put his death scenario into motion."

"The physical description provided by the survivors is all over the map in terms of height and weight," Kaminsky said, "but we know he is male, and that he wears all black clothing and what is probably a mask over his face that makes it look unnaturally white and skeletal. And he drives, owns, or has access to an old blue or gray van."

"So who are we looking for?" Tony asked.

"I have no idea," Kaminsky said as Crane shrugged. Kaminsky glanced at Charlie. "Fortunately, our team now includes a highly educated expert to help us figure this out. Any insights you care to share, Dr. Stone?"

The look Charlie gave Kaminsky should have withered her. It didn't.

Transferring her gaze to Tony, Charlie said, "Like I said, the first group of victims needs to be checked out: something about them as a group, or one of them as an individual, has meaning for him. I feel fairly confident that at the time of the murders of that first group he was living or working within a twenty-mile or less radius of the kill site. Also, the method of coercion—how he terrified his victims into killing one another—is important. Why did he choose those methods? Were they particular fears of the victims, and, if so, how did he know about them? Are they fears of his, and if so, how did he come by them? Did he, perhaps, have an experience mirroring one of the scenarios? Or did a close family member? For example, did his father drown? Or was the Gingerbread Man himself, at a tender age, the victim of something involving a propeller, such as a lawn mower accident? Or—"

"Or maybe he's just plain evil," Michael interrupted. "No cause and effect, no traumatic childhood experience: just evil. That's where your soft heart's steering you wrong, buttercup: you want to think that people do bad things because bad things were done to them, and they're broken as a result, which means that they can be fixed. That *you* can fix them. I'm here to tell you that it ain't necessarily so, and that's the kind of thinking you want to be careful of because it can get you killed."

Charlie saw that for once he was being absolutely serious, and her brows contracted. A lightning-fast whisper of a question flickered through her mind—*Is he warning me about himself?*—before she noticed the gathering frowns on the faces of the three living beings she'd been talking to before Michael had butted in.

"Charlie?" Tony prompted. The look he was giving her was kind of weird, kind of questioning, and she realized that as far as Tony and Kaminsky and Crane were concerned she had totally spaced out in mid-spiel in front of them.

Damn it.

"Sorry, I had to stop for a moment to gather my thoughts," she said, as with her peripheral vision—because she was absolutely not looking his way again—she watched Michael smile with what she had no trouble identifying as sardonic enjoyment of her predicament. But she was *not* going to be distracted again, be that smile ever so maddening. Instead, she concentrated on Tony, and on getting out the rest of the facts about the killer that had been coalescing in her head.

"What we are dealing with here is a highly organized killer. He is almost certainly a white male, aged twenty-five to forty, intelligent, plans everything in advance, is a perfectionist with no tolerance for mistakes," she continued. "He sees himself as dominant, controlling, and powerful, so I would expect to find him in a job where he has quite a bit of authority. He is a sadist with a God complex. He enjoys having the power of life and death over his victims."

"If what that means is that he gets everything into place ahead of time, before he snatches the victims, then it's probable, even likely, that by now he already has the killing grounds for the next group of victims prepared, is that right?" Tony frowned thoughtfully, her brief lapse forgotten, she thought.

"Yes," Charlie replied. "He has almost certainly already prepared the killing ground for both groups of victims that remain to allow him to complete this year's ritual."

Tony slapped a palm down on the counter with satisfaction. "There you go. That gives us another possible way of finding him: find those killing grounds."

Charlie nodded. "They should be within a few miles of the next two experts he's planning to send a message to."

"Only we don't know who those experts are," Kaminsky objected.

"No." Charlie shook her head. "We don't."

"But you can make some guesses, right? Identify some possibilities?" Tony was looking at her intently. "That should help us narrow the places where we mount a search."

"Yes, I can," Charlie said. "But I have no way of knowing if I'll be accurate. With the first three groups, he didn't send a challenge to anyone at all that we know of. After that, he chose a reporter, a geneticist, a university professor, and a researcher. What the last three have in common is an interest in and a certain expertise in the workings of the mind of a violent criminal. But he could change his parameters for selecting the next individual he wants to involve in this case at any time."

"Understood." Tony's eyes met hers with a touch of humor. Charlie realized that she was probably sounding a little pedantic.

"The thing is, this is such an anomalous case," she explained. "I'm not sure how many of the rules apply."

"Understood," Tony said again, and slid off the bar stool. "If you're ready, I'd like to get going for that interview with Jenna Mc-Daniels."

Charlie stood, too, and automatically began gathering mugs. "Give me a minute, and I'll be right with you."

"We've got this covered." Crane took the mugs away from her.

"Then let me get my purse," she said to Tony. As she left the kitchen, she heard him giving a brief recap to the others, prioritizing what they needed to do. With Michael trailing her—"I feel like a damned puppy on a leash," he muttered, which made her smile—she was back with her purse and jacket in no time. All traces of breakfast were cleared away. Kaminsky stood at the breakfast bar tucking her laptop into its case, Charlie saw as she reentered the kitchen. Crane sat on a bar stool beside Kaminsky fiddling with the controls on a video camera. Tony was over near the sink talking on his cell phone, and as he saw her held up a finger to indicate that he would just be one more minute. Charlie nodded at Tony, then headed for the kitchen table. There was something she needed to do.

"So, are you going to be working with us on this one all the way through?" Kaminsky asked her, her tone making it clear that she was hoping the answer was going to be *no*. Kaminsky was keeping her voice low, Charlie surmised, so as not to interfere with Tony's conversation. It sounded to Charlie as if he was giving a superior a brief overview as to where the team was and what it was doing, but Charlie didn't actually listen as she packed the DVD and letter that had come with Michael's watch safely into a zippered compartment of her purse, then moved the rest of the mail to the console table.

Besides those items, nothing was urgent; even the bills could wait a few days.

"Looks like it," Charlie replied, while Michael, having observed what she had tucked into her purse, said, "No point in wasting your time with that. What's done is done."

Last night's anguish was totally absent from his tone. It was cool, casual. Equally, there was no trace of emotion that she could perceive on his face.

Even if he really was that indifferent to what was on the DVD, she wasn't. And suddenly she was very sensitive to the cool weight of his watch on her arm.

Her eyes met his.

I owe it to you to check it out.

But, of course, she couldn't say it aloud.

"We're honored to have you, Dr. Stone," Crane told her, with a reproving look at Kaminsky. "You're a real asset to the team."

Charlie smiled at him. "Thank you. And call me Charlie, please."

"Charlie." Crane was stowing the camera away in a case full of miscellaneous equipment. "And why don't you go ahead and call me Buzz?"

His bright blue eyes gleamed at her from behind his glasses.

"Oh, please." Kaminsky rolled her eyes. "What are we, the Waltons? Let's try to keep it professional, people."

"Hey, *Lena*, guess what?" Crane's (no, Buzz's) voice was as low as Kaminsky's but that didn't blunt the edge on it. Knowing how Kaminsky felt about being addressed by her first name, Charlie almost winced: nothing good was likely to follow. "Nobody thinks being reasonably friendly with coworkers is unprofessional except you."

Kaminsky glared at him. "I don't notice you going around calling Bartoli *Tony*. Or would that be because you're only interested in getting *reasonably friendly* with Dr. Stone here?"

"Holy Mother of God, Lean Cuisine, you need to get a grip," Buzz snapped. He and Kaminsky were exchanging glares when Buzz let loose with an only partly masked yawn. For a moment Kaminsky stared at him in astonishment. Then, very softly, she began to laugh.

"Hours getting too long for you, *Buzz Cut*?" she jeered.

Buzz looked embarrassed. "I'm a little sleep deprived, okay?" He glanced at Charlie. "You might want to get your computer checked out. It kept turning on all by itself the whole time I was trying to sleep."

Michael chuckled. As Charlie made the connection—Michael had been on her computer in the room in which Buzz had been trying to sleep—her eyes widened with guilty knowledge. What Buzz or Kaminsky might have made of her expression she fortunately didn't have to find out, because Tony had finished his call and was coming toward them.

"If you two don't knock it off, I'm going to fire one of you." Tony gave both of his subordinates warning glances. Kaminsky, still looking mad, didn't reply, but Buzz muttered *"Sorry"* and Tony, with another hard look at Kaminsky, nodded.

"Ready?" he asked Charlie. Charlie nodded, and they headed toward the hall. He added, "I'd apologize for that little by-play, but you've seen it before."

"It's okay. I think they're kind of cute," Charlie replied.

Tony grinned. "For God's sake, don't let Kaminsky hear you say that. I really will have to fire her."

Charlie laughed. "Don't worry, I won't."

"Do you mind if we take your car?" Tony asked. "I'd like to leave the rental for Kaminsky and Crane."

"That's fine." She was fishing in her purse for her keys as they approached the front door. Tony reached around her to open it for her.

"You planning to drive?" Michael inquired as she produced them. "'Cause I can tell you right now that Dudley'd like to have the keys, but I'm betting he's going to be too politically correct to ask."

Charlie's fingers clenched around her keychain. Whether she'd been about to hand them over or not she had no idea, but now that he'd put the issue of gender equality into play she definitely would not. Lips compressing, she stepped out into the hot, brilliant sunlight, squinted a little, shaded her eyes with her hand, and shot Michael a blistering look as he appeared beside her.

"You'd want to drive, too, you—you man," she mouthed, piling a fair degree of venom on that last word. With Tony so close behind them, her voice wasn't even as loud as a whisper. But when Michael grinned, she was perfectly sure that he had understood.

"You're right, but the difference is that *I'm* not worried about being politically correct," he answered. "I'd just tell you to hand the keys over."

Unable to reply because Tony, clearly assuming that she had stopped to wait for him, was sliding a proprietary hand around her arm now as he joined her, Charlie gave Michael a fulminating look. It was wasted. He wasn't looking at her—or Tony. He was looking toward the street.

"Damn," he said in a totally different tone, and then as Charlie followed his gaze she found herself staring in horror at the tide of reporters rushing at them.

CHAPTER THIRTEEN

Ken Ewell and Howie Martin, another deputy sheriff whom Charlie knew vaguely, had been parked in their marked cruiser outside of her house since shortly after dawn. They were ordered there by Sheriff Peel when media types had first started arriving in town. (That would be shortly before dawn.) Their mission was to keep the press on the public streets and off private property (such as Charlie's yard and the yards of her neighbors), and to keep one of Big Stone Gap's residents (that would be Charlie) from being harassed as the eyes of the nation that had been following on TV the effort to find Jenna McDaniels now turned to where and how she had been found. Although for the last hour there had been satellite trucks and carloads of reporters parked out in front of Charlie's house, everything had been completely under control until Charlie herself stepped through her own front door.

Then all hell broke loose.

This Ken explained to Charlie in a breathless rush as he and his partner tried and failed to keep the press from completely surrounding her and Tony as they fought their way toward her garage, a detached, shedlike structure at the top of her driveway. By the time they reached it, Tony had his arm wrapped tight around Charlie's waist and she had her head bent against his shoulder to avoid the intrusive cameras.

"Dr. Stone, is it true that you rescued Jenna McDaniels?"

"What can you tell us about her ordeal, Dr. Stone?"

"Hey, Charlie, look this way!"

"Wait, aren't you the FBI agent who worked with Dr. Stone on the Boardwalk Killer case?"

"Yeah, you're right, it's Special Agent Anthony Bartoli! Is this another serial killer case, Agent Bartoli?"

The press yelled those and what felt like a hundred other questions at them until Charlie and Tony (and Michael) reached the relative safety of the garage. With Ken and Howie trying to clear reporters from in front of the garage door—she and Tony entered through the people-sized one on the side of the small building—Charlie forgot about asserting her equality and being politically correct and whose car it was anyway and all other possibly pertinent issues except expediency, and handed Tony the keys to her blue Camry.

Bottom line was, he had more practice driving through a horde of reporters than she did. Besides, she understood herself well enough to know that if somebody jumped in front of her bumper, she would hit the brakes. And she'd seen Tony drive a sufficient number of times to further know that he would not; she liked to think it was because he trusted whomever it was would get out of his way.

"That was a cluster fuck," Michael muttered as the Camry made it out of the garage, around Tony's rented dark blue Lincoln that was clogging up her driveway, and into the street, where it sped away from the media, all of whom had rushed to return to their vehicles to give chase. Ken and Howie had successfully blocked the pursuit by turning their car sideways in the street, but that wouldn't hold the reporters back long, Charlie knew. Still, it might give them enough time to get to the hospital unimpeded. "Good call letting Dudley drive, by the way."

The car was small, with lingering traces of new car smell (she'd bought it right before she had moved to Big Stone Gap, so it was only a few months old). It was as stiflingly hot as a blast furnace as the air-conditioning struggled to make a dent in the heat. Michael was in the backseat. Unwilling to do more than cast a quick glance around at him under the pretext of looking out the back window for chasing reporters, Charlie flipped down the passenger-side visor, which came equipped with a small mirror. Of course, she couldn't see him in it: she had forgotten. But it didn't matter: the image she'd gotten in that one glance was engraved indelibly on her mind. He was way too big for the cramped space. His legs were folded up in a way that would've been uncomfortable if he were alive, and his forearms rested on his knees. The disgusted expression on his face would have made her want to smile if she hadn't been battling off shivery little flutters of déjà vu. This degree of media interest was actually not as bad as the frenzy that had engulfed her when she had been the teenage survivor of the murder of Holly and her family. It was not as bad as what she had been through in the aftermath of the Boardwalk Killer's resurgence. But the memories it evoked—the terror, the helplessness, the sense of being both trapped and at bay—made her wonder, suddenly, if maybe Michael wasn't right. Maybe she should simply walk away from her work at Wallens Ridge, abandon her research, forget about her determination to find out the building blocks of a serial killer and how such monsters could be identified and stopped, and make a whole new life for herself in which serial killers were part of her past, not her present, and not her future.

The thought that it might be possible for her to do that briefly dazzled her.

But then she thought, *No. If I do that, if I walk away, all those horrible things that happened will have been for nothing. The deaths of Holly and her family, of the other victims, will be just that many more senseless killings. If what I am doing can save even one more life, then that's what I have to do.*

"You okay, babe?" Michael seemed to be able to read her thoughts with uncanny accuracy. She wasn't sure she liked that. No, she was sure: she didn't like it. Then she realized that, while she couldn't see him through the mirror, he could see her. He was reading her face, not her mind.

Frowning, she gave a barely there nod by way of a reply. And snapped the visor back up against the ceiling so that he could no longer see her eyes.

Hah!

"If you can give me directions, I won't have to stop and fiddle with the GPS," Tony told her, and, glad of the distraction, Charlie did. Past the church where Michael was buried—as far as she could tell, Michael didn't even give it a glance—and the Farmer's Market and Miner's Park, through the small downtown with its antique-style street lamps on every corner and Little Stone Mountain rising like a hulking, blue-gray sentinel above it, left at Traffic Light five (the lights were numbered one through eight), and finally into the hospital parking lot.

Unlike the town itself, which was light on traffic on Saturday mornings, the parking lot was crowded with vehicles. The hospital was a long, low structure of brick and white stucco with only sixty beds. There were at least that many cars in the parking lot. Charlie's eyes widened as she saw the crowd of reporters gathered in front of the entrance. Satellite trucks from stations as diverse as their local WAPK to CNN had set up shop on the sweltering blacktop.

"Oh, boy," Tony said, glancing at her. "I'm afraid there's nothing for it but to brave the gauntlet."

"Sneaking in the back isn't going to work, either: looks like they got the place surrounded," Michael added. Charlie could feel his eyes on her. "Look, you know you don't have to do this. Dudley and the gang have been catching serial killers just fine without you. You can hole up in a hotel or something until this is over. If you want to help them, you can do it over the phone."

She was tempted, of course she was, but only for a second. She gave a quick, negative shake of her head, and Michael said, "Fuck."

By the time they reached Jenna's room, Charlie was seriously wishing that there were another choice she could have made. Even after they fought their way through the reporters—the hospital's security guards had been supplemented by deputies and local cops to keep the media out of the building—there was still the hospital itself to deal with. The area around the emergency room in particular was thick with the phantoms of the recently, violently departed. Even with Michael playing bodyguard, two of them rushed her the moment they realized she could see them. She never did find out what they wanted, because Michael scared them off before they reached her, and with Tony at her side she had to continue on. To make things worse, she found that she was the object of a great deal of unwanted attention from the living, too. At first she couldn't understand all the sideways glances and nudges and not-quite-discreet-enough pointing fingers. Even though it seemed like almost everyone in the hospital recognized her and was interested enough to watch her for as long as she was in sight, that was, surely, only her own paranoia at work.

Or so she told herself.

But then, as she passed a half-filled waiting room and caught a glimpse of her own face on TV, she understood. It was starting up all over again. Just as Michael had said, she was the girl who had lived: a never-ending story, apparently, especially considering what she had grown up to become.

The knowledge made her feel cold all over.

Detective Sager was standing outside the door to Jenna's room, along with a second man—who Charlie assumed was another detective—and two uniformed cops.

"Since that initial interview last night, she's clammed up. We've been ordered to keep a guard on the door, but not to enter the room or let anyone else in—unless authorized by the parents. But only a few minutes ago we got a call telling us that you were on the way up and we should let you through," Sager informed Tony with barely concealed ire. "So I guess that makes you and Dr. Stone here special." His eyes slid over Charlie, and not in a friendly way.

Seeming to take no offense, Tony frowned at him. "Family has some clout, I take it?"

Sager grimaced. "Her father's a federal judge. He's in there now, along with her mother and somebody I think is the family lawyer. What I want to know is, why don't they want her to talk to us?"

Charlie was pretty confident she knew the answer.

"Teen Queen's feeling guilty," Michael said, echoing her own thoughts. Charlie knew he was remembering Raylene Witt's accusation just as she was. If Jenna had killed Raylene, and possibly Laura, too, she very well might not want anyone to know. Telling Jenna up front that having his victims kill one another was part of the Gingerbread Man's MO might or might not make her feel better about what she had done, but it would also taint any account that she gave of what had happened. When it came time for trial, defense lawyers would have a field day painting investigators as having led the witness. Tony had explained this on the way over, and Charlie knew it was true. She only hoped that Jenna knew what had happened was in no way her fault.

Tony shrugged. "Couldn't say." Then, with a nod at Sager and a brief knock, he opened the door for Charlie and followed her—and Michael—into the room.

It was a typical hospital room, small, cool from the air-conditioning, bright from the overhead light, and smelling of antiseptic.

"Special Agent Bartoli?" A tall, silver-haired man in a dark suit was the first to react to their presence. He stood on the opposite side of the hospital bed alongside another man, who was shorter, stockier, with thinning gray hair, in another dark suit. A well-dressed woman of around fifty was seated on the near side of the bed. She had short, expensively styled red hair, and as she looked sharply around at the new arrivals, Charlie saw that her features were remarkably similar to Jenna's: delicate, pretty, upscale. Jenna herself was in the bed, in a semi-sitting position which allowed her to see and be seen without obstruction. She was still pale, but aside from that and the bandage on her forehead there were no outward marks of her ordeal that Charlie could see. Her long, inky black hair hung in a single thick braid over one shoulder, and she wore a satiny pink bed jacket on top of her hospital gown. A blue hospital blanket covered her from the waist down. An IV was in her left arm, and her expression as she looked at the newcomers was both nervous and wary.

"Hello, Jenna," Charlie said softly as Tony and the silver-haired man, who introduced himself as Jenna's father, Judge Alton McDaniels, shook hands. For a moment Jenna's eyes locked with hers, and Charlie could see the horror lurking in that golden brown gaze. Jenna was going to see a lot of people who would talk to her about putting what had happened behind her, about moving on, about forgetting. Charlie knew the girl never would.

Jenna simply looked at her without replying.

"Who are you?" Jenna's mother asked sharply.

"I'm Dr. Stone. We talked on the phone last night, remember? Your daughter ran to my house for help." The woman's face wasn't exactly hostile, but it wasn't encouraging, either. However, it was

Jenna Charlie was interested in, Jenna she hoped to help. "I'm a psychiatrist. I'm working with Agent Bartoli"—she nodded at Tony, who was talking to Jenna's father and the other man—"and his team to help catch the man who did this."

"Why did the freak send me down to your house?" There was an edge of suspicion in Jenna's voice. *The freak,* Charlie knew, was Jenna's way of referring to the Gingerbread Man.

"Did he specifically send you down to my house?" Even as Charlie asked the question, she knew the answer: of course he had. "How did he do that?"

"He said that the only place in the world where he wouldn't kill me was the big white house at the bottom of the path. He said if I could make it there before he caught me, he'd let me live." The rising emotion in Jenna's voice caught the men's attention.

"He wanted to get me involved," Charlie told her, at the same time as Jenna's father said, "Jenna, are you all right?"

As Jenna nodded, the man looked at Charlie with narrowed eyes.

"And you are?"

His wife told him. Charlie allowed herself to be distracted by introductions, shaking hands with Judge McDaniels; his wife, Jill; and Clark Andrews, their family attorney, in turn.

"Thank you for letting us talk to Jenna," Tony said when the last of the introductions was finished.

"Only as long as she doesn't get upset." Jill McDaniels was holding her daughter's hand. Beneath the strain on her face she, too, looked wary, and Charlie wondered exactly what Jenna had told her.

"We're going to do everything in our power to catch the person who did this," Tony promised them all. He looked at Jenna, and his voice gentled. "It would help us a lot if you could answer a few questions. We'll stop whenever you want."

After a moment's hesitation, Jenna nodded.

Tony asked, "Do you mind if I record this? So I don't have to try to remember everything." Jenna looked at her father. Both parents looked at the lawyer. He nodded.

"As long as you're prepared to turn it off if I tell you to," Clark Andrews said.

Tony said, "Absolutely." Reaching into his pocket, he pulled out a small tape recorder and set it on the bed table alongside the glass of water and other miscellaneous objects that were already there. Pressing a button, he turned the machine on, and looked at Jenna again.

"Okay, here we go." Tony smiled at Jenna. Charlie found herself impressed by the air of calm reassurance he projected. "Can you tell me where you were and what you were doing when you were abducted?" Charlie knew that he wanted to get some concrete information under their belts as quickly as possible, in case the session had to be stopped.

Jenna took a breath. "In Hampton. On Pembroke Avenue, near the intersection with Mallory Street. We—my sorority—were having our run. You know, the No Excuse for Child Abuse 5k. I was handing out water at the three-mile mark. I gave out all my water, and everybody had passed, and then one of the golf carts came by and gave Skyler—the girl I was with, she was feeling sick—a ride to the finish line. They were going to come back for me, but it was getting dark, so I started walking on in by myself. There were other people from the race heading in, too, and I was kind of following them, so it didn't feel like I was really alone or anything. I remember the strap on my sandal came unfastened, and I sat down on a curb to fasten it, and everybody else was still walking and talking on up ahead. Then . . . I don't know, I . . . blacked out." Her mouth started to shake. "When I woke up I was in this—cage."

Tony asked: "While you were walking, did you see anyone suspicious? Anyone you now think could have been the man who grabbed you?"

Jenna shook her head. "No. Nobody unusual, nobody who stood out that I can remember. I only just—I heard a voice, okay? Then later, when . . ." Clamping her lips together, she swallowed.

"One of the doctors who examined her last night said that there are marks on her that are consistent with the use of a stun gun," Judge McDaniels told Tony. His face was rigid, and his eyes were alive with anger at what had been done to his daughter.

Tony nodded acknowledgment.

"You said you heard someone speak. Do you remember what he said, Jenna?" Tony's voice was incredibly gentle.

Jenna closed her eyes briefly. "Last thing I remember hearing before I blacked out was a man saying in this kind of weird voice, *'Hi, there.'* Like, behind me. I never saw who it was. Then, when I woke up in the cage, I started screaming. I screamed my head off. He—I couldn't see him. It was so dark. All I heard was this disembodied voice again. He told me that if I didn't shut up, he would cut my throat. I believed him. I shut up."

Even from where she was standing, Charlie could see the girl's shiver.

"Would you recognize the voice if you heard it again?" Tony asked.

"I—think so. Like I said, it was weird."

Tony's gaze was intent on the girl's face. "Where was the cage, Jenna?"

"In some sort of vehicle. A van, I think, or maybe one of those small camper trucks. The cage took up almost the whole back. It had sleeping bags. And—kind of a toilet." Jenna stopped, and took a deep breath. "There was food—packages of peanut butter crackers. And a two-liter of water. After the first day, we—we rationed it."

"We?" Tony questioned carefully. This was a sensitive area, Charlie knew.

"The other girls—and me."

"You were kept in the same cage?" Tony asked. "How many of you?"

"Three."

"Including you?"

Jenna nodded.

"Did you know the other girls previously?"

Jenna shook her head.

"Were the other girls put in the cage before or after you?"

"I don't know. I kind of kept passing out and waking up, but at some point I remember seeing them and realizing I wasn't alone. They were just—lying there, even when I was screaming, and later I figured out that they were passed out, too. Then we finally all woke up at about the same time."

Drugs? Charlie wondered. *Possibly a gas that was pumped into the back of the truck?* The autopsy on the two deceased victims, which if all was going according to schedule would be under way at that very moment, should tell them what substances the girls had been exposed to. Jenna's blood had certainly been drawn last night for testing, and the analysis might be able to tell them the same thing, although it was possible that whatever it was had already metabolized out of her system.

Tony asked, "Did you talk to the other girls?"

Jenna nodded again. "They were . . . nice. Whatever happened, we made a pact to stick together. When he came—we knew he would come—we were going to attack him. Raylene—Raylene . . ." Jenna's voice shook. "She was tough. She made a weapon out of this big metal comb she had in her hair, by bending over some of the teeth and holding it in her fist. Sort of like brass knuckles with spikes. She said she was going to go for his eyes. Only—she never got the chance."

Breathing hard, Jenna stopped.

"Oh, baby," her mother whispered, and Charlie could see how tightly their hands were clasped.

"Why didn't Raylene get the chance, Jenna?" Tony's voice was soft.

Jenna was lying back against her pillows now, looking at him out of eyes that were stark with remembered horror.

"We agreed to never sleep at the same time, that one of us would always stay awake to keep watch so that he couldn't sneak up on us. But—we must have all fallen asleep anyway. And . . . and when we woke up we were at the bottom of this well." She took a breath, glanced at her mother. "I was so scared."

"Jenna," Mrs. McDaniels said piteously.

"What happened then, Jenna?" Tony prompted.

"I won't have her getting upset," Mrs. McDaniels flashed at him.

"Jill, let her talk," Judge McDaniels told his wife.

Mrs. McDaniels cast her husband an angry look, then focused on her daughter. "Honey, do you feel like you want to go on?"

Jenna looked at her mother. They were holding hands so tightly now that Mrs. McDaniels' knuckles showed white. Jenna wet her lips. Then she nodded, and looked at Tony again.

"Last night—I can't believe it was just last night. Oh, my God." She paused, and swallowed. Then she went on. "Anyway, it was really dark. We could barely even see one another. At first we didn't know what was happening. We didn't know where we were, or any-thing. Only that we were in this moldy-smelling place that was wet. We got up and started feeling around, feeling the walls, to see if we could find a way out. Raylene's the one who said she thought it was a well, and I think she was right. It was really deep, with curved stone sides that were slimy and disgusting and impossible to get a grip on. Way up above we could see this little circle of night sky. There was nothing we could do, no way we could climb out or escape. We were screaming but it didn't help. It just echoed back at us, and nobody came. There was this rushing noise, and we looked up. Then water started pouring in on us, nasty cold water, like from this giant hose, gushing, and we tried to get away from it and we did, kind of, by hug-ging the edges of the well. But the water kept pouring in and getting deeper and deeper and Laura started crying and saying that she couldn't swim."

Jenna broke off. Her eyes closed.

"Everything's all right now. We've got you safe," Mrs. McDan-iels told her daughter.

Taking a deep breath, Jenna nodded, then opened her eyes and looked at Tony. "That's when we saw him: when the water started getting up to our chests and Laura was freaking out and crying and we were trying to tell her how to swim. He leaned over the top of the well and shined a light down on us. At first I thought it was somebody come to help us and I was begging him to get us out of there. Then he must have slipped up with the light and I saw him. He was wearing a black hoodie or cloak or something with one of those Guy Fawkes masks, you know, all white with the creepy smile. And he said—and he said—"

When she broke off again, Tony waited a few seconds and then asked, "What did he say?"

Charlie could almost see the chill passing over Jenna's skin. The girl gave a long, shivery sigh, then squared her shoulders. She looked straight at Tony. "He said, 'Two of you are going to die here tonight. Maybe all three of you are. I'll let one of you live—*if* you kill the oth-ers. Kill the others, and I'll let the last one alive go home.'" Jenna's voice was cold and clear suddenly, as if she was repeating words that had burned themselves into her brain. Which those had, Charlie knew. She also knew that they would haunt Jenna for the rest of her life.

Charlie's heart ached for the girl.

"Then what happened?" Tony prompted.

"Then he threw a knife down into the water, and he said one of us should grab it and go after the others, but none of us would. He kept filling up the well. He'd fill it and leave us swimming in it for a while then let it drain, and each time he started to fill it up was worse than the last because he left the water in longer and we knew what was coming. Raylene and I could swim but it was awful and scary and the water was so cold and it kind of swirled around, which made it worse because there was a current that felt like it was trying to suck us down. We started realizing we couldn't do it forever. Laura kept trying but she really couldn't swim and she was getting tired and we were getting tired from trying to help her. After what I think was the fourth time, when most of the water had drained out again, and Laura, like, collapsed on the bottom, Raylene said, 'She's not going to make it,' and when I looked around she had picked up this rock. She was kind of sneaking across the bottom of the well toward Laura, and I looked at her and she said, 'She's going to drown anyway,' and then she hit Laura in the head with the rock. Laura started screaming, but Raylene kept hitting her and hitting her in the head with that rock and there was blood everywhere and her brains were coming out and then Laura just—she just curled up in the mud and died."

Jenna drew her knees to her sharply and covered her face with both hands. Charlie could see the shudders that wracked her.

"Baby." Eyes welling, Mrs. McDaniels rose from her chair.

Jenna's hands dropped. Tears spilled from her eyes. "Oh, Mama, that's when I—"

"Jenna," the lawyer interrupted. "That's enough for now. Agent Bartoli, please turn off the tape recorder."

CHAPTER FOURTEEN

Jenna started to sob. Mrs. McDaniels wrapped her daughter in a hug, which Jenna returned. The sight of mother and daughter so lovingly entwined made Charlie's throat tighten—her overly emotional reaction was, she knew, the result of her own mother issues, and nothing to do with the case. Tony turned off the tape recorder as requested, although as he punched the button he said, looking first at the lawyer and then at Judge McDaniels, "It would really help us to hear the rest of her story. We're all on the same team here."

When the lawyer shook his head and the judge answered with, "That's all my daughter has to say," Tony said, "Could I talk to you two for a minute in private?" and when they agreed the three men went into the hall.

Out of the corner of her eye, Charlie was aware of Michael moving protectively closer to her, and supposed that with Tony gone he felt he had to up his bodyguard-to-the-vulnerable-female game. But he didn't say anything. He just leaned against the wall near her, his arms crossed over his chest, a stalwart sentinel she knew she could count on to have her back. As her glance found him, and their eyes held for the briefest of seconds, she immediately felt calmer, more centered. She recognized the ridiculousness of it: how screwed up was her world when the ghost of Michael Garland served as a grounding presence? That's when Charlie remembered that he might be—*might be*—the exact same kind of monster as the one they were hunting.

A chill slid down her spine.

I have to know the truth. No matter what, she had to ascertain to her own satisfaction whether Michael was innocent or guilty. Not knowing would eventually tear her apart.

The door opened. Judge McDaniels poked his head into the room. "Jill, could you come out here for a minute?"

"I'm not leaving her." Mrs. McDaniels was shaking her head even as she looked around at him. With her head on her mother's shoulder now, Jenna was crying in deep, shuddering gasps. Listening to her, Charlie remembered the fear and the pain, the shattering guilt, the desperation, she herself had felt all those years ago, and her heart broke for the girl.

"Mrs. McDaniels?" Charlie moved closer. "If you need to go talk to them, I'll stay here with Jenna. She won't be alone."

"It's important, Jill," Judge McDaniels insisted.

Jenna let go of her mother and wiped her eyes. "Mama, I'll be all right."

"Are you sure?"

Jenna nodded, and with a searching look at Charlie, Mrs. McDaniels joined the others in the hall.

"So is this some kind of trick to get me to spill my guts to you now that we're alone?" Jenna's eyes still brimmed with tears. Her voice was shaky in the aftermath of her sobs. It was also faintly hostile.

Charlie shook her head. "No, I promise. Anyway, I'm a doctor. All you have to do is claim doctor/patient privilege and I can't repeat anything you say to me."

She watched Jenna absorb that.

"Last night you kept talking to . . . some invisible person. What was up with that?"

Luckily, Charlie had already anticipated that Jenna might ask her that particular question.

"I don't like to talk about my beliefs, but I will tell you that when

I'm under a great deal of stress, as I was last night, I tend to pray out loud," she said with dignity.

"Oh."

Out of the corner of her eye Charlie saw Michael's wry smile. She saw Jenna digesting her words, saw the last of her hostility fade away. Jenna's eyes were red-rimmed and still wet with tears, and the occasional soblike breath still shook her. Charlie remembered way too vividly how it had felt to be in Jenna's shoes: terrifying, disorienting, soul-crunchingly lonely. As if her whole life had just been destroyed, and she had been left in a place she didn't recognize, in a place that didn't even feel as if it was real, with nobody who knew her, or that she knew. And she made a decision.

"Jenna," she said. "I know what you're going through. Fifteen years ago, I survived an attack by a serial killer, too."

The girl dashed away a tear that had started to slide down her cheek and stared at Charlie suspiciously. "What are you talking about?"

"When I was seventeen, my best friend and her whole family were murdered by a serial killer. I was in the house. I had a chance to save my friend, but I was too afraid that he would catch me and kill me, too. I—ran away and hid." Charlie hadn't expected the punched-in-the-gut feeling the confession would give her. She had to stop talking and breathe.

"Is that the truth?" Jenna demanded.

Get a grip, Charlie ordered herself fiercely, and nodded. Then she told Jenna about Holly.

By the time she was finished, she was sitting on the side of the bed and she and Jenna were holding hands.

"You'll experience survivor's guilt," Charlie told her. "There will be days when you wonder why you lived and the others died. You're going to feel depressed, and you're going to feel afraid, and you're going to feel angry. You may have nightmares. You may find yourself having flashbacks, or revisiting every little detail of what happened obsessively. You may lash out at the people who are trying to help you. All these things are normal reactions to the trauma you've been through. You'll never forget what happened, and you are never going to be the same person you were before it happened. There will always be a before and an after. But I'm here to tell you that you can get through this, you can get your life back, you can go on and be successful and be happy and fall in love and—"

Charlie broke off when the door opened and the McDanielses, Mr. Andrews, and Tony filed back into the room. As they gathered around the bed, Charlie squeezed Jenna's hand and relinquished her place to Jenna's mother.

"So are you going to tell me what the summit meeting was about?" Jenna looked from one parent to the other.

Her father cleared his throat. "After talking to Agent Bartoli, we think it's best if you tell him exactly what happened, exactly the way you told it to us."

Jenna sucked in air. She seemed to shrink, like a child caught doing something wrong. "Dad . . ."

"You can tell them, baby," Mrs. McDaniels said.

"I want you to start where you left off," Tony said. "What happened after Laura died, Jenna?"

Jenna met Charlie's eyes.

"It's all right, Jenna," Charlie said. "You can trust us."

Jenna nodded and closed her eyes. As she started to talk, with a nod at Judge McDaniels, Tony quietly turned the tape recorder back on.

"After Laura died, Raylene was kneeling there beside her holding that rock. The freak job at the top of the well yelled, 'Only one more, and you get to go home,' in, like, this gloating voice, and I knew he was talking to Raylene. I knew he meant she should kill me next."

Jenna broke off then, and wet her lips. Her eyes opened, and she looked at her mother, whose face was tight with love and anguish. As she continued, her voice was barely above a whisper. "So when she stood up, I grabbed the knife out of the mud and I stabbed her with it. I stabbed her and stabbed her and stabbed her until she was dead. Then the freak job yelled down, 'Congratulations, we've got a winner!' and he lowered a ladder into the well and I climbed out and he told me to run. And I did."

By that time she was utterly white and tears were sliding down her cheeks.

"You only did what you had to," Mrs. McDaniels sounded as if the words were wrenched out of her.

"All right, you've got enough," Judge McDaniels said abruptly to Tony, as his wife wrapped her arms around their daughter and Jenna burst into noisy sobs. Watching mother and daughter clinging together, Charlie had to turn away. The moment felt too private to witness.

"Thank you for your cooperation." Tony spoke to Judge Mc-Daniels in a low voice as he scooped up his tape recorder and dropped it into his pocket. "We'll be in touch."

Charlie, meanwhile, pulled a business card from her wallet and scribbled her cell phone number on the back of it. By the time she and Tony had said their goodbyes to Judge McDaniels and Mr. Andrews, Jenna was once again leaning back on her pillows while her mother sat beside her clutching her hand. Jenna's breathing was still ragged, her eyes still gleamed with tears, but there was determination in the tilt of her chin and a new strength in the firm line of her mouth. Jenna, Charlie felt sure, would be all right. Holding the card up so that Jenna could see it, Charlie put it down on the bed table, within her reach.

"Call me if you want to talk," she told Jenna.

"Thanks." Jenna's voice was wobbly, but she managed the smallest of smiles.

"Yes, thank you, Dr. Stone," Mrs. McDaniels echoed over her shoulder, and Charlie nodded by way of a reply.

"You know what? You're a real nice person, Charlie Stone," Michael said in her ear as they were leaving the room. "And take it from me, that's a rare thing."

Charlie couldn't respond, because right at that moment Tony was exchanging a few quick words with Sager and the men with him, and with Special Agents Flynn and Burger, who had just shown up to relieve Sager and crew from door-guarding duty, and she was surrounded by the living. Then Tony took her arm and ushered her toward the freight elevator. He'd made arrangements for Kaminsky and Buzz to switch cars with them, leaving the rented Lincoln near the loading dock and driving off in Charlie's car. That worked like a charm—half the media types present were busy chasing Kaminsky and Buzz, and the other half, the half that held their positions, paid no attention to the Lincoln when Tony nosed it out of the parking lot. As they drove, she and Tony talked—for one thing, she asked, "What *was* the confab in the hall about?" and he told her that he had decided to tell the McDanielses and the lawyer about the Gingerbread Man's MO so they wouldn't be afraid Jenna would face legal problems if she confessed to killing Raylene. All the while Charlie was conscious of a warm little glow pulsing deep inside her. It served as a small but steady counterpoint to the cold wave of horror that the visit to Jenna had evoked, and it came, she knew, from Michael's words.

It wasn't so much what he had said, as how he had said it: there had been, she thought, genuine admiration in his tone. Approval and, yes, affection had been mixed in there somewhere, too.

His opinion of her meant something to her. Actually, it meant a whole lot.

The realization didn't exactly make her happy. Bottom line, though, was that it was a new fact of her life with which she was just going to have to deal.

She and Tony grabbed a quick lunch at the Mutual Drug Store and Cafeteria, which was so crowded with members of the Powell Valley High School football team who were having a meal after practice that they were able to eat undisturbed except for a few friendly waves. They talked shop throughout, although Tony did throw a couple of would-be-flirty comments her way. Given that Michael was lounging beside her listening to every word that was said, flirting with Tony was impossible, so she didn't follow through and that part of the conversation went nowhere. Which didn't exactly please her—a relationship with Tony was something that she really did want to explore—but under the circumstances what could she do? She did manage to consume her lunch without worrying too much about Michael, who was looking increasingly disgruntled as he listened to their conversation. But he did nothing more disruptive than make the odd annoying remark, which she, of course, ignored, and watch them eat.

Tony was paying the bill—Bureau expense account, he teased—when Charlie's cell phone buzzed. Having set her phone on vibrate, she'd been letting her calls go through to voice mail but this one, she saw, was from Tam.

Tam was different. Tam was important. Tam's call—and Charlie hated to think what that said about how her priorities were now ordered—might very well be about Michael. This call she needed to take.

Excusing herself to Tony, she headed for the ladies' room.

"You can wait out here," she told Michael at the door. A pair of elderly women walked out of the restroom at that moment. Michael glanced at them, then looked back at her.

"You see me arguing?" He settled his broad shoulders against the wall beside the door.

Charlie went inside and called Tam.

"Oh, cherie, I am in such a state!" Tam exclaimed without preliminaries when they connected. "Where are you?"

Charlie told her.

"You're safe? You're not in any kind of danger?"

Charlie looked around the small, blue-tiled restroom. The last stall was occupied by a woman and her little girl—Charlie knew, because she could hear them talking—but other than that she was alone.

"No. I'm fine."

"Well, you listen up: there's danger around you. Terrible danger. Ever since I talked to you, I've been getting visions of you being swallowed up in this giant gray cloud. It makes my blood run cold."

"What kind of danger?" Charlie tried not to let her voice change. She knew Tam: Tam was the real deal. If Tam said she was in danger, then Charlie was prepared to take her word for it.

"I don't know. It isn't clear. I just know it's close—closer than you think. For some reason you can't see it. It's like you're blind to it, or the wool is being pulled over your eyes or something." Tam's voice had an urgent undertone. "I wish I could be more specific, but I can't. Not yet anyway."

"Okay." Charlie felt as if a cold hand was gripping the back of her neck. She caught herself looking warily around the bathroom. It was no more than two sinks, three stalls. Wherever the danger to her lurked, she was pretty certain it wasn't in there. "Thanks for warning me."

"I'm focusing on you real intensely. I'll have a breakthrough soon." Tam was breathing hard; Charlie could hear it through the phone. "You be careful, you hear?"

The sound of the toilet flushing made Charlie jump. A moment later, the little girl and her mother emerged to head for the sink.

"I'll be careful." Charlie instinctively made sure her back was to the wall as she watched the mother and daughter at the sink. The knowledge that Michael was right outside was comforting. If she yelled, he would hear.

But then, given that he was as solid as mist, what good would that do?

"I'll call you, cherie, the moment I get more," Tam promised, and, as Charlie said, "Thanks," she disconnected.

Dropping her phone back in her purse, Charlie's first instinct was to run as fast as she could to first Michael and then Tony and tell them what Tam had said.

But as she considered it, the thought of telling Tony that her psychic friend had warned her she was in danger made her uncomfortable: how far on the nut-job side of the equation did she really want him to think she was? As for Michael, there was the solid-as-mist factor to consider. Plus he was already in overprotective mode, and did she truly want to risk having him start harping again on how she needed to find a new job?

As the mother and daughter left, Charlie washed her hands, splashed a little cool water on her face, then took a moment to brush her hair and smooth on lip gloss. All the while she was thinking the matter through.

She couldn't tell Tony. But Michael?

Charlie hadn't made up her mind when she exited the bathroom to find Michael, as she had expected, still stationed outside the door. Straightening to his full height as she approached him, he swept her with a sardonic look. Then his eyes narrowed on her face.

"So what's with you?" he asked.

Charlie's lips pursed. She walked down the short corridor toward the main dining room, where she knew Tony would be waiting for her. Michael fell in beside her.

"Something's up," he persisted. "In case you still don't get it, your face is as easy to read as a neon sign. You can either go ahead and tell me what happened in there, or we can play twenty questions until I get an answer. Your choice."

Charlie flicked him a look. Could he really read her that easily? The answer was: apparently so. Then she sighed and gave up. The truth was, she almost certainly had been going to tell him anyway. She badly needed to tell somebody, and Michael was the only one around who would not only believe her, but, because he'd had firsthand experience with Tam's gifts, appreciate the seriousness of the warning.

"Tam called." The corridor was deserted. Charlie stopped walking, turned to look at him.

He stopped, too. His eyebrows went up. "The voodoo priestess?" Then he frowned at her, as if it had occurred to him that he might have been the subject of the conversation. "What did she want?"

Charlie hesitated. While she'd been tangentially absorbing how tall and powerfully built and absolutely staggeringly good-looking he was, a horrible little niggle of a suspicion inserted itself into her brain. Once it was there, there was nothing she could do about it. It squirmed around taking on a life of its own. "She called to warn me. She said I'm in danger."

His eyes narrowed. His jaw tightened.

"What kind of danger?" he asked carefully.

She shook her head. "Tam didn't know. She simply said I should be careful. She said she saw me being swallowed up by a big gray cloud, and that that was bad."

Even as she said it, Charlie felt that creeping chill on the back of her neck again.

Michael swore. Then he said, "You take her seriously?"

Charlie nodded. "Yes. I do."

His face softened fractionally. "You don't have to look so worried, buttercup. I got your back. And from here on out, I'm not letting you out of my sight."

"Yes, but what if *you're* the danger Tam saw?" That was the niggling little thought that had been squirming around the edges of Charlie's mind, and now she'd come out with it. After all, it wasn't as if there was anything physical he could do to her even if the wool had been totally pulled over her eyes and he really was the psycho killer she had first thought him. She didn't think.

"Me?" He first looked surprised, then disgusted. "As in, you think you're in danger from *me*?"

The look Charlie gave him brimmed with all the latent mistrust she'd been arguing herself out of since he had died.

As he met her gaze his eyes cooled. Then they hardened. Then he gave her the smallest of mocking smiles. "If that's the case, then I guess I'd have to say that makes you shit out of luck."

Two more women appeared at the top of the corridor, clearly heading for the ladies' room, and Charlie started walking again. Michael stalked—that was the only word for it—at her side, and a glance at his face told her that he was seriously angry.

"You don't scare me, Casper," she hissed beneath a hand she lifted to ostensibly cover a yawn.

"Watch it, Doc," he said. "You're pissing me off. Lucky for you I don't have access to a ghost knife."

"*That* was out of line," she flared at him as they proceeded into the dining room, completely aware that they were no longer alone but hoping that amid the football team's rowdiness no one would notice her talking to empty space. "Tam said the wool was being pulled over my eyes. I'd be a fool not to be cautious."

"Oh, right, and that would be by me." His eyes glinted at her. "But you've figured out that you don't have to be afraid of me because I'm dead, right? It'd be different if I was still alive."

Before she could respond to that, Tony, spotting her, called her name, and she had to look away from Michael to smile at him.

Two hours later, she, Tony, Buzz, and Kaminsky (plus a still obviously ticked off Michael) were on board the team's private plane on their way to Columbia, South Carolina, where David Myers lived. He had agreed to meet with them at four. After that, they would talk with local investigators, interview the surviving victim, who still lived in the area, and tour the kill site. Then they would fly on to Charlotte, North Carolina, where they would spend the night. In the morning they would interview Eric Riva, tour the Group Four kill site (there was no surviving victim in that group), then drive the eighty-three miles to Winston-Salem, where they would meet the final expert, Jeffrey Underwood, and visit the Group Five kill site. The Group Five survivor, then-seventeen-year-old Andrew Russell, had since moved to Seattle, Washington. It was agreed that the most time-efficient method of talking to him and other geographically distant survivors was via Skype.

On the plane, they all got busy doing their respective jobs, and for a while, except for the hum of the engine, quiet reigned. Charlie compiled a list of possible experts whom she guessed the Gingerbread Man might target next. By limiting herself to the general geographic area that seemed to be the killer's comfort zone, and doing her best to extrapolate what might draw the Gingerbread Man to a particular expert's résumé, she came up with a list of ten possibilities. It wasn't by any means comprehensive, as she told Tony when she presented it to him, nor did she have any idea if the Gingerbread Man would actually choose any one of the experts on the list. But as Tony said, it was a place to start, and he immediately alerted local FBI offices to keep a watch on the people she had named, and to start searching within a ten-mile radius of their locations for possible future kill sites.

There was no time to waste. None of them ever forgot for a minute that the clock was ticking. In approximately twelve more days, the Gingerbread Man would collect his newest victims, and the killing cycle would begin again.

"He would've needed some kind of equipment—an industrial-grade hose and pump, presumably—to siphon water from the secondary pit to the primary one," Tony said. By that time, they were all seated together in the cushy leather seats surrounding the small oval pop-up conference table in the middle of the plane. Kaminsky had her laptop on. The rest of them relied on their own notes or devices—or memories—to keep up. The day was beautiful if hot, the flight was smooth, and outside the window at Charlie's elbow the sky was endlessly blue above a layer of frothy white clouds.

"The secondary pit was fed by an underground stream, so it was always full," Kaminsky said. "Continual flooding was one of the reasons the site had been abandoned."

"Can we try to identify and trace the equipment?" Tony asked.

"On it," Buzz said, and pecked a note into his tablet. "It's probably a rental. If it is, this'll be a piece of cake."

"What we have here is a power seeker killer," Charlie said

thoughtfully. "There is no sexual component to the murders at all, and no gain motivation, either, as far as I can tell. But I think there is a purpose behind the killings other than the thrill he gets from acting as God to the victims. Of course, it might be something as simple as him getting a charge out of the challenge of coming up with and then acting out these death scenarios. Or it might be something else."

"The guy's a sick fuck." Michael was stretched out on the couch opposite the area where Charlie and the others were sitting. His blue eyes were impossible to read. His mouth had a hard look to it. "There you go, babe. End of story."

"We just got preliminary results back on the objects left in Dr. Stone's kitchen." Kaminsky was looking at her computer. "The knife was the weapon used to kill Raylene Witt. The only fingerprints on it belonged to Jenna McDaniels, which confirms her account of what happened. And the handwriting on the *You can't catch me* letter is consistent with Laura Peters'. Her fingerprints were all over the paper and envelope. There was no one else's."

"So the unsub made Laura Peters write the note," Tony said. "He's toying with us. He knew we'd be salivating at the idea that we had a sample of his handwriting. And I'm one hundred percent convinced that he left that knife because he wanted to make sure we knew that Jenna McDaniels killed Raylene Witt."

"Like I said, he's a sick fuck," Michael said. Charlie flicked him a glance—with one arm tucked behind his head he looked comfortable enough, although his broad shoulders were too wide for the narrow couch—then focused her attention on the others, who actually were trying to contribute something productive to the discussion.

"Omar's—the bar Laura Peters left right before she was abducted—is right around the corner from Pembroke Avenue, where Jenna McDaniels was picked up." Kaminsky was still peering at her computer screen.

"Which leaves us with the question: did he go there targeting them, or did he pick them at random?" Tony asked.

"There has to be a common denominator among the victims." Because she was basically thinking aloud, Charlie looked at Tony without really seeing him. "What makes him choose them? Laura

Peters couldn't swim, for instance, and he chose to subject that group to death by drowning. The question we need to ask is, did he *know* Laura Peters couldn't swim? And if so, how did he know it? And what about the others? Did he choose the death scenarios he placed them in according to their fears? If so, how did he know his victims, and what they were afraid of?"

"Raylene Witt was a manicurist at Hollywood Nails in Hampton. Maybe at some point she did the other girls' nails," Buzz offered.

Tony looked at him.

"I'll check it out," Buzz added hastily. Then he made a face. "She couldn't have done them on the day they disappeared, though, which was the only time Jenna McDaniels was in Hampton. Raylene had called in sick on Wednesday, which is the day she disappeared, and wasn't scheduled to work again until Saturday. Only, because she lived alone, no one knew she had disappeared."

"Maybe there's a twenty-four-hour clinic or pharmacy or something over there near that bar where Laura got nabbed and the street where Teen Queen got picked up. Maybe the screamer was over there because she was sick. Because it makes sense that they were all taken from the same area." Michael was frowning up at the ceiling rather than looking at Charlie. She knew that, she realized crossly, because *she* was looking at *him*. But his comments bore repeating, so she did.

"I'll check that out, too," Buzz said.

"You know what, I think I may have just found a common denominator for these last three victims." There was barely suppressed excitement in Kaminsky's voice. "They were all in terrible car accidents when they were young. Raylene Witt's mother was killed when a drunk driver hit the family car. Raylene was six years old. Her injuries were minor. Laura Peters was in a car crash when she was twelve. A friend's mother was driving a group of four girls to a birthday party. Kylie Waters and Sara Goldberg—who were both twelve, too—were killed." ("There you go," Michael said, his gaze shifting to Charlie. "Kylie and Sara." Remembering the two little girls who had come for Laura, Charlie thought, *Yes, that sounds right.* Those little girls, who were presumably her close friends at the time they were killed, would have come to take Laura to the light. Presumably.)

"Then there's Jenna McDaniels. At the age of sixteen, she was on her way to a dance when there was a rollover accident. The boy driving, Tommy Stafford, who I'm assuming was her date, was killed."

"Could be coincidence," Buzz cautioned.

"Ain't no such thing as coincidence," Michael said. He was looking at the ceiling again.

"All right, we want to check into first responders, hospital personnel, anybody who might have been on the scene of all three accidents," Tony said. "If that's a coincidence, it's a pretty big one."

"I'll get on it." Kaminsky typed something into her laptop.

The pilot's voice came over the intercom, telling them to prepare for landing. They were on the ground not long afterward.

"Oh, for God's sake, are you still pouting?" Charlie hissed at Michael, taking advantage of a semi-private moment as Tony talked to the flight crew, Kaminsky placed a phone call, and Buzz went to fetch the rental car. Michael was standing grim-faced and silent on the tarmac beside her.

"Pouting?" The look he slanted down at her was sharp with disbelief. "I don't pout."

"Oh, yeah? You could have fooled me."

Then Buzz pulled up in the rental car and any chance of further conversation, at least on her part, was gone.

"Just so you know, babe, fooling you ain't that hard," Michael said by way of a parting shot. Surrounded by the living again, Charlie couldn't do more than skewer him with a dirty look in reply.

A little more than forty-five minutes later, with Tony at the wheel of their rented SUV, they were on the University of South Carolina's campus driving down Sumter heading for their meeting with David Myers. Charlie cast a fond look at the Horseshoe, the quadrangle that was home to some of the campus' most historic buildings, admiring the huge oaks with their festoons of gray Spanish moss and the lush lawn where a handful of students lounged in the shade. Then they rounded a corner, and a moment later they were pulling into the parking lot of the very modern building that housed David Myers' office.

"So, you went to college here, huh?" Michael asked as they walked through the suffocating heat of the parking lot into the welcome chill of the building. "What, was this guy your college sweet-heart?"

Glad as she was that he seemed to have gotten over being mad at her, Charlie didn't care for the subject. Since it previously had been raised right after Michael had seen Laura go off with her two dead friends, and he hadn't commented at the time, Charlie had been hop-ing he'd been too wrapped up in what he had just witnessed to pay attention when she'd been admitting to a relationship with David Myers. Obviously, no such luck.

A firming of her lips was her only reply. Clearly he took that for the *yes* she really didn't want to give him, because interest sparked in his eyes.

When the door to David Myers' office opened in response to To-ny's knock, Charlie thought she was prepared.

She should have known that she wasn't.

CHAPTER FIFTEEN

For a moment, for the briefest sliver of time as she found herself looking at David, Charlie was twenty-one again and achingly vulnerable. She had an instant mental image of herself, slim in blue jeans with her waist-length hair pulled back from her face by a barrette so that the silky fall of it rippled down her back, as she had looked on the first day of spring semester of her senior year in college. That was when she'd come to work for Dr. David Myers as his research assistant. By the end of that semester she had absolutely hero-worshipped him.

At least now she was mature enough to realize just how young and foolish she had been. But still, as she came face-to-face with David again, the memory was more embarrassing than she had expected it to be.

"Charlie!" He greeted her with apparent delight, smiling broadly as his gaze swept her. "You look fantastic."

"Hello, David." Burningly conscious that she was the object of the undivided attention of every other member of her group even if none of them (except Michael) was blatant enough to be openly watching her, she smiled her coolest, most professional smile and held out her hand. When he shook hands with no more than the appropriate degree of friendliness, she found herself devoutly glad that he seemed determined to keep things professional, too. "I'd like you to meet—"

"Holy hell, he wasn't a student when you were here anymore than I was," Michael said in her ear as she, trying her best to tune her bête noire out, performed the introductions. "What, were you boinking your professor?"

Actually, yes, she had been. Her psychology professor, to be exact. Only a few times, toward the end of the semester. And the last time they had set eyes on each other, when he had broken off their budding relationship because he was getting married to the woman he'd been engaged to, unbeknownst to her, all along, and then going to England to accept a fellowship at Oxford, she had told him she loved him and begged him to stay.

None of which she said out loud. That last part at least she never intended to share with anyone. Seen in the bright light of eleven years later, it was downright humiliating. Worse, it was stupid.

It was also one more example of her unerring instinct for choosing the absolutely wrong man.

His office was different than the one he'd had when she'd worked for him. Bigger. Not quite as messy. Of course, he was a full professor now, instead of a freshly minted, thirty-year-old Ph.D. in his first year as an assistant professor. Except for a well-trimmed mustache and goatee, he looked pretty much the same: a shade under six feet tall, with a slim build that showed no signs of softening around the edges and short coffee brown hair. A few gray hairs at his temples and some lines at the corners of his eyes and mouth that hadn't been there before were the only real indications of the passage of time. Even the Gamecocks tie and blue dress shirt he wore tucked into blue jeans could have been the same.

Charlie took comfort from the knowledge that she looked—and was—totally different from the academically accomplished but otherwise clueless girl that he had known.

"The Columbia Police Department took the letter the day after I got it," David answered Tony's question, which referred to the whereabouts of the *You can't catch me* message David had received. Tony sat in the chair across from David, who was ensconced behind his cluttered desk in what Charlie, in psychiatrist mode, recognized as his deliberate assumption of the power position. Charlie and Kaminsky sat on a tweedy love seat in front of the window. Buzz perched atop a small stool nearby. Michael leaned against the wall near Charlie. "I don't know if they still have it, or if they passed it on to the FBI. At first the detectives here thought they were dealing with just a bizarre double homicide. It was a couple of weeks before the connection to the previous murders was made and the FBI was called in. I spent quite a bit of time working with the detectives and the FBI to try to identify the killer"—he glanced at Charlie with the faintest of smiles— "and I even tried to enlist the help of the illustrious Dr. Stone here, whose work with serial killers I have followed with interest and admiration, but the fact is we made no appreciable headway. Of course, now that your elite team of serial killer hunters is on the job, presumably we can hope for better luck."

"Do you have any idea why you were chosen to receive that letter?" Tony asked.

David shook his head. "No, not really. I mean, I'm fairly certain it was because of my book. I'm the author of *Criminal Psychology: Understanding the Deviant Mind,* you know—it's the textbook of choice in most criminal psychology courses, so there's wide access to it."

"A fifteen-year-old boy survived the attack," Charlie said. "Had you ever met him before?"

"Saul Tunney." David turned his attention to her, and Charlie recognized that particularly intent gaze as the one he got when something truly interested him. "A remarkable young man. No, I'd never met him before, but we stay in fairly regular contact now. He's actually planning to matriculate here at USC when he graduates high school." He made a face at her. "I had to do quite a bit of talking to get him into regular counseling, but I did it. I've been acting as kind of a mentor to him. As horrible as what happened was, it doesn't seem to have done any permanent psychological damage to him."

"What about the two deceased victims?" Tony asked. "Had you ever met either of them?"

"No." David shook his head. "I'm sorry."

"Did you know Dr. Jeffrey Underwood or Eric Riva prior to receiving that letter?" Kaminsky asked.

"I knew *of* Dr. Underwood, of course." David glanced at Charlie. "I've been aware of his work for years, as I'm sure Charlie has. It's really very impressive." Charlie nodded in agreement. "I did not know him in any other capacity. And I had never heard of Eric Riva until I found out—weeks after I was dragged into the case—that he had been the first recipient of the killer's taunt."

"Do you have any idea why the Gingerbread Man chose a Charlotte newspaper reporter to send that first letter to?" Tony asked. "It doesn't seem to mesh with his selection of three widely heralded experts in the criminal psychology field as the recipients of the next three letters."

David's expression brightened. "Now, that I can tell you. We— the previous investigators and I—believe it was because Mr. Riva had written several newspaper stories about the ordeal suffered by the three boys in an earlier attack. I posited that the killer had read those articles, which I felt meant that at that time he had to be living somewhere within the readership area of the *Charlotte Observer.* I still think that."

Tony nodded. Remembering the file David had sent her to look at when he had asked her to consult and that she had sent back when she'd declined, Charlie said, "Could we get a copy of the file you put together on the case, do you think? As well as anything else you have that you think might help us."

"Yes, of course," David said. Then he smiled a little ruefully at Charlie. "Once the killer is caught, I'm hoping to turn my experiences with this into a book. So if you would treat everything in that file as confidential I would appreciate it."

"We will," Charlie promised, and Tony nodded agreement.

David summoned his newest research assistant—a pretty college senior who seemed just as eager to please David as Charlie, inwardly wincing, remembered she once had been—to make a copy of the file, and they all stood up to take their leave. David took advantage of the fact that the other three had moved ahead of them into the hall to pull Charlie aside and ask her quietly if she'd like to go out to dinner with him that night, "for old times' sake."

When foolish little girls grow a brain, was what Charlie thought, in the spirit of *when pigs fly.* What she said, with scarcely any acidity at all, was, "Don't you think your wife might object?"

"I'm divorced. Three years ago." He smiled at her. "That's one of the reasons I reached out to you when I got pulled into these murders. I've never forgotten you, you know. In fact, I've followed your career with great interest. And pride, I might add. After all, you were once my star pupil. I was hoping we could get reacquainted."

"We're leaving town tonight," Charlie said. Then she added, very gently, "And David—even if we weren't, I'm not interested."

She wouldn't have been human if that softly spoken rejection hadn't made her feel a little bit better. As far as her pride was concerned, it evened the scales to some small degree. But the other truth was that she would have refused even if there hadn't been a history between them that needed avenging. She no longer felt the slightest interest in him as a man: the girl who had thought that he was the greatest thing since sliced bread was long gone.

"Guy's a douche bag," Michael said as they joined the others in the hall and observed the adoring smile the research assistant gave David as she handed him the file she had copied for him. "One of these days you're going to have to tell me how you ended up hitting that."

The look Charlie shot him said *Not in this life*. And for the first time since lunch, he smiled.

Saul Tunney was waiting for them in his mother's home in Ballentine, a Columbia suburb. He was now sixteen, although he was still round-cheeked and faintly baby-faced, which Charlie thought he tried to counter by sporting a blond crew cut that looked almost defiantly masculine. At about five-eight and a hundred thirty pounds, his size wouldn't have posed much of an obstacle to someone bent on kidnapping him, especially since, a year ago when the crime had occurred, he'd presumably been even smaller. Having apparently told his story dozens of times, he related it to them in a few terse sentences. He had been snatched off a Columbia street after a baseball game. He'd found himself in a cage, and, later, a grain elevator with two other kids: Isaac Stein, fourteen, and Sofia Barrett, eighteen. If they wanted to know what had happened in the grain elevator, they could read the police reports: he was done talking about it. What it came down to was, in the end, he had lived, the other two had died.

No, he hadn't known them previously. No, he couldn't identify his attacker: he'd just caught a glimpse of the guy, who had worn black clothing and a white Halloween mask, with a Joker kind of grin. No, he had no idea why he had been targeted.

He did have two things of interest to tell them: he thought the attacker had used some kind of voice synthesizer to disguise his voice; and, four years previously, Saul had been out hunting with his uncle and cousin when his uncle had accidentally shot his cousin dead.

That last had been in response to Kaminsky's question about any other violent deaths he had witnessed in his life.

"I think that's the answer, it really might be our common denominator," Kaminsky said with barely suppressed excitement once the interview was over and they were on their way to meet with the local detectives and FBI agents who had worked the case, to see the Group Six kill site.

"Now all we need to do is uncover a violent death in the pasts of seventeen other victims, tie them all together, and figure out what it all means, and we'll have solved the case," Buzz said dryly.

"At least it's a place to look," Kaminsky snapped.

Their subsequent visit to the abandoned grain elevator that only Saul Tunney had escaped alive was, for Charlie at least, heartrending. At the time, the silo had been full of corn. Standing on the surface of the stored grain was much like standing on quicksand, one of the local agents who was walking them through what had happened explained. When none of the victims had done anything in response to his warning that he would kill them all unless they started killing one another, the Gingerbread Man had opened a floor hole, which was designed to speed the flow of grain from the silo to a loading chute. The girl, Sofia, had been swept away. Her body was found with grain clogging her throat, her nose, her eyes. It was, the detective said, a particularly hideous death. The boy, Isaac, had subsequently been killed by Saul Tunney. With a pickaxe, the kind that was sometimes used in grain elevators to break up hard clumps of grain. The silo had since been emptied of its contents, but traces of Isaac Stein's blood still stained the walls.

Looking at those rust-colored speckles, Charlie felt sick.

It wasn't until much later, when they were getting ready to land at the Charlotte airport, that Charlie finally realized what had been bothering her so much about this case. She'd been listening with only half an ear to the various discussions swirling around inside the plane while she mentally twisted the facts that they knew like the pieces of a puzzle in hopes of getting something to fit, when it clicked.

"I think," she said, looking at the others as if she was really seeing them for the first time in a while, "that he's killed before. Before these group murders began, I mean. This whole thing is too elaborate. He has to have worked up to it. This is his escalation. We need to start looking at unsolved single murders." She paused to let her thoughts settle. "We should probably begin in the same geographical area in which the first Gingerbread Man murders occurred. We should work backward from the date of those murders. He will have an MO, although it will be different from what he's doing now. There will be a pattern. There should be a series of single murders, because this— these death scenarios with multiple victims—represents a major escalation."

For a moment everyone simply looked at her.

"Makes sense," Michael said. He was lying on the couch again, and his eyes had been closed until he looked at her as he spoke. Charlie hadn't even realized that he had been paying attention.

"What kind of time frame are we talking about?" Tony asked.

Charlie shook her head. "If he is at the upper age limit for serial killers—and with this severe an escalation I'm guessing that he is— we're probably looking at the last twenty years."

Buzz whistled through his teeth. "What's the geographical area?"

Kaminsky consulted her laptop. "The first Gingerbread Man murders occurred right outside Clarksville, Virginia."

"Buggs Island Lake," Charlie said suddenly. She looked at Michael, started to say, *Remember, Laura said,* swallowed that, and quickly switched her gaze to Tony. By leaving off the first three words, the rest of the sentence was perfectly acceptable. "The van Jenna McDaniels and the other girls were put into smelled like fish, remember? Buggs Island Lake is this huge fishing destination. And part of it is near Clarksville, Virginia. We should check it out."

"That's in Mecklenburg County," Kaminsky said. "And how do we know the van smelled like fish?"

"We just do," Charlie said impatiently.

Kaminsky eyed her askance.

"Okay, we look for unsolved murders with a single MO in the vicinity of Clarksville, Virginia, and this lake," Tony summed up as the pilot announced they would be landing in Charlotte in five minutes. "Starting around the date of the Group One murders and going back twenty years."

"Got it," Buzz said, and Kaminsky added, "Not that this is going to be hard or anything."

"Look at it this way." Tony smiled tranquilly at the pair of them. "If it was easy, none of us would have a job."

It was full dark by the time they got to their hotel, which in late August meant that it was after ten p.m. Charlie was tired, wired, and a little on edge. They grabbed a quick dinner in the hotel restaurant—Charlie had salad and a bowl of soup—and then they went up to their rooms, which were in a block on the eleventh floor. They each had their own, with Tony on one side of Charlie and Kaminsky on the other. Crane's room was next to Kaminsky's. For security reasons (actually, Charlie knew it was for *her* security), Tony had requisitioned a local FBI agent to stand watch in the hallway all night.

She appreciated it. Now that it was night again, Tam's warning was crowding in on her. The thing was, she had never known Tam to be wrong.

"I've stayed here before," Tony said to Charlie as they walked along the hallway to their rooms. "They've got a great jogging track up on the roof. I'm going to go make use of it. Want to come?"

"Yes," Charlie said instantly. Running was what she did for relaxation, and tonight she badly needed to relax.

"You notice he's not inviting us," Buzz said to Kaminsky, only partly under his breath, as they passed Charlie.

"I noticed," Kaminsky agreed. They were moving on to their respective doors, while Tony had walked Charlie to hers and stopped.

"I heard that," Tony called after them good-naturedly. "And it's because you don't run. But you're welcome to come along if you want."

Declining, they both disappeared inside their rooms.

"I'll be back in ten," Tony told Charlie, who nodded. Then he waited until she was inside and closed the door.

Flipping the switch beside the door caused a lamp to come on, which allowed Charlie to see her surroundings. Decorated in soothing earth tones, the room was typical hotel: two queen beds with a night-stand holding said lamp between them, an armoire containing a TV and, on its lower level, a mini-fridge, an armchair with a floor lamp in the corner by the heavily curtained window, a bathroom, and, op-posite it, a closet. Having preceded her inside, Michael now stood in the middle of the room, giving her an unreadable look.

"What?" Charlie said.

"Not a thing," he answered. She didn't probe further. Instead she extracted her running clothes and her small cosmetics case from her suitcase and went into the bathroom to change. When she emerged a few minutes later, she was wearing silky black running shorts, a pale pink tee, and sneakers. Her hair was pulled back into a ponytail.

"Cute," was Michael's comment as his eyes swept her. "Dudley's going to think he hit the jackpot."

Charlie glared at him. She was carrying his watch—she didn't feel like having it slide around on her arm while she ran.

"Is there something you want to say about me going running with *Tony*?"

"Nope."

Walking over to the nightstand between the beds, she set the watch down by the phone. His eyes tracked her.

She gave him another inimical look. "Good. Then I'd appreciate it if you'd just let me enjoy my run in peace."

"Whatever you want, babe."

Then Tony was at the door and the three (!) of them were heading for the roof.

The track ran along the perimeter of it, which was thirty stories high and provided an excellent view of the glowing skyline of down-town Charlotte. In the middle was a swimming pool, lounge chairs, and a few fake palm trees all decked out in white Christmas lights. There were a couple of people in the pool. Otherwise, the roof was deserted. Almost as soon as Charlie started to run, she felt the tired-ness and tension and, yes, even the fear, start to ebb away. The warm summer breeze smelled faintly of chlorine. The black sky and full moon and twinkling stars overhead seemed almost close enough to touch. Street sounds drifted up from below. There was an occasional laugh or splash from the swimmers in the pool.

"I hate it that you're caught up in this, of course, but I have to admit I was glad to get the chance to work with you again," Tony said as they rounded the far side turn for the eighteenth time. They'd been talking about the case in a desultory way without coming up with anything new. A seasoned runner herself, Charlie appreciated the fact that they were at the four and a half mile point and he wasn't even breathing hard yet. She also appreciated how good his lean, fit body looked in his shorts and tee. It made a nice change from his FBI agent suits, and she thought for what must have been the thousandth time that she was a fool if she didn't at least give this budding attraction between them a chance.

Of course, the fact that she was afflicted with the ghost from hell was quite a deterrent. Especially given the fact that he was within easy earshot, keeping pace without the slightest difficulty. Not that she would describe what he was doing as running, exactly. She wasn't even sure his feet were touching the ground. But he was indisputably there, glancing at her from time to time with mockery in his eyes.

"I'm glad to have the chance to work with you again, too," Charlie replied. It was absolutely true. The seeds of a promising relationship were there, she thought: they simply needed nurturing.

Hard to do when she had a ghost on a leash.

This is my life, and I owe it to myself to make an effort.

"Oh, yeah? I got the impression, last night, that you were kind of in a hurry to get rid of me."

And that would have been because of a blaring TV and a blast of hope that said ghost had managed to stay earthbound rather than move on to his just rewards.

"It's only—I believe in taking things slow." That wasn't really a lie. At least, it had been part of the reason she'd sent Tony swiftly on his way. Okay, a really tiny part.

"You're not seeing anybody right now?" he persisted.

Charlie ignored the slash of a pair of sky blue eyes in her direction. "No, I'm not."

She'd definitely said it a little too firmly. Tony didn't seem to notice, though. In fact, he smiled. "Me either. So maybe we could take it slow together."

A sky blue eye roll. Which Charlie pretended she didn't even see.

"Maybe," she replied, and Tony laughed.

"You sound like you might be a little bit gun-shy."

"Just a little," Charlie agreed.

"Some bad relationships, huh?"

Charlie nodded. "A few."

He chuckled ruefully. "I hear you. I've had my fair share of those, too."

They reached the five-mile mark and pulled up. They were both breathing hard by this time, and Charlie at least was feeling one hundred percent better as they headed toward the elevators.

"How about we start with dinner again, the first chance we get?" Tony was smiling at her as the elevator doors opened and they stepped inside. Returning his smile, Charlie registered how handsome he was. With his dark, even-featured face and hard, athletic body, he would make any right-minded woman drool. *Plus, he's sweet and smart and I like him a lot,* she thought.

By turning her back on the six-foot-three-inch, sardonic-looking ghost who leaned, arms crossed, against the back wall of the elevator, Charlie was able to concentrate on the real, live man with whom she would truly like to begin a real, live relationship.

"I'd like that," she said. Tony's eyes moved over her face. Then, to her surprise, he slid a hand around the back of her neck, pulled her closer, bent his head, and kissed her.

There was nothing about the kiss that fell under the heading "taking it slow." Instead, there was tons of tongue action, tons of heat. Getting into the spirit of it, Charlie kissed him back, and thoroughly enjoyed the pleasant little tingle of excitement that chased around inside her.

The ping of the elevator announced that they had reached their floor, and Tony reluctantly let her go.

Charlie smiled at him. And to hell with her glowering ghost, who had straightened to his should-have-been-intimidating full height and had squared his impressively broad shoulders and was looking at Tony with violence in his eyes.

She didn't flick so much as a glance in his direction. The crux of it was, she had her life to live. And she refused to let *him* throw her off. He was an affliction with which she had been saddled. What she had with Tony—what she might be able to have, if she let herself, and put some effort into it—was real.

The borrowed FBI agent/security guard glanced at her and Tony as they emerged from the elevator. Tony lifted a hand in greeting as they passed him, then waited a beat before whispering to Charlie,"I don't suppose you'd want to stop by my room for a candy bar from the mini-fridge?"

Despite the semi-hopeful tone, it was so obviously said with no expectation of having her take him up on it that Charlie smiled.

"No," she said.

"Got it. We're taking it slow."

They had reached her room by that time. Tony waited while she unlocked the door and walked inside.

"See ya," he said, smiling at her, the memory of that kiss there in his eyes.

It had been a very nice kiss. One she wouldn't mind repeating.

She smiled back at him.

"Good-night," she said, and he nodded and turned away. Then she closed the door—right in the face of her pissed-looking ghost.

Of course, she should have remembered that unless he wanted it to, closing a door on Michael did absolutely no good at all.

CHAPTER SIXTEEN

He walked right through it.

The look he gave her when he did should have made her shiver. It should have made her quake in her sneakers. He was in full badass mode, all hard-eyed and hard-jawed and radiating barely suppressed hostility. Add an orange jumpsuit and some chains, and he would have been every bit as scary as the death row convict she'd first met.

Only he was Michael to her now, and whatever he had or had not done in the past, and however menacing he might look in the present, he and she were way past the point where he could actually scare her. Tam's warning about having the wool pulled over her eyes notwith-standing, she was now as sure as it was possible to be that the threat Tam had been warning her against didn't emanate from Michael.

In fact, Charlie realized, she was absolutely convinced that he would never hurt her, even if he could. At least not physically.

In other ways? Well, that was a different matter.

He stopped just inside the door. With the next item on her agenda being a shower, she had moved no farther than the bathroom door-way. As he came through she turned to face him, so that they now stood way too close to each other in the narrow space that marked the entrance to the room.

She didn't like being reminded of how tall he was, of how much bigger he was than she. She didn't like having to look so far up to meet his gaze.

Her first impulse was to take a couple of steps back, so she wouldn't have to tilt her head so far. Then she thought, *To hell with that*, and stood her ground.

Chin up, arms folded, challenge in her eyes, Charlie waited for him to fire the first (verbal) shot. He didn't say a thing. Instead he simply looked at her.

With grim eyes and a tight mouth.

"I can do whatever I want. I don't need your permission," she snapped. And knew as soon as she said it that she should have kept her mouth shut and gone into the bathroom without a word. But she hadn't been able to do it. Something about the way he was looking at her made her feel guilty, like she needed to defend herself.

Which was complete baloney.

He still said nothing.

She narrowed her eyes at him. "Just so you know, I'm going to be dating Tony for the foreseeable future."

Still nothing.

"Damn it, you and I are not a couple. If I didn't have this horrible cosmic curse, I wouldn't even be able to see you. You wouldn't be here. Because, you know, you're *dead*."

"He turn you on?" Michael's voice was perfectly even. Without that gravelly undertone, from his voice alone she wouldn't have even suspected he was mad.

"Yes," she answered defiantly.

"If he turned you on, you'd be sleeping with him already."

"What, did you miss that part of Tony's and my *private* conversation? We're taking it slow."

"Oh, is that it?" He smiled. She knew what that mocking smile meant, and it sent fury sizzling through her veins.

"Okay, so maybe I didn't take it slow with you. Big deal. Bad decision. Anyway, I'm not even sure that the sex we had was real."

His smile got nastier. "Oh, it was real, Doc. Every little thing about it was real. You were on my side of the barrier that night. Remember how my shirt got wet when Laura leaned against me? That's because she and I are both as solid over here as you are right now over there. Remember me taking that knife in my back for you? That happened because I was able to cross the barrier for a second and be solid on the same side of the barrier as you. So yeah, when I fucked you, when you made that bad decision, you and I were both solid and on the same side of the barrier and it was real. And it was a big deal. Remember how many times you came? I do."

Lucky for her she wasn't prone to blushing, because, yes, she (unwillingly) remembered that, too. She also noticed something: he had called her Doc, which he rarely did now. Only, she deduced as she thought back, when he was seriously bent out of shape with her.

He added: "You really think Dudley can make you come like that?"

"Yes," she lied, caught herself as she was about to wet her lips, and clamped them together. His eyes were on her telltale mouth and some of the grimness had left them as she put an end to the (useless, infuriating) conversation by saying, "I'm going to take a shower."

Turning on her heel, she walked into the bathroom and closed the door. Gently. When what she actually wanted to do was slam it.

He stayed on his side. Not that she'd expected him to come barging in after her, but she was relieved when he didn't.

Too bad she had forgotten to bring her nightclothes into the bathroom with her. When she got out of the shower, she wrapped herself in a towel and studied her reflection in the mirror for a moment, less than pleased at what looked back at her. Then, because she knew he was out there, because sharing a room and a life and a sizzling, unwanted attraction with a man (?) meant that she actually cared what she looked like when she was around him no matter how much she might want to pretend to herself (and him) that she didn't, she muttered a curse under her breath and whipped the towel off her head and blew her hair dry until it curved soft and smooth around her shoulders. She rubbed lotion into her thirsty skin. She brushed her teeth, and even applied cherry Chapstick because she wanted her lips to be smooth in the morning (and, yes, all right, to give them a little flattering color). After that, after there was nothing left for her to do that wouldn't look too obvious, she discovered that she had the option of putting on her sweaty workout clothes again or of walking into the bedroom wrapped in a towel to retrieve her nightgown and robe from her suitcase.

For a moment she hesitated. Then she thought, *Screw it.*

When she walked into the bedroom, it was to find Michael stretched out fully dressed on the bed closest to the window. He appeared lost in thought, and whatever they were he didn't seem to be enjoying them particularly: he was frowning, and his mouth was tight. His eyes flicked her way, widened. She had on a white hotel towel, standard issue, and it was wrapped around her in perfectly adequate fashion, covering her from approximately the armpits to the tops of her thighs. He would have seen more of her if she'd been wearing a bathing suit. Still, there was something about slim, tanned legs and a hint of cleavage and bare shoulders and arms emerging from a towel that made her feel ridiculously self-conscious. His eyes stayed glued to her, and his frown smoothed away. She didn't say a word. Instead she walked (as opposed to stomped) to her suitcase, which was on the little folding suitcase stand at the foot of her bed, opened it, and started digging down for her PJs.

She couldn't help it if she could see him perfectly well even if she wasn't deliberately looking at him. She couldn't help it if the damned man (?) was drop-dead sexy enough to make thoughts of doing him almost impossible to keep from popping into her mind at odd moments (like now). She couldn't help it if said thoughts made her body tighten and burn.

But she could get mad at him all over again.

The merest suggestion of a smile touched his mouth. "You want to make nice with me, you could try dropping the towel."

She shot him a withering look. "In your dreams."

His smile widened. But she didn't care, because she'd found what she was looking for. Turning her back on him, she retraced her steps to the bathroom. She could feel his eyes on her every step of the way.

It was unfortunate that her favorite blue bathrobe had been too bulky to fit in her suitcase. Because the silky pale peach one that matched her silky pale peach nightie was a lot slinkier than she had realized when she packed it. It had long sleeves instead of the nightie's spaghetti straps, and it ended at mid-thigh instead of at the tops of her thighs like the nightie did, but the shimmery silk was thin, and clung because she was still faintly damp, and when she tied its silk ribbon of a belt around her waist it left way too little to the imagination.

When she'd been packing her PJs, she hadn't yet totally gotten her head around the concept that the ghost from hell was going to be seeing her in them on a nightly basis.

Reality bites.

Her only option was to wrap a towel around herself over the robe, and that was too ridiculous even to think about.

She thought *Screw it* again, and walked out into the bedroom.

Michael's eyes slid over her. As she headed around the end of *her* bed—i.e., the one he wasn't on—she watched them go dark and hot, and to her annoyance felt herself going all dark and hot inside, too.

The good news, she told herself savagely as she started to pull the covers back prior to climbing into bed, was that no matter how worked up either one of them got, sex wasn't going to happen.

"Okay, you're killing me here." His voice was husky. His eyes hadn't left her since she'd walked out of the bathroom. It occurred to her as she saw the look on his face that when she'd turned her back to him and leaned over the bed to free the far side of the covers, then tossed the decorative pillows to the floor, maybe he'd gotten more of a view than she'd meant to give him.

The possibility made her cross. "So close your eyes."

"Feeling a little bitchy, babe? I've noticed before that kissing Dudley has that effect on you."

"Ever think it might be *you* who has that effect on me?"

"Nah. We both know what kind of effect I have on you. You ever have phone sex?"

That was so unexpected she shot him a suspicious look. "No."

He had turned on his side and was watching her with his head propped on a hand. "That's where I tell you all the dirty things I want to do to you and you tell me all the dirty things you want to do to me and we both get off without either one of us laying a hand on the other," he explained helpfully.

She might not have had it, but she knew what it was. At the erotic images that flooded her mind in the wake of his words, her knees went weak.

"Not happening, Casper."

She climbed into bed, and pulled the covers up to her chin, and turned off the light.

His voice came out of the dark. "Sleeping in your robe tonight?"

Damn it, she'd forgotten to take it off. There was just enough light filtering in around the edges of the curtains to allow her to see the big, dark shape of him. Which meant that he could probably see her, too. Which meant that she was going to be taking her robe off under the covers, and dropping it discreetly off the far side of the bed.

Which she did.

"Dudley doesn't turn you on."

Punching a pillow into submission, she turned onto her side with her back to him and laid her head on it. "How would you know?"

"I know what you look like when you're turned on. And you don't look like that when you're kissing him."

"I'm not having this conversation with you. In fact, I'm not having any conversation with you. I'm going to sleep."

"If he doesn't turn you on when you're kissing him, he's not going to turn you on in bed."

She rolled so that she was facing him. "Damn it, Michael—"

"You don't want to have a relationship with a guy who doesn't get you hot."

"Are *you* giving *me* relationship advice?"

"If that's what you want to call it. Bottom line is, you deserve a guy who gets you hot, babe."

"I'm not talking to you anymore. Good-night." She closed her eyes.

"You like sex, Charlie. You know you do. You don't want to shortchange yourself in that department."

Actually, most of the sex she'd had could be classified as lukewarm rather than hot. If she had to come up with an adjective to describe it, it would be *fine. The sex was fine* would cover almost every relationship she'd ever had.

It didn't cover sex with Michael, though. In fact, it was about the last description she would use to cover sex with him.

Sex with Michael was not fine. It was—oh, no, she wasn't going there. Not even in her thoughts.

But her body went there anyway. She could feel its hungry tightening, feel her blood starting to steam.

"There's more to a relationship than sex," she growled.

He laughed. "You keep telling yourself that, babe."

Her eyes popped open of their own accord.

"Mutual interests. Mutual respect. Common goals. A shared life plan." She enumerated the building blocks of a good adult relationship.

"If I could come over there and put my mouth on your breast and my hand between your legs, I guarantee you wouldn't give a damn about any of that."

As her breath caught and her pulse rate surged and her bones liquefied, she sat straight up in bed and glared at him through the darkness. "Stop. I mean it."

"What? We're having a discussion. You know, you make your point, I make mine."

"I don't want to talk to you."

"I can think of lots of things I'd rather be doing to you, too—like, oh, I don't know, getting you naked and pushing up inside you and making you come for me."

Caught by surprise by an undulating wave of desire that was hot enough to make her press her thighs together and squirm a little, Charlie fought to keep her breathing under control so her tormentor wouldn't have a clue.

"Listen, you jackass, if you don't shut up I'll—" Since she couldn't think of anything that he might reasonably believe she would do to threaten him with, she broke off until something occurred to her. "Go knock on Kaminsky's door and tell her the air-conditioning's not working in my room and ask to sleep in her spare bed."

She could sense rather than see his smile. "And there you go: you just proved my point. You're not threatening to run to Dudley, because you're half afraid I'll do something that'll make you have to follow through, and you won't do it. And you won't do it because you don't want to make him think you want to sleep with him, because you don't, and that would be because he doesn't turn you on all that much. If he did, you'd already be over there in bed with him."

"That is a total crock."

"Anyway, even if you did run to Sugar Buns for protection, I'd come with you. Remember that short leash you've got me on? The only difference would be that with Sugar Buns there you wouldn't be able to answer back when I said dirty things to you."

"You know what? I don't have to listen to this. I'm going to sleep." She flopped back down and turned her back to him again.

"You wearing any panties under that nightgown?"

Charlie practically ground her teeth, but she didn't reply.

"Nah, I already know you're not. Tell the truth, babe: did you bend over that bed on purpose, to drive me crazy with a glimpse of your sweet—"

"Enough!" Charlie catapulted into a sitting position again and practically shot napalm at him with her eyes. "You want to talk? Is that it? Fine, I'm in. Why don't you tell me about"—it took her a second, but then she had a topic that she felt was pretty much a sure bet to redirect his thoughts—"your watch?"

There was a moment's silence. "What about it?"

Hah. She had him. She could hear the difference in his tone. "Where'd you get it? Was it a gift? What's with the engraving on the back? That kind of thing." She said it very much in the spirit of taking the battle to the enemy.

He rolled over onto his back. She could see his hard profile, see the firm musculature of his chest and the flat plane of his abdomen and the bulge in his jeans and the powerful length of his legs, all in outline against the curtains. *God, I want him.* The thought came out of nowhere, and she was helpless against it. If he'd been alive, if he'd been a man instead of a ghost, she knew as well as she knew anything that she wouldn't have been able to stop herself from crawling into bed with him and wrapping herself around him and letting him do anything he wanted to her while she sated herself with that hard body. But since he was a ghost, since doing what she was dying to do wasn't possible (which was, she told herself, a good thing), she firmly ignored the hot, insistent throbbing deep inside her body and the too rapid beating of her heart and every other physical manifestation of her inner-slut-where-he-was-concerned. Instead, she was going to take advantage of this opportunity to try to get some answers from him. Even if she still wasn't a hundred percent sure whether she could believe what he told her or not.

"Some buddies gave it to me," he said.

"What kind of buddies?"

"Marine buddies. Look, I don't feel like talking about my watch right now. What the hell difference does it make at this point anyway?"

"Oh, so we can talk about what you want but not about what I want? Is that it?" Crawling to the end of her bed, Charlie retrieved her laptop from its compartment in the top of her suitcase and clambered back up to the head of her bed with it. "So how about we don't talk at all, then?"

"What are you doing?" he asked as she pulled pillows into position, propped herself up against them, opened her laptop case, and turned her computer on. The soft glow of the screen allowed her to see that he was giving her a narrow-eyed look.

"I was sleepy, but now I'm not. So I'm checking something out." She clicked through to the file she was interested in.

"What?"

"None of your business." It was Michael's file, the digitalized combination of the boxes of papers and the Internet records and the medical and psychological assessments and everything else with his name on it that had been sent to Wallens Ridge when he had been acquired by her as a research subject. She'd had everything scanned and uploaded and cataloged into a master file which was kept on her office computer, and which had also been downloaded to her laptop for convenience, just as she had done with the files of all of her research subjects. Everything that was officially known about each of their lives, and their crimes, was in there somewhere.

Charlie located the section she was interested in, and started scrolling through the images.

"That's my damned file." Michael had rolled to his feet and was now looming over her as he frowned down at the screen.

"You're right, it is."

As the page she sought came up, Charlie sucked in her breath: three photographs recording a silver man's watch, its wristband

twisted and broken, the glass covering its face shattered, with a terrifying brown staining that she knew was dried blood darkening the
cracks and crevices. Taken from different angles against a white background, the photographs were labeled State's Exhibit 27A.

Reaching out, Charlie turned on the bedside lamp and picked up
from the nightstand the man's watch she had worn all day. Then she
held it up beside the screen, comparing the object to the images. As
far as she could tell, the two watches were identical.

The pictures on the screen did not show the back of the face of the
broken watch, where the words *Semper Fi* had been engraved on the
watch in her hand.

"Checking out my story?" There was an element of careful control to Michael's voice. She glanced up at him, too engrossed in what
she was doing to register the look in his eyes.

"The watches appear to be identical." Her tone made it a concession. She once again mentally checked off every similarity she could
find: brand, features, size. "Of course, any engraving on the back of
the face on this watch"—she tapped the screen—"is concealed by the
angle of the pictures."

"There's no engraving on the back of that watch. I got a real good
look at it at my trial. Like I told the stupid motherfuckers then, and
like I'm telling you now, it ain't mine."

"Citizen men's 860 stainless steel watch, found beside the body of
victim number seven, Candace Hartnell," Charlie read aloud. She had
shifted into researcher mode. Her earlier tiredness—and arousal—
was forgotten as she concentrated on the file. At the bottom of the
page was a blue, underlined cross-reference number.

As she clicked on it, Michael settled himself beside her on the bed.

A moment later a video file labeled State's Exhibit 27B came up
on the screen. She clicked on the play arrow. For a second the screen
went black.

Then Charlie found herself looking at a grainy picture of Michael
smiling a slow and seductive smile at a pretty dark-haired woman in
a bar.

CHAPTER SEVENTEEN

It could have been any bar: dark gleaming wood, a long mirror fronted by a jumble of bottles and glasses, a heavyset bartender filling a mug with beer from a tap. Busy, with every bar stool occupied and more patrons crowding up to the counter. Dimly lit. Blue-collar and rowdy.

Charlie found herself absolutely mesmerized by what she was watching. There was no sound, only poor-quality footage taken from a security camera above the bar. Other patrons were visible, but Charlie had no interest in them. Her attention was all on the extraordinarily handsome blond guy as he laughed and chatted and bought drinks for pretty, twenty-five-year-old Candace Hartnell, whom Charlie recognized from the photos in Michael's file. She was obviously in the process of being swept off her feet. He was knocking back drinks himself at a rate that told her he was feeling no pain, and chasing the booze with an occasional handful of peanuts scooped up from the dish on the crowded counter. Watching the way Candace looked at him, the way she smiled, the way she first laid her hand over his and then playfully trailed her fingers down his muscular arm, Charlie saw with no surprise that the interest was at least as high on her part as it was on his. Finally, when he put his hand somewhere out of range of the camera, which Charlie thought from the angle of both their bodies must be her thigh, and in response she leaned toward him to whisper in his ear, Charlie could tell she was ready to leave with him whenever he wanted. The footage practically crackled with heat, but it was Michael who captured her attention. This younger, happier, deliberately charming version of him made her breath catch and her heart ache a little.

At least, until she recollected that the young woman he was using his devastating good looks to seduce so successfully would be dead before morning, her nude body found horribly slashed and mutilated in the tangled sheets of her own blood-soaked bed.

Once she remembered that, it was almost like watching a python toy with a mouse. Gritting her teeth, Charlie pushed emotion as far away as she could, and set herself to looking for details: Michael was dressed exactly as he was right now, white tee and jeans, and—she was willing to bet, although she couldn't see his feet—boots. The same outfit he was presently wearing, she was almost sure. On his wrist, plain to see and absolutely unmistakable in the context of what she now knew, was his watch. She looked at it closely. It appeared identical to both the intact one she was holding, and the broken one in the photos.

As she watched, video Michael rolled to his feet, snagging Candace with an arm around her waist and pulling her up with him. Laughing, she leaned into him while he nuzzled her neck. Then, close as a stamp to an envelope, she walked out of the frame with him. He seemed slightly unsteady on his feet. She was clingy and had both arms around his waist.

Candace Hartnell was slashed to death later that night. Early the following morning, Michael Garland was arrested and subsequently charged with the crime. Shortly thereafter he was linked with six previous knife murders of young women. The night she was watching had been the last night of freedom in his life: the five subsequent years had been spent in an assortment of jails and prisons. Charlie knew all that, knew, too, the overwhelming nature of the evidence pointing to his guilt that had been presented at his trial. The video she'd just watched, for example, was damning. It even showed him wearing the watch that had been found tangled in the covers with Candace Hartnell's dead body: State Exhibit 27A.

Only Charlie was holding an identical watch in her hand. One, moreover, that had been identified as belonging to Michael by the Mariposa Police Department, which had arrested him hours after Candace Hartnell's murder and had presumably taken it from him then as intake material. Michael had correctly described the engraving on the back to her before he'd ever gotten a look at it. It was sized to fit his larger than average wrist, and he insisted that it, and not the one in the pictures, was his.

That, to Charlie, raised at least a flicker of reasonable doubt as to his guilt.

Clicking off the video, she glanced his way. He was lying on his back beside her now, his head on a pillow, his hands laced behind his head. Instead of watching the video, he'd been staring up at the ceiling. As if he felt her eyes on him, he looked at her.

"After that, I took her back to her house and went psycho on her. Raped her. Cut her to ribbons with my handy-dandy hunting knife that I subsequently got rid of where no one could find it. Only I was too damned dumb not to get myself arrested, so I got nailed for her murder and six other murders besides. Does that answer the question you're getting ready to ask me?" His tone was *almost* casual. His eyes were savage.

Charlie sighed. She'd read those details in his file when he'd first become a subject of her study and, up until less than a week ago, had seen no reason to question them. Now she discovered that she was ready to consider other possibilities.

"You want to tell me what really happened?"

"What, you don't believe I went psycho and killed that girl? That's the conclusion a jury of my peers reached. They were so damned sure of it I got sentenced to death."

Tired of holding his watch, she slid it onto her arm. His eyes tracked the gesture, narrowed.

"I want to hear the truth, whatever it is," she said.

His lips compressed. "Does it matter? At this point, what the hell does it change? Unless you've got some cure for dead I don't know about."

"Michael. Please. Tell me what happened."

The look he gave her glittered with anger and frustration and a whole host of other emotions Charlie didn't even try to analyze.

"You want the truth? Here it is: I had a few drinks, I picked up a girl in a bar, I went home with her, we got it on. No rape involved. Hell, I never raped a woman in my life. When I woke up, it was about four in the morning. She was asleep—not dead, no blood, not a hair on her head harmed; in fact, last time she had anything to say she gave me to understand that she was feeling pretty good. I wasn't in any mood for the whole morning after thing so I put my clothes on and left. No, I didn't wake her up to say goodbye. Hell, at that point I couldn't even remember her name. But she was *alive.* So I'm driving home, and I guess I was speeding or something because I got pulled over by this damned little pissant of a cop. He arrested me on suspicion of drunk driving—no Breathalyzer or anything, but he said I flunked his damned field sobriety test, which I didn't. I guess he could smell the booze on me. So he takes me in and they lock me up, and while I'm asleep in their damned cell somebody comes across Candace—I found out her name pretty quick—sliced to pieces in her bed." He grimaced. "After that, things went downhill on a greased slide."

Charlie was remembering the evidence. "They found your DNA all over her, and her DNA all over you, which I guess makes sense if you'd just slept with her. There were dozens of eyewitnesses to you leaving the bar with her, as well as that video footage. Your watch—a watch that appeared identical to yours—was found in bed with her dead body, looking like it was ripped off your arm and broken as she fought for her life. According to all the evidence, you were the last person to see her alive. Plus, if I recall, she had your skin under her fingernails and you had scratches on your body."

"The scratches were on my back! She was wild as hell, and when we were having sex, she scratched my damned back! That's the kind of thing the prosecutors did: they twisted everything to make it sound like I was guilty. But I didn't kill her. Why the hell would I kill her?"

At something he must have seen in Charlie's face, his brows snapped together. "Oh, that's right: I'm a murderous psychopath. Who needs a reason?"

"Serial killers are compelled to kill," Charlie explained with automatic precision. "The compulsion is their reason."

The look he gave her was grim. "Like I said, she was alive when I left her."

Charlie clicked back through the file for the information she wanted. "Her body was found at eight a.m. by her sister. Time of death was estimated at three to four hours previous to that." She frowned. "That means she was killed between four and five a.m."

"Like I said, I woke up around four and left her house—with her alive in it—as soon as I got my clothes on. Probably around 4:10."

She was scrolling through his file. "You were logged in to the jail at 5:30 a.m."

He made an impatient sound. "That dick of a cop kept me on the side of the road for a good hour."

"If you left Candace Hartnell alive at 4:10, that means somebody else had to have entered her house and killed her within the next fifty minutes." It might be unlikely, but it wasn't impossible, Charlie decided.

"Yeah, I worked that out." His voice was dry.

Having run through the pages of photos of the evidence and not found what she sought, Charlie frowned. "What about the clothes you were wearing? I don't see them here, but they should have been introduced as evidence. The crime scene was apparently extremely bloody. You should have been covered in blood."

"You'd think, wouldn't you?" he said with disgust. "These are the clothes I was wearing—at least, the ghost version. Last civilian clothes I ever wore, except for a suit the lawyers scared up for my trial. They weren't any more covered with blood when I got arrested than they are right now. The prosecution claimed it was because I killed her while nude, then showered, then dressed."

Charlie considered: if there was no blood on his clothes, then the prosecution's theory was the only one that fit. "You were convicted of killing six other women over the two and a half years previous to Candace Hartnell's murder. How many of *them* did you sleep with?"

He snorted derisively. "None. Not one. Never even laid eyes on any of them. I swear to God. Yeah, I know they said my DNA was all over them and all that shit, but that's not possible. Either one of those testing labs fucked up big-time, or somebody framed me. Why? How the hell do I know? Maybe some asshole cop or FBI agent wanted to clear up some old cases and I was the best option they had for sticking 'em on somebody. Or maybe somebody didn't like me. Like I said, I don't know."

Charlie watched him carefully. "Every single murder was within a four-hour drive of where you lived."

"I don't know what to tell you."

"The murders started right after you got out of the Marine Corps, and continued over the entire period between then and your arrest. And you didn't have an alibi for any of the nights those women were killed."

He sighed. "I did have an alibi for some of them. I was living with a girlfriend for something like the last six months before Candace Hartnell was killed. We broke up the day before I hit that bar and the shit hit the fan. On the nights of two of the other murders I know for sure I was asleep in bed with Jasmine. Hell, I'd just opened my garage and I was trying to get that business going. I was working maybe eighty hours a week and I was tired—too tired to run around slicing up women in the middle of the night. Only the damned cops messed with Jasmine until they got her to agree it was possible that I snuck out of bed while she was asleep, killed those women, then got back into bed before she woke up in the morning. Which was total shit. But she was pissed at me anyway because of the breakup, and then they scared her to death of me. They kept telling her, 'You've been sleeping with a serial killer. Do you know how lucky you are to be alive?' That kind of crap."

Charlie glanced back at the file. "So why'd you and Jasmine break up?"

"Not because she was afraid of me. Nothing like that. She wanted to get married, and I didn't. Hell, I didn't even mean to start living with her. She just sort of moved herself in."

Charlie looked at him again. And realized only as she did so that she had been deliberately *not* looking at him as he talked about his girlfriend. She hated to admit it even to herself, but ever since she and he had started getting, uh, better acquainted, she'd been mentally poking around the fact that he'd had a girlfriend at the time of his arrest. The question that had burned unacknowledged in the back of her mind was, had he loved her?

From the tone of what he'd said, the answer was no, he hadn't.

Not that it makes any difference, Charlie told herself hurriedly.

"You got no call to be jealous of Jasmine, babe."

His words were so on the money that they almost made Charlie jump.

"What?" Her eyes flared at him indignantly. "I am *not* jealous of your girlfriend. You've got to be kidding me."

The hardness that had been hovering around his eyes and mouth relaxed as he gave her a slow, teasing grin.

"*Ex*-girlfriend. And I told you I could read your face like a neon sign."

"You are the most conceited—" She broke off, flustered, hoping he couldn't tell. The more she protested, the more convinced he would be that he was right, she knew. So she shot him a withering glance, and went for the best distraction she could think of: the DVD that the Mariposa PD had sent along with the (his?) watch. She had transferred it from her purse to her laptop case when she'd been packing for this trip, and now, with Michael beside her so that she could gauge his reaction to whatever was on there, was the moment to watch it. Whether or not Michael was a serial killer was something she needed to have settled in her own mind before this . . . this *connection* that seemed to be growing between them went any further. Most of the time, whether he was being charming or annoying or overprotective or sexy as hell, she didn't think about what he had done, and that, she decided, was due to the sheer force of his personality. But when she did, when she actually allowed herself to remember the seven women he had been convicted of slaughtering, the chill of fear and revulsion that went through her was enough to stop her in her tracks, enough to make her think she needed to get out of the way and let divine justice take its course where he was concerned.

"What's that?" he asked as she inserted the DVD into her laptop. She told him. Neither one of them said anything as the screen sprang to life. The first shot was an identifying one: date and time, which placed the footage as running from 9:31 to 9:35 a.m. on the morning after Michael had left the bar with Candace Hartnell.

Then the camera was focused on Michael—the same younger, video Michael from the bar security tape. He was now seated in a small, gray police interrogation room, dressed exactly as he had been the previous night, exactly as he was right at that moment on the bed beside her, as a matter of fact. Only the smiling seducer of the bar footage was replaced by a still to-die-for hot, but now obviously angry, man with bloodshot eyes and a night's worth of stubble. Each wrist was cuffed to an arm of the straight-backed metal chair on one side of a small metal table, and almost the first thing Charlie noticed was that the watch he'd been wearing the night before was missing.

Which didn't mean anything, she reminded herself as her pulse quickened a little in response. Whether the watch had been taken from him at the jail or whether he had left it behind at the crime scene, by this time it would have been missing in either case.

"So what did Candace do to piss you off?" The blue-uniformed cop on the opposite side of the table was leaning forward in his chair, his forearms resting on the smooth metal surface as he stared at Michael. The angle of the camera, which was positioned to capture the person being interrogated, recorded the cop's beefy back, and the left side of a florid face beneath a close-cropped cap of reddish hair.

"What? Who the hell is Candace?" Glaring, Michael rattled his cuffs against the metal arm rails. "Look, I got things to do. How about you tell me how much the fine is and let me pay it and I'll be on my way."

"The lady you were with last night." Ignoring the last part of Michael's speech, the cop looked at him intently. "We both know what women can be like. She must have pissed you off pretty good. What'd she do?"

Michael's eyes narrowed. "I don't know what the hell you're talking about."

"Oh, come on, now, Mr. Garland. We both know you do. Why don't you just tell me what happened? Whatever the reason was, if you tell me about it now, I guarantee things'll go a lot easier for you."

A commotion in the hall caused both men to glance in the direction of the open door. A split second later, a woman burst through it, crying, "Michael! Oh, my God, Michael, what did you do?"

The woman was in maybe her mid-twenties, with a pretty, sulky-looking face enhanced by lots of mascara and bold scarlet lips, a riot of long black hair, and a va-va-voom figure in tiny shorts and a low-cut tank top.

"Jasmine!" Michael sat straight up as she flew toward him, her high-heeled sandals clattering on the industrial gray floor. Before she could reach him, the cop behind the table leaped to his feet and interposed himself between her and Michael, and another cop barreled through the door to catch her by the arm.

"Sorry about that! She got away from me—" the second cop said to the first as, drowning out the rest of what he had to say, Jasmine screamed at Michael, "You fucked another woman? We're broken up one day and already you're out fucking another woman? You . . ." The string of expletives she let loose with made the florid-faced cop whose chest she had run into, and who was at that moment backing her toward the door while the other cop pulled her in that direction with a hand on her arm and another on her waist, wince.

Charlie couldn't see Michael—the cops and the woman blocked the camera's view of him—but in the background she could hear him growl, "Jesus H. Christ, what the hell did you bring *her* here for?"

"Miss Lipsitz! You can't talk to him!" said the cop, urgently pulling Jasmine out the door.

Jasmine strained to get away. Every bit of her focus was on Michael. "You fucked her and then you killed her! That's what they're saying! Some bitch you picked up in a bar! Is it true?"

Although the camera's view of him was still blocked by the beefy cop who was shoving Jasmine out the door, Michael could be heard saying, "What the hell?"

Jasmine was once again screaming expletives as she was forced into the hallway and the door was shut on her.

The camera had an unimpeded view of Michael then. He was staring at the beefy cop, who'd turned back to look at him.

"That girl I was with last night . . . she's dead?" Michael asked slowly.

The cop didn't say anything. But even Charlie, watching grainy footage on a laptop, could read the answer in his body language: *yes*.

"I want a lawyer," Michael said. And that was it. The footage ended, and the screen went blank.

"Like I said, after that it went downhill fast," real, live (well, dead) Michael said. Charlie looked at him without really seeing him: she was too preoccupied with analyzing what she had just viewed. The news that Candace Hartnell was dead had definitely seemed to come as a surprise to him. Could he have been acting? Her best judgment said *no*, but she realized that she couldn't be sure. The psychology of serial killers was complex enough to preclude her being able to count on the veracity of his reaction, and her connection to him was too personal to allow her to count on her own reading of it.

"So that was Jasmine," she mused, and only realized that she'd said it aloud when Michael grinned at her. Immediately she wanted to bite her tongue.

"She was cute," he said. "And even fun for a while. Not the brightest, but then, I didn't keep her around to perform brain surgery on me."

"I bet." Charlie couldn't help it. That bit of sarcasm simply came out.

His grin widened. "Like I said, you got no reason to be jealous of Jasmine, babe."

Charlie gave him a look, decided she wasn't going there, and concentrated again on the evidence: the watch was the key.

She said as much, then added, "If that watch they found at the crime scene wasn't yours, and if that could be proved because it didn't have the engraving on the back that yours did, wasn't there anybody who could testify that it *wasn't* your watch because *your* watch had *Semper Fi* on the back of it?"

His eyes returned to the ceiling. "Everybody who could testify to that is dead."

"Everybody?"

"Yup."

Clearly, Charlie saw, she was touching on what was, for him, a sensitive area. Or else he was smart enough—and he *was* smart enough—to know that he could get around her by pretending it was a sensitive area. That she was so *softhearted* she wouldn't probe further if she thought the questions she was asking caused him pain.

Yeah, to hell with that.

"You want to elucidate on that a little?" she asked.

He smiled faintly as his gaze slanted her way. "You trying to confuse me with that big word?"

That didn't fly, either. "Michael."

The smile vanished. "The watch was given to me by members of my unit, who were killed in Afghanistan, all right? They're the only ones who knew what was engraved on it."

From the sudden tension in his jaw, she could tell he didn't want to talk about it. And, damn it, she discovered that she *was* too softhearted to push him to a place that was obviously (unless he was very, very good at faking it, which was possible) hurtful to him.

Kicking herself for her own lack of toughness, she moved on to something else that had occurred to her. But now that it had, it loomed large as a mountain right smack in the middle of the winding road she was traveling on the way to maybe actually believing him.

Her eyes skewered him. Her tone sharpened until it teetered on the edge of being accusing. "So tell me this: if you didn't kill those women, then how did you wind up in Spookville when you died?"

His expression turned grim. "Babe, I never said I didn't deserve to be where I was. What I said was, I didn't kill those women."

Charlie frowned at him. "So what in the world did you do to deserve Spookville?"

He shook his head at her. "I'm done talking about what I did or didn't do. The only reason I even told you any of this is because it pisses me off when every now and then you start looking at me like you think I'm Jack the Ripper. What it comes down to at this point is, either you believe me or you don't. Your call."

He sat up, and she was surprised at how physically close that brought him. As big as he was, he took up way more than his fair share of space on the bed, and her field of vision was suddenly full of his broad shoulders and wide chest. Their arms almost brushed, and she could see the muscles flexing in his, and in his torso beneath his shirt. They were both sitting on top of the covers, but she had her legs tucked beneath her and her laptop in her lap while his long legs in their jeans and boots stretched out almost to the end of the bed. He looked as solid and alive as it was possible for a man to look. Charlie was conscious of her idiot heart speeding up again just from his proximity.

"So?" he said, and she knew what he was asking.

She had to look up to meet his eyes. As she did, they darkened, and his mouth firmed. Searching his hard, handsome face, she realized that she had to consider the possibility that her original diagnosis of him might have been influenced by the fact that she had known he was a convicted serial killer. If she turned the thing on its head, if at the time of diagnosis she had been introduced to him as a normal, law-abiding citizen, would she have concluded that he was a charismatic psychopath capable of the ultimate in horrific violence?

Or would she simply have seen a gorgeous guy with a charming smile?

At this point, it was impossible to know.

"Okay, I believe you," she told him.

His eyes slid over her face. One side of his mouth quirked up in a wry half-smile. "With reservations, huh?"

He'd said he could read her face like a neon sign: here was more proof of it. She was still mentally sorting through the factors for and against his version of what had happened with Candace Hartnell.

"I haven't seen any overwhelming evidence that you're innocent," she told him honestly. "On the other hand, I've seen enough to make me think you could be."

"Your faith in me is staggering, babe." The dryness in his voice made her smile a little.

"What we need to do is find somebody who is willing to testify that this watch"—her voice was brisk with determination as she touched the watch on her arm—"is yours. Somebody who knows about the engraving on the back."

He smiled at her, a slow and ultimately dazzling smile that made her breath catch and her toes curl. Nobody, but nobody, looked like Michael when he smiled like that.

"There goes that savior complex of yours kicking into gear again," he said. "We don't need to do shit. There's no point in it. I'm dead, remember? Whether I'm innocent or not doesn't matter a damn anymore to anybody but you."

"But . . ." Knowing that he was right defeated her.

"You got to go with your gut here, babe. What's it gonna be?"

Looking into those sky blue eyes, Charlie silently acknowledged that for quite some time she had been having trouble picturing him as a merciless slaughterer of young women. It just didn't fit with the man she was getting to know, she felt, pretty well.

But there was no way to be sure. All she could do was go with—not so much her gut, she realized, as her heart.

Her stupid, soft, and way-too-vulnerable heart.

"I thought so," he said with satisfaction, and she knew he had once again successfully read on her face what she was thinking.

"Fine," she told him. "I believe you."

"You could sound happier about it."

"I probably could." If her response was tart, it was because she was disgusted with herself for being such a sucker where he was concerned. No good could come of it. She knew that, and was a sucker for him anyway.

As he watched her face his eyes darkened. Then his head bent, and she felt a shivery little thrill of anticipation when she realized that he was going to kiss her.

Despite all the reasons why she shouldn't, she closed her eyes and tilted her lips up to meet his. Meanwhile, her heart pounded and her pulse raced and her stomach fluttered like a thousand butterflies were taking wing in it.

Then her lips got hit with the slightest of electric tingles and he said *"Fuck"* and her eyes flew open.

To find his gorgeous blue eyes mere inches away, blazing down into hers.

In a flash she realized what had happened: for a moment there, they had both forgotten that he was nothing more than a spirit with no physical substance whatsoever. He'd bent his head to kiss her like he'd thought he actually could, and she'd lifted her mouth to his like it was really going to happen.

"Yeah," he said in grim acknowledgment of reality, and got off the bed. He was already on the move when he told her over his shoulder, "I'm going for a walk."

"You can't," she began in instant warning, reminding him that they were tethered.

"I won't forget that I'm on a fifty-foot leash. If nothing else, I'll probably pace back and forth in front of your door. You should go to sleep." His eyes slid over her, and then a quick, wry smile touched his mouth. "You look sexy as hell in that pretty nightgown, by the way. Not being able to do a thing about it is driving me out of my mind."

That was when she realized that ever since she'd clicked on the bedside lamp he'd gotten an up-close and personal view of her slinky little gown with its loose, cleavage-baring neckline that gave the impression of being barely held up by satiny spaghetti straps. A quick glance down at herself confirmed it: the shimmery peach slip clung to her full breasts and lay whisper close to her narrow waist and flat stomach, leaving little to the imagination before, lower down, her laptop obstructed his view of her slender legs. Her nipples stood up in taut supplication beneath the thin silk. He had to know, as she did, that they were like that because of him.

"I want you like hell," he said, his tone making it almost a throwaway line.

Then he strode out of view.

Charlie just sat there looking after him. Her lips still tingled in anticipation of that thwarted kiss. Her heart still pounded. Her pulse still raced. Deep inside, her body pulsed and burned. But even though she was now almost entirely convinced of his innocence, the hard truth was that the potent attraction that sizzled between them was still as impossible as it had ever been. If he was innocent—and she realized that on some deep, cellular level she had felt he was almost since he had died—that was terrifying in a whole new way. Because it meant there was now nothing to stop her from falling absolutely head over heels in love with him. Except for the fact that the only way falling in love with Michael could end was with her own heartbreak.

Because he was still dead, and there was still no future in it.

It took Charlie a long time to fall asleep.

CHAPTER EIGHTEEN

The next few days were grueling. Michael seemed preoccupied, and Charlie was glad that he didn't have a whole lot to say. Tony was sweet to her, but there was no time even to work in a run and they were rarely alone. The pace of the investigation was such that they were simply too busy to pursue a personal relationship further at that point, for which she was both glad and sorry. Glad because Michael—get real, her feelings for Michael—presented a definite obstacle, although she told herself fiercely that she was a fool to let that happen. Sorry since she really *did* want to pursue a personal relationship with Tony, because he was exactly the kind of guy she could see herself having a long-standing, mutually loving and supportive relationship with. Kaminsky and Buzz were their usual bickering selves, but nobody had time for much conversation that wasn't directly related to the case. As the hours flew by without anything turning up in the way of solid leads, frustration threatened to set in. All of them were too aware of the ticking clock. Like the others, Charlie couldn't rid herself of the tension-producing certainty that if they didn't succeed in discovering the identity of the Gingerbread Man soon, more innocent victims were going to die. That was enough to keep her pushing doggedly ahead.

Eric Riva was the first known recipient of the Gingerbread Man's *You can't catch me* letter. When they stopped by to interview him at his office at the *Charlotte Observer* he was glad to walk them through the circumstances surrounding the series of articles he had written on the Group Three (crossbow) murders two years previously. They had been published before he was contacted by the Gingerbread Man (which had happened in conjunction with the Group Four— propeller—murders) and before anyone had even realized that the killings were the work of a serial killer. Riva's focus in the articles had been on the three victims, and included detailed accounts of each of their lives before the crime, and, in the aftermath, the effect the crime had had on the murdered boys' families, as well as the survivor and his family. The articles, which Charlie and the others had read before meeting with Riva, packed a real emotional punch. Riva agreed with them that the articles were probably what had prompted the Ginger- bread Man to send him the letter in the first place. Riva'd had unusual access to inside information on the victims because one of them, fourteen-year-old Brad Carson, had been the son of a former girl- friend. The articles detailed the murders, in which three boys had been forced to vote on which of them would be the first one to die, in terrifying detail. The boy chosen had been killed by an arrow shot from a crossbow from outside the enclosure in which they had been imprisoned, presumably by the Gingerbread Man himself. After that, the two remaining boys had been given the choice of firing crossbows at each other until one of them was dead, or of both being killed. There had been a survivor in that group—sixteen-year-old Matt Hayes—but he no longer lived in the area. Immediately after the kill- ings, he had been charged with the murders of the two other boys, because at the time the authorities hadn't believed his story of a white- masked, grinning sadist who had forced him to kill. It had taken al- most a year, and the commission of the Group Four murders along with the Gingerbread Man's taunting letter to Riva, for authorities to believe that Matt had been telling the truth about what had hap- pened, and to come to the conclusion that he should not, after all, be held responsible for the deaths of the other two boys. When Matt was finally exonerated, his parents took him and his three siblings and moved out of state. For which Charlie didn't blame them a bit.

When the team reached Matt on the phone, he declined to talk to them. His mother told Tony, who had placed the call, that he had worked hard to put the horror behind him, and to please not contact them again.

Charlie didn't blame them for that, either.

"Kelly—Brad's mother—was totally devastated by the murder of her son. She gave me access to everything she knew about the case. Plus I did a lot of research," Riva told them. Thirty-nine years old, of average height, with the kind of overmuscled build that told Charlie he spent a great deal of time lifting weights, he perched on a corner of the table in the newspaper's glass-walled conference room. His brown hair was thinning and worn overlong to compensate, his khakis were rumpled, and the knot on his tie hung a couple of inches below the unbuttoned collar of his shirt, making him, in Charlie's view, look like the quintessential reporter. "It was bad enough when she thought he had been killed by another teenage boy, but it was absolutely terrible for her to realize that he had been the victim of a serial killer. What made it worse was when she found out the same killer had struck in similar fashion at least twice before, and no one had known anything about it. She felt that if there had been any publicity about the previous killings, she would have kept Brad closer to home and he wouldn't have been taken and subsequently killed."

"Did Kelly Carson approach you about writing the articles?" Tony asked. Unlike the rest of them, who sat around the table, he stood in front of the long windows that provided a panoramic view of Charlotte's downtown. Tall and clean-shaven, he looked every inch the FBI agent in his dark suit and tie. The sun pouring through the window made his black hair gleam. Michael stood close by, a shoulder propping one of the struts between the windows, arms crossed over his chest, looking big and tough and gorgeous, a tawny-maned Sun God. Charlie couldn't help the thought that popped into her head as she looked at the pair of them: handsome and handsomer.

Then she determinedly refocused on the case.

"Kelly DeMaris," Riva corrected. "Brad's father died, and she remarried. She turned to me as a friend when Brad was killed. It was my idea to write the articles, so people would know that a monster was at large in our community."

"How and when did Brad's father die?" Kaminsky's eyes had sharpened with interest. Like Tony, she and Buzz were in their FBI suits, but Kaminsky's hair was still faintly damp from her shower and was slicked back from her face and tucked behind her ears. She'd slept through her alarm, she told the three of them with a glower when she joined them in the hall at the appointed time, and hadn't had time to blow-dry her hair. Since then, she'd been snappish, and Charlie, and the others, too, had done their best not to provoke her.

"He was killed in a small plane crash when Brad was nine," Riva said. "Brad and Kelly were with him and were injured, but they recovered."

"Where did the crash happen?" Kaminsky asked with an uptick of excitement as she typed something into her laptop, no doubt noting one more victim who had witnessed the violent death of someone close. The list was far from complete, but it was shaping up to be one of the best—or at least most tantalizing—leads they had.

Riva frowned. "In Indiana somewhere, I think. Why?"

Kaminsky made a face. "No reason."

See, that was the problem with this particular lead: it encompassed too much. The number of first responders, emergency room personnel, doctors, nurses, chaplains, etc., involved was just too large, and the geographic areas of the deaths were too diverse. In trying to track down exactly who had been present at each of these possibly case-related death scenes, they had found it was almost impossible to be as precise as they needed to be to draw any meaningful conclusions. The medical personnel could be identified with a fair degree of accuracy from the patient charts, but it was much harder to pin support staff to the same time and place as a particular patient. Plus they felt there was a very good chance that a number of unaccounted for people were in and about the accident sites, emergency rooms, and other venues where these patients had been cared for. And if compiling a list for each individual site was difficult, cross-referencing with other sites, which they needed to do to find any individual who might have been present at multiple deaths, was so inaccurate as to be practically worthless.

In other words, the lead was promising, but as far as useful results were concerned, they had zilch.

"Did the boys know one another prior to the murders?" Charlie asked. There had to be a common denominator: she was certain of it. They just hadn't found it yet.

"They weren't close friends, but they were acquainted," Riva replied. "They were all from Mooresville—it's a pretty small town—and they had all played in the same baseball league."

Charlie could see Kaminsky typing something into her computer, and guessed she was reminding herself to look into the other victims' sport team affiliations. After all, Jenna had been participating in a run when the Gingerbread Man had grabbed her. Perhaps they could turn up a similar link with the others. Because there had to be *something*.

"We have them, thanks," Tony replied to Riva's offer to get them copies of the articles under discussion. "What we'd like are copies of the notes you used in writing the articles, if you'd let us have them."

Riva agreed readily, but when Charlie saw the hundreds of pages of his photocopied notes, some of them of handwritten originals, that a staffer handed over a short time later, she felt her expectations plummet. Going through so much material as thoroughly as it needed to be gone through would clearly take a lot of time, and time was in increasingly short supply. What it came down to now was a matter of prioritizing what was most likely to yield results.

"When Kelly came to me, after Brad's death, I started trying to help her find out who did this," Riva said. "Then, when that next batch of kids was killed, when I got that letter from the bastard who did it, I did everything I could to track him down. I'm still working on it. I've consulted with the local cops and the FBI agents who were working this case before you guys were brought in. I've run down a thousand possible leads, and explored so many theories that I can't even remember most of them. And I don't think I've come anywhere near identifying him. I hope you have better luck."

"We will," Tony promised grimly. Charlie felt heartened by his confidence.

After that, they met with the local police and FBI agents, toured the Group Four (propeller) kill site, then drove to Winston-Salem and the Wake Forest campus. Charlie had long been familiar with the work of Dr. Jeffrey Underwood, who had a made a career out of studying the genetic makeup of violent killers and, most recently, serial killers. They met him at the medical school, where he was a distinguished professor.

"It's a pleasure to meet you, Dr. Stone. I'm a big fan of your work," was how Dr. Underwood greeted them when they joined him in his lab, where half a dozen graduate students labored diligently over implements ranging from microscopes to computers. Smiling at him, flattered at his words, Charlie returned the compliment. After shaking hands with her, and making a few remarks on her latest research paper, which had been published two months previously in *The American Journal of Psychiatry,* he turned his attention to Tony, Buzz, and Kaminsky.

"I have no idea who could be behind these atrocities," he said in response to Tony's question. Balding and bespectacled, distinguished in his white lab coat, he looked older than his forty years. He was a tall, thin man with a restless air who stood shifting from foot to foot, watching his assistants with eagle eyes even as he answered questions, and rapping out the occasional instruction or rebuke to his underlings as he felt the need.

"How was the letter from the Gingerbread Man delivered to you?" Tony asked.

"It was slipped under the door to my office," Dr. Underwood said. "I came in one morning, and there it was. Needless to say, I immediately contacted the police."

Tony looked at Kaminsky.

"We already have a copy of it," she answered, correctly interpreting his unspoken question. "Like the others, it was written by one of the victims, Liza Gill, under what we are sure was some sort of coercion. That was the group killed in the trash compacter, if you remember."

"Are there security cameras in the building?" Buzz didn't look particularly hopeful. Because even if there were, by this time the footage would have been about a year old, which meant that unless it had been deliberately preserved, it almost certainly no longer existed.

"There are," Dr. Underwood replied, "but I understand that nothing usable was found. By the time police thought to check, the images had been taped over. I think the cameras are set to do that every seventy-two hours."

That came as a slight disappointment, but no surprise. As they went through their litany of questions, Dr. Underwood answered readily, but he had very little new to tell them.

Still, Charlie found much of what he had to say fascinating, but that was because he kept getting away from Tony's questions to explain to her where he was going with his research.

"Right now we're doing DNA tests on a number of samples of genetic material to see if the CHRNA7 gene, which is often missing in schizophrenics, is also missing in serial killers," he told Charlie. "I'm hoping to get funding to do a large scale study on the subject, which includes mass killers as well, such as the Colorado movie theater shooter."

"Do you feel that mass murderers and serial killers will be found to have the same mutation?" Charlie asked, immediately interested. It wasn't often she had the opportunity to talk shop with someone whose area of expertise so closely paralleled her own.

Dr. Underwood nodded. "I think so."

"I'm not convinced that we'll ever find one single component that creates a serial killer," Charlie said, totally drawn into the discussion. "It may be that a number of factors have to be present. Genetics may certainly play a role, but I am leaning toward the theory that environmental factors may be as important."

"Perhaps we could collaborate on a paper at some point," Dr. Underwood suggested. "I'd be very interested in incorporating the work you're doing into my research."

"I'm open to that," Charlie agreed. A stray glance that happened to encompass the faces of Tony, Buzz, and Kaminsky reminded her that, involving though the discussion was, it wasn't their reason for visiting Dr. Underwood. Michael was smiling faintly as he watched her. As she met his eyes she thought that what she saw might be pride in them . . . for her. Silly as it undoubtedly was to let the thought that he was proud of her affect her, she felt the beginnings of a tiny little glow. It occurred to her that having someone show pride in her was a rare thing in her life: she didn't come from that kind of background. Funny (sad?) that it took her impossible bête noire to open her eyes to the fact that she had wanted that.

"I only have one more question for you, Dr. Underwood," Tony said. "We know that the Gingerbread Man is going to strike again, and soon. Do you have any suggestions as to which experts working in fields similar to yours and Dr. Stone's he might be planning to send his next letter to? Whoever it is will be within the three-state area of North Carolina, South Carolina, and Virginia."

Dr. Underwood thought for a moment, then named two researchers who were on the list of a dozen names that Charlie had already compiled. In response to the same question, David Myers had also given them a couple of different names that were already on Charlie's list, so the information was not particularly helpful.

"You kicked ass in there, babe," Michael told her as they left. Having forgotten herself so far as to glance at him in response, she caught the look in his eyes and knew that she hadn't been mistaken: he *was* proud of her. She couldn't help it: she smiled at him. Sometimes, having Michael in her life actually felt good. And she meant good in a way that had nothing to do with sexual attraction.

"At least we've got a sort of consensus about the probable next experts he'll contact," Buzz said gloomily when they were in the air again, en route to Hampton, Virginia. That was the town from which Jenna, Laura, and Raylene had been kidnapped, and the team hoped to find something there that linked the three girls. They were armed with fresh details of how Jenna had spent the hours before she was kidnapped, gleaned from another interview with her via Skype, into which her mother, hovering anxiously in the background, had continuously interpolated comments. They had also acquired comparatively fuzzier details about how Laura and Raylene had spent that day, which they compiled from interviews with family, friends, and the team's own reconstruction of events. Once the plane landed, they would be back to beating the investigative bushes in hopes that something substantive would turn up.

"We've got local teams conducting round-the-clock surveillance on the experts on your list, including their offices and residences," Tony said to Charlie. Like the rest of them, he was seated around the airplane's pop-up table. Since they were doing so much traveling, the sleek Gulfstream V had become their de facto War Room. "If the unsub delivers a letter to one of them, we should have him."

"The problem with that is, by the time he drops it off, he'll have already kidnapped and probably killed his next victims," Kaminsky pointed out.

"And it's possible that he won't personally drop off the letter," Buzz said. "He could mail it, like he did to Riva. Or convey it to the intended recipient in any number of ways."

"Or the list could be wrong," Charlie reminded them. "We wouldn't have put Eric Riva on it, for example."

"At least it's a starting point," Tony said. "If he's casing the expert ahead of time, surveillance should pick up on it. We've got helicopters and ground personnel looking for possible kill sites in the vicinity of the names on the list. If he shows up at any of them, we've got him."

"Here are the key points to keep in mind." Kaminsky had set up what amounted to a PowerPoint presentation for their delectation. They'd already gone over several facets of the investigation, but the discussion had for the last few minutes gotten diverted. Now she called their attention back to the slides she was projecting on a pull-down screen above the couch where Michael lay. Since Charlie was the only one who could see him, she was the only one who found his presence there distracting. To all appearances, he was napping, although, of course, he didn't nap.

"We know that the unsub is a white male between the ages of approximately twenty-five and forty. We know that he possesses or has access to a blue or gray van with an interior that may or may not (because it might not be permanent) be outfitted with a cage and that smells like fish. We know he spoke on the telephone to someone he called Ben. We know a stun gun was used to initially subdue at least some of the victims, and that later a sedating gas was used to keep at least some of them either semi- or unconscious. Blood work on the last three victims identified that gas as nitrous oxide, so the unsub will have access to it. We know that the murder scenarios he plans are unusually complex, and require significant prior preparation. We know that he somehow knows or knows of Eric Riva, Dr. David Myers, Dr. Jeffrey Underwood, and our own Dr. Stone. We know that all of the sites of the murders and kidnappings are no more than a seven-hour drive apart, which means he lives or is staying within

that area, at least during the time the murders are being carried out."
Kaminsky flipped to the next display, which was a bulleted list of
names. "We know that these victims witnessed or were present at the
violent death of someone close to them before they were involved in
this case. That's more than half. A large enough percentage to be sta-
tistically significant. In the case of the victims where we have not
confirmed close exposure to a violent death, it's because the information isn't available, not necessarily because it didn't happen. Which
means the incidence rate is likely to rise. So I think we can assume
that close exposure to violent death in victims is important. Also important is how the unsub knows of the violent death in the victim's
past. We need to determine how he has access to that information."

"Any insight into that?" Tony looked at all three of them in turn.

"Checking the medical personnel and hospitals involved," Buzz
said. "So far nothing's jumping out."

"I think we're going to find that our unsub was exposed to a
similar violent death at a young age," Charlie said. "So that gives us
one more marker to look for. It's possible his exposure will correlate
to the ages of the first victims, which was between twelve and fourteen."

"How about checking obits for past accidental or violent deaths
for something like ten years before those first murders?" Michael suggested without opening his eyes. "There can't be that many newspapers in North and South Carolina and Virginia. And they all keep
archives."

Charlie almost said, *Good idea*. Catching herself in time, she instead repeated his suggestion.

Tony looked at Buzz.

"On it, boss," Buzz said.

"What about trying to find out where he gets his nitrous oxide?"
Tony asked.

Buzz shook his head. "You'd be surprised how many uses for nitrous oxide there are: dentists use it, race car drivers use it in their
engines, it's used in cooking and in aerosol products like whipped
cream, it's also used illegally, as in, teenagers inhaling it. All that
makes it fairly easy to come by."

"Suppliers?" Tony asked.

"Not that many, but the distribution is so widespread that it's taking some time to check," Buzz replied. "We're talking about going through thousands of individual bills of sale. Then there's the secondary market."

"Keep on it," Tony said.

Buzz nodded.

"People." Kaminsky's voice drew their attention back to her presentation. The screen changed again to show pictures of the five survivors, with a bullet list beneath each. Certain items were highlighted in red. Indicating it, Kaminsky continued, "We've talked to all the survivors now—well, Matt Hayes wouldn't talk to us, but all the other survivors—and their accounts are consistent: they were kidnapped, drugged, forced to kill, released, and ordered to run for their lives as the sole survivor. They describe the unsub as wearing all black with a white, grinning mask. Estimates of height and weight vary significantly. At least two thought he was disguising his voice with some sort of digital device."

"Does that mean the unsub knows the victims, do you think?" Buzz asked.

Tony shook his head. "It might just mean that he doesn't want the survivors to be able to identify his voice later."

Buzz nodded. Charlie concurred: that made sense.

"What about unsolved single murders in the Buggs Island Lake area around the time and previous to the first Gingerbread Man attack?" Charlie asked.

"Going back ten years from that date, there are two unsolved murders, neither of which seem to fit our criteria. One was thought to have resulted from a bar fight and one appeared to be a professional hit," Kaminsky said. "But there are a number of accidental deaths that might be something more. I'm still working on it."

"So what've we got?" Tony asked.

Kaminsky made a disgusted sound. "Not as much as you'd hope. Our best lead is a violent death in the victims' pasts. Like Dr. Stone said, we're looking for a common denominator, and that's the closest thing we have."

"Okay," Tony said as the pilot came over the intercom and advised them they were getting ready to land. "Let's keep digging. We'll figure it out."

Charlie was stepping down onto the blisteringly hot tarmac when it hit her. Her mouth fell open. Michael, beside her, saw the expression on her face and said sharply, "What?"

"Holly," she answered before she thought, and then as the others looked at her she pulled herself together and refocused on them. "I was exposed to a violent death at a young age, too. You remember, my friend Holly Palmer."

Who had died at the hands of the Boardwalk Killer, while Charlie had survived.

"Holy cow," Buzz said.

"That's a link." Kaminsky sounded excited.

"Check the other experts. See if Riva, Myers, or Underwood had exposure to a violent death in their pasts." Tony looked at Kaminsky. "Maybe that's how he selects the experts."

"If so, then finding the next expert just got a lot easier." Buzz sounded almost as excited as Kaminsky.

"And the next kill site. Because it will be within close proximity to the next expert," Kaminsky chimed in. She looked at Buzz. "You take the list of experts he's likely to target, and I'll take Riva, Myers, and Underwood. Let's see if this pans out."

Charlie missed Buzz's reply to that, because at that moment her cell phone went off. Glancing at it, she saw that the caller was Tam. Her heart sped up. This call was not likely to be anything good.

"Excuse me a minute: I need to take this," she said. Then she walked a few yards away from them for privacy's sake while staying within the shadow of the plane, and within their view.

"Hey, Tam," she said into the phone.

"Cherie," Tam greeted her. "Oh, cherie, I have something I need to tell you. First, are you someplace safe?"

Tam's tone made Charlie feel cold all over. A quick glance around found Tony and Kaminsky talking to each other and, hopefully, paying no attention to her, while Buzz was walking away from them, presumably going for the car. Michael was beside her, looking down at her with a frown. She was, she realized, glad he was there. He had somehow become a bulwark in her life.

"Yes," she said, while Michael drawled, "If that's the voodoo priestess, ask her if she knows a way to make this damned leash I'm on a little longer."

But Charlie didn't have a chance to ask Tam anything, because the other woman burst out, "I know where the danger comes from. It's water. You are in terrible danger around dark water."

CHAPTER NINETEEN

"You're getting Dudley all worked up, you know." Michael walked through the closed bathroom door, then stopped to watch her with hard eyes as she smoothed on fresh lipstick. Charlie flicked a look his way.

"What part of *the bathroom is off-limits* did you not understand?" she asked tartly.

His lip curled. She took that to mean, *it's only off-limits if I want it to be,* and frowned at him.

The bathroom they were in was a small, elegantly appointed ladies' room right off the Marriott's patio, where she, Tony, Kaminsky, and Buzz had not so long ago finished having a late, badly needed dinner. A little while earlier Kaminsky and Buzz had gone upstairs, where the team had four adjacent rooms on the twentieth floor, while Charlie, at Tony's invitation, had chosen to stay on for coffee and dessert. He'd ordered key lime pie and she'd ordered mango sherbet, which they'd eaten. They had been waiting for the server to bring the check when she had excused herself to go freshen up. Since the door to the ladies' room was visible from where they sat, neither of them had seen any need for him to escort her. The restroom contained a single stall, divided from the sink area by a partition, and once inside

Charlie had locked the door. Nobody was getting to her in there—except, of course, for Michael.

He'd been bent out of shape ever since Tam's phone call. He wanted her to tell Tony about Tam's calls, about the danger Tam said she was in. He wanted her to leave the investigation and go hole up somewhere until the Gingerbread Man was caught. He wanted her to abandon her entire career and find an alternative use for her medical degree that did not involve serial killers.

And he wanted her not to get involved with Tony. That one he hadn't said in so many words, but she didn't have any trouble interpreting the increasingly grim set to his mouth, or the antagonistic glint in his eyes, as she and Tony had talked more and more exclusively to each other over dinner, while Kaminsky and Buzz did the same. Then, when the others had been leaving and Tony had asked her if she wanted to stay on for coffee and dessert, and she had agreed without so much as a glance thrown at the frowning ghost sprawled in a chair across the table from her, Michael had started to radiate hostility like rays from the sun.

She'd felt that hostility all but scorching her as over dessert she and Tony had completely abandoned shop talk and he'd told her self-deprecating stories about his days as a college football player that made her laugh. Then when she had excused herself to go to the restroom and Michael had (of course) followed her, her back had practically blistered from the heat.

"The bathroom is off-limits," she had warned Michael out of the side of her mouth as she reached the ladies' room door, in an effort to avoid the discussion (fight) she had a pretty good idea was coming.

So much for that. At least he'd had the decency to wait until (she assumed) he'd heard the buzzing of the air dryer that had told him she was drying her hands.

The dress wasn't helping.

The thing was, she was wearing one. It was a sundress, a beautiful deep red print, with a thin strap over each shoulder and smocking that kept it snug to the waist and a floaty, tea-length skirt. She'd bought it in the hotel's upscale gift shop, when the four (five) of them had come in from walking Hampton's sidewalks as, straight off the plane, they had followed the route Jenna said she'd taken before being grabbed. Evening had fallen as they went inside each of the establishments Jenna would have passed, and examined the spot where the abduction had occurred, but the temperature stayed in the nineties, and the humidity was thick. By the time they returned to the car and drove to the hotel, besides being cross from listening to Michael without being able to answer back, Charlie had been hot and sweaty and heartily regretting the way she was dressed. Her sleeveless silk blouse had been clinging unpleasantly to her skin and her lightweight slacks felt like they were heavy wool and plastered to her legs. No surprise: she'd packed work clothes, but what she had failed to consider was that her work clothes had been chosen with an indoor, air-conditioned office in mind. They weren't suitable for being outdoors in so much heat and humidity.

So when she had seen the pretty, lightweight summer ensembles in the hotel gift shop, she'd left the men to check in and, with Kaminsky following on her heels, headed for the clothes. If anything, Kaminsky in her fitted suit was even more inappropriately dressed for what they'd just been doing and were planning on continuing to do the next day than Charlie was. They had a brief meeting of the (female) minds and Kaminsky, too, had indulged in some shopping.

The result was that Kaminsky had worn a sleek, knee-length (she told Charlie with a wry twist of her mouth that she couldn't go longer because of her height) black linen shift with a nifty little short-sleeved bolero to hide her shoulder holster, plus her own stilettos, which she refused to forsake, while Charlie had worn the sundress, and a pair of embellished sandals with delicate kitten heels that she'd purchased to go with the dress.

Having of necessity followed her into the gift shop, Michael in typical male fashion had displayed little interest as she had riffled through the clothing. So when she'd emerged from the bathroom of her hotel room to find him draped over one of the two wing chairs on the other side of the single king bed, desultorily watching TV, the night sky black behind him through the opened curtains and the room itself softly lit by the floor lamp between the chairs, his eyes had widened in surprise as he glanced her way.

"You look beautiful," he said. Fresh from her shower, with her hair twisted into a cool updo that left a few tendrils loose to curl around her face and neck, and her makeup subtle but there (it had all but melted away earlier), she felt so much better that she smiled at him, which, because she'd been hot and cross and tired of him telling her what she needed to do, she hadn't done for a while.

"Thank you," she said.

He stood up and came toward her, his gaze sliding over her before lingering on her nearly bare shoulders. "All this for Dudley?"

Her brows twitched together. "All this because the dining room closed at nine, so we'll be eating outside by the pool, and it's hot out there." She reached for his watch, which she'd left beside her purse on the console table that ran along the wall opposite the beds, and slid it onto her arm. Then she picked up her purse and turned to head for the door.

"Listen to what you just said: you'll be eating outside by the pool. You know it's night, right? That makes the pool dark water. For that matter, this hotel's on the beach. The ocean is right there. More dark water."

Already having had the same thought and conquered it, and aggravated at having all that latent fear stirred up again, she turned around to glare at him. "If I stay in the room and run a bath, and turn the light out in the bathroom, the tub will be full of dark water, too."

His lips thinned. "The difference is, there's not likely to be a serial killer who knows your name in the bathroom with you."

"No, he'll be right outside the door," she retorted.

"Oh, ha-ha." From his expression, he clearly didn't find that amusing. "Your friend the voodoo priestess says you're in danger. You say the voodoo priestess is generally right on. How stupid is it to stay here in harm's way when it would be the easiest thing in the world to stay in your room tonight, hop a plane tomorrow, and fly somewhere safe?"

Charlie sighed. "That's the problem, don't you see? There isn't anywhere safe. I'm as liable to be running into danger as I am to be running away from it. Tam says I'm in danger near dark water. If you think about it, there's dark water everywhere. For my money, the reason I'm in danger near dark water is almost certainly because there's a serial killer out there who knows my name. Therefore, the way to make me safe is to catch the serial killer. And at a guess, I'd say I'm safer surrounded by three armed FBI agents than I would be on my own."

Their eyes met. *You'd be with me,* his said, and hers replied, *You can't protect me,* and his narrowed and his mouth tightened in angry acknowledgment.

"You're scaring me to death here, all right?" His words were abrupt. His face was tight. "At least tell Dudley about what the damned woman said so he's on his guard, would you please?"

"Fine," she snapped, annoyed at herself because it touched her that he would disregard the rivalry she knew he felt with Tony to try to make sure she was protected. "I'm scared, too, you know. I'm always scared, all the time. I live with this constant, low-grade fear and have since my friend was killed and I found out what kind of evil exists in the world. What Tam said simply cranked it up a couple of notches. But what I've learned over the years is that the only thing to do when you're scared is stay cool and keep moving ahead."

Even as the words left her mouth, Charlie realized it was the first time in her adult life that she had ever admitted to anyone that she was afraid. Fear had been her constant companion for as long as she could remember; she had learned to hide it, to deny it, to hold her head high in the face of it and carry on.

But she had never admitted to it out loud until right now—to him.

Her ghost.

And what did that say about the state of her heart where he was concerned?

"Charlie." His eyes darkened and slid to her mouth, and she knew he wanted to kiss her. And she knew that if there had been any way, any possible way to make that happen, she would have walked straight into his arms and slid her own around his neck and kissed him until kissing wasn't enough. And then she would have gone to bed with him.

Because that's what she was burning to do.

Just thinking about it made her go all soft and shivery inside.

Her face must have given her away, because his eyes blazed at her. Suddenly passion beat in the air between them, as tangible as the pounding of her heart.

A knock at the door broke the spell.

"That'll be Tony," she said, and saw his eyes flare.

She was still aching for Michael when she turned and opened the door to find Tony standing there.

"Why, Dr. Stone," Tony greeted her on a note of surprised pleasure, doing an exaggerated double-take as she stepped out into the bright light of the hallway and he took in her dress. He wasn't his usual FBI agent-correct self, either, having lost the coat and tie and rolled the sleeves of his white dress shirt up to his elbows. The tail end of his shirt was out, too, and she presumed that was to hide his gun.

"Why, Special Agent Bartoli," she echoed on the same note, giving him a copy of the exaggerated once-over he had given her, and he laughed and caught her hand and brought it to his mouth and kissed it. The brush of his lips on her skin was warm and pleasant, and the casual grace of the gesture made her heart hurt a little.

Because it served to underline the fact that she was never going to have that with the man (?) she really wanted. The simple pleasures of casual physical contact were never going to happen between her and Michael.

But, she decided as she smiled at Tony and he tucked his hand around her arm—it felt warm and strongly masculine against her skin, and she was suddenly acutely conscious of it—and they started walking side by side toward the elevator where Kaminsky in her new dress and Buzz in rolled-up shirtsleeves were waiting, she wasn't going to let her heart get broken. Having it break over a dead man would be stupid. Because it wouldn't change a thing: he would still be unavailable for the life she wanted—he would still be dead.

There was a phrase from a song her mother used to listen to: *love the one you're with*.

She liked Tony a whole lot. She found him attractive, sexy. His kisses turned her on.

Tony she could kiss. Tony she could have sex with. Tony she could even, eventually, if things worked out, make a life with.

Stupid she wasn't. She knew enough to choose the possible over the impossible.

So that's what she made up her mind to do.

They joined Kaminsky and Buzz at the elevators just in time for

Charlie to overhear Kaminsky saying to Buzz, "So where'd you go last night?" to which Buzz replied with a startled, "What?" while Kaminsky pinned him with a censorious look and answered, "I was in the room next door, remember? I heard you go out," before they both shut up as Charlie and Tony reached them. Charlie had the fleeting thought that Kaminsky's oversleeping that morning was thus explained: she'd obviously stayed awake listening for Buzz to return from wherever he'd gone. Which meant that the situation between them was getting interesting. Charlie realized that she hadn't been paying much attention to them, which wasn't surprising: she had her own (way complicated) situation going on, after all.

The elevator came, and the four (five) of them piled in.

When they emerged on the ground floor to head across the cavernous, marble-floored lobby and through the big glass doors into the covered outdoor walkway beyond, it was full night. A ruffle of strategically placed potted palm trees blocked the patio from view. Soft romantic music filled the air, along with the sounds of conversation and laughter from their fellow late diners. The moon was a tipsy crescent high in the sky and thousands of stars twinkled like tiny rhinestones set into midnight velvet. A few steps down took them to the wide patio with its wrought-iron tables and chairs. It was enclosed on two sides by smaller buildings connected to the hotel, but the front was open. The surrounding landscaping was lush and fragrant, and the flickering lights from dozens of jewel-toned hurricane lanterns glowing on the tables and on tall, willowy stands around the perimeter added a magical beauty. It was still hot outside, but the humidity was made bearable by a slight, salt-scented breeze blowing in off the ocean. In the distance, across a stretch of pale, barely seen beach, Charlie glimpsed the roll of whitecaps on the gleaming black water. Much closer at hand, down a path that led from the patio to the beach, the hotel's grottolike pool still accommodated a few die-hard swimmers. Dark water, Charlie thought, and felt a cold finger of fear slide down her spine. Her step faltered for a second—but really, what was there to do, run back to her room and stay there until Tam gave her the all clear? Saying, "At least stay away from the damned water" in a goaded tone, Michael moved in close beside her, placing his big body between her and the pool and the sea, but it was Tony's hand that slid around her arm again. It was Tony's touch she felt, Tony who was solid and warm and as physically present as she was. Refusing to even glance at Michael, Charlie deliberately leaned into Tony a little, just enough so that their bodies brushed, and looked up at him and smiled.

Over dinner, Charlie concentrated on the man she could have, and pretended the one she couldn't have wasn't there. Because in a world that didn't absolutely suck, he wouldn't have been, and she could have fallen in love with Tony without any damned infernal interference.

Which was why, when Michael joined her in the restroom, she was braced for him to be ticked off at her. And she already knew that, his anger notwithstanding, she was going to hold to the course she had chosen, and not back down.

She was choosing Tony, and Michael was simply going to have to live (or not) with that.

So now Michael was in the bathroom scowling at her. "You got him thinking he's going to get lucky tonight."

Finishing with her lipstick, giving herself a final check in the mirror, Charlie turned to face him. No point in beating around the bush. The thing about it was, with Michael attached to her like a tail to a kite there was no way he wasn't going to know. Not only about Tony, but about everything she ever did in her life from that point on until either she died or he disappeared. The knowledge was unsettling. No, terrifying. But all she could do was find a way to deal with it—him—on terms she could live with.

"Maybe he is." She gave him a level look. "I'm thinking about it."

"What?" To say Michael looked astounded was an understatement.

"At some point, if my relationship with Tony continues, we're going to have sex. I'm thinking about making it tonight."

Astounded gave way to flabbergasted, which was replaced almost instantly by plain mad.

"The hell you are."

"You don't have anything to say about it. I'm telling you as a courtesy, so you can stay out of the way. In other words, if I go into a hotel room with Tony, you stay outside, got it?"

"In your fucking dreams."

"I thought watching wasn't your thing."

"Baby, I'm telling you up front that if you go into a hotel room with Dudley with the intention of having sex with him, that's going to turn into the most haunted hotel room you've ever been in in your life."

Her brows snapped together. "Guess what, Casper: since I'm the only one who can see or hear you, if I simply shut my eyes and tune you out there's nothing you can do."

"Try me."

"Oh, I'm going to. I get to have a life."

His eyes narrowed at her. "You got turned on, didn't you? In the bedroom earlier. I turned you on, and now you're wanting to get your rocks off with Dudley. Just so we're clear, that ain't going to work for me."

"You're disgusting," Charlie hissed at him, her cheeks flaming. She started walking toward him, because she wasn't wasting any more breath arguing, and he was blocking the door.

"It's the truth and you know it. I'm the guy you want to fuck, not him."

"Get out of my way."

He folded his arms over his chest. "Uh-uh."

Her blood boiled. What he seemed to forget was that she could walk right through him, which was what she did, and the electric tingle be damned. Yanking open the door, she realized a couple of long strides beyond it that she was stalking instead of walking, and moderated her gait. By the time she reached the table, she was able to smile at Tony, who was signing the check and handing it back to the waiter, as if all was right with her world, and never mind Michael's honey-infused voice at her back growling, "You ever try eating a turkey sandwich when what you really want is a pizza? When you finish the sandwich, you're still craving that pizza."

Of course she didn't reply.

"In case that went over your head, I'm the pizza."

Oh, she'd gotten it, all right. And she still didn't reply.

"Damn it, Charlie," Michael said, planting himself in front of her. Narrowing her eyes at him, she veered around him. Walking through him was possible, as she'd just proven, but the truth was it was something she didn't like to do.

"Hey." Tony stood up as she reached the table. "This was dinner," he said, smiling at her, and she remembered that they'd agreed to dinner as a first step in their take-it-slow pact. "Want to try for a dance before we go up?"

There was a cleared area on the far side of the patio, over by another ruffle of potted palms that almost hid the solid brick wall behind it. Couples were dancing there, eight or nine, ranging in age from young professionals to grandmas and grandpas. Nothing fancy, no *Dancing with the Stars* glitz, simply all of them holding each other close as they swayed and turned and circled the floor to the music.

"You don't want to do this," Michael said.

"I'd love to," Charlie told Tony with determination, and when he smiled at her and took her hand she followed him onto the dance floor and turned into his arms.

She had danced with him before, but only as part of working on a case. It had been a careful and formal dance, under the watchful eyes of Kaminsky and Buzz and a camera. This dance was different. This was her plastered right up against Tony, with his arm tight around her waist and his body hard and unmistakably masculine against hers. It was personal. It was romantic. It was *real*.

"You look good," Tony told her, his mouth close to her ear. "You smell good, too."

"Thank you," Charlie said. She tipped her head back to smile at him. The moonlight made his eyes seem very dark as he met her glance, and highlighted the lean hard bones of his face. He looked good. He *felt* good. He *was* good. Really, what was not to fall in love with?

"You actually think you can have a relationship with him? You can't even tell him about the things you see," Michael spoke in her ear. "You're afraid to tell him that you've got a voodoo priestess friend who's saying you're in danger. He has no idea that you're looking at a ghost over there in the corner who's got half his head blown away. And we both know you're sure as hell never going to tell him about me."

Of course Michael was going to be a pain in the ass. So what else was new? Yes, she did see the spirit in the corner, a young man standing over an upscale-looking sixtyish couple talking earnestly over dinner, who clearly had no idea he was there. But so what? She saw ghosts all the time, and this particular one was keeping his distance, and that meant he was none of her business. Just like what she told or didn't tell Tony was none of Michael's business.

As a movement of the dance turned her around, she glared at Michael over Tony's shoulder. And mouthed, *"Go away."*

"So tell me how you came to be an FBI agent," she said to Tony. Manhunting 101: get the guy to talk about himself. It had been a while, but she remembered the drill. Anyway, he knew all (well, almost all) about her from the damned background check he'd run on her. If she was going to start a real relationship with him, it would probably be a good idea to learn a little more about what made him tick.

"It was either be an FBI agent or a lawyer," Tony said. "What would you do?"

She laughed. "FBI, definitely."

His arm tightened around her waist. They were swaying together, turning a little, basic box step stuff. His cheek—she thought it was his cheek, but it could have been his lips—brushed her hair.

"There you go," he said. "They lured me in with the great government salary. And the hours. Then they clenched the deal when they told me that occasionally people might shoot at me with a gun."

She laughed again. She *liked* him. And she felt safe with him. Those were two sturdy pillars on which to begin to build a relationship. *I can do this,* she told herself, as the prospect of the normal life she had always wanted but been afraid to reach for shimmered tantalizingly in her mind's eye. All she had to do was keep her mouth shut about the woo-woo stuff in her life, pretend it (most especially Michael) didn't exist, and she could build her own future just the way she wanted it.

"So did you pick your own team, or were Buzz and Kaminsky assigned to you?" Charlie asked. Tony's hand slid down below her waist, not quite to her butt but getting there. He wasn't quite as tall as—he was tall enough so that they weren't crotch to crotch, but she could still feel what was going on below his waist, and registered it with an interested tingle.

"Didn't your mama ever tell you that classy women don't let men feel them up on the dance floor?" Michael's drawl had an edge to it. He was behind Tony again, so all she had to do was look over Tony's shoulder to see all six-foot-three infuriating inches of him.

She turned her head instead to admire the clean line of Tony's jaw.

"Crane was assigned to me," Tony told her. "Kaminsky was a cop when Crane recommended we use her for a case because she speaks fluent Bulgarian, which we needed. She did an amazing job, not only with the language but with everything. So I told her that if she joined the Bureau, I'd hire her. She did and I did."

Those were definitely Tony's lips brushing her ear, Charlie thought, and then nuzzling the hollow below it. The sensation was pleasant, and as she closed her eyes to enjoy it she could feel herself warming up inside. Sliding her hand along the width of his shoulder, she enjoyed that sensation, too. Beneath the smoothness of his shirt, his shoulder felt muscular and firm to the touch, just like the body she was pressed against felt muscular and firm. She moved a little, wriggling experimentally, and as her breasts pushed harder into his chest she felt a pleasurable little throb.

"Babe, you shouldn't ought to have to work that hard to get turned on. Why don't you give up and admit that Dudley ain't lighting your fire tonight?"

Charlie's eyes shot open. Michael was behind Tony, watching her like a hawk hunting for rodents. His tone was mocking, but the skin over his cheekbones was hard and tight as he focused on her face.

She glared at him. Then she turned her face into Tony's neck and pressed her lips to the smooth warm skin there. It felt good. She was *definitely* getting turned on.

"Charlie," Tony whispered huskily, and she lifted her head and he kissed her mouth. Not a full-out kiss, because they were, after all, on a dance floor, but more of a tasting.

She liked it.

Crash.

The noise was so unexpected that Charlie jumped. So did everyone else, including Tony, whose arms dropped away from her as his hand shot behind his back toward where, she imagined, he had stashed his gun, probably in his waistband. Looking through all the moving shadows that played across the patio, she saw that one of the hurricane lanterns had fallen from its stand to shatter into a million ruby red shards on the stone at the edge of the dance floor.

She saw, too, that Michael was standing next to the stand where, seconds before, the lantern had flickered. Her eyes widened. Was it possible that he had . . . ? As she remembered the remote he'd learned to work, and the computer he'd managed to operate, and the two or three occasions when he'd actually manifested for a few seconds in solid form, her blood pressure skyrocketed. Yes, she grimly answered her own question, it was possible. In fact, knocking that hurricane lantern from its stand was exactly what he had done.

"Yo, babe." Seeing her eyes on him, Michael gave her an insolent little wave.

With Tony able to see her, there was no possible response she could make.

"Whoa," Tony said. His hand had never actually reached his gun, and now it slid around her waist again. "I didn't realize the wind was that strong."

"Me either." Charlie registered that her tone was acerbic only after the words had left her mouth. By then, there was nothing she could do.

The music, which was piped in rather than live, hadn't stopped, and as a server ran off, presumably for a broom, everybody started dancing again. Tony pulled her back into his arms, and Charlie nestled there, determined to re-establish the sensual buildup exactly where she'd left off.

Tony seemed to be on the same page. "You've got the softest skin," he murmured, dropping a kiss on her shoulder.

Crash.

Charlie didn't even jump this time. She'd been expecting it. But Tony did, at least enough to let her go and look around at the second hurricane lantern to crash to the ground.

The dancing stopped as everyone around them once again stared at the broken glass.

"I can do this all night long," Michael called to her.

Every muscle in Charlie's body hummed with tension. She caught herself glaring at him, and instantly forced the anger from her face.

Two can play at that game, was the thought she sent winging Michael's way.

"It *is* getting windy. Why don't we go on up?" she said sweetly to Tony. And took his hand.

The flaring of Tony's eyes was the ocular equivalent of a *hell, yes* fist pump: as Michael had so maddeningly put it, Tony thought he was about to get lucky. It was only there for the briefest of instants, but Charlie saw it and was conscious of feeling slightly nettled. She knew masculine sex-on-the-brain when she saw it, and Tony was exhibiting classic symptoms.

Which, she told herself, was exactly what she wanted.

"Good idea," was what Tony said, his voice perfectly bland, his eyes now no more than warmly encouraging.

Men, she thought savagely, and smiled at him as they walked hand in hand to the elevators.

"Something the matter?" Michael was with them. Smirking.

Of course the minute the elevator doors closed Tony pulled her into his arms and kissed her. A deep kiss. Hungry. Promising.

Wrapping her arms around his neck, Charlie shot a one-fingered salute at the devil watching her and kissed Tony back.

The shrilling of the emergency alarm made Tony jump like he'd been goosed.

Having been expecting—not precisely that, but *something*—Charlie didn't jump. Finding herself dropped, she took advantage of her sudden freedom to turn her back to Tony and shoot her nemesis a look that would have killed him if he hadn't already been dead.

"What the hell?" Tony said over the shrilling of the alarm, turning to examine the control panel in obvious hopes of shutting the damned thing off.

Leaning back against the wall, folding his arms over his chest, Michael gave Charlie a malicious grin. "I got to say, this is the most fun I've had since I died."

Charlie was still working on rearranging her features into a reasonably pleasant expression for Tony's benefit when the elevator, alarm still trilling wildly, reached their floor and stopped. She walked out first. Catching up with her, Tony slid a hand around her arm.

It took an effort, but she smiled at him.

Michael said, "Watch out, babe, you're shooting poison darts out of those big blue eyes."

She kept the smile, and tried not to clench her teeth.

The guard Tony had scared up to stand sentinel in the hall was nowhere in sight. Had Tony arranged for him to be elsewhere until he was summoned? Because he was astute enough to realize that she would find it embarrassing to invite him into her room under the eyes of an audience?

Charlie didn't know. She didn't really care. Glancing down, thrusting a hand into her purse, she pulled out her room key.

Tony saw it, and his hand tightened possessively on her arm.

"Think I could get the sprinkler above your bed to go off?" Michael asked in a tone that, if Charlie hadn't known better, would have indicated he was just idly wondering. "Well, guess we won't know till I try."

Charlie shot him an evil look. The three of them had reached the door to her room by that time. Turning her back on Satan's spawn, she paused with her key card in her hand to look up into Tony's now subtly gleaming brown eyes.

CHAPTER TWENTY

"So, am I coming in?" Tony asked her with the smallest of crooked smiles.

Charlie's hand tightened on the key card. She looked up into the lean, dark face of the absolutely-perfect-for-the-life-she-wanted man standing so close to her. She did not so much as glance in the direction of the tawny-haired curse with which she was afflicted.

The sad, infuriating truth was, she had no choice.

"We're taking it slow, remember?" Smiling apologetically at Tony—the apology at least was genuine—she slid her key into the lock. And tried to keep a lid on the fury she felt welling up inside her as Michael—not that she was looking at him—responded to that with a wide grin.

Only for a second did Tony's face reveal his disappointment.

"Slow," he said. Then he smiled a little wryly at her. "I got it. Slow."

Then he cupped her face with both hands and gave her a long, lingering kiss good-night.

Gripping his wrists, Charlie responded. Lots of tongue. But, damn it, thanks to the looming presence of the ghost from hell, not so much heat.

When at last Tony let her go, she smiled at him, sweetly apologetic still, then walked into her room and shut the door in Michael's face. She took three strides, turned, and waited.

He strolled through the door just as she'd known he would and grinned mockingly at her.

"Dudley get you turned on yet?"

Charlie felt her whole body quiver with anger. She felt the burning heat of it rising through her veins like red-hot lava. She could feel her face flush with it. She could feel her eyes blaze with it.

"You do not get to ruin my life," she said through her teeth, advancing on him with a pointed finger aimed at the center of his wide chest. She stopped short before she reached him, but once again she made the mistake of coming too close: she had to tilt her head back to glare into his face. His eyes still mocked her. The slight curve of his mouth was—sexy as hell. "I want normal. I want easy. I want happy. I want to do my work in peace, and find a man I can fall in love with, and maybe even get married to and have kids with. If you interfere with that one more time, I'll find a way to send you back on your way to hell, I swear."

His eyes narrowed at her. "You know what I want? I want to be able to eat a nice steak dinner like you had tonight. I want to drink a couple of cold beers. I want to feel the sun on my face when I'm outside. I want to sleep. I want my damned life back. And I want to fuck the hell out of you."

By the time he finished, his eyes were a hard, glittering blue. Charlie glared into them with true fury, but even as she did she could feel the electricity arcing between them, feel the air around them turning to steam. Her heartbeat sped up. Her pulse started to pound. Deep inside, her body quickened. Her nipples suddenly felt all hot and prickly as they pushed against her dress' built-in bra, which inexplicably seemed to have gotten a couple of sizes too tight. Inside the silken scrap of her panties, she felt dampness, and heat.

As he watched her face, his pupils dilated until his eyes were almost black.

"Pay attention, babe: that's what being turned on feels like," he said softly.

Charlie looked into those hot-for-her eyes. She took in the hard, impossibly handsome face—the strong jaw, the sensuous curve of his mouth, the Sun God hair; and then, lower, the veritable mountain of sleek, powerful muscle that was pure sex-on-a-stick. And she felt a fresh burst of anger at him, at herself, at the damned universe, along with another wave of infuriating, overpowering, all-but-irresistible desire.

He hadn't even touched her, and she was melting inside. She wanted to start ripping off her clothes.

And he could tell. She saw it in his eyes.

"I didn't ask to get saddled with you," she threw at him, clenching her fists as she turned sharply away. "I want you out of my life."

"I didn't ask to get saddled with you, either," he growled. "But you're mine now, Doc."

To Charlie's astonishment, before she could take more than a single step, hard hands gripped her waist, and she was spun around and lifted off her feet like she weighed nothing at all until he— Michael!—set her down with her back against the door.

She gaped at him. Eyes flaming, he loomed over her, his hands so solid on her waist that she felt the size and strength of them clear through her dress.

"You're—" Anger forgotten, she started to tell him that he was solid, that he'd somehow crossed the barrier and was in her world now, but she never got the chance.

He pushed up against her, letting her feel every powerful inch of him as he crowded her back against the door. His big hand curved around the vulnerable nape of her neck. His fingers burrowed into her hair. Then he dropped his head and took her mouth.

This was no gentle kiss.

His lips were hard and hot and hungry. And angry. And incredibly, mind-blowingly arousing. As his tongue took bold possession of her mouth, Charlie made a helpless little mewling sound deep in her throat and slid her arms around his waist and her hands up under his shirt and kissed him back with a burning intensity that, until she had met him, she would have said was utterly foreign to her nature. His skin felt warm and satiny to the touch. The flexing muscles beneath were firm and smooth. He was far bigger than she was, far stronger than she was, and he was letting her know it. She couldn't have gotten away from him if she'd tried, which she didn't. Instead she plastered herself against him, arching her body to fit the powerful length of his. Pathetically primitive creature that she apparently was, she felt a rush of mindless pleasure, a blast of torrid heat. Her heart seemed to go haywire. Her blood sizzled. Kissing him with reckless abandon, she slid her palms up over his shoulder blades, reveling in their breadth and strength. She could feel every inch of him: the muscular wall of his chest, the bump of his belt buckle, the unmistakable hardness below. She could feel the brush of his jeans against her bare calves. Her toes touched the tip of his boots. If this was a war, he had already won hands down. The warm, wet invasion of her mouth made her shiver. It made her quake and melt inside. He was kissing her so hot and deep that she was dizzy.

I want you.

If he hadn't been kissing her like he was, she would have said it aloud. But she couldn't talk, could barely think or breathe.

His hand was on her breast, flattened on top of it, rubbing her, caressing her through the thin fabric of her dress. Her body's searing response caught her by surprise. Her nipples tightened. Her breast surged into his palm. If her dress had had buttons, she would have been ripping them open for him. If it had had a zipper, she would have been yanking it down. But it didn't. The only way out of the thing was to pull it over her head, which she couldn't do because he was leaning against her, pressing her back into the door with enough force to keep her pinned there, holding her in place with his body.

He weighed a ton; he radiated heat.

Then he solved her dilemma for her by sliding a hand inside the neckline of her dress.

It was big and hot and masculine, and it covered her breast completely. Her nipple instantly puckered into a small hard nub that quivered against his fingers, then jutted into his palm. She made a little sound of abject surrender into his mouth as his thumb brushed back and forth over the sensitive point, and when he did it again her insides turned to jelly and her knees went weak.

He lifted his head, and she opened her eyes to find that he was looking down at her. His eyes were heavy-lidded and burning hot. His lips were parted, and damp from her kisses.

"Charlie," he said, his voice rough with passion. Then his eyes flickered. Then they widened, and his mouth twisted into a pained grimace, and the big, solid body that was holding her in place shivered. He groaned, a harsh, grating sound that seemed to be dragged out of somewhere deep inside him. The next instant he was gone. Vanished.

She was left clutching air.

"Michael," Charlie said blankly, still stupid with desire, still aching and burning and not quite grasping what had happened. Then in a burst of terrible clarity she knew: for a few moments he had managed to materialize, managed to become as real and solid as he had been when he was alive, and now he was paying the price.

The horrible, painful price.

Pushing away from the door, she glanced a little wildly around the room. There was no mistake. He wasn't there.

Her heart pounded like a kettledrum. But this time it was from fear.

"Michael!" Even as she called his name, she knew it was useless. He wasn't anywhere where he could hear.

Calm down. Try to think.

The last time he had materialized so fully it had been to take a knife in the back for her. After that, he had been gone for four days.

There was no reason why this time should be any different.

All I have to do is wait.

She still felt shaky with the aftermath of passion, and faintly disoriented, and afraid. Her legs were unsteady. Taking the few steps necessary to reach the nearest bed, Charlie sank down on the foot of the mattress.

Michael. There was no point in calling out to him again, though, so she took a deep breath instead, and fought to clear her head. The last lingering effects of passion dissipated. At the thought of where Michael almost certainly was at that moment, she felt cold all over.

From everything he'd told her, and her own brief personal knowledge of it, Spookville was a terrifying place.

What if he can't get back?

That was the thought that made her insides clench.

He was way past the after-death date when most spirits permanently left this plane. The universe already had been on the verge of taking him away to meet whatever eternity awaited him when she'd intervened with her candle and glass. It had him now.

This time the question came as almost a shriek inside her head: *What if he can't get back?*

Assessing the likelihood of that, Charlie felt stark fear. She'd known it all along: ghosts can't stay.

She felt as if a giant hand had grabbed her heart and was squeezing it.

The universe knows what it's doing. He won't get worse than he deserves. He's tough. He'll endure.

Charlie realized she was shivering, and wrapped her arms around herself.

You'll get your life back. You'll get your chance with Tony, if that's what you want. You won't have a ghost that you never asked for chained to you forever.

Even as she reminded herself of those things, Charlie found herself battling the urge to scream. To the universe, to send him back. To God, to have mercy.

He had gone so fast.

Her chest was suddenly so tight that she could hardly breathe.

Maybe he'll make it back, she told herself. After all, he did before.

What she needed to do was stay calm. Turn the process over to whatever part of Divine Providence handled such matters. Trust in the ultimate rightness of all things.

She sat perfectly still, taking deep, hopefully calming breaths, searching for her inner Zen.

Then she thought, *To hell with that.*

Her legs still felt unsteady as she pushed to her feet. Snatching up her purse from the floor where it had fallen when Michael had grabbed her—she didn't even remember dropping it—Charlie fished inside it for her phone and called Tam.

"Cherie, I was just getting ready to call you" was how Tam greeted her. "I have more: in the dark water, there is a gray house. The danger is inside the gray house."

It sounded screwy. Lots of times, Charlie recalled, Tam's visions sounded screwy, until they worked out exactly the way Tam said they would. But at the moment, she didn't care.

"Tam," she said, and it was a struggle to keep her voice from cracking. "You remember that ghost you told me how to keep here? A few minutes ago, he"— kissed me senseless—"materialized. All the way. As real and solid as if he was alive. Then he groaned, and looked like he was in terrible pain, and disappeared. It was—fast."

"Spirits shouldn't be materializing," Tam said sharply. "It goes against the way things are supposed to be."

"Well, he did. And now he's gone. I think he's been sucked into Spookville—well, that's what he calls it. A place that's all cold, purple twilight."

"The Dark Place." Tam's tone was stark with horror. "The spirit you wanted to keep earthbound is from there?"

"Yes."

"He should not have materialized. He broke the bond." Tam paused. "Which is probably just as well."

"I need to help him get back."

"No and no and no. If I had known before—"

"Tam. Please."

"But, cherie, if he is of the Dark Place, then you need to leave him be. *He—is—not—good.*" Tam said that last forcefully.

"Tam, for God's sake, if there's anything I can do to help him get back here, tell me what it is."

"Really, cherie?" Tam sounded as disapproving as Tam ever sounded, which Charlie realized ordinarily would have made her think twice about what she was asking. That saying about only count-ing the sunny hours? That was Tam. She always chose to embrace the light.

"Yes. Really." Charlie heard the desperation in her own voice, and briefly closed her eyes. *"Please."*

"Hmm." Tam sighed. "All right, well, let me see. You closed the passage to keep the spirit earthbound, if I recall." Charlie made an affirmative noise. "There is no sure method to bring spirits back from the Beyond, much less from the Dark Place, I must tell you. My best suggestion to you would be that you open the passage again. You have a candle?"

"Yes."

"Light it to open the passage, then call the spirit's name. The spirit may hear, and find the passage, and return."

Charlie heard the second possibility in the other woman's voice loud and clear: or he may not.

She tried to control her too-rapid breathing. "Is there anything else I can do?"

"That's all I know, cherie," Tam said.

"Thanks." As Charlie was disconnecting, she heard Tam call to her, "Take the utmost care."

Charlie never traveled without her Miracle-Go kit, to which she had added a small, heavy glass for the closing of spectral passages since she had realized such a thing might become necessary. Now she grabbed a lighter and one of the squat, round jasmine candles from the kit. Then she pulled out a second and a third candle. It hit her that turning on the water might help, too, so she took the candles into the bathroom, set them on the counter, and lit them. As the scent of jasmine started to fill the air, she closed the door to keep the aroma in and turned the cold water tap in the sink on full blast.

Then she turned off the bathroom light and looked into the flickering flames and called, "Michael."

Again and again and again.

He didn't come.

The terror she felt for him frightened her.

Minutes ticked past, blurred into hours.

Finally Charlie was sitting on the bathroom floor, still in her dress, with her knees drawn up almost to her chin and her back against the cold hard side of the tub. She was growing hoarse. Her eyelids were heavy as lead.

She gave up on calling his name only because she fell asleep.

At first she thought the creeping tendrils of fog that snaked toward her were smoke from the candles. Then she noticed that they were purple and thick. As they reached her they started slowly swirling around her like multiple lariats. Even as she blinked at them, they rose, enveloping her in a way that the puny smoke from her candles never could. Instead of jasmine, they smelled of—rotting things and damp. Eyes widening, Charlie clambered to her feet. Everywhere she looked—and she got the impression that she was confronting vast distances in all directions—the landscape was overlaid with billowing clouds of purple mist.

She shivered, suddenly cold. Her arms and shoulders and legs were bare, and her feet were, too. It took her a second to realize that she was still wearing her red dress, minus the shoes. It seemed to be twilight—there was no sun, but it wasn't quite dark, either. The ground beneath her feet—she couldn't really see it because of the fog—seemed to be composed mostly of solid sheets of rock, with a few patches of what looked like slimy moss.

Where am I?

But even as the question popped into her mind, she knew.

Spookville.

Michael.

Oh, my God, how did I get here? An instant later the more pertinent question brought a thrill of fear with it: *How do I get back?*

In the distance, a bloodcurdling scream tore through the mist. Charlie jumped and looked fearfully all around as a sense of utter dread filled her. Closer at hand, she heard a kind of shuffling, lumbering sound as if something huge was moving toward her at a fast pace. That rhythmic wheezing gasp was its breathing, she realized with horror a split second after she became aware of it.

She caught a glimpse of a huge dark *thing* shrouded by the mist as it rushed past her.

Now the screams were so close that they sent icy ripples of fright coursing through the center of her being. It sounded like a creature was being torn to shreds not more than a stone's throw away, and Charlie thought that the nightmarish shrieks came from something the thing had caught. She barely managed to swallow her own answering scream.

Then she saw another horror in the mist: what looked like two unblinking yellow eyes luminescent enough to glow through the swirling fog, turning in her direction.

She knew, instinctively, that she was in terrible danger.

Swallowing another scream, she ran.

Not far to her left, there was a scrabble of feet, a barely seen leap through the mist as if something pounced, another deathly scream.

Fear washed over her in waves.

Michael. She dared not cry his name out loud, not with whatever these things were so near. He was there somewhere, she was sure. Instinct—a sixth sense, an insistent psychic pull—told her so. It sent her fleeing in a certain direction, but whether it was right or not she had no way of knowing. If she was wrong—the thought made her shake. Creatures bounded past her. Horrific screams pierced the air. Feet bruising on the rocky ground, she fled past stands of what seemed to be shaggy, misshapen trees, past boulders bigger than she was, past a fissure in the ground spewing a sulfurous gray steam.

An orange glow, blurred by the mist but still a beacon in the gloom, drew her. As she neared it, gasping for what little air there was, feeling as though her heart would burst from her chest, she saw that she was running headlong toward the dark edge of a cliff and slowed abruptly. The orange glow came from a fire far below, she discovered as she drew cautiously closer, a roaring, raging conflagration from which screaming people fled while flames consumed them.

Charlie recoiled in fear.

At the edge of the cliff overlooking the horror, a man crouched, his back against a boulder the size of a bus.

His face was turned away from her as he looked down into the abyss, but there was no mistaking those broad shoulders or that tawny hair. Limned in orange, his big body was no more than a dark shape against the glow, but she would know him anywhere.

"Michael!" This time, as she flew toward him, she did cry his name aloud.

He looked sharply around, surged to his feet, leaped toward her. "Charlie!"

She threw herself against him, and he caught her. His face was all sharp planes and angles, and his eyes were as black and fathomless as hell's deepest pit. For a moment the intensity of emotion she felt at having found him swamped everything else. He hugged her tight, and she wrapped her arms around him and clung to him as if he was the only hope of salvation she had left.

"Jesus Christ." The stark fear in his voice penetrated a split second before she heard the growl. It was a low, guttural, threatening sound that had to have come from something huge, and it was close behind her. She looked up at Michael: what she saw in his face made her blood run cold. Whatever could make him look like that, she didn't want to see.

CHAPTER TWENTY-ONE

Michael whirled with her so that his back was turned to whatever it was. Curling himself protectively around her, he pressed her head to his chest. Tensing, clinging close, silently reciting every prayer she had ever learned in her life, Charlie cowered in his arms.

"Think of somewhere safe, quick," he told her urgently.

Even as Charlie did, the growl turned into a roar. She felt a rush of air as the creature leaped at them and they passed it while it was in mid-jump.

The mist swirled. She had the sensation of being hurtled forward, and closed her eyes against a rushing wind. She could feel Michael warm and solid against her, and she held on to him for dear life. The very air seemed to writhe, and suck at her skin. Then the cold was gone, along with the smell, and with those things went the clingy dampness of the fog. Entwined together, the two of them tumbled in what felt like a free fall through the infinite blackness of time and space. Clinging to Michael as if he was the only solid thing left in the universe, Charlie felt as if she were being crushed; as if she couldn't breathe. Then, suddenly, everything around them was still. There seemed to be solid ground beneath her bare feet. Carpet, from the texture of it.

Charlie opened her eyes. They were in her hotel room, in the narrow hall between the bathroom and closet, near the spot where he had disappeared. The room was awash in moonlight that spilled inside because the curtains over the big window across the room were open to the night.

Safe. Thank God.

"You okay?" Michael's voice grated. She looked up at him. Her arms were locked around his waist. His were wrapped tight around her shoulders. His face was harsh. His eyes were still black, blacker even than the night outside the window, but some of the horrible soulless glitter left them as he looked down at her.

Charlie took a deep breath, glad to be able to fill her lungs. "Yes." Then as he closed his eyes she took another breath and added, "What about you?"

He didn't answer, and she frowned. He was his usual handsome self, but—not. He seemed bigger than usual, and badder. Savagery radiated from him like rays from the sun. Ruthlessness was there in the set of his jaw, brutality in the curve of his mouth. There was a hardness around his cheekbones and closed eyes. *This is what a man capable of killing looks like,* was the thought that came to her unbidden, and her mind flicked uneasily back to what Tam had said about the Dark Place, to the question of how innocent or guilty of the heinous crimes that had been attributed to him she really believed him to be. She became fully aware of how solid and real he felt in her arms, and faced all the ramifications of what that meant. There was no cosmic shield between them to protect her, no lack of substance on his part to keep her safe.

They were on the same side of the barrier now, and for better or worse she was locked in his arms.

Charlie faced the terrible truth: there was no place else on earth she would rather be.

"Michael." Her hands unclasped from around his waist to gently stroke his back. Whatever the Dark Place had brought out in him, she chose to attribute to the place, not him. She hoped her touch would remind him that they were away from that horrible place and safe. Beneath the softness of his shirt, his back felt warm and firm. Her hands slid beneath it: his skin was hot and faintly damp. She could feel his back heaving beneath her hands. She asked him again: "Are you okay?"

His eyes opened. She was relieved to see that more of the black had retreated now. But there was a hard, predatory glitter in them still that alarmed her as they raked her face.

"You afraid of me, babe?" he asked. "'Cause you're looking at me like you are."

"Of course I'm not afraid of you," she answered firmly, unsure if right at that moment it was strictly the truth. Dark energy rolled off him in waves. The look on his face, coupled with the rasping voice and the steely prison that his arms around her had become, made her heart beat faster. She could feel his strength, feel the power in the big body that held her, and knew that if he didn't want to let her go, she wasn't getting away.

"Maybe you should be." He drew in air through his teeth, and Charlie got the impression that he was fighting for control. "That place—it does things to people. Bad things."

His hold on her tightened until, if she had been afraid of him, she would have struggled. His body was taut with tension, and she could feel the aggression flowing through him. Her hands flattened and stilled on his broad back, but she didn't let go of him. Didn't want to let go of him, even though every instinct she possessed screamed *danger*. But no matter how menacing he might seem, this was Michael, and she was in his arms, and that by itself was enough to make her go weak at the knees. Instead of trying to pull away from him, she pressed closer still, letting him feel her softness, her femininity. Her breasts swelled against the unyielding wall of his chest; she could feel the delicious prickle as her nipples tightened. She settled her hips more intimately against his. As her breath caught and her body quickened at the rock hardness she found there, she felt the long muscles of his back tense beneath her hands. She looked up then, and met the fierceness of his eyes, which were still only sky blue rims around a center of glittering black.

"I'm going to fuck you all night long," he said, still in that harsh voice.

A shiver went through her as all around them the air turned to steam.

She had no chance to reply before his head dropped and he took her mouth, kissing her like he was a marauder and she was his captive, like he owned her, like she had no say. His hands, big and possessive, closed over her bottom, pulling her up on her toes, cradling her so closely against him that she could feel in graphic detail how aroused he was.

As he rocked her against him her body caught fire, just went up in flames.

"Michael." She moaned his name into his mouth, kissing him back as fiercely as he kissed her, molding her lips to his, meeting the hot deep invasion of her mouth with a passion that matched his. She was shivery with lust, lightheaded, eager. As urgently as he needed to take, she needed to give. He kissed her ear, ran his mouth down the side of her neck, and she felt her bones dissolve.

"You're mine, Doc," he growled just as he had earlier, and even though part of her knew she should protest that women in general and she in particular were not something that could be owned, she was too turned on to do anything except cling to his broad shoulders for support as he bent her back across his hard-muscled arm. Then his mouth was on her breast, opening over her nipple so that she could feel the heat and wetness of it even through the cloth of her dress. Toes curling into the carpet, she arched her back and threaded her fingers into his hair. His hand went beneath her dress to stroke its way up over the smoothness of her bare thigh, then moved between her legs and caressed her through her silky panties, making her gasp, making her burn. Then he was kissing her again, his lips hard and hot and hungry, and his fingers slipped inside her panties to push into the hot, wet center of her so that she turned to liquid fire in his hands and moved with helpless pleasure for him.

"God, I've wanted you," he said thickly, letting her go before she was ready, leaving her wanting more as he caught her dress and pulled it up and over her head. She was naked now except for her panties, and the air in the room felt cool on her overheated skin. Following his gaze, looking down at the pale globes of her own breasts with their dark, eager nipples, at the slender indentation of her waist, at her flat stomach and long slim legs, Charlie felt a wave of desire so intense that she trembled. Her head spun; her pulse drummed in her ears. His eyes were all over her, burning in their intensity, and she felt her muscles liquefy beneath their heat.

"I've wanted you, too," she confessed, and knew even as she said it that it was an understatement. She had ached for him. Burned for him. Still did.

She slid her panties down her legs, stepped out of them. Her heart was hitting about a thousand beats a minute. Her legs were unsteady. Deep inside, her body throbbed.

Watching, dark color suffused his face. He made an inarticulate sound. Then he yanked his shirt over his head, and she reached with shaking fingers for his belt buckle. She barely got it unfastened before he pulled her against him, kissing her with a fierceness that made her dizzy.

His hard-muscled arm curled beneath her bottom, and he lifted her off her feet as if she weighed nothing at all, pushing her back against the door to the hall, spreading her thighs and positioning himself between them. Bending his head, he claimed each nipple with quick, succulent tugs of his mouth. Shivery with desire, she clung to him. His skin was hot and damp with sweat, and his broad shoulders were corded with tension. As his mouth found hers again, and she returned the kiss with wild abandon, Charlie felt the cool smooth wood of the door to the hall against her back. A wave of scalding heat washed over her even as she wrapped her legs around his waist. She felt his hand between them, heard the rasp of his zipper, and her pulse went haywire. Then he pushed himself inside her, huge and hot and urgent, making her cling to him, making her cry out.

"You like that," he growled in her ear as he held himself buried deep. It wasn't a question. He knew.

She told him anyway. "Yes. *Yes.*"

Kissing her, he thrust into her again and again with a ferocity that set her on fire. She could feel the door at her back, and the hard strength of his arms around her and his body pounding into her, and the combination made her spiral out of control. What they were doing felt so unbelievably good that she cried out over and over again. Her body burned and clenched and trembled. It was sex at its rawest, most carnal, most intense. The end, when it came, was explosive.

"*Michael!*" Charlie gasped. Then as he thrust inside her one last time and groaned she came so violently that her body convulsed in a quaking wave of heat.

A moment later, he kissed her again, deeply. As she kissed him back, she felt a shiver run through him, and opened her eyes. A subtle transformation in his face told her that whatever had been going on with him before, he was now at least near to something approaching his usual self. As if he could feel her eyes on him, he broke the kiss and lifted his head. His eyes opened, and she was relieved to see that, except for slightly enlarged pupils, they were once again their normal sky blue as he frowned—not glared—down at her.

"Did I scare you?" He sounded faintly penitent.

Charlie shook her head, still not sure whether or not she was telling the truth. Her heart was beating way too fast. "No."

"It's that damned place. It does things to me." He stepped back to let her slide to her feet. "No matter what happens, I don't ever want you following me into Spookville again, understand?"

"If that's your version of pillow talk, you should probably know that it could use some work," she responded tartly, telling herself that she had *not* been hoping for a hearts and flowers kind of speech from him but realizing even as she did so that, obviously, she had. She leaned back against the door, boneless and still a little shaky, watching him with secret, silent pleasure as he pulled up and refastened his jeans.

His mouth curved in the merest suggestion of a smile. His eyes slid over her, and the sudden hot gleam in them reminded her that she was naked. Her dress was somewhere on the floor. There it was, by his feet.

"You're beautiful," he said. "Sexy as hell. Just what I always wanted."

"That's better." She nodded toward her dress. Since he stood between her and it, asking him for it seemed the best option. "Could you please hand me my dress?"

"No." He stepped closer, imprisoning her with his hands braced against the door, on either side of her as his big body rested on top of hers and he kissed her, a slow, hot sampling that made her heart start to pound again and her body quicken. "I meant what I said about Spookville: stay out."

He gave her a hard look, and Charlie tried to concentrate on that, not his mouth, which next slid across her cheek to nuzzle her ear—or his hand, which found her breast. Or the heat of his bare chest against her breasts, or the abrasion of his jeans against her legs, and her stomach, and the most sensitive, responsive part of her.

Oh, God, can he really turn me on again this fast?

Focus on what he said. Before the part about Spookville.

She narrowed her eyes at him. "What do you mean, no?"

"I like you naked."

That made her heart skip a beat. If she'd really wanted her dress, she would have insisted, but the truth was that being naked in the moonlight with him made her go all quivery inside. Her hands, which had been pressed flat against the door, rose to press flat against his chest instead. Not that she was thinking about pushing him away or anything. No way.

She loved how his chest felt under her hands: warm and strong and satiny smooth.

"About Spookville: I didn't mean to go there, believe me. It just happened." She sounded faintly breathless, and that would be because she found his powerfully muscled chest so sexy to touch. Plus, his mouth on the sensitive hollow below her ear was hot and wet. And his hand was big and warm. And arousing, as it cupped and caressed her breast. "Anyway, if I hadn't followed you, that—that *thing*—would have gotten you."

"Nah. I've gotten pretty good at getting away."

He was kissing the side of her neck, his mouth crawling down the sensitive cord. His thumb brushed back and forth across her nipple. Lightning bolts of sensation shivered through her. Her knees went weak. Carrying on a conversation with him under the circumstances was growing increasingly difficult, but she persevered, because this was something she truly wanted to understand.

"I saw two yellow eyes looking at me through the fog," she said. Remembering the horror of it made her shiver. He lifted his head to look at her, and her blood started to steam at the hot, dark gleam in his eyes.

"That was a hunter. They catch us poor unfortunate souls that wind up in there and drag us off to hell."

Charlie's heart gave an odd little hiccup when she thought about that in relation to him. "Really?"

"I don't know. I've never been caught by one. But I think it's a good guess."

"You know"—she was sounding way too breathless, and that would be because of his hand on her breast—"this would probably be a good time for you to tell me why something would want to drag you off to hell."

Because any and all possible reasons that she could come up with made her go cold all over.

Michael shook his head, refusing to answer. He radiated a hard sexual tension, and Charlie shivered and quaked and burned in instinctive response. The truth was that she was weak with longing, hungry for him again, embarrassingly needy. His eyes flamed at her, and she remembered him saying that he could read her like a neon sign. Then he bent his head and kissed her again.

It was intended as a distraction, she knew. Charlie felt the insistent molding of his mouth to hers, felt him parting her lips, felt the hot slide of his tongue, and considered her situation. She thought about the black soullessness she had seen in his eyes, and the crimes he denied having committed, and what it might take to get a man sent to hell. And the conclusion she came to was that it didn't matter: whatever he was or wasn't, whatever he had or hadn't done, she was now so ensnared in the web they had gotten caught in together, there was no breaking free.

She closed her eyes and slid her arms around his neck and kissed him back. His mouth was hot, and unhurried now, and so mind-blowingly expert that it made her wild all over again.

Still kissing her, he picked her up and carried her to bed.

His heavily muscled shoulders and arms looked silvery in the moonlight, she saw as he laid her down on the mattress and she opened her eyes. When he would have straightened away from her, she held him with her arms around his neck, and pressed her open mouth to his wide chest, kissing and licking the firm, warm flesh. He shuddered against her, and she flicked a look up at him.

His eyes were hot and dark. "Let me take off my pants," he said, his voice hoarse.

As he stood up and unfastened his jeans, she moved to the edge of the bed. Then she stood up, too, in front of him, and slid her hands down inside his shorts to close around him.

He was huge, and hot, and velvety soft and hard as steel at the same time.

She wasn't a child; she knew what to do. As her hands tightened on him, did what she knew he'd like, he groaned. But that was all he could do, because he was busy pulling off his boots, and then shoving his jeans down his legs. By the time he got his clothes off, she was on her knees in front of him, her hands on his ass, pleasuring him with her mouth.

Naked, he stood very still, his body rock solid while sexual tension rolled off him in waves. His hands slid into her hair. By this time it was loose, falling around her shoulders, and she could feel the tug at the roots. She knew he was watching her because she could feel the weight of his eyes. She wanted to make him come, and would have done it, too, if in the nick of time he hadn't freed himself and picked her up by the waist and tumbled her back on the bed. He pushed inside her instantly, thrusting deep, and she cried out.

He kept driving into her, hard and fast, and kissing her breasts and then her mouth, while she wrapped her legs around his waist and her arms around his neck and let the delicious waves of dark, hot passion catch her up until at last they broke and he came and she came for him again.

After that, she lay boneless and pleasantly drifting in his arms as they talked about everything and nothing, really. Until he turned her onto her stomach, and brushed her hair aside to kiss the nape of her neck, which made her sigh a little because she liked the way the touch of his lips on her skin made her feel. He followed that kiss with another, and another, until he was trailing kisses down the length of her spine, licking and nibbling, tracing its curving pathway with his mouth all the way to the cleft in her butt. Then he kissed her bottom, too, his mouth crawling over every inch of the soft round curves until he had her squirming against the mattress and digging into it with her nails. Finally he spread her legs and knelt between them, and pulled her up to meet him. He entered her that way, with fierce demanding strokes and his hand between her legs.

She came so hard for him then that she screamed his name.

"Michael! Oh, my God, *Michael*!"

Lucky no one but him could hear.

Afterward, he pulled her against him, and kissed her mouth. She kissed him back, all languid heat now, then settled in with her head on his shoulder and a hand resting in the center of his wide chest, while his arm curved around her, keeping her close. Already she could see, through the open window, the first pink fingers of dawn creeping across the dark sky. It was beautiful, but as she watched it her heart hurt.

A glance at Michael's face told her that he was watching it, too. The chiseled planes and angles were gorgeous as ever, but there was a bleak cast to them that said he was as aware of the passage of time as she was. Then he must have felt her eyes on him because he looked at her, and rose up on an elbow so that his powerfully built torso blocked out most of her view of the window. She had just a second to absorb the fact that his beautiful mouth was hard now and that grimness lurked behind the hot dark gleam in his eyes before his mouth was on hers and he was rolling on top of her and pushing inside her again.

There was a fierceness to their lovemaking, because they both knew that they would have only this one night, and it was drawing to an end.

She came with a hot rippling pleasure that had her gasping and trembling, and, finally, made the night explode like fireworks against her closed lids. He came with his mouth pressed to the tender curve between her shoulder and neck, and a groan that was muffled against her skin.

When the alarm on her phone went off, it wasn't like it was unexpected, so Charlie didn't know why the sound jolted her so. But it did, catapulting her out of the unlikely sanctuary she had found in his arms, jarring her senses, making her heart leap.

"Michael—" Her eyes flew to his face, but even as his eyes widened and his arms tightened around her, the room seemed to fold in on her. Everything went black as she was buffeted by a blast of cold wind. She lost all conception of time and space until she felt a sudden jarring impact. Her heart leaped, she sucked in air, and then her eyes snapped open.

She was in the bathroom, lying curled on the floor in front of the tub, with only the fluffy white bath mat protecting her face from the tile. The bathroom was dark, not black but gloomy, and there was a rushing sound that she couldn't quite place. For a second she blinked at her shoes, which were under the sink directly within her line of vision, and she recalled kicking them off sometime during last night's long vigil. Then she remembered the candles, and pushed herself into a sitting position to check: sure enough, there they were on the counter, flames now out. The wicks were black and burnt, and from the hollowed-out look of the candles they had guttered on melted wax.

The rushing sound came from the water still running in the sink.

She must have made some small noise, because all of a sudden there was Michael barging through the bathroom door then stopping to look down at her as she sat on the floor. From the speed with which he had arrived, she thought he must have rushed to find her there. For a moment she detected a flicker of relief in his eyes— probably he had been worried about where she had gone when she had vanished from beside him—but then he simply looked grim. She guessed that he was wrestling to come to terms with the fact that their idyll was over, just as she was. They were on different sides of the barrier again. Looking at him, she felt an aching sadness, as though she had lost something precious. Their relationship had been impossible from the first, but knowing that there was no future in it was even harder to bear now. Her heart stuttered as she considered that any physical contact between them was quite possibly over forever, unless she learned how to control the astral projection thing, which was clearly what she had done again last night. But before she could decide if trying to become an expert at astral-projection-on-demand was even something that she wanted to do, much less if it was feasible, she realized exactly what she was looking at, and blinked.

Michael was naked.

Michael was gorgeous.

As her eyes slid up his long, muscular legs, paused for a second to register once again how impressively well endowed he was, then moved on to admire his washboard abs and wide chest and heavily muscled arms and shoulders before stopping on his hard, handsome face, she felt her pulse pick up the pace and her body, which had been feeling a little cold from lying on the floor, start to get warm again. After the night they'd just spent, she would have thought she'd be past getting turned on by anyone or anything for a good long while, but she would've been wrong. Simply looking at Michael was enough to do it. And not only because naked—or not naked, for that matter—he was the hottest guy she had just about ever seen. There was something between them—a sizzling chemistry, a potent sexual attraction— that had been there from the beginning, when she had conducted her first interview with the scary, insolent, way-too-gorgeous convict in chains.

Now, merely the sight of him was enough to make her heart go pitter-pat. Charlie would have told him so if some tiny, self-protective part of her hadn't warned against it: no point in taking this debacle in the making any further than she already had. So if she wasn't going to say something on the order of *every time I look at you I get turned on,* she realized as she met his gaze that she was at a loss. Because, really, what do you say to a naked man you have no future with after a night of truly epic sex with him? She had no clue.

He saved her. Having spent much less time looking at her than she had spent looking at him—she guessed that, in her crumpled red dress, which covered her from her armpits to her knees, and with her hair hanging down in a tangle around her face, she wasn't as much to look at as he was at the moment—he had taken in the candles and the running water, too. He knew what they were for; she didn't have to explain.

"Next time I get sucked in to Spookville, you leave it the hell alone," he warned again. His eyes had turned unreadable. His voice was hard. His words made it clear: he expected to wind up in Spookville again at some point. The terrible truth was, she expected that he would wind up there again, too. Just thinking about it made her feel all raw and vulnerable inside, so she dragged her thoughts away. "I can take care of myself. And there's no telling what might happen to you in there."

Okay, so tender words of mutual affection—or even a classic was-it-as-good-for-you-as-it-was-for-me conversation—seemed to be out. Well, for both their sakes, that was probably a good thing.

"You seemed happy enough to see me last night," she retorted, glad to skip any emotional heartburnings in favor of getting their relationship back to what felt more or less like normal. Scrambling to her feet, she turned off the tap. A glance in the mirror confirmed it: she looked a mess. Surprisingly, she didn't feel all that tired. While her spirit was having world-class sex, apparently her body had gotten some rest.

"I wasn't," he said grimly.

"Probably it would help if you did *your* best to stay out of Spookville." The look she gave him was severe. Or, actually, it started out that way, but then the realization that they were having this conversation while he was leaning a broad shoulder against the wall and standing there casually nude affected the quality of her severity a little, so that she had to give herself a tiny mental shake before refocusing. The sad truth was, she could feel herself starting to get turned on *again*. "For one thing, you can't materialize anymore. Tam said it weakens the bond. That must have been why you got pulled in like you did."

"Brought the voodoo priestess into it, did you?" The slow smile he gave her made her heart beat a little faster. "You must have been worried about me."

There was no point in denying that. The evidence was too clear. Besides, he knew.

"I was."

There was a lot she could have said after that. A lot she would have said if she was foolish, like *I was scared to death that I was never going to see you again,* or even, *Yes, okay, you were right, I am crazy about you,* but neither one of those felt smart—in fact, not only did they not feel smart, they felt stupid and even downright dangerous—so she didn't. Instead she contented herself with a monitory, "Don't materialize, okay?" Then, with the brisk air of getting down to necessary business she stepped toward him, and the light switch, which she flipped on. The sudden brightness made her squint a little as she looked at him. "We should probably go ahead and do the whole light-the-candle, close-the-passage thing again. Then I need to take a shower. I'm supposed to be out in the hall at seven." She glanced at his watch, which dangled braceletlike around her wrist. "Which is in forty-three minutes."

For a moment he simply looked at her. Then he said, "Let me put my pants on first," which she got the impression wasn't what he had been going to say at all, but made her think about when he had taken them *off,* until he turned away and she got distracted by the very nice view that she was afforded of his broad back and small, tight butt.

Watching so much flexing muscle and rippling sinew was making her start to feel all soft and squishy inside. Fortunately he disappeared through the door before she got so hot she dissolved into a steamy little puddle on the floor. Opening the door in anticipation of his return, she found him scooping his clothes up from the floor beside the bed.

When Michael returned, he was fully dressed, down to his boots, and she had a glass and a candle ready to light.

"Fuck," he said, eyeing the setup, and she took that to mean that he was ready.

The ritual went much the same as before, although they were both better prepared for his pain. When it was over, she ordered him out.

"I'm going to take a shower. And the bathroom is still off-limits," she reminded him, just in case he had some notion that last night had changed the rule. "Shoo."

The slightest of wicked smiles touched his mouth. "Babe, at this point I've seen it all. And touched it. And licked it. And—"

Charlie gave him a withering look. She should have known he wasn't going to let her simply forget about everything they'd done. "Go, all right?"

Even as she shut the door on him, he grinned at her.

She was in the middle of her shower before she remembered that, once again, she'd forgotten to bring her clothes into the bathroom with her.

When, wrapped in a towel with another towel wound around her head, she walked out into the room, it was to find him standing in front of the dark TV, frowning. That frown changed to an interested look as he spotted her, which changed to a hot gleam as his eyes slid over her. It was just as well that she was in a hurry, she thought, because that meant she didn't have time to respond to the look in his eyes with more than an inner quiver. Which she immediately ordered herself to ignore.

If she was going to get turned on every time she looked at him or he looked at her, this would be bad.

"You know, you *can* get dressed in front of me," he said dryly when she grabbed clean undies from her suitcase then walked to the closet to extract the clothes she had hung there the night before. "It's not like I can do anything but look."

Actually, merely the thought of him looking was all it took to turn that inner quiver into a delicious melting quake, which was alarming. Charlie had a sudden terrible suspicion that last night's sex-a-thon might have conditioned her to respond to him automatically, like Pavlov's dog.

"Yeah. No," she said.

"Your call. I'll still be around when putting your clothes on in the bathroom gets old, though."

Probably true, but like lots of things concerning him she mentally filed it away under "Stuff to worry about later." Clothes in hand, Charlie was heading back into the bathroom when she noticed the disgusted glance he cast at the remote, which lay on the console table beside the TV. Frowning, she paused to ask, "Is something wrong?"

"I can't work it. The remote." Reaching for it, he demonstrated: his hand passed right through, no traction at all. "I'd gotten to where I could. Before last night. Now I can't."

He looked so bothered by his failure that she would have said something comforting, like *Hmm,* if a knock hadn't sounded on the door.

"Charlie?" It was Tony's voice. Michael immediately looked sour. "You up?"

"Yes. I'll be right there," she called back, and rushed into the bathroom to dress. When she emerged, Michael was leaning against the wall beside the door, waiting for her. As he straightened, his eyes skimmed her. Her hair was twisted up in a loose knot, lots of tendrils which made it, she hoped, both cool and elegantly sexy, and she was wearing another purchase from the gift shop, a sleeveless, knee-length yellow linen shirtdress with a skinny belt around her waist, and last night's kicky little sandals. She thought, with pardonable satisfaction, that she was looking pretty good. When his eyes rose to meet hers again, he smiled.

That slow smile was enough to make Charlie's heart skip a beat. *Oh, boy.*

Well, she'd known she was in trouble.

"You look good enough to eat," he said. Then, right as a quick *thank-you* smile was curving her lips, he added, "Just so we're on the same page, you start making out with Dudley again and it's going to royally piss me off."

Here it was. She'd known this was coming. It was tempting—oh, so tempting—to ignore it, to brush it off, to save this cold splash of reality to be dealt with at a later, more convenient time. But she felt she needed to make herself very clear, for her own sake as well as his.

The scary thing was, she was dangerously close to losing her heart to him, and she wasn't about to let that happen.

Her life would be ruined forever.

"You have no right to object to anything I choose to do," she said evenly. "Last night was only a night. We can't be together; you know that. And I have to live my life. So if I want to make out with *Tony*—or anybody else, for that matter—that's what I'm going to do."

Then, before he could erupt—and it was clear from his face that an eruption was imminent—she turned and walked out the door.

CHAPTER TWENTY-TWO

"Are you fucking kidding me?" Michael's furious growl sliced through the conversation as Charlie headed with Tony, Buzz, and Kaminsky for the elevators. "An hour ago I'm fucking you into next week, and now you're throwing this shit at me?"

Tony was laying out the game plan for the day, so Charlie's reply to Michael was minimal: she narrowed her eyes at him. He stalked along beside her, looking all badass and mad, but she wasn't about to back down. For her own self-preservation, she needed to draw a line in the sand with him while she still could.

"I just heard back from Eric Riva. He was in an ATV wreck as a teenager that killed the friend he was riding with," Kaminsky said excitedly. She was checking her e-mail as they stopped to wait for the elevator. Like Charlie, she was wearing one of her gift shop purchases: a short-sleeved orange blouse worn loose over a white tank and skirt. Charlie presumed the blouse hid Kaminsky's gun.

"You want to get it on with Dudley? Is that it?" Michael had planted himself directly in front of her. "What, did I give you a taste for hot sex last night and now that I can't come through you think you'll get him to pinch hit? Here's a heads-up, babe: it don't work like that." His eyes blazed at her.

Entirely unaware of Michael practically oozing menace over the pair of them, Tony, who was standing beside her, smiled at Charlie. "Did you have a good night?"

"Yes," she replied with an answering smile, while Michael snarled, "You want to see him turn tail and run, tell him how good your night really was."

They were in the elevator on the way down by that time, and Tony was close enough so that if she leaned slightly to her left their arms would brush. But she didn't. Right at that moment she didn't feel in the least little bit like doing anything to further her relationship with Tony. She had just wanted to make her position clear to Michael. To leave her options open, so that when the memory of last night's lust-fest had faded enough, she could move ahead with her life. If not with Tony, then with someone else. Some living, breathing man.

Michael said, "Let's see, how many times did I make you come? Three? Four? Hell, I lost count long about the third time you sucked my—"

"Did you find any more possible single murders around Buggs Island Lake?" Charlie asked Kaminsky before Michael could finish, in a deliberate effort to not hear that last word. Because the scorching memory it conjured up was, in the bright light of day, embarrassing. It also turned her on a little, but she wasn't even going to let herself think about that.

"Oh, so you think you can fucking ignore me now?" Michael growled, and slammed a hand down on the elevator alarm. But instead of going off, as it had last night, nothing happened: his hand passed right through it.

Michael looked totally pissed. Charlie almost smiled.

Kaminsky grimaced. "Right now, four of the accidental deaths could possibly be murders. But what's really interesting is that ten kids between the ages of eleven and seventeen have gone missing from around that lake over the ten years before the Gingerbread Man killings started. That I've found so far. I mean, it's a big area with a lot of people, and ten in ten years isn't actually all that many, but—"

"They're important," Charlie told her, her attention effectively refocused, at least temporarily.

"What I thought was interesting is that Buggs Island Lake is no more than a four-hour drive from any of the grab or kill sites," Buzz said. "If the area we're looking at was a wheel, the lake would be almost in the center of it."

"He started there," Charlie said. "I'm almost sure of it."

"Keep looking into those deaths and disappearances around that lake," Tony said to Kaminsky, who nodded. They reached the lobby, and Kaminsky sheared off toward the hotel conference room which she had set up as a kind of ad hoc War Room, with her computers in place. The rest of them headed for the waiting SUV. Tony and Buzz started comparing notes on which of the victims had confirmed having been exposed to a violent death at a young age, and Charlie tried to stay tuned in to what they were saying, but it was hard with Michael practically vibrating with anger beside her.

"Fine, babe," he said as they all stepped out into the wall of sweltering heat that was the day. "You want to give me the cold shoulder, you do that. For now. But I'm not going anywhere, and neither are you."

That sounded so much like a threat that Charlie flicked a look up at him. He was cold-eyed and hard-mouthed, his tall, powerfully built body sending out waves of aggression. If she'd met him as a stranger in a dark alley right now, she thought, she would have shrunk back into the shadows and tried to escape his notice. But he wasn't a stranger, and she wasn't afraid of him.

What she *was* was teetering on the brink of falling hopelessly, madly in love with him, she realized with dismay. Last night she'd gotten a glimpse deep beneath the gorgeous golden surface, into what lurked in the furthest reaches of his soul. What she'd seen there had been dark and violent and dangerous. And the truth was, as far as the way she felt about him was concerned, it hadn't changed a thing.

And that, she thought, was the scariest thought of all.

They grabbed coffee from a McDonald's, parked the SUV, and started walking along Mallory Street, which was on the route of Jenna's 5K run. They went from store to store, interviewing the workers. The heat was oppressive even so early in the day, and a number of the stores weren't yet open. Buzz was marking those down on a map so they could catch them on the way back up the street, and Tony was thanking a voluble restaurant owner for his cooperation, when Charlie noticed the spirit. It was a well-dressed but blood-drenched elderly man who was following an equally well-dressed (living, not blood-drenched) elderly woman along the sidewalk. Nothing special: she saw spirits like him all the time. At a guess, he'd died in some kind of accident, certainly within the last seven days. But a little farther down the block she saw the spirit of a teenage boy with the blue lips of someone who had died from a lack of oxygen following a middle-aged couple going in the same direction as the elderly pair. And behind him came the spirit of a little girl of maybe five, blond with a pink bow in her hair and not a mark on her that Charlie could see, following a woman of about thirty who had tears running down her face and looked so much like the little girl that Charlie assumed she had to be her mother.

Three spirits of the newly, violently dead on the same block, heading in the same direction, was unusual enough to make Charlie frown.

"So, you got a clue what this whole spook parade going on out here is about?" Michael asked in her ear. He hadn't spoken a word to her since his "I'm not going anywhere" comment, and she knew he absolutely wasn't over being mad at her. That meant that what he was seeing was extraordinary enough to compel him to mention it to her. She didn't think the three spirits she could see would constitute a spook parade in his book, so after a glance to assure herself that Tony and Buzz were still preoccupied Charlie did a quick pivot so that she was facing Michael.

"I see three spirits," she told him, mindful of the other people on the crowded sidewalk. "What do you see?"

The look he gave her bristled with barely contained hostility. But then he glanced around and came back to her with, "I count eleven of 'em. All walking down the street in the same direction, following somebody who's alive."

Charlie frowned thoughtfully. Then, as she saw Tony finishing with the restaurateur and Buzz looking in her direction, she quickly said, "Could you ask one of them where they're going?"

He snorted. "You really think I'm going to keep doing your dirty work? News flash, babe: I ain't the damned ghost whisperer's apprentice."

"We're trying to catch a guy who murdered a bunch of kids here," she hissed.

His lips compressed. But as Tony caught up with her and Buzz came trailing behind, Michael left her to apparently walk beside someone she couldn't see.

"You get anything?" Tony asked Buzz as he joined them. Buzz shook his head. Michael, meanwhile, appeared to be engaging in conversation with the unseen spirit.

"Not a thing." Buzz sounded discouraged. "If Jenna, Laura, or Raylene went inside any of these places, nobody remembers seeing them. Maybe we'll see something on the security camera footage from the ATM at the corner. What about you?"

Tony shook his head. "Nothing. You check the security video from Omar's?"

One corner of Buzz's mouth quirked up. "Yeah. Lena—uh, Kaminsky—and I looked at it last night. We got Laura Parker on it, all right. She's competing in a wet T-shirt contest with about twenty other girls." The quirk turned into a full-blown grin. "It was something to see." At the look Tony gave him, Buzz added hastily, "Kaminsky did facial recognition on all the guys caught on tape watching, but there was nobody who jumped out."

Michael was back. The look he gave Charlie as her eyes turned on him questioningly was dark.

"Damn it." Tony glanced around at the surrounding buildings in frustration. "There's got to be something here. I just don't think he chose those three girls at random, and this is the only place that we know they intersect."

"They're following their loved ones to a grief counseling group session," Michael told Charlie, who sucked in a breath as the connection suddenly became crystal clear in her mind. "Apparently there's a meeting on the second floor of that building on the corner."

He pointed, but he didn't have to: Charlie watched the blood-drenched elderly man follow the elderly woman into the building, and grabbed the sleeve of Tony's jacket.

"It's grief counseling." Charlie could feel the excitement coursing through her veins. "*That's* the connection. I'm sure of it. We'll find that all the victims were with someone who suffered a violent death and then went to *grief counseling*."

"What?" Tony said as he and Buzz gave her identical surprised looks.

"They're getting ready to have a session right now on the second floor of that building on the corner." Charlie tugged on Tony's arm. "Come on."

"You're welcome," Michael said sourly, and Charlie forgot herself enough to give him a quick smile even as she was practically frog-marching Tony toward the building. Michael didn't smile back. Watching her with Tony, his eyes had gone all flinty, and his mouth was grim.

Tony frowned at her questioningly. "What made you think of grief counseling? And how do you know there's a session getting ready to start in that building?"

"I can't wait to hear this." Michael's voice was dry. "Go on, buttercup, tell him how you know."

"The universe speaks to me, remember?" she said lightly, throwing Michael an *eat dirt* look. "Plus, somebody walking past was carrying a brochure."

"Yeah, I thought so," Michael said.

The look Tony gave her was searching. Of course, he knew she *was*, ahem, a little bit psychic, even if he didn't know the half of it. One day, Charlie told herself, she might even sit him down and tell him the whole truth. Minus the part about Michael, of course.

She was never going to be able to tell anybody about Michael.

The Grief Connection was the group's name. It was printed on a sign affixed to the open door of a room that was already filling up with people, dead and alive. Rows of molded plastic chairs, a speaker's podium, a table with coffee and pastries, that was it. According to the social worker getting ready to lead that day's session, open meetings were held every weekday from nine to ten a.m. It was run like an AA meeting. People came, shared the source of their grief, and found comfort. No, there were no records of who attended the meetings, and there were certainly no security cameras. But she was able to give them a list of the meeting leaders, and a number they could use to contact the parent organization for more information.

"What are the chances that Jenna, Raylene, and Laura all ended up in one of these sessions together?" Buzz whispered as they stood at the back of the room watching the meeting get under way.

"It's the only thing that fits." Tony's gaze swung to Charlie. "You want to give Jenna a call when we get out of here and see if she can confirm being at one of these meetings the day she was kidnapped? I'd do it, but I think it'd be better coming from you. Crane, when we get back to the hotel, see if you can find out if any of the other victims went in for some kind of grief counseling."

Charlie nodded, and Crane said, "Will do, boss."

As they watched the elderly woman Charlie had observed on the street stand up and start to share her story of loss—her husband of fifty-two years (who she had no idea was right beside her) had been killed in a traffic accident the previous week—Charlie said thoughtfully, "The Gingerbread Man almost had to be at that same session. How else would he know that those girls had suffered that kind of loss?"

"Maybe they have regulars, and one of them will remember a weird guy who stared at all the participants, trying to decide who he was going to kidnap and kill." That was Michael, who was standing beside her looking both pissed off (that would be at her) and seriously formidable, which she assumed was his way of making sure that the spirits she couldn't see steered clear.

None of the participants in that morning's meeting looked as if he could remotely fit the bill, Charlie determined with a glance.

After the organized part of the meeting was concluded, when the participants were milling around the refreshments table, Tony asked the social worker about regulars. She pointed them out, and they went to talk to them. They got nothing.

They were just leaving the meeting when Tony got a call from Kaminsky, who'd been kept abreast of the possible grief counseling connection via a text from Buzz. Charlie, who was in the act of phoning Jenna, knew instantly from Tony's expression that something was up.

"Kaminsky thinks she's figured out the identity of the next expert the unsub's going to contact," Tony said as he disconnected. "We need to head back to the hotel."

Jenna wasn't answering her phone. As they sped back to the hotel, Charlie left a message asking the girl to please return the call as soon as possible.

The makeshift War Room was a small conference room down a short hall off the lobby. It was windowless, and Kaminsky had set it up with a system that had her facing a half-dozen laptops placed side by side on the long table that, along with the eight chairs around it, was the room's only furniture.

"It's Dr. Steven Pelletier," Kaminsky burst out excitedly as the others walked into the room. She was seated in a padded leather chair, but stood up as they entered. On one of the laptop screens was the frozen face of the esteemed neuropathologist who had made a name for himself studying the effect of brain disease on criminal behavior. From the look of him on the screen, Kaminsky had hit pause in mid–phone call. "He's the only one of the experts on the list you gave me who was involved in a violent death when he was young. His eighteen months' older sister was killed in a house fire when he was seven. Apparently the two of them were found unconscious at the bottom of some stairs by firefighters. Dr. Pelletier was able to be revived; the sister was not."

"Sounds like you got it," Tony said, nodding at Kaminsky to resume the call. "No way can that be a coincidence."

Kaminsky hit a button, said, "Sorry to put you on hold, Dr. Pelletier. Here's our team leader, Special Agent Anthony Bartoli."

"Dr. Pelletier." Tony slid into the seat beside Kaminsky. "I'm sure Special Agent Kaminsky has filled you in on what's going on."

Pelletier nodded. Charlie had never met him, but she was familiar with his work. In his late thirties, with a round, jovial face and short, reddish hair, he looked like anything but the distinguished researcher he was.

"Everything's been fine," Pelletier said in reply to Tony's question about whether he'd noticed anything out of the ordinary over the last few days.

Tony nodded. "We're going to be putting surveillance on you. I'll have people in place within the hour. Around your home, office, you personally. They'll stay out of sight, but they'll be there."

Pelletier looked a little startled. "You really think a serial killer's going to be contacting *me*?"

"Yes," Tony said uncompromisingly. "And right now you're our best hope of catching this guy, so we'd appreciate your cooperation."

"Sure," Pelletier agreed, and they ended the conversation with him looking alarmed but game. No sooner had he hung up than Jenna called Charlie back: she hadn't attended the Grief Connection counseling session the morning of the run, she said, which caused Charlie momentary consternation. Then Jenna added that she had stopped by the session briefly to drop off flyers about the run, and had stopped to talk to a couple of people near the door about the tragedy in her own life. It was possible that she could have been overheard, she said, although she didn't remember anyone who seemed particularly interested in her. She also didn't remember seeing Laura, or Raylene, although they could have been there. She hadn't been paying much attention, and she hadn't stayed long.

"That's got to be it," Charlie said as she recounted the conversation to the others, who agreed.

"All we can do is look at any security video we can find from the surrounding streets that morning," Tony said. As it had already been collected and was in the process of being reviewed, that base was pretty well covered.

"Look who I've talked to this morning," Kaminsky said as Tony, after refusing Kaminsky's offer to contact the deputy director of the Bureau on Skype, went out to make the call to set up the arrangements for what needed to happen with Pelletier.

Kaminsky punched a button, and immediately faces appeared on all of the screens.

Charlie recognized four of them at a glance. The other two she had no clue about.

"I left messages for Dr. Underwood and Dr. Myers yesterday"— Kaminsky pointed to two of the screens—"and both called back this morning to confirm that at a young age they were present at the violent death of someone close. Dr. Underwood had a friend hit in the

chest with a ball at a baseball game—I know, bizarre—and Dr. Myers'
cousin was accidentally shot and killed when they were together."
She looked around at Charlie and Buzz. "Which means all four of our
experts share that common experience. Include Dr. Pelletier—
although he is not technically one of our experts *yet*—and we've got
a clean sweep. *Plus,* I've talked to Ariane Spencer"—she pointed to
the pretty blond teen on the third screen—"who was, if you recall,
the surviving victim from Group Two . . . (that was the snakes)—"
Kaminsky broke off to shudder. "—and Andrew Russell, the Group
Five . . . trash compactor, remember? . . . survivor"—she pointed to
the fourth screen—"and Saul Tunney, the Group Six . . . grain silo . . .
survivor"—his was another of the faces Charlie recognized—"and
they all confirm that they were present at the violent death of someone close, previous to what happened to them with the Gingerbread
Man."

"What about grief counseling?" Buzz asked. "Did they get any?"

"I don't know." Kaminsky sounded faintly aggrieved. "When I
was talking to them, grief counseling wasn't part of the picture." She
made a face. "Well, I guess I get to call them all back."

"You called Ken Ewell?" Charlie was frowning at one of the faces
on the screens. The deputy sheriff from Big Stone Gap seemed like an
unlikely contact for Kaminsky to need to make.

"He called me," Kaminsky corrected. "Apparently they have a
surveillance video of what looks like a gray van on the road leading
into Big Stone Gap on the night of the murders. He's e-mailing it to
me."

"Maybe we can get a license plate," Buzz said hopefully.

"Like our luck is ever that good," Kaminsky replied. Then she
pointed to the last screen. "This is a parent of—"

She broke off as Tony came back into the room. An envelope was
in his hand, and the expression on his face as he looked at Charlie—
directly at her, instead of at the three of them in general—was concerned.

"This came for you," Tony said as he handed the envelope to her.
"It was delivered this morning. The clerk at the front desk thought it
might be urgent, so he gave it to me to give to you."

Charlie accepted the envelope. It was one of the cardboard overnight delivery envelopes from FedEx. The name on the return label was unknown to her, she saw as she ripped it open.

Inside was another envelope, a white business-sized one. On it, in spidery black handwriting, was nothing more than her name: Dr. Charlotte Stone.

The flap was unsealed. Inside that was a single sheet of paper. Even before Charlie unfolded it, her heart started to slam in her chest.

She knew, *knew,* in every cell of her body, who it was from.

CHAPTER TWENTY-THREE

YOU DIDN'T CATCH ME was what the message said.

"The Gingerbread Man," Kaminsky breathed, as Michael, who had been looking over Charlie's shoulder, said, "Fuck," and Charlie looked down with growing horror at the small, stiff square of paper that had been tucked inside the folded sheet.

It was a Polaroid photograph of three young girls lying, apparently unconscious, in a wire cage.

"Oh, my God." Charlie dropped the picture like it stung her fingers. The images of the girls—they looked to be young teens—burned itself into her brain. Someone—Buzz—took the letter from her, while Tony picked up the photo, holding it very carefully by the corner with a tissue he'd acquired from somewhere, and positioned it so they all could see.

"He's escalating again," Charlie said. For the first couple of seconds she'd looked at it, she'd thought—hoped—that what she was seeing was one of the groups of victims he had attacked in the past. But she didn't think so. In fact, she was as sure as it was possible to be that this was a new group of victims.

"Find out who those girls are," Tony ordered, and Kaminsky nodded.

"Since we know Dr. Pelletier is the expert the Gingerbread Man's most likely to contact, we can catch him," Buzz said. "Pelletier's at the Virginia Tech Carilion School of Medicine, right? Isn't that in Roanoke? We can be there in a couple of hours, catch the SOB when he drops off the letter."

"Unless he's smart, and mails it, like he just did to you," Michael said dryly to Charlie.

Charlie repeated that, minus the snark.

Frowning, Tony was looking down at the photograph he still held in his hand. "Even if he drops it off in person, by the time he does, at least two of these girls are going to be dead. And we may be totally wrong about the identity of the expert. Or he may not even contact an expert this time. As the change in timing proves, he's flexible enough to make adjustments to his game plan."

"I think our best bet is to try to identify him, and the place we need to look is where the first Gingerbread Man murders occurred." Charlie was thinking it through as she spoke. "He'll have some kind of roots there. Probably a connection to one of the first group of victims."

"We don't have time to dig into all that." Kaminsky's voice was tight as she looked up from the laptop, where she had been frantically working. "He's already got those girls. That means we have—at most—two more days. Or we might not even have that. He's already changed the timing on us."

"You got anything on the identities?" Tony asked Kaminsky while he passed the photo to Buzz, then said to him, "We need to get that, and the letter, to the lab."

"I'll see to it," Buzz said, while Kaminsky answered, "Nothing yet. I'm checking all the databases, but nothing's instantaneous, you know."

"I have a psychic friend whom I know to be very accurate," Charlie said. With lives at stake, and possessing information she felt might be important, concealing her chats with Tam no longer mattered. "She called a couple of days ago to warn me that I'm in danger near dark water. It seems to me that if I'm in danger near dark water, then any water that can turn dark—like Buggs Island Lake, for example—is where the danger has to be. It's possible she's gloamed on to a different danger, but I don't think so. I think the danger I'm in comes from the Gingerbread Man, and the Gingerbread Man will be found near water that is or can be dark."

For a moment everyone else in the room stared at her silently.

Then Kaminsky said, "Well, that sure clinches it for me."

Michael gave a snort of amusement. Charlie shot Kaminsky an unappreciative look. Tony said, "I'm not willing to discount any psychic help we can get." He looked at Charlie. "You got the grief counseling connection pretty much out of nowhere. How strongly do you feel about tracking the unsub down through the Buggs Island Lake connection?"

Charlie hesitated.

"I've got a hit on the girls." The tension in Kaminsky's voice was palpable as she looked up from her laptop. "Diane Townsend, Kim Oates, and Natalie Garza. All fourteen, all reported missing this morning from Twinbrook, a girls' camp in Rocky Mount, North Carolina, that specializes in—get this—grief counseling. Apparently this week's program caters to survivors of school shootings."

"Looks like our guy was in a hurry," Michael said. "Instead of cherry-picking 'em, this time he went straight for the all-you-can-eat buffet."

"Notify the agents down there that we may have a lead on the girls," Tony told Buzz, who nodded, then asked, "Should I tell them we're on our way?"

Tony grimaced. "As I see it, we've got three ways we can go here. We can head for Roanoke and sit on Pelletier. We can head down to Rocky Mount and join the search there. Or we can take a quick trip to Buggs Island Lake and see what we can dig up."

Buzz said, "Dr. Pelletier's covered. If the unsub shows up there, we'll have him."

"Too late for the girls, though," Kaminsky put in.

Buzz continued as if she hadn't spoken. "I'm guessing that they've got half the Bureau, plus the state police and all available local law enforcement, on the scene in Rocky Mount."

"We'd be the only ones looking at Buggs Island Lake," Tony said.

Kaminsky looked up from her computer. "A friend of a girl who went missing at Buggs Island Lake five years ago reported that in the days leading up to her disappearance a man had been following them. She told police she could describe him, although if she ever did, it didn't make it into this file. The witness still lives in the same house, near the lake."

"We could go interview her, get a description, check out any local police records," Buzz said. "If it doesn't look like anything will pan out down there, we could move on."

Tony made up his mind. "Sounds like a plan. Get packed. I want to be in the air in under an hour."

Buggs Island Lake (as they call it in Virginia), which is also known as Kerr Reservoir (to the folks in the Carolinas), was a fifty-thousand-acre swimmers', boaters', and fishermen's paradise. Long and narrow, it ran along the Virginia/North Carolina border and was one of the most popular summer resort areas in both states. Erin Hill, the friend of the disappeared girl, who lived in the little lakeside community of Clarksville, was indeed able to give them a description: a dark-haired man, maybe in his early thirties, who had followed them around in a gray van. The part about the gray van hadn't made it into the police report, and it sent a shaft of excitement through the team. The lead was promising enough that they turned Erin over to a local police sketch artist.

While they waited for the results, in an empty office off the small squad room, Kaminsky was busy checking out a map of the lake area that hung on the wall. Charlie, who like the others was acutely aware of the swift passage of time, was starting to realize that she hadn't gotten as much rest the previous night as she had supposed. She was sitting in one of the hard metal chairs and chugging stale police coffee as she went over the missing persons reports that Kaminsky had thought might be relevant to the case, which the agent had e-mailed to her. Buzz was combing through the police files on the four supposedly-accidental-but-deemed-by-Kaminsky-to-be-suspicious deaths that she had identified in the area during the time period in question. Having stepped outside because the reception was better, Tony was on the phone, talking to agents at the scene of the kidnappings in Rocky Mount, and then to those assigned to conduct surveillance on Dr. Pelletier. Michael was on his feet staring out the window at the beautiful blue water of the lake. It was early evening by this time, but the sunlight was still strong enough to make the surface sparkle. Charlie could read in Michael's body language his longing to be out there as part of the living world again, but he was still palpably angry at her and for the most part wasn't talking. Under the circumstances, she wasn't, either. What could she say? There was nothing in what she had told him that she would take back. And she badly needed to put him in his proper place in her life, which should probably be, as he had sneeringly described it, the ghost whisperer's apprentice and nothing more. But the sad truth was, just letting her eyes run over him evoked feelings in her that were disturbingly sexual. One look at his broad shoulders and muscular back, at his tight butt and long, powerful legs, and she was back in last night's darkened hotel room with him again.

He makes me hotter than any man I've ever known.

That was the thought that was floating through her mind when Kaminsky glanced around at her and asked, "What did that psychic friend of yours tell you, exactly?" Charlie was caught off guard enough so that she had to think for a moment.

"She said I was in danger near dark water." Which—Charlie had noted, to her relief—Buggs Island Lake was not. At least at that moment, its waters were the approximate shade of Michael's eyes. "She said the danger came from a gray house in the dark water. I'm wondering if maybe we'll find our unsub on a houseboat."

"You know I'm fluent in a number of languages, right?" Kaminsky said. "One of them is Algonquin. About fifteen miles from here on this side of the lake is Pocomoke Village. In Pocomoke Village is Pocomoke Street." Buzz was looking at Kaminsky, too, at this point. "In Algonquin, *pocomoke* means *dark water.*"

At that, Michael also swung around to stare at Kaminsky.

"Oh, my God," Charlie said. At the same time Buzz said, "Wow," and Michael said, "Shit."

"It's probably a coincidence." Kaminsky turned away from the map to head for her laptop, which rested on the desk. "But there it is."

"There's no such thing as coincidence," Michael said, and narrowed his eyes at Charlie. "You don't go anywhere near that place."

As Kaminsky plopped herself behind the desk and Buzz rose to look over her shoulder while she called something up on her laptop,

Charlie gave Michael a hard look that could be roughly translated as, *You're not the boss of me.*

He folded his arms over his chest. "Babe, here's a tip: don't mess with me right now. I ain't real happy with you."

Bite me, was what she silently replied.

"I've got it here on Google Earth. Pocomoke Street is dotted with what looks like little fishing cottages. They're far apart, and the area seems really rural," Kaminsky drew her attention by saying.

"Laura said the van smelled like fish," Charlie said before she thought.

"Who?" Kaminsky frowned at her, while Michael, with a taunting smile, said, "Oops."

"Somebody. It doesn't matter." Charlie covered her misstep hastily, and covered herself even further by refusing to look at Michael again. "The point is, someone said the van used in the kidnappings smelled like fish."

"I think I heard that," Buzz said.

"One of the cottages is painted dark gray." Kaminsky got to the point. "What we have here, then, is a gray house on the equivalent of Dark Water Street."

"There are a lot of gray houses on a lot of streets with Indian names," Tony cautioned when he stepped back into the office after finishing his phone calls and Kaminsky's discovery was explained to him. "Who owns it?"

Kaminsky tapped a few keys on her laptop. "Benjamin Motta." Her tone was portentous.

I can't talk right now, Ben.

That's what Laura said she'd overheard the Gingerbread Man saying to someone on the phone.

"Let's go check it out," Tony said.

"Oh, no," Michael said, pointing a finger at Charlie. "Not you."

But she was already on her way out the door with the rest of them.

"Can you say 'death wish,' Doc?" Michael growled as they all piled into the car, a rental that had been waiting for them at the airport.

Charlie's mouth tightened. She hated to admit it, but he had a point.

"What about Ms. Hill, boss?" Buzz asked from the backseat, where he and Kaminsky now sat as a matter of course. Ms. Hill was the witness who was at that moment working with the sketch artist.

"One of the locals can give her a ride home if we're not back by the time she's finished. We'll pick up the sketch later." From the little side street they'd been on, Tony pulled onto the main drag that ran along the lakefront even as he glanced at Kaminsky in the mirror and added, "Kaminsky."

"Taking care of it." Kaminsky pulled her phone out.

"You're not really stupid enough to go to a gray house on dark water, are you?" Michael snarled at Charlie from the backseat, where he was sandwiched between Buzz and Kaminsky, his invisible presence making them both crowd toward their respective doors, which still left him with not near enough room. "Hell, I know you're not."

Actually, much as she might feel like annoying Michael, now that she had a chance to think about it, Charlie wasn't. Reluctantly she said to Tony, "You know, I think I'm going to have to sit this one out. If you could drop me at a restaurant or something . . ."

"Smartest thing you've said all day," Michael said.

"Don't worry, I wasn't going to take you anyway," Tony told her reassuringly. "Even aside from the dark water thing, you're a civilian, and if this pans out it could get ugly. In fact, I think we're going to want the local police with us as backup. If we should need to go in, if there should be some indication that the missing girls might be at this location, we're going to want to have a perimeter set up and plenty of firepower available. Kaminsky, check your Google map or whatever it is you check and find us a place where you and Charlie can hole up while this thing gets done."

"I hate to say this, but I'm actually kind of liking Dudley right now," Michael said.

"What?" Kaminsky screeched, then immediately moderated her voice to add, "I'm not sitting this out."

"No, you're not. You're doing your job, which is to protect our expert." Tony gave her a cool look through the mirror. "Get on it, Kaminsky."

Charlie felt the sizzle of Kaminsky's glare on the back of her head.

"The Bluefly Inn is a small hotel located right outside Pocomoke

Village. They have a good, down-home-style supper buffet Tuesday through Sunday, clean, well-appointed rooms and two conference rooms available for family reunions or any larger groups." Kaminsky sounded like she was reading the words off a virtual brochure. There was no missing the bitterness in her tone.

"Sounds good," Tony said, then got on his phone to make arrangements with the local cops for what he needed.

The Bluefly Inn looked exactly like what it was: an old-fashioned hunting and fishing lodge. Built of dark, unpeeled logs with a green-shingled roof and a covered porch complete with rocking chairs that ran the length of the front of the building, it was set well back from the street in a gravel parking lot. There were a number of cars in the lot, and Charlie realized with a glance at the dashboard clock—it was almost 8:30, she saw with a sense of shock—that this was probably the tail end of the dinner rush.

She also realized two completely disparate things: she was hungry, and the girls they were hoping to save were running out of time.

In the end, she felt like coming here was on her shoulders. The gray house on the dark water owned by Ben Motta was a good lead, but was it right?

There was no way to know. Only, if it wasn't, those girls might very well die tonight.

Charlie sent a wordless prayer for their safety winging skyward.

"This is complete sexist crap." Kaminsky glared at Charlie across the table as they both sat down to eat. Tony and Buzz had been gone maybe ten minutes, and Charlie and Kaminsky had elected to make the best use of their time by having a meal while they reviewed files that had just been updated by the support staff at Quantico on their respective laptops. ("Let 'em starve," was Kaminsky's reaction to Charlie's suggestion that perhaps they should wait for the men to return before they ate.) Located at one end of the lodge, the dining room was dark, log walls, a long steam table set up down one side. The deepening twilight seen through the partially closed blinds covering the two large windows and the glass tops of the front and back doors didn't help the gloom. The smell of fried chicken and fried fish, the main dish staples, was more than enough to make up for it: it was so appetizing that Charlie's stomach growled. Their table was a small four-top pushed against the wall. The only illumination was provided by the steam table, a tiny candle in a small, brown glass globe on each table, and the red glimmer of two signs that labeled the ladies' and men's rooms, which were down a short hall that opened up behind Kaminsky and which Charlie could see faintly sputtering as if their bulbs were about to go out.

There was also the light from their open laptops: the pale glow from Kaminsky's made her look like something out of *The Walking Dead*. Not that Charlie meant to tell her so, and not that she had any hope that the glow from hers made her look any better. Anyway, except for Michael and the waitress who brought their drinks, no one was paying the least attention to either her or Kaminsky.

Maybe a dozen diners remained.

"I agree." Charlie took a bite of fried catfish, and almost closed her eyes at the delicate cornbread flavor of the crispy crust. Even Michael's wry expression as he watched her eat couldn't dim her appreciation.

Kaminsky bit into the catfish, too, but seemed to be in no mood to appreciate it. "He assigns me to you because we're both *women*."

"I'd rather have Buzz," Charlie assured her. "I'll be glad to tell Tony so."

Even the coleslaw was superior, Charlie decided as her gaze drifted down to the file she had been perusing: a detailed background check on Jeff Underwood. Reading it felt like an invasion of privacy, but with the lives of those girls on the line they couldn't afford to overlook any possible clue. She was going over the experts' files, and Kaminsky was reading through the victims' files, and then they were going to switch, because fresh eyes were always a good thing. They were looking for anything, *anything*, that might lead them to the killer.

"Like Bartoli'd listen." Kaminsky gave her a hostile look. "Anyway, that makes me sound like I'm being difficult. Like I'm not a team player."

Charlie didn't say anything. Despite her ire, Kaminsky was eating in a way that made Charlie think she was enjoying her food, too.

"I'd file a complaint, except I like Bartoli. I like our team." Another hostile look that Charlie translated to mean, *Especially when you're not on it.*

Charlie shrugged. "If I were you, I'd just shut up and sit tight. After all, I'm not a permanent fixture."

Her eyes returned to Underwood's file. Reaching the end of it, she clicked onto the next one: David Myers'. At the idea that she might come across details of her own youthful involvement with him inside the next few pages, she barely managed not to grimace.

"Bartoli would like you to be," Kaminsky shot at her. "He thinks you're a real *asset.*"

Michael snorted. "He wants to bang your brains out," he corrected with a sneer.

Charlie ignored that.

"I am," she told Kaminsky serenely, and kept her smile to herself as the other woman almost choked on her food.

"We were doing fine without you," Kaminsky retorted as soon as she finished swallowing a restorative sip of water, but by then Charlie wasn't listening: her attention was riveted on the file in front of her.

"I think I may have found something." Charlie's pulse pounded in her ears as she looked at Kaminsky. She felt a weird, almost light-headed sensation, like her blood was draining toward her toes. "I've always felt that the first Gingerbread Man murders were the most significant. His victims were boys between the ages of twelve and fourteen, remember? It's been my theory that our unsub's original exposure to violent death occurred at that same age. I've also felt that he would have roots, or a connection, to this location, because the first murders occurred near here."

Kaminsky scowled at her. "So you want to cut to the chase?"

Charlie did: "According to this file, David Myers was thirteen years old when he shot his cousin in Granville, which is about twenty miles from here."

Kaminsky's eyes widened. "Are you saying you think *Dr. Myers* might be the Gingerbread Man?"

As hard as it was for her to process, Charlie gave a jerky nod. "I think it's possible."

"Holy shit," Michael said. "That little worm?"

Charlie already had her phone out and was pushing the button that dialed Tony's number.

"You telling Bartoli?" Kaminsky asked with a glance at the phone.

Charlie nodded. But Tony didn't pick up.

"He's not answering," Charlie said tensely.

As Charlie left Tony a message, Kaminsky snatched up her phone, saying, "I'll try Crane.

"Thank God," Kaminsky said as Buzz answered. From where Charlie was sitting, she could hear his end of the conversation as well as Kaminsky's. The other woman's voice was quiet and urgent as she spoke into the phone. "Listen up: Dr. Stone thinks the Gingerbread Man might be Dr. Myers."

"*What?*" Buzz sounded shocked. "How? Why?"

"We'll explain later." Kaminsky broke into his sputtering impatiently. "Just tell Bartoli. Dr. Stone tried to call him, but he's not answering his phone."

"He's got it turned off," Buzz said. "You caught me right as I was turning mine off, too. *Hey, boss!*" It was a loud whisper. "Damn it, he can't hear me. You slowed me down: he's already up there by the garage." From the sound of Buzz's voice, he was now on the move. "We're at the house. The local police have a perimeter set up, and Bartoli and I and a couple of detectives are getting ready to go in. Doesn't look like it's going to amount to much, though. The house is dark and looks deserted. We don't even have to break in. One of the detectives has a universal garage door opener and he's using it to open up the—"

BOOM.

The explosion came out of nowhere. It was loud enough to hurt Charlie's ears, to make the room shake, to rattle dishes and cutlery, to bring everyone in the room, including Charlie, leaping to their feet. Outside one of the big windows, Charlie could see a not-too-distant geyser of black smoke and scarlet flames shooting upward over a jagged skyline of trees.

She gaped at it in shock.

"What the hell?" Michael's eyes were riveted on the mushroom-

ing fire. Everyone rushed toward one of the two doors, clearly meaning to pour out into the parking lot to get a better look at what was
going on.

"Crane! Buzz!" Kaminsky cried into the phone. She gave Charlie
a stricken look. "I could hear the explosion over the phone. I think—
either it knocked out reception or—*Buzz! Buzz!* My God, was it
them?" She started toward the nearest of the doors at a run, her eyes
wild. "Let me see if the reception's better outside. You stay here."
The last part of that, which she threw over her shoulder at Charlie,
was fierce.

Charlie nodded, but Kaminsky, already thrusting through the
door, didn't see. Heart thumping, cold with dread, Charlie felt like
she'd been rooted to the spot. She'd heard it clearly, too: the sound of
the explosion had come through the phone. Which meant that Buzz,
and Tony, had been on the scene.

Oh, my God.

"This ain't good." Michael had moved over to the nearest window, and was staring out at the billowing cloud of smoke and fire as
it reached for the sky.

Out of the corner of her eye, Charlie saw that the last remaining
diner, a man who'd popped out of the restroom at the sound of the
explosion only to drop his briefcase at the sight that greeted him
through the windows, was on one knee hastily gathering up his papers.

Please let Tony and Buzz be fine.

Probably the reception had been knocked out.

Taking a breath, getting a grip, Charlie moved to help him. Giving in to the panic that was surging through her body did no one any
good. Crouching, she scooped up a handful of papers, which looked
like pages of a manuscript. The title page was one of a number in her
hands, and as she glanced at it the title leaped out at her. In large,
bold type it read, *Causative Factors: A Treatise on the Nature of
Evil.*

Charlie blinked at it, then glanced up at the man crouched on the
other side of the briefcase. He was holding a handful of papers, too,
and as their eyes met he looked as astonished as she felt.

Her heart gave a great leap. Every tiny hair on the back of her neck shot upright.

"David," she breathed.

That was all she said, because his name had no sooner left her mouth than he punched her in the face as hard as he could.

Charlie felt an explosion of pain, and everything went black.

CHAPTER TWENTY-FOUR

"Charlie!"

The voice yelling her name was loud enough so that she would've winced if she could have. Michael's voice: she would recognize it anywhere.

Opening her eyes, Charlie nearly blacked out at the pain, and let her lids drop.

My face hurts.

"Michael?" she whispered.

"You need to wake up, babe. Right now."

The urgency of it made her try to open her eyes again. This time, since she was prepared for the pain, it wasn't quite so debilitating. But for whatever reason, her eyes wouldn't quite open all the way, and so she peeped out through narrow slits.

Michael leaned over her. His face was the first thing she saw. It was hard, fierce even. She smiled anyway, or at least made a pathetic attempt at it. That hurt, too, so she stopped.

He didn't smile back. She could feel tension rolling off him in waves.

"Hey," he said. "You with me?"

"Mmm." At least, she was trying. Then she remembered. "You're mad at me."

"No," he said. "Not now."

Relieved, she tried smiling again. It still hurt.

Michael said, "I know you're hurting. But you got to snap out of it."

He moved away from her, out of her line of vision. She tried to track him but failed because it hurt when she moved her head. Wherever she was, it was dark. Not pitch dark: she could see shadows, and flashes of light that seemed to come out of nowhere. The lights ran across the walls—curved metal walls—only to vanish. It took her a second to realize that what she was seeing were the headlights of passing vehicles slicing through the one she was in. She *was* in a vehicle: she knew that for sure because of the movement and the sounds. She was lying down on her side, on a hard, uncomfortable surface, in a moving vehicle. Something warm pressed close against her back. Her face—her nose and cheekbones and eye sockets—ached and throbbed. The skin over them felt swollen, a little tingly, mostly numb.

Charlie realized that she would have been afraid if Michael hadn't been there.

"Michael?"

"Shh." From the sound of his voice, he wasn't very far away. "Keep your voice down. I'm right here."

"What . . . happened?" Whispering, she moved a little, trying to locate him. A quiver of pain shot like an arrow behind her eyes, and her head swam, but she persevered. Breathing through her nose, she discovered, was hard. Clearly she'd been in some kind of accident.

She tried to think, to remember, but the effort made her head pound so she gave up.

"I missed part of it—I was looking out the damned window—but best I can tell you ran into that bastard Myers, and he punched you in the face and knocked you cold." Michael's voice was grim. "You remember any of that?"

"No." Charlie saw Michael now, as a big solid shape in the darkness, through a grid of metal bars mere inches from her poor damaged nose. He was crouched about three feet away, and appeared to be examining the tall metal grid that inexplicably seemed to stand between them. She tried to make sense of what Michael had just said. "David?"

"He's the Gingerbread Man."

"What?" Woozy, she was unable to think clearly. As long as she kept her head relatively still, moving her arms and hands didn't cause her pain, Charlie discovered as she reached out to curl her fingers around the metal wires, each of which was approximately as thick as her pinkie finger. The whole grid felt as sturdy as if it was made of solid steel. "What . . . is this?"

"It's a cage. You're in a damned cage."

That still didn't make sense. Nothing made any sense. She forced out an inarticulate questioning sound.

Michael glanced her way. "Okay, here's the situation as it stands: you're in the back of that gray van you've been looking for, locked in a cage. That bastard Myers is driving. The cage takes up nearly the whole back of the van, it's bolted to the floor, it's got a padlock on the door, and right at the moment I'm not seeing any way to get you out of it. Those three missing girls are in the cage, too, lying next to you. They're out for the count. There's a tank—I think it's empty, thank Jesus—out here, with a hose going into the cage. I'm guessing from its presence that the girls were gassed. Oh, and Sugar Buns is in there with you, too. She got zapped with a stun gun when she went outside hunting for you. From the look of her, she'll be coming around any minute."

Charlie began to frown. Frowning hurt. She stopped. A hard knot of fear formed in her chest. She could feel her heart starting to beat a little faster. Her brain was still missing some of its spark, but at least it was starting to function, bathed by an icy infusion of adrenaline.

"David," she said with horror, as the truth hit her like a slap in the face: David was the Gingerbread Man; David had kidnapped her; David had her locked in the back of his van—

"Charlie, is that you?" A familiar, almost jovial voice from the front seat responded, and she realized that she had forgotten to whisper.

Fear made her blink. Blinking hurt.

"Son of a bitch," Michael said.

"David?" Charlie's gaze slanted in the direction of the voice. Even as she said his name again the memory of looking up over the manuscript pages in her hand to see David staring back at her surfaced. A split second later, had he slammed his fist into her face? Yes, Charlie concluded as anger joined the fear that was turning her icy cold inside, he had. She moved a little, careful to shift her whole body rather than only her eyes, and strained to see him. The dark shape of his head was just visible on the other side of what appeared to be the curved edges of a sliding plastic door similar in type to that which separates the back of a limo from the chauffeur. At the moment, it was open. He could talk to her, and obviously to some extent hear what was going on in the back of the van. He was driving, and past him, through the windshield, she got a slight glimpse of inky sky. Indignation filled her voice. "You hit me!"

It was such a stupid thing to say. Clearly, since he had locked her in a cage in the back of a van that smelled (she was a little relieved to realize she could still smell) of fish, with, according to Michael, the three kidnapped girls and Kaminsky unconscious beside her, the fact that David had punched her in the face was a small thing. But it felt like such a violation of the relationship they'd had that, yes, she was angry.

"Don't worry, babe. I'll kill him for you later." Michael's tone was so even that for a moment she almost missed the deadly promise that ran beneath it. Glancing at him, registering his tall, powerful body, she knew he meant it, and knew, too, that he could break David in half with no trouble whatsoever. Then she remembered that he was dead, and there was, actually, nothing he could do, which he was apparently forgetting, too, and she felt cold sweat start to prickle to life around her hairline.

"You saw me," David said. "It was the only thing I could think of to do. I could see in your face that you knew. I stopped at the Inn to grab a quick dinner before I hit the road, and I went to the restroom, and when I came out there you were. If I'd had any idea you were around—but I didn't. And then after I put you in the van, when I was going back for my briefcase, your cop friend saw me, too."

By cop friend, Charlie knew he was referring to Kaminsky.

Charlie caught her breath, sucked in air.

"You're the Gingerbread Man." Again, it was stupid. She even said it with a touch of incredulity, because, she supposed, she was still hoping that this was all some huge mistake, and he would deny it. But then reality set in, and she knew that however unthinkable, however terrible it seemed, it was true.

As she faced the reality of that, her mouth went sour with fear.

"Have bad taste in boyfriends much?" Michael asked grimly from the other side of the cage, which he was slowly circling like a predator trying to get in. Under other circumstances, the sight would have made her smile. She didn't.

In this case, it wasn't that he couldn't get in. It was that he couldn't get any of them out.

The knowledge was terrifying. It settled like a rock in her stomach. She was already battling back a creeping tide of panic. *Tony and Buzz. The explosion.* Oh, God, she remembered everything. Had they been hurt? Were they even alive? *Please let them be okay.* But she had to be careful: the last thing she wanted to do was let David think she and Kaminsky were now alone.

"David, *why?*" she asked when he didn't say anything. Talking felt funny, but it didn't really hurt, and her nose had, thankfully, gone numb. What hurt was blinking, or trying to move her eyes.

"Because I wanted to find out what makes people into killers," David replied as if it was the most natural thing in the world. Charlie saw that he was watching her through the rearview mirror, and goose bumps raced over her skin. What would it take to provoke him to kill? Because hard as it was to get her mind around it, that was clearly what he intended: to kill her. And Kaminsky, and the three girls as well.

The certainty made her shiver. The question was, how much time did they have?

I have to try to get out of here.

She made an abortive movement to sit up, lifting her head, pushing down against the uneven metal floor beneath her with an elbow.

Pain shafted through her head. It hurt too much. She stopped, sank back, rested her eyes.

Michael's voice was tight as he said, "Babe, you want to stay kind of still, and when Sugar Buns wakes up you want to tell her to stay still, too. He's got the ability to incapacitate you, either with that stun gun of his or more of whatever he used to knock out these girls, and you don't want to give him cause to do it."

Charlie felt her blood turn to ice at Michael's words. She could tell from his tone that he was trying not to scare her, but that he was expecting something bad to go down soon. And if they were all incapacitated, none of them would stand a chance.

She tried to think, tried to concentrate, tried to come up with a plan. But all she could focus on was the relentless pounding of her pulse in her ears.

"There's a reason people become killers," David continued, and she opened her eyes and forced herself to pay attention. Maybe, if she listened, she could latch on to something that she'd be able to use to talk him out of killing them. He sounded perfectly normal, perfectly rational. Hearing the familiar voice under such circumstances was surreal. Charlie's stomach turned inside out. Her mouth went dry. "There's always a reason for everything. I wanted to find out what it is. It's the same reason you do your research."

Pull yourself together. Use what you know.

"Causative Factors: A Treatise on the Nature of Evil," Charlie enunciated each word precisely. The title, she had discovered, was branded on her brain. Easing onto her back so that she could get a more complete view of her surroundings, feeling the wire grid beneath her digging into her shoulder blades and butt through the thin linen of her dress, she was able to see all three of the girls. They were right beside her, sprawled across one another as though they had been huddling together when they'd collapsed, limp as fresh corpses now, although Charlie could see—and hear—that they still breathed. Little girls, really, two with blond ponytails, one with long, loose dark hair. Shorts and tees and tennis shoes. Children. Innocents. What were their names? Oh, yes: Natalie and Diane and Kim. Beyond them, on the far side of the cage, lay Kaminsky. Her breathing had changed; she was moving a little.

"I wish you could read it." David sounded enthused suddenly, and proud as well. Charlie realized that in his mind he had been doing serious work. "My working theory is, there's something inborn in some people that makes them more able to kill than others. I could never tell who in each group the killer was going to be, though."

Searching for some way to reach him, working hard to keep the fear that was making her feel all shaky inside at a manageable level, Charlie remembered the violent death they'd uncovered in his past. Could she use it to try to throw him off balance? The last thing she wanted him to do was get into his groove, his serial killer mode. They all had them: every serial killer she had studied had presented as perfectly normal until something triggered the monster within.

"Did you kill your cousin on purpose, David?"

She could see his eyes on her in the mirror.

He said, "I was never sure. Tommy—that was his name—was my best friend as well as my cousin, you know. I stayed at his house near the lake here every summer when I was a kid, and we hung out together. One day when we were thirteen, we found his dad's—my uncle's—pistol in a drawer. We were looking at it, and I pointed it at him and pulled the trigger. It was loaded. It killed him. Everybody thought it was an accident, but to this day I'm not sure." He paused. "All I know is I liked watching him die."

There was the serial killer talking. Charlie felt as if an icy hand had just closed around her heart.

"So you killed again." It wasn't a question: Charlie knew the answer too well from her own work. They were called serial killers for a reason: they killed serially. Insatiably, one victim after another, again and again and again.

"I did, once I started coming back to the lake in the summers. For a number of years after Tommy's death, though, I didn't. My uncle and aunt sold the house Tommy died in, everything changed, and I didn't really have the urge. But then, when I was in college, I got a summer job working for one of the marinas here. And it suddenly came back to me: Tommy's death, and how it had felt to watch him die. I kind of considered myself like a shark: I'd had a taste of blood, and I needed more."

"Who did you kill next?" Charlie asked. As long as she didn't move her head too quickly, she could do what she needed to do, she decided. The pain behind her eyes had subsided into no more than a dull throb. The middle of her face felt swollen, but the good news was it was also numb.

Shifting positions a little, she was able to see Michael. He was on his feet, back bent to accommodate his height to the van's ceiling as he feverishly examined every inch of the cage's door. From his strained expression the result wasn't pleasing him.

"A girl. A stranger. She was swimming. I drowned her. Everybody thought that was an accident, too. No one knew I was involved." He drew in an audible breath. It was a sound of excitement, and she realized that he was taking pleasure in remembering. Her heart gave an odd little kick. Her life's work was studying serial killers. She knew the signs: David was getting worked up for the kill. "After that, I just kept killing. One or two a year. If I couldn't make it look like an accident, I'd hide the bodies. But as I got older and began teaching and doing research, and people started looking up to me, I realized I had a lot to lose, and I tried to stop. But I couldn't. I simply had this compulsion to kill. I can't give you a reason for it. Except—I like watching people die."

Charlie's heart was pounding, as if her body had finally processed and recognized the extent of the danger she was in. Kaminsky stirred again, and her breathing was lighter and faster. Charlie hoped it wouldn't be long before she regained consciousness: a highly trained FBI agent was a valuable ally. Was it possible that Kaminsky still had her gun? Charlie thought about what she knew of David, and answered herself: no, it was not.

He was intelligent, methodical. A highly organized killer. He would never be that careless.

Keep him talking. Keep him remembering who he's talking to.

"So you decided to conduct some experiments to learn why you felt the need to behave as you did," Charlie said. She actually could understand that: she'd run experiments on subjects (serial killers) herself to understand why they behaved the way they did. Only her tools involved things like inkblots, not murder.

The van jolted, and Charlie felt something jab hard into her left shoulder. She was, she saw as she cautiously shifted position again, lying on one of the bolts that fastened the cage to the floor. That was the least of her concerns: the quality of the ride had changed. It was now rough and bouncy, and Charlie could hear the rattle of gravel beneath the tires.

"Hell, he's turned off the road." The savage note in Michael's voice scared her to death. She knew he sounded like that because of her. Because he was afraid for her.

"Yes, I did," David responded, pleased that she understood. "My first theory was that it was purely genetic, so I took my nephew—he was the closest I could come to someone who shared my genes who was of an appropriate size and weight to work with easily—and two other boys, and locked them in an abandoned tractor-trailer with an abundance of weapons but without any water, and told them that if one of them killed the other two, I would let that one live. I was hoping that stress would cause my nephew's relevant genes to surface. But it didn't. They all just—died." He sounded disgusted. "So then I started wondering if environmental factors played a role."

"You thought that killing your cousin might have been the trigger that caused you to kill others," Charlie said.

"That's right." His tone was that of a teacher pleased with the performance of a star pupil. Charlie remembered him sounding exactly the same when she'd been in his class. "So I started looking for subjects with a similar trigger. But it was difficult to find young, malleable people who had actually killed someone else, so I settled for suitable subjects who had firsthand exposure to sudden, violent death."

"You found them at grief counseling sessions." It wasn't a question. Charlie knew the answer. Beside her, one of the girls gave a sudden little gasp, and moved her arm.

"Keep 'em quiet," Michael warned, even as Charlie felt a rush of fear. If David thought he needed to, he would knock them all out again, she was sure. Her worst fear was that he had more of the oblivion producing gas, because if he used it to knock them all out it would be game over.

David said, "My parents made me go to a lot of grief counseling sessions after Tommy died. People spill their guts at those things. All I had to do was go to one and sit and listen. Hearing what they had to say—they talked about nightmares they had, terrible experiences, everything—gave me some ideas for certain modes of death to threaten them with that played on their deepest fears. I hoped that might act as a trigger as well. I even followed the survivors of my experiments, like Saul Tunney, to see if the trauma of being forced to kill might turn them into killers afterward. It didn't. Not one." He shook his head. "That's the fascinating thing. What I found is, you never can tell. Some people just have it in them to kill, and others don't."

Kaminsky's eyes were open now. Charlie watched them widen in sudden alarm as Kaminsky started to take in her surroundings. With a quick glance at the rearview mirror to make sure David wasn't watching, Charlie waved a hand to get her attention. As Kaminsky looked her way, Charlie shook her head at her.

"Stay down. Don't move," Charlie mouthed. Kaminsky blinked and frowned.

Then she nodded.

Thank God.

"You kept records," Charlie said to David, thinking of the manuscript. "You wrote it all down."

"It's the greatest research project I've ever done," David agreed happily. "I wanted to bring other researchers in on it, but it took me a long time to figure out how. Then I read the newspaper articles by that reporter—Eric Riva. I was impressed with some of his conclusions. So I thought I'd get him to contribute some more of his thoughts by inviting him to try to catch me. That worked so well I decided to invite the researchers I most respected to contribute to the project as well." Charlie could see him looking at her in the rearview mirror again. Feeling his eyes on her made her skin crawl. How had she missed the fact that he was insane? The only excuse she could come up with for herself was that she had known him years ago, before she'd gone to medical school, before she'd become a psychiatrist and started studying serial killers. "You've come the closest to catching me. I should have expected it. You were my most brilliant student, Charlie."

"Thank you," she said, doing her best to keep the irony out of her voice. Charlie reached past the pain in her head and the dread that was making her feel shaky all over and forced herself to concentrate. Wherever David was taking them, when he got there he was going to turn into the monster he was at his core. If she had any chance of talking him out of killing them, she was going to have to do it soon. "You know, I could help you with your research, David. We could continue it together. It takes my work and expands on it in a way that is truly groundbreaking. I feel you are on the verge of some major break-throughs. I could help you get there."

To her dismay, David laughed. "You can't pull that one on me, Charlie. I know you through and through. I watched you when you were my student, when you were my intern. I knew you had that en-counter with the serial killer who murdered your friend in your past. I thought maybe you were like me. But by the end, I knew you weren't. Then, when I started to think about including you in my project, I started watching you again. You know how many nights I spent out-side your house looking in? A lot. That night I sent that girl running down to you I hung around to observe how you'd handle it. I thought maybe you had developed more—let's call it ruthlessness—over time. But you took care of her, stayed with her until the ambulance people took her away. I was right there, looking in the back window at first, standing by your front door later, watching as you put yourself at risk for her."

He paused to shake his head, and Charlie thought, *Raylene*. He'd been outside her door when Raylene had appeared, and Raylene had been attached to him. If Charlie had gone out her front door, if she had seen him then, she would have known.

"But you're still not what I hoped you'd become," David con-cluded almost sadly. "You're one of those people who doesn't have it in them to kill."

There was a change in his voice that made Charlie fear he was starting to get jazzed by the prospect of killing her. Beside her, one of the girls gave a little gasp and turned her head. Charlie didn't know whether to hope they woke up or not. It all depended on what was going to happen.

Talking past the tightness in her throat, she tried a new tactic. "David, I can help you if you'll let me. You know my friend and I aren't here alone. Special Agent Bartoli and Special Agent Crane are here, too." Charlie prayed once again that they were all right. She didn't know what had blown up, but it had been big and the men had been close. Thankfully, David wasn't aware of that, and she wanted to keep it that way. "They already know you're the man they're look-ing for. You've been using Ben Motta's house as a staging area, haven't you? There will be all kinds of evidence there: DNA, fingerprints, the works. They have other evidence, too, that points to you. Irrefutable evidence. What I'm telling you is, you can't get away with this. You're going to get caught no matter what happens to me, to us. I'm a psychiatrist. I can testify on your behalf. I can help you avoid the death penalty, help you stay out of prison. I know you. I can be your friend, and your doctor, and your advocate. And I will."

David looked at her in the mirror again. "You're trying to talk me out of killing you, I know. And I don't want to. I never meant to. But now I have no choice. I knew yesterday, when your friend back there called me to ask about Tommy's death, that the FBI was on to the connection with traumatic deaths at a young age in the researchers' pasts. I knew they only would have started looking into that if they'd found out about the link to violent deaths in the victims' pasts. I knew they would find Dr. Pelletier, whom I intended to be the next researcher I invited to join the study, and the study site I had set up for the next set of subjects. I was afraid if I didn't take steps, they might keep digging until they found me. So I've decided to quit for a while, and let things die down. The plan was to keep them—you—busy by taking these three girls so everyone would be frantically searching for them, while I cleaned up a few odds and ends around here. You almost spoiled things for me."

Charlie could hear it in his tone: time was growing short. The objectification, the coldness, the distancing—he'd lumped her in with "them"—necessary for him to kill her was coalescing.

Kaminsky's eyes were wide open. Charlie could hear the controlled quality of her breathing. One of the girls made a sound, a whimper. She glanced that way: the girl's eyelids were moving. She was one of the blondes, the second one down. If she woke up, what would David do? If the girl got agitated, started moving around, maybe cried or screamed, that might be all the trigger he needed. Kaminsky was looking at the girl, too: Charlie's eyes met Kaminsky's, held. *"Keep her quiet,"* she mouthed. Kaminsky nodded. The other woman was frightened, she could see, but had herself in hand. Charlie's gaze was drawn to Michael, who was cursing a blue streak as he tried, and failed, to grab hold of the padlock.

Another of the girls stirred.

The sense that the situation was getting ready to spiral out of control was strong.

Dread wrapped around Charlie like a pall. Putting a hand on the arm of the moving girl in hopes of keeping her down and calm if she should awaken, Charlie did the only thing she could think of to do: she talked.

"David, you're overlooking something." She kept her tone very even, very sure. "Special Agent Bartoli and Special Agent Crane *know your identity*. And they'll be looking for Special Agent Kaminsky and me. Every law enforcement agent in the state will be looking for us. If you harm us, every law enforcement agent in the country will be looking for you. You can't possibly get away."

David laughed. "Oh, Charlie. Do you think I didn't consider the possibility that this day might come? I have a second identity, a second life that I can go to. David Myers is going to disappear tonight." He laughed again. "Trust me, I've thought of everything. No one will find me."

"Bartoli and Crane already will have missed us." Charlie fought to keep her growing desperation out of her voice. "They probably have every police officer in the area looking for us right now. They'll put up roadblocks. They'll send up helicopters. They'll watch the airports. They *are* going to catch you. Your only chance is to let me help you."

"Your FBI special agents aren't doing anything right now." David sounded almost gleeful. "I heard your friend back there screaming about them being in an explosion into her phone right before I zapped her. That explosion was my house going up. I disconnected the hose from the gas stove, and as I was leaving, gas was already filling the house. All it took was a spark to set it off. I knew it would happen soon, although I have to say I didn't expect it to happen *that* soon. I was thinking pilot light from the water heater, but I doubt it was that." He paused a second. "I'm guessing your special agents set it off. Yes, I bet that's what happened. In that case, they're most likely already dead. So I don't have to worry about them."

The garage door opener. Horror widened Charlie's eyes. An indrawn breath from Kaminsky told Charlie she was thinking the same thing.

Please let Tony and Buzz still be alive.

"If that's the case, I really did clean up after myself." David sounded highly pleased.

"Oh." One of the girls was definitely waking up. It was the brunette: she rolled free of the others and, before either Charlie or Kaminsky could do anything to prevent her, sat up. She was plump, with a snub nose.

"Oh," she said again, looking around. Then she began to scream like her fingernails were being pulled out.

The hair stood up on the back of Charlie's neck.

"Holy shit, shut her up," Michael barked. "He's got another can of gas back here."

"No, it's all right," Charlie cried to the girl at the same time as, moving almost simultaneously and with Charlie resolutely ignoring the shooting pain in her head, she and Kaminsky scrambled to crouch beside her.

"Hush, hush, you're all right," Charlie babbled at the girl, grabbing one arm, while Kaminsky grabbed the other, shook it, and snapped, "Shut up, you little idiot."

When the girl didn't, Kaminsky hauled off and slapped her across the face.

Charlie felt as shocked as the girl looked, but at least the screaming stopped. Eyes wide and tear-filled, her breath coming in gasping sobs, the girl stared at Kaminsky. Charlie slid an arm around her, and the girl collapsed against her shoulder and, more quietly this time, wept.

Across her shaking shoulders, Charlie and Kaminsky exchanged speaking looks.

"That didn't suit me, that didn't suit me at all," David said. "I think I'm going to have to give you ladies another little dose of gas." Charlie could feel him looking at her, and she glanced up to meet his eyes in the mirror. "It'll make things easier for you," he told her comfortingly. "I won't wake you up."

Charlie's blood ran cold. Then, when he reached behind him to slide the plastic door closed, her heart shot into her throat.

"What's he doing?" The girl jerked upright in Charlie's arms. Her voice shook with fear. Her head swiveled so that she was looking at Charlie. "I want to go home! I want my mom!"

"*Shut up,*" Kaminsky and Michael roared at the same time, and when the girl did, burying her face in Charlie's shoulder and shaking silently in her arms, Charlie could hear the soft, sibilant hiss of gas.

"It's coming through the vents." Michael was making valiant attempts to close them, but Charlie could see his hands passing right through the black plastic slots. She could feel his frustration, his terror for her. Realizing that he was helpless to help her, helpless to save her, Charlie felt cold sweat wash over her in a wave. "Babe, you've got to get out of that cage. It's weakest in the corners. You and Sugar Buns are going to have to try to kick your way through. Try the one on the back left, near the door."

An instant vision of her kitten-heeled sandals and Kaminsky's towering pumps flashed through Charlie's mind, along with the conclusion, *At least it's better than bare feet.* Charlie looked at Kaminsky. "We've got to try to kick through one of the corners of the cage." She pointed at the one Michael had indicated. "That one there."

Kaminsky scrambled toward it. Charlie said, "It's going to be okay" to the girl, released her—she crumpled into a sobbing ball—and scrambled after Kaminsky. The other woman was already slamming her foot in its high stiletto heel against the wire when Charlie reached her.

"We need to do it together," Charlie cried, and Kaminsky nodded. "One, two, *three.*"

They were just slamming their feet against the wire strut in unison when, so loud it made them jump, they heard the wail of a police siren. Revolving red lights flashed through the van.

"Thank God," Kaminsky breathed, and she and Charlie stopped kicking the cage and looked at each other.

"Thank God," Charlie echoed. She was already starting to feel a little dizzy from the gas.

"Did I ever say I don't believe in miracles? I take it back. Two cop cars are right behind us." Michael, jubilant, came to crouch in front of them. "It's going to be okay, babe."

With a screech of tires, the van sped up as if it had been shot from a gun. Charlie was thrown back onto her butt. Kaminsky was spared the same fate only because she grabbed hold of the wire grid. The van rocketed down the road; Charlie could hear the spray of gravel hitting the sides.

"He's making a run for it," Michael groaned as the wail of the sirens seemed to fall behind. He rushed toward the cab, for what purpose Charlie didn't know. The gas was starting to make itself felt: everything Charlie could see was starting to spin. Kaminsky coughed; the girl whimpered, a high, keening sound that grated on Charlie's nerves.

"It's a bridge." Michael was back, roaring. "He's driving us off a fucking bridge into the lake! *Hold on!*"

Even as he said it, there was a tremendous jolt, and the van seemed to jump forward.

For a moment, Charlie got the terrifying impression that they were suspended in space. Then the front of the van tilted down, and with a tremendous splash and enough force to send all of them flying, it plunged into the lake.

CHAPTER TWENTY-FIVE

Charlie tumbled head over heels, crashing into bodies, bouncing off the sides of the cage, which had broken loose from its moorings and was tumbling around, too. When the violent motion stopped, water was already pouring inside the van. It was gushing in through the cab, and from the angle she realized they were going into the water front end first. Unsecured now, the cage lay snugly against the plastic doors that divided the driver's compartment from the cargo area. A glimpse of night sky at the rear told her that one of the cargo doors had flown open on impact. The strip of starry sky she could see provided the only illumination.

What had become of David she had no idea. She, Kaminsky, and the girls were tangled together in a barely moving heap on what was now the bottom of the cage.

We're still locked in the cage.

As Charlie realized that, panic sent a rush of adrenaline shooting through her veins.

Cop cars had been close behind them. Rescue had to be on its way.

Charlie felt cold water gushing over her ankles, and knew they dare not wait.

"Get up! You got to get out! *Now!*" Michael bent over them, yelling, and Charlie, dazed and hurting as she was, still knew he was right. Water was already rising around her, rising around all of them as it filled the cargo area from front to back. It was cold, fishy-smelling, and shiny black as oil.

Dark water. Her heart lurched.

Even as Charlie had the thought, she was scrambling upright, grabbing at the wire grid. She couldn't see much, only the pale shapes that were Kaminsky and the girls. Pain stabbed her behind her eyes; her head swam. She ignored all of it. The van was sinking into the water; if they didn't get out, they would die.

"Help! Help!" One of the girls shrieked as she struggled to her feet. "Somebody, help us!"

"What's happening?" another cried. "Diane, where are you?"

Two of them were on their feet now, screaming and clutching each other as they tried to keep their balance in the rising water. As water edged up around her knees, Charlie ignored them, frantically rattling the grid, seeking an area of weakness. There just wasn't any give—

"Charlie, do you see any way out?" The cry came from Kaminsky, who was sloshing around to her left. Charlie saw that she was hauling the third girl's head clear of the water, and thrusting her into the arms of one of her friends with the admonition, *"Hang on to her."*

"Babe, there's a hole in the wire where the bottom of the cage was fastened to the floor of the van. Right here."

With the water swirling around her thighs now, Charlie followed Michael to the hole. It was small, with jagged edges, but she thought they could fit through it.

"Here," she called to Kaminsky, holding on to the grid as the van tilted forward a little more and water rose almost to her waist. "Give me one of the girls."

An instant later, a small cold hand clutched hers.

"This is Kim," Kaminsky said. "Get her out of here."

"Oh, my God! Oh, my God!" Kim—she was one of the blondes—gasped over and over again as Charlie helped her wiggle through the hole.

"Go out the door back there and swim," Charlie ordered when Kim was free. She watched the girl scramble on all fours up the slippery floor toward the open cargo door, and realized that the van was tilting more.

"Come on, Diane," Kim cried, stopping to look back as she teetered at the edge of the open door.

"Jump!" Charlie yelled at her. With one last look over her shoulder at the girl Kaminsky was thrusting toward Charlie, Kim did. The sound of the splash told Charlie that the rear of the van was still a good distance above the water.

The problem was, it was sinking fast.

"Hurry," Michael said urgently.

"Hurry," Charlie repeated to Kaminsky as she thrust the second girl—the brunette, who had regained consciousness first—through the hole.

"I'm not a very good swimmer," the girl—Diane?—cried, looking back.

"Go! We'll be up there to help you soon," Kaminsky yelled. She was struggling with the third girl, a delicately built blonde, who, although her eyes were open and she seemed responsive, was still clearly under the influence of the gas.

"You go through and I'll hand her up to you," Charlie said, ignoring her pounding heart in favor of holding on to the girl as the water swirled ever higher around them. The angle of the van was increasingly precarious, and keeping her footing was growing ever more difficult.

Nodding, Kaminsky pulled herself through the hole, then reached down for the girl.

"Hold your hands up," Charlie ordered, then when the girl looked at her blankly she snapped, "Natalie! You're Natalie, right?" The girl nodded. *"Hold up your hands!"*

Natalie did. Kaminsky grabbed them—"I've got her!"—and despite the girl's apparent inability to help much, with Charlie pushing from beneath they managed to get her through.

"Take her on out." Charlie was already working her way through the hole. "I can manage."

Kaminsky nodded and started half-helping, half-pushing Natalie toward the door, where Diane, poised in the opening like a swimmer on the block, hesitated, looking back at them.

"Jump!" Kaminsky yelled at her.

Diane did. Seconds later, Kaminsky and Natalie reached the door.

"I'm out," Charlie called to Kaminsky as, having made it through the hole, she knelt on top of the cage preparatory to standing up. "Go!"

With a glance back to make sure Charlie really was through, Kaminsky locked a hand in the back of Natalie's shirt and they both disappeared. A splash an instant later told Charlie they were in the lake.

"Goddamn it, babe, move your ass," Michael snarled at her.

With a terrifying slurping sound, water reached the top of the cage as Charlie scrambled to her feet. Her heart thudded when the van tilted, and she almost lost her balance.

"*Go,*" Michael roared, and Charlie pushed off from the top of the cage, meaning to follow the others to the door and jump into the lake.

But something cold and hard latched on to her ankle, snatched her back. A hand! David! Circumstances—like, say, a short in the electrical system caused by the water which prevented him from operating the doors or windows—must have left him with no choice but to exit the cab through the plastic doors, and force his way into the cage, which he had to pass through to reach the open cargo door. Charlie looked down to see the pale circle of his face glaring up at her through the water as he pushed his way through the hole after her, and her heart gave a great leap.

"Let go!" she cried, kicking at his imprisoning hand. The water rose around her ankles even as David's head burst through the hole. He only had one arm through. His shoulders, she saw, were too big to fit. "Michael, help!"

David's head cleared the surface of the water, and Michael saw what was happening. "Fuck!"

Even as Charlie fought to yank her ankle free, Michael was at her side, throwing punches, stomping at David's head, but David never felt a thing. Realizing that Michael really, truly couldn't materialize, Charlie felt her stomach drop clear to her toes. Her heart pounded. Her pulse raced.

"Help me get out of here," David groaned. His eyes were wild as they fixed on her, and Charlie fought the urge to scream. She was afraid that if she did, it would incite him, push him into the kind of frenzy that serial killers were typically capable of. Already he was horrifying to look at: his expression made his face a grotesque parody of his usual good looks. His hair was plastered to his skull. Water streamed down his face, running dark on one side, and Charlie realized that his head was bleeding: he must have been injured in the crash. But his hand gripping her ankle felt stronger than it had any right to be, and she remembered that serial killers, when in the zone, often had far greater than normal strength.

"Let me go and I'll help you!" she promised, tamping down on the hysteria that bubbled into her throat, fighting to stay calm in the face of burgeoning terror, but he laughed. The van swayed, and as he struggled to force himself through the hole the water rose to lap at his chin.

"You better get me out of here! If I go down, you're going with me," he threatened her, and she could tell he meant every word. His fingers dug into her flesh, hurting her. Water inched up her calves, the van rocked, and panic surged in an icy tide through her veins. Talking him into letting her go might work, given enough time. But time was what she didn't have. If she didn't get free, soon, she was going to drown. To hell with inciting him into a frenzy: she screamed—please God, let Kaminsky hear and come to her aid—and kicked at his face.

Yanking her ankle hard, he knocked her off her feet. Charlie landed on her back with a splash. Surprise widened her eyes, made her suck in air. The water slurped around her. The van swayed.

"No!" Charlie screamed as David started pulling her toward him, and she realized that he meant to drag her back down through the hole. Holding on to the grid for dear life, kicking and struggling with every ounce of strength she possessed, she fought to get free even as he inexorably dragged her closer, inch by desperate inch.

"Babe! Behind you!" Michael yelled. Charlie glanced frantically around to see moonlight glinting on a metal canister the size of an oxygen tank that had floated—with Michael's help?—within her reach. "Grab it and bash him in the head! Now! Quick!"

To do it she had to let go of the grid. She did, snatching the canister up with both hands. It was heavy, solid.

"Got you!" David screeched, jerking her toward him. The lubrication of the water beneath her caused her slide to be terrifyingly fast.

"Hit him!" Michael yelled.

Screaming, Charlie smashed the canister into David's head with all her might. The thud was sickening. The look in his eyes was worse. They went wide and black. His fingers slackened on her ankle. Shaky with terror, she jerked her leg free, and scrambled out of his reach.

The van slid another few inches into the water.

David just had time to gasp out, "Charlie!" before the water covered his mouth, and then his nose—

"Get the hell out of here!" Michael screamed.

Blocking the horrible sounds of David's frenzied flailing from her mind, Charlie pushed off from the top of the cage and scrambled toward the strip of night sky she could see through the open cargo door.

Even as she struggled to climb the now nearly vertical floor, the water gave a great gurgle. Her heart jackhammered. She clawed frantically for the door as the van sank, taking her with it as it plunged with terrifying speed toward the depths of the lake. Quick as a blink, the water closed over her, swallowing her, rushing up her nose, blinding her.

Holding her breath, she tried frantically to swim up through the sudden fierce suction that pulled at her from below.

Lungs burning, heart pounding, pulse racing, she fought valiantly as she was dragged down and down and down into the dark, swirling water. Soon her lungs felt as if they would explode and she opened her mouth to suck in air because she couldn't resist the urgent need any longer, only there was no air anywhere and what she sucked in was water.

Lost in blackness, dizzy and weak, struggling until she couldn't any longer, Charlie saw beautiful shimmery stars pinwheeling through the darkness in front of her eyes and felt the cold water rushing past her turn warm and comforting, like a lover's arms.

She could hear Michael screaming, "No, no, no," in her ears as she died.

CHAPTER TWENTY-SIX

Seen from the green, grassy shore, the lake at night was beautiful. Its smooth dark surface rippled in the moonlight, reflecting the icy white sickle of the moon itself, and the glitter of thousands of stars. The breeze blowing in off the water was warm and smelled of flowers.

Charlie felt happy. She felt at peace.

Even so, there was a tremendous amount of commotion around her. The red flashing lights of police cars ringed an area not far away. She could hear voices, cries, weeping. She looked closer. Although she was not physically near, she recognized the three young girls huddled together, the woman and two men kneeling around a second woman lying supine in the grass.

She even remembered their names: the girls were Natalie and Diane and Kim; the kneeling woman was Lena, and the men were Tony and Buzz.

The supine woman in the soaked yellow dress, with the heavy man's watch glinting silver on her slender, motionless wrist, pulled at her. Charlie felt a drift of gentle sadness as she realized: that woman, drenched and drowned, lying unmoving and pale in the moonlight, was her.

Dr. Charlotte Stone.

She drew closer.

"I thought she was right behind me." Lena sounded as if the words were being ripped out of her throat. She was wet and shivering despite the warmth of the night. Moonlight gleamed on what looked like a tear sliding down her cheek.

Buzz slid an arm around Lena. His clothes were dirty, ripped. A grayish powder—ash, she remembered there had been an explosion—dusted his hair. "It's not your fault. We should have come back faster. By the time we got to the Inn, saw your laptops still on the table, and figured out what had happened, Myers was long gone."

"If one of the waitresses hadn't remembered seeing a gray van tearing out of the parking lot and been able to tell us which way it went, we never would have found you." Tony's voice was hoarse. His white shirt was torn and smeared with grime, and he had a cut on his cheek. Like Buzz, his black hair was full of ash. His face was white with shock, twisted with grief. "I can't believe we got to you too late. *Charlie*. Dear God in heaven, how could I have let this happen?"

The raw pain in his voice made Charlie want to reassure him. But Buzz and Lena already were, and then more people joined them, police officers and others, official types. She heard one of them say, "We've got divers down there trying to extract Myers' body. It's still trapped in the van," and then because she didn't want to hear anything more about that, she moved away.

"Charlie!" From out of the shadows Michael appeared, tawny hair washed silver by the moonlight, tall body powerful as ever, handsome face solemn and unsmiling as he walked across the grass toward her.

She knew him instantly, as she knew she would always know him in any realm, in any universe, in any dimension, in any time.

"Michael," she said, and smiled at him as the slight uneasiness Tony's pain had caused her gave way to pure joy.

He opened his arms to her. She walked into them. They closed around her, hugging her close. She could feel every hard, muscular inch of him. She lifted her face to him, and he kissed her, his lips hot and slow. Sliding her arms around his neck, she kissed him back.

She could feel every thrilling nuance of that kiss.

She never wanted it to end.

They were on the same side of the barrier now, and he was hers, just like she was his. Nothing to separate them any longer.

Ghosts couldn't stay. But what she hadn't realized was, she could go. With him.

"I'm dead?" It was both a question and a statement, asked when he stopped kissing her at last.

"Charlie." His honeyed voice was husky, low. She was in his arms still, with her cheek resting against his wide chest, knowing there was no place else in heaven or hell where she would rather be. When he hesitated, when he said nothing more beyond her name, she tilted her face up so that she could see his eyes. They gleamed down at her, their usual sky blue veiled by moonlight.

A faint tinkling of chimes blew in on the breeze. Charlie turned her head to listen.

Not too far away, in a clearing in the middle of a copse of tall trees, a sprinkle of falling moonbeams turned into a column of solid light.

Her mouth fell open as she looked at it. The light was beautiful, celestial, divine.

She knew what it was. The gateway. The passage.

The light mesmerized her. Drew her. It was everything she could do to tear her eyes away to look up at him, to draw his attention to it. All of a sudden it occurred to her that maybe she could take him with her into it, that maybe its power would hold his weight as well as her own, that maybe there could be an eternity for them together, after all.

"Michael." Pulling out of his arms, she caught his hand instead, tugging him with her toward it. "There's the light. Come with me into the light."

"Charlie." He resisted. He was too big, she couldn't budge him against his will. "No."

"You see it, don't you?" she asked in sudden consternation, because she remembered then that he'd never been able to see it before.

"I see it."

"You can walk into it with me. It's strong enough for both of us. I can feel it. I'm"—*almost*—"sure it will take us both."

"Maybe." His tone was grim. "Whether it will or not, babe, you don't want to go."

Charlie frowned at him. "What? Yes, I do."

He shook his head. "No, you don't. Being dead sucks. You want to stay here. You want your life."

She answered almost piteously: "No."

"Yes." He was inexorable. "They're over there giving you CPR again. You can still go back."

"No." But then she thought of her house, and her work, and her mother, who would grieve. So, it seemed, would Tony, and Buzz and Lena, too. And—others. Her colleagues. Her friends. Then there was Michael. What if he couldn't walk into the light with her? What if he was torn away from her, and she never saw him again?

Until that moment, she hadn't really noticed that the breeze had turned into a gentle suction, wafting her toward that poor drowned body in the grass.

She looked up at him, undecided, and he pulled her into his arms and kissed her. Kissed her as if he was promising her forever, as if he had found eternity in her arms. Clinging, she kissed him back, and was still kissing him when—*swoosh*—he was no longer there.

A moment later, she was lying in the grass coughing and sputtering and spewing out lake water like a fountain.

Michael stood where she had left him.

The feel of her was still in his arms. The taste of her was still on his lips. She was back in her body. He could see her moving over there in the grass. She would be fine, he knew. She would live, and have her life.

He wished with every glimmer of his being that he could say the same.

The light was still there. The white light that she'd been talking about for so long. It had come for her. Not for him.

But he could feel it pulling at him. He walked toward it, curious. It waited for him, beautiful and shimmering. He could feel the hope of it, the promise of it. Looking at it, he was tempted. Just to try.

For a long moment he stood there, resisting the pull, deep in thought. Then he turned his back on the light and walked away.

There was a woman he wasn't yet ready to leave.

Have you read the first paranormal romantic thriller to feature
sexy serial killer hunter Charlotte Stone?

KAREN ROBARDS

The Last Victim

Dr Charlotte Stone sees what others do not.

An expert in criminal pathology, Charlie regularly sits face-to-face
with madmen. She's been obsessed with learning what makes human
monsters commit terrible crimes since she was sixteen, when a man
butchered the family of her best friend Holly, then left the girl's
body on a seaside boardwalk one week later.

Charlie kept quiet about her eerie postmortem visions of Holly
and her mother. And even years later, knowing it might undermine
her credibility as a psychological expert, she tells no one about the
visits she gets from the spirit world.

Now all-too-handsome FBI agent Tony Bartoli suspects the
Boardwalk Killer is back. A teenage girl is missing, her family
slaughtered. With time running short for the innocent girl, Bartoli
turns to the only person who could stop this vicious murderer.

But Dr Charlotte Stone sees what others do not. And she sees the
Boardwalk Killer coming for her.

HODDER

The next in the paranormal romantic thriller series featuring
Charlotte Stone:

KAREN ROBARDS

Her Last Whisper

The last time criminal psychology expert Dr Charlotte 'Charlie'
Stone helped capture a serial killer, it was nearly the last thing she
ever did. Now she's determined to stick to research – and leave
risk-taking to the law. But when dangerous duty calls, she can't
refuse. And there's no greater danger than the 'Cinderella Killer',
a charming predator who lures beautiful, single women to their
deaths.

FBI agent Lena Kaminsky fears her missing sister has fallen prey
to the seductive psychopath, and desperately needs Charlie's unique
skills before it's too late. Joined by Special Agents Tony Bartoli,
Buzz Crane – and her ghostly bad-boy lover, Michael Garland –
Charlie heads to Vegas to track down Lena's sister before the
Cinderella Killer seals her fate.

But it's Charlie who ends up gambling with her life, when the
lethal lothario decides she's just his type . . .

HODDER

KAREN ROBARDS

Hunted

Caroline Wallace is one of New Orleans Police Department's top hostage negotiators, and she's never failed to get every hostage out alive. But this time, it's different: the hostages include her father – the superintendent of police – and the mayor. And this time, she's trying to negotiate with Reed Ware, a former co-worker who left the force in disgrace, and who is considered to be volatile and extremely dangerous.

As police snipers arrive on the scene, Caroline has only a few moments left to persuade the hot-headed, reckless (and extremely handsome) Reed to turn himself in before anyone gets hurt. But when the SWAT team runs out of patience and launches an attack, Reed manages to escape – taking Caroline hostage in the chaos. He then tells her he's uncovered corruption at the highest levels of the police department and city government, and those involved will stop at nothing to keep him from exposing what he knows . . . including murder.

Now Caroline must question everything she thought she knew about her job and her city and join Reed on the run . . . putting both her life – and her heart – in jeopardy.

HODDER

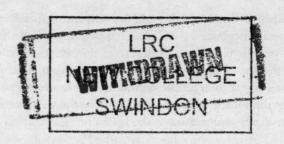

KAREN ROBARDS

Shiver

When she swore off love, he was the last man she imagined would steal her heart.

If driving a tow truck through the seediest part of town with a gun beside her means putting a roof over her son's head, then single mother Samantha is going to be the best repossession woman on the books. But when she hooks her truck up to a flashy BMW, the last thing she expects is to find a beaten, bloody man in the trunk – or to be catapulted into a terrifying fight to survive.

Daniel knows the drug runners who kidnapped him from protective custody will stop at nothing to see him dead. With his life on the line, his only option is to take his pretty saviour hostage and force her to help him.

Sam and her four-year-old son are in too deep. With ruthless killers on their trail, she must reluctantly trust this handsome, menacing stranger. And as Sam relinquishes control, she feels an unmistakable desire. But what is the price of falling for a man who operates on the edge of danger – her heart, her life . . . or both?

HODDER

KAREN ROBARDS

Sleepwalker

When rookie cop Micayla Lange arrests a man she discovers breaking into her old family friend Nicco Marino's mansion, her troubles have only just begun.

Because, as she pulls a gun on professional thief Jason Davis, he drops the bag he's stolen – and it spills open to reveal photographs of Micayla's genial 'uncle' Nicco handing money to a number of Detroit's most powerful politicians and law-makers.

No one was meant to see those photos, least of all a police officer. And – with close circuit cameras capturing every moment of Micayla's realisation that Uncle Nicco is seriously involved with the mob – she may now be in mortal danger.

But Jason has a suggestion. Perhaps if they team up – then maybe there'll a chance they'll both get out alive . . . He's her only hope. But can she trust him with her life?

HODDER

In the best books, the ending often comes as a shock.
Not just because of that one last twist in the tale,
but because you have been so absorbed in their world,
that coming back to the harsh light of reality is a jolt.

If that describes you now, then perhaps you should track down
some new leads, and find new suspense in other worlds.

Join us at www.hodder.co.uk, or follow us on
Twitter @hodderbooks, and you can tap in to a
community of fellow thrill-seekers.

Whether you want to find out more about this book,
or a particular author, watch trailers and interviews, have
the chance to win early limited editions, or simply browse
our expert readers' selection of the very best books,
we think you'll find what you're looking for.

And if you don't, that's the place to tell us what's missing.

We love what we do, and we'd love you to be part of it.

www.hodder.co.uk

@hodderbooks

HodderBooks

HodderBooks